I0819237

# Seven Sisters

# Seven Sisters

## Captives and Rebels in Revolutionary Europe's First Family

Veronica Buckley

VIKING

VIKING
An imprint of Penguin Random House LLC
1745 Broadway, New York, NY 10019
penguinrandomhouse.com



Image credits may be found on pages 495–96.

*Designed by Meighan Cavanaugh*

ISBN 9780525561903 (hardcover)
ISBN 9780525561910 (ebook)

Printed in the United States of America
1st Printing

The authorized representative in the EU for product safety and compliance is
Penguin Random House Ireland, Morrison Chambers, 32 Nassau Street,
Dublin D02 YH68, Ireland, https://eu-contact.penguin.ie.

*For my own dear six sisters*

*—of course*

# CONTENTS

# PROLOGUE

It was a brief announcement, just fifty words or so, printed in old Gothic letters on the front page of a popular Vienna newspaper on a chilly Friday morning, the fourth day of February 1814:

> After a long and arduous journey, accompanied by a small retinue, Her Majesty the Queen of Sicily arrived in this imperial city on Wednesday the second of the month, descending from her coach at the imperial residence, a guest of Her Majesty the Empress-Queen. The illustrious traveller will sojourn here a few days before continuing her journey to Pressburg.

The Queen of Sicily was Maria Carolina, sixty-one years old, last surviving child of Maria Theresia, the great Empress-Queen of Austria, dead and buried thirty years and more. The Empress-Queen who greeted her now was Carolina's twenty-six-year-old niece Ludovika, determined to extend the warmest possible welcome despite her own frail health and the opposition of her husband and his powerful first minister, Prince Metternich, preoccupied as they were, forging a new European order out of the bloody shards of revolution and war. The royal visitor, aunt as well to the Emperor-King Franz, had been given to understand that her stay was to be brief. For a few days she might sojourn in the city of her birth, in the house of her royal forebears, but longer than that she was not to remain.

Prince and emperor regarded her as meddlesome. She had her own claims to press in the *mêlée* of demands enveloping them now from the head of every European state, whether crowned or elected or imposed by force. After decades of fighting, there were armies still in the field, with the city of Paris under siege and Napoleon Bonaparte, self-proclaimed emperor of the French, at large in the countryside, evading final defeat.

Metternich had not waited to witness that. For months he had been engaged on a plan of his own brilliant devising, a plan of phenomenal ambition, to reconstruct, no less, the entire political map of Europe. It was a plan of counterrevolution, undoing the tremendous changes of the preceding quarter century. Monarchies were to be reinstated and social hierarchies largely reestablished. Any threatened rebellion would be stopped in its tracks by a strong police state. Above all, there must be no more war in Europe. Governments would be stable and property secure; borders would be fixed and peace assured throughout the continent. There would be no more challenges to the power of priests and aristocrats, and no more guillotining of kings.

Or of queens, Carolina might have added. For in the upheaval of revolution, the death knell had sounded for her most beloved sister. All her sisters, all her family had paid a price, losing coronets and fiefdoms, territory and treasures. Carolina herself had lost her kingdom, driven from it by the new political necessities. But it was Marie Antoinette who had lost the most: her crown, her dignity, her husband, her children, and finally her life.

There was to be no more of it. Metternich was intent on turning the clock back to the supposed certainties of his youth. Carolina wanted her share in this, for herself and for her descendants, but it was not the share that others had in mind.

It was a brief announcement, but for the people of Vienna, reading between the lines, its fifty words contained a hundred stories.

A hundred stories, beginning half a century before, in the year of comparative peace, 1764.

# INTRODUCTION

In which we visit a small imperial city, and meet a large imperial family.

On a broad plain in Central Europe, between two mountain ranges, lies the city of Vienna. Nourished by the great Danube River on its way east from the Black Forest to the Black Sea, the once Celtic, then ancient Roman settlement was a minor outpost until the early middle ages. But in the fifteenth century, the Habsburg family made it their royal residence and the seat of the Holy Roman Empire, and by 1764, with some two hundred thousand inhabitants, Vienna was the largest city in the German-speaking world, though still only roughly half the size of Naples, a third that of Paris, and a mere quarter the size of London.

At the centre of Vienna, then as now, stood the grand old *Stephansdom*, the Cathedral of St Stephen. Built largely in the fourteenth century on a site hallowed since antiquity, it towered above palace and town, affirming the significance of the Roman Catholic Church in the lands of the Habsburgs. Though revered, the *Stephansdom* was not greatly loved. As a work of architecture, it was unremarkable, "a dark, dirty, and dismal old Gothic building," in the words of an English visitor. For imposing state occasions, it served very well, but for regular services and more private celebrations the imperial family had long preferred the smaller, fourteenth-century Church of St Augustine, its Gothic bones now fleshed out with the plump features of the Baroque. It stood in the centre of the city alongside their royal residence, the Hofburg palace, where Maria Theresia herself had been born.

Maria Theresia was an archduchess of Austria and the Queen of Hungary and Bohemia. Her father, the Emperor Karl VI, had had no sons, and in 1713, he had had to wrest agreement from the other European powers to allow a daughter to succeed him as ruler of the Habsburg lands. But on Karl's death in 1740—from a too-large helping of poisonous mushrooms—a twenty-three-year-old Maria Theresia had found herself at war: Overturning their previous agreement with her father, a powerful alliance of states, including Louis XV's France, had challenged her right, as a woman, to inherit the royal throne. The ensuing war of succession had lasted eight years, before she was finally affirmed as ruler in 1748.

Karl's death had also left a second throne vacant, that of the Holy Roman Empire. Founded by Charlemagne in the year 800, this was a supposed re-establishment of the western empire of ancient Rome. Though it was, in Voltaire's famous dictum, "neither holy, nor Roman, nor an empire," it had lasted in its various forms, shaping the political and cultural development of much of Europe, for almost a thousand years. It was a mosaic of some three hundred kingdoms, principalities, free cities, bishoprics, and estates, bound to one another more or less closely, depending on the diplomatic requirements of the day. All these territories, including Austria itself, were both part of the Empire, and officially independent entities within it. There was thus an overlap between the Austrian Monarchy and the Holy Roman Empire, although, being its most powerful member, Austria generally managed to keep the Empire subservient to its needs. At the Hofburg palace in Vienna, there were separate wings for the administration of Monarchy and Empire, and ministers might find themselves in one wing in the morning and the other in the afternoon.

By convention, the Holy Roman Emperor was almost always a Habsburg, though the throne did not necessarily pass from father to son; rather, the new emperor was chosen by seven Electors, all princes of the Empire, who weighed the competing claims and advantages of the candidates. As a woman, Maria Theresia was automatically excluded; in consequence, she had made strenuous diplomatic efforts to have her husband, Franz Stephan, elected in her late father's place. In 1745, she had succeeded.

As consort of the Holy Roman Emperor, she herself was now an empress as well as an archduchess and a queen, with a score of other, lesser titles to other, lesser lands. Contemporaries found it too much of an effort to be correct, and generally referred to her simply as the Empress: and to her collective territories, with their population of some forty million, as the Habsburg Empire (though it was not technically an empire at all), or Austria (though it included Hungary and Bohemia and many other lands), or simply the Monarchy. Franz Stephan, both Holy Roman Emperor and nominal co-regent of Austria, had little interest in political affairs; he left the business of empire largely to his imperial chancellor, and the government of Austria, at her own insistence, to his purposeful and capable wife. This state of affairs garnered the Emperor much criticism and the Empress much praise, with Prussia's King Friedrich II, "Frederick the Great," berating Franz Stephan's laziness and lack of ambition, and eulogizing Maria Theresia as "a woman you could call a great man."

In her father's day, a stiff atmosphere had prevailed at the royal palace of the Hofburg, aping the funereal etiquette of the Spanish court. But with Maria Theresia's accession and her marriage to the easygoing Franz Stephan, most of the gloom had been swept away. Visitors were charmed by the unaffected manner of the Viennese court and the affability of the imperial couple themselves. Their entertainment-loving children and their many young companions enlivened things further, so that, as a visiting prince observed, "Despite the war going on elsewhere, in Vienna, at court and in the private palaces of the aristocracy, it was all pleasure and gaiety." Even in the streets, the nights were bright, with thousands of oil lamps burning from dusk until one in the morning.

"The war going on elsewhere" was the recently concluded Seven Years'

War. Fought on many fronts and reaching halfway around the world, it had involved all the great European powers and many smaller ones, and it had brought about some important changes: France had lost its preeminent place, overtaken by Britain, particularly as a colonial power. Friedrich II's Prussia, supported by London bankers, had moved into the front ranks of the continental states; it was now a match for Maria Theresia's Austrian Monarchy, and bent on surpassing it. Austria's own efforts in the war, at times a fight for very survival, had in the end been largely for nothing. Broad areas of the Monarchy had been laid waste; three hundred thousand military and civilian casualties had been sustained; and every year, the war had consumed some 40 million florins, so much that, before the end of the conflict, after pawning her own jewellery, the Empress had even had to send some of her soldiers home, being without the wherewithal to feed them. By 1764, Austria's state coffers were empty.

Fortunately for the Habsburg family, their private purse was not. For apart from his imperial crown, the Emperor Franz Stephan also possessed a good bourgeois three-cornered hat: In short, he was an excellent businessman. As a young man, he had inherited substantial property from the last survivor of the great Medici dynasty, who happened to be his aunt, and childless. From this, and from his Grand Duchy of Tuscany, his coal-rich Silesian Duchy of Teschen, and numerous smaller territories, including some of Maria Theresia's Bohemian lands, he had built a more future-oriented and vastly more wealthy empire. By 1764 it was enormous, encompassing not only traditional agriculture and forestry but factories and mines as well. Intelligent reforms and astute investments had spurred its growth and spread its scope, so that its products now reached every part of the Monarchy.

Franz Stephan now had many millions in the banks of Italy and Amsterdam but, having been shrewd enough to borrow initially from his wife, he had remained shrewd enough to lend nothing back to her. "And I even have it from a very good source," reported the Prussian ambassador, "that they have several times argued about this." Maria Theresia needed cash for the frequent gifts she made to her ministers and favourites as part of her traditional system of court patronage. Franz Stephan, by contrast, held more modernizing views, paying his own staff well enough to allow a cadre of professionals to develop and obviating the need for constant handouts. This provoked accusations of tightfistedness, but the outgoings from his accounts were regular and predictable, and he was never in debt. From these very different examples, the couple's children would in time draw their own different lessons. But their father's exertions had built a prodigious fortune, and it was to ensure the Habsburgs' prosperity for centuries.

For three hundred years the Habsburgs had been the most powerful family in Europe. Astute positioning of their many princesses and princes in other royal houses had vastly increased their territories and their influence across the continent. Often avoiding the need for open conflict by strategic betrothals to potential enemies, they had earned, over the centuries, the blessed historical dictum: "*Bella gerant alii, tu felix Austria nube.* Others make war; you, happy Austria, marry."

To this old injunction Maria Theresia and Franz Stephan had responded heroically, aided by an eagerness to marry each other in the first place. Now, at the age of forty-seven, the Empress was the mother of sixteen children, five of them already gone to God, as her firm Catholic faith taught and consoled her; there remained to her four sons and seven daughters. Her own marriage, through the course of its twenty-eight years, had become almost legendary: Alone among European monarchs, she and her husband shared a single bedroom, and spent every night in it together. One bold courtier, consulted by Franz Stephan as to the best way of persuading the Empress to a particular course of action, advised him to refuse to sleep with her until she came round to his way of thinking. The Prussian ambassador, who relayed this story to his sovereign, assured him the Emperor would not have long to wait.

Centrally located at the top of a grand staircase in the Hofburg palace, the imperial bedroom symbolized the duty and purpose of all Habsburg lives: to proclaim and continue the dynasty. Like their ancestors, Maria Theresia's eleven surviving children were expected to place the demands of their exalted family before any preference or need of their own. Their mother, intensely conscious of her own place within so illustrious a house, was making her arrangements for each of them now with characteristic determination.

Visiting Vienna at about this time, Madame Geoffrin, a handsome *dame d'un certain âge* and a leading light in advanced Paris circles, reported that the Empress had "introduced to me, with an inexpressible grace, all the archduchesses one after the other, and the young archdukes; this family is the loveliest thing you can imagine." Of the two adult boys, twenty-three-year-old Joseph matched his parents in height—his mother at least was above average—while lanky Leopold, at seventeen, towered already over them all. All seven girls were tall for their age. The eldest of them was Marianna, a fine artist, scientifically-minded, once an enthusiastic hunter—a sweet portrait exists of her at the age of seven, already riding side-saddle on a piebald pony—and an attendee at all court balls and theatrical performances, but now, at twenty-five, living a rather quieter life, and likely to remain unmarried owing, it was generally thought, to her indifferent health. Twenty-two-year-old Marie Christine, also interested in art and a particularly good linguist, was the acknowledged favourite of their empress mother; twenty-year-old Elisabeth, volatile of temperament, quick-witted, sharp-tongued, and flirtatious, was the beauty of the family; Amalie, just turned eighteen and also remarkably pretty, was their Amazon, a lover of horses and hunting, but somehow a little apart, too young for her three elder sisters, too old for the three below her—Josepha and Carolina, thirteen and eleven, Josepha not so bright but perhaps a little artful, Carolina clever and spirited; and the youngest, delicate of health and rather neglected by her mother, eight-year-old Antonia, sandwiched between two little boys of nine and seven, Ferdinand and Maximilian.

Unusually for a royal mother of the period, Maria Theresia had been quite involved in her elder children's education, not teaching them herself, of course, but deciding what they were to study, setting out hourly routines for them, and personally checking their progress every day. The three eldest sisters had all had the benefit, in their *aya*, of the exceptionally able Princess Caroline von Trautson. A close friend and advisor of the Empress, this cultured woman was also a fluent French speaker, and this facility she had passed on to her charges, an important asset for them, since French was the *lingua franca* of Europe's courts, and within the family they spoke only their native Viennese German. But whether the demands on the Empress' time had increased or her own enthusiasm had waned, by 1764 she was paying less attention to what was going on in the schoolroom, and taking less care in the appointment of *aya*s. The results were predictable, with the younger girls in particular being indifferently educated compared to their siblings.

There is a delightful series of coloured pastel portraits of all the imperial children, painted at about this time by Jean-Étienne Liotard of Geneva. It shows the three elder sisters in blue-grey silk, the four younger ones in pink, and their brothers in white, and it gives us a glimpse of their everyday activities, if only indoors, and only for the girls. Marianna is reading; Marie Christine is dipping a paintbrush into little coloured pots; Elisabeth gesticulates, as if in mid-conversation; Amalie is embroidering; Josepha is playing on a double keyboard; Carolina poses with a pink rose matching her gown and neck-ruff; Antonia pulls a thick-threaded bodkin through a heavy fabric. Their four brothers, two of them still little boys, stand or sit in powdered attitudes of proto-authority.

Joseph's future and that of his three brothers had already been decided. As the eldest son, he was expected to succeed his father, and to this end he had just been crowned King of the Romans. Since there was in fact no Kingdom of Rome, and the eternal city itself was ruled directly by the Pope, Joseph's title, with a nod to the seven Electors, signified only that he was heir to the Holy Roman Empire; in time he would also inherit his mother's crowns. As the second son, Leopold was to have his father's Grand Duchy of Tuscany, with its seat at the massive Palazzo Pitti in Florence. Just turned seventeen and still sighing for a little Hungarian countess, he had recently been betrothed to a daughter of the King of Spain. Ferdinand, not quite ten years old, had been promised for five years already to a wealthy Italian duchess, and seven-year-old Maximilian was to have the Governorship of Hungary, currently held by a local noble.

Each of the brothers could thus look forward to a handsome establishment. For their sisters, however, a great deal of diplomatic work remained to be done. It was largely in the hands of Maria Theresia's formidably intelligent chancellor, Prince Anton Wenzel von Kaunitz-Rietberg, fifty-four years of age, tall and lean, a widower with a passion for Vienna's theatres and also their actresses. Kaunitz hailed from a far from wealthy Bohemian noble family, and his ancestral lands, such as they were, lay near Austerlitz in Moravia. His exceptional talents had raised him, and the residual sensitivities of his comparatively modest birth had left him disdainful of men of greater family and lesser ability. His elegance of dress and speech and his fastidious personal habits, to say nothing of his hypochondria—in his youth he had suffered from a weakness of the lungs—made him an easy target for those who had cause to resent or fear him. His residence in Vienna was "the most arrogantly aristocratic house" in the city. And he was vain, sporting epicene suits of pink and silver, and "unable to pass a mirror without standing for a moment in front of it."

Whatever his foibles, Kaunitz was beyond doubt a man of rare gifts, widely regarded as "first minister of all the first ministers of Europe." Devoted to the Monarchy and unimpeachable in office, he also had the habit, unusual for the time, of prioritizing domestic development over foreign entanglements. For the moment, however, his focus was outwards: The Empress had half a dozen marriageable daughters; half a dozen marriage contracts advantageous to the Habsburgs remained to be concluded.

WHAT THE HABSBURGS considered advantageous to themselves had lately changed. For more than 250 years, since 1500, their dynasty had largely defined itself by a violent hereditary enmity with the French. Originally, neither Austria nor France had had much to fear from the swampy and disordered region of Prussia to their north and east, but a succession of ambitious Hohenzollern princes had ensured that the once minor state had gradually become one of the continent's Great Powers. In recent years its expansionist king, Friedrich II, had joined forces with a globally rapacious Britain to challenge the dominance of the Habsburgs on the continent and the French overseas, and in 1756, the two ancient enemies had been forced to come together to meet the new threat.

This overturning of centuries of policy, masterminded by Chancellor von Kaunitz and the French King's politically powerful mistress, the marquise de Pompadour, was known as the Diplomatic Revolution, or *le renversement des alliances*. Though in Austria it had been generally accepted as a necessary adjustment to new realities, Franz Stephan himself had not supported it. His mother had been French and his upbringing in Lorraine strongly Francophile, and he doubted that centuries of enmity could be written out of millions of hearts by a few royal signatures on calfskin parchment.

In France itself, the *renversement* had never been broadly popular. The defeats of the Seven Years' War, causing colonial losses in India and Canada and enormous, politically destabilizing debts at home, had only increased the general dissatisfaction with it. It had been all too easy to lay the blame on the new alliance with Austria: The enfeebled Habsburgs, it seemed, no longer had strength enough to restrain the dynamic young giants of Prussia and Britain. By 1764, a year after the war's end, it was widely agreed in France that the country had taken a serious misstep in joining forces with Austria. But the alliance had held, and diplomats on both sides had remained active, seeking to match the Habsburgs' daughters with princes of the House of Bourbon.

These were not by any means all Frenchmen. Half a century before, the armies of the Sun King, Louis XIV, had defeated the Habsburgs' Spanish cousins, imposing Bourbon rule over not only Spain itself but its Italian territories as well. Now, in 1764, three of the four Bourbon thrones were occupied by Spaniards, all direct descendants of Louis XIV: Carlos III in Madrid; his son Ferdinando in Naples; and his nephew, also called Ferdinando, in the Duchy of Parma in northern Italy. On the throne of France itself sat Louis XV, the Sun King's great-grandson.

Franz Stephan's misgivings notwithstanding, three Habsburg-Bourbon marriages had already been arranged, increasing Austria's influence in Italy as much as in France. Two had been for his sons, but the most prestigious of them all was that of his youngest daughter, Antonia, with the little duc de Berry, grandson of Louis XV. To the eight-year-old girl herself, still playing with her dolls in the spring of 1764, this meant little, but political observers considered it the consummate achievement of the Diplomatic Revolution. In time, marriages with junior Bourbon houses would also be arranged for three of Antonia's sisters, while three others, within the Austrian Netherlands and the crown lands of Hungary, Bohemia, and Austria itself, would serve the dynasty's long-term project of centralizing its power.

For the Habsburgs themselves, this centralization was a progressive undertaking, an attempt to modernize the Monarchy's diverse economies and standardize its administration; this in turn was to make it more competitive and ensure its overall prestige within a changing Europe. For its individual regions, however, centralization meant a loss of local power and long-standing traditions, political and religious. The three eldest sisters would be caught up in the resulting tug-of-war between Vienna and its satellites. For Marianna and Elisabeth, despatched to enhance the Habsburgs' presence in newly strategic regions of Austria, the challenge would be to manage institutions once part of an all-powerful Church, now subject to decreasing funds and increasing restraints. For Marie Christine, far to the north in the Austrian Netherlands, the battleground would be political as well as religious, a prolonged trial by combat between the forces of reaction and revolution. Like their younger sisters in the Bourbon palaces of Italy and France, they would walk a path of thorny compromise between obedience to the old dynasty and loyalty to their new families and subjects, with all sides attempting to form and confine each sister's developing sense of self.

As women in an age of fierce constraints, they would begin as pawns on the Habsburg dynastic chessboard, in time, whether willingly or not, becoming players themselves. The diplomatic *renversement* intended to ensure the Habsburgs' security and standing would itself be *renversé*, returning France to its ancient pinnacle as the greatest of all their enemies. Revolution and the expansionary nationalism of the Napoleonic era were to present the sisters with fearful new challenges, to be met by each of them according to her character and talents.

Each unique in passions and temperament, all seven sisters would be shaped, and all shaped differently, by the powerful personality of their empress mother. Their stories are in many ways a response to her own. Attempts to escape her, to placate or emulate her, even to take revenge on her, these form, for many years, their strongest impulses. They are fused as time goes by with wider fears and desires, with the will to power, ambition for children, and the love of men. The sisters' interwoven lives reflect and also catalyze the ideals and events of their rich and turbulent age. Often, and often despite themselves, they would become its symbols, positive or negative: Adulation of their patronage, piety, and dynastic continuity would have its counterpoint in accusations of abuse of privilege, hypocrisy, and betrayal. As women, they would be particularly vulnerable to instrumentalization as anti-models of filial and wifely disobedience, sexual promiscuity, and political overreach.

Seven sisters, seven daughters. Four wives, three mothers, two queens. Two abbesses, in name at least. Marianna the seeker after truth; the *grande dame* Marie Christine; Elisabeth, the malicious, disfigured beauty; Amalie, troubled and troublesome; Carolina the politician; the tragic bride Josepha; and Antonia, youngest of the seven, sacrificial offering to the gods of revolution. Theirs is a story of many layers: It is the story of a great European family, the story of seven women, at once ordinary and extraordinary, and the story of a brilliant world collapsing, in a fearful time.

# I

# 1764

In which two secret loves emerge,
and Elisabeth loses a king.

Among the piles of marriage files stacked within the gilded cabinets of Chancellor von Kaunitz's apartments, there was not a single page concerning the eldest, Marianna. Alone among the seven sisters, owing to her state of health, she appeared to have been excused the primary dynastic duty of marriage and motherhood. During her childhood, various matches had been considered for her, but at the age of eighteen she had collapsed with an infection of the lungs, brought on by "too vigorous movement while dancing," or so at least thought Court Treasurer Khevenhüller, who was keeping a detailed journal of court events. Whatever the case, the infection had almost killed Marianna. Fearing the worst, the Empress had written to her long-standing friend, the Countess Maria Walpurga Lerchenfeld, that "the loss of this daughter, so dear to me, her wretched condition and the pain in which I see her, have brought me extremely low. . . . God's holy will be done. . . . I confess this is the child I loved most of all."

Saved from death, supposedly by suckling at the breast of a wet-nurse four times a day, Marianna had been left with a permanently weak chest and a pronounced curvature of the spine. "Her ribs are so bent," Khevenhüller had confided to his eldest son, "on one side you feel they might almost pierce her lungs," and in the eight years since then, though her posture seems to have improved somewhat, her brother Joseph had taken to calling her "hunchbacked Marianna." This first daughter was Franz Stephan's favourite, who, unlike his son and heir, shared his love of hunting and his interest in the scientific developments of the day. She was a skilled artist, too, garnering the praise of professionals for her copper engravings and drawings. As well as portraits and still lifes and genre scenes of daily life, she also produced arresting seascapes and moonlit landscapes in an intense, early Romantic vein, for Marianna had something of the seeker in her, always striving, never quite at ease in herself.

Unusually for the time, Maria Theresia had permitted her four eldest daughters to attend some of their brothers' lessons alongside them: Keenly aware of the deficiencies in her own education, and blaming her father roundly for this, it seems she had determined to avoid the same shortcomings in the next generation of Habsburg women. Less happily, this did not extend to any training in general affairs of state, to say nothing of the actual day-to-day business of government. In time, this lack of preparation would leave the more highly placed of the sisters floundering in deep political waters.

Marianna herself felt that her "masculine and rather unsystematic" education had not been altogether positive for her. It had encouraged, she said, the "inborn fire and intensity of my passions," which she felt might have been brought under firmer control. But her illness at eighteen had done what her education had not: It had put a stop to her hunting all day and dancing all night. Instead, she admitted, she had taken to reading novels all day and playing cards all night—apparently for very high stakes—and whenever she felt her health allowed it she had returned to her more active pleasures, "and with them new kinds of nonsense, one leading to the next; I immersed myself completely in delights," often enough paying for them with a painful relapse of her illness. At twenty-five, she was by no means the saintly invalid that some would later seek to make of her.

But although her doubtful health had made the prospect of any match unlikely, Marianna was still prey to "the intensity of my passions," for, unknown to almost everyone at court, she was—and had been for some years already—deeply in love.

As so often, love had arrived when least expected. In the earliest years of womanhood, Marianna had lived, as she said, "much too occupied with pleasures to think of love; for a long time, my birth and a certain haughtiness of manner protected me from the danger of being addressed in that way; I had never been vain and didn't consider myself able to attract anyone, so I didn't suspect that I had done so." Though not a striking beauty in the way of her younger sister Elisabeth, Marianna was tall and graceful, with refined features, her eyes full of intelligence and humour and, as everyone remarked, particularly beautiful hands—at that time an important feature in the assessment of female beauty. She was perfectly able to "attract" someone; most probably she had not thought of love because no one had yet attracted her. But in the late winter of 1760, when she was twenty-one years old, she had met the man she was to love for the rest of her life. He cannot be identified with any certainty—even Khevenhüller's informative journal is missing for these years—but, as she herself was to write, twenty years later, "Once I fell in love, I never thought of anyone else."

In the four years and more since then, Marianna and her "friend," as she always referred to him, had enjoyed a time of cautious happiness, though they had taken care their feelings should not be generally known. "We were so discreet and careful," she wrote, "I never wanted the kind of comedy I had seen being played so often." There were no doubt passionate exchanges and stolen kisses, but they wanted no gossip and no furtiveness, and they are unlikely to have consummated their love—with servants everywhere, it would have been almost impossible to keep such a secret. Had Marianna been a widow or a married woman, or even a single woman of far lower rank, that might have been the natural course of events, but she was an unmarried archduchess; apart from any religious or moral scruples, the fear of a scandalous pregnancy would have been enough to persuade her to chastity. It may even be that, apart from an evident meeting of minds, this unconsummated sexual tension had kept the flame between Marianna and her "friend" burning longer than it might otherwise have done.

Why had Marianna not married this man? It may be that he was already married. Perhaps he was living apart from his wife—a common situation in an age of arranged marriages, often between near-strangers. Even so, in the eyes of the world, a relationship with such a man would have been scandalous and, crucially, in the eyes of the Church, deeply sinful.

In these years of her early twenties, Marianna was not particularly devout. She was close to her father, who took a relaxed view of his faith, advising his children there was more to be learned of good and evil by observing the world than by listening to confessors. Marianna would have known of his affairs and his way of accommodating them to his Catholicism—his favourite mistress, the Princess von Auersperg, "for whom the Emperor displays his passion quite openly," was in fact a noted freethinker who believed, following the ancient philosopher Lucretius, "that religion was simply to keep the common people under control." Still, between what a man might do and what an unmarried woman might do, there remained a deep gulf. Franz Stephan's mistress, though the same age as Marianna, had been married for some years: Her "value," as it were, could not depreciate, since she was no longer on the marriage market, and any pregnancy arising could simply be imputed to her husband. Marianna was wise to be "discreet and careful" in her behaviour.

But she seems to have seen nothing sinful in the relationship, and it is more likely that the man she loved was not married, but rather a single man in modest circumstances, probably of considerably lower rank than herself. Such a man would have been regarded as presumptuous in the extreme to raise his eyes to the daughter of an emperor, and Marianna would have been ridiculed for paying attention to him. An engagement, or even an acknowledged understanding, would have been out of the question.

Perhaps the man was not Catholic. Within Maria Theresia's Monarchy, no public career, let alone marriage into the family, was possible for anyone who was not. Or perhaps he was a member of one of the influential Catholic orders, charitable or military, whose members, both priests and laymen, were vowed to celibacy—the Order of Teutonic Knights, for instance. If he had no private fortune, he may have been unwilling to compromise his prospects by withdrawing from such a brotherhood in order to marry.

Marianna's secret love was never named by her in writing. It is known only that he was a nobleman, and it seems he lived, at least part of the time, in or near Vienna. They could not, or did not marry, but years and decades into the future, Marianna herself would be found lamenting the "very tender but not changeable heart" that had kept her love for him alive "for twenty-one years, the last just as the first."

THROUGHOUT THIS SAME SPRING of 1764, Marianna's younger sister, twenty-two-year-old Marie Christine, was sighing after a secret love of her own. This young man, twenty-six-year-old Lieutenant Prince Albert Kasimir of Saxony, had arrived in Vienna in 1760, together with his younger brother, Clemens. It had then been the middle of the Seven Years' War and, although they were sons of the late King of Poland, both brothers had been serving as officers in the Austrian army. It was common at this period for aristocrats to volunteer as officers in the armies of other states, provided they were not at war with their own.

Prince Albert's heart had been lost to Marie Christine on the very evening of his arrival, when he had heard her, together with Marianna, singing and playing at the Hofburg. "They were both very beautiful," he noted in his memoirs, "but the second one had, as well as an absolutely perfect figure, the loveliest possible face and such a lively and intelligent expression, quite individual. That was all it took. The moment I saw her I fell in love with her." Delighted to find himself seated beside Marie Christine on a sleigh ride by candlelight through a snowy palace park, he was equally charmed by her conversation "which enchanted me even more." The die was cast, though Marie Christine herself was to recognize it only gradually.

Albert's passion was all the more intense for being apparently hopeless.

Marie Christine seemed unreachable. The daughter of an imperial house, she far outranked this sixth, uninheriting son, even if his father had been a king, and their grandfathers had been brothers. His despair may have lifted earlier had he guessed that eventually Marie Christine had fallen in love with him, too. But, knowing that her father had long had another man in mind for her, she had for almost two years betrayed to Albert only an impeccable friendliness. By 1764, however, her heart had long been open to him; even the Empress had guessed the truth, though she in her turn was doing her best to conceal it from the Emperor.

The Prince Franz Stephan favoured for Marie Christine was his nephew, the Duke de Chablais, scion of the powerful House of Savoy, a useful connection for the Habsburgs in their manoeuvring for control of northern Italy. As yet, however, nothing had been concluded. The idea of a match remained secret, while Marie Christine and Albert struggled to keep their own love the same.

In this they were supported by the Empress, for Marie Christine, as was only too well known, was Maria Theresia's favourite. This second daughter, known within the rest of the family simply as Marie, was "my dear Mimi" to her doting mother. She was the fifth child and the fourth daughter born to the Empress (two had died in infancy), and she had arrived one evening in spring, in the middle of a palace ball, on the latter's twenty-fifth birthday. Significantly, when Marie Christine was born, there was already an elder brother safely tucked up in the nursery, a hearty little son and heir, fifteen-month-old Joseph. Though the war of succession for Austria's crown had been still raging across Europe, it was the first time the Empress had felt able to welcome a daughter into the world.

But this was not the reason Marie Christine had become her mother's favourite. From her childhood there is actually no evidence that she was preferred at all. In those early days, it seems rather to have been Marianna who took prime place in her mother's as in her father's heart. She was, after all, the first of the Empress' children to survive infancy, and not surprisingly, perhaps, during her childhood her mother "loved her to the point of idolatry." The special affection continued, however, for she was also the fruit of Maria Theresia's happy, early married life, before her husband had turned his gaze toward other women. "Listening to Marianna sing," she had written, when the girl was twenty-one years old and Marie Christine already seventeen, "I was moved almost to tears, and I felt I loved her more than the others."

For a time Marianna's star had dimmed beside that of Joseph's first wife, the dazzling Isabella of Bourbon-Parma, who had besotted not only Maria Theresia but Franz Stephan as well, usurping Marianna's role as dearest child as well as her precedence, as first archduchess, at court. It was only after Isabella's early death in 1763 that the Empress' active affections had been transferred firmly and finally to Mimi. Marianna remained no less beloved: The Venetian ambassador could still write that "she of all her sisters is regarded with particular fondness by the Empress Queen, and she well deserves it for her exceptional mind and for the sweetness of her manner." But her uncertain health had circumscribed her future, and so the Empress had begun to project her ideals of marital happiness and worldly success onto her second daughter.

The transfer had been planned and promoted by Isabella herself, impossibly in love, as she had been, with her sister-in-law. Still in her early twenties and believing her own death to be imminent, indeed longing for death, she had instructed Marie Christine how best to ingratiate herself with her mother once she herself was gone: "You have enough intelligence and perception to manage this for yourself," she had told her. "Look to win her heart, look to insinuate yourself in her mind, show love and gratitude to her always and at every moment, and you will be sure to be adored and esteemed for it. In everything and everywhere you can, pay your court to the Empress, and pretend to do it with pleasure. You will replace me in the Empress' heart and that will recompense you for everything. Adieu, I kiss your adorable arse." Though she had not returned Isabella's passion, Marie Christine had followed the advice of her frustrated and designing sister-in-law with extraordinary success. As a visitor to the court observed, "She can, when such is her pleasure, temper her demeanour with the most gracious and winning condescension." The Empress' favouritism toward her now, evident in constant gifts and attentions, was naturally resented by the rest of the brood. Joseph behaved particularly coolly to her, no doubt also because, after his wife's death, he had found in her writing-desk a number of unsent letters, sapphic in tone, addressed to his sister. Even the Empress had confided to a friend that there were papers of Isabella's that Joseph should never see.

Some observers thought Marie Christine "naturally distant and haughty," and over the years there were to be many accusations of pride levelled at her. But this stance may have been partly defensive: In her childhood she had suffered from an embarrassing speech defect, "as if her mouth was full of porridge." Whether resolved naturally, perhaps through her many lessons in singing and reciting, or corrected systematically by her determined *aya*, in Marie Christine's adult life, at least, there was to be no mention of it; no doubt it had played a part nonetheless in the forming of her always controlled public demeanour. Marie Christine was on her way to becoming an acclaimed "great lady" of the highest circles; though she was not without deeper impulses, she rarely allowed them to crack her elegant surface glaze.

> *I also want to speak to you about your marriage; it's an essential matter for you. An intelligent and sensible woman would contribute a good deal to your success. I don't know whether it would be more advantageous for you to make a foreign alliance, or to marry one of your subjects?*

The young man in receipt of this advice was thirty-two-year-old Stanisław August Poniatowski, Grand Duke of Lithuania and, owing to the efforts of the Russian Tsarina Catherine II, newly elected King of Poland. His correspondent was the Parisian literary hostess Madame Geoffrin, a long-standing friend of Stanisław's family and indeed of the young King personally—in their letters they addressed each other as *My dear son* and

*My dear Mamma*. Stanisław, able and very handsome, had spent several years at the Russian court, partly in diplomatic service, partly in plain intriguing, and a good deal of the time as the preferred lover of the then Grand Duchess Catherine herself. Until recently he had been hoping to marry her, but Catherine had had other plans: Stanisław was to take the throne of Poland and ensure the country's continuing subordination to Russia—in this, however, he was doing his best to disappoint her.

The "foreign alliance" that he was now considering, early in 1765, was with Maria Theresia's third daughter, the Archduchess Elisabeth. Stanisław had met her several times before during his visits to the Viennese court, but she had been only a child, and there had been no thought then of his marriage with any of the archduchesses: Although through his mother he belonged to the powerful Czartoryski family, Stanisław would not then have been of sufficiently high rank to marry the daughter of an emperor. But he was now a king, and Elisabeth a highly attractive girl of twenty.

Madame Geoffrin had met Elisabeth as a young girl, but she did not really know her; if she had, it is doubtful that she would have seen in her the "intelligent and sensible woman" she felt would suit her "dear son." Stanisław was a passionate reader and a significant patron of the arts and sciences; in the months since his election, he had already revealed himself to be an ambitious political reformer as well. Elisabeth had no interest in things of the mind or in the duties and challenges of government, though she was beautiful and in good health, and might have produced the many children always desired in a ruling family. The marriage might have been a dynastic success, but it is unlikely to have been happy.

Though not without native ability, Elisabeth generally deployed her wit and vivacity only to make caustic jokes at the expense of her siblings, or to flirt with one or other of the young men at court. There was an indolence about her that left her mother decidedly not amused, with the Empress complaining of "Elisabeth with her beauty. She only wants to be liked by some guardsman or prince, she is satisfied with that and cultivates nothing else." But though it is true Elisabeth liked to enjoy herself without having to make too much of an effort, she may have felt she had enough to do in any case with the manifold duties—diplomatic, religious, charitable—imposed on her as a daughter of the ruling house.

A nephew of Stanisław was later to claim that it was Maria Theresia who had initiated the discussions about a possible match. But Stanisław himself had been eager for a Habsburg bride, and he had also been encouraged by the British, pushing for a stronger alliance between Poland and Austria to offset the rising power of Prussia. Negotiations were purposefully pursued, but they did not last long. Though Maria Theresia was well disposed toward Stanisław personally and wanted to remain on friendly terms with him, she believed that the Tsarina Catherine, who had brought him to his throne, after all, would hold too great a sway over him. Since Stanisław was already trying to pursue an independent line, the Empress did not wish to offend him by pointing this out too clearly. Instead, she conjured up a financial obstacle: Stanisław did not have sufficient means to keep Elisabeth in a manner befitting her rank; if he should leave her a widow, she would have even less to live upon.

This at least was the Venetian ambassador's opinion of the situation. And it seems the Empress also had her doubts about the prospect of a resurgent Poland to her north. The ambassador thought the marriage might have been concluded all the same, had it not been for the intervention of Catherine herself. But Stanisław's commonwealth, comprising the Kingdom of Poland together with the Grand Duchy of Lithuania, the whole largely encircled by Russia, Prussia, and Austria, was too strategically important; Catherine wanted to keep it weak and under her own control. An alliance with Austria would mean a considerable shift in the balance of power, a shift by no means to Russia's advantage. The Tsarina forbade Stanisław outright to make the match, and he, mindful of the past or fearful for the future, duly capitulated to her.

Maria Theresia's instincts had been right. And whatever Elisabeth may personally have felt about the loss of a Polish crown, not to mention a most attractive husband, given the trials Stanisław was soon to face, her mother can only have thought it a good thing the diplomatic romance had ended as it did.

# II

# 1765

In which two matches are made, one good and one bad, and an emperor meets his end.

As heir to the Habsburg Monarchy and also to the Holy Roman Empire, twenty-three-year-old Joseph was regarded, within the family as without, as the most important of the eleven siblings. Already a widower, and the father of a tiny girl named, unavoidably, Maria Theresia, Joseph was now under pressure to marry again and produce a male heir of his own. He had no personal wish to do so, startling his mother by insisting his physical needs could very well be met without the bonds of matrimony. After a time, he had agreed to remarry, but only on condition that the bride be the Princess Maria Luisa of Bourbon-Parma, younger sister of his late wife, Isabella.

This princess was already betrothed to her cousin, the Prince of Asturias and heir to the Spanish throne. Worshipping Joseph and desperate for an heir to the Monarchy, Maria Theresia humbled herself, pleading with the King of Spain to annul that betrothal. Carlos' reply was floridly diplomatic, but negative nonetheless. Maria Luisa, still only thirteen, was packed off to Madrid, where she was later to be immortalized, with minimal flattery, by that court's great painter Francisco Goya. It was perhaps as well for Joseph that he did not succeed in marrying her: On her deathbed Maria Luisa was to confess that of the fourteen children she had borne, not one had been fathered by her husband.

With his preferred princess unavailable, Joseph announced he would leave the matter entirely to his mother: If she could find a suitable match for him, he said, he would do his dynastic duty. "And I would prefer a German Catholic princess," the Empress declared, "having for more than one reason too great a repugnance for a Protestant."

Maria Theresia was a deeply committed Catholic. In the absolutist tradition of the *ancien régime*, she regarded her throne as the direct gift of the Almighty, and the promotion of Catholicism as part of her duty as ruler. She allowed no confessional dissent among those who served her in any senior post: Protestants or Jews seeking advancement at court or in other prominent professions were simply obliged to convert to Catholicism. But within the bounds of the Catholic faith, she was by no means in thrall to Rome. Instead, she favoured a progressive or at least unorthodox trend within the Church, which had decided undertones of Protestantism: This was the Jansenist movement.

As a girl, she had absorbed the sterner and simpler practices of Jansenist Catholicism through her mother, a convert from Lutheranism. Franz Stephan, too, had grown up with Jansenist thinking at his French-speaking court in Lorraine, for though it had originated in the Netherlands, Jansenism was largely a French phenomenon. It was in effect a kind of Catholic puritanism or, as the Jansenists themselves called it, "rational Christianity," emphasizing bible reading, good works, and a resigned stoicism rather than traditional Catholic devotions, many of which were held to have degenerated among the common people to superstition and even idolatry. The Empress herself observed most of the old devotions, and her children had been taught to say the rosary and attend mass every morning, and to celebrate the traditional feast-days and festivals, but theirs was what was known as "enlightened Catholicism," which in Austria was Jansenist-dominated. Though always with recourse to prayer, they were to take practical action rather than waiting for miracles to occur; and there was to be no nonsense about witchcraft, which Maria Theresia considered an ignorant superstition—this at a time when, in neighbouring Germany and Switzerland, "witches" were still being burned at the stake.

In moral teaching, in any case, there was little difference between traditional and enlightened Catholics, or even Protestants, at least where the education of girls was concerned. "You know that we women are subject to our husbands," the Empress told her daughters, "that we owe them obedience, that our only end in everything must be our husband, to serve him, to be useful to him, and to make of him our best friend, while always regarding him as our master." Whichever princess she chose for her son would have been brought up with this view of her duties, but, as the Empress observed, "Among the Catholics in Germany, the choice is very slim and is limited to the princesses of Bavaria and Saxony. The first has considerable advantages in the hope of her succession to the allodial lands of Bavaria . . . but she has not yet had the smallpox."

In the end, the hope of increased territory won out over the fear of disease, and the princess chosen for Joseph, tempting Providence as it turned out, was the twenty-five-year-old Maria Josepha of the House of Wittelsbach. In a markedly ungallant letter to the father of his late first wife, Joseph described the lady who was shortly to become his second: "She has not had the smallpox, a disease of which I have a frightful memory; a short, fat figure; no youthfulness; a common face; on it, some little pimples with red spots; bad teeth."

The wedding took place in January 1765 at the newly rebuilt palace of Schönbrunn, just outside Vienna. Though it was an important day for the Habsburg dynasty, little public celebration was permitted, Isabella's death being still too recent. The festivities were confined to court circles, with Joseph's siblings, all of them musical, playing a prominent part. Two paintings survive, both by the court painter Johann Georg Weikert, illustrating the family's talents, as displayed at Schönbrunn on the day after the wedding. The first shows four of the bridegroom's sisters performing in the specially commissioned serenata *Il Parnaso Confuso* (Parnassus in Turmoil) by court composer Christoph Willibald Gluck, fifty years old and in the full flower of his genius, to a libretto by the elderly court poet Pietro Metastasio. This lovely and accessible comic opera was staged in a single act lasting more than two hours. Amalie took the starring role as the god Apollo, with Elisabeth, Josepha, and Carolina as three less energetic muses. Both Amalie and Elisabeth had inherited their mother's beautiful voice, but the work reveals Amalie's superior technique; it also suggests that Carolina had a mezzosoprano or even contralto voice, in contrast to her three soprano sisters. Court musicians completed the ensemble, with brother Leopold, eighteen years old, conducting the whole from his seat at the clavichord.

Court Treasurer Khevenhüller, not usually an enthusiast for Gluck's music, called the *Parnaso* "honestly and *sans flatterie* perhaps one of the best performances yet seen at a court." Afterwards the three youngest children made cameo appearances in a famous old ballet from the court of Louis XIV. Ferdinand and Antonia danced together as shepherd and shepherdess, improbably decked out in silks in the Bavarian colours of blue and white, with music-loving Ferdinand distinguishing himself "really marvellously, beyond expectations and to general admiration," and Maximilian, just turned eight and appropriately plump, appearing in the role of Cupid.

To his new bride, short, fat, and pimpled, Joseph behaved throughout the celebrations with civility but no warmth. And though Maria Josepha, with increasing desperation, did her utmost to please him, his feelings for her were not to change. "She never sees him at all," Marie Christine wrote to Albert a few months later. "He told me she sends her valet every morning to ask how he is. I told him in no uncertain terms that if I had the honour to be his wife and he treated me like that I would have already fled or hanged myself from one of the trees at Schönbrunn."

**Maria Theresia had known** for almost a year that Marie Christine and Albert were in love and hoping, if rather against hope, to marry. But Franz

Stephan's wishes on the matter were clear and, unusually, the Empress had not tried to impose her own: Marie Christine was expected to marry the Emperor's nephew, the Duke de Chablais. And in the spring of 1765, Chablais made a visit to Vienna "incognito," as the Empress confided to her close friend and former lady-in-waiting, the Countess Sophie Amalie von Enzenberg. In a classic instance of insult added to injury, Albert was obliged to vacate his apartment in the Hofburg to make way for his rival; he himself went to stay with his brother for the duration.

Chablais arrived, "a very well brought up and rational gentleman, with quite a good figure, somewhat like [Joseph]," as the heartily built Court Treasurer Khevenhüller recorded, "but his voice is somehow misplaced, as if coming out of a double pipe, however it mostly strikes a *falsetto* tone, arising from an internal defect of the throat, which he has inherited from his royal father, who is well known to have a very fat and, to use a good German expression, lumpy neck"—a prominent adam's apple, perhaps.

Marie Christine was unnerved by Chablais' visit. It suggested that her mother was still in two minds about whom she should marry. But more likely the Empress was concerned to keep up appearances until she could persuade the Emperor to accept Albert as a son-in-law. In a letter to Marie Christine of about this time, she took pains to emphasize her sincerity with her, conveniently omitting to mention her lack of it with regard to her husband.

"I need time," she wrote, "and I can take no steps before we return from Innsbruck"—which meant that Marie Christine would have to wait, giving no public hint of her feelings, until later in August, after her brother Leopold's wedding in the Tyrolean mountains. People had begun to talk, all the same, and the Empress urged her daughter to behave with more discretion, to "act naturally" and "play the role you have to play, and no little confidences or private chats, not with your sister [Marianna], not with anyone. Don't trust anyone with this, for the whole world is watching you."

Where Marianna was concerned, at least, it was almost certainly too late for such a warning. As the eldest in the family, she was long used to keeping the secrets of her younger siblings. As she herself said, "I was everyone's confidante." Franz Stephan kept making jokes and insinuations about Chablais, with Maria Theresia complaining about "the jealousy this provokes within the family"—a reference, perhaps, to Elisabeth, disappointed of her Polish crown. And in an unwitting echo of her late daughter-in-law, Isabella, she urged Marie Christine to "manipulate your father's tenderness by a thousand attentions, and don't give him any grounds for suspecting you with my protégé, because he notices everything."

The Empress had by now given the lovers permission to write and send flowers to each other, to be partners at evenings of cards at court, and even to meet in each other's apartments. It is more than likely that the observant Franz Stephan, along with everyone else at court and in the town, was well aware of the undeclared romance. What he apparently did not suspect was his wife's determination to bring about a marriage between the two. But if she had had any doubts at all, the pitiable situation of Joseph's unloved wife may have settled the matter for her: Three months after that wedding, Maria Josepha's misery was only too apparent, with the sole ray of light in her otherwise friendless life the kind attention of Franz Stephan. As she wrote, perhaps naively, to her sister, the Emperor regarded her "not only as a daughter-in-law, but as a true friend."

As for Marie Christine having to wait until after Leopold's wedding, there would simply be no time to arrange everything before then. Once Franz Stephan had come around to the idea, Albert would require a formal position, the couple would need some kind of establishment, the wedding itself would take time to prepare, and the Empress, as always, would be wanting to control every detail.

**Leopold's bride, whom** as yet he had not met, was the Infanta Maria Luisa, daughter of the King of Spain. At nineteen and a half, she was a year or two his senior. The wedding had been fixed for the fifth of August 1765 and, to the dismay of the great and good in Vienna, the Empress had decided it would take place in Innsbruck, 250 miles away. Khevenhüller's diary contains a little rant about "this unpleasant journey," a round-trip of almost a week by stately carriage, with the Court Treasurer's annoyance overcoming his usual deference toward the Empress: "No one can understand why this woman, against the wishes and advice of the Emperor and ministers and to her own very considerable discomfort, wants to undertake this lengthy journey," and he marked down indignantly all the other places that would have been closer or easier or cheaper.

Court rumour had it that the Empress wanted to revisit the convent in Hall, a little town near Innsbruck, with a view to retiring to a holy life there "in case anything human were to befall the Emperor," as Khevenhüller's picturesque phrase had it. Franz Stephan, still in apparently robust health for his fifty-six years, personally found Innsbruck oppressive, encircled as it was by high mountains. There was no doubt also a strategic element in Maria Theresia's decision: Innsbruck had once been an important centre of Habsburg power, but now, for a hundred years exactly, there had been no prince of the family resident there. A loud and lengthy sojourn in this mountain city, far to the southwest and usefully close to Italy, could only emphasize the family's strength and further the Empress' larger scheme of gathering the disparate structures of the Monarchy into a modernized and centralized whole.

The support of the common people for this ongoing project was to be encouraged by civic improvements in time for the wedding: All the streets and little alleys were to be cleaned and newly cobbled, street lighting improved, and the town's stinky moat drained, but, as the Empress instructed her friend, the Countess Enzenberg, who was the wife of the local Governor, "I don't want our arrival to raise the cost of everyday things, and your husband should arrange some little extras for the town, for the better off and others, so that they're left with an agreeable memory of their masters' visit." None of it, in any case, made any difference to Khevenhüller, whose grumblings continued in his formal despatches—"You can read all about it there," he concluded.

As was usual during the summer months, the whole imperial family had been staying at the palace of Schönbrunn, but in early July they returned to Vienna to allow Leopold to make his farewells to the imperial city and its people. Joseph's wife had remained at Schönbrunn, feeling unwell or, as the Empress confided to the Countess Lerchenfeld, with any luck, pregnant:

> *Thank God we have every reason to hope she won't come with us. For the past fortnight she's been saying she's ill, and for the past week she's been late with a certain something. . . . It would be another miracle on the part of the good Lord, and we need one, for really my son is to be pitied; she's neither pretty nor agreeable, but at least she'll give us an heir, provided it's a prince.*

Joseph did at least drive back from Vienna to have supper with his wife, though "not so much of his own volition, rather on his mother's orders." He returned to the city directly afterwards.

At half past four the next morning, following a public mass at St Stephen's Cathedral, and a breakfast of hot boiled trout "which the Emperor ate with considerable relish," the party set off, planning to cover the first fifty miles before the day was out. It was a lengthy caravan of princely carriages and service wagons, but the imperial family itself was rather reduced: just the Emperor and Empress with their four eldest children, Marianna, Joseph, Marie Christine, and, naturally, the bridegroom Leopold. The deliciously beautiful Princess von Auersperg went along, too, officially as a lady-in-waiting to the Empress and unofficially as the Emperor's long-standing mistress. And also of the party was Prince Albert, at Maria Theresia's insistence. He had not wanted to go, having no formal function and not being a family member, but his younger brother, Clemens, now bishop of Regensburg, was to serve as the officiating priest, and the Empress regarded this as excuse enough for Albert's presence. The Duke de Chablais was also to be there, and she may have wanted Franz Stephan to see the two compared at close quarters: Handsome Albert, witty and friendly, already a general favourite, would be certain to have the advantage.

Everyone else had been left behind at Schönbrunn with Joseph's woeful wife, and if the sisters were disappointed, the two youngest boys were not: Ferdinand and Maximilian had as yet little interest in the comedy and drama of weddings, though eleven-year-old Ferdinand had been betrothed for six years already to the Italian Duchess Beatrice d'Este, an only child and sole heiress to her ancestors' valuable territories in Lombardy. From Milan, Beatrice had been penning anxious letters to the Empress to ask how much her future husband was likely to grow: Four years her junior, Ferdinand was still much shorter than the large-featured fifteen-year-old Duchess herself. Maria Theresia, knowing that "this point will be of some interest to you," had replied reassuringly that he had "grown a great deal this year."

THE CARAVAN DID NOT TAKE the most direct route southwest, via Linz and Salzburg, to Innsbruck. An imperial wedding and a court *en passage* provided too rich an opportunity to display the power and cohesion of the Habsburg dynasty in other, less visited cities. So they drove far to the south, through Graz and Klagenfurt, stopping at the castles of local nobles, appearing in public at religious services and hunting parties and illuminated festivities in the towns. As they moved into the mountain regions, labouring up the indifferent roads, the hot July weather gave way to rain and snow; inside the heavy carriages, at once stuffy and drafty, the squeezed and perspiring passengers turned shivery and frozen-footed. For the bridegroom himself, ill with a nasty gastric problem, the journey was a torment.

On the sixth day after their departure from Vienna, just as the sun was sinking, they pulled into Klagenfurt, since late medieval times the principal town of the province of Carinthia. They were to stay at the elegant baroque palace of Count Franz Xaver von Orsini-Rosenberg, built a hundred years before in the "new" town square. Rosenberg, a confirmed bachelor in his early forties, was a scion of the Bohemian grand nobility, a former diplomat, and a man of the highest abilities. The Empress trusted him absolutely, and Leopold had expressly asked that he be appointed senior advisor to his own new court in Tuscany: Rosenberg was to prove his remarkable talents by serving them both at the same time, and both of them capably and honestly. He was not at home for this visit of the imperial family; a facilitator of Leopold's marriage with Maria Luisa, he was at that moment escorting the bride from Spain, via a rough sea voyage to Genoa and a jolting coach ride across the Brenner Pass and through the Alps, to Innsbruck.

The following morning, after mass, the Empress and her daughters paid a visit to the local convent of the Sisters of St Elisabeth, a nursing order caring for the city's poor. They found the convent in a sad state, with only eleven nuns living there, and the hospital building itself in disrepair. Visiting convents, in Vienna and elsewhere, was a regular duty for all the women of the imperial family, and no one but Marianna seems to have found this one to be of any particular interest. She admired the sisters' useful work, and her approachability encouraged the Mother Superior to appeal to her for help. The dilapidated hospital had only nine beds; a new building was desperately needed. Marianna relayed the appeal to her mother, and that very evening, the Empress despatched one hundred gold ducats to the convent.

Though a handsome sum, this was by no means enough to replace or even properly repair the hospital; it was rather an ordinary charitable gift intended to repay some debts and keep things going much as they had been. It was Marianna herself who was to provide continuing support for the Sisters of St Elisabeth, modest at first but gradually more substantial until, in time, their work would form the cornerstone of her life.

ON A MID-JULY afternoon in 1765, ten days after their departure from Vienna, the imperial party was formally welcomed to the city of Innsbruck beneath a nascent triumphal arch, erected in haste out of wood and linen. Maria Theresia was evidently tired from the travelling and exasperated with all the formalities; she turned away "with much impatience" to go to her evening meal, fortunately nothing more elaborate than a light supper, just with those closest to her, plus Albert and his brother, "who were regarded as part of the family."

Before and after the wedding there were to be days and weeks of festivities, from most of which Leopold absented himself. Still far from well, he had retreated to his apartments in the palace. Good news reaching him about his bride may have made him feel a little better: Maria Luisa arrived in Innsbruck three days before the wedding and, to the happy surprise of the whole court, "since we had heard this princess was ugly and red-haired and badly brought up," she turned out to be a vivacious and charming blue-eyed blonde. If her pretty face looked familiar to Leopold already, he would not have been much surprised, since her mother and his own were first cousins. Khevenhüller thought she looked just like Joseph's late wife, Isabella, even in her way of walking—but then, they had been first cousins, too.

On the wedding-day itself or, as the Court Treasurer described it, "the designated day for the Act of Copulation," the bridegroom's family were unexpectedly slow getting dressed in their gala uniforms and gowns, so that the bride was left waiting outside the Cathedral of St Jacob. She descended from her carriage only when Leopold arrived, and the pair walked up the aisle together, his lanky, slightly stooping form and serious demeanour quite at odds with her easy charm and the exuberant baroque interior of the cathedral itself. A local priest rather dampened the proceedings by giving a sermon on the likelihood of unexpected death for all the imperfect Christians of the attendant congregation—a prescient theme, as it turned out. But the stars were otherwise well aligned; Leopold and Maria Luisa were to have a long and happy and very fruitful marriage, producing sixteen children in twenty-one years, though in this they made something of a late start: Leopold's gastric illness had not by any means run its course, so that on the Act of Copulation day itself and for some time afterwards, he and his new wife were obliged to sleep in separate rooms.

· · ·

FOR SEVERAL FURTHER WEEKS after the wedding, the imperial court, already a month absent from Vienna, was to remain in Innsbruck. While Leopold languished in his sickbed, and Joseph, who loathed any kind of ceremony, did his best to avoid any engagements at all, the rest of the family was kept busy with the various pleasures and duties afforded or required of them. Maria Theresia took the opportunity to spend some time privately with Madame Enzenberg, while Marianna and Marie Christine paid dutiful visits to local convents and churches. Marie Christine was maintaining a careful decorum whenever Prince Albert was nearby, which was often, he and his brother dining regularly with the imperial family. Meanwhile, his rival, Chablais, was being distracted by the Court Treasurer's elder son, Karl, invited expressly for the purpose: Young Khevenhüller had been instructed to spend all unscheduled hours showing the Duke the sights of Innsbruck. What these might have been, over a spell of six weeks in a town of three thousand people, is perhaps best left to the imagination, but "from excess of goodness," or from excess of determination to keep Chablais away from Marie Christine, the Empress had given Karl 1,000 ducats to make sure the Duke enjoyed them.

There was a theatre, of course, performing ballets and plays new and old, with the enthusiastic Emperor in frequent attendance, and on the eighteenth of August he was there again in the evening to see one of each. He had been feeling a little unwell during the day but, fortified with anti-flatulence drops, he had gone to see the new ballet, *Iphigenie*, by Florian Gassmann, court ballet composer in Vienna and teacher of a very young Antonio Salieri, and Carlo Goldoni's play *Il Tutore*, already thirteen years past its first performance. Neither one appealed to Franz Stephan, who spent most of his time examining the ladies in the opposite boxes through his opera glasses.

At half past nine he returned to the palace to take supper with the Empress. Stepping up to the great doors, he suddenly collapsed. Servants carried him inside and laid him on a camp-bed belonging to one of them; they called Joseph, who rushed to his father, cradling him in his arms as they opened a vein to try to relieve his blood pressure, but the Emperor was dead within minutes.

From her own apartments, Maria Theresia now sent to tell her husband she was ready for supper. A servant returned to say the Emperor had been taken ill and would not be joining her that evening; no one dared tell her he had died. But she knew he had not been feeling well even before he set out for the theatre, and she became suspicious; she tried to go to him; she was stopped, and had to push her way "violently" out. She actually walked, in fact ran, past her husband's body as it lay on the little bed, concealed behind a pair of nervous courtiers. It seems those present tried to persuade her to return to her own apartments; she refused, and as she had rushed forcefully out, so now she was brought "almost violently" back in. There, gently, Joseph told her what had happened.

It had been a stroke. Maria Theresia retreated to her bedchamber. No one was allowed in. Through the night she remained alone, but toward morning a chambermaid and one other trusted servant were permitted to enter the room. Though four of her children were waiting, anxious and weeping, outside her doors, she refused to see any of them.

When she did emerge, she began railing against herself for allowing the Emperor's death to happen: She should never have left her physician behind in Vienna, it was only because of Joseph's wife; she should have insisted Franz Stephan be bled before going to the theatre, she had known he was not well; she should never have come to Innsbruck in the first place. Khevenhüller tried to persuade her that the Emperor's death could not have been prevented, that it was the will of God, but she would not be consoled.

For three days, in the black-draped ballroom of Innsbruck's royal palace, Franz Stephan lay in state, encircled by priests reciting continuous masses. At the end of the third day the coffin was carried to a boat on the Inn River, to sail downstream to the Danube and on to Vienna. On the last evening of

August, after a grand and sombre Requiem mass, Franz Stephan was laid to rest in the dynasty's vaulted crypt of the Capuchin Friars.

Maria Theresia herself was not present; she had remained in Innsbruck to be with Leopold, who was still unwell, and she had given orders that none of the women or children of the imperial family were to attend—a practice not uncommon at the time. Quite forgotten, but not least affected among them was Joseph's wife, Maria Josepha. In the seven sad months since her marriage, Franz Stephan had been her only friend. His death had made her an empress, but that elevation was as nothing to her compared with his loss. "How can I accept your compliments on this?" she wrote to her sister. "It has come at too high a price. I would a hundred times rather have died Queen of the Romans than survive such an honourable father who showered such kindness on me. . . . I loved him like my own father."

THOUGH FRANZ STEPHAN'S death had been unexpected, it had not found him unprepared. More than a decade earlier, with his three youngest yet to be born, he had composed a document of advice for his children in their spiritual and temporal life. Writing in fluent but eccentrically, almost phonetically spelled, French, with a personal copy made for each of them in his own dreadful handwriting, he had urged them to view the salvation of their souls as the ultimate purpose of their lives. He advised them to start every day with a prayer and end it with an examination of conscience, and encouraged them to observe the traditional forms of Catholic worship. Religious processions and other extravagances, however, they were to understand as masquerades—as he said, like coronations. A kindly man himself, known for his easy manners with his ministers and servants and his warmth toward his children, Franz Stephan emphasized the need for *douceur*, gentleness or kindness, here perhaps graciousness: It was an attribute of God, he said, and should be an attribute of every ruler and every husband—advice that Leopold and Ferdinand were to take to heart, though Joseph, emphatically, was not. And all the children were to remember that, despite their own exalted worldly rank, all souls were equal in the sight of God.

So far, so acceptable to Franz Stephan's grieving widow. But he had also left a will, and this was less to her liking. At first no one had been able to find it, but after a good deal of searching, Joseph had discovered it inside an old, rusty-locked cabinet, sealed in a red leather case. It was dated 1751, and it bequeathed the bulk of the late Emperor's vast personal fortune, some 25 million gulden, to the eldest of his sons who should be alive at the time of his death—in other words, to Joseph himself.

Maria Theresia was disagreeably surprised by her own modest placing among the beneficiaries. She was always in need of ready money to maintain her old-fashioned system of court patronage, preferring this to the emerging practice, championed by her late husband, of fixed salaries for senior appointees. In due course Joseph would follow his father's example, as part of his effort to create within the Monarchy a professional bureaucracy, taking no account of "age, ancestors, connections, friendships, sexual morals or bigotry." In his immediate response to the will, however, he revealed himself to be a very different man, at least where money was concerned. Where Franz Stephan had made clever use of state funds to increase his own private fortune, Joseph now did precisely the opposite, announcing that everything he had personally inherited was to be used to pay off part of the enormous state debt, some 300 million gulden borrowed at high interest, that had been incurred during the Seven Years' War.

Selflessness beyond the call of duty this may have been, but Joseph did not limit it to himself. Arguing that when the will was made, Franz Stephan had been Grand Duke of Tuscany, he insisted that 2 million gulden that Leopold had received, as the current Grand Duke, in fact belonged to himself as well. The resulting furore took months to resolve and was a foretaste of trouble to come, with Joseph seeking to contain Leopold's independence and Leopold nursing a private but growing animosity toward his brother.

As for Maria Theresia, disappointment over the will proved the least of her griefs. Her husband's death had changed everything. As she herself, inconsolable, declared, "Even the sun seems black to me." She was now the Empress Widow, and for the rest of her life, her appearance and habits were to reflect this sad new reality. One of Maria Theresia's first acts was to call for her chambermaid and to have her cut off her hair. She then donned a black widow's bonnet and, as the maid's daughter recorded, "she put aside all her colourful finery and all her jewellery, shared her gowns out among her women, had her bedchamber draped with grey silk and grey curtains hung in her lonely rooms, and in her manner, too, she showed that life and the world had lost its appeal for her."

The imperial family and indeed the whole Monarchy entered a period of mourning that was expected to last till the end of the following year. During those sixteen months there were to be no balls given, no public theatre, and no court entertainments. A new opera, *La corona*, that court composer Gluck had written for the sisters to sing on their father's name day, with soprano Amalie in the virtuoso role of the huntress Atalanta, was simply cancelled; it was not to see the light of day for more than two hundred years. To add to the general gloom, the Empress even forbade the women of the city to wear rouge, and released a flock of cawing church commissioners to enforce the prohibition.

Though Joseph was now Holy Roman Emperor, he was always to prioritize the affairs of his family's Habsburg Monarchy over those of the Empire. In Tuscany, eighteen-year-old Leopold was about to embark on the reforms that would make him famous as one of the wisest and most enlightened princes in Europe. Their two younger brothers would in time acquire territories of their own to govern, and as for their sisters, their role remained straightforward and not negotiable: to marry as instructed and produce the next generation of male rulers.

## III

# 1765-1766

In which two new matches are considered,
and the Empress kills several birds
with one Hungarian stone.

Precisely one month before Franz Stephan's death in Innsbruck, another ruler on another family wedding visit had met his own end, suddenly, from smallpox. He was Don Felipe, Duke of the Bourbon Duchy of Parma in northern Italy, a younger brother of King Carlos of Spain and father of Joseph's first wife, Isabella—it was to him that Joseph had complained of his pimply second bride.

Felipe had left behind him a fourteen-year-old son, Ferdinando, already an Infante of Spain, who now became Duke of Parma, together with the nearby city of Piacenza and the little Duchy of Guastalla. Parma had once belonged to the Habsburgs, if only for a short time, but since 1748 it had been ruled, in name at least, by the Spanish crown.

Along with his coronet, Don Ferdinando had inherited a formidable First Minister in the person of Guillaume Du Tillot, and it was Du Tillot himself who had long held the real reins of power in Parma. He was naturally concerned that this situation should not change, and to this end had persuaded King Carlos in Madrid to declare his young nephew already of age to rule, so that no regent would be imposed to dilute his own power as First

Minister. Maria Theresia had encouraged this, advising the boy to "hold fast to the people employed by your dear late father, especially that incomparable man, the faithful Tillot," but as Don Ferdinando was later to complain to her, "I was a child, he knew perfectly well he would make of me whatever he wanted."

A ruler come of age must have an heir; it was clear that Don Ferdinando must marry. Through his Spanish father and his French mother, he was already a Bourbon twice over; the diplomatic *renversement des alliances* dictated, in consequence, that his wife should be a Habsburg. This suited the Empress very well. Parma, the only Bourbon court in northern Italy, was an important link in the chain of Austrian-French alliances. Isabella's death had broken this link; the sooner it was replaced, the better. Du Tillot himself was anxious that the bride, whoever she might be, should bring a substantial dowry with her, since Parma's public finances were in a parlous state.

The Empress wrote to Don Ferdinando's French grandfather, Louis XV, and summoned Chancellor von Kaunitz to consider the possibilities. Marianna, in indifferent health, was quickly exempted. Marie Christine was unofficially committed, whether to Chablais or to Albert; Elisabeth was too much older than the Duke. Nineteen-year-old Amalie, however, was deemed suitable, as in due course, to her surprise and dismay, she would discover.

THE NEXT MATCH to be considered, that of Marie Christine and Albert, had nothing to do with the *renversement* at all, though Franz Stephan would not have approved it for all that. At court, though the romance was widely rumoured, a marriage had been thought unlikely, with uncharitable tongues sniggering at "the subsidized prince," third surviving son of an ousted king, living on a limited allowance and the charity of Maria Theresia. But Albert was the Empress' first cousin (once removed), and a general family favourite, and Marie Christine loved him. This was enough for Maria Theresia. By the autumn of 1765 "the subsidized prince" from Saxony found himself possessor of the Silesian Duchy of Teschen, once Franz Stephan's, and from him inherited by a now despoiled Joseph. The chastened Hofburg courtiers adjusted their bows accordingly for the newly made Duke of Sachsen-Teschen.

In November of the same year, the Empress finally gave her permission for Marie Christine and Albert to marry, surprising even Joseph, who "would not have suspected it myself a week ago." He was delegated to convey the happy news to Albert. "For a long time he would not believe I was speaking seriously to him," Joseph wrote to Leopold in Florence, "but once convinced of it, I leave you to judge his expression, seeing his hopes crowned after six years of constant passion. . . . The joy of the two parties has been inexpressible."

Joseph was not usually known for his generosity, and Khevenhüller was convinced he had resisted the transfer of his Duchy of Teschen to Albert, but his satisfaction about the marriage itself was genuine. As he told Leopold, the match would be to his own advantage, providing him with "good company for my whole life; since I am unhappily without resources in my own house, this new family will be a great comfort to me, and I shall spend my moments of recreation there. I love the mistress and am a friend of the master of the house." "Good company" from his own wife Joseph had long ceased to hope for: After ten months of marriage, as he told his brother, "I live almost as a bachelor, seeing my wife only at table and touching her only in bed."

By February 1766, the engagement news was an open secret, and Albert had moved to the little Hungarian capital of Pressburg, fifty miles upriver east of Vienna, where he had just been appointed governor or *locum tenens* of the Kingdom. The position had been being informally reserved for the Empress' youngest son, but with Maximilian still only nine years old, the issue was not pressing; in due course it was intended that Marie Christine and Albert together would succeed Franz Stephan's brother Karl in Brussels, as joint governors of the Austrian Netherlands.

Albert had been rather taken aback by the Hungarian appointment, having, in his own words, "studied nothing but warfare until that point, and having only the weakest and most superficial notions of everything to do with matters of government, and none at all about the law, and above all, I knew nothing about Hungary . . . and as for Latin [the official language], I had only studied the syntax and could not speak it at all. . . . But it would have been against all my principles just to play a ceremonial role, and as the Empress also wanted me to carry out all the functions of the position zealously, I worked even harder and applied myself all the more to acquire the necessary understanding of things."

The appointment was typical of a time when birth or favour could place an inexperienced or incompetent man in a position of power. But it was also typical of Albert's own mind and character, of his determination and pragmatic sense of responsibility, that he should buckle down now, at the age of twenty-eight, to the hard work of making a good ruler of himself. It suited Maria Theresia to have him in the governor's position: For some time she had been looking to tilt the levers of control away from the Hungarians themselves. She thought highly of Albert, indeed really loved him, but she was not above misleading him now, and he did not perceive the truth: that she did not want him to "carry out all the functions" of his office, or indeed any of the important ones. While he earnestly set to preparing himself for the business of government, she kept real power in her own hands, appointing her own minister plenipotentiary, and positioning Albert for a largely ceremonial role. It was "against all [his] principles," but it was to be his fate.

At the time of Albert's appointment in 1766, the Kingdom of Hungary included a large part of Romania and parts of Serbia and Croatia—almost as much territory as all the rest of Maria Theresia's hereditary lands together. Its total population of some six million, less than half of it ethnic Magyar, was mostly rural, with only about twenty thousand in the little capital of Pressburg, far to the west. Such modest urban centres as existed were inhabited largely by skilled immigrants from "Swabia" or traders from "Greece"—blanket terms used by the Hungarians for any German or vaguely Balkan region. The Magyars themselves remained mainly in the central areas, though the nobles among them, particularly those of considerable wealth, were generally to be found in Pressburg or Vienna. As an old saying went, not all the Magyars were noble, but all the nobles were Magyar.

Unlike the Habsburgs' other hereditary or "crown" lands, Hungary possessed a constitution of its own, an anthology of laws and customs surviving from medieval times which overwhelmingly favoured the tiny nobility, some 5 per cent of the population, over the small bourgeoisie and the large, impoverished peasantry. In the Hungarian Diet, or parliament, the greatest magnates wielded almost complete control, with their first advantage a total exemption from taxes.

Maria Theresia had a soft spot for the Hungarians, as well she might. In 1741, in the dark early days of her reign, with the combined armies of Prussia, France, and Bavaria arrayed in the field against her, all determined to oust her, a mere woman, from her father's throne, the twenty-four-year-old Queen of Hungary had made a desperate appeal to her noble subjects in the ancient castle of Pressburg. Legend has it that, holding up the six-month-old Joseph—vitally, a male heir after the birth of three daughters—she had implored them for military help in a powerful and moving Latin oration accented with eloquent tears. In fact, she had not had Joseph with her—he had been brought into the Diet some days later—but imaginations had been stirred, and the image of the beautiful young Queen, babe in arms, beseeching the chivalrous, mustachioed Magyars in their romantic traditional dress, proved too potent to be abandoned, begetting countless politically useful pictures and stories. As the Empress now declared to Albert, "I am a good Hungarian; my heart is full of gratitude for this nation."

But in the years following her dramatic appeal in Pressburg, despite her general efforts toward reform throughout the Monarchy, living conditions for the overwhelming majority of her Hungarian subjects had only gone from bad to worse. In 1764, the peasants had broken out in protest against their forced service in border militias and the casual brutality of their overlords. In an early show of organized civil disobedience, whole villages had refused to obey the local authorities and had deserted their hovels to live in the forests. A group of them had even walked to Vienna to present their grievances in person to their queen.

Generations behind other European regions in agriculture and commerce, with transport interrupted by often impassable roads and the spread of technical knowledge hindered by a lack of schools, Hungary was also bedevilled by an absentee landowning class who had long ago converted to Catholicism, learned to speak German, and largely decamped to the Habsburgs' entertaining and opportunity-laden courts, taking with them huge proportions of the Kingdom's wealth, though Chancellor von Kaunitz, himself something of a Bohemian *arriviste*, felt able to condescend to them all the same, complaining that "the Hungarians weren't as distinguished as they should be."

Maria Theresia had arguably aggravated the absentee situation by binding the Magyar nobles ever more closely to her, installing those from the grandest families in high diplomatic and military posts and even, on occasion, paying their debts. But those of her Hungarian subjects who lived beyond court patronage, struggling to develop small industries or improve their farms, were hampered by unbalanced trade tariffs which worked very much against them: Goods coming into Hungary from elsewhere in the Monarchy were tax-free, while anything moving in the other direction was subject to high duties. And the burden of ordinary taxes was still being carried by the peasants on their meagre subsistence farms.

Maria Theresia had now been on the throne for almost twenty-five years, fifteen of them harsh years of war. She had learned that a state organized by uneven regional authorities, as hers had been, would always be hard pressed to defend itself: Modernization, which in her view entailed a centralized administration, was the clear path forward. But the Hungarians' peculiar constitution had prevented this within their country. Austrian and Czech nobles, for instance, had already surrendered their tax exemptions and implemented reforms in education, agriculture, and religious and legal practices, but the Diet of Magyar nobles had refused to do the same, and Maria Theresia had had no legal power to force them. In the same year, she had decided to circumvent the problem by simply refusing to convoke the Diet, instead sending some ten thousand direct instructions every year to her Hungarian lieutenants. The Hungarian nobles' last avenue of protest would once have been their Palatine or *Nádor*, a man traditionally elected by themselves to represent their concerns to the sovereign, but Maria Theresia had abolished the position, replacing it with a governorship, to be filled by a person of her own choosing—namely, Albert.

Bereft of their Diet, the Magyar nobles could cling at least to their tax exemptions, observing from their palaces in the capitals as reforms in their homelands were carried through at the direction of Vienna. They made no very loud protest. Their queen had judged shrewdly: As expected, personal advantage had proved more important to them than constitutional principle.

It was a clever decision to appoint Albert governor of Hungary. At a stroke, Maria Theresia had settled his uncertain status at court, and ensured that her favourite daughter, once married, would still be living within easy travelling distance. Pressburg was only fifty miles upstream on the Danube River, and the Empress, though not in good health, was to make the journey frequently, at times simply to pass a few hours in Marie Christine's company. The couple were also to spend a great deal of time, including much of every winter season, in Vienna, in the newly refurbished little baroque Palais Tarouca; in due course this would house the great art collection that the two were to build together. If, on the other hand, they preferred to stay at the Hofburg nearby, they were to find Maria Theresia's own apartments at their disposal—these she now vacated especially for them.

AT TWENTY-THREE, MARIE CHRISTINE felt as assured as any mortal could be that a lifetime of happiness lay before her. For twenty-seven-year-old Marianna, too, a grand position seemed in store, as abbess of the Theresian Foundation for noble ladies in Prague. This was a *Damenstift*, the most prestigious religious institution of its kind in the Monarchy: No woman could enter it as a nun or lay resident unless all sixteen of her great-great-grandparents had been nobles—in other words, unless she belonged to one of the oldest established families. Its abbess even had the right to crown the queen of Bohemia, a title that Maria Theresia herself possessed.

Though the convent had been founded in 1755, it had as yet had no abbess at all. The Empress had taken enormous care with its constitution, overseeing every article herself, intending it to serve as a model for other similar foundations. But it was not Marianna whom she had originally ordained to be its first abbess. Years before, from a castle in Bohemia, she had written home to Vienna, to the then twelve-year-old Marie Christine: "I have had to promise Prague a daughter and as they have asked me for one who is not a child, this can only fall on you. Marianna, the eldest of all, I cannot give; Elisabeth is still a child [in fact only one year younger than Marie Christine], so I have promised you; I hope you will not deny me this." But for Marie Christine, there was now Albert, "and Marianna should be happy with the position," she told him, a little tartly, in January 1766, "since all her life she's enjoyed giving orders and there she'll have plenty of opportunity." All the same, she added, "I think there'll be more objections and questions." The Empress was still "up to her ears in conversation with Marianna over this Prague business." Albert teased her about swapping places with her sister, saying he would rather like to see Marie Christine herself dressed as a nun, an idea the lady found "somewhat extraordinary for a lover"; she suggested he turn his mind to learning Hungarian instead.

There was in fact no question of Marianna becoming a nun; indeed, the Empress regarded the idea of celibate life with distaste. Though some of the girls and women entering the Prague *Damenstift* took holy orders, others led bright secular lives, and they could marry or simply leave if they so wished. As abbess, Marianna would effectively be holding court in Prague, doubly so as the primary representative of Habsburg power in Bohemia.

And though Albert's tone here was teasing, he was actually feeling quite insecure about Marie Christine, as other letters of this time show. The very next day, he received news of the death of a close friend, and Marie Christine's condolences released a flood of petulant letters from him, questioning her love. "I'm very sad to hear you say he was the only real friend you had in this country," she had written. "Could you have any friend more sincerely and truly attached to you than I am?" Albert took strong exception to her use of the word "friend," accusing her repeatedly of having no stronger feelings toward him. She defended herself spiritedly: The name of "friend" did not imply "a kind of distancing"; rather, "it's to that very name that I aspire the most, because the passion of love passes and if our union is not based on friendship the tenderness between us will soon be extinguished. Note that I'm only talking about you"—a reference to Albert's more overtly sexual feelings, which she admitted she shared, while remaining "sufficiently mistress of myself to avoid expressing more to you than it suits me to do." If she had disappointed him in that respect, he had offended her, too, as her little postscript, a sardonic repetition of her mother's advice, now revealed: "Pardon me if I've chosen you for my best friend and hope you think the same about me. Of course for yourself I reserve as well the quality of lord and master. Obedience is no trouble to me where people I love and esteem are concerned. So that's what I think. Condemn me if you can, or consider for a moment which of us loves more genuinely."

Albert might have let the matter rest there, had not a new challenge been presented to both of them just two days later. For several months already, Marianna had been in markedly low spirits and rather peevish. Her mother had expected her to be delighted with the handsomely remunerated *Damenstift* appointment, and indeed, Marianna had begun to do the administrative work belonging to it. But she was making no plans to leave Vienna. It appeared she did not want to go to Prague, "and I do not think I can compel her on this," the Empress confided to Madame Enzenberg. At length Maria Theresia had insisted on knowing the cause of Marianna's malaise, and had found, "to her great surprise," as Marie Christine told Albert, "that not only is she not content with her situation, she is complaining about it with astonishing bitterness, even viciousness." Marianna, it transpired, wanted an establishment like her sister's, "but since the Empress cannot provide two of that kind, she has offered me to switch places with Marianna, to calm her down and make her content. Knowing how I feel, you can judge what an effort it cost me—I told the Empress I was obliged to obey her in all things but that I couldn't consent to anything without you and I didn't think you would want to do that. She said she knew you were affectionately attached to her and you wouldn't refuse her if she asked you to take one daughter instead of another, especially one who wanted it so much. . . . She ordered me to write to you and ask what you decide. I made so bold as to say you could only be happy with me and I said if you accept this switch I won't oppose it because if you don't prefer me to all others then you don't deserve me. So that's how it stands. Think about it and make your decision. You have three days. My happiness now rests in your hands."

Did the Empress really expect Albert, after loving Marie Christine for years, to set aside his engagement to her and marry Marianna instead? The betrothal had not yet been formally signed and sealed, but it was widely known, and Albert had already been appointed governor in Pressburg. If it was a test of the couple's love, it was late and surely unnecessary, and if a test of their obedience, it was markedly cruel. Marie Christine's response had revealed her strong sense of self. She knew her duty, she knew her own feelings, and she also knew her own worth. She was almost sure Albert would refuse, though "I remember," she told him, "you said recently you found Marianna so beautiful and talented and agreeable that perhaps the sacrifice will not be so great."

And what of Marianna herself? By her own declaration, she was in love with another man. Was she so jealous that she wanted to destroy her sister's happiness without achieving her own? It is more likely that, in the fury of a woman scorned, she wanted to spite her "friend" for not marrying her himself. Though she had loved him for six years, it was only in recent months that she had become so sullen and irritable. Perhaps, after so long, he had abandoned hope and married someone else. Perhaps he had even been given a hint to do so by the Empress, who was now seeking to make amends to Marianna, or at least to pretend she had tried.

For Albert, of course, refused at once. And although "she saw you were very angry with her," the Empress praised him for it, reducing Marie Christine almost to tears by telling her that, after all, her love for Albert must be her strongest feeling in life, with her love for her mother taking "only second place in my heart. You're right not to swap your Mimi," Marie Christine told him, "because there's no one in the world who would love you as she does and the good Lord has already made it clear we are destined for each other."

Marie Christine remained in her apartments that evening, in order to avoid attending a dinner hosted by Marianna. But on a cold Lenten Sunday late in February 1766, after a service in the Church of St Augustine, she joined the rest of the family and all the courtiers as they trooped back into the Hall of Mirrors at the Hofburg, where the Empress installed her eldest daughter as the first abbess of the *Theresienstift* in Prague.

The letters between Pressburg and Vienna continued, twice a day, morning and evening, with Albert still a little insecure, Marie Christine's more loving tone notwithstanding. He was now afraid, on no evidence whatsoever, that her mother had simply commanded her to love him. The Empress was certainly following the courtship closely, with every letter from either party appropriated for her own perusal. "Remember," Marie Christine wrote, "if you want to send something for my eyes only, it needs to be on a separate sheet"—to be delivered in secret by a recompensed courier. Joseph was also trying to read at least Albert's letters, pressing his sister for them at table and even at late hours in her apartments. Mostly she rebuffed him, but one she did let him read, "and he let his soup go cold while he almost devoured the whole four pages, then he only said his style as a husband had been different"—evidently he was thinking of his late wife, Isabella, rather than his living wife, Maria Josepha.

That unhappy lady, "the other Empress," as she was referred to, had been making no progress in Joseph's, or indeed anyone else's, affections. "It's true she's insufferable," Marie Christine wrote now. She had gamely allowed Elisabeth to sneak away early from after-dinner cards, and had found herself trapped with her tiresome sister-in-law out of politeness until half past eleven—"She bored me to death." She was repaid only by the grateful young Empress insisting on seeing her again the next day. "I'm really quite upset about it," she wrote, though she was kind enough to accompany Maria Josepha again on other occasions when Elisabeth, and Marianna, too, had made themselves scarce.

IN HER EAGERNESS to see her "dear Mimi" happily settled, Maria Theresia had crossed two important boundaries, ignoring the demands of her new diplomatic alliance with the Bourbons and playing a deceitful game, over a period of years, behind her own husband's back. With the marriage arranged, she now stepped quickly across yet another, interrupting the court's period of deep mourning for Franz Stephan so that the couple might marry a full eight months before its official end. This meant recalling the Imperial Council, suspended after the events in Innsbruck, and it caused quite a scandal, as Khevenhüller noted in his diary, "since *d'une certain façon* it offended the memory of the late Emperor," and the whole story was printed "in our German and French newspapers and [Vienna's] so-called Diarium."

But whatever the courtiers or the rest of the family might have felt, there was no one, not even the new Emperor Joseph, who had the authority to oppose Maria Theresia. The formal betrothal took place in the Hofburg on the second day of April 1766, with most people pointedly dressed in mourning black. But Marie Christine's three brothers appeared in their officers' uniforms, Albert sported a colourful and richly patterned coat, and the bride herself wore a pink gown, "with layers and layers of Brussels lace." Since the wedding itself was not to be in Vienna, the betrothal was celebrated "as if it was the wedding-day, and the banquet as well." Listed informally in the news-sheets in order of their ages were those of Marie Christine's siblings who had attended—all apart from Leopold, already installed in Florence, and Marianna, troubled by her weak chest perhaps, or, more likely, by the wounded heart within it. Three days later, the articles of marriage were officially signed.

Had "our French and German newspapers, and the so-called Diarium" been able to get hold of these articles, it would certainly have caused another scandal. But the articles, flagrantly favouring Marie Christine over all her siblings, were kept secret, "since the Empress, who harbours an exceptional partiality to the bride, is indulging her excessively, in that, apart from all the other valuable gifts in jewels and rich accoutrements, she is giving her a dowry of four million [gulden], partly *in specie* as the county of Altenburg in Hungary." This 4 million was fully half of the total sum that the Empress had nominally set aside for all seven of her daughters and her two youngest sons. Moreover, to Altenburg were subsequently added two further Hungarian counties. Albert himself was promoted from lieutenant to full field marshal with command of the Hungarian army, and dubbed a knight of the Order of St Stephen, receiving, to complete the picture, a golden fleece, with sword, belt, buckle, hat, and ring, all set with diamonds.

The newlyweds could thus count on an annual income of about 1 million gulden—not counting the fifty thousand that Albert had been left by his father, or the one hundred thousand that Marie Christine had been left by hers. Maria Theresia was more than happy to indulge them. To Madame Enzenberg she wrote of the pleasure she took in seeing the two of them together, saying, "They often remind me of my own early marital happiness."

THE WEDDING OF MARIE CHRISTINE and Albert took place a few days after their betrothal, at Franz Stephan's lovely old hunting manor of Schloss Hof, some thirty miles east of Vienna on the way to Pressburg. Maria Theresia had insisted on a quiet wedding in the countryside, perhaps to avoid further recriminations about the untimely relaxation of mourning for her late husband. The Empress was dressed in black, as she had always been since Franz Stephan's death; the gentlemen were in grey or black uniforms, but the court ladies wore only black armbands on their taffeta gowns, and at six in the evening, the bride herself entered the round-vaulted chapel wearing a white muslin dress embroidered with silver flowers and many jewels. The ceremony was followed by a supper, from which, perhaps still feeling a little guilty, Maria Theresia excused herself. And the next day, to please the local people, there were the usual public festivities—"country fair and amusements, such as [a staged] peasant wedding, mock battle, dancing etc.," as Khevenhüller, bored and grumpy, scratched into his little book.

A few days later, Marie Christine and Albert moved on to Pressburg to meet the local nobles—a perfect scroll of Hungarian history, with Pálffys, Esterházys, Batthyánys, and others, including Count Bethlén, or "Bethlehem" as the Empress called him, the newly appointed Court Chamberlain, who happened to be Khevenhüller's son-in-law. The old diarist was happy about that, at least.

# IV

# 1766-1767

In which a melancholy Marianna seeks distraction in religion and science, and Chablais' falsetto voice is heard again.

Marianna had been among the first to return to Vienna after her sister's wedding. She was in no frame of mind for festivities. In later years, overlooking the anguish of her lost love, she would write in her *Confessions* that it was her father's death the previous summer that had "put an end for a year to all my enjoyment of social life and entertainment." It is true she had been Franz Stephan's favourite, and his fondness and attention had been her consolation for periodic ill health, the loss of many pleasures, and perhaps, too, the abandonment of any hope of marriage. He had been, in her memory at least, "my only support, my only delight. His death felled me to the floor, and I began, in my silence and loneliness, to turn inwards. I found no one to help me and I made my way through it by myself, alone."

It is a sad picture of a once vibrant young woman, though not, perhaps, without a trace of melodrama. Marianna said she was "everyone's confidante," but she was perhaps unwilling or unable to confide in others herself. Her former Mistress of the Household, the excellent Princess von Trautson, was still at court, now, at sixty-five, a lady-in-waiting to the Empress; she would surely have given her a kindly hearing, had she been asked to do so. In her place at the head of Marianna's household was the Polish Countess Isabella Salmour, a woman of her own age, known for her intelligence but also for her piety; it may have been she who persuaded Marianna now to a deeper engagement with her own religious faith.

For she had become anxious about her father's immortal soul. Though the obsequies for Franz Stephan had been many and long and all in accordance with the highest Catholic rites, it had not been enough to reassure her of his salvation. Following orthodox teaching, she had begun to fear that his soul would now have entered a fiery purgatory in expiation for the "disordered life" he had led—namely, his love affairs. Moreover, she had convinced herself that she was partly to blame, having failed to restrain him and even helping him to sin—though how this might have been, she did not say—perhaps no more than by behaving with civility to his mistress, the Princess von Auersperg, who, as one of the Empress' ladies-in-waiting, was often to be seen at court. Still, she said, "reproaches of this kind tormented me day and night," and she began a regime of stricter religious observance for herself, hoping to redress the moral balance and release the soul of her beloved father more quickly into heaven.

She gave up all her pastimes except her very favourite (card-playing), and largely withdrew from society in order to spend more time in prayer and self-examination. Doubting her own self-discipline, she had let the rest of the family know, for "I knew myself weak enough that this would keep me to it more than all my good intentions." As she had foreseen, her family, and indeed her servants, all made fun of this, though her friends did not, and there was one man in particular, her unidentified "friend," who argued fiercely against her retreat from the busy life of the court, albeit to no avail.

This was the time, as she writes in her *Confessions*, of her greatest spiritual test. In the face of the strenuous objections of "my friend," she embraced the consolations and, more especially, the demands of her religion, turning away from the life of the court, seeking to conquer her "stubborn and unruly spirit" and stifle her "blameworthy passion," in penance and prayer. Marianna speaks often of her passion, and it is not always clear what she means by this. It may have been the passion of grief, which kept her from submitting to God's will in "taking my father from me," but more probably it was the passion of love, which she says she continued to feel. She had not earlier described it as "blameworthy," but if her "friend" had indeed married, then it would have become so: She would now be, in the biblical phrase, coveting another woman's husband.

Marianna admits she passed her spiritual test only middlingly, and certainly she did not persist long in this first retreat from the world. Within a few months, she had got up from her prayer stool and was hosting scientific meetings several times a week. She had begun them, she said, as a way of distracting herself, even forcing herself from her feelings. "I knew myself to be too weak to overcome my passion by myself, so I restrained myself, I gathered a circle of women around me so that we would have to spend these hours together"—not conducting experiments, however, but reading and discussing published texts and the circulating letters of science enthusiasts across Europe.

It was an old pursuit of hers, newly revived to serve a pressing new purpose. Her father had been the first to encourage her interest in the natural sciences, and Pater Richter, her Jesuit confessor since her girlhood and now a personal friend, was also an amateur astronomer. And after Franz Stephan's death, his brother Karl in Brussels had stepped into the breach to support his favourite niece, at least in terms of her intellectual interests. His journal is dotted with mentions of seashells and rock crystals and butterflies and marine plants and other "natural curiosities," purchased expressly for her at very considerable sums.

Marianna was to continue her scientific salons with ladies of the court, every other day, for the next six years and more. After two years of physics, there followed a year of mechanics, another of geometry, a further in chemistry and botany, and finally, "natural history," a catch-all expression covering every scientific investigation from insect biology to astronomy. Berating herself, as she often did, for lack of self-discipline, she insisted this was something she could not have done alone, even if it had involved no more than reading. She needed the other women, she said, since then "I had to turn up even if I didn't feel like it. I would have been ashamed to appear frivolous."

The Empress had successfully flouted her late husband's wishes by arranging Marie Christine's marriage to Albert. By the summer of 1766, perhaps feeling a little guilty toward Franz Stephan's memory, she had resurrected his plan to marry his nephew, the high-voiced, lumpy-necked Duke de Chablais, to one of his daughters—to Elisabeth, perhaps, or to Amalie. "I can't resist telling you this, in the greatest secrecy," she wrote in July to Madame Enzenberg. "It would give me great pleasure, since he is the only nephew I have. I would leave the King [Chablais' father, Carlo Emmanuele III of Sardinia] to choose between the two of them. I am more inclined toward Elisabeth, but if one is considering only the well-being of the nephew and the acceptability to his family, then I think Amalie would be more welcome."

Elisabeth was not quite twenty-three. Being the elder sister, it was natural that her mother would want her to be married first, though Amalie, at twenty, was also of an appropriate age for the twenty-five-year-old Duke. Madame Enzenberg had a definite preference. "I know how much you want the marriage of Amalie (your favourite) with the Duke of Chablais and their establishment in the Tyrol," said the Empress, and her own concern about "the well-being of the nephew and the acceptability to his family" suggests that she understood why. In a letter of some years before to Madame Lerchenfeld, asking her to consider the position of *aya* to the two sisters, she had pointed out that "the first [Elisabeth] would have far greater need of your direction."

Elisabeth was known to be coquettish and lazy, and she could certainly be cutting, but why she might need more direction than a sister three years younger is not clear, especially since Amalie herself had not exactly proved an ideal pupil. "There is plenty to be said against her, too," Madame Lerchenfeld had told her son, before declining to become *aya* to the two. "They are both too wilful and volatile to put up with for any length of time. Only an idiot or a martyr would accept the position."

From all that can be gleaned from letters and journals of the period, it seems that Amalie was the most fractious of the seven sisters. Portraits of her as a girl show a pretty face, without the too prominent Habsburg chin, and a slightly diffident expression, as if she were not quite sure of herself. It may well have been so. In her mother's presence she was generally "very obliging," but the Empress could be formidable and, as Antonia was to remark, though she did love her mother, "even at a distance, I am afraid of her." Amalie was a fine horsewoman and huntress, which suggests she was not naturally timid, and there is an often repeated story of the strong will she had evinced as a nine-year-old, after suffering some kind of fit: The physicians of the day had decided this called for a *clystère*, a saline enema administered via a large metal syringe. The girl had resisted; the physicians had used violence, injuring her rectum and almost provoking a bacterial abscess which might have killed her. This injury would later give rise to rumours that she could not bear children, a near slanderous suggestion for the daughter of a ruling house.

Amalie had her defenders. Maria Theresia herself admitted that, though she was not very practical and would not exert herself where she had no interest, she did have a good character and plenty of patience with other people and "when you want to, something very touching about you that is hard to resist." She was a favourite of the Empress' friend, the Countess von Enzenberg, apparently less for her "obliging" ways than for her spirited nature. Marianna, more than seven years older, had also taken Amalie under her wing; perhaps she saw something of herself in her restless younger sister: Their brother Joseph, no hunter himself, had reported in 1765 that these two "hunting sisters" had between them shot "more than 1,400 wild boar this year." It may be that the "something touching" about Amalie was a certain vulnerability, springing from some instability in her constitution. Like others in the family, she could certainly be impulsive, but in Amalie there was emerging an unpredictability and even self-destructiveness that was to make her path through life the harder.

Why, then, might volatile Amalie be more acceptable than Elisabeth as a wife for Chablais? A letter that survives from a few years before may provide an explanation. Maria Theresia had written to Marie Christine from Schloss Hof, where Marianna and Amalie were on a hunting trip with their father. Elisabeth was then eighteen years old, and though Marie Christine herself, one year older, was in poor health at the time, their mother had chided her nonetheless for her behaviour toward her sister. "As for Elisabeth," she had written, "after keeping a most rigorous silence for thirty hours, she returned to normal; yesterday I spent four hours alone with her and d'Herzelles and Lodron at Niederweiden. You were not forgotten, and I think you are often wrong in your dealings with her, for one must regard her as someone who is ill, have pity on her, but not push her."

The marquise d'Herzelles was Elisabeth's current Mistress of the Household, the eighth she had had so far, since no one was willing to remain in the post for long. The Countess Lodron was one of her ladies-in-waiting. Niederweiden was a small and rather dilapidated baroque palace near to Schloss Hof, where the three ladies had retreated for some private talk—apparently a four-hour discussion of Elisabeth's "silences."

Maria Theresia was not the woman to indulge a day-long sulk on the part of a daughter. Her response to Elisabeth's withdrawal, surprisingly empathetic, as she was often very critical, suggests that she understood her problem to be a severe form of "melancholy"—in other words, depression. The Empress herself was no stranger to this powerful malady. Long before her husband's death, which had stolen so much strength from her, she had admitted to feeling periodically "like a dumb animal, I am so overwhelmed I cannot think, nor can I speak, because if I do I become over-excited to the point of rage, and I feel utterly desperate. . . . All I can do is lock myself away alone." Elisabeth also experienced these moments of over-excitement, but was unable to remove herself from the scene as her mother might have done; instead she would lash out, offending her siblings, her ladies-in-waiting, and anyone else in her way, afterwards leaving the embarrassed Empress to apologize on her behalf.

Marie Christine had evidently had something less understanding to say about Elisabeth's moods. The Empress, though often exasperated by Elisabeth, was at least able to recognize "someone who is ill." And though in recent years Marianna had been regarded as the family invalid, Elisabeth had also once been sickly and weak. Indeed, or so the story was told at court, as an infant, being unable to take any food at all, she had only survived by the intervention of the aptly named Doctor Engel (Angel), who had thought to feed her chocolate, "which was finally something she could keep down, and since then she really seem[ed] to get better."

Elisabeth's physical health had long been stable; she was now in the flower of youth and beauty. Perhaps the prospect of marriage to the unappealing Chablais, after the glorious promise of King Stanisław of Poland, had unsteadied her once again. In any case, her volatility remained. As her mother had noted, "I intend to treat her as a madwoman whom one must approach with caution. . . . At the moment, everything is well, but I don't trust that, I've had too much experience."

Regardless of who Chablais' bride turned out to be, a match with a Habsburg princess was in itself very much in Sardinia's interest. King Carlo Emmanuele had been dismayed by the *renversement des alliances* bringing Austria and France together, since it had long been a cornerstone of his foreign policy to play them off against each other. His son's marriage would bring his kingdom into the newly unified and now doubly powerful fold. Chablais would be set up as governor of the Austrian province of Tyrol, as Albert had been (admittedly rather more grandly) in Hungary. This would extend Sardinia's reach further into the continent.

But Maria Theresia hesitated. It would cost a good deal to establish Chablais in the Tyrol, and she had already paid out a vast amount for Albert.

Moreover, Joseph was against the match. He objected to the use of state funds for the furthering of his sister's marriage, and he was suspicious of Carlo Emmanuele's longer-term aims. Since Maria Theresia's accession to the throne in 1740, the Sardinians had had some claim to the Austrian territory of Lombardy in northern Italy, young Ferdinand's promised fiefdom by his future marriage to Beatrice d'Este. Chablais was already a cousin to the Empress' children; as the husband of one of them, his claim could only be stronger.

In the end, Joseph's doubts and the anticipated costs proved greater than the Empress' fondness for her nephew-by-marriage. Though Elisabeth would be considered again in a year or two, Chablais' prospective match with a Habsburg cousin came to nothing. In due course he married one of his very young nieces instead, fathering no children and proving a cold and neglectful husband. As Albert later observed, he seemed to prefer the company of men.

FIFTY MILES UP the Danube in Pressburg, Marie Christine and Albert were settling into a sedate provincial luxury. Their principal residence was the massive white stone Pressburg Castle, perched fortress-like on a hill above the town. It had been in place, in parts at least, for seven hundred years, but there was still building work going on, the renovation of old rooms and construction of the new, for though it belonged by long inheritance to the great Pálffy family of Hungary, it was now to declare itself more loudly as a Habsburg court, with a Habsburg archduchess its prime denizen, her husband's post as governor notwithstanding. To this end, sumptuous private apartments had been prepared for the pair, the small park was being improved and a fashionable "naturalistic" English garden added, and the presentation rooms extended and ornamented according to designs of the high priest of courtly architecture, Franz Anton Hillebrand. In his spacious "Theresianum" hall, almost a hundred of Marie Christine's own works of art would be displayed, reminding visitors of the archduchess' standing as a lady of culture.

The Empress had imposed her own choice of minister plenipotentiary for Hungary, but Albert had also invited some of his own old friends, including several Protestants from his home city of Dresden who had not been permitted to serve at Maria Theresia's court, and a good many Freemasons, too—Albert himself had recently joined a Dresden lodge. The Brotherhood of Freemasons had its origins in medieval communities of actual stonemasons, but over the centuries it had developed into more of an intellectual society, and by now its values were broadly aligned with those of the European Enlightenment. Its members were men—and a tiny handful of women associates—with a generally progressive outlook on social and political questions. They supported the scientific investigation of the natural world, and in matters of religion were markedly tolerant, often themselves being freethinkers or Deists, rather than adherents of a traditional Church or faith. The insistently Catholic Empress, doubting their religious reliability, had this very year banned all members of the Brotherhood from employment in the Monarchy's service, though Freemasonry was almost a family tradition: Franz Stephan had been a member, as were Joseph and Leopold as well as Albert, and Marianna was known to be a supporter.

Like her sister, Marie Christine shared many of the Freemasons' ideals, and she welcomed them easily into her new Pressburg circle. She had also brought some of her own closer personal staff with her from the Hofburg, but nonetheless, she was not feeling quite at ease: Though married for only three months, she was "miserable" at not having yet conceived. "One sees there is no such thing as perfect happiness," the Empress remarked to Madame Lerchenfeld. In the event, Marie Christine did not have long to wait. In May 1767, a year after her wedding, she was brought to bed with her first child.

Her birth pains began on the Friday, and lasted through the night; at nine the following morning, after a particularly difficult delivery, a baby girl was born, "but she came into the world so weak that [Albert's brother] Clemens saw fit to baptize her at once, in all haste." It was as well he did, for the little girl lived only until the Sunday. Two days later, Marie Christine fell dangerously ill with childbed fever, a bacterial infection carried by the unwashed hands of her physicians. On hearing the news, Maria Theresia fell into "a state of the most extreme agitation." The imperial family's usual public attendance at mass was immediately cancelled, and they heard the service all together in their private chapel. Though they could not know it, this was the last time they were to do so.

Marie Christine survived the fever, but it left her sterile: She was never to conceive again. Her daughter, Maria Christina Theresia, was buried in the imperial crypt, near her infant aunts, the first daughters of the Empress, in their own tiny grey coffins.

# V

# 1767

In which two unhappy princesses escape their fate, only to meet a worse.

In the middle of May 1767, a courier from Naples arrived at the Hofburg, bringing a letter for the sixteen-year-old Archduchess Josepha. It was a courtly letter, signed by her intended husband, the young King Ferdinando, though it had undoubtedly been dictated by his regent, First Minister Tanucci—a copy of it was subsequently bound into a leather folder of the Minister's personal correspondence. As yet there had been no formal request for Josepha's hand in marriage, but she was already considered Ferdinando's Queen Consort, and he addressed her now, or Tanucci's secretary addressed her, as "Madame my Sister, Spouse, and Cousin." Kings and queens regarded themselves as siblings, and all royal persons were considered cousins, which, often enough, they were: Josepha and Ferdinando themselves were both descendants of the French King Louis XIII. And though the two had never met, the letter followed protocol in indicating that from now on they were to present themselves as passionate lovers, too: "My marriage to Your Majesty has now become my greatest comfort," wrote the King. "I feel that, once I am assured of Your Majesty, I will be forever happy."

Josepha was not deceived by the flowery language. Every Hofburg tongue was wagging about Ferdinando's deficiencies, and every ear shrivelling from the sound of his "sister, spouse and cousin" sobbing behind the doors of her regal apartments. To her fifteen-year-old sister, Carolina, she now blurted out the unfairness of it all: Marie Christine had been allowed to marry the man she loved, "and I have to marry someone I've never seen, and besides that everyone knows he's already making love to the Princess Belmonte!"—the latter a famed Neapolitan beauty.

Josepha's bitterness at Marie Christine's good fortune was double-edged: Not only had her sister married the man she loved, she had married the man Josepha herself loved, too—a visitor was later to record the gossip at court about it. Josepha had not originally been Ferdinando's intended bride. That honour, or duty, had fallen to an elder sister who had died in childhood, and since then the Empress had been working "behind the scenes," as she put it, to slot Josepha into the place left vacant, with the girl herself knowing nothing of it. And her language lessons had been expanded: To German, Latin, French, and Italian, Spanish had been added—in secret, however, until the terms of the betrothal could be properly signed and sealed.

The Empress held no very high opinion of Josepha. A few years before, she had provided Madame Lerchenfeld with a summary of the girl's appearance and qualities. It is an unflattering picture. "Her facial features are not attractive," she had declared baldly, "and neither is her manner; there is something rough about her." Portraits of princesses generally err on the side of gallantry, but the girl did have the infamous jutting Habsburg chin, a trait she shared with her younger sister Antonia, though the latter was considered very pretty all the same. Josepha was flighty and gossipy, her mother continued, and inclined to be stubborn, and her apparent piety was not genuine. She was a dissembler, though admittedly this might be useful to her "in that country"—meaning Naples—but it was a perilous tendency all the same, since if allowed to go too far, it could degenerate into a general untruthfulness.

Maria Theresia's critical tone was not unusual; she judged all her daughters harshly, particularly while they were growing up, and in her advice to them and to those who cared for them, she rarely dwelt on the positive. But if Khevenhüller, recently promoted to Court Chamberlain, is to be believed, the intervening years had found Josepha much improved, both inwardly and outwardly. In his journal of court life, he has left an admiring description of the girl at sixteen, dark-haired, already tall for her age and still growing, and evidently more emotionally mature than she had been. "She is nicely formed," he wrote, "her features not regular, but her demeanor majestic and at the same time approachable, a heart and temperament of the best, high-spirited, though from her early youth she ha[s] learned to suppress this, also *de ce qu'on appelle un bon esprit* [a touch of wit], benevolent and generous; *enfin* she ha[s] inherited the best qualities of both her parents. . . . Her love, her deference, and her respect for Madame her mother could not [be] greater."

Josepha's qualities, in fact, were currently the subject of some discussion at Ferdinando's Neapolitan court. Though any one of the Habsburg Empress' daughters would have been an acceptable bride for him, some in Naples were pleased, and others less so, that Josepha seemed to be a strong-minded girl who would comfortably dominate her childish spouse.

On the one hand, the intellectual "Neapolitan" faction wanted her to take over the official reins of government, since, as they insisted, "His Majesty lacks both the will and the competence" to rule. The new Queen, they felt, would simply be following the lead of her mother, whose reforms within the Austrian Monarchy had been gathering pace for some years already, while in Naples itself, there was the precedent of the late Queen Amalia, Ferdinando's mother, who had been very politically active, though it was true she had not been popular. With these progressive examples before her, or so the "Neapolitans" thought, Josepha would let them get on with their own programme of root-and-branch reform of the kingdom, currently "in such miserable condition."

On the other hand, there were the conservative "Sicilians," led by Ferdinando's confessor, who were determined to fix the reins securely in the young King's hands—or rather, in their own. Hoping to add an extra *pinta* of red blood to Ferdinando's machismo, they were emphasizing what a disgrace it would be if he allowed himself to be governed by his wife, who was, after all, just a young girl.

Perched solidly above both factions was the First Minister, the marchese Bernardo Tanucci, a loyal lieutenant of Carlos III since 1734 when, as a young man coming into that kingdom, Carlos had wanted to make Naples independent of Spain, then ruled by his elder half-brother. With the passing of a generation and his own assumption of the Spanish throne, Carlos' views had changed, though Tanucci's loyalty had not. The First Minister's concern now was to ensure Naples' continuing dependence on Madrid. A Habsburg alliance would be advantageous, certainly, provided the Austrians did not gain the upper hand.

TANUCCI HAD A VERY PARTICULAR concern about Josepha. The wedding was to take place in mid-October, and she was expected to arrive in Naples well before Christmas. Her arrival, he feared, would interrupt a long-laid plan very dear to his heart, as he informed Carlos in Madrid: "This Princess, or so it is reported, will be very favourably disposed toward the Jesuits, which suggests that if the work of expulsion has not been completed before November, it will not be completed at all, as there will be no one here who dares to resist the [new] Queen's declared protection and will."

This "work of expulsion" had been gathering pace in Europe for some time. A few months before, the Spanish Jesuits, to their astonishment and almost everyone else's, had been arrested and driven out of Spain itself and from its vast overseas colonies, "on pain of death." In Austria, there had been a milder turn against them; they had encountered rejection rather than outright repression. The Empress still had her Jesuit confessor, though she also had shelves of anti-Jesuit books, with a quick little curtain that she drew whenever she was to meet with him.

Like most of Europe's thinking men, Tanucci had himself been educated by Jesuits, and his objections to them now were less religious than political.

He was committed to the establishment of a secular state, with the sovereign's authority above that of the Church. "In all countries," he had told the young Ferdinando, "the Jesuits seek wealth, power, temporal goods for themselves and for the Court of Rome, with all means, even the most iniquitous and the most seditious and wicked; they enter everywhere, they contaminate all the Organs of State; they subvert the judges, the nobility, the ecclesiastics, the women, the common people, in a thousand ancient ways; they subvert religious confessions, confraternities, missions, with a vast force, extending everywhere."

No wonder, then, that Tanucci was anxious about Josepha. But his information was incorrect. Though the Empress had permitted her elder daughters, all now well into their twenties, to make their own decisions about their confessors, and each had remained loyal to the Jesuits, by now the four younger daughters had been given Jansenist confessors. At one time Josepha had affected a rather showy piety, though her mother had insisted it was not genuine. Whatever the case, by now she had no pronounced religious leanings in any direction.

Alongside his efforts to drive the Jesuits out of the Kingdom of Naples, Tanucci was busy arranging Josepha's entry into it, or as he put it, "the delivery of the bride-Queen." This was no straightforward matter, since, as Ambassador Ernst von Kaunitz reported to his chancellor father in Vienna, the roads leading to Naples were "in the most pitiful condition and completely dilapidated." This was not just a question of national embarrassment: For a vast royal cortège, the roads might actually be impassable. Tanucci had already set fifteen hundred men to work repairing them, but for the moment, this multitude of fractious labourers was proving less troublesome to him than their own undisciplined King.

Ferdinando, jaunty and careless, was insisting on making an extravagant formal entrance to the city with his bride, which Tanucci calculated would cost 40,000 florins, though some of this might be recouped, he thought, given "all the horses, carriages, mounts, liveries, and everything else that would have to be sold off after having served for this one morning." On top of that, the sixteen-year-old King wanted a huge party for that evening, and this was expected to cost an extra 5,000 florins—a higher sum, the Minister noted pointedly, than had recently been paid for a similar event in that most extravagant of cities, Paris. Moreover, the young Emperor Joseph was planning to escort his favourite sister to her new home and, with his intense dislike of ceremony, was expecting the simplest arrangements possible; to this, Ferdinando was putting up a determined resistance.

Tanucci was now a toad-like sixty-nine, thickset and grumpy-faced. Beset by the Kingdom's financial problems, attacked for the inadequacy of his economic reforms, demoralized by "my hypochondria . . . and my by now habitual melancholy," he was beginning to feel overwhelmed. His energies—"this little effort that the divine mercy allows me still in my declining age"—were, he feared, no longer equal to the tasks required of him.

While Marie Christine lay feverish and grieving the loss of her baby in Pressburg, oblivious to the world outside her chamber, a tragedy of greater scale was gathering pace at the Hofburg. In late May 1767, Joseph's unloved wife, the twenty-eight-year-old Empress Maria Josepha, had taken to her bed, saying she felt unwell. Joseph was not concerned; to this day it remains unknown where he was over the next few days, but at no time did he find it worth his while, or worth his reputation as a husband, to visit Maria Josepha or even to enquire after her.

Maria Theresia, who disliked her daughter-in-law, nevertheless possessed a sufficiently strong sense of duty, or of guilt for her previous neglect, to call on her now. She entered Maria Josepha's room as the physicians were about to bleed her—a common intervention of the time for most medical ailments, practised on the assumption that it would either restore a proper balance to the patient's vital fluids, or release infected blood. She approached the bedside just as the young Empress held out her arm, and it was Maria Theresia herself who was the first to see the tiny red spots on the outstretched limb. A hasty examination revealed many more spots on the body.

The conclusion was clear and alarming: Maria Josepha had contracted the smallpox.

The physicians announced she must be isolated at once. The dowager Empress must leave. With heroic kindness, or perhaps as an act of penance, Maria Theresia, who had no immunity to the disease, now leaned toward the distraught young woman and, "careful to conceal how little particular inclination she felt for this daughter-in-law, made the effort, not without repugnance, to embrace her as she left." Chancellor von Kaunitz reported that "Her Imperial Highness, out of the exceeding goodness of her heart," had not only put her arms around Maria Josepha, but had kissed her, too. Whether humane or contritional, the Empress' gesture had been enough to infect her.

Smallpox was the most deadly killer of the age. A single epidemic could take thousands of lives. Those who survived it were left disfigured, more or less seriously, or even blinded. Maria Theresia had already lost three children to the disease; three of Franz Stephan's brothers had died of it; Khevenhüller and the imperial physician Gerard van Swieten, too, had watched children of their own perish from it, covered in sores and wracked with pain.

Van Swieten believed there was no remedy for the smallpox. As a medical student in Leiden, he had learned that bleedings and enemas and a particular diet could help, but he was not convinced of this. Instead he believed that, since "the smallpox poison . . . is so tiny it cannot be perceived by any of our senses, the only thing the physician's arts can do is to weaken the patient's life itself: for it is life that allows the poisons to work."

Travellers from West Africa and the Ottoman lands had long brought tales of a miraculous means of smallpox prevention that was commonly used outside of Europe. As early as 1717, Lady Mary Wortley Montagu, wife of the British ambassador in Constantinople, had reported the practice to friends at home:

> *The small-pox, so fatal, and so general amongst us, is here entirely harmless by the invention of* ingrafting, *which is the term they give*

> *it. There is a set of old women who make it their business to perform the operation every autumn. . . . The old woman comes with a nutshell full of the matter of the best sort of small-pox, and . . . rips open [the vein] you offer to her with a large needle . . . and puts into the vein as much venom as can lie upon the head of the needle, and after binds up the little wound. . . . I am patriot enough to take pains to bring this useful invention into fashion in England; and I should not fail to write to some of our doctors very particularly about it, if I knew any one of them that I thought had virtue enough to destroy such a considerable branch of their revenue for the good of mankind.*

The "best sort of small-pox" was actually a sample of the live virus taken from the pustules of a person already infected with a mild form of the disease. As far as Lady Mary knew, this "ingrafting," or inoculation, was harmless, producing nothing worse than a couple of days' mild fever. In Ottoman lands, the practice had been known since medieval times, and it may be that the "old women" were able to administer the virus without much risk, but the inexperienced European physicians who had since attempted it quite often only killed their patients. Hence, even in 1767, inoculation in Europe remained a rare and dangerous practice; van Swieten was strongly opposed to it. Those who looked to the Church for guidance were met with ambivalence: Some priests viewed it as a blasphemous interference with the will of God, yet only ten years before, the scientifically-minded Pope Benedict XIV had himself been inoculated against smallpox. With so perilous a disease, a good deal of resistance to half-understood treatments remained, not least on the part of the physicians themselves, whatever the state of their revenues.

THE PROGRESS OF SMALLPOX is swift, and Maria Theresia grew quickly ill. For four days she lay feverish and stabbed by kidney pain, until the pustules broke out on her hands and feet, and on her eyes and mouth, so that she could neither see nor speak clearly. Twice she was bled; she grew ever weaker, and it was feared she could not survive. But, conscious throughout, she insisted on being kept informed of her daughter-in-law's state. When the news came of the young Empress' death, Maria Theresia worsened suddenly; "putrid matter began to burst from her mouth, mixed with globules of blood." Joseph, overwhelmed, declared it was the worst day he had ever lived through. He had returned to watch over his mother, and he stayed with her even as his wife was buried, unmourned, her personal tragedy overshadowed by that of a woman more admired, and more cherished.

On the first day of June, the Empress was administered the last sacrament. She had been calm enough to request this herself. Albert startled everyone by showing apparent symptoms at first but, like his brother Clemens and Marianna and Amalie, he was immune from infection, and all four of them remained at her bedside throughout, deeply moved by the Empress' spiritual strength. Vienna's churches were filled with her subjects praying for her life, and through the streets of the city thousands processed behind holy relics, with the same plea in their hearts. Others, needing their own part in the drama, stood outside the Hofburg, waiting for news.

And after two days, the tide turned. The fever receded, the ghastly pustules broke and then faded. By the fifth of June, the Empress was well enough to pen a pageful of shaky lines to Marie Christine in Pressburg, herself now weakly recovering from the childbed fever which had almost killed her. Given her own condition, she had not previously been told of her mother's illness, but within a week she was well enough to travel the fifty miles from Pressburg to Vienna, and was herself at her bedside.

All the bells of all the churches in the Monarchy were set to pealing in loud thanksgiving for the Empress' recovery. But it was more than a month before she appeared in public again for the first time, at a service at St Stephen's Cathedral, with the royal purser strewing silver coins for the people along her path back to the Hofburg afterwards. Twelve little orphans, handpicked weeks before to pray for her recovery, received comfortable lifelong pensions of thirty gulden a year. And on the same day, although—or perhaps because—he had done nothing particular to intervene in her illness, Maria Theresia's physician Gerard van Swieten became a Knight Commander of the grand new Order of St Stephen of Hungary.

The hypochondriac Chancellor von Kaunitz was quick to issue an imposing new order of his own: From now on, no member of his staff was ever to mention the word *smallpox* in his presence. And if that word should appear in any official despatches, it was to be struck out utterly before the offending sheet was handed to him.

THE TURBULENT MONTHS of the midsummer of 1767 were followed by a quiet August, much of it at Laxenburg, some fifteen miles from Vienna, "a small town in the hollow part of the great plain, with an old chateau, newly patched up, and a strange low palace, the residence of the imperial family." So much for the two connected royal buildings, at least in the opinion of the young English traveller Henry Swinburne. The grounds, however, with lakes and an island and a large deer park where Marianna and Amalie had often hunted with their father, Swinburne considered "a true oasis of enchantment and pleasure." There was still hunting at Laxenburg; those not riding followed the hunt in open carriages, with everyone coming together for a picnic lunch in one of the modest little houses dotted around the park. At the end of the day, the air still mild, they would gather in the garden for an outdoor performance of some light-hearted play.

There is a portrayal of them there at about this time, painted by an unknown hand, the Empress seated on a satinwood armchair, plump in her shapeless widow's weeds, the sisters in brightly coloured, panniered gowns, their wide whalebone undergarments exaggerating waists and hips *ad absurdum*, and spreading out the patterned fabrics to display their full beauty. Though the sisters are all still young, their hair is grey—not dyed, but intertwined with false pieces to make for greater volume, and the whole powdered over, to conceal the blending of nature and artifice.

With autumn came the return to the city, and the resumption of dynastic duties, and early in September, the formal request was made for Josepha's hand in marriage to the young King of Naples. Marie Christine and Albert's wedding had been celebrated fairly quietly. Josepha's was the first royal wedding to take place since the end of the two-year official mourning period for Franz Stephan, and consequently, extravagant festivities were in order. These included, as always for important dynastic occasions, a specially commissioned opera and ballet, to be performed at the Burgtheater, which adjoined the Hofburg: Rebuilt some twenty years before, it allowed the imperial family to step directly from their own palace apartments into their large private box at the theatre.

The ballet was watched with particular interest by the Archduchess Antonia, perched on a stiff chair alongside her siblings in the imperial box. Though almost twelve years old and destined for the exacting court of Versailles, she had never yet had the benefit of a first-rate dancing master—during her childhood, the excellent Franz von Wewen, who had taught her elder sisters so well, had been working at the Russian court. But now the great Parisian choreographer Jean-Georges Noverre had arrived in Vienna, enticed by an enormous annual salary of almost 7,500 gulden, plus a private carriage and a bountiful supply of wine.

Maria Theresia moved quickly to appoint him Antonia's teacher. It was important for a princess to be able to dance well, and the Empress was anxious that her youngest daughter should not appear provincial when she eventually took her place among the legendarily fashionable ladies at Versailles. Antonia had always moved with instinctive poise, and under Noverre's wing she was to develop a graceful and unaffected style of dancing that would garner praise from all who saw her. In due course, she would poach him for her own court at Versailles.

A few days afterwards, in the pretty baroque town of Salzburg, not yet part of the Austrian Monarchy but an independent prince-archbishopric of the Holy Roman Empire, the Mozart family could be seen mounting a public coach for the two-hundred-mile journey to Vienna. There were four of them: father Leopold, a composer and violin teacher of some repute and considerable ferocity; his wife, Anna Maria; and their two surviving children, sixteen-year-old Maria Anna, a keyboard *virtuosa*; and the dazzling Wolfgang Amadeus, eleven years old. They were hoping to be invited to perform at some of Josepha's lesser wedding festivities, and having recently completed a successful tour of capital cities, they even thought the Vienna concerts might result in a formal appointment for one of them at least. Once arrived in the city, they took up lodgings with a goldsmith's family near St Stephen's Cathedral.

The Mozart children had performed in Vienna before; in 1762 they had even played for the imperial family at the Hofburg. According to father Leopold, a baby romance had sprung up between Wolfgang and the Archduchess Antonia, both then six years old, and the Empress herself had taken the boy onto her lap. Whatever the truth of this, it is certain that Wolfgang had left the Hofburg with a suit of fine mauve fabric that had been made for the Archduke Maximilian; the Salzburg court painter Lorenzoni has left a roly-poly portrait of the little genius wearing it.

Since Albert had been already living in Vienna, Marie Christine had had the unusual pleasure, for a royal bride, of marrying her husband in person. King Ferdinando, by contrast, was far away in Naples, so that Josepha was to marry him by proxy in the Church of St Augustine, with her younger brother, thirteen-year-old Ferdinand, representing him. A succession of black-clad Spaniards had arrived in Vienna to ensure the wedding would proceed in accordance with their own very formal rituals. Not all went smoothly; Spaniards and Austrians could not agree on who should take precedence—a young queen of Naples, or a middle-aged Habsburg empress. In the event, it was agreed that Maria Theresia and Josepha should walk up the aisle together.

For the proxy bridegroom Ferdinand, it was a form of practice for his own wedding, still some years in the future. His betrothed, the *duchessa* Beatrice d'Este, herself already seventeen, had been concerned for some time about the figure he was likely to cut as a grown man. Maria Theresia had been doing her best to reassure her: Ferdinand had been riding a lot and exercising with his battalion, and this was making him "more robust," and he was growing, though she was obliged to admit she "could wish him a head taller." But now, as he was being fitted for his surrogate's costume, his mother had the satisfaction of informing Beatrice that he was growing lean and lanky like his brother Leopold. As for the boy himself, pseudo-bridegroom to his sister Josepha, Ferdinand had apparently adopted a pseudo-role toward his unknown betrothed as well. "He always calls you his little sister-in-law," reported the Empress, charmed.

The wedding-day was fixed for Wednesday the fourteenth of October 1767. But at Schönbrunn, on the morning of Sunday the fourth, Josepha mentioned she was feeling unwell, and the next day found her no better. Though the planned formal receptions were reduced, two opera performances were still performed that evening at the newly refurbished Schönbrunn palace theatre. One of the works was Gluck's "lugubrious" tragedy—the description is Khevenhüller's—*Orfeo e Euridice*, the first of the composer's "reform" operas in a simpler dramatic style. By an unfortunate coincidence, *Orfeo* had had its *première* while Joseph's first wife, Isabella, had lain ill with the smallpox, so that, as Khevenhüller noted, "this peculiar choice was almost regarded as an evil omen."

And indeed the following morning, Wednesday the seventh, the couriers could be seen saddling up to carry the news to Naples and Madrid. For Josepha's illness had been identified: Once again, it was the smallpox. With such a disease no one could say what the outcome would be, but it was clear that the wedding journey, planned to begin in only eight days, would have to be postponed until the spring at least.

No one was more put out than Joseph, though not so much out of concern for his favourite sister, whose bout of the capricious disease he considered not serious. Rather, he was annoyed that his own journey through Italy would now have to be delayed. For one thing, he had been looking forward to escaping his mother for a time—since his father's death and his own elevation to the Empire's throne, her behaviour toward him had become rather overbearing. For another, he had wanted to see the sights, to converse with his admired brother Leopold in Florence, to visit Naples and Pompeii and Rome and Venice, cities he had never seen. And now "through this sorry incident it has all been spoiled and relegated to the lowest priority."

Joseph and four of his sisters—Marianna, Amalie, Carolina, and Antonia—had already had a mild form of the smallpox in childhood: They were safe. But Elisabeth, together with Ferdinand and ten-year-old Maximilian, were despatched at once to the Hofburg in Vienna. At Schönbrunn, the Empress, immune to the disease since her own infection in May, moved to an upper floor to be nearer to Josepha. Marie Christine and Albert arrived from Pressburg at the little palace of Hetzendorf outside Vienna; here they would stay for the time being, nearer to the family, yet safely distant. Josepha was doing fairly well; she seemed to have the same mild form that her sisters had had; there were red pustules on her face, but not on her body, and she was not delirious. Courtiers and family members allowed themselves a measure of cautious optimism.

But she quickly grew worse. On Saturday the tenth her condition was so poor that at five in the afternoon she was administered the last rites of the Church, with the "extreme unction" of holy oils. Marianna and Joseph accompanied the priest from the chapel downstairs back up to Josepha's bedside, but the Empress remained waiting for them on the landing, "since she had great trouble walking . . . and to see this grieving mother, tears streaming, moved all our hearts, especially as now, knowing the progress of this disease, there could be no hope of recovery, or only very little."

Indeed, on Sunday, the eleventh, it was announced that Josepha was dying, and within hours, that she was dead. But the news was false; she had simply lost consciousness. She came to, breathing with difficulty, to spend an easier night, then two easier days. By the morning of Wednesday the fourteenth, ten days after she had first been taken ill and her once intended wedding-day, those who loved her were beginning to hope again.

It was only on the afternoon of the same day that the course of "this treacherous illness" turned for the last time. Josepha became desperately cold; she could hardly breathe. The pustules, now spread to her hands, began to lose their redness. They became pale, shrinking inwards, "and we could not doubt, alas, that she no longer had the strength to drive the pox outwards again, to let the pustules erupt."

The physicians, uselessly, resorted to a purgative. A repentant Joseph had a bed made up for himself near his sister's. The Empress remained with them through most of the night. On Thursday, the fifteenth, Joseph gave orders that carriages should be readied for a sudden return to Vienna in the event of the worst. For some minutes, Josepha came to herself, and asked her mother if it was not the feast-day of her patron saint, Theresia. The Empress confirmed that it was. Josepha had the presence of mind, and the grace, to offer her mother her regret that from now on, her feast-day should be a day of mourning. Had she been able to choose, she said, she would have waited until the next day to take her leave.

At five in the evening in the Schönbrunn chapel, a service of Exposition of the Blessed Sacrament was held, the consecrated host in its jewelled monstrance held up to be viewed and adored by those present. And at six, Josepha died.

By morning, the roads out of Vienna were choked with people desperate to flee "the infected Viennese air." Leopold Mozart was able to secure two places in a northbound carriage; he took his son with him, leaving his wife and daughter to manage as best they could. It was to be a week before they could escape the city.

Those who had cared for Josepha at Schönbrunn were now quarantined there. Those who had had the smallpox before, and consequently could not infect others, returned to Vienna. Here they found a rumour circulating that Josepha had caught the disease from the unburied corpse of her sister-in-law, Joseph's wife, Maria Josepha. It was true she had visited the imperial crypt shortly before falling ill. She had gone with her mother to pray before the tomb of her late father, a dutiful gesture of farewell before setting out for the distant Kingdom of Naples. It had been more than five months since Maria Josepha's death from smallpox but, in a further, sad indication of her unimportance to anyone at court, no coffin had as yet been built for her. Her body lay in another part of the crypt, covered only with a thick veil, and with the windows open, so that "the poisonous exhalations" wafted through to Josepha and the Empress. Given the incubation period of the disease—at least a week and usually longer—Josepha could not have been infected in this way, but the rumour became legend, and the legend can be heard in Vienna still.

# VI

# 1767-1768

## In which tragedy strikes Elisabeth, and the King of Naples chooses a new Queen.

In Naples, plans for Josepha's arrival were for the moment in abeyance, but not because of the tragedy in Vienna. As yet, First Minister Tanucci had not even heard that Josepha had been taken ill. He had in any case more immediate concerns. From the British envoy, thirty-six-year-old William Hamilton, a careful observer of nearby Mount Vesuvius, Tanucci had been receiving warnings of the volcano's imminent eruption.

Hamilton's warnings were to be taken seriously. His scientific work was well regarded; indeed, his reports on the Vesuvius eruptions of the previous year had earned him a Fellowship of the Royal Society in London. Since his arrival in Naples in 1764, he had been monitoring the volcano, long famous to every European schoolboy through Pliny's eyewitness account of its eruption in the year 79, which had spelled the end of the ancient city of Pompeii. Over the past three years, Hamilton had spent hundreds of hours clambering over the blackened slopes of the mountain, knee-deep in ash, picking up salts and samples to examine and to send to other geological enthusiasts across the continent, each of them a cog in the wheel of the great international movement of discovery and analysis that was the scientific Enlightenment.

The Vesuvius eruptions of 1766 had lasted "about nine months in all." Now, it seemed certain, they were about to begin again. The volcano had been rumbling and spewing out stones; at night, reddish smoke could be seen furling out of its peak, and "by degrees, the smoak took the exact shape of a huge pine-tree, such as Pliny the Younger described in his letter to Tacitus." On the nineteenth of October 1767, at seven o'clock in the morning, the volcano erupted, this time in a vastly more powerful explosion than any of the year before. The seventeen-year-old King Ferdinando was at his palace at Portici, at the very foot of the mountain, and "the concussion of the air from the explosions was so violent, that, in the King's palace, doors and windows were forced open; and even one door there, which was locked, was nevertheless burst open." Ferdinando and everyone else fled Portici for the city, which was already in a state of terror, as Hamilton reported:

> *The confusion at Naples this night cannot be described . . . all the churches were opened and filled; the streets were thronged . . . the prisoners in the public jail attempted to escape. . . . Ships at sea, twenty leagues from Naples, were covered with [ashes]. . . . In the midst of these horrors, the mob, growing tumultuous and impatient, obliged the Cardinal to bring out the head of Saint Januarius, and go with it in procession toward Vesuvius; and it is well attested here, that the eruption ceased the moment the Saint came in sight of the mountain.*

Unlike the young King Ferdinando and his superstitious Neapolitans—"horrible fanatics," as the Empress viewed them, "far more to be feared than the whole eruption," who were only too eager to experience a miracle—the scientifically-minded Hamilton saw no operation of cause and effect in evidence here. But he was honest enough to admit that "it is true, the noise ceased about that time, after having lasted five hours, as it had done the preceding days"—the last phrase a vital empirical qualification in a report on its way to the Royal Society.

The ash fell thick on the city and the countryside for miles around it, inflaming the lungs and eyes of those who breathed it in. Such a vast quantity of it had been projected into the air that for days afterwards, the blue Neapolitan skies were completely obscured, and "the sun appear[ed] as through a thick London fog, or a smoaked glass."

With Vesuvius still erupting, a heroic or foolish Tanucci returned to the palace of Portici and sat down to pen a letter to his sovereign King Carlos in Madrid. He had only just learned of Josepha's illness. "You will know already of the Royal Spouse's smallpox, which postpones the wedding until March," he wrote. "I pray God, and we all beg God's mercy to make her well soon."

The courier despatched from Vienna on the seventh of October, announcing Josepha's illness and the wedding's postponement, had taken twelve days to reach Naples, with riders travelling at top speed in relays from post-house to post-house. By the time Tanucci received the news, five days had already passed in vigils and masses for her departed soul. Two members of the imperial family had absented themselves from the final obsequies: twenty-four-year-old Elisabeth, who had been feeling unwell and had retired to bed, and Joseph, who had elected to go hunting instead. Perhaps he had felt unequal to this ceremony for his favourite sister: As a friend observed, "though he may not have been aware of it, his attachment for the Archduchess Josepha was quite out of the ordinary, and her death has only distanced him further from any other woman."

Elisabeth's fever and weariness, assumed to be symptoms of chickenpox, did not abate. She developed an intense headache and pains in her back; she began to shiver; she was overcome with nausea. After two days, red spots appeared on her face and body, not the small red blisters of the chickenpox, however, but the poisonous pustules of the smallpox—"the same illness and of the same bad kind" as her deceased sister.

They appeared so suddenly and so severely that Elisabeth's death was thought imminent, but she was stronger than her sister had been. As the Empress had done for Josepha, so now she watched day and night beside another daughter, praying and in tears. "My heart is hanging by a thread," she declared. "My courage is completely gone. With God all is possible. I place myself entirely in His hands."

On the sixth day, Elisabeth herself gave up hope, and asked that the last sacrament be administered to her. For five further days she suffered and struggled, until at last, on the third day of November, her relieved, exhausted, yet still fearful mother was able to write a few lines to Ferdinand's betrothed in Milan: "I have the consolation of being able to inform you that my daughter is out of danger. . . . I ardently hope that my sons will not be attacked by the same illness."

Ferdinand and Maximilian, believed to be at risk of infection even from their immune mother, had had to remain at a distance, greeting her from the nave of the church as she sat in her balcony, or waving from beneath the windows of their sister's room. In due course, after much anxious reflection on the Empress' part, they themselves would be inoculated against the disease. The two archdukes would survive the often fatal operation, as their physician expected them to do: As was common throughout Europe at this time, he had been practising on the city's poor.

Elisabeth, once she was well enough, began to talk and to eat a little. After a time—how much time is not recorded—she bravely asked for a mirror. The image reflected back to her revealed the end of the life she had delighted in: an end of pride and admiration, an end of flirting and trifling with hearts, an end of coquetry and charm. Her once beautiful face, more beautiful than that of any of her sisters, was now covered in lumps and scars, some red, some pale, none ever to vanish.

Though her mother, and her eldest brother, too, would continue to haggle over her on the royal marriage market, Elisabeth's value had fallen drastically. The daughter and sister of emperors she remained, but without her lovely face, she would never be sought for herself. Even if she were to marry, she would be no more than a name on a deed of contract, an object of scorn and horror, neglected by her husband, no doubt, as her sister-in-law had been.

She was not present at the formal reception, a kissing of the Empress' hands, that was held at the Hofburg to mark her recovery. She appeared for the first time only late in November, on an ordinary day, among her family and the senior courtiers. Court Chancellor Khevenhüller allowed himself one brief remark about it in his diary: "I found her very much changed," he wrote.

**In Naples, with the prisoners** locked back in their cells, and the ash and stones being slowly cleared from the roofs and streets of the city, a weary Tanucci picked up his pen once again to commiserate with King Carlos in Madrid. His letter contained "the most bitter news"—not of Elisabeth's personal tragedy, since it would be some weeks before anyone heard of that so far from Vienna, but of Josepha's death, for after another twelve days of hard relay riding, the couriers announcing it had only just arrived. Despite "my declining age," Tanucci had energy and sagacity enough to press directly for "a new marriage . . . as similar, as nearly equivalent as can be."

It was not unduly heartless of him to do so. In Vienna, Chancellor von Kaunitz, who had known Josepha well, had already suggested the fifteen-year-old Carolina as her replacement: "She is no less suitable," he had written to Madrid, "and she has the advantage of having had the smallpox already, so that her beauty is not at risk from this cruel disease." It was a delicate matter, as Kaunitz's ambassador son in Naples admitted to his father: It could not be seen to be arranged with undignified haste, but at the same time, if it were too long delayed, some other princess might be found for Ferdinando, and the Habsburgs would lose Naples altogether. Meanwhile, he reported, the townspeople had decided for themselves who they wanted as their queen: not Josepha's younger sister Carolina, but her elder sister, twenty-one-year-old Amalie.

Ferdinando himself was in no state to offer an opinion. He had been furious at the news of Josepha's death: It had robbed him of a day's hunting, and now there would be months of dreary mourning. He took his revenge, or indulged his grief—perverse in either case—by staging a mock funeral procession, his attendants all in black, traipsing through the royal palace behind a wooden coffin, in which lay a young boy dressed as the late Archduchess, his face spotted with drops of chocolate in macabre imitation of the deadly pox.

His father's response was as straightforward as the son's had been bizarre. The Empress had other daughters "in stock." In mid-November, Maria Theresia received a letter from Carlos in which the King made his intentions clear: "It is up to us to make good this loss, in so far as it is possible. I am so eager to join my House with that of Your Majesty . . . that I ask you, without hesitation and without losing a moment's time, to approve another of your daughters for my son in Naples. We shall simply imagine we have changed the name, and Providence will bless our good intentions."

The Empress, indeed, had five other daughters "in stock." Marianna, however, was *hors de combat*, and Antonia was promised already. Elisabeth, at twenty-four, was probably too old for the seventeen-year-old Ferdinando, and as her mother said, "I am keeping her out of the affair; she has been ill enough in any case." That left only Amalie and Carolina. If the Neapolitans favoured the former, Tanucci favoured the latter, emphasizing that she was at least "safe from this tremendous Austrian danger of the smallpox." But Amalie was also immune, and the Empress thought her a better choice. Given the reports of Ferdinando's childish and wayward character, she felt an older bride would be more of a steadying influence on him. And as Court Chancellor Khevenhüller observed to his eldest son, "She is much more beautiful than her sister and will probably be more to the Neapolitan's liking."

True, there were plans already afoot for Amalie: There was still the Duke de Chablais, Franz Stephan's old favourite, and now, behind the scenes, the Infante of Parma as well, the brother of Joseph's first wife, Isabella. But nothing was certain. The Empress shrugged her shoulders. The King of

Spain should choose for himself. She wrote to tell him so, sending an envoy to Madrid with portraits of both girls, not forgetting all the same to emphasize Amalie's robust health, "which announces the likelihood of a numerous progeny."

And as Maria Theresia had left the decision to Carlos, so Carlos now left it to his son. From Tanucci's correspondence, it seems that Ferdinando did not care who his wife was to be, provided she was a Habsburg princess. When he saw the two portraits, however, his choice was immediate. She was less pretty than her sister, perhaps, but still, she had big blue eyes and rosy red lips, and she was just fifteen years old, nearly two years younger than himself: He chose Carolina.

Known within the family as Charlotte after her father's sister, Carolina was a strong-minded girl with none of the timidity in her mother's presence felt by some of her sisters. Though ready to praise a docile demeanour in others, Maria Theresia in fact rather liked this confident aspect of Carolina, remarking to Madame Lerchenfeld, "of all my daughters, she is the most like me." Carolina does seem to have had, even so early in life, her mother's sturdy sense of her place in the world and of her duty toward her family, and also a certain tenacity, enduring despite physical illness: through all the challenges of ruling and waging war and reforming a vast administration and bearing sixteen children, Maria Theresia had at times allowed herself to complain, but she had never given up. This stamina Carolina had inherited, along with some of her mother's less useful qualities, including her tendency to over-reward her favourites. The Empress, however, was not openly affectionate, and this trait Carolina possessed to a fault, with the prime beneficiary until now being her petted little sister, Antonia.

Unlike Josepha, Carolina made no objection to the match with Ferdinando. She was by no means without ambition, and was fully aware of the prestige and influence she would have as a queen, outranking all her sisters and equalling their mother in social position. No doubt she had understood, too, that her fate in any case was to be delivered, sooner or later, into the hands of some unknown man, whose age or appearance or habits or qualities of mind would count for next to nothing against the political advantages of her marriage with him.

There was no need to prepare a new contract of marriage between Ferdinando and his replacement Habsburg bride. Josepha's name and the proposed date of her wedding were simply scratched out of the thick parchment, and Carolina's inserted in its place. "I tremble for her," wrote the Empress to Madame Enzenberg. "She is so determined and bereft of any help or advice, and still such a scatterbrain, still only a child herself."

# VII

# 1767-1768

In which the Empress regains her zest for command, Amalie finds love only to lose it, and a Habsburg heir arrives at last.

*I am very fat, and also red, especially since the smallpox, but my feet, chest, eyes are wearing out; the first are very swollen; I am daily expecting them to split open. My eyes are almost completely gone; the worst thing is that I can use neither [magnifying] glass nor spectacles. I think I have the beginnings of damp in my chest, since breathing is difficult when I walk and even when I am lying down.*

Everyone at court, and all her friends elsewhere, had long been used to Maria Theresia's complaints of ill health and advanced age—she was now fifty years old. Her physician van Swieten was concerned about the dropsy swelling, a sign of heart trouble, but he was reluctant to bleed her; unlike most of his colleagues, he held that bleeding served only to weaken the patient. And she was suffering from pain in her right arm, which van Swieten supposed to be rheumatism, which gave her great trouble when writing—though she dictated much of her correspondence, she penned many personal letters in her own rounded hand. The Empress trusted her physician, but she was not an easy patient. As Marianna observed, "She didn't like to need anything."

And in fact, since her recent peril, in spirit at least she was feeling quite rejuvenated. For some time after Franz Stephan's death, she had been ready to abandon the arduous business of government for a quiet life in Innsbruck, but now, even if she couched it in terms of renunciation, she had rediscovered her zest for command. "Since the smallpox," she wrote, "I have made the sacrifice of reappearing and dedicating the rest of my sad days to my states and, as far as I am able, of devoting my last efforts to serving and being useful to them."

Though her recovery had been cause for general rejoicing, and her eldest son, Joseph, had been as relieved and thankful as anyone to see her well again, he was not pleased by his mother's full return to government. Now aged twenty-six, twice widowed and resolved never to marry again, he had fully committed himself to the business of state. Since his father's death more than two years before, he had become not only Holy Roman Emperor but also, at his mother's behest, formal co-regent with her of the Austrian Monarchy. He had relished this first stretching of his ruler's wings, and had been frustrated to find himself in practice less co-regent than sub-regent. And in his mother's experienced and implicitly trusted Chancellor von Kaunitz, officially responsible for foreign affairs but in fact dominating every ministry in the land, he had been confronted with a counterweight hardly less powerful than the Empress herself.

Joseph had nonetheless managed to introduce a handful of the many reforms he was wanting to make. If public policy was kept largely beyond his reach, in matters of court etiquette he had a freer hand, and here he had done much to curtail the ceremony that he himself so disliked. He had abolished the last trappings of Spanish court dress, halved the number of formal church attendances, prohibited gambling at card games ("which he doesn't know how to play in any case," as Khevenhüller noted sullenly), and, to the dismay of the French ambassador, eliminated almost all gala festivities.

Ongoing expenses, he insisted, were to be minimized. Military expenses could not be curtailed without compromising the security and standing of the Monarchy, but there were many discretionary expenditures, such as hunting and court entertainments; these Joseph reduced at no cost to himself, since he had always done his best in any case to avoid them. Subsidies were continued for the German theatre, which the Emperor promoted, and decreased for the French theatre, which he did not like. Some respite from their many formal commitments was probably welcome to his sisters; the reduction in pleasanter pastimes was no doubt less so.

By the autumn of 1767, it was clear the Empress was not going to retire to Innsbruck, or even to her favourite palace of Schönbrunn. Joseph was obliged to retreat into his old role of dutiful son, playing the ruler only when and where his mother allowed. Though she was not above threatening to abdicate when things did not easily go her way, Maria Theresia was not to lessen her grip on power in the years to come. Joseph would have to wait until he was almost forty before he could come into his own as sovereign.

JUST BEFORE THE NEW YEAR of 1768, in one brief sentence above a long disquisition on the treatment of genuine and fraudulent beggars—the former to be fed, the latter to be driven out of town—Vienna's twice weekly news-sheet announced the arrival in the city of a young Rhineland prince, heir to the Electorate of Bavaria. He was to lodge for the duration of his visit in the "House of God's Eye" on the Tuchlauben. The name of the little street, a stone's throw from the Hofburg, called to mind an earlier time when it had been a market arcade for fabrics and draperies; the house itself, still known by its old name, had so far escaped the new bureaucratic efforts to quantify and categorize all the Monarchy's persons and possessions: As yet it had no number.

The Prince was the twenty-one-year-old Karl August of Zweibrücken, and he was making his first visit to Vienna. On the very day of his arrival, he was presented at court, and Khevenhüller reported him as "a really very good figure of a man, markedly averse to French culture and manners"—in other words, disdaining the effete styles of the other, Frenchified courtiers in favour of a determined manliness, evidently to the Chancellor's approval.

There were many reasons for a young man to leave his little baroque town in the Rhineland for a sojourn in cosmopolitan Vienna, but it was rumoured that Karl August had come now with a specific purpose in mind: Maria Theresia wanted to arrange a match for him with the Archduchess Amalie. Though his father had recently died, he was not free to choose a bride to please himself, but the two uncles to whom he owed allegiance both supported the idea of his marrying a Habsburg princess. Amalie, not quite twenty-two, chestnut-haired, tall like her sisters, was about seven months older than the Prince. In the candlelit rooms of the Hofburg, on this winter's evening, they set eyes on each other for the first time.

It was love at first sight, as the Princess Eleonore von Liechtenstein told her sister, the Countess Leopoldine von Kaunitz, in Naples. Leopoldine was the wife of the Viennese Ambassador Ernst von Kaunitz, eldest of the Chancellor's six sons and the only one of any use, as his father had stated baldly. The two sisters, born Princesses of Oettingen-Oettingen and Oettingen-Spielberg (*sic*), were exceptionally close; their mother had died giving birth to Eleonore and they had no other siblings. They wrote to each other several times a week, with their thousands of confiding and informative letters, written over almost thirty years, becoming an important testimony of their times. Now, in January 1768, Leopoldine learned that Karl and Amalie had been driving out together in the same carriage, a clear indication of the Prince's purpose. "I'm pleased to see it," she replied. "I would like to see them married. It would be a good establishment for her, and a grand match for him."

In the first week of February 1768, with the formal contract of marriage between Carolina and King Ferdinando of Naples signed and sealed, the court's attention turned to Amalie. The announcement of her own betrothal was every day expected, not least by Amalie herself. Joyfully in love and loved in return, she had convinced herself that her mother would do for her what she had done for Marie Christine—and had plainly not done for her younger sisters—namely, give her blessing to a marriage, as the saying went, of inclination.

Amalie's feelings were clear to everyone, and the court took her part. Karl August was more than the proverbial handsome prince. Energetic and strong-minded and likeable, he was a man of wide-ranging interests, from military matters to painting and architecture. Joseph thought highly of him, and had predicted that "if he has a good brain, he will play a very great rôle in Germany one day. . . . In territory he will be as powerful as the [expansionist] King of Prussia, though I hope he won't have the same ideas."

The Prince departed, but in the first week of March an ambassador from his Palatinate uncle Maximilian arrived in Vienna with a formal proposal for the hand of the Archduchess Amalie in marriage. Amalie was ecstatic. Maximilian had even added to the offer by making Karl August immediate ruler of Neuburg on the Danube, a neighbouring principality within the Holy Roman Empire. There a court was to be established for them, "appropriate to the high birth and dignity of the couple, drawn in large part from the great noble families of Neuburg," and an infantry regiment garrisoned, "for the Prince's amusement."

The match looked settled. "It would ensure the Prince the two Electorates of Bavaria and the Palatinate," noted Leopoldine von Kaunitz. "If he married his sister, the Emperor would not contend with him over them." It was true that the Prince was heir apparent to all these broad lands; the two Electorates alone would give him two votes out of seven in the appointment of any future Holy Roman Emperor.

But this was a long way in the future, if indeed it would come to pass at all: Both the Prince's uncles, Maximilian of Bavaria and Karl Theodor of the Palatinate, were still only in their forties, and might yet have sons of their own. Karl Theodor indeed had a string of children installed near Cologne already, though admittedly all were illegitimate. And the little principality of Neuburg, garrisoned or not, could hardly be an adequate seat for the daughter of an empress.

Neither this meagre offering for the present, nor the possibility of power in the future, was enough to sway Chancellor von Kaunitz. He urged Maria Theresia and Joseph to decline the Prince's offer. Amalie's feelings were not considered, and could in any case have held no sway over Kaunitz's cool politicking. The enormously influential "first minister of all the first ministers of Europe" had little trouble in persuading the hopeful bride's mother and brother to his own point of view. Two days after the ambassador had made the proposal, Kaunitz informed him it had been rejected.

Marie Christine's sympathetic husband, Albert, had been watching the drama unfold. This quondam "subsidized prince" noted the nub of the problem in his diary: "Since he had not the means to offer a suitable establishment to the Archduchess, the Empress herself would have had to supplement their income, as she had done in the case of my wife. However, this sovereign lady did not see any need to lend her support to this idea." Albert understood the difference. Marie Christine was her mother's favourite. Rules could be bent and purses stretched to ensure her happiness. Amalie was in no such position. Her happiness would have cost more than her mother was willing to pay.

Like many aristocrats of Bohemian origin, Chancellor von Kaunitz had made his career in Vienna, and his refusal of the Prince's offer now was the quintessence of Viennese disingenuousness, as he relayed smoothly to the Empress:

> *I did not hesitate, consequent upon Your Majesty's orders and those of His Majesty the Emperor, to make him a very positively negative reply, although perfectly honest, and for that I made use of the phrasing that seemed to me most appropriate. The candidate's supposed brilliant prospects . . . can be set at so little value, and his current situation, which is scarcely that of a moderately comfortable private person, renders the whole proposition so absurd that one has difficulty in restraining one's annoyance at it. But happily it is so ridiculous that one can confine oneself to laughing about it. . . . I*

*most humbly beg Your Majesty's pardon for these little observations which have escaped me.*

Amalie, for one, did not confine herself to laughing about it. She wept and protested furiously, and from this point she thrust aside the role of dutiful imperial daughter to become ever more insubordinate, erratic, and self-indulgent, until some were ready to declare her a madwoman.

And behind the scenes it was rumoured there was quite another reason for the refusal: Despite Kaunitz's disapproval of military ventures abroad, twenty-six-year-old Joseph was already nursing ambitions to take Bavaria for himself. His marriage to a Bavarian princess, after all, though he had loathed and neglected her, had given him a pretext to do so. But, as Leopoldine had observed, Joseph could hardly contest Karl August's claim to Bavaria if they were brothers-in-law. Kaunitz was against any Bavarian venture. He had been responsible for the Monarchy's foreign affairs since Joseph was a boy of ten, and he was convinced that Austria should be expending its energies on internal reform rather than territorial expansion. Joseph was a young man still, and Kaunitz's power was for the moment almost absolute, but in time, both factors would change. The question of Bavaria would arise again, and Karl August would be swift to answer it.

On receiving news of the refusal, he had not been seen to laugh either. He was humiliated, and a slow-burning vengeance took seed in his broken heart. "He will be as powerful as the King of Prussia," Joseph had written, "though I hope he won't have the same ideas." But between them, Joseph and Kaunitz and the Empress had made of Karl August an implacable enemy. In his determination to strike back at Austria, he was to have very much the same idea as the King of Prussia. Indeed, within a decade, with Friedrich II at his back, he was to take the field against the Habsburgs in a futile and wasteful war over Bavaria.

His Elector-uncle, Karl Theodor, was not quite ready to abandon the idea of a Habsburg match for him. Over the next two or three years, he was to approach the Empress several times about it: It seems he thought that if

Prince Karl was not good enough for Amalie, he might be acceptable for the devalued Elisabeth, with her smallpox-scarred face, whose marriage prospects must necessarily be lesser. His insistence, in the face of repeated refusals, occasioned an embarrassed correspondence between Baron Neny, the Habsburgs' negotiator, and the Elector's own Count Lehrbach. "We are still somewhat deterred by the very meagre propositions that Monseigneur the Elector made two or three years ago," Neny told Lehrbach, "and for the present we do not expect His Royal Electoral Highness to make any offers of an establishment such as the rank and dignity that Madame the Archduchess Elisabeth would require." Lehrbach understood, and took it upon himself to offer more, up to 100,000 florins per annum, given "the great desire the Elector has, and which he will not relinquish, to obtain Her Royal Highness." Whether Elisabeth would have been content to accept Prince Karl on these or any other conditions is unknown. The Elector, fearing a second humiliation, or wanting to keep other possible matches in play, had stipulated the negotiations must be kept secret, with Neny duly informing Lehrbach, "Your Excellency may assure Monseigneur the Elector that upon this object an inviolable secrecy will be maintained." And so it appears to have been, very probably even from Elisabeth herself.

**Whatever Amalie and Elisabeth** may have felt, Kaunitz and his sovereigns were confident that in rejecting Prince Karl of Zweibrücken, they had preserved the integrity of the House of Habsburg. But their satisfaction was not unqualified. No marriageable daughter, no matter how closely controlled, could guarantee the succession of that same illustrious House. For that, a son was needed—in fact, the son of a son.

In this most vital duty of an heir, Joseph had so far proved a failure. Though he did have a daughter, another little Maria Theresia, now almost six years old, there was no likelihood of her eventually inheriting the Austrian and Hungarian crowns, let alone the throne of the Holy Roman Empire. The Pragmatic Sanction of fifty years before, which had allowed a daughter to inherit in the absence of any male heirs, would not necessarily be honoured in the future; it had not even been honoured in 1740, when France, Prussia, and other powers had turned on the young Maria Theresia, challenging her for the succession. The ensuing war had lasted eight years, sharpening the Empress' preference for sons into an obsession. The simple fact of a male heir now could prevent a similar war in the future.

Yet after the brief but miserable years of his second union, Joseph had declared he would never marry again. In consequence, with Ferdinand and Maximilian not yet out of the schoolroom, all eyes were on twenty-year-old Leopold, whose wife, Maria Luisa, already the mother of an infant daughter, was about to give birth again. Maria Theresia had persuaded herself that the baby would be another girl but, tempered by the family's recent losses, or perhaps not wishing to tempt Providence, she remained, at least outwardly, dispassionate: "Provided the father and mother are well," she insisted, "we can wait for everything else."

Her temperance was rewarded: In mid-February 1768, at the imposing Palazzo Pitti in Florence, Maria Luisa was safely delivered of a son, Franz Joseph Karl of Habsburg-Lorraine. When the news arrived at the Hofburg, the joyful Empress at once rushed across to the Burgtheater, interrupting the performance and astounding the spectators by shouting out, in broad Viennese dialect, *Der Poldl hat an Buam!*—Leopold's got a boy! It was the first time she had appeared in the theatre since Franz Stephan's death two and a half years before, but her elation was warranted, and the public responded by cheering to the rafters. Eleonore von Liechtenstein was among the audience. "It was a really moving spectacle," she told her sister in Naples.

As for Joseph himself, he could not have been happier, seeing himself freed at last from the obligation of yet another marriage of state. Instead, his royal and imperial inheritance could eventually pass to the family of his able and, in his view, more deserving brother—Leopold, known to his siblings as "Doctor," had always maintained an intellectual and moral dominance within the family. Within months, another baby was on the way; Joseph wrote delightedly to Leopold: "Excellent populator, dear brother, what do I not owe you! Your wife is pregnant yet again. You render a service to the state, and I'm eternally obliged to you as well. Carry on, dear brother, don't slacken the pace, bravely give the monarchy as many children as you can. If they're like you, there will never be too many of them."

From the perspective of the Monarchy, there could indeed never be too many, and Leopold himself was to be conspicuously happy among his children. Over the course of twenty-one years, Maria Luisa would bear no fewer than twelve sons, plus a further four politically useful daughters, uncomplainingly fulfilling her dynastic duty, again, and again, and again.

THE BIRTH OF A SON to Leopold and Maria Luisa had assured the Habsburg succession, and the matches made with Naples and France had strengthened the Bourbon alliance, but there remained the question of Parma. Though small and far from rich, it was the only Bourbon court in northern Italy, and it remained an important foothold for political control of the region. Its reigning Duke, Don Ferdinando, was still in search of a bride, or rather, his overweening first minister, Guillaume Du Tillot, was still seeking a bride for him. Three years before, Elisabeth had been considered, then ruled out as being too much older than the Duke, but the idea of a match had persisted. In April 1768, with Prince Karl of Zweibrücken out of the way, it was decided this dynastic duty should fall to twenty-two-year-old Amalie.

Though dominated by Du Tillot, Don Ferdinando was officially the ruler of Parma. As an heir, though not direct, to the Spanish throne, he also held the title of Infante, and it was by this appellation that he was generally known. And if overshadowed in government, he was already highly regarded for his fine intellect and liberal character—rather too highly, as it transpired.

From a distance, at least, Don Ferdinando seemed an ideal prince, but Amalie did not care. She regarded him as a mere schoolboy; at seventeen, he was five years younger than she was. Her Prince Karl had been a man, full-grown, a soldier in the making. And if the Duchy of Zweibrücken had been dismissed as insignificant, what was so important, it seemed to her, about the Duchy of Parma? And Don Ferdinando was only a duke; she was an archduchess, above him in rank as she was in age. Her younger sisters were marrying kings; she was effectively being demoted. Only weeks before, she and Karl had been together at the Hofburg, looking to Marie Christine and Albert as a happy auspice for their own love match. Now she was to be parcelled off to a place she did not want to go, to be subservient for the rest of her life to a juvenile husband whom she had never met.

Maria Theresia had promoted the match enthusiastically. Joseph, less enamoured of the Bourbon alliance, had disagreed with his mother's choice, finding it "very strange that I should sacrifice my daughter. If I have done so," the Empress insisted to Leopold, "it is for reasons of state . . . and knowing the abyss into which my daughter was about to fall, I wanted to save her while there was still time."

The "abyss" before Amalie does not seem to have been any looming scandal; there had been no thought, for instance, of her eloping with Prince Karl. Rather, the abyss seems to have been one of serious ill health, probably mental as well as physical. But in administering the medicine of a forced marriage, Maria Theresia was feeding her daughter poison. The effects were immediate, and they were never to disappear entirely, as the exasperated and rueful Empress was to lament in letter after letter.

The consent of the Pope was required for the marriage, and to this end she now appealed to His Holiness, Clement XIII. Amalie registered a desperate protest to the whole business by withdrawing to her rooms and refusing to eat.

# VIII

# 1768

## In which Carolina becomes Queen of Naples, and hundreds of people make a thousand-mile journey.

*The King of Spain remaining constant in his intention of uniting his House ever more closely to the House of Austria, initiated, after the death of the Archduchess Josepha, a new negotiation with this court. . . . In consequence, on the seventh of April 1768, the Archduke* Ferdinand *married by proxy, in the name of the King of the Two Sicilies, his sister the Archduchess Carolina, and the new Queen departed Vienna the same day to journey to Naples.*

Thus the text composed by Marianna for her copper engraving of a large bronze medallion marking Carolina's marriage to King Ferdinando. She was producing a book depicting all the medals minted to commemorate the major events of her mother's reign—all the official ones, at least, with any unflattering medals struck by the Empress' opponents simply omitted. The idea for such a collection of engravings had originally come from Marianna's grandfather, the Emperor Karl VI, who had admired the *histoire metallique* compiled to commemorate the reign of

Louis XIV of France. Karl had produced no such collection, but he had passed the idea to his daughter, and so it had survived into the third generation, and Marianna, possessing the necessary time and talents and moved by a wish to please her mother, had brought it all into being.

Copper engravings were particularly popular at this time. Attractive works in themselves, they also served as portable reproductions of larger works—oil paintings, sculptures, and architectural marvels—that could not otherwise be widely seen. Marianna herself was a fine engraver. She had been trained by two celebrated exponents of the art, and had recently been elected a member of Vienna's Imperial Academy of Copper Engravers. Her skill was such that she was now making the medallion engravings "exactly after the originals," guided in her selection by an elderly French numismatist, and assisted by a twelve-year-old apprentice named Adam Bartsch, later to serve as advisor to Marie Christine and Albert as they assembled their own spectacular collection of prints and drawings. It may have been the presence of young Bartsch who inspired Ferdinand and Maximilian, thirteen and eleven, to take an interest in commemorative coins and medals themselves: They now had a press set up to allow them to make their own.

Marianna's engravings were a major undertaking that no doubt helped to bring a sense of purpose to her often rather lonely days. She had the eventual hefty book of three hundred copper plates, with a parallel description in German and French adjoined to each, bound in blue morocco leather embossed in gold. On the front there was an image of Maria Theresia, and on the back, one of Marianna herself, feather pen in hand, drawing a medallion. She sits before a Greek temple, opposite a statue of Pallas Athena, goddess of handcrafts—and heroic endeavour.

LIKE ALL WEDDINGS in the imperial family, Carolina's took place in the Church of St Augustine, decorated for the occasion with extravagant displays of bright spring flowers. Marie Christine's, two years past, had been an event of great happiness; Josepha's reluctant wedding, only six months before, had turned to tragedy. Carolina's feelings were at neither extreme: More politically minded and more stoical in temperament than Josepha, she had stepped into her sister's role with some nervousness, no doubt, but also with determination and pride. She understood, at least in theory, that she was about to be delivered to a man everyone knew to be an ill-bred buffoon, perhaps an imbecile. "She is very well aware how difficult her situation is," her mother had said. "One feels sorry for her." But she was also going to become a queen, the first of her sisters to equal their mother in personal rank. By marrying the Bourbon King of Naples, Carolina was strengthening Maria Theresia's most vital diplomatic alliance, and extending Austria's influence in Italy. Indeed, she would be, in a measure, reclaiming the kingdom once held by her grandfather, the Emperor Karl VI, before he lost it to the Bourbons.

Her realm would be large, encompassing the whole of southern Italy and the island of Sicily, and her palaces far grander than anything to be found in the Habsburg lands. Her seat in Naples itself, the old Renaissance-style Palazzo Reale, had recently been embellished in anticipation of her arrival. Built early in the previous century, from one side it looked out across the bay to Vesuvius, and from the other, to a grand public piazza alive with noise and movement and colour. The other three royal residences, all built by her father-in-law, King Carlos III of Spain, were even more impressive: Capodimonte, a vast edifice of red volcanic rock on the hills above the city, pretty Portici, along the coast on the slopes of Vesuvius, and the stupendous palace of Caserta, built by "an army of labourers and Muslim slaves captured on the coasts of North Africa," the largest royal residence in the world, with five floors and some twelve hundred rooms—no one was quite sure of the exact number.

By contrast, the living standards of the Kingdom's people were miserably low. Two centuries of rule by the Spanish Habsburgs, exploiting the region's natural riches but developing nothing for the local population, had left many of them living like "the most miserable savages." With the arrival of the enlightened Bourbon Carlos in 1734, a period of reform had begun, but the entrenched interests of the nobles and the Church, together with a marked local tendency to inertia, had limited its success. Carolina had learned of these difficulties from Chancellor von Kaunitz, who had recently been instructing her in the history and politics of the Kingdom, and, as he reported to her mother, she had responded with intelligence and enthusiasm—and no doubt a degree of confusion as well: While Kaunitz had been impressing on his charge the importance of her outwardly deferring to Naples' powerful First Minister Tanucci, he not been able to conceal his own mistrust of the man. Tanucci was and always had been a servant of King Carlos of Spain; between Spain and France, though both were Bourbon powers, there was a marked rivalry, and France was now aligned with Austria. Though marrying into the Spanish Bourbons, behind the scenes, Carolina was expected to continue serving the Habsburgs.

CAROLINA'S HEART WAS TENDER, and she shed many tears at the prospect of leaving her family. "She does nothing but weep. It's costing her infinitely more to leave us than it did the other one [Josepha]," the Empress confided to her friend Count Rosenberg. Yet there was also a certain ambition in her, even at fifteen, and in her character a willingness to sublimate her feelings into a rewarding sense of doing her duty, which Josepha had lacked. As their mother had said, "Of all my daughters, Carolina is the most like me," though there may have been another factor in this assessment: The Empress had admitted to Marie Christine that, "after you, she is the one who has always shown the most real concern to seek and follow my advice."

So if apprehensions about King Ferdinando's personal failings came to Carolina now, they were not necessarily uppermost in her mind. Today, in any case, in making her vows, she had only to see the friendly face of her brother Ferdinand, who was acting the part of proxy bridegroom, as he had been intended to do for Josepha. Ferdinand was now almost fourteen years old, and since that fatal day, he had grown taller and his physique had begun to fill out, a satisfying state of affairs for his anxious fiancée in Milan, whom the Empress felt she could now reassure: "If he is not marred by the smallpox," she had told the well-built Beatrice, "he will be handsome enough." The Princess von Trautson, an elderly lady-in-waiting, was less convinced. "He is growing," she admitted, "but he'll always be a pretty little miniature compared to the lady destined to be his life's companion."

He was tall enough at least for a proxy bridegroom, and he escorted his sister elegantly to the high altar. She looked very pale and, like Marie Christine, wore a white gown embroidered with exotic myrtle flowers in silver thread. But where her elder sister's had been muslin, a modest choice in a time still marked by mourning for their father, Carolina's was of the finest silk satin, and the bride herself was "draped in jewellery of inestimable value." The ceremony was conducted by the papal nuncio, surrounded on the altar by a quasi-angelic host of ecclesiastics, all of them also in nuptial white. After the exchange of vows—Carolina's preceded by a deep bow to her mother—the men of the choir gave resounding voice to a thanksgiving psalm in ancient Ambrosian plainchant, a thousand years older than the church itself.

The long journey to Naples was to begin that same afternoon. After the ceremony, the family returned to the Hofburg to partake of a last meal all together, but there were many tears, and neither the bride nor her mother was able to swallow a morsel, with the Empress confessing, tellingly, to Rosenberg, "I love my children very much, but I only really feel it when I have to lose one." Carolina left the table, and went to her apartments to change into her travelling clothes.

It may have been now that she sat down to compose a brief letter to her new father-in-law, the King of Spain. Certainly, the letter is dated on her wedding-day, but it is a formal, indeed formulaic note, penned in her clear schoolroom handwriting with a few celebratory flourishes, and she had probably prepared it beforehand, to be sent from the Hofburg on this day: "I have just been united to the King your Son by the sacred Bonds of Marriage," she wrote, "and I am departing, to take my place by His side, filled with the Desire to constitute his Happiness, which will constitute all my Felicity. . . . My foremost Study will forever be to convince Your Majesty of my perfect submission and tender attachment." Had she been able to see even a few months into the future, Carolina might have phrased the letter more equivocally. Tender attachment was very much in her nature, but, unluckily for the King, and his son and the ministers of Naples, perfect submission was not.

Downstairs, her family and friends, her servants and her beloved *aya*, Madame Lerchenfeld, stood waiting for her. She returned to them wearing a gown of vibrant blue, trimmed with gold. Both colours featured on her new coat of arms as Queen of Naples and Sicily, and all those travelling with her now were dressed in the same.

It was time to go. In tears, Carolina embraced her mother and, one after the other, her weeping sisters and brothers. Ferdinand handed her into her carriage. The Neapolitan ambassador had wanted her to have it to herself, so that she could travel in solitary royal splendour, as befitted, in his view, her exalted new rank. But Maria Theresia had brushed aside this forlorn Spanish etiquette and instead ensured her daughter would have good company on her long journey: Waiting inside the carriage now was the Countess Antonie Paar, not quite fifty, a capable princess of the great Esterházy family of Hungary and also, had Carolina known it, a reliable informer to the Empress. Carolina took her seat, but no sooner had she done so than she jumped up and out of the carriage to embrace her mother once again, and then, repeatedly, her precious youngest sister, Antonia. Then, to the sound of rumbling wheels and the cracking of whips, and farewells spirited or mournful, she was on her way.

**It is near** to a thousand miles from Vienna to Naples, much of it over difficult terrain or hazardous rutted roads. For a vast train on wooden wheels, it was an arduous undertaking. To cross the Alps, the very carriages had to be dismantled, with the more highly ranked of their passengers hoisted in litters onto the shoulders of frozen-footed servants. Half the distance might have been covered more comfortably by ship from the Monarchy's own port of Trieste, or even along the western coast of Italy, from Genoa, and this idea had rather appealed to Maria Theresia, but in the end, ease of travelling could not be the main consideration for a royal and imperial cortège. Apart from the actual "delivery" of the bride, Carolina's slow procession southward was to serve as a celebration of Habsburg splendour for those who were the dynasty's friends, and a reminder of its power for those who were not. Consequently, it was to be as grand as possible.

It was very grand indeed. Some 350 carriages and wagons preceded and followed the new Queen's royal coach, her entire Vienna household, with ladies-in-waiting, liveried footmen, and servants of all kinds, trailing carts loaded with food and clothes and silver and linen, the whole escorted by a troop of dragoons (mounted infantry), with a prestigious company of German soldiers as her personal guard. To keep the vast caravan rolling, 370 fresh horses stood waiting at every post station along the way.

It had originally been intended that, as he had planned to do for Josepha, Joseph should accompany Carolina to Naples, but, detesting all formalities, he had excused himself, confessing to Count Rosenberg, "The truth is that I am not on such intimate terms with the others as I was with my late sister." In his place, Leopold was to escort Carolina at least part of the way through Italy, with his wife, Maria Luisa, elder sister to Carolina's new husband, travelling with them.

It was only in Innsbruck, ten days after setting out from Vienna, that Carolina had a moment to herself to pen a first informal letter home. It was to her former *aya*, Madame Lerchenfeld, and after details of the journey, she asked for news of her favourite sister, Antonia, herself a notoriously reluctant letter writer: "Tell me," she implored, "all the smallest circumstances of Antonia, what she says, what she's doing, almost what she's thinking too. I urge and beg you to love her dearly for I care about her terribly, every kindness you show to her you will be showing to me. . . . Adieu my dear *Aya*, I love you doubly in gratitude for all you've done for me and in advance for all you will do for my dear sister."

From Innsbruck, Carolina's enormous wedding train travelled directly southwards, through the spring alpine passes, still heavy with snow, to Bologna, a border city of the papal states, and here she was welcomed by her brother Leopold, Grand Duke of Tuscany. It had been almost three years since the two had last seen each other, before his own wedding in Innsbruck and their father's sudden death. Leopold was pleased to find the lively schoolgirl he remembered matured into an engaging young woman, blue-eyed and rosy-lipped, and eager, too, to learn about politics and government. He did slip back into his old family pose of "Doctor" to caution her against chatting too freely with the young guardsmen, however, and though she seemed to understand the need for discretion, for the onward fifty-mile journey to Florence, he took the precaution of replacing them with greyer men.

Leopold held court in the Palazzo Pitti, a vast Renaissance edifice established by a Florentine banker in the days of Cosimo de' Medici. Since then it had become the seat of the Grand Dukes, but if its exterior was forbidding, the life of the court within it was unceremonious and full of interest. Politically, Leopold's palace was a hub of the latest Enlightenment ideas; still only twenty, he had already begun the work that would make him one of the great reforming rulers of his age. Culturally, the palazzo was a treasure house, the immense acquisitions of its Medici owners over the previous centuries having filled every room with beauties and glories. Carolina found the imposing Renaissance buildings of Florence "more beautiful than Vienna, but for me they don't have any of the other's charm and softness," but she was drawn at once to the gentle countenance of her "really amiable sister-in-law," Leopold's twenty-three-year-old wife, Maria Luisa.

Not having been present at their wedding, she had not met her before, but despite the eight-year difference in their ages, a warm friendship developed between them in the days they spent together in Florence and on the week-long journey down to Naples. Though Maria Luisa was the sister of Carolina's new husband, she did not know him well: On her father's accession to the throne of Spain, she had moved to Madrid with her parents, leaving the child Ferdinando behind in Naples. Consequently, there was not much she could tell Carolina about him. Not three years married, the equable Maria Luisa was already the mother of two small children, both "very pretty," as Carolina reported, "the girl is walking and the boy," the future Emperor Franz II, just three months old, "is very strong and never cries."

The warmth of Leopold's family circle was a comfort to Carolina, for by now, almost a month after her departure, she was feeling homesick. Her letters to Madame Lerchenfeld are full of queries about goings-on in Vienna and greetings to people left behind. "But above all," she wrote, in her own wayward script and imperfect French, "I beg you, love Antonia and let her write to me in her dreadful handwriting and bad style, only it musn't be a nuisance to her and she must enjoy writing to me. I would really like it if she could . . . Adieu dear *Aya*, you will see how much I like talking to you since I can't finish."

Passing through Rome, just 150 miles distant from Naples, they pointedly avoided any audience with Pope Clement XIII, for between the Holy See and Naples there was a deep diplomatic rift. As far as the Pope was concerned, the Kingdom of Naples and all who belonged to it were his subjects, and had been since a papal power grab more than five hundred years before. But in recent years, the Neapolitans, led by First Minister Tanucci, had refused to recognize that authority; in their view, Naples was an independent kingdom owing no political allegiance whatsoever to the papacy. Following the example of the French, they had taken many of the Catholic Church's former powers into their own hands and confiscated much of its property. The Pope had responded by excommunicating Tanucci, but the tough old minister had held his ground. The kings of France, Spain, and Portugal were on his side—by now, indeed, the Church's political power was declining in all parts of Europe. Naples would not submit to Rome.

"I am well," Carolina told Madame Lerchenfeld as she left the Eternal City, "but my heart is sad and oppressed, being so close to its destiny. . . . More than ever I would like to return to my homeland and see my family again and my dear compatriots. I beg you, tell my sister [Antonia] that I love her tenderly." The nearer they came to Naples, the more sombre her mood became. The pace of approach to Carolina's "destiny" in fact increased as she went, thanks to the now excellent roads leading to Naples. Tanucci's fifteen hundred fractious labourers had risen at last to the challenge, and they had overlain part of the ancient Appian Way, "already dilapidated in the days of Horace," with small square stones, covered with "a kind of earth found in these parts that seems to condense, and it gives the road a consistency that can somehow withstand the inconveniences that roads are normally subject to elsewhere."

And as the pace quickened, so did Carolina's nervousness. Leopold, concerned, reported to his mother that she was hardly sleeping, and that the demands of the journey and constant receptions by local dignitaries had so exhausted her that at times she could not even speak coherently. As they neared the port of Terracina, which marked the border of the Kingdom of Naples, she began to tremble so violently that Maria Luisa thought her about to faint. Her state of mind was not improved by the sisterly conversation that followed their arrival in the bleak little harbour town. The Empress had asked Maria Luisa to explain to Carolina what she was to expect on her wedding-night.

There were some who were already persuaded that a traumatic experience awaited her. Count Rosenberg, Leopold's Grand Chamberlain and general right-hand man (and Maria Theresia's own spy at his court), had been sent on ahead to Naples, and the report he sent back now to Terracina did nothing to inspire confidence. Ferdinando was ugly and clumsy, he said, with a dreadfully loud voice: "When he speaks, he shouts, and he waves his arms about . . . I very much fear the effect the first sight of him will have on the young Queen."

Though unmarried himself, the forty-five-year-old Rosenberg was sensitive enough to imagine the repulsion Carolina would feel at the prospect of sex with Ferdinando, and he urged Leopold and his wife to prepare her very carefully. "After the first quarter of an hour of tears and anguish, she will calm down and accept her misfortune with patience. It is vital that your good lady wife and all the ladies give her courage to endure her wifely duties without displaying any disgust. On this point the whole happiness of her life could depend." Though thin, the King was tall and well-proportioned and healthy, and likely, Rosenberg thought, to transfer his appetites to other women if the Queen did not keep him sexually satisfied.

Carolina, of course, did not see this letter, nor would it have helped her if she had. Over the next few days there were more fits of trembling and sobbing. At Portella, at the moment of "delivery," where her own household staff and guards retreated and those arriving from Naples took their place, she absolutely collapsed, recovering only to throw her arms repeatedly around the young Countess von Trauttmansdorff, now returning to Vienna with the 250 courtiers and servants who had accompanied her thus far. Carolina's own distress swept through the whole assembly, until among the Viennese, there was only weeping and dismay, and among the Neapolitans, only embarrassment. The Prince Belmonte, Ferdinando's Grand Chamberlain and husband of his supposed mistress, attempted to console or at least distract her with a sumptuous pearl bracelet and a diamond necklace, but she could barely give him a few words of thanks. As Leopold wrote to Joseph, "I would not witness such another scene for an entire kingdom."

In the event, Count Rosenberg's fears proved more than founded. Carolina experienced a traumatic wedding-night. Spanish court custom required her to go to bed heavily clothed, in a tight-laced bodice and even wearing gloves. It was early summer in steamy Naples, and the following morning her husband baldly remarked to his hunting companions of his new wife, "She sweats like a wild boar."

Distraught, Carolina relayed the grim details to Maria Luisa. The King had behaved "very roughly and very reluctantly"—perhaps, at seventeen, he had not had much idea what to do with a virginal girl even younger than himself. Heroically, Carolina took the blame on herself, but Maria Luisa had other ideas: She took her brother to task about it, and to his credit, he responded well, bringing Carolina a gift of large diamonds and—an astounding step to those who knew him—cancelling his daily hunts to spend time quietly with her. His wife was greatly to his taste, he said.

In response, Carolina exerted herself to please him. "The King is very ugly, but one gets used to it," she told Madame Lerchenfeld, "but apart from that his character is better than people said. What annoys me most is that he thinks he's handsome and suave, and he's neither one nor the other. Honestly I must confess I only love him out of duty, but I'm doing all I can to make him think I'm passionately in love with him, I behave very sweetly and patiently. He says he really loves me, but he never does anything I want."

# IX

# 1768–1769

In which Amalie is demoted, the French monarch is disappointed of vicarious pleasures, and Elisabeth loses two more kings.

*My very dear grandson . . . I am expecting a courier from Spain bringing me news of your marriage. I have been looking forward to it for some time, as you know, and afterwards, I expect to hear how you found attaining knowledge of a woman.*

Thus King Louis XV of France to the seventeen-year-old Duke of Parma, revealing a rather hasty prurience, for though the marriage had been agreed by both families, it had not yet received approval from the Pope. The betrothal was formally announced on the last day of April 1768, to the satisfaction of Louis at Versailles and Carlos in Madrid and seemingly everyone in Vienna apart from Amalie herself. Informed that her betrothal was to be announced, "she threw herself at the Empress' feet," weeping and railing. Maria Theresia was impassive. Amalie implored her to at least give her a year to get used to the idea. The Empress rebuffed her. Amalie became defiant. She flatly refused to marry the Duke; if her mother absolutely ordered her to do so, she warned, she would be miserable for the rest of her days.

The Empress stood firm. "Everyone here is talking anew about the marriage of the Archduchess Amalie with the Infante Duca di Parma," the Venetian ambassador reported. "The tales they tell here of this prince could not be more advantageous."

Don Ferdinando had been educated with assiduous care by two French pedagogues, the first, Auguste de Keralio, a former military engineer with a passion for mathematics, and the second, one of the most famous figures of the Enlightenment, the long-faced, sharp-eyed Étienne Bonnot de Condillac. Keralio had been Don Ferdinando's *ayo*, and thus responsible for his moral education, since the boy was six; Condillac had arrived some years later to oversee his intellectual training. Both were believing men, Condillac indeed an abbé, but their Christianity was similar in nature, if not in name, to Maria Theresia's Jansenism—simple, unpolemical, and far from the superstitious old ways of *le petit peuple*. In this respect they were progressive men, but that had not prevented them from imposing an exceptionally strict discipline on Don Ferdinando, including confinements and beatings.

Amalie, still refusing to eat, was growing thin and ill. Envoys and spies in Vienna reported the new development to Versailles, and an anxious correspondence ensued between First Minister Du Tillot in Parma and his envoy in France, the Baron d'Argental, a squat little man known to his intimates as "Tubby." Du Tillot told D'Argental that he had heard, through not quite official channels, that Amalie might not be able to bear children. D'Argental doubted the truth of it. "That would be more worrying than a real illness, which would give us the right to abandon the match," he replied. "We must try by all possible means to discover the truth. No one could object if the uncertainty over the Archduchess Amalie's condition should bring him, despite the disproportion in their ages, to seek the Archduchess Elisabeth."

The idea that Amalie could not bear children may have originated in concern about her refusal to eat, which might have interrupted her menstrual cycle; anecdotes may have resurfaced about the injury she had sustained as a girl of nine, when she had resisted the enema and her rectum had been injured; or the rumour may have come from Amalie herself, still trying, at this late stage, to avoid marrying the Infante. Among the Bourbon ministers, a suspicion arose that the Empress was deliberately putting forward an infertile princess for their duke, since by law, if he should have no heirs, the Duchy would revert to direct Habsburg rule. Eventually D'Argental concluded that Du Tillot had invented the whole story, hoping to cancel the match and marry Don Ferdinando instead to the heiress Beatrice d'Este, currently betrothed to Amalie's brother Ferdinand: Her vast inheritance would easily have filled the hole in Parma's public finances.

Had anyone enquired with any interest in solving the matter, the cause of Amalie's malaise was clear enough to see. Whether her sisters now comforted or chided her, or merely sympathized in silence, is not known. She had always been close to Marianna, and this was never to change, so it can be assumed that her eldest sister at least was ready to help dry her tears and, probably, to recommend resignation and the consolations of religion. Maria Theresia herself had not long remained "very pleased indeed" about the match. As empress, she had made a calculated decision that would benefit the Austrian Monarchy, but as a mother, her heart could not remain unmoved by Amalie's distress. Even at this late stage, she appeared to hesitate, instructing Count Rosenberg to ride the hundred miles up from Florence, where he was serving as Leopold's right-hand man, to make a close inspection of the Duke and his Parma court.

"Amalie has been persuaded of some very strong prejudices against him," she wrote. "She thinks he is a hunchback, and stupid, and Parma a horrible place and the establishment there very insignificant. She will do her duty, but if that's all she has, along with her prejudices, then I admit I feel very sorry indeed to have to sacrifice my daughter. So I want you to inform me, as soon as possible and very precisely, about the *appearance, health, and character* of this prince, about his income and *the life* they lead there, and let me have *your personal opinion* as well." The despatches of her envoys would have given the Empress almost all this information already; as for the Duchy's revenues, they were dependent, as she knew, on French and Spanish largesse. Rosenberg's report, concerning precisely the points that concerned her, was probably intended simply to reassure Amalie.

It did not. Eventually, her mother was exhausted by her continuing resistance. "I am dried out inside," she told Madame Enzenberg. "I feel terribly aged and weakened and very low. . . . Everything weighs on me, and in the end I simply let things take their course."

It was too late to stop the marriage, too late to recall Prince Karl, too late to make things right for Amalie. And even had it not been too late for the young people concerned, it would have been diplomatically impossible. There was nothing obviously wrong with Don Ferdinando. On Amalie's part there was no "real illness" to offer the Bourbons an easy way out of their contract, and the Habsburgs could not risk her permanent removal from the marriage market by inventing one.

Don Ferdinando himself had as yet no stated opinion about the whole affair, but at least his grandfather, daydreaming salaciously at the palace of Fontainebleau, was looking forward to his marriage. "I will send you further details about it once everything is arranged," Louis wrote, "and I hope you will send me details too, down to the very smallest ones, when it is consummated."

SEVEN YEARS BEFORE, Joseph's first wife, the brilliant and beautiful Isabella, had sent a letter, one of many, to Marie Christine, the woman she loved, lamenting the fate held in store for all young princesses. Exceptionally, Marie Christine had escaped this fate, but Carolina and Amalie and young Antonia had not been so fortunate. "What should the daughter of a great prince expect?" Isabella had asked:

> *Her fate is without question the most unhappy. At birth she is a slave of the people's prejudices. . . . Eventually they seek to find her*

> *an establishment. And there she is, condemned to abandon everything, her family, her country, and for what? For an unknown man, for a person whose character, whose way of thinking, she knows nothing of, for a family who perhaps regard her only with jealousy. . . . She is a sacrifice, supposedly for the public good, but even more for the sorry politicking of a minister who can find no other way to ally two houses. . . . She departs, leaving everything most dear to her, uncertain even of pleasing the man she is destined for.*

Isabella's lament could have been written with Amalie herself in mind. She had passed a miserable spring and a miserable summer, though with the autumn had come a temporary respite. The wedding had been due to take place before Christmas 1768, but the absence of papal consent had forced a delay.

This had nothing to do with the state of Amalie's health, whether her illness was "real" or otherwise. It concerned, at least on the surface, the Church's laws forbidding consanguinity. Through their French ancestors, Amalie and Don Ferdinando were cousins, not first cousins, but close enough to breach the prohibition. Consequently, in order to marry, they needed a papal dispensation. This was not unusual for royal marriages; it was recognized as a regular source of income for the papacy and normally would have been provided as a matter of course. But Pope Clement XIII was not well disposed toward the young Infante of Parma, even refusing to recognize his ducal title. As far as the Pope was concerned, the Duchy of Parma was the same as the Kingdom of Naples: both were subject to himself. In his view, Don Ferdinando was merely an Infante of Spain, and as for the secular powers within the Duchy, all edicts and laws issuing from them were null and void and were to be disobeyed, on pain of excommunication. In January 1769, he despatched a letter to this effect; First Minister Du Tillot at once issued a public statement denouncing the Pope's claim to the Duchy. It was reported in Parma that when Clement read it, "he wept and, as was his wont, addressed his complaints to his crucifix." It did not help him, at least not in this world. The very next day, he suffered an apoplectic fit, and died.

Clement XIII had been a mild and in some ways quite progressive soul, but the decade of his pontificate had coincided with a series of assaults on the Church through much of Catholic Europe. The expropriation of Church property to the state was one aspect of this, but its greatest fury, less religious than political, had been spent on the Jesuits. There had already been expulsions in Portugal, France, Spain, and Naples; now they began in Parma. And, as elsewhere, a single overnight raid on their Houses proved the most effective method: all Jesuits within the Duchy's jurisdiction were arrested and confined in pens at the city gates, awaiting deportation. Only those too ill to travel were allowed to remain—plus one priest for each of the Society's Houses, who was forced to help draw up inventories of the possessions about to be confiscated.

Pope Clement's departure coincided with the arrival in Rome of two temporal princes: Joseph and Leopold. They met at the Villa Medici, the latter's own elegant residence on the Monte Pincio, adjoining the famous Borghese Gardens. Maria Theresia was uneasy about this meeting of the two brothers: It would be the first since their father's death, almost four years before, and their argument over his will. Worse, she feared they might join forces against her. Consequently, she had taken the precaution of sending a number of informants to observe and report on their movements.

While in Rome, the pair sat, or rather stood, for a double portrait by the celebrated Pompeo Batoni; though not young, Batoni had made his name quite recently by painting wealthy tourists visiting Rome as part of their European Grand Tour. The two brothers are shown side by side, Joseph taking Leopold's hand in his, and turned toward him. Though Leopold is the younger by six years, he is taller and his expression is less engaged. Batoni may have divined something of the actual relationship between the two, for Joseph always sought Leopold's friendship, often praising his abilities and achievements, while Leopold was rather disdainful toward Joseph, and resisted any influence on his part.

The portrait at least was applauded on all sides, and it earned Batoni a title of Austrian nobility. Careful viewers of it would have noticed, draped across an elaborate writing-table, a manuscript of the Baron de Montesquieu's *De l'esprit des lois*, written twenty years before, a seminal text in political science. Its presence in the portrait marked Joseph and Leopold as men of the Enlightenment—though only Leopold, of all Europe's princes, was ever to approach in practice the most daring of Montesquieu's precepts: that the ruler himself is subject to the law of the land.

Joseph spent a crammed fortnight in Rome, mainly visiting places of practical interest such as hospitals, colleges, and workshops, but also seeing many of the Eternal City's greatest sights, and proving himself no philistine: After five hours' wandering through St Peter's Basilica, he declared he would need months to see it properly. And after Rome, he made his way 150 miles southward down the coast, to visit his sixteen-year-old sister, the new Queen of Naples.

THREE YEARS HAD PASSED SINCE the Russian Tsarina had halted negotiations for Elisabeth's marriage to the King of Poland. The Duke de Chablais had turned his attentions to architecture, and was busy modernizing and embellishing his little palaces in northern Italy. But in Madrid, the widowed King Carlos III was looking toward Vienna for a new queen. In his youth, a match had been planned for him with Maria Theresia herself; now, at fifty-two, he was considered still young enough to choose one of her daughters as his bride. But, from the numerous flock once available, only Elisabeth and Amalie remained, and the latter, though she was still resisting it, was already spoken for. That left only Elisabeth.

Little is known about the negotiations, but they did not last long. Perhaps Carlos felt he had sons enough to continue his dynasty; perhaps he was deterred by reports of Elisabeth's disfigurement, or by rumours, perhaps a reflection of Carolina's apparent ambitions in Naples, that she was personally keen to wield political influence in Spain. In any event, he decided not to marry again. But one king had no sooner left the scene than another made an entrance: the fifty-eight-year-old Louis XV of France.

Louis' pious Polish wife, Queen Marie Leszczyńska, was actually still alive, but she had been ill for some time and her death was believed to be imminent, not least by herself. Marie was a popular queen, who had borne the King ten children. Their marriage, when Louis was just fifteen years old, had naturally been arranged by their families, but though Marie was then already twenty-two, the pair had fallen genuinely in love, and had enjoyed happy and faithful years together before the King had embarked on a new role as womanizer *extraordinaire*.

Now, as Marie lay dying, Louis had returned to her side with a fond devotion. His influential mistress, Madame de Pompadour, had died several years before, and despite a few dalliances, no woman had since emerged to take her place. At court, this was taken to imply that, after more than thirty years of infidelities, Louis was on the brink of mending his ways. As the Viennese ambassador, the Count Florimond von Mercy-Argenteau, reported to Chancellor von Kaunitz, it seemed that "the King, led to a reform of his morals, would in the case of widowhood perhaps think of uniting himself with an amiable young wife who could procure him the repose of his conscience and happiness for the rest of his days"—in other words, he would be able to have as much sex as he wanted with a pretty young woman, without entering into a state of sin for transgressing his marriage vows.

The young Henriette Genet, currently a reader of approved books to Louis' daughters and later, as Madame Campan, a celebrated chronicler of the Versailles court, claimed it was Mercy-Argenteau himself who first had the idea that Louis should marry Elisabeth. Since the autumn of 1768, together with Kaunitz and the French Foreign Minister Choiseul, he had been colluding to arrange the match.

No one considered it necessary to inform Elisabeth about the matter. More surprisingly, for some time the triumvirate had also concealed it from

Maria Theresia, and even from the King himself. Once informed, Louis demurred, but the Empress was enthusiastic. It would be one more link in the French-Austrian chain, and it would be good for Antonia, so very young as she was, to have her elder sister there at Versailles with her. Joseph was in favour of the match as well, as long as it did not cost him anything. As he explained to his mother, "I would very much like my sister Elisabeth to find so honourable an establishment, but at the same time, not at a cost to the State, which a match with the King of France would be." Before the end of the year, however, an obstacle to the plan had appeared in the person of Louis' new, as yet unofficial mistress, Marie-Jeanne Bécu, the comtesse du Barry.

Madame du Barry had come a long way since her early days in Lorraine. The illegitimate daughter of a seamstress and, supposedly, a Franciscan friar, she had been pushed into a marriage of convenience to the comte du Barry by his enterprising brother Jean-Baptiste, who had seen in the beautiful and biddable eighteen-year-old a potential mistress to the King, and hence a channel to his own advancement. Before the marriage, Marie-Jeanne had been living with Jean-Baptiste himself; he had supplemented his uncertain income by prostituting her to his friends whenever a bill was pressing.

By late 1768, he had got her to court and into the King's bed, and it was now his principal business to push her one important step higher, and see her declared the King's official *maîtresse-en-titre*, first among all his mistresses, a formally recognized position of considerable influence at the French court. This was the position Madame de Pompadour had had, and she had used it to further her own political interests, far from the confines of the court itself. Madame du Barry had so far evinced no bent for politics, but that was no guarantee for the future. She was now twenty-five years old; Louis was still only fifty-eight; once installed as *maîtresse-en-titre*, she could remain for decades. But she had not yet been formally presented at court. For Foreign Minister Choiseul, it was vital to prevent this, for without it, it would be impossible for her to advance to the position of *maîtresse-en-titre*. Her potential influence could be forestalled, and Louis might be persuaded to remarry.

However, there were other obstacles to the King's remarriage. As Mercy explained to Kaunitz in Vienna, the French court also harboured a corrupt and powerful faction who opposed the whole idea of it, fearing that "a judicious queen could open [Louis'] eyes to the disorder and the enormous abuses existing here in every department and so cause a great deal of embarrassment to those in charge of them." While robbing the King's coffers at every turn, they sought to persuade him that if he married again, he would not have money enough to provide for his existing family. The parlous state of his finances, as Mercy reported, lent easy weight to this duplicitous argument.

Despite her designing relatives, the amiable comtesse du Barry had seemed to pose a lesser threat than a potential new Queen of France, especially an Austrian Queen of France, for few at court had been friends of the *renversement des alliances*. But Madame du Barry's reputation as a woman for sale, and the vulgar grasping of her brother-in-law, to say nothing of his police record, was enough to change most minds. And in Louis' daughters at least, there was piety enough to make them wish for a Church-sanctioned outlet for their father's unflagging appetites. They harassed him day and night with prayers and protestations, "with such success," Mercy reported, "that the King told them positively that he would ask for the Archduchess' hand in marriage, *provided her face did not displease him*."

Everyone at Versailles knew that Elisabeth had been scarred by the smallpox, but this was no uncommon thing: Even Antonia's pretty face had its blemishes from the mild form of the disease she had had as a small child. It was, after all, an age of illnesses and accidents whose effects could not be repaired. Physical perfection was the more valued, perhaps, because it could so rarely be expected, and because, in most cases, its hour was so brief. The Englishwoman Lady Mary Coke, visiting the Hofburg, found in any case that there was still much to admire in Elisabeth; she had been watching her as she moved elegantly through the lofty rooms with her sister Marie Christine. "The two Arch Duchesses I thought extremely handsome," she wrote, "tho' the Arch D: Elisabeth had the small pox two or three years ago which has deprived her of her great beauty, but as the figure is the principal thing at a distance & as nothing can be more perfect than both those Princesses, tis no wonder I was so struck with their appearance."

Louis was naturally less concerned with Elisabeth's appearance "at a distance." Nor was he much interested in her interior qualities—a religious disposition and a good mind, though admittedly undeveloped owing to her distaste for intellectual effort of any kind. If there was a depressive tendency, this was unknown outside the Empress' narrowest circle. Well known, however, was Elisabeth's quick wit, which made her often very lively company, and if it had sometimes an unkind bent, this would not have been out of place among the sharp-tongued courtiers of Versailles. When she chose, her manner was graciousness itself, as Lady Mary noted.

But Louis wanted to see her face. His daughters persuaded him to send a painter to Vienna with the French confessor and Parisian hairdresser who were setting off to attend to the Archduchess Antonia. Portraits, however, could be deceiving, as the King well knew. Long before any painting had arrived, and almost certainly to invalidate it in any case, he announced that, before he could make a decision, he—or at least someone whose judgement he trusted—must see Elisabeth in the flesh. This would have to be handled with great delicacy: An archduchess could not be paraded and appraised like a porcelain vase or a prize cow, but Choiseul persuaded the King that it could be arranged. Perhaps the Empress could concoct a state visit to the Austrian Netherlands, he suggested, and Elisabeth could form part of her train; perhaps the Archduchess could accompany Joseph when he brought Antonia to Versailles, or perhaps she could simply pay a visit to Brussels to see her Aunt Anna Charlotte, Franz Stephan's sister, secular abbess of the grand Abbaye Remiremont in the Vosges mountains. Any of these might provide an occasion for Louis, or his *député*, to catch sight of Elisabeth under apparently unrelated circumstances.

Mercy was shocked at the very idea of it. But he dutifully relayed the proposal to Vienna, adding his own opinion that "Her Imperial Royal Apostolic Majesty" was a woman of "too exalted a mind and too tender a heart" to subject one of her own royal daughters to such a demeaning exercise. He was right, and in due course the Empress' reply came back to him: He should disabuse Choiseul of any hope whatsoever of such an *entrevue*, "since Her Majesty will never agree to sanction anything that is not absolutely in keeping with protocol and propriety."

It would in any case have made no difference, for Louis himself had all along been playing a languid double game, enjoying the company of his mistress while holding his daughters and his ministers at bay with continuing talk of a match with Elisabeth, whose lumps and pockmarks had in fact disqualified her from the outset. The comedy had lasted a year, or eighteen months, or two years, depending on the orations of the various actors who crossed the stage at different times. What Elisabeth herself thought about it is unknown. Certainly it would have been a very grand match for her; her prestige across Europe and within her own family would have risen enormously, and half the pain of her loss of beauty might have been assuaged. Joseph sent a disgusted letter to the Empress, bewailing the state of things in France: "What a misfortune to have to deal with these intriguers," he concluded, "and to live in a country where things are conducted on that footing." Kaunitz agreed, remarking to Mercy with double-facing *hauteur*, "I assure you, when I see these horrors, I congratulate myself on being here, though here one is bored, rather than where you are, though there one is amused."

# X

# 1769

## In which Carolina misbehaves, Joseph visits Naples and Parma, and Amalie's fate is sealed.

In her long letter of advice to the newly married Carolina, the Empress had cautioned her against taking any political role in her new realm: "You will not involve yourself in affairs of state unless the King wishes, and unless you believe you can be more useful to him than others. This is a very delicate point; another mother would urge you to try to participate in affairs of state, but I know too well all the weight and all the delicacy of it to want to set you on that course."

It had been an ambiguous caution, all the same. How was Carolina to judge, in the inexperience of her sixteen years, whether she would be more useful to the King than other people—than First Minister Tanucci, for instance? The Empress had advised her to defer to her brother Leopold, and he had advised her to defer to Tanucci. Joseph had at first believed she should feel her way cautiously into political involvement in case her husband proved incapable, but after seeing the situation at first hand, he had overcome his reservations about the First Minister's pro-Spanish views and given her the same advice.

In these early days of her marriage, Carolina had no personal right to involve herself in the business of government, but by the terms of her nuptial contract, once she should bear a son, she would be entitled to a seat, and a voice, in the Kingdom's Council of State. Though Tanucci was to protest this strenuously, she herself was looking forward to it: In the rather hasty political instruction she had received from Chancellor von Kaunitz in Vienna, she had proved an eager pupil. At the same time, she had accepted her novice status, and more than once in the months after her arrival had declared that, with her husband behaving like an undisciplined juvenile and Tanucci bent on maintaining Spanish ascendancy in Naples, she needed guidance from some other capable person, "a minister or a lady who seems to merit your trust," as her mother had put it. But, as the Empress had observed, "people of this kind are very rare."

There was in fact one lady, in Naples five years already, who might have served the purpose: Leopoldine von Kaunitz, wife of the Viennese ambassador and daughter-in-law of Maria Theresia's chancellor. But Carolina's brothers had vetoed her. Leopold at least admitted the lady to be clever, but he regarded her as bigoted and ignorant, declaring she knew no more of politics than she knew of Chinese. No doubt she was simply too conservative for his enlightened tastes; certainly she disapproved of Carolina's forthright and impulsive ways, describing her only a few days after her arrival as "a silly little headstrong thing who will give us plenty of trouble."

But at that point, Carolina had been worn out by the journey and still tearful for her family, to say nothing of the trauma of her wedding-night. Within three weeks, Leopoldine had changed her opinion. "The Queen is behaving perfectly and getting on very well with the King," she told her sister, Eleonore von Liechtenstein. "Certainly when she has a mind to she will work more than miracles, for she is highly intelligent and very good-natured. Though I'm a little afraid she might be led astray; there's some kind of entertainment every day, suppers, balls, dinners, little parties," adding a sighing little postscript, "I'm always obliged to go, too."

Soon after her arrival Carolina had thrown in her lot with what Leopoldine regarded as "the worst ladies of the court," notably the talented marchesa

Catarina di San Marco, one of her ladies-in-waiting. Born a Medici, the marchesa was just twenty-one, young enough to share Carolina's liveliness yet old enough to maintain an easy influence over her. She was intellectual and politically minded, a student of mathematics and "natural philosophy," and a vocal supporter of progressive ideals—indeed, a Freemason and active participant in a ladies' lodge, to which she soon introduced the Queen. Saddled with a husband forty years older than herself, she had taken as a lover the thirty-one-year-old Austrian ambassador Ernst von Kaunitz, which is unlikely to have endeared her to Leopoldine, who was his wife.

Under the aegis of the marchesa di San Marco, the Queen had begun spending extravagantly and socializing with a pleasure-loving set of young courtiers, sharing their diversions, making fun of the local grandees, ignoring the ordinary social proprieties, and even forgetting her religious duties. At one point, larking about in a boat out in the bay, she fell into the sea and had to be rescued—and manhandled—by three men, a hilarious incident to Carolina herself, but scandalous to most others, including Leopoldine, who by now had reverted to her original judgement of her. "She's not ill-intentioned," she told Eleonore, "but she's the flightiest, most thoughtless girl you could find."

Carolina had just turned sixteen. A thousand miles away from her dominating mother, queen of a disordered and sycophantic court, encouraged by her rule-averse husband, it is hardly surprising that she took some missteps. But though her elders made a tremendous fuss about it, even the worst of her failings was not so very depraved. It seems she and Ferdinando had been taking little boat trips out in the bay late in the magical summer nights, returning a little too noisily. It was unorthodox and no doubt undignified—Leopoldine von Kaunitz called it "shameful"—but everyone else at court simply shrugged their shoulders, and the worst criticism Carlos and Maria Theresia could levy was that it was bad for the young couple's health, and consequently likely to delay the arrival of an heir.

The Empress had been apprised of her daughter's every movement, for she had in fact engaged Leopoldine to spy on Carolina from the outset. The ambassador's wife was to send a monthly report, "and if there is something particular, be so kind as to write more often, even by dispatch rider . . . Rest assured I will never inform my daughter or anyone else of this." Ten years older than Carolina, Leopoldine had dutifully, and duplicitously, slipped on the persona of friendly elder sister, and the girl herself, glad to have someone of her own background to lean on, had responded to her with liking and an unwarranted trust. "Please don't stand on any ceremony when you write to me," she told her. "I love you unlimitedly and I can't wait to see you again."

Leopoldine did manage to bring about some improvement in the young Queen's behaviour, at least temporarily. "My very dear friend," Carolina wrote to her, sounding not entirely repentant all the same, "I received your dear letter this morning and I promise your words will have an effect. I am quite resolved to become a good and well behaved princess, only I beg you, my dear little countess, don't lose patience. I would give my life not to have ever done such childish things and I could die of shame that people know all about it."

And there was news from Vienna: Amalie's stubbornly resisted marriage had been indefinitely delayed, at least until the election of a new pope. Knowing her sister's feelings, Carolina was happy to hear this, though the accompanying news was less cheerful. "Amalie is having headaches again and is losing all her beauty and youth and is thin and ill."

On the very same day, Eleonore had written to Leopoldine, telling her that, "between ourselves, the Archduchess Amalie is behaving very badly," having retreated to her room on the pretence of a bad cold. "I'm curious to see whether she'll succeed. As far as I can tell she's caught this cold from the Duke of Parma. I'll try and see what else I can find out about it."

Carolina had now been married almost a year, and as yet there was no sign of a pregnancy. Joseph blamed this on the fact that she had been learning to ride a horse. Like most of her sisters, with the decided exceptions of Marianna and Amalie, both keen hunters, Carolina had never learned to ride properly. Even their mother had learned only as an adult, and she had then taken to it with a fury, speeding ahead of her attendants at a thrilling, alarming pace. But once in Naples, Carolina, too, had begun taking lessons, and Joseph, no exceptional horseman himself, had written to warn her against it: "You are riding horses without considering the anatomical reasons why that is not healthy for women who are to bear children. I assure you that in general your sex does not appear to me to be made for this exercise, and however fine a woman may be upon a horse, she is never graceful. . . . I hope you will moderate your enthusiasm which, if I know you, would make you quite forget any danger and could even lead you to imagine yourself some kind of hussar."

Sister and brother met on the last day of March 1769, in the full flower of a Neapolitan spring, at the pretty royal palace of Portici at the foot of Vesuvius. Joseph arrived earlier than expected, and surprised Carolina in her private rooms overlooking the magnificent Bay of Naples, where she was sitting with Ferdinando and a few ladies-in-waiting. She leaped up and threw her arms around her brother, overjoyed, hugging him again and again. When Joseph attempted to embrace the King, whom he had not met before, Ferdinando responded coolly, assuring him "between his teeth" that he was pleased to see him.

An uxorious man, Ferdinando was used to having Carolina to himself; he may have been a little put out by her excessive warmth toward her eldest brother. He may also have been intimidated by Joseph, ten years his senior and an emperor, after all, whose reputation for intelligence and self-assurance had undoubtedly preceded him. Joseph managed to break the ice by suddenly lying down full-length on the floor to view the bay through a low-standing telescope, and suggesting Ferdinando do the same. Thus a rather lopsided amity was born. An hour or two later, the King asked Joseph to forget all formalities and call him simply *Don Fernando*, and without waiting for a reciprocal invitation, dubbed the disconcerted Emperor *Don Pepe*.

Joseph was on the whole unimpressed by Ferdinando's court. Like the Hungarian magnates clinging to Vienna, the great lords of Ferdinando's kingdom clustered around Naples, leaving their country estates, and the thousands of peasants dependent on them, effectively to fend for themselves. Though agriculture had for centuries been the basis of their wealth, they found it easier now to beg for money, and the court was swarming with princes and dukes and counts, as a disdainful Leopoldine von Kaunitz reported to her sister in Vienna, "bowing and scraping before the King and his ministers for years and years to get some little office that no honourable man would take." Apart from being the locus of patronage, the court was the liveliest place for a noble to be, and where the nobles went, the commoners followed, Figaro-like, to serve and supply them. It was an old circle of ever less productive activity, so that by now only one sixth of the ordinary people of Naples were living by steady work, with the rest hanging from the fraying tailcoats of the aristocracy.

Before his first day was out, Joseph had sat through a private three-hour audience with First Minister Tanucci, now seventy-one, and looking more like an aged court jester than the feared and powerful man he was. Joseph found him furiously anti-papist and anti-Jesuit, and strangely reluctant to discuss his two young sovereigns, but from what he could glean, he concluded that Tanucci was rather afraid of Carolina. Her energy and strength of mind, plus Ferdinando's evident sexual infatuation with her, all posed a threat to the Minister's heretofore comfortable control of the young King. For a decade, Tanucci had dictated everything of importance within the Kingdom, answering only to Carlos in Madrid and, as Joseph thought, manipulating him into the bargain. Though Ferdinando's marriage to a Habsburg princess had strengthened the Bourbon alliance with Austria, it had also potentially weakened the influence of Spain, and consequently that of Tanucci himself.

Despite this, Tanucci was still regarded by both detractors and admirers as the most important force in the Kingdom of Naples. Since his arrival in 1734 with Ferdinando's father, King Carlos, he had devoted his talents to reforming the legal and economic structures of this poor and backward region. Both had been held in a dual stranglehold, centuries old, by the local nobility and the Church, and both powers had naturally resisted Tanucci's reforms. He had succeeded in curbing the power of the Church, but reform of the region's chaotic economy, particularly agriculture, had proved beyond him. Meeting him in the spring of 1769, Joseph had found him still ambitious and, though admittedly able, a cunning man full of tricks and feints, mistrustful of the Habsburgs, duplicitous toward his master in Madrid, and determined to keep Ferdinando under his personal thumb.

**JOSEPH SPENT NINE DAYS** in Naples. Though invited to do so, he did not stay at Portici or at the Palazzo Reale in the city itself, but rather at the less formal Austrian embassy, and each day he rode the easy four miles out to the palace at the foot of Vesuvius. Though always most interested in the practical aspects of government—roads and hospitals, industry and trade—he was here effectively as an agent of his mother: Unable to travel herself, Maria Theresia used her children wherever possible as personal informants. Joseph accordingly sent her a seventy-nine-page report of his visit, detailing the manners of the court and the habits of his sister and the King.

Carolina appears to have been on her best behaviour while he was there. In his report, in any case, she came out well. "The Emperor is enchanted with the Queen," Maria Theresia told Leopold, "he supports her in everything; he hardly looked at her when she was here, but since he has been in Naples, he is her greatest admirer." The "worst ladies of the court," supposedly his sister's bosom friends, had been conspicuous by their complete absence during Joseph's visit, though it would not take long after her brother's departure for Carolina to revert to her unregal ways. But for the moment, her pastimes, horse-riding notwithstanding, were not such as to compromise her health: Though she did have occasional attacks of fever, her periods, vitally, were regular. She had as yet managed to suppress her interest in political affairs, and Joseph commended her forbearance with the vulgar, clumsy, at times repellent man who was her husband; though he had eyes already for the lively young marchesa di San Marco, in public Ferdinando was markedly lascivious toward his wife.

Maria Theresia had never met her son-in-law, and she appreciated Joseph's physical description of him—the fact of it, at least, if not necessarily the details:

> *The King would be five feet seven thumbs tall, so a good thumb taller than I, he is very thin, wiry and bony, round-shouldered, with very long arms, very thin, skinny thighs and legs, very long feet . . . his knees are always bent, but they are not knock knees, and he has a loping walk. The King's hands are very brown, rough and dirty, since he never wears gloves, and his fingers are very long. On top of this body quite a small head, a forest of hair, the colour of café au lait, which he always wears unpowdered. A nose that starts in his hair and gradually grows in a straight though not aquiline line down to his mouth, which is very large, with a puffy lower lip, his teeth are quite a nice ivory but crooked, a low forehead, little piggy eyes, sunken cheeks and a very long neck. . . . He has an extremely high, thin voice, almost like a high falsetto, painful to the ear, you could distinguish him among a thousand persons.*

Thus *Il re nasone*—"King Bignose"—at eighteen. But though he wearied and embarrassed Carolina, she was above self-pity. With the dauntlessness of extreme youth, she was determined to make a success of her life as the Queen of Naples, with the King unavoidably at its centre. She was not without personal pride, and it cost her considerably to endure his public fondlings and practical jokes, but endure them she did, brushing them off as the harmless faults of "her good fool," as she called him. She deferred to all his daily wishes, often following him on his hunts, tedious and uncomfortable as they were to her, but she took an interest in affairs of state and noticed political opportunities where he did not, and he observed this with both relief and resentment, complaining of it often to his father in Madrid, while at the same time relying on it from day to day, yet disrupting her efforts by interfering impulsively whenever the mood struck him.

Joseph saw clearly enough that his brother-in-law possessed a native ability that his woeful upbringing had prevented him from developing. But he himself lacked the emotional intelligence to sense Ferdinando's annoyance at his condescension to him. The young King was not proud: He accepted the Emperor's superiority in education and experience—apart from anything else, there was a ten-year age difference between them. But to the British envoy William Hamilton he insisted he was naturally as clever as Joseph himself, or even Leopold. And Joseph had few defenders in Naples. To the courtiers, he seemed patronizing, even egotistical. As Hamilton later confided to his compatriot, the memoirist Nathaniel Wraxall, "Joseph did not, indeed, inspire any very high admiration by his deportment or general conduct. . . . He was irritable, and even irascible, where he should have shown good humour or command of temper." Joseph himself remained unaware that he had offended anyone. He was content with his visit, content with his sister, content with himself. As for Ferdinando, as he reported to his mother, "at least he doesn't stink."

**JOSEPH HAD NOT THOUGHT** much of Carolina's husband, but he preferred him in any case to the man Amalie was about to marry. On his way home from Naples, in mid-May 1769, he stopped for three days in Parma to make the acquaintance of his brother-in-law-to-be. If King Ferdinando had been difficult and embarrassing, Don Ferdinando proved insufferable, as Joseph reported to the Empress from Bologna, sitting down to write at eleven o'clock in the morning:

> *He has quite a handsome face, but his figure is poor, very fat and squat. He limps with his left leg, which looks somewhat crooked. . . . He is extremely well brought up, completely inexperienced, knows a*

> *lot, but seems to have no genius or much intelligence, and is as tiresome as can be, holding on to my arm and never leaving me alone for a step. . . . If the King of Naples had had his education, it would have succeeded infinitely better than with [the Infante,] and I would much prefer to spend eight days with the King than with him.*

Joseph was diplomatic enough to send a completely different report to the Infante's grandfather at Versailles, and Louis was vain enough to believe it. He wrote to Don Ferdinando of "all the fine things he said to me about you and his enduring feelings for me. Really I love him as my own son."

The Parma court was very much to Joseph's taste. Though ruled since 1748 by the Spanish Crown, French tastes had long been in the ascendant before being firmly and finally established by Don Ferdinando's late mother, Elisabeth. The eldest daughter of Louis XV, she had held far more political sway than her retiring Spanish husband Don Felipe, so that Don Ferdinando had grown up in what was effectively a small French court, and now, in 1769, the influence of France was still paramount. And if not politically minded, Don Felipe had been a man of high intellect and deep culture and, together with his enlightened First Minister Du Tillot, he had promoted these interests to such an extent that his little duchy had become known as "the Athens of Italy."

Joseph was consequently not surprised to find the men of the court intelligent and entertaining, and he was quite captivated by Du Tillot, a Frenchman by birth and, at fifty-eight, still slender and suavely handsome. Joseph liked the court ladies, too, all dressed *à la française*, their faces rouged and pretty, all of them amiable and rational, a good many of them actually Frenchwomen. But he was particularly taken by the beautiful Italian marchesa Anna Malaspina, forty-two years old, "exceeding all the others in gifts of the mind." La Malaspina had already been appointed Amalie's *Grande-Maîtresse*, Mistress of her Household, and though Amalie herself had not been consulted, Joseph thought her an excellent choice. He also approved of the ladies-in-waiting, all of them French, all designated in advance, and "some of them very capable. So apart from her confessor she will not need to bring anyone with her," he wrote to the Empress. "I can assure Your Majesty that my sister, if she is sensible, will be able to live very agreeably in Parma."

Joseph did not need to mention that the marchesa Malaspina was Du Tillot's mistress. Nor was he concerned that their personal closeness might prove problematic for Amalie and her young husband. If he thought of it, he probably considered the older couple's interference, not to say determination to control, no very bad thing, at least in the short term; certainly he had no high opinion of Don Ferdinando's capacity to rule, and even less of his sister's. Du Tillot was a Frenchman, it was true, but the French were now Austria's allies. The Empress was aware of the potential for trouble, but thought it would help rein in Amalie's impetuosity. "I am quite aware of the trouble Madame Malaspina may cause my daughter by her attachment to the Minister," she wrote, "but I find more good than ill in that, since it is the way to make her more careful about what she says, and to make her leave off her bad habit of saying too much or just whatever comes into her head."

As a brother, all the same, Joseph might have spared a thought for Amalie's feelings. He had enjoyed conversing with the ministers and ladies of the court but, like his three eldest sisters, he spoke French well, and Italian to boot. By contrast, Amalie's French was poor, as the Empress, despite disavowals, was now reproving her: "It's not my fault; how many times have I preached at you and provided you the means of improvement, but without effect. I am not at all reproaching you, but I'm afraid you will often think of me and regret the time you wasted."

Maria Theresia may have been feeling somewhat defensive: None of her younger daughters had good French. The three eldest had all had the benefit, in their *aya*, of the capable Princess Caroline von Trautson. A close friend and advisor of the Empress, this cultured woman was also a fluent French speaker, and that facility she had passed on to her charges, an important asset for them, since French was the *lingua franca* of Europe's courts, and within the family they had spoken only their native Viennese German.

Maria Theresia's less than helpful advice to Amalie now was for her to avoid speaking at all: "The less you speak, the better it will be. . . . I know your way of telling stories, and I tell you as a friend, it is most annoying, in fact you should confine yourself to relating things that happened in your childhood or on your journey. You still have the fault of thinking in German and translating word for word."

On his way home from Parma, Joseph stopped in Florence, where Leopold was recovering from a smallpox inoculation; in Venice, where he cancelled the elaborate celebrations arranged in his honour; and in Milan, where he made the acquaintance of the Princess Beatrice d'Este, the betrothed of his fifteen-year-old brother, Ferdinand. One afternoon, he allowed her to accompany him on a stroll along the famed city walls, built by the Spaniards in the sixteenth century. She impressed and disappointed him in equal measure: He found her intelligent and sensible but, at nineteen, much older-looking than she actually was and, on the whole, very ugly.

By mid-May 1769, the conclave of cardinals in Rome had reached a decision: The new pope was to be Clement XIV Ganganelli, a Franciscan friar educated by Jesuits. Though a compromise candidate, he had gained the support of the Bourbon courts, who expected him to take a stand against his former teachers. Dissolution procedures were duly initiated; in 1773, the Society of Jesus would disappear from Catholic Europe, though in the Protestant countries, where the Pope held no authority, the fathers would continue their teaching work.

With Parma and its Bourbon cousins victorious, Clement XIV was easily persuaded to sign the dispensation allowing Amalie and Don Ferdinando to marry. In an additional gesture of submission, he even had a large cross of diamonds and emeralds sent to the Hofburg, to congratulate the unwilling bride. On the first day of June 1769, the marriage contract was concluded. Amalie's dowry was to be 60,000 gulden, less than a third of Carolina's and a fraction of what Marie Christine had received. Unlike Carolina, Amalie would have no personal right to rule in the event of her husband's death. And she was even upstaged by her youngest sister, thirteen-year-old Antonia, who shortly after the dispensation, made her first formal appearance, at the palace of Laxenburg, as a future princess of France. She enchanted all who saw her.

Amalie's wedding by procuration took place at the end of the month, in the Church of St Augustine, as Josepha's and Carolina's had been and, as Marianna inscribed in her book of copper engravings marking the great events of her mother's reign, "once again it was the Archduke Ferdinand, who married his sister the Archduchess Amalia in the name of the Duke of Parma." It was the third time he had served as proxy bridegroom, and Maria Theresia took the usual opportunity to inform Beatrice in Milan about his height, but the pace of Ferdinand's growth had slackened, and this time there was no talk of lanky Leopold, though the Empress insisted, "My son grows every time one sees him: he will not be much shorter than the Emperor [Joseph], and if he continues as he is doing, he will be taller"—though in the event, Ferdinand was to remain very small. About Amalie herself she was less reassuring, writing to Madame Enzenberg, on the day of the wedding itself, "May God bless her; but I am not entirely easy about her state of health."

# XI

# 1769

In which Amalie meets her husband, and causes a great deal of trouble in Parma.

Amalie spent the day after her wedding privately, but the following day was crowded with ambassadorial receptions and flowery formal congratulations, before brother Ferdinand handed her into the carriage for the first stage of her journey south to Parma. In her pocket, and no doubt burning in her memory, too, was the lengthy *Instruction* her mother had given her, to be read, supposedly, at least once a month. Amalie was exhorted—prematurely, as it happened—to follow Carolina's example of moderation in her spending and restraint from involvement in politics. Though the letter was not entirely negative, it cannot have increased Amalie's confidence as she was driven away from everyone and everything familiar to her, toward a country she did not know and a man she had never seen:

> *What will you be able to do when you are face to face with a prince so accomplished, so well informed as your husband? You know very well you have never had any taste for those useful, common studies and disciplines that are almost necessary these days in this world . . .*

*You are older than your husband and master, and you must not give any grounds for suspicion that you want to dominate him. . . . You can be very attentive to other people, you are even really helpful; and when you want, you have something really touching about you that is hard to resist, and you are very patient and your character is good. . . . Take care not to get excited, then you don't speak very coherently, especially in French.*

For more than a fortnight, as far as Mantua, Amalie was to follow the same route as Carolina had done, making the same pause at Innsbruck to pray in the room where Franz Stephan had died, and to visit her mother's friend, Madame Enzenberg, who had always been particularly fond of her. Amalie's train was also grand, and farewelled with "many thousands of wishes for happiness and blessings from the innumerable people lining the streets," but where prestigious German dragoons had led the new Queen's guard of honour, the new Infanta, now downgraded from archduchess to mere "espoused Duchess," was obliged to be contented with an escort of lower-status Hungarian hussars.

Beyond Mantua, on the southern bank of the broad Po River, a nervous Don Ferdinando stood waiting for his bride. No record has survived of Amalie's impressions as she first set eyes on him. He was five years younger than she and several inches shorter, blond-haired, his body agile enough though rather on the podgy side, his face also plump but with a generally pleasing expression, and his bearing, as befitted a grandson of Louis XV, assuredly aristocratic. The voice that issued from his sensual mouth was deep and rich. Though he had learned some German, it is not clear how well he spoke it, and he probably addressed Amalie now in French, which he would certainly have expected her to know. No doubt she made some stuttering replies, then kept to her mother's advice and said as little as possible.

Don Ferdinando had felt his spirits lift as Amalie stepped from the boat, tall and slender, with "a majestic air," as the Baron de La Houze, the French ambassador, reported two days later to Versailles. "She has big blue eyes, chestnut hair, and beautiful, regular features. She is already the whole happiness of the Infante, who adores her." It was only a few miles further to the palace of Colorno—splendid enough, though, like Amalie's dowry, only a third as big as Carolina's royal palace, with four hundred rooms to Caserta's twelve hundred. Here, beneath the pink Corinthian columns of the chapel, the marriage was confirmed. But if Don Ferdinando was fast losing his heart to his silent bride, Amalie evinced no more enthusiasm than she had for her brother in the Church of St Augustine.

And from his summer residence of Compiègne arrived the inevitable letter from Louis XV, wanting to know all about the wedding-night: "My very dear grandson, Today or tomorrow will be a great day, and very pleasurable for you, I await confirmation of it most impatiently. The letter I receive from you next Thursday will be full of it, I hope."

Thursday brought only disappointment. Far from pages replete with salacious details, Don Ferdinando had sent only a bare letter confessing there had been no consummation at all. Gallantly, he blamed himself, and appealed to Louis for advice. There was no mechanical problem per se, and Ferdinando was apparently more than well endowed—his valet had remarked that he was "apt, very apt to have *numerous and healthy offspring*"—but erections were painful to him, and he feared he was suffering from "the king's disease," so called not because it was a particular affliction of those of royal rank, but rather because it was widely believed to be something only a king could cure. Physicians called it scrofula; it was a form of tuberculosis producing unsightly lumps on the skin.

Louis' reply to the letter was immediate and quite sensible. "It is true, my dear grandson," he wrote, "that at my consecration I acquired the gift of becoming the instrument of God's grace to cure the scrofula, but for that I would have to be there myself, and it has been some time since it last happened. We have remedies here to cure this malady. If you wish I will send you some with instructions for their use."

Whether Don Ferdinando declined the remedies, or they arrived and were of no use, the situation did not change. Amalie was in good health overall and fully recovered from the fatigues of her journey, but now it seemed there was a hardening of the glands in her breast. This was to be a recurrent problem for her, and though not serious it was often painful. Don Ferdinando dutifully relayed the information to Louis, who replied quite sharply: "What is this pain in your wife's breast? Is she very buxom? They say she's thin. Do you find her attractive? It seems to me this little pain shouldn't prevent the rest of it. . . . Whose fault is it if there has been no full consummation? Perhaps you need a little operation. Your cousin here may need it, too; it's quite common." Louis was referring to circumcision, which it seemed Antonia's future husband might eventually need as well. "The pain in your member is only because your foreskin is too long and you cannot pull it back properly."

Amalie's breast pain grew worse, then metamorphosed into constant headaches. By mid-October, three months after the marriage, there had still been no consummation. Informed of every detail by spies posing as servants, the Empress even began to think a divorce might be necessary, "though the scandal would be most disagreeable." A physician was finally summoned—an indiscreet physician, whose gossip made its way, via Ambassador La Houze, to everyone at Versailles—to investigate the cause of the Infante's erectile pain. It was not phimosis, as Louis had thought, which indeed might have been repaired by circumcision, but something much simpler, requiring no operation apart from thorough washing: Don Ferdinando's penis was encrusted with filth.

It was probably the reticence of extreme religiosity that had prevented him from keeping it normally clean. Despite the licentiousness prevailing in some eighteenth-century courts—Louis' own was a prime example—the religiously inclined maintained a prudish, even punitive attitude to sex. Don Ferdinando, raised by the affectionate but strict moralist Keralio, would have been discouraged from touching himself at all; his own finickety piety had evidently ensured that he had not.

Soap and water worked their usual magic. Don Ferdinando took full advantage of his new ability to maintain an erection without pain. "I am very pleased that your generative member is better, and that you are doing your best to enjoy yourself," his grandfather wrote from Fontainebleau. By December Don Ferdinando believed Amalie had conceived. Louis was sceptical: "Your wife would need to be very susceptible indeed to be pregnant already, and I very much doubt it," he wrote to his excited grandson. "Perhaps next week we'll know more."

Louis was right. It was to be more than a year before Don Ferdinando became a father.

*The present Royal Family of Parma are much beloved: the Infanta is lively, active, and of great courage; is very fond of the chase, as well as an admirable marks-woman, and will pursue the game frequently on foot, when the frozen snow lies on the ground. She is extremely humane and generous: her allowance is a thousand sequins a month, and she gives the greater part of it away. The Infanta is a perfect mistress of music, has a charming voice, and reads a good deal. She is tall and fair; never wears rouge or fard. The Infant is of a mild, indolent, unambiguous disposition, totally devoted to his minister Tillot.*

Thus the letter of a voluble visitor, on a chilly November night, to a friend at home in England. The visitor, Mrs (later Lady) Anna Miller, a woman of about thirty, was travelling in Italy in a paradoxical effort to reduce her expenditures, the cost of elegant living in London having reached unattainable heights. Mrs. Miller's information was not entirely accurate: Amalie, unpowdered, was a brunette rather than a blonde, and her husband was not only indolent but completely, indeed irresponsibly uninterested in government. Moreover, if he had ever been devoted to the First Minister, this had stopped within weeks of his marriage.

That had been Amalie's doing. She had arrived in Parma with a prejudice against Du Tillot, knowing that he had opposed a match with her on financial grounds. Amalie had since accepted her duties as a wife, but she had never reconciled herself to the demotion in status her marriage had implied. In the months since then, her bitterness toward Du Tillot had not lessened, nor had the meagre sum of her dowry helped him to change his mind.

At the time of her arrival in July 1769, the fifty-eight-year-old minister had already been active in the government of Parma for over twenty years. Though modestly born—his father had been a *valet de chambre*—he had recently been ennobled, and was now the marchese di Felino. A convinced man of the Enlightenment, his personal library graced with Diderot's daring new *Encylopédie*, he was at the height of his powers, a "fine courtesan, a lover of every beautiful and exquisite thing, a most assiduous intendant-general of the royal household, a Parisian, not by birth, but all the more by education and sentiment." Despite his French instincts, Du Tillot had well understood the Duchy of Parma's own specific needs and, like his counterpart Tanucci in Naples, he had attempted to adapt his general reformist ideas accordingly, reorganizing the important agricultural economy and improving education and local administration across the region. In so doing, he had made many enemies among the Duchy's old establishment. Landowners and others resentful of his reforms had joined forces with the weakened men of the Church in an effort to drive him out of power. Don Ferdinando had been too lazy to serve as the figurehead of their resistance, but in Amalie they had found the force of character they needed.

Maria Theresia had foreseen how it would be. "I know there are many people hoping to bring about a change in the ministry through you," she had told Amalie in the letter of *Instruction* on her marriage. "You can and must tell them, calmly and kindly, that you do not involve yourself in the business of government, and you do not want to know anything about it. . . . I tell you again and I cannot tell you often enough, you are not equipped to rule. Leave this care to those whom God has charged with it. . . . It is a terrible responsibility, and for a single moment of satisfaction there are a hundred troubles."

To those she sent to advise Amalie, however, the Empress told a different story. Within a few months of the wedding, she had admitted that Don Ferdinando's now very clear ineptitude would in time push Amalie forward. "I myself believe that in the long term my daughter will have to rule," she confided to Count Rosenberg, "but this must be with the consent of both Kings [Carlos and Louis], and they must be the ones to demand it."

Amalie's ears had been deaf, in any case, to her mother's warning. She was dismayed to find her husband so meek in relation to his First Minister. Though her inferior in rank, Don Ferdinando was, supposedly, a sovereign ruler, and she felt his subservience as a further humiliation for herself. She had no real interest in day-to-day politicking or even political ideas in the abstract; the grievances of landowners and clerics meant little to her. But she wanted to make her husband stand up to Du Tillot, and she wanted respect for herself. She gladly accepted the role the First Minister's enemies offered her, and began to present herself as Parma's supposed liberator from Spanish and French tutelage and, to a lesser extent, champion of its realignment with Austria.

In theory, this meant little. Since the *renversement des alliances*, Austria was already allied with France and, by extension, its satellite court in Parma. Amalie, petulant or careless, had expressed her hostility to Bourbon tutelage in a series of petty insults and a general defiance of courtly norms: obliging her household to wear Austrian colours, riding out on horseback unaccompanied but for a handful of young guardsmen, or simply walking about the little town, minimally attended and chatting informally with the local people, a habit derided by the French and Spanish ambassadors as evidence of her unsophisticated Austrian upbringing. Above all, no doubt still smarting from her own demotion from archduchess to mere duchess, she paid no attention to distinctions of rank, undermining the basis of half the life of the court.

Don Ferdinando, easily dominated, raised no objection to his wife's imprudent behaviour. It accorded in any case with his own predilection for clowning about with noisy friends of low rank, or reneging on his court responsibilities to spend hours praying with the Dominican friars he favoured and at times even daydreamed of joining.

News of the pair's outlandish behaviour had been disseminated in the scandal sheets of Europe, horrifying the Empress, astounding Louis at Versailles, and outraging Carlos in Madrid: Within two months of the marriage, he had sent a flinty reprimand to his great-nephew: "They say you have blindly submitted to the Infanta's wishes. Her mother the Empress informs me that her intention had been to give you a wife and not a governor. You should understand that your well-being and your security depend on Us, and that if the King your grandfather and I were to abandon you, other courts would take little interest in your affairs."

It had made no difference. Don Ferdinando had gone on roasting chestnuts in the park and racing his friends to ring all the bells of the town's churches. Amalie had carried on riding out with the guardsmen and casually dispensing largesse that the Duchy could ill afford. The people loved her for it, but it compromised her seriously in the eyes of her powerful relatives, and in the hearts of her nearer family, too.

**Amalie's behaviour had been** no better than Carolina's, each case exacerbated by a husband's weakness of character. Like the King of Naples, the Duke of Parma was at once annoyed and relieved to find the smaller decisions of his life made for him by his strong-minded wife, just as he had been to see the larger decisions made by his First Minister. In both cases, animal infatuation had played its part as well: It was easier for two eighteen-year-olds to accommodate their wives' flaunting of regal dignities when the prize was uncomplaining sex.

The scolding letter sent from the King of Spain to Parma had been to no avail. The Empress accepted it was her turn to act. Austria had no permanent representative to the Duchy, but Maria Theresia had high hopes of the special envoy she selected now: Baron Philipp von Knebel, an intelligent man of exceptional moral probity, whom she sent in the autumn of 1769. But Knebel was tenderhearted by nature and, moreover, only thirty-two years of age, and the Empress had reckoned without his susceptibility to the charms of an attractive young woman. Though he dutifully reported back to Vienna all Amalie's indiscretions, in Parma itself he quickly took her part, attributing her behaviour to faults in her education, to the strength of her feelings, and rather daringly, to her mother's lack of love for her.

"My mother hates me," she had declared to him, and he had relayed this information immediately to the startled Empress. Nonetheless, as he reported, the Infanta was willing to do whatever her mother wanted, "as long as she loves me a quarter as much as she loves the others." Knebel begged the Empress to temper the tone of her letters, since "for some time now she has been receiving only reprimands, so severe that she trembles every time the post arrives."

Amalie wanted Maria Theresia's approval, but she also wanted to be free of the constraints and demands that would have imposed on her. The contradiction could not be resolved, and it is not surprising that she vented her frustration in impulsive outbursts of one kind or another. But Knebel's sympathy did not help. In fact he made things worse by encouraging her illusions of independence, telling her, as he artlessly reported to the Empress, "that having left her mother's house, she was no longer dependent on Madame her mother in her everyday life, and that she was now mistress at Parma just as Your Majesty is at Vienna."

Amalie's everyday life, however, was the life of a Bourbon court. As her mother would sharply remind her, owing to her marriage she was "required to conform her way of thinking, her attitudes, and even more her behaviour and conduct, whether in private or in public, to the court customs or other conventions of the Houses of Bourbon." And it was in the very details of her everyday life that Amalie was coming to grief. Her disputes with Du Tillot were not, on the whole, about policy or government, or even about any significant leaning away from Spain and France and toward Austria. They concerned the smaller matters of staffing and spending and protocol within her own household, matters unfortunately well suited to accusations of petty interference on both sides.

The Minister was not singling Amalie out. All court expenses needed to be reduced; Parma's expenditures greatly exceeded its income. But Amalie was intractable, regarding every suggested change as a personal attack on herself, and presenting her resistance as a defence of Habsburg honour. "The Minister is already alarmed about her impulsive interfering," the Empress complained to Knebel. "The Queen of Naples is also taking up arms against Tanucci. If this goes on, what will people say about my daughters' behaviour to their ministers? They may blame me. In any case they are sure to say they both have a decided liking to dominate, and what they extrapolate from that could very easily affect the future of my dauphine"—who was still in Vienna, awaiting the formal announcement of her marriage. Following the early death of his father, the fifteen-year-old duc de Berry had become dauphin of France. Louis-Auguste now stood next in line to his grandfather to inherit the throne, with fourteen-year-old Antonia beside him.

KNEBEL HAD DONE his kindly best for Amalie, but his velvet glove had failed: It was time for the iron fist. From Versailles, Louis now instructed his man in Turin, Monsieur (later the marquis) de Chauvelin, to make the 150-mile journey across to reinforce his ineffectual ambassador, La Houze.

Chauvelin was a tough old soldier who had overseen the recent French conquest of Corsica. In Amalie he saw intelligence and good governing potential; in her husband he saw neither, but he approached them both in the same manner, and bullied them into submission in no time, threatening them with the loss of their subsidies from Spain and France if they did not comply. Amalie was obliged to dismiss those of her staff who were most bitterly opposed to Du Tillot, and to accept that courtiers and guests would from now on be seated and treated according to rank. Don Ferdinando was made to promise to refrain from any involvement in the government for the next four years, and to banish his cherished Dominican friars altogether from all official meetings. Both signed their names to the appropriate documents, and both seemed sincere, but with Chauvelin's departure, things swiftly returned to the disordered status quo ante.

Early in November 1769, the Empress ordered Count Rosenberg to travel down from Leopold's court at Florence. He managed, to some degree, to bring Amalie to reason. Her mother, refraining from any comment on their relationship, still held Du Tillot and the marchesa in high regard. Like Louis and Carlos, she saw them, not incorrectly, as intelligent and experienced people, thoroughly familiar with the government and court affairs, and she remained broadly in favour of their many reforms, including those restricting the power of the Church. For now, she said, Amalie had only to support Du Tillot and follow the marchesa's advice, turning her back on those who opposed them, and making no decisions whatsoever of her own. In a general way Amalie conceded this, but Rosenberg was not satisfied. Returning to Florence, he told the Empress that, in his opinion, "the only person in the world who could persuade Amalie" to step back into line was her eldest and favourite sister, Marianna.

Marianna was at the Hofburg, where she had recently received an invitation to become a member of the Grand Ducal Academy of Arts in Florence. This was not likely to have been brother Leopold's doing, though the academicians may have made their decision with a glance in his direction. But in a rare confluence of opinion with Joseph, Leopold was not fond of Marianna, and he had shown no interest in the fine copper engravings and drawings and watercolours that had brought her this honour now. He was in Vienna at this time, echoing the rest of the family's disparagement of her plan to retire to the Sisters of St Elisabeth in Klagenfurt. Maria Theresia had been particularly opposed to the idea, but Marianna had made up her mind, and a small classical-style palace, with a formal garden, had been being constructed for her there. Land being needed for the new building, nearby acres had been simply appropriated. Compensation had been paid to the farmers and other tenants, but the Sisters had been inconvenienced, too, losing some of their rooms and part of their own garden, and even having to move the little cemetery "for our departed patients," as one of them recorded.

It was only after Amalie's wedding, and possibly because of it, that Marianna had finally decided to go to the convent in Klagenfurt instead of to her *Damenstift* in Prague: The two sisters had always been close, and the distance to Klagenfurt from Parma was less than half that to Prague. Amalie, restless by nature, was constantly making plans to travel, but for Marianna, given her uncertain health, the effort was generally considerable, and she did not make the five-hundred-mile journey from Vienna now to help her sister or persuade her to change her behaviour. She would almost certainly have written to Amalie at this point, though no letters are known to have survived, but whatever she may have said, she might have saved her breath: Amalie carried on just as before.

# XII

# 1770-1771

## In which Maria Antonia becomes Marie Antoinette, not yet a queen and not quite a wife, and Amalie issues further challenges in Parma.

On the sixteenth of April 1770, after five years of informal engagement, the betrothal was announced of the Archduchess Antonia to the dauphin Louis-Auguste, heir to the throne of France. The ceremony itself was followed by two gala dinners, at which the guests polished off 1,430 bottles of champagne and 1,340 bottles of burgundy, the elegant wines introduced to Vienna long before by the Francophile bon vivant Franz Stephan, plus an untallied number of other less refined libations.

Antonia had not been the first princess chosen for the dauphin by his grandfather, King Louis XV. As a child, she had shown no particular talents, so that on the advice of Joseph's late wife, Isabella, Louis had initially selected her spirited sister Carolina, two years older than the dauphin. But the boy had been slow to develop, and the King had decided a match with someone younger than himself would be better for him. For some years, however, he had not permitted a formal betrothal, in case "a physical disfigurement should occur in the years before the wedding." This did not mean the smallpox, since Antonia had already had a mild form of the disease; indeed, slight traces of it still marred her pretty face. But Louis was a connoisseur of the female form; he felt it was important that his grandson's wife should be attractive to him, and the betrothal had in any case to be postponed until Antonia had started her periods, since an infertile dauphine would be useless.

At the age of thirteen, at the summer palace of Laxenburg, Antonia had made her first public appearance as dauphine-to-be. At the tail end of a numerous family and largely overlooked in her childhood, she had quite suddenly become the object of everyone's attention. Her educational routines had been a good deal intensified and her indulgent *aya* replaced by the more demanding Countess Lerchenfeld. To improve Antonia's inadequate French, the Empress had rather hastily engaged a pair of native speakers—two roving actors who had proved less than courtly in manner and idiom. They had been quickly dismissed, and in their place, deeply flattered by this unexpected opportunity, had come the thirty-three-year-old abbé de Vermond. Though a man of no great brilliance, Vermond had been quick enough to take the measure of his new pupil. "She is more intelligent than anyone has thought her for a long time," he reported. "Unfortunately, up to the age of twelve she has had no intellectual discipline at all. She is a bit lazy and a bit flighty, and that has made her more difficult to teach. I believe she can only be brought to apply herself by being entertained." Humbled and fatigued by her mother's belated efforts to improve her education, Antonia had been at the same time excited, and her head a little turned, by the courtiers' predictions about the life she would lead at the incomparably fashionable court of Versailles. As Eleonore von Liechtenstein told her sister Leopoldine, "The little soul is completely ruined here; they talk to her incessantly and only about all the dazzle and parties awaiting her in France."

At her grand palace in Naples, Antonia's own sister Carolina had been thinking of something very different awaiting the little dauphine. Memories of her own ghastly wedding-night made her anxious for her favourite, as she told Madame Lerchenfeld:

> *I have always had a particular tenderness for her, and when I think that her fate may be like mine, then I want to write her whole*

> *volumes about it, and I really hope she will have someone, as I did, at the start, because without that, frankly, it's desperate, you suffer a martyrdom, and it's even worse because you always have to pretend to be happy. I know what it is, and I really pity those who have yet to go through it. I can say, and I'm not exaggerating, if Religion had not told me to think of God, I would have killed myself; to live another week seemed like hell to me, I would have wanted to die. I'm sure that in the first few days after my sister's arrival I'll shed many tears imagining what she will suffer.*

Three days after Antonia's formal betrothal, at six o'clock in the evening, the fourteen-year-old bride arrived at the Church of St Augustine for the wedding by procuration. She walked down the aisle with her mother, swishing and shining in a beautiful gown of silk interwoven with silver threads. At the altar, brother Ferdinand stood waiting in his regimental uniform, proxy bridegroom to his youngest sister as he had been for Carolina and Amalie. He was now almost sixteen and, as the Empress informed his fiancée in Milan, he was "as tall as [his stocky steward] Crivelli, but very slim and slender." Beatrice knew Crivelli, having received all the Empress' letters from his hand; the comparison was expected to reassure her.

Antonia left Vienna on the twenty-first of April. Surprisingly, the Empress had discouraged her from keeping in touch personally with her siblings—"I don't think you should write to your family"—with the exception of the Emperor Joseph, and of Carolina in Naples, who had expressly asked her mother's permission to correspond with her. "I don't see any difficulty with that," Maria Theresia had written. "She will tell you nothing that isn't reasonable and useful . . . so you may write to her, but make sure everything is of a nature to be read by everyone."

Antonia's train set off at a quarter past nine in the morning. With this early departure, the Empress had hoped to avoid a heartrending farewell such as Carolina's had been, but it was of no real help. Maria Theresia remained fairly composed: "Having seen less of her than the others," the Princess von

Trautson observed, "she is less attached to her." But for Antonia herself, every beloved face provoked a fresh outburst of tears. She clung to her old wet-nurse, wailing, "I will love you all my life. Don't forget me!" and the nurse fell at the feet of the new dauphine, both of them sobbing desperately. The scene was so emotional that the two had to be separated.

The hour was in any case not early enough to prevent the whole of Vienna, or so it seemed, turning out to make their adieux. They stood in the streets and squares of the town, packed and straining for a sight of Antonia's gold-painted carriage parading the double-headed Habsburg eagle of her past and the Bourbon *fleur de lys* of her future. At first they waited in a solemn silence. But when they saw Antonia herself, in tears, "hiding her eyes now with her handkerchief, now with her hands," craning out the carriage window for a last glimpse of the Hofburg, "then arose not only tears; but piercing cries, on all sides. Men and women alike abandoned themselves to such expression of their sorrow, until the last Courier that followed her disappeared, and the crowd melted away."

**It was an eighteen-day** journey from Vienna to the French border, and even when upholstered in velvet, a sprung carriage drawn by six horses over indifferent roads and hilly terrain was not a comfortable conveyance. Travelling with Antonia on the opposite bench of her coach was the observant and informative Countess Paar, who had also travelled with Carolina and Amalie on their wedding journeys. It was her job to keep the new dauphine company and, with one day's drive as much as nine hours at a stretch, to distract her from melancholy or anxious thoughts.

Antonia spent the first night of her long westward journey at the Baroque Abbey of Melk, sixty-five miles from Vienna, where Joseph awaited her. He was still in mourning for his little daughter, who had died of rheumatic fever a few months before, and it may have been this association that drew him now to his youngest and still very childlike sister, fourteen years of age to his twenty-nine. Until her early death, Josepha had been his favourite;

from now on, Antonia took that place. From Melk the train of fifty-seven carriages—Carolina, as a reigning queen, had had five times as many—travelled westward through Bavaria. The last stage of the journey took them through the dense and mountainous Black Forest to the great Rhine River, ancient boundary between the German lands and France. Like the Po River for Amalie, the Rhine marked for Antonia the point of *consegna*—delivery of the bride from her old court to her new.

On the neutral territory of an island in the middle of the river, Antonia was to be formally handed over to the French. A large wooden pavilion had been rather hastily built to house this *consegna*, with an Austrian side room and a French one, and an extravagantly decorated central room, all of which had been opened to view by any well dressed visitor. In the French side room, Antonia was now divested of all her clothes, down to her stockings and undergarments. The various pieces of her beautiful bridal trousseau were snatched up as perquisites of office by her four new *dames de palais*, all of them strangers to her, before they reclothed her in the tight-corseted French fashion. From this ordeal she emerged on the west bank of the Rhine, and for the first time, as Marie Antoinette.

A local girl reported watching her coming out of the room with her light step. "She was weeping abundantly," she wrote, "for the Empress, for the archduchesses her sisters and for her friends." She was leaving the last traces of her Austrian life behind her: almost all the Viennese courtiers who had accompanied her thus far, her own German language, her servants, her clothes, even her pug dog, Mops, a sad-faced little symbol of the pathos of the day—though the thoughtful Austrian ambassador was later to have the dog sent on to her at Versailles. Seeking the comfort of even a vaguely familiar face, she ran at once to the comtesse de Noailles, whom she had met for the first time only the evening before, and threw her arms around her. As she had clung to her wet-nurse on her last day in Vienna, so now she clung to the startled comtesse on her first day in France.

It was quite the wrong thing to do. In a telling sign of the extreme formality of French court life, Madame de Noailles coolly extricated herself from the precipitate embrace, and Marie Antoinette, abashed and confused, humbly begged her forgiveness and her guidance. She was unfamiliar with French ways and, at this point, far from perfect even in the language itself. Madame de Noailles was not unkind, but her thinking was inflexible and her personality without warmth. Her knowledge of the conventions and courtesies of the French court was faultless but, as a lady-in-waiting observed, "she wore the young princess out with it, without showing her why it mattered." The harassed dauphine would soon be referring to her, irreverently, as "Madame Etiquette."

She made an excellent first impression at least on King Louis XV, who met her some days later at his hunting château of Compiègne, still under renovation in the newly fashionable neoclassical style. Shortly afterwards he penned a reliably suggestive note about her to his grandson, Amalie's husband, Don Ferdinando, in Parma. "The dauphine has been in my hands for hours now," he wrote. "I am very pleased with her and my grandson is too, but he'll be even more pleased in a day or two." In his own rather baldly kept journal, the dauphin himself recorded only that he had met *Madame la dauphine*. Marie Antoinette's thoughts at this first meeting with her husband are unknown.

Among the courtiers presented to her at Compiègne was the Savoyard Princesse de Lamballe, already a widow at twenty years of age. Her marriage had lasted just a year, but her husband had left her, along with an immense fortune, a reminder of himself in small unsightly scars on her otherwise pretty face, marks of the venereal disease that had killed him. As a Belgian courtier noted, "Marie Antoinette's tender heart needed friendship," and it was Madame de Lamballe who at once assumed the place Madame de Noailles had instinctively resisted—of an affectionate confidante to the uprooted dauphine. Maria Theresia, suspicious of the potential for gossip and political intrigue, had warned all her daughters against having favourites; in this case, the princesse hailed from the House of Savoy, Austria's rival, and this had spoken doubly against her. But it would have been diplomatically difficult to exclude a person of such high rank from the dauphine's circle and, as Ambassador Mercy subsequently reported, she was a steady and good-natured young woman, with no apparent interest in the constant little stratagems of the court. The Empress was reassured, and Marie Antoinette was permitted to keep her new-found friend.

The wedding ceremony itself took place in the vaulted royal chapel of Versailles, with the bright May sun streaming through its large windows. Lady Elizabeth Percy, Duchess of Northumberland, attending as part of a late-in-life Grand Tour, described the dauphin, in his extravagant ceremonial attire, in the journal she was keeping of her travels. "I expected to have found him horrid," she wrote, "but on the contrary his figure pleas'd me very well. He is tall & slender with a Countenance tres interessant & a look of good Sense. . . . As he pass'd by he look'd quite fatigued, he seems very delicate & to have the appearance of a Boy who had out grown his strength." Of the diamond-draped bride herself, Lady Percy noted, "She Blushed, is very little & slender. I should not have taken her to be above 12 Years Old. She is fair & a little mark'd with the Smallpox." As for her wedding gown of white brocade puffed out with hoops, "the Corps of her Robe was too small & left quite a broad stripe of lacing & Shift quite visible, wch had a bad effect"—but which no doubt provided a good subject for court gossip in the days to follow.

The rest of the royal family "were all excessively magnificent" in gold and other sumptuous cloths that "I do not exactly recollect." The dauphin's youngest brother, the twelve-year-old comte d'Artois, supposedly a very clever and winning young man, resembled most of his relatives in being "extremely fat," and surprised Lady Percy by his "very vacant Countenance . . . though the [fourteen-year-old] Comte de Provence, next Brother to the Dauphin . . . has a most pleasing sensible Countenance. . . . The Dauphin's sisters are two little fat things," with Elisabeth, just turned six, "as round as a Ball. I dare say her Circumference considerably exceeds her height. She was almost cover'd with Pearls." Three of the dauphin's middle-aged aunts were present, too. Lady Percy found Madame Sophie as lean as her nieces were fat, "& Horridly ugly." Victoire showed the family tendency to *embonpoint* but was nonetheless still pretty, and the shrewd eldest sister, Adélaïde, who dominated them all, "looks decay'd but not ugly, & there is something sensible & good natured in her Countenance."

The bride was offended, however, to see the comtesse du Barry among the six thousand wedding guests. In her innocence, she had not at first understood Madame du Barry's function at court. She was unaware of the formal French position of the King's *maîtresse-en-titre*, there being nothing similar at the Hofburg. For her part, the worldly Lady Percy was disappointed in the comtesse. "She is rather of a tall, middle size, full breasted, and is pretty but not to be call'd handsome . . . & has a strong Look of her former profession."

Though the morning had been lovely and the weather had held into the afternoon, soon after the ceremony it broke with a drenching rain, forcing the cancellation of the planned fireworks, and providing superstitious observers with the grim satisfaction of a bad omen for the future.

"[THE DAUPHIN'S] WIFE has had her periods properly for the first time since we have had the pleasure of possessing her. I am delighted that your own wife is well and without her headaches." Thus Louis XV at Versailles, evidently informed of all the details and not above a double entendre, to his grandson Don Ferdinando in Parma.

Whatever Louis may have been daydreaming of throughout the summer since Marie Antoinette's wedding, the bridegroom himself had not yet had any such pleasure. In fact he had not even attempted to consummate the marriage, as Count Mercy-Argenteau, the Viennese ambassador, informed Maria Theresia. Mercy had been at Versailles for some years already, and his current remit included basically spying on Marie Antoinette, who had been instructed to trust him absolutely.

At first the lack of consummation caused no great concern. Allowance was made for the couple's extreme youth and the dauphin's "subdued and reserved character." In Marie Antoinette's words, "he loves me and is well intentioned, but there's a nonchalance and laziness about him that never goes unless he's hunting." She was seen to be gaining his confidence, and each had admitted they liked the other. "The only real happiness in this world is a happy marriage," the Empress had told her. "I know what I'm talking about. Everything depends on the woman; she must be obliging, gentle and amusing."

Three months after the wedding, the methodical dauphin informed his wife, and she informed Mercy, who informed the Empress, that "he was not ignorant of anything relating to the state of marriage, that from the very beginning he had formed a plan about it from which he had not wished to deviate, that the time had now arrived, and that at Compiègne he intended to live with Madame la dauphine to the fullest extent of intimacy appropriate to their union." It seems the boy had, sensitively and sensibly, wanted to get to know his wife a little before making love to her. But even the plans of princes go awry. Six months after the wedding, things were no further along, as half the smirking court seemed to know.

Why was there no pregnancy? It is true Marie Antoinette's periods had been irregular; indeed, she had not long finished growing: At the time of her marriage, she had been "very small and child-like," as her mother admitted. But she was now past puberty, and her husband was spending some nights and many mornings alone with her. Maria Theresia concluded that the lack of consummation was entirely her daughter's fault. The dauphine was doing everything wrong. At night she was staying up too late, by day she was going horse-riding—"which I do not approve of at all"—evidently the Empress shared Joseph's view that riding was "not healthy for women who are to bear children." And she was not making herself sufficiently attractive. She was not wearing the right gowns, not cleaning her teeth properly—in a word, she was letting herself go. Even the good news was not really good: The "very little & slender" bride, looking like a twelve-year-old, had by now grown taller and filled out somewhat, but this had only led her mother to worry she might be developing "the body of a woman without really being one."

There was no suggestion that Marie Antoinette might have been able to help her husband with the act of sex itself. Bereft of the least information about it, she also seems, at just turned fifteen, to have had little libido, despite an apparently determined temperament. As the Empress told Mercy at precisely this time, "I know my daughter well enough to be convinced she will succeed in doing whatever she wants, and she will dare to do a lot." Though Marie Antoinette certainly wanted to do her duty and produce an heir, it seems she did not particularly want sex in itself.

King Louis, for his part, well aware that to every man she encountered, the dauphine was perfectly attractive just as she was, felt there must be some physical problem on his grandson's side. He thought the dauphin's foreskin might be too long; he had conveyed as much to his Parma grandson, Don Ferdinando. Or it might be a case of phimosis: The foreskin might be too tight, as Dr. Lassonne, Marie Antoinette's physician, believed. In either case, erection and ejaculation would still be possible, and if there was pain, the dauphin could be circumcised, a minor operation even in the eighteenth century. Dr. Lassonne conducted a thorough examination, to which the patient submitted without embarrassment, but no evidence of any physical problem was found. Simply and sensibly, Lassonne concluded that the dauphin had not fully understood the mechanics of the sexual act, but less sensibly, he took no steps to enlighten him.

IT DID NOT HELP Marie Antoinette to know that her sisters seemed to be managing their marriages perfectly well. It was true that, after two and a half years, Carolina was not yet pregnant, but her husband had been sleeping with her regularly, indeed enthusiastically, from the very beginning. As for Amalie, her husband's erectile dysfunction having been cured by the straightforward application of a little *acqua di Parma*, in November 1770, after an arduous labour, she had given birth to her first child—to everyone's disappointment, a daughter.

She wanted to breastfeed the baby. This was a rather daring practice at the time for women of her rank, who typically relied on wet-nurses, women of lesser means who had themselves just given birth and were prepared or obliged to pass their own babies into less assiduous care elsewhere. Amalie may have been seeking to gain her mother's approval—the Empress was known to approve of breastfeeding—but she needed her husband's permission in any case, and in his turn, Don Ferdinando had appealed for advice to his grandfather, at his summer palace of Marly. Louis had been discouraging. "It is not the custom here at court that mothers breastfeed their infants," he had replied, "though some of our young women have been taken by this idea; some of them have found it good, others not. I cannot advise for or against it. I will tell you, however, that husbands should not be in favour of it since it deprives them of their wives for eighteen months, and afterwards their breasts are thoroughly spoiled, and they are a very agreeable feature if they're pretty, as I'm sure your wife's are."

A self-declared connoisseur of women's breasts—by his own admission it was always the first thing he noticed in a woman—Louis shared the then common misapprehension that breastfeeding would deform them, when in fact it helped to retain their firmness. This error may have been circulated by confessors appealing to the vanity of the women in their charge, for the Church itself had long forbidden breastfeeding. Its prohibition was based on the floundering physiology of the time, according to which all bodily fluids were mixed together. A husband's semen, for instance, would join with his wife's blood, supposedly making her stronger. But if the wife were lactating, the semen would also enter her breastmilk, so harming her baby. As a husband's rights were held to preempt those of a child, so his right to sex preempted the baby's right to food; hence the Church's prohibition.

Don Ferdinando being a man of particular piety, it was perhaps for this reason that in the end he forbade Amalie to breastfeed. Indeed, before the infant Carolina was two months old, he had decided his attractive wife was perfectly recovered from the difficult birth, and was expressing his impatience for her to provide him with a son.

It was at this same point, in January 1771, that the infighting between

Amalie's supporters and Du Tillot's faction came to a head, when a phial containing five drops of what might have been poison was found in the possession of one of Amalie's ladies-in-waiting—the girl had concealed it beneath her bodice. She confessed she had been given it by the Infanta's enemies, and from this Amalie concluded that Du Tillot had ordered an attempt on her life. She urged her husband to appeal to his uncle in Madrid, and for good measure Don Ferdinando accused Du Tillot of corruption and outright theft. Du Tillot himself believed he was on the brink of arrest, which indeed Don Ferdinando was considering, supposedly for the Minister's own safety.

Carlos consulted with Louis, and the two Kings initiated a formal inquiry. It lasted for months, sapping energy and patience in all three Bourbon courts and at the Hofburg as well. Amalie fell ill, believing, or possibly pretending, that she was pregnant again. By the spring, five more French, Viennese, and Spanish envoys had arrived in Parma with instructions to effect a reconciliation between the warring parties.

They were all to fail.

*I'm writing now, my dear daughter, with your picture in front of me, but to me it seems you've lost that youthful air you had eleven months ago, and unfortunately that's not because of the change in your marital state. That news I await with great impatience, but I can't say it often enough: don't make a fuss. Caresses, cajoling, yes, but too much pressure will ruin everything. Use only sweetness and patience. Everything will be fine: you're both so young; it's even a good thing for your health, you're both still building up your strength. But it's only natural for your old relatives to wish to see the thing accomplished.*

Thus the importunate Maria Theresia to Marie Antoinette in the spring of 1771, with the consummation of the marriage still to be accomplished almost a year after the wedding. The Empress could not resist a further little prod a few months later, when, after twelve years of preparation, the Archduke Ferdinand finally married the "sensible but ugly" Milanese heiress Beatrice d'Este. Marie Antoinette had the humiliation of being informed that her brother's bride had "become his wife" on their actual wedding-night, "and the two of them are clearly in love." "My new sister-in-law can only make me jealous of her marriage," she had replied to her mother coolly.

King Louis had taken more overt action. Anxious about the Bourbon succession, he had brought forward the marriage of the dauphin's fifteen-year-old brother, Louis-Stanislaus, the fat and bookish comte de Provence, with a princess of the powerful House of Savoy, Austria's rival for control of northern Italy. Eighteen years old, the new comtesse de Provence was, in the words of her grandfather-in-law the King, "very nicely made, not tall, with an awful nose. . . . The comte de Provence is very pleased with her, and I believe he is already further advanced than his brother. Though not pretty, she is very nice, and having seen her, if I were a few years younger, I would have taken her for myself."

Louis was evidently persuaded by Provence's boasting about his sex life with his new wife, which was largely to taunt his still virgin elder brother. But six weeks after the marriage, the comtesse confided to Marie Antoinette, who in turn conveyed it to Maria Theresia, that "her marriage has not been consummated at all." "I am not displeased to hear that the comtesse de Provence is no further advanced in the state of marriage than the dauphine," the Empress replied. "These princes are simply too young. It requires patience and a great deal of tenderness. Too much haste only leads to discouragement."

Soon enough there were whispers that Provence was sleeping with a young duke, and the comtesse with one of her ladies-in-waiting, but though the two were to live largely separately and were never to have any children, the rumours of homosexuality, as indeed of anything else at gossip-ridden Versailles, were to be taken with a pinch of salt, at least as far as the comte was concerned. In due course, he would install another of his wife's ladies-in-waiting as his mistress.

AT VERSAILLES, MARIE ANTOINETTE had welcomed her rival in the heir-producing stakes with the best grace possible. To her own rival for political influence in Parma, her sister had taken quite the opposite approach. In July 1771, Amalie had announced the summary dismissal of Du Tillot's mistress and accomplice Madame Malaspina, and despite the lady's appeal to the envoys of France and Spain and Austria with all the eloquence of her "elevated soul," exiled her to her country estate. Amalie did at least agree to continue paying the emoluments due her.

La Malaspina was gone, but Don Ferdinando's appeals for a similar dismissal of Du Tillot—"He's a villain. He has neither Religion nor decency. I demand to be set free of him!"—proved fruitless: The Minister remained *en poste*. Amalie resolved to incite a riot against him. On the thirtieth of the month, with Du Tillot due to drive into Parma, she ordered soldiers into the town to call out as many of his opponents as possible: They were to surround his carriage and compel him to resign. "At this news," it was reported, "the common people, a great part of the nobility and numerous ecclesiastics came running"—even the wet-nurses joined the demonstrators. The carriage was forced to a halt, the crowd threatened violence, and Du Tillot was on the brink of capture. He was saved by the intervention of Ambassador La Houze, and little by little the crowd dispersed, spitting abuse at the Minister and all things French as they went.

Amalie's coup had failed. Maria Theresia despatched Rosenberg once again to Parma. He arrived in mid-October 1771, just in time to hear the verdict of the formal inquiry against Du Tillot. Though the First Minister was found innocent of all charges, it was clear there could be no cooperation between him and the ducal pair. Reluctantly, Carlos dismissed him. At the age of sixty, after twenty-two years of service to the Duchy, he was placed under house arrest at his Colorno residence. Within five days he had fled and was on his way to France.

From Versailles, Louis penned a somewhat overdrawn letter to Don Ferdinando. "I saw Du Tillot yesterday," he wrote. "I hardly recognized him. Your wife is of a very strange cast of mind and I will not conceal it from you, no one in her family has ever loved her. She may mend her ways and I hope she will do so with all my heart, especially for your sake, my dear grandson." As for Marie Antoinette, "I cannot tell you how embarrassed I am by the Infanta's behaviour," she told the Empress. "It's astonishing that she's learned nothing from what you and Rosenberg have been saying to her. Of course I will do all I can to lessen the bad impression it's having here. But really," she added, with the sincerity of her own compliant and easily scandalized nature, "if I were in her unfortunate position, the wish to spare my dear maman any trouble would be enough to reform me."

# XIII

# 1772-1774

## In which the Empress contends with the troubles of four daughters, three greedy neighbours take a bite out of Poland, and Marie Antoinette becomes Queen.

My poor daughter in Parma is really beginning to worry me," the Empress wrote to her new daughter-in-law Beatrice in the spring of 1772. "Her health is of the worst. It's all the more astonishing since here she enjoyed perfect health, though she was never merry. I fear there's a good deal of melancholy." Two years and more of constant provocation had not turned Maria Theresia against Amalie: She persisted in thinking her unwise and untutored rather than vicious or worthless, but Joseph and Kaunitz had been urging her to take a firmer stand, and now, for the third time, she instructed Rosenberg to ride down from Florence. He arrived armed with a stern document for Amalie, imperiously entitled *Rules of Conduct.* It contained twenty-three articles, not of advice but very much of command, concerning court etiquette and the management of her personal household, as well as her own behaviour and her influence on Don Ferdinando.

Amalie was taken aback, but she made a spirited riposte to each point, admitting she had been wrong to borrow money and get into debt, and acknowledging the obedience she owed her husband, but otherwise insisting on her right to decide her own way of life. Forbidden any hand in managing the ducal stables, for instance, she insisted she would continue to be involved, "seeing that no one here knows how to do it, and they're negligent in their work"—a reasonable reply, given her considerable experience with horses; in fact, she was soon to start a stud farm of her own.

As for the very formal Bourbon customs she had been forced to observe, "from the very beginning I found it completely ridiculous that a prince with such a little state should have to conform to the same ceremony as the Kings of France and Spain"—in fact, in Vienna, her own father and brother had done away with the same solemnities. She rebuffed a suggestion that she exploited her ill health to manipulate her husband, and for good measure, managed a little dig at her mother: "There is nothing lower than listening to informers and spies; these sort of people betray one person today and someone else tomorrow. Perhaps if certain persons hadn't listened to such people, a great many misfortunes might have been avoided." And she concluded roundly, "From the moment of my arrival here, I have said that I recognize no authority apart from the Infante's; and therefore, provided he is not displeased, I want my freedom."

Rosenberg was shocked by her tone of extraordinary defiance. "She wants to shake off every yoke and all dependence on the Kings of France and Spain and Your Majesty," he reported to the Empress. "She has informed me that Your Majesty is only making things worse by always wanting to interfere in things that have not been Your Majesty's concern since her marriage. Judge of the insurmountable stubbornness of Madame the Infanta." It is true that Amalie's tone was impudent, even insolent, if indeed she was addressing her mother. But she suspected Rosenberg and the marqués de Llano, Du Tillot's Spanish replacement as First Minister, of having compiled the list themselves, and her reply betrays her indignation that they should have dared to dictate to her at all.

The Empress, aggrieved, responded starkly. From now on, she announced, no member of the family was to maintain communication with Amalie. No letters were to be sent to her; any arriving from her were to be returned unopened; she was not to be received at any family court or residence, nor was anyone to visit her in Parma. "I know what it will cost me, but I will do my duty," she told Rosenberg. "She is dead to me." The state of incommunicado between Amalie and her family was still in force at the end of 1772, by which time Don Ferdinando had sacked the upright de Llano and replaced him with a local man, the conte Giuseppe Sacco, who appears to have considered it his first duty to enrich his family at the Duchy's expense.

Briefly, the Empress even considered armed intervention, but neither Austria nor France, nor even Spain, had any legal right to intervene in Parma's governance. It was a sovereign duchy, and Don Ferdinando was its ruler; there was only the claim of family ties to justify any interference from outside. And after all, the couple's faults were not heinous, simply irregular and foolish, "to be pitied rather than reproached," as the Empress accepted with a sigh. The only solution was to abandon them to their own devices, withdrawing all financial support, sending no further envoys, and forbidding Amalie to set foot anywhere in the Monarchy's territories, or in Tuscany, which she particularly wanted to visit. In time, her mother hoped, "the thick veil through which they see only our power, without noticing our tenderness and amity," would fall from their eyes. And if not, their need for money would no doubt bring them around.

The unedifying scenes and stories from Parma were naturally relayed through all the courts of Europe, to Amalie's severe disadvantage. Some saw, in her outlandish behaviour, the mischievous hand of Maria Theresia, trying to sow discord at a Bourbon court, and certainly the Empress was concerned it would reflect badly on herself. But other observers suspected Amalie was mentally unstable, and it was this view that was to gain ground from now on, at Parma, at other courts, and within her own family, with ever sadder consequences for herself.

CROSS WITH AMALIE, far from well with chest problems and "overwhelmed by fatigue," as she herself admitted, the Empress had fallen prey to morbid thoughts. "Why didn't I die in the smallpox," she sighed to Madame Enzenberg, "how happy I would have been!" In fact, she had been sewing her winding-sheet, only half metaphorically, for some years already. Lady Mary Coke, visiting from London, had observed that "the Empress is always making a sort of chain of red silk, which they told me is used in some sort of embroidery." This was a mourning chasuble that she had begun to make soon after Franz Stephan's death, a sumptuous red and gold vestment to be worn by the priest who would eventually officiate at her own funeral. The firmness of Maria Theresia's religious faith allowed her to think of the end of life without great fear, "though not without trembling at the terrible account I will have to render," a result of the great responsibilities attendant on her powerful position now. "There is only God's great mercy and my own good intentions which reassure me," she concluded.

Despite her protestations, the Empress' strong sense of duty and her personal taste for control made it unlikely she would ever surrender her reign. Habit and instinct drove her on, with Chancellor von Kaunitz guiding her and Joseph at her side, the latter often more hindrance than help. In his urgent twenties, chafing at the bridle of co-regency, the young Emperor was dismissive of his mother's long experience and impatient with the Chancellor's careful methods. He wanted the Monarchy to change internally and expand externally, and he wanted everything to happen as swiftly as possible.

Revelling in army life and yet not battle-scarred, he had no dread of armed conflict; where an immediate advantage might be gained, the stately quadrille of conventional European diplomacy, maintaining the balance of power for the sake of general peace, could be interrupted in an instant, he felt, by the blast of a military trumpet. And in August 1772, in an episode from which Maria Theresia's reputation was never to recover, she allowed him to override her habitual caution by his avidity, even recklessness, in the inglorious first partition of Poland.

In the seven years since his abortive plan to marry the Archduchess Elisabeth, King Stanisław had devoted his efforts to reforming his haphazardly governed and weakly defended Commonwealth. This geographically enormous sovereign territory, the largest in Europe at this point, comprised not only the Kingdom of Poland and the Grand Duchy of Lithuania, but also Belarus and a large part of Ukraine, plus substantial lands on the Baltic Sea. Stanisław's powerful neighbours, Russia and Prussia, viewed his reforms with displeasure: The Tsarina Catherine regarded his Commonwealth as her natural sphere of influence and wanted it to remain so, while Friedrich's more ambitious intentions were to devour the most savoury parts of it himself, "like an artichoke, leaf by leaf."

Austria was uneasy with both points of view, and for a time had joined the French in opposing Russia and Prussia, so effectively supporting Stanisław's independence: Poland was, after all, a useful buffer between the Monarchy's territory and that of the other two Great Powers. But at the end of 1770, despite the hapless attempts of the then fifteen-year-old Marie Antoinette to protect him, the duc de Choiseul, architect of the Franco-Austrian alliance and her own marriage, had been dismissed from the Foreign Ministry, and Friedrich had seen his opportunity to shake the entente and convert Maria Theresia to his own way of thinking: He tempted her with the handsome prize of the Kingdom of Galicia and Lodomeria, with the ancient city of Lviv as its capital. Though she was at first reluctant, Joseph egged her on, pushing for even more territory than Prussia had at first been offering.

In the end, Austrian fear of Russian and Prussian aggrandizement and the temptation of a fine new crown land had proved too much to resist: By September 1773, the Monarchy would have gained some thirty-three thousand square miles of land and more than two and a half million new subjects, among them, for the first time, to Maria Theresia's "horror and disgust," a substantial population of Jews. Though ambitious Protestants were also required to convert to Catholicism, and though certain Jewish entrepreneurs were, for a price, permitted access to the court, the Empress maintained a harsh prejudice against Jews as a whole, driving them pitilessly out of her crown lands despite pleas from her ministers and even the Pope, and infamously declaring, "I know of no plague worse for the state than this nation for fraud, usury and money dealing, for driving people to beggary and for engaging in low activities that any honourable man would despise. As far as is possible, they are to be kept at a minimum and kept away from here."

With her juicy chunk of Poland, they came nonetheless. Cartoons of the time depicted the plump Empress sitting at table with Catherine and Friedrich, shedding hypocritical tears for the dismembered country while accepting her own generous piece of the pie.

France had proved too weak to influence the power games in the heart of the continent, even to protect one of its oldest allies. At Versailles, those who had opposed the *renversement des alliances* felt vindicated by Austria's treachery, and throughout Europe the Monarchy's trustworthiness declined. Marie Antoinette felt the chill of French disapproval, and repeatedly sought reassurances from Mercy that the relations between Austria and France had not been affected, to such an extent that he thought it might even be time to "begin to explain to her some idea of the intent, the origins and the purpose of the alliance between the two courts"—a startling indication of the ignorance in which the Empress had allowed her to be left until now.

Maria Theresia instructed her to curry favour with her grandfather-in-law the King, and Mercy explained to his ingenuous pupil how this was to be done: "I went into detail about the way to captivate this monarch, about the need to pay court to his favourite [Madame du Barry] and the ministers." The frightened dauphine—"Where would I be if there was a rupture between my two families?"—at once acquiesced. "She told me she would do all that Your Majesty required of her," Mercy reported, "that I had only to suggest what she should do, that she would lend herself to anything."

Their combined efforts were to no avail. Louis XV told Marie Antoinette never to mention the subject of Poland, then turned his back on the matter, ignoring Stanisław's continuing pleas for help. The three invading powers of Russia, Prussia, and Austria, concerned to whitewash their rapacious land grab and the unprovoked destruction of a sovereign state, tried to present it all as a voluntary cession on Stanisław's part. Backed into a corner of his shrunken territories, the last King of Poland could only denounce their claim for the outrageous lie that it was.

THE EMPRESS WAS FEELING her age. Not that she was so very old, still in her fifties. But in Maria Theresia the impulse to life had weakened. The years since Franz Stephan's death had not lessened her grief for him, and in that time she had lost Josepha, too, and waved three other weeping daughters off into unknown lives with unknown husbands. Those of her children still at home were not entirely satisfactory, either. The arguments between herself and Joseph had been increasing in frequency and even in volume, and he had recently had the Belvedere palace renovated "so that he can remove there and live as he pleases," as a French envoy expressed it, "given the unfortunate incompatibility of temper existing between mother and son." Nor were his sisters behaving quite as might be wished: Elisabeth was constantly wailing about headaches and toothaches and having no proper establishment, and Marianna was wearing herself out with correspondence for the Prague abbey and her big medallion engraving project and wasting her ladies' time with rocks and electricity and other useless things, and now she had fallen into a depression.

It was true that Elisabeth had cause for complaint. Five possible matches had slipped through her fingers, and now, almost twenty-nine and disfigured as she was, it was unlikely that a sixth would eventuate. Even Maximilian, aged just fifteen, had already become Coadjutor and Knight of the Teutonic Order, guaranteeing him a handsome income and a useful occupation in adult life. His position would be prestigious enough: Together with the Knights Templar and the Knights of Malta, the Teutonic Order was one of the three great medieval knightly orders founded to defend the Christian faith.

Becoming a knight meant taking a vow of celibacy, however, and this had given the Empress reason to pause. She had originally intended Max Franz, as she called him, to have the Governorship of Hungary, but this she had by now given to Marie Christine's husband, Albert. She justified Maximilian's fate by insisting on his lack of tenderness, little suited in any case "to make a wife happy." In due course he would be further promoted, occasioning an outburst from Elisabeth, as the Empress told Marie Christine: "She started sobbing, saying that everyone has an establishment and she is the only one left out and she will have to stay on her own with the Emperor, which she will never do. We had a great deal of trouble to make her keep quiet; it's a sorry thing to see her being so unreasonable."

Elisabeth's complaints were not so unreasonable, all the same. No provision had yet been made for her, though there was one obvious possibility. Since Franz Stephan's death in Innsbruck in 1765, Maria Theresia had been restoring the Hofburg there, intending to establish in his memory a religious foundation for noble ladies similar to Marianna's *Damenstift* in Prague; Marianna was to include the Innsbruck commemorative medal "struck to perpetuate the conjugal piety of the immortal Sovereign" in her hefty volume of engravings.

The Innsbruck Hofburg had once been a royal residence, but for the past hundred years or so, there had been no Habsburg prince resident in the Tyrol, and the palace had gradually fallen into disrepair. Now it was being rebuilt in the late baroque style favoured by court architect Nikolaus Pacassi, who had already refashioned Schönbrunn, and the Empress was personally setting down its constitution of mostly religious requirements, including daily prayers to be recited by twelve noble ladies, dressed in mourning black, for the soul of her late husband.

But there was no thought at this time of Elisabeth becoming its abbess, though Marianna, five years older, had had her foundation in Prague for years already, and she was also actively involved with the Elisabethan convent in Klagenfurt. She had no intention of ever living in Prague, though she was doing some administrative work for the abbey, for which she was receiving 80,000 gulden a year, in addition to the money her father had left her. It is easy to see why Elisabeth might feel herself unprovided for by comparison.

Why did her mother not reserve the Innsbruck foundation for her? It was still being renovated; if she was not yet ready to assume the role of abbess, she would have years to prepare for it. She went readily enough to church, and it was not as if she would have had to become a nun—indeed, Maria Theresia's distaste for celibacy had led her to expressly forbid the *Damenstift* from ever becoming a convent. The position of abbess was primarily representational, and perhaps administrative if the abbess was so inclined; if not, such responsibilities could be left to the local governor. There would be an income attached to it, and a good deal of respect, which would not go amiss given Elisabeth's decreased value on the marriage market. And the Habsburg presence in the Tyrol would as easily be boosted by her residence there as by Marianna's. Indeed, Innsbruck was dynastically much more important than Klagenfurt, as the splendour of the palace's representation rooms would show.

The Empress may still have been hoping that, against the odds, Elisabeth would marry, but her reluctance was probably rooted in her own unsettled plans to leave command of the Monarchy in Joseph's hands and herself withdraw to Innsbruck, "where I am always yearning to be and where my last happy days came to an end." Certainly when it suited her, in the middle of a sticky political situation, she would sometimes threaten to retire immediately, a trick that Chancellor von Kaunitz, too, was not above playing to get his way. Her friend Madame Enzenberg was a permanent resident of Innsbruck, and the Empress' letters to her at this time are full of regrets that she cannot be there with her, away from the court, where "my worries increase by the day."

But it seems Innsbruck would have held less appeal if Elisabeth were to be there, too. By now the Empress was finding her third daughter something of a trial, and it is true that she was less self-reliant than her sisters and given to complaining a good deal more. But her mother, critical of all her children, was quick to blame her even when sympathy might have been more appropriate. Elisabeth had trouble with her teeth, a thing of horror in the eighteenth century. Decay from one tooth had spread and produced infection, and infection had led to an abscess inside her cheek. This had been lanced, from the outside, three times, and three of her teeth had been extracted; and, having secretly taken some primitive painkillers, she had not recovered from the ordeal in time to accompany the rest of the family to Laxenburg. "I'm sorry for her," her mother declared unconvincingly to Ferdinand in Milan, "though she brought it on herself by taking strong things that weren't compatible so as to finish more quickly, without anyone knowing. Nothing could be more dangerous. I hope that will teach her to be more careful in future."

Clearly something had to be done for Elisabeth, and just as clearly, the Empress could not decide what. Innsbruck had to be reserved for herself, even if it meant moving a great distance away from her beloved Mimi. But for once, even Mimi was behaving less than irreproachably, if rumour could be credited. It seemed that, at her lovely summer retreat of Schloss Hof, with its gardens laid out on sloping land leading down to the Danube River, she was engaging in "a little intrigue" with the Prince Karl von Liechtenstein. A lieutenant field marshal serving as military attaché to the Hungarian court, the forty-two-year-old Prince was looking for promotion to a grander post: Paying attention to the *châtelaine* was "a means of advancing his prospects," as he assured his wife, the Princess Eleonore, and as she relayed to her sister, Leopoldine von Kaunitz, wife of the former Viennese ambassador in Naples, now resident in Moravia. Evidently the liaison, whatever its precise nature, was not new. "My husband says he knew about it already in Vienna," Leopoldine told her now. "I suspected it myself though I wasn't sure; I think Madame's passion is greater than Monsieur's."

A woman of her calculating time, Eleanore was not stirred to jealousy. She herself had been married at eighteen to a man almost twice her age whom she did not love. Her expectations had never been romantic. It was not the first time her husband had taken a mistress, and if he was going to do so, as her sister pointed out, "he could hardly find a prettier woman, and she's so well in with the Empress and so manipulative that far from harming him, this could actually be of some benefit." "Yes, it's an advantage to him,"

Eleonore agreed, "and I admit I think it's a very good idea, especially since there's nothing underhand about it and it's concealed beneath the veil of friendship. And to be honest she looked ravishing today, she was wearing a dress of the most beautiful rose colour with gauze finishings, no bodice, half-décolleté, hair looped up and hardly powdered, almost no diamonds, the most engaging behaviour in the world. . . . So be it," she declared stoically, "I'll have to drink the cup to the dregs."

Had she wished, she might have consoled herself with an affair of her own, since her own husband "allows me to do as I please," and for some time she had been being pursued by the thirty-one-year-old Emperor. Joseph had vowed never to remarry, but only days before he had declared to Eleonore "that he regarded me as his wife, that he had that kind of feeling for me. 'A man isn't in love with his wife,' he said to me, 'but he takes an interest in everything that concerns her. It seems to me that you belong in this.' I told him I understood nothing of his metaphysics of feelings, but that I was very far from belonging to him in any way. He's very likeable in a social setting, certainly, but it's very difficult to have anything to do with him, his behaviour changes according to how the mood takes him."

Perhaps surprisingly, Maria Theresia appears to have encouraged her son's penchant for Eleonore. In letters of this time to his brother Leopold, Joseph admits he has been visiting prostitutes regularly, exposing himself, despite the silk and fish-skin prophylactics of the day, to dangerous venereal diseases. Since he refused to marry, the Empress may have felt he would be safer sleeping with an otherwise virtuous married woman, one indeed whom she knew and liked. But Eleonore was not tempted. She was a devout woman in her way, and besides, Joseph was so singular: "He's a funny specimen," she went on, "I've never seen anything like him in the world." "What can you do, he's made like that," Leopoldine replied. "It's just not in him to act like other people."

Joseph had also spoken to Eleonore about the situation with her husband and Marie Christine. Albert, driving out regularly with them both, with the lady always seated snugly between the two gentlemen, appeared to regard the relationship as entirely innocent. Others reached different conclusions, with Maria Theresia even turning up unexpectedly at Schloss Hof. She stayed five days, and shortly afterwards, whether to end the affair or to nip it in the bud, she appointed Prince Karl military governor of Vienna. This would keep Eleonore in the imperial capital, which would please Joseph and prevent him from taking a less suitable mistress; and if Marie Christine should encounter the Prince in Vienna, the Empress herself was sure to be interferingly present.

But Marianna was unwell again. "She has been bled three times in nine days," her mother reported to Ferdinand. "She's better, but it will take her some time to recover properly." So often ill, she was used to exerting herself to meet her commitments at court and within the family, and she carried on now. From Versailles, Marie Antoinette told her mother, "I was touched by the friendship of my sister Marianne, who has written to me by this mail in spite of her illness." The dauphine had a paradoxical new anxiety of her own. Yearning for a pregnancy, she was also now worried about her figure, no longer thin but too fat: "This fasting food has been disgusting," she wrote in the Lenten season of 1773, "but I've got used to eating it. It hasn't harmed my health at all, I've even put on weight. I hope I don't put on any more."

With the winter not quite past, Marianna had reached a nadir. It was perhaps at the suggestion of Madame Salmour, the devout Mistress of her Household, that she now began, at the age of thirty-five, an "ascetic diary," an ongoing examination of conscience, more berating, however, than consoling.

It makes sad reading. On the twenty-fourth of February, the first day of Lent, having received the annual *memento mori* of a cross marked in ashes on her forehead, she recorded "my far too great longing to be dust and ashes already." Over the next forty fast days, the diary reveals a near unrelenting lethargy and bitterness, "my spirit . . . beaten down." She tries to pray, but is "so utterly depressed" that she cannot say the least prayer with any concentration. She performs acts of charity, then undermines them by attributing them to human kindness rather than piety; this, she believes, discounts their value in the spiritual economy. In any case, she writes, "My own mind is so depressed that I cannot help myself, much less help other people."

Except on her "lost days," when she cannot get up at all, she goes every day to church, "but heard the word of God with so little understanding of any of it," unless the sermon is preached in Italian, "which moved me very much, unfortunately only because this language more easily makes an impression in my heart." She has constant headaches; she loses her temper; she feels sick and weak and cold; she chides herself for laziness; she cannot climb even one flight of stairs; she makes a spiritual offering of her pain; she longs for death; she makes a will.

Occasionally she is able to summon a little strength. She exerts herself to go out driving in the fresh winter air, "which lifted my mood a little," to see a few friends, even to appear in public—"I cannot describe what this cost me." In the evenings, she usually sits for a while at cards, preferring those games requiring least communication among the players; if sharp-tongued Elisabeth is present, there is more chance of malicious gossip. Pushing herself to attend a little party for Joseph's birthday, she is met by taunts from the others about her Lenten regime of strict self-denial, which Elisabeth and Maximilian have also begun, but failed to maintain. Their ridicule puts her in a bad mood and she quarrels seriously with one of her ladies-in-waiting, who promptly resigns her service and withdraws to a convent. When one is alone, Marianna concludes, one offends God less.

It is an echo of the Empress' own resigned response—"All I can do is lock myself away alone"—to her own depressions. But when Marianna approaches her mother and opens her heart to her, she only succeeds in distressing her, too, "leaving me in such confusion and dejection that I couldn't lift myself out of it all day." Things go from bad to worse to impossible; as she sits thinking of a recently deceased friend, his grieving widow arrives, "which left me even more dejected than ever and made the whole day useless." Now and then she has a calmer day, and then there are no thoughts of death. But most entries in the journal reveal Marianna bludgeoned by depression, perversely going to her bed "with joy, since I am one day nearer my deliverance."

Joseph had insulted Chancellor von Kaunitz. The state of affairs in the new, formerly Polish territory of Galicia, he had said, was wholly unacceptable. The situation in Milan was far from adequate, and even the prosperous and trouble-free Austrian Netherlands required attention. The Chancellor's office should henceforth be subject to the control of an independent cabinet. The Chancellor proffered his resignation. The Empress rejected it. Joseph asked to be released from co-regency of the Monarchy. The Empress declined, and announced her own intention to retire to Innsbruck.

Bluff after bluff was called. No one resigned. Everyone remained precisely where they had been, stubbornly unsatisfied. But at least the dynasty was expanding: Four new arrivals were expected before the end of 1773. In Florence, Leopold and Maria Luisa welcomed their seventh child and fifth son—a brilliant result after only eight years of marriage. Ferdinand and Beatrice in Milan, after a promising start—she had "become his wife" on their actual wedding-night—had rather fallen behind in the stakes: It had taken them two years to produce a child, and only a daughter at that, one more little Maria Theresia. The news from Naples was equally disappointing: another girl for Carolina. The mother herself was enchanted with the baby and unconcerned about the still missing heir. "She is as much in love with this second daughter as she was with the first," the Empress relayed to Ferdinand. But the grandmamma was not. "I was sorry to hear about the girl in Naples," she went on. "The Queen is more philosophical than I am: that's because she's just starting and I have finished."

The news from Parma was better, too: Almost three years after the birth of her daughter, Amalie was about to have a second child. Her first delivery had been long and difficult, and she was no doubt concerned about the ordeal to come: Whether to please her husband, or placate her mother, or appeal to the Almighty, she summoned her intermittent piety now to write, and have published, a little orison, *Seven Prayers for Pregnant Women*. One way or another, it seems to have helped, and on the fifth of August 1773, without too much ado, she produced baby Ludovico, a squalling heir to the Duchy. King Carlos was delighted. He at once announced three days of festivities in Madrid, dubbed his great-nephew a Knight of the Golden Fleece, and declared that, provided Don Ferdinando and Amalie agreed to reestablish the marqués de Llano as first minister, all the disagreements of the past would be forgiven.

The Empress' response was cooler. "The Infante has let us know of the birth," she told Ferdinand. "I shall reply, but that will be all. We have had no celebrations and sent no compliments, since there is no communication between us, and there will not be until the King of Spain resumes his correspondence with them." "Those who deserve it least have the most happiness; that's the way of the world," she remarked peremptorily to Chancellor von Kaunitz, adding, however, "a mother's heart doesn't cease, in spite of offences. I hope he will be a child of peace."

And indeed the arrival of a son and heir in Parma did bring redemption. Royal feelings warmed, with Amalie and her husband persuaded to obedience, as predicted, by their need for French and Spanish money. By the autumn of 1773, de Llano had been reappointed and the remittances resumed. The Empress had yielded, too. "The reconciliation with Parma is complete," she told Madame Enzenberg. "I know you are always interested in what's happening there. I hope it continues." As for Amalie's children, "Her daughter is as lovely as an angel, and the son looks as though he will be too, but she has sent me a portrait of herself; if it's a good likeness, she cannot live two years. She looks consumptive; no colour, even ugly, which she never was."

Amalie was not consumptive, though Don Ferdinando's correspondence with his grandfather at Versailles shows that she was certainly not well. An ongoing fever, malaria perhaps, had left her thin and pale; the breach with her family had weakened her psychologically, and in the absence of de Llano, the Duchy's chaotic government and increasing indebtedness had made for an atmosphere of general anxiety at court. Moreover, Amalie's relationship with her husband, never good, was growing worse. "Wherever there are men and women, there are arguments," Louis told his grandson, philosophically. But only four years after the wedding, a separation seemed imminent.

IN THE AFTERNOON of the tenth of May 1774, his face swollen and blackened from smallpox, Louis XV died. As he gave his last breath, a candle in the window of the apartment was extinguished, signalling the end of his reign. Henriette Campan, a lady-in-waiting to Marie Antoinette, recorded that a few moments later, "there was a terrible noise, absolutely like the noise of thunder. . . . It was the crowd of courtiers deserting the late King's antichambre, to make their obeisances to the new King Louis XVI." Hearing this sound, Louis-Auguste and Marie Antoinette understood what had happened: They threw themselves onto their knees, beseeching the help of God, weeping that they were too young to rule. The old King of France had been sixty-four; Louis XVI was nineteen years old; his frightened queen was eighteen.

It was not customary for the royal family to remain at Versailles while the late sovereign's body still lay there. Preparations for their departure had already been made, and at four o'clock in the afternoon Louis and Marie Antoinette set out for the smaller château of Choisy, some fifteen miles distant. Seated in the carriage with them were the King's two brothers and their wives. They drove for some time in an awkward silence, until the little comtesse d'Artois, unable to restrain her natural liveliness a moment longer, made a witty remark, and the six of them burst out laughing.

# XIV

# 1774-1776

In which Maximilian yawns his way through a Grand Tour, an heir to the Bourbon throne is born, and Marie Christine and Albert discover the glory and chaos of Italy.

"I'm sure if he doesn't have quite the right manners or way of speaking, he will make up for it by his good education and his other qualities." Thus Marie Antoinette's hopeful response, in the autumn of 1774, to the Empress' concern about her gauche youngest son, Maximilian. Soon to turn eighteen, he was about to embark on a Grand Tour of Europe, the indispensable finishing touch for every young aristocratic man with pretensions to culture or intellect, or plans to cut a fine figure in elegant social circles. Maximilian's social graces, such as they were, still required a good deal of finishing, and his religious devotions more attention, as his mother now elucidated for him in a stern letter of many, many pages. She expressly forbade him to visit England, where he could be corrupted by "the contagious society of London," since, as she said, "The English are almost all Deists, Infidels, and Free Thinkers." And finally, he was to keep a full account of his journey, for her later perusal, "according to the example style attached."

Before the end of this year of 1774, accompanied by the ever-reliable Count Rosenberg, now in his early fifties, Maximilian had arrived in Brussels. Marie Antoinette was disappointed to learn that he would not reach

Versailles before February. She was missing her family and was eager to see this brother, just one year younger than herself. From Naples, too, came bittersweet news: In the first week of January 1775, Carolina gave birth to her third child and, vitally, her first son—an heir to the Kingdom at last. Though happy for her favourite sister, Marie Antoinette could not help but feel diminished by comparison: After almost five years of marriage, she was no nearer to that all-important accomplishment than she had ever been.

By now, Louis' younger brother, the fat comte de Provence, had himself been married for four years; his "awful-nosed" comtesse had also failed in her dynastic duty. But a new threat had emerged in the person of her lively sister, diminutive in all respects other than her exceptionally long nose—noses being evidently no point of pride in the family—who at the end of 1773 had married Louis' youngest brother, the comte d'Artois. This pair, married at the respective ages of sixteen and seventeen, were to succeed where the others had not.

At the beginning of August 1775, after a labour of just two hours, the proud little comtesse d'Artois was delivered of a healthy son. Marie Antoinette had been present throughout, and afterwards was pursued across the great Versailles courtyard to the very doors of her apartment by fishwives shouting at her "in the most obscene language, that it was her job to produce heirs to the throne."

"It's useless to say how much I suffered to see an heir who is not my own," she told her mother. "Nonetheless I did manage to pay every possible attention to the mother and the child." The Empress applauded her generosity of spirit—"I recognize my dear daughter in this"—but increased the pressure on her all the same. A princely nephew was all very well, but a son in the direct line of inheritance would be much better, "and it is a long time since I heard anything on this important matter. It seems to me you are not taking it very seriously, and you are not doing enough to bring it about."

Marie Antoinette defended herself: "It isn't as if I weren't very concerned about it and didn't often speak to the King about it, though gently and carefully. I'm working at persuading him to have the little operation we've already spoken of, and which I believe is necessary." But Louis did not want to be circumcised, and his physician was not in favour of it. The life of the French royal family being so public, and the courtiers' taste for gossip so general, everyone at Versailles and beyond knew there had been no consummation. Even before the birth of Artois' son, she and Louis had been the target of libellous pamphlets criticizing their childlessness, though the blame had been laid squarely on the King: He was assumed to be impotent through some "fault of nature." The Queen emerged nonetheless as the villainess of the piece, ambitious as only an Austrian could be, acutely aware of the precariousness of her position, ready to produce a son at any cost in order to establish herself securely as "mother of a prince who could claim the throne in the event of the King's death." The Bourbons were warned it was in their "most vital interest to examine scrupulously the designs and conduct of the young Queen of France, lest she secretly place a stranger in the King's bed, and the son of that stranger on the throne."

There was no danger of any such thing; the couple had, if anything, grown closer in recent months. But sadly, Marie Antoinette was by now seeking out other people's children, "to surround herself with illusions that could console her heart," or so Henriette Campan understood the situation. The Queen had become very fond of her youngest sister-in-law, Elisabeth, now eleven years old, "a charming child full of intelligence and character, and very poised," as Marie Antoinette told her mother, adding, "I'm afraid I'm becoming too much attached to her." Madame Campan said that her mistress had long wanted to bring up a child herself, "to make it the object of her constant care," and in this same summer of 1775, she found a little boy to meet this need.

He was a blue-eyed peasant child of four or five who had run out into a country road in front of her carriage and narrowly missed being struck down. He was an orphan, with four other siblings, and his overwhelmed grandmother was only too happy to give him into the Queen's care, in return for ongoing support for the rest of the family. The boy himself was less enthusiastic, and was carried kicking and screaming back to Versailles, where he was very thoroughly washed, reclothed in silks and laces, and even given a new name: Jacques Gagne became Jacques Armand. Outwardly, at least, he adapted to his altered circumstances, and for the next five years or so he was constantly to be seen at the Queen's side.

Some no doubt rolled their eyes at the irony of it, others perhaps shed a sympathetic tear, but no one, including the King, seems to have objected to the presence of this compensatory child. It was in any case a common practice, in an age of great inequalities in wealth, for the "surplus" children of the poor to be adopted by the childless rich. In time the Queen would adopt three more children, including a little Senegalese boy rescued from slavers and presented to her as a gift.

Less generally tolerated than these small adoptees was another new arrival in Marie Antoinette's circle that summer, the violet-eyed comtesse Gabrielle de Polignac, sister-in-law of a prominent lady-in-waiting, Diane de Polignac, who was herself a clever behind-the-scenes manipulator of court affairs. The comtesse Gabrielle was by all accounts completely charming in appearance and manner and conversation, and the Queen fell instantly under her spell. She was accompanied by her husband, Jules, an impoverished military man a few years older than herself. Marie Antoinette was insistent the pair should remain at Versailles, and Louis, seeing the happy effect of the engaging newcomer on his wife's mood, encouraged the idea. But life at Versailles was expensive, too much so for the Polignacs, and besides, the couple were already in debt to the tune of 400,000 livres, a hundred times the amount of the comte's military stipend. Like her mother and her sisters Amalie and Carolina, Marie Antoinette was, with her favourites, generous to a fault. In this instance, the fault was considerable: Against the loud protestations of the reforming Comptroller-General of Finances, Baron Turgot, she paid the Polignacs' debt from the royal purse, and established them both in prestigious positions.

Ambassador Mercy was not impressed. "The comtesse de Polignac, her favourite, has neither the intelligence nor the judgement nor even the character necessary to enjoy the confidence of a great princess," he declared to the Empress. Others at court were equally critical or resentful of the Queen's partiality, with one lady observing, "She makes as many jealous people as there are courtiers."

But away from Versailles, even during the dangerous Flour War in the spring of 1775, when shortages and soaring prices led to protests and rioting in and around Paris, and Louis was compelled to send in troops to quell the unrest, Marie Antoinette remained popular. "Every time she has come to the city," Mercy assured the Empress, "she has been received with great acclamation by the public, despite the high cost of bread and the misery of the times, which makes the people very restless." After decades of mismanagement under the reign of Louis XV, the present "misery of the times" had been inflamed by an ill-timed laissez-faire decision on the part of Comptroller-General Turgot to lift controls on the price of bread. In Paris itself and throughout the country, profiteering had increased, causing hardship and hunger, and though he had been on the throne for only a year, the twenty-one-year-old King was being held answerable for it. A pamphlet of the same time gave him warning: "If Louis XVI does not remedy this sea of evils promptly," the writer prophesied, "if he leaves so many crimes unpunished, he who is not their author could well end up one day their victim."

**Maximilian had been** keeping his Grand Tour journal dutifully, dictating it day by day to his secretary. The first part of it, which included his visit to Versailles in the late winter of 1775, has not survived, but there are records enough to tell the story, and they reveal that the Empress had been right to be anxious about his behaviour, at least in this earlier part of his *Kavalierstour.* Marie Antoinette met him in early February at the pretty château de la Muette, just outside of Paris. It was the middle of carnival, the two months of festivities before the beginning of Lent, and it could not have been a worse time for an aloof and unrefined brother of the new Queen to arrive. Maximilian was prudishly disdainful of the social life of Versailles, always sparkling and at carnival time positively glittering; he was indifferent to the many beauties and glories of French art and architecture, and unimpressed by the exaggeratedly polished ways of the courtiers surrounding his sister. His visit embarrassed her and, though it was hardly his fault, even compromised her via a diplomatic tiff about precedence which emphasized her own status as an outsider who, Queen of France though she might be, would never belong to the Bourbons.

Marie Antoinette was nonetheless sorry when, in mid-March, after three weeks of awkwardness, it was time for him to go. He had been, after all, the first family member to see her in five years. "I was deeply affected by my brother's departure," she told their mother. "It's a cruel thing to think we may never see each other again."

After Paris, Brussels, Frankfurt, Prague, and a dozen other places of interest or protocol, Maximilian had returned to Vienna to pause a few weeks before embarking on the second stage of his *Kavalierstour.* His mother had welcomed him warmly, before starting out on further criticisms. Though touched to see her youngest child again after an absence of eleven months, she could not relax her sense of duty, and she sent him off for a further year with reminders to stand up straight, not hold his hand over his mouth when he spoke, and to attend to his personal cleanliness, "especially in Italy, where the heat is considerable."

He was indeed on his way to Italy, a leisurely southwestern way down to the peninsula where four of his siblings had made their home. En route he stopped in Salzburg, where a new opera, commissioned especially for his visit, was to be performed: *The Shepherd King*, by the nineteen-year-old Mozart. Archduke and composer had met before, at the Hofburg in Vienna in 1762, when they were both little boys, and Mozart had been presented with a mauve silk suit of Maximilian's. In Salzburg, on the following evening, after a keyboard recital by two local ladies, Mozart himself sat at the instrument and "played various pieces out of his head, exquisitely," as Maximilian recorded.

On the tenth of May, he reached the Duchy of Parma. Brother and sister met on the banks of the Po River, Amalie receiving him "most joyfully," and they drove back together to the ducal palace, "which is completely run down," where the greatest part of the local nobility awaited him, elaborately decked out. Here he also met "the little masters, consisting of one prince and two princesses"—Amalie's children, four-year-old Carolina; the ducal heir, Ludovico, not quite two; and baby Antonia, just six months old.

Maximilian spent three days in Parma, and he does not seem to have enjoyed them much, displaying the same indifference, not to say boredom, that had blighted his reputation in France. In the journal he was keeping for his mother's perusal, he described how Amalie and Don Ferdinando went "in great pomp and style whenever they drive out, in an elaborate coach-and-eight, with horse-guards and a suite of carriages after them, always according to Spanish court etiquette," but neglected to mention that by now they were no longer living together: Amalie, together with the children, had moved the year before to the nearby district of Sala Baganza, having renovated a ramshackle country house there.

Despite their separate residences, and rumours of the Duke fathering an illegitimate daughter, relations between the couple were apparently amicable; they sometimes dined *à deux*, and Don Ferdinando made regular visits to her Casino dei Boschi at Sala Baganza—indeed, a further thirteen children, including three sets of twins, were to be born to them, though only four would survive childhood. Living apart, however, they were easy targets for those who wished to discredit them: In due course the adventurer and spy-for-hire Count Giuseppe Gorani would publish slanderous and well paid gossip about them both, with the Duke's absence supposedly suiting the Duchess very well, "since it allowed her to enjoy a liberty of which she makes ample usage." Their very meetings were only a cover, the Count suggested, "to allow the Duke to pretend to the honours of paternity."

Content to omit all reference to his sister's separation of abode from her husband, Maximilian also reported nothing to his mother about the political situation in Parma. But all was not well. Du Tillot's Spanish replacement, the marqués de Llano, had not been successful: He had been unable to remedy the incompetence or restrain the greed of the ministers installed by Don Ferdinando and Amalie. Worse, he had misjudged the public mood in the Duchy, posting notices insisting on his own authority and denigrating Amalie's capriciousness and interference. But, mindful of her regular showers of coins in the streets, the people had remained loyal to her. Early in 1774 de Llano had been recalled for the second time to Madrid, with Carlos washing his hands of Parma altogether.

Since then most attempts at reform had been abandoned. Don Ferdinando had returned the religious authorities to their old positions of influence, and had even reestablished the Inquisition, though mercifully, the new Grand Inquisitor was a man of temperate views. But piety was back in fashion, to a near burlesque degree. The English traveller Henry Swinburne, himself a Roman Catholic, dismissed the reigning sovereign of Parma as "a fat fool, who doats upon the Dominican friars, gets up at daybreak to go to matins, and plagues the poor priests out of their lives if they do not attend to all their duties."

And if overreligiosity was Don Ferdinando's weakness, overindebtedness was Amalie's: "His wife is a very bad paymistress," Swinburne continued. "She buys a horse one day upon tick, to sell it the next for half price, to raise the wind [money for something else]." Slow to pay her own debts, Amalie also took no more interest in the financial administration of the Duchy than did its sovereign duke. She did manage to impose some new taxes, though not to make any material improvements: Instead, or so she claimed, she used the money to repay debts she had incurred getting rid of Du Tillot. Despite a handful of satirical notices pasted up in the town, it was not enough in any case to turn the people against her.

Maximilian departed Parma for Milan, to meet brother Ferdinand; from there he would make his way to Naples for a visit of three weeks, a stark comparison to the mere three days he had spent in Parma. Others of the family had done and would continue to do much the same, emphasizing

Amalie's sense of her comparatively low importance in her unenticing little duchy.

CAROLINA WAS AS delighted to see Maximilian as Amalie had been, though by the time he reached Naples it was mid-June, and the heat was intense. The Queen had driven out to meet him five miles north of the city, and she insisted he join her in her own carriage for the drive back to Naples. Once arrived at the royal palace, she took him directly to the loggia leading from her apartments to admire the view. For once, Maximilian was impressed, and he spent the whole afternoon there, chatting with his sister and admiring "the whole great sweep of the city itself, stretching out in two half-moons along the sea," though he was less impressed with the presence of the galleys and galley-slaves along the waterside.

There was a lot more to see in Naples than there had been in tiny Parma. With more than four hundred thousand souls, Naples was the third-largest city in Europe, and twice the size of Vienna. Though populous, it had not been particularly cosmopolitan, but now, owing to the unearthing of ancient Pompeii and Herculaneum twenty years before, it was becoming part of the celebrated Grand Tour. The still active volcano of nearby Vesuvius also provided a kind of open-air laboratory for natural philosophers, the proto-scientists of the day, as well as a spectacular subject for artists inspired by the new Romantic passion for landscapes.

No Grand Tour would have been complete without a visit to Pompeii, but though Carolina had attended excavations and took an interest in the diverse objects being unearthed there, she did not join her brother now; having delivered her third baby only five months before, she was already four months pregnant with the next. The King also exempted himself, going off to play football, despite the game having been banned by the Pope as meriting excommunication. But in the evenings, the family staged little musical *soirées*, as there had been so often at the Hofburg, with Carolina's well trained contralto joining Maximilian's pleasant manly tones, and Ferdinando, less happily, singing along in the "extremely high, thin voice, almost like a high falsetto, painful to the ear," that Joseph had earlier described.

**Maximilian returned to Vienna** to begin his military training, and in the new year of 1776, Marie Christine and Albert, accompanied by an appointee and informer of the Empress, departed Pressburg on their own southward journey to Italy. The roads were bad and the weather dreadful, and for nine days they rattled along, huddled in furs, with Marie Christine's warm little Bolognese dog Azor on her lap, as the snow beat against the panes of their coach. Their escort was large and well armed, since the way between Ljubljana and Trieste was the haunt of bandits, but nearing Venice they took ship, and on the sixth of January they sailed into La Serenissima.

The pair were overwhelmed by the architectural glories of the incomparable city, though they were disappointed by the poor quality of the local theatre and opera, and appalled by the dirty streets. But the most important aspect of their visit was probably their reacquaintance with the Viennese ambassador, Count Giacomo Durazzo, now nearing sixty and a leading light in Venetian cultural and intellectual circles. Hailing from a wealthy trading family in Genoa with substantial financial connections to the Habsburgs, the count was also an old personal friend of Chancellor von Kaunitz, and had held several important artistic posts in Vienna before turning diplomat in 1764. Since then he had devoted much of his time to improving his already extensive art collection.

Durazzo had visited Pressburg a few years before, and there the three had initiated plans for a major new collection of prints and drawings to be kept in Vienna. Though Albert had long been a capable draughtsman, particularly of military plans and maps, it was a volume of copper engravings given to him during their engagement by Marie Christine, familiar with fine art since her childhood, that had opened his eyes to this second most enduring passion of his life, and the one that would make him famous. Like Albert, the count was a Freemason, keen to advance a scientific understanding of the world. Like the Swedish "father of taxonomy," Linnaeus, ordering and classifying all his plants and animals, so Durazzo had been categorizing his many artworks. Now he was writing a little *discorso* outlining the basically regional organization of the future Viennese collection, and also affirming its progressive purpose: to serve not so much as a representation of its owner's taste, but rather as an educational tool, to help all who viewed it to a broader knowledge of art and a deeper understanding of art history.

Durazzo had carried the first cache of prints and drawings with him on his journey to Pressburg; now he brought several thousand further examples to sell to the delighted pair. Given the number of works, it is unlikely they enquired too closely into their provenance, though another aficionado did report that Durazzo had acquired them by employing "people who, without raising suspicion, knew exactly how to inveigle them at little cost from their ignorant or penurious owners."

From Venice, Marie Christine and Albert made their way southward, along very bad roads and through miserably poor villages, to Bologna. Visiting the city's university, the oldest in the world, Marie Christine was startled, as a woman, to be invited to attend the dissection of a female corpse. The authorities assured her that, until very recently, the chair of anatomy had itself been held by a woman. This lady had just died, though the corpse, it seemed, was not hers. Marie Christine declined the invitation nonetheless, and went to examine a collection of antiquities instead.

And so on to Tuscany. The roads improved as they approached Florence, the result of investment by Franz Stephan during his early days as Grand Duke. At Leopold's Palazzo Pitti the couple were to spend a full six weeks, resting from the exertions of travel, admiring the fabulous Medici collections, and getting to know their brother's large and lively family. Leopold had greatly extended the improvements begun by his father, and he and Albert spent many hours together in the countryside around Florence discussing "various highly interesting new ideas about culture and the rural economy, the latter at such a high point of perfection here—the Grand Duke was in command of every last detail to do with it, and since on top of that he was a very good walker," the pair covered a good deal of ground. They also visited several of the farmers' cottages, conversing amiably with them, and Albert noticed how fond Leopold's tenants were of him—evidently he had not forgotten his father's recommendation of graciousness as a vital attribute of every good ruler.

Albert and Marie Christine's visit to Florence coincided with that of the painter Johann Zoffany, a favourite of Maria Theresia's who was currently preparing for her a life-sized portrait of Leopold and Maria Luisa and their seven surviving children. Demandingly, the Empress now commissioned a portrait of Marie Christine as well, expecting the artist to complete it within three months, before making his way to Naples to paint another, this time of Carolina. In the event, the artist's journey to Naples came to nought, with Zoffany protesting it would take him a year just to complete the portrait of Marie Christine, but in fact he finished it in record time, and it is a lovely work of informal elegance, with the Archduchess in silver-white silk, pearls at her throat and in her grey powdered hair, her little dog on her lap, and on the table beside her, a small statue of the goddess Athena, the sitter's "patroness," as she was, too, for her elder sister, Marianna. The portrait shows Marie Christine, at thirty-four, in the bloom of womanhood, an almost ironic smile on her full, fashionably oval face. The relaxed life she had been leading in the bosom of her brother's family evidently suited her; she had been putting on weight, though not yet enough to please her mother, who insisted, "your fatness does not yet reassure me."

Leopold, acutely aware of his duty to the dynasty, was proud of having produced so large a brood in a mere ten years of marriage—and Maria Luisa was already expecting again. He was proving to be the kind of warmhearted father Franz Stephan had been. Albert remarked that the children were all "well made and healthy," providing a good part of "the happiness of this household. There's not one of them who doesn't seem to be very intelligent," and as they were being brought up "less with severity and constraint than with persuasion and reason," he was confident they would grow up to be "useful to society" and happy adults, too, particularly if their emotional training was correct. In this respect, however, he had his doubts about the eldest boy, seven-year-old Franz; though an astute and reflective child, he had about him a certain reserve "which could turn to falseness and hardness, if they don't take care in time to form his heart for kindness and charity." It was a perceptive and, as it was to turn out, almost clairvoyant observation, given the coldness with which Franz, once grown to man's estate and become emperor, was to treat his aunts in their hour of need.

Maria Luisa, too, now thirty years old, seemed to have found her element. Within the imposing palazzo, she was the centre of a full and boisterous life of conspicuous domestic happiness. Marie Christine was enchanted by it, writing to her mother with details of all the children, none of whom their grandmother had ever seen, "and especially of Karl," Leopold's third son, whom she particularly doted on. At this time a little blond boy four and a half years old, he is depicted in Zoffany's portrait sitting on the floor with his favourite black spaniel. Marie Christine went so far as to send the Empress a separate portrait of him. This was met with a polite thank you and a request for a picture of his seven-year-old brother, Franz, Leopold's heir, and heir to the Monarchy and the Holy Roman Empire, too, "who is in any case of most interest to me." Indeed, a very fine Zoffany portrait of young Franz as ruler-in-waiting was shortly to be despatched to the Hofburg, with the satisfied painter reporting to a friend in England, "I have Gust sent a portrait of the Grand Duck's to Wiena."

# XV

# 1776

## In which a lively sojourn in Naples is followed by a dispiriting visit to Parma.

The southward road to Naples led across the peninsula to Rome, and here the travellers settled for more than a month to drink in the many wonders of the Eternal City. Marie Christine kept a 150-page descriptive journal of all they saw: the sites of antiquity, the *piazze* and *palazzi*, the villas and churches, bridges and galleries, and all the greatest works of art in the smallest detail, for as she herself told Albert, "You know whatever Marie Christine does will be well done or not undertaken at all." At the Vatican, she received a golden rose from the hands of a friendly Pope Clement XIV, "a handsome man with a good healthy colour to his face, which gave him a youthful air quite unusual for a pope," before travelling on through the poor and poorly administered territory of his papal states—"and how could it be otherwise," Albert noted disdainfully, with industry strangled by monopolies, "and only priests managing everything, and any man with any talent or brains or knowledge of what the country needs excluded because he isn't one!" At twilight, they drove into the little town of Fondi, where a crowd of local people swarmed around their carriage, screaming with excitement, "leaving us in no further doubt as to which country we had just entered." They had arrived in the Kingdom of Naples.

Weaving back to the coast along roads still studded with Roman ruins and lined with fig and orange trees "and other trees that at home you find only in gardens and glasshouses," they came to Mola on the Bay of Gaeta. They spent the night in a pretty house by the sea, nestled among other modern houses, all built on the ruins of the dwellings of antiquity, and lapped by the waves at high tide. In one of these, as Albert recorded in a moment of historical *frisson*, the Roman statesman Cicero had been assassinated, eighteen hundred years before.

It was mid-April, full springtime in the bright southern climate. The couple were entranced by the beautiful countryside, lush and fresh, and the glorious vistas of the Amalfi Coast. They arrived at the little town of Aversa at the very moment that Carolina herself was arriving. Albert tried, in vain, to do justice to the emotional scene that followed:

> It would be most difficult, if not impossible, to find colours sufficiently vibrant to paint a picture of the meeting between the two sisters in this town. They jumped down from the coach, pushed their way through the crowds of people in the street and, taking no notice of the horses and carriages in their way, ran into each other's arms.

Marie Christine and Albert joined Carolina in her royal coach for the twenty-mile drive to Naples, arriving as the church bells were striking noon. The newcomers noticed little of the city itself, overwhelmed as they were by the thousands of people milling and pushing around them, so many indeed that it was all the guards could do to make a path for them to drive through the streets. They pressed on to the edge of the city, there to change horses and take the road to the palace of Portici, but before they could complete that eight-mile journey, they encountered a mounted party coming from the other direction. It was led by the King himself: Carolina's husband had come out to meet them on the road.

This meeting was as effusive as the first had been, with Ferdinando himself hardly less emotional than Carolina. Marie Christine and Albert had not met him before, and they were taken aback by the warmth of their reception. They were also surprised to find his appearance and manners much less disagreeable than they had been led to expect; Leopold and Joseph and young Maximilian, too, had all given them the impression that Ferdinando was at best a very rough diamond and at worse a kind of grubby buffoon. But seeing him in person "contradicted that infinitely." He climbed back into Carolina's carriage with them, and the four drove together on to Portici, where the whole court had assembled to welcome them. Ferdinando disliked formal occasions—Albert thought he felt inadequate to their demands—and he pulled the family members through to the Queen's private rooms, where the four of them took a quiet supper together.

Marie Christine and Albert spent three weeks in Naples, seeing all the famous sights and revelling in the superb art collections. But they found their greatest pleasure in the warmth of Carolina's family life—even, it seems, in its smallest details, at least where Marie Christine was concerned. "She went into everything," Carolina later complained, "my books, my private life, *toilette*, expenses, charities, my domestic life, I was just so angry, and I had to repress it all the time, and that made me ill, I had to be bled and I developed a serious fever."

Carolina herself also surprised the expectations of her sister and brother-in-law, for the better and for the worse. Now almost twenty-four and the mother of four children, she had blossomed from the fifteen-year-old girl they had last seen on her wedding-day in Vienna, with Albert, never slow to admire a pretty woman, confessing that "her personal attractions, in my opinion, have greatly increased since she has been here." In its place had emerged another, no less passionate sentiment: a devotion to her children, "whom she loved beyond all expression." Most of her time was spent with them, caring for them, instructing them and playing with them: Ferdinando was a fond and proud father, too. One of their daughters would later recall: "All of us were always together and we were lucky enough to respect our father and mother and to consider them as our best friends and confidants, whether in troubled or happy times. None of us came first or second with Papa and Mamma, we were all equally their children and nothing could make them happier than to see we were doing well."

In the previous year of 1775, Carolina had in fact borne two children, in January the all-important heir, Carlo, and in November a third daughter, Anna. But when her husband attempted to have sex with her shortly afterwards, she had pushed him away, shouting at him, "I refuse to be pregnant again for at least a year, and I don't care if you die or burst!" Ferdinando evidently did not give up, indignantly reporting the ensuing scene to his father. "In bed," he wrote, "she became a fury, she began to scream and slap at me, she said I was the lowest kind of brute there could ever be and then—I can only think she was having convulsions—she jumped on me like a dog and bit me on the hand, and I still bear the scars." Since then, however, she had resumed her "wifely duties."

But since Anna's birth, Carolina had often been unwell, and this had prevented her taking any physical exercise, even walking or driving out for fresh air. As she herself confirmed in countless letters—as Joseph quipped, "My dear sister writes more than my cabinet"—she was reduced to spending most of her days in the same sedentary way, indoors, *en famille*. Marie Christine and Albert felt it was not good for her; it seemed to have drained her natural vivacity, and Albert thought it "most unhealthy for her excessively sensitive soul." The gaiety that had been such a particular mark of her personality they found quite gone.

Her marriage, however, appeared to have stabilized. For whatever reason, in this year of 1776 there was, indeed, no pregnancy, though the King seemed to be as fond of his wife, or at least as sexually drawn to her, as he had ever been. That was a very good thing, in Albert's view, since he thought Ferdinando "unequivocally formed to attract the attention and appreciation of the fair sex." As yet, he noted, there was no sign of his indulging in "those excesses which could make one greatly fear for his health"—an oblique reference to venereal disease, and a portent, if the Duke could have known it, of what lay in store. But Albert was mistaken. His brother-in-law had already engaged in a long affair with the "prodigiously beautiful" (the phrase is Casanova's) Irish memoirist and quondam serving maid, Sarah Goudar. Carolina had managed to drive this lady out of Naples—she took refuge in Florence, and there became the mistress of the marquis de Sade—but many other affairs were to follow, endangering not only Ferdinando's own health, but Carolina's, too, and that of their fourteen children yet to be born.

THE BIRTH OF CAROLINA'S first son had not only given the Kingdom of Naples an heir; it had also given the then twenty-two-year-old Queen herself the right to a seat in the Council of State, as agreed in her original contract of marriage. The Council met three times weekly, supposedly to hear Ferdinando's decisions on the matters brought before it, but in fact it had long been little more than a signing ceremony, with First Minister Tanucci presenting every decision already made by himself, and requiring only the compliant King's signature on the documents. At first Tanucci had not expected Carolina's arrival to change this—he was a declared misogynist with a reluctant respect for Maria Theresia and Catherine the Great, alone among their sex—but gradually he had understood that she was made of sterner stuff than her husband, and after her son's birth he had repeatedly delayed her accession to the Council, knowing that her arrival would mean the end of what had effectively been his own government.

Ferdinando had not always agreed with his wife about Tanucci. Though without any interest in government himself, he resented her attempts to restrain the Minister's scope of action and had often complained to his father about it. The arrangement in place since 1759 had suited all three of them: Ferdinando had been only eight years old; Carlos had left the reins of the

Kingdom in the hands of a man he regarded as a trustworthy regent, and Tanucci had clutched them eagerly. Ferdinando was now twenty-five, but no more willing, and no more able, to assume real power than he had been in his boyhood. He would have been content for Tanucci to retain control, leaving him free to spend his days hunting and fishing and generally pleasing himself.

But Carolina thought differently, and she would not let the matter rest. Like Amalie, she believed her husband should rule his own kingdom—or at least, that he should be seen to be ruling it, whatever her own influence behind the scenes might be. Further, she felt Naples should have a greater presence of its own in Europe, and not be just a fiefdom of Spain: When Carlos himself had been king there, he and Tanucci had made strenuous efforts toward real independence, but since Ferdinando's accession they had reversed this process appreciably. Finally, after seventeen years with Tanucci at the helm, there was much that was still wrong in the Kingdom: The economy lagged far behind that of comparable powers, the administration remained chaotic and the justice system corrupt, and certain important responsibilities had been neglected almost entirely.

Chief among these, in terms of the Kingdom's status and security, was the condition of the armed forces. On paper, Naples had a standing army of thirty thousand men, though less than half that number were available for service. Worse, for a supposed sea power, was the state of the navy: It had just eighteen ships, sixteen of them dilapidated, and three slave galleys, and every vessel was poorly commanded. On a recent sailing to Sicily, the royal flotilla had been overpowered and plundered by the hardboiled crew of a single pirate bark. In theory, in the event of an attack, Naples could call on Spanish warships, but this was only to reinforce the Kingdom's vassal state.

Visiting Naples in 1769, Joseph had judged Tanucci to be not quite honest in his dealings with Carlos in Madrid, and had thought him already rather afraid of Carolina, or at least of her power over Ferdinando. He had sided with her in wishing to see the Minister's power in the Kingdom diminished. Now, more than seven years later, Marie Christine and Albert thought the same, and when the Minister threw down his heaviest gauntlet yet before Carolina's feet, they were at her side to help her pick it up.

Until now, Tanucci's disagreements with her had mostly concerned Spanish court protocol: Like her parents and brother before her, and her sister in Parma, too, she felt burdened and confined by its heavy formality. The Minister was not such a stickler for the old ways, but in Carolina's determination over the lesser matters of etiquette—such as abolishing the cumbersome trains on the ladies' gowns, which dragged little loads of dust with them, threatening Carolina's lungs, as the Empress herself complained—Tanucci had seen the formidable opponent he would have over the more substantial questions brought before the Council of State.

Carolina wanted reform: She wanted to change the Kingdom of Naples into something resembling the economically advanced Grand Duchy that her revered brother Leopold was creating in Tuscany. Tanucci had long been counted a purposeful political reformer himself, but in his forty-three years of pushing and pulling among Naples' recalcitrant nobles and priests and peasants, he had often had to admit defeat, particularly in the poorest rural regions of the Kingdom. As he had found, reform was good in theory; in practice it was endlessly difficult, if not impossible. But the Queen had now been in Naples for eight years herself, and her influence was growing. The Minister decided he must secure his own predominance once and for all, and he decided to stake everything on the outcome of a single issue. He chose the Brotherhood of Freemasons.

He thought he could hardly lose, since in legal terms there was no debate to be had. In 1751, the otherwise forward-thinking Pope Benedict XIV had banned the anticlerical Brotherhood throughout the Roman Catholic world. In Naples, the Freemasons, like their young king, had been loud proponents of reform, but this had not prevented their criticizing Carlos, and he had welcomed the Pope's ban in that it had silenced an articulate opposition to himself. The Freemasons had continued to meet in secret, and after 1759, when Carlos assumed the Spanish throne and left Naples for Madrid, they had gradually come out of hiding.

Since then, though their meetings remained illegal, policing had been lax and the lodges had continued, including some that admitted women. Encouraged by her liberal-minded lady-in-waiting, the marchesa di San Marco, Carolina herself had taken to attending meetings. Ferdinando complained to his father that the Queen had been urging him to join as well, though it seems he was put off rather by the prospect of reading the required texts than by any objection in principle. Carolina numbered several Freemasons among her close acquaintances, and also attended banquets hosted by them. Tanucci had friends among the Brotherhood, too; his only real grievance against them was that they were operating under the Queen's protection, and so, in any area of dissension, were inclined to support her against himself. In Carolina's absence, he persuaded Ferdinando to sign a new edict, banning them once again.

A week later, the people of Naples gathered, as much festively as piously, to celebrate the feast-day of their patron, Saint Januarius. Those early or assertive enough to find a place in the city's cathedral expected to observe a miracle: the liquefaction of the saint's own blood, preserved in a glass jar; this he had supposedly been performing since his death almost fifteen hundred years before. But this time, the miracle did not occur.

Tanucci was no devotee of the old beliefs, but he knew how to manipulate the people's superstition. He started a rumour that the miracle had failed since the saint was displeased at the large number of Freemasons still living in his city. The predictable commotion ensued. Warning of possible riots and quietly alerting his own friends, Tanucci persuaded Ferdinando to have the Freemasons arrested. Informed by police spies, a squadron of guards, led by an over-eager captain in a flaming scarlet cloak, staged a symbolic storming of one lodge just as a new member was being initiated: All present were arrested, and a trial set up.

It proved a farce. Carolina, with the marchesa di San Marco behind her, was too well organized. "A horde of powerful protectors from the army, the nobility and the Court" descended on the chambers to "confuse, tempt and terrify the judges." They included the Queen's own sister and brother-in-law, Marie Christine and Albert, with "a swarm of other exalted Masons," among them the duchesse de Chartres, rich, influential and outraged, who had travelled all the way from Paris to attend the trial. The duchesse, a relative of Marie Antoinette's friend, the Princesse de Lamballe, was *Grande-Maîtresse* of all the ladies' lodges of France, and she was welcomed in Naples with pomp and splendour. Carolina, at pains to show herself a more serious friend of advanced thinking than her beloved but incorrigibly frivolous sister at Versailles, invited her to view her personal library of eight thousand blue-bound volumes. These were in German, however, which may have prevented the lady from grasping the decidedly unserious nature of most of them: A bookseller had effectively been building the collection by sending a regular selection of the latest Viennese publications, with Carolina privately admitting she had scarcely time enough to read their titles.

Madame de Chartres' arrival added weight to others' warnings that the whole of enlightened Europe was watching the Freemasons' trial in Naples. The intimidated judges gave way to their social overlords, who denounced the whole proceedings and took it upon themselves to declare the prisoners innocent. To his opponents, exulting prematurely, it seemed Tanucci's fate was sealed. To Ferdinando, it was clear where his own interests now lay. His wife had triumphed over the Minister; it was no longer worth supporting him against her. In letters to his father, some of them almost certainly dictated by Carolina herself, he revealed his new position: Tanucci was an old man, he said, well over eighty, forgetful and dithery; it was time for him to go. But Carlos was still receiving regular letters from the Minister himself, and he knew quite well that Tanucci, who had incidentally just turned seventy-eight, was still comfortably in possession of all his mental faculties. He had been a long and loyal servant, and he had done nothing wrong. The King ordered the Minister to stay where he was.

IN THE FIRST WEEK of June, before six o'clock in the morning, Marie Christine and Albert arrived in Parma. Weary from the journey and not wanting all the fuss of a palace welcome at such an early hour, they quietly put up at an *auberge* in the town, and ordered refreshments. But news of their arrival could not be kept secret: Hearing of it from her servants, Amalie immediately left her own country residence at Sala Baganza and drove to Colorno to collect Don Ferdinando. Together they proceeded to the *auberge*, where they startled the travellers, still dusty from the road, having "hardly had time to tidy ourselves up and make a decent appearance."

Amalie's own appearance was not much better. The portrait she had sent to her mother more than two years before had not been deceiving. She had changed, "to the point that she was unrecognizable. There was no trace remaining, none whatsoever," wrote Albert sadly, "of the vivacity and beauty that one had admired in her, and though her lovely figure wasn't entirely spoiled, the carelessness of her dress and manner made her even less attractive."

It was not a happy visit. Don Ferdinando appeared to the new arrivals much as he had to Joseph and Maximilian: polite, impassive, superficially educated, indolent, particularly in political affairs, and rather embarrassingly devout. Amalie was "just as decided as ever in her opinions," though she maintained she was no longer interested in political arrangements within the Duchy. She spent her time walking or hunting in the countryside, and supervising her three children, without much warmth to any, however, except three-year-old Ludovico: This little boy had suffered a fall, striking his head against a marble table, and since then had been subject to epileptic seizures. Don Ferdinando took little interest in the children, either; relations between husband and wife were distant; and Albert noticed in the eldest, five-year-old Carolina, "the most beautiful child you could imagine . . . an air of sadness that was very affecting to see."

With Du Tillot five years gone, with Amalie withdrawn and Don Ferdinando indifferent, political life in Parma had stagnated. The current ministers, in Albert's view at least, were limited men and not widely respected; First Minister Sacco was still in place, still channelling what he could of the Duchy's wealth to his own family. There was not much active government;

even the collection of state revenues had been delegated to private individuals, with the usual corruption ensuing. But the people's fondness for the old Catholic ways kept them loyal to Don Ferdinando, and Amalie's liberality with money supplied by France and Spain had kept them on her side as well. There was little progress or prosperity in Parma, but equally, there was little sign of dissent.

There were rumours, however, that Amalie had a lover, namely the forty-one-year-old marchese Cavriani, a regular riding companion: Unexpectedly, and at Amalie's instigation, he had been made lieutenant-colonel of the Parma cavalry. For Cavriani, the relationship was amicable and no doubt useful, but for Amalie it was a close and vital friendship, to the extent that, in a letter to Joseph of this time, she felt able to describe Cavriani as "perhaps the only friend I have." As so often, she was being histrionic: The day before she had been telling the marchese that one of her court ladies had lent her 3,000 sequins for a trip to Venice, adding with a sigh, "At least I have found one person to take pity on me and who wishes me well." The trip to Venice was not to eventuate. The fate of the sequins is unknown.

There are many letters extant between Amalie and Cavriani over a long period of years, but none reveal the slightest hint of a romance between them. Maria Theresia knew enough about the patterns of palace gossip to dismiss whatever she may have heard to the contrary, and in due course Don Ferdinando, evidently without suspicion, was to appoint the marchese his own Court Chamberlain. The rumours of an affair were likely no more than the customary attack on a prominent woman by impugning her sexual virtue. Cavriani himself never married, had no mistresses, and left no known descendants. He may simply have preferred the company of men.

**Marie Christine and Albert** had been six months travelling. It was time to think of home. Early in July 1776, they set off, via Venice and Ljubljana, for Vienna, where a small family gathering had been planned. Amalie had not been invited, though she had pleaded with her mother repeatedly to be allowed to come. "I feel most sorry for poor Amalie, she's the most unhappy of all," the Empress wrote to Marie Christine, "though I haven't given up hope of seeing her some other year, but never in Vienna."

It seems Amalie now asked the marchese Cavriani to intervene for her. He was quite often in Vienna, either on official business, or simply to visit his relatives, long established there; at court he was well known and always well received. Evidently he had brought the matter up with the two eldest archduchesses, with no happy result. Hurt and insistent, Amalie replied to his letter, in her markedly poor French, "I don't understand what you're trying to say, of course Marianna and Marie Christine have different feelings, the first loves me very much and I can't imagine she wouldn't be very pleased to see me, the second doesn't love me at all and she believes everyone thinks the same as she does." The Empress had evidently instructed both her daughters to discourage Amalie's attempts to visit.

It was probably not her constant social improprieties, embarrassing though they were for the Empress, that formed the reason for her banishment from Vienna. More damaging was her continuing insolence toward her French and Spanish in-laws. At a recent military inspection, she had knocked a French officer's hat clean off his head, since it displayed no Austrian feather. Appealed to for an appropriate response, Don Ferdinando had simply shrugged. "What can I do about it?" he said. "My wife is mad. The best thing to do, is to do nothing."

For the Empress, traces of guilt still lingered about the marriage she had forced on her daughter. "There is nothing to be done about it," she wrote, defensively, to Marie Christine, "and there's no point at all in going back over the past. Your sister's situation, for which really she has no one to blame but herself, is disagreeable, almost intolerable, especially for one of her frame of mind. I feel really very sorry for her, and I would like to make things better, but there's no simple remedy." Her delusions about Don Ferdinando, at least, had long been lost. "This poor Infante," she went on, "is it possible that his incomparable sister [Joseph's first wife, Isabella] could have such a brother? Often I can't believe what I hear about him, apart from the

Dominican business. Another man would have his mistresses, or hunting, gambling, horses and so on and so on. He has no money for such things; he must have something. We all have our weaknesses."

What did the Empress mean by Amalie's "frame of mind"? She was volatile, certainly, with sudden rages on the one hand and impulsive generosity on the other. And though she was, at this point, rather neglectful of her children, she constantly sought closeness with her own family: A French envoy declared the post to France never left without a letter from the Infanta to Marie Antoinette, and she is known to have written often to Marianna and Carolina as well. She took regular vigorous exercise, riding and walking long distances, yet her physical health remained poor, and at times she would withdraw completely, refusing to eat.

Amalie herself, at the age of thirty, had a simple understanding of her own "frame of mind." "I have been unhappy since I came into the world," she wrote to her friend Cavriani, "and I will be until my death is upon me. Since I am only halfway through my life, I hope I shall find some recompense in the next life. For now it's enough just to live, and not die."

# XVI

# 1776-1777

*In which the travellers return to the Hofburg, Carolina despatches Tanucci, and young Louis finally learns the facts of life.*

Marie Christine and Albert were almost home, rushing through the post stations and forgoing meals in order to reach Vienna by the date Maria Theresia had stipulated. Leopold and Maria Luisa were travelling with them, and though none of them really wanted to, they made a brief stop in Klagenfurt, "only to see the palace and garden the Empress has had built on the outskirts as an eventual home for the Archduchess Marianna." They found the new construction no more appealing than the town itself, "which has nothing remarkable to offer," though no doubt they agreed among themselves not to say so directly to the Hofburg ladies. En route they also drove past "a shabby gloriette or so-called country house, built on a small hill not far from the town; apparently they've called it Annabichel, since it's also intended for her use." This was to be Marianna's summer house, modest certainly, but hardly shabby, though no doubt it seemed so after the fabulous residences of her siblings in Italy.

At eight o'clock on the sultry evening of the thirteenth of July 1776, the two couples drove across the grand courtyard of Schönbrunn palace. The Empress was nervous and overexcited—in her impatience to see them, she had even denied them a night's sleep at Laxenburg, but she was surprised all the same to find none of them looking particularly well. "I find my son [Leopold] very much thinner and his wife the same, though that's not surprising, given the number of children she's had. She's an angel with no will of her own," she told Beatrice in Milan. "It's a quality rather to be admired than imitated. As for Marie Christine and the prince, I find them just as thin as they were when they left, if not thinner."

Chancellor von Kaunitz was unwell, too, with his frequent trouble of catarrh. And the good old Court Chamberlain was no more. At fifty-nine, the Empress' own age, Khevenhüller had departed his own well-provisioned dining-room to taste of lighter fare at the table of the Lord. He left behind him eight volumes of diaries detailing almost forty years of Hofburg life, and eight grown children to continue his loyal service to the Habsburgs.

Marie Christine and Albert had brought back portraits of the family in Italy, plus four other paintings, "very expensive and interesting," as well as their valuable cache of prints and drawings, and the Empress engaged the young German painter Heinrich Füger to produce a group portrait of everyone admiring them. Füger's painting, just fifteen inches square, shows Maria Theresia seated in her black widow's weeds and, standing behind her, admiring the family portraits, Marie Christine, with Albert in dashing red breeches, Maximilian sporting his knight's cross of the Teutonic Order, Marianna, the rather taller Elisabeth, and Joseph, shorter than his sister, tactfully depicted leaning forward as if to speak to his mother.

Leopold and his wife remained two months in Vienna before making a slow journey home to Florence—with her ninth baby just six months old, Maria Luisa was once again pregnant—"and I do fear for her," wrote the Empress, "suffering from the heat as she does." While "the Tuscans" kept the Empress company, Marie Christine and Albert drove through the heat and dust of high summer to wave the dynastic flag at Pest, across the Danube River from the old Hungarian capital of Buda, and Joseph rode off to inspect his soldiers in Bohemia, glad of any excuse to escape his mother's Hofburg. Amalie, banned from that desired place, was hoping to visit Milan instead, "and if you are willing to extend this pleasure to her," the Empress told Beatrice, "it would be a work of charity. She has hardly any resources, but that makes her only the more to be pitied, and I confess she is very dear to me. But I must warn you both not to get caught up in anything with her. . . . She's reckless, not as much as Elisabeth, but still."

At least Marianna, feeling in better health, did journey down to spend a friendly week with her, and Joseph, too, no doubt compelled by the Empress, stopped briefly in Parma to see her. Little is known of this visit, though Joseph does not seem to have enjoyed it unduly. As Amalie told Cavriani, "The Emperor said my dogs stink."

In Naples, though Tanucci had been granted a reprieve, his contest with Carolina was by no means over, with the Minister periodically threatening to resign if he did not get his way. Like Maria Theresia herself, and Chancellor von Kaunitz, too, he had used this tactic often throughout his career, his high standing and supposedly indispensable contribution to government making him each time confident of success.

But things had changed. Toward the end of October 1776, after a dispute so minor that no one could afterwards recall it, Tanucci proffered his resignation once again, sighing, as he had often done before, that after so many years of arduous service, he wanted only the peace and quiet of private life at his little farm near Portici, in the company of his aged spouse. Carolina called his bluff. On the following Saturday morning, with the Minister still in his bed, he received an unscheduled visit from a nobleman known to be among the Queen's supporters. This envoy brought with him Ferdinando's acceptance of the Minister's resignation. "I have heard nothing about this from King Carlos!" Tanucci is said to have exclaimed. "Your Excellency has made this request so often," the nobleman replied, "that King Ferdinando has at last decided to grant your wish."

Carlos was no less stunned than the Minister himself when he was finally informed of what had happened. But though he sympathized, he did not seek to overturn the decision; the Minister was an old man, after all, and there was clearly no possible path to peace between himself and the Queen. Tanucci bewailed his dismissal as a symptom of modern decadence and departed Naples "like an exiled monarch retiring to the country from the odious sight of man." Ferdinando had enough sway, and enough respect for Tanucci, to retain for him an advisory seat in the Council, though in the event neither made much use of it.

Tanucci's swift replacement as First Minister was the marchese della Sambuca, a man of "heavy and inanimate" appearance, fifty years old, a native of Palermo, and, not coincidentally, a former ambassador to Vienna. Where Tanucci had been Carlos' man, the opportunistic Sambuca, at least for the moment, was Carolina's. The tilt from Spanish to Austrian influence was recognized instantly, with Marie Antoinette at Versailles particularly proud of the coup her favourite sister had staged. "I was delighted for the Queen of Naples to learn of M. Tanucci's departure," she wrote to the Empress. "Although she always behaved perfectly correctly toward him, it's still a great advantage to be rid of him. I find my sister and the King have managed this affair very cleverly." This was true enough, at least when compared with how Amalie and Don Ferdinando had despatched Du Tillot and de Llano, but the consequences in Naples were to prove not so different from those in Parma. Sambuca, like Amalie's conte Sacco, was mostly concerned to exploit his new position for his own advantage. Where he did attempt to serve the state, he was to prove "impolitic and blundering." Carolina had traded intransigence for incompetence, and to that, in the longer term, Sambuca was to add a measure of sly opposition.

**Despite some backbiting** and occasional snide comments about the lack of an heir, the dauphin's two brothers and their wives had on the whole been good companions to Marie Antoinette. They had plenty of money and few responsibilities, and if most of the money was borrowed, they were not concerned about ever having to repay it, relying instead on the generosity of their eldest brother Louis-Auguste: As they saw it, in due course he would be king, with all the resources of the country at his personal disposal. Though the tiny comtesse d'Artois had tested Marie Antoinette's generosity by producing an heir where the latter had not, her husband had managed to become the young Queen's principal *chevalier servant*, taking charge of her excursions and entertainments. Unlike the gauche dauphin and the beefy comte de Provence, Artois was an exceptionally elegant young man, tall and handsome, and everything he arranged was touched with his charm and flair.

The dauphin's two sisters were rarely of the party. Elisabeth, ten years younger than her brother, serious and strong-willed, was a favourite of Marie Antoinette, but she was only a child, and on most of their outings could not accompany them. Clotilde, heavily built like her middle brother and consequently known as Fat Madame, was of an age to take part, but had no inclination to do so. A devout girl, she was intending to enter a Carmelite convent; operas and gambling parties were not to her taste, and besides, Marie Antoinette did not like her.

More significantly, the dauphin himself had no interest in day-long country picnics and late-night carousing in Paris. He preferred to sit quietly reading, in half a dozen languages, or working at his locksmithing, a popular gentlemanly pursuit of the time. He followed the news of scientific expeditions to the Americas and the Pacific, and kept up with current intellectual and political ideas—he was even a subscriber to the London *Spectator*. He had a real passion for history, and was a particular admirer of the Enlightenment philosopher David Hume, whom he had met personally; he actually recommended Hume's six-volume *History of England*, with its controversial sympathy for the executed King Charles I, to Marie Antoinette, and she read it, certainly slowly, but apparently attentively. The dauphin had no interest in music, a great lack as far as his wife was concerned, but rather surprisingly, he did enjoy amateur theatricals, with the two of them performing together for their own court circles.

But there was not much else that she shared with him. Formal appearances were required of them together, which neither could bear. Mrs. Hester Thrale, friend of London's famous Dr. Johnson, was among the audience at a banquet one autumn afternoon at the Renaissance château of Fontainebleau: "It is a mighty silent ceremonious Business—this dining in publick," she observed. Louis and Marie Antoinette "sat like two people stuffed with straw."

Exactly a year after the birth of her son, Louis' youngest sister-in-law, the comtesse d'Artois, had presented her husband with a healthy daughter. By the spring of 1777, she was pregnant again, and Maria Theresia's harangues to Marie Antoinette resumed with renewed force. There were to be "no separate beds, and no late-night parties, and above all no gambling," the latter being the main reason, according to Ambassador Mercy, why the twenty-one-year-old King wasn't sleeping every night with his wife: He was an early riser, and he went early to bed; she stayed up half the night playing cards, and he never knew when she would return. Moreover, Mercy had heard that certain "wretched people in the perverse whirlwind of this court" were plotting to ensnare Louis with a mistress, and had even "dared to speak to him" of a young star of the *Comédie française*.

Marie Antoinette defended herself. Her husband "doesn't like us both sleeping in the same bed," she retorted. "I make sure there's no complete separation. Sometimes he does come to spend the night with me. I don't feel I should torment him to come more often, since he comes to see me every morning anyway in my private room." The Empress was annoyed to learn that Louis disliked sharing a bed: "I regard this as an essential point," she wrote, "not for having children, but for being more united and closer and more confiding, having a few hours alone together every day." But she conceded all the same that her daughter was right "not to torment him about it."

And, in any case, help was at hand. Joseph was planning a visit to France, with one of its goals "to judge of [the Queen's] present situation, and get some idea of her future, however that should eventuate, and how my own benevolent opinions might be of assistance to her." The Empress was all approval. "Speak quite openly to your brother about the state of your marriage," she advised her daughter. "I can answer for his discretion and can assure you he is well placed to give you good advice."

In his ceremony-avoiding alias as the Count von Falkenstein, Joseph arrived in Paris in the middle of April 1777. He would have liked to make the journey with his brother Leopold—"What discussions we'd have together, and how we'd talk behind closed doors about everything we'd seen!"—but the extensive reforms which Leopold was himself overseeing in his Grand Duchy of Tuscany, not to mention the demands of his family—Maria Luisa had just delivered her tenth child in as many years—meant that for him, a journey of such length was out of the question.

Since Louis' ascent to the throne of France three years before, Joseph had asked to see Ambassador Mercy's Versailles reports for himself, and the Empress had acquiesced, "keeping only the secret ones for myself (not even Kaunitz sees those)," as she told Mercy. Joseph had been writing to Marie Antoinette, too, but in German, and by now Mercy was having to translate the letters into French for her. Though he did say she had not quite forgotten her mother tongue, it seems she no longer had occasion to speak it, and after seven years in France, she was finding it difficult to read or write; possibly she could no longer manage the singular *Kurrent* script used at the time for handwritten German. At least her own babyish French handwriting had by this time begun to take on a more adult form, to such an extent, indeed, that the Empress was suspicious of it, and supposed she had been dictating the letters to her confessor Vermond.

Perhaps advised by Carolina, who had kept her own liveliest friends at bay during Joseph's visit to Naples, Marie Antoinette had prepared for her brother's visit by temporarily relinquishing La Polignac and most of her other pleasure-seeking companions, and installing the sedate duchesse de Duras, daughter of the formidable Madame Etiquette. It did not help her much. Ten days after his arrival, Joseph reported disparagingly to Leopold of their twenty-one-year-old sister, "The Queen is a pretty woman, but she's a featherbrain who as yet cannot make use of her advantages. She spends every day going from one dissipation to the next, all of them perfectly permissible in themselves, but dangerous all the same since they prevent her from the serious reflection of which she is in such need."

Joseph in fact thought the whole court, if not the entire country, was in need of serious reflection. "Everything is done for the sake of appearance," he wrote, "but when you go further and really look for what's useful, you're very disappointed." He admitted the "astonishing luxury" of Paris, and was amused by all the ceremony and fuss at Versailles, but by what he could judge of the civil and military administration he was very much less impressed, seeing it as poorly organized in itself and sclerotically resistant to change.

He had hoped to meet Turgot, the Comptroller of Finances, of whom Leopold and Albert were also admirers, but the reform attempts of this dynamic man had ruffled too many highly-perched feathers, and he had been forced out of office the year before. The King was intelligent enough to have appreciated Turgot's insights: The public purse was almost empty, and strong measures needed to be taken. He had defended him, but he had not proved strong enough to resist his wife's pleading: Turgot had tried to curb spending in the royal household, and had opposed the appointment of one of the Queen's favourites to an important diplomatic post, and in the self-assurance of her then twenty years, Marie Antoinette had insisted he must go.

Her action had been prompted by an instinctive and rather naive loyalty to her friends, rather than by any imperiousness attendant on her rank. She showered gifts on her favourites, as her mother had always done, but she failed to understand the political significance of those gifts in a system built on strategic patronage. As for her favourites themselves, most were simply happy to take, without any thought of reciprocal obligation. "They were shallow people who wanted positions for themselves and their families," noted the comte de La Marck. "They knew their way around the tricks and games of the court. The Queen was far superior to her usual entourage, but she needed friendship. . . . Above all, she was very tenderhearted and was always wanting to oblige those who applied to her. People took great advantage of this."

Joseph saw that, like himself and his sisters Carolina and Amalie, Marie Antoinette disliked ceremony and often went about accompanied by only a handful of people, "without the trappings of royal dignity." This he could approve, up to a point. "Her virtue is intact," he told Leopold, "she is even rather prudish by nature, and there is a simple air about her that would be good in any ordinary woman, but she's not fulfilling her functions as Queen, and that could have consequences in future."

As for Louis, "He's physically strong and it seems he should be able to become a father. On that subject there are incomprehensible mysteries. He has good hard erections apparently." Thus Joseph to Leopold, three weeks after his arrival at Versailles, on the vital subject of the non-consummation of their youngest sister's marriage. The thirty-six-year-old Emperor had been strolling out with the twenty-two-year-old King, discussing this very question with brotherly frankness. He had been speaking in similar vein with Marie Antoinette, but it was to be a further month before he plumbed the depths of the couple's ignorance, and their remarkably weak sexual urges. On the ninth of June 1777 he relayed it all to Leopold:

> *He's not impotent, not physically, not mentally, but the* fiat lux *has not occurred, darkness still covers the earth. Imagine it—in his marriage bed, this is the secret, he has strong erections, perfectly firm, he introduces the member, stays there for perhaps two minutes without moving, withdraws still erect, without ejaculating, and bids good night. It's unbelievable, because sometimes he has night-time emissions too, but never when he's actually in the act. He's quite happy, he says frankly he only does it out of duty and has no inclination for it. Ah! if I could have been present once, I would have fixed it, I would have whipped him, to make him ejaculate in a fury, like a donkey. And my sister isn't very ardent, either. The pair of them are two absolute incompetents.*

Happily, as the Empress had predicted, Joseph was well placed to give them good advice. He did so, and finally, after seven years of marriage, the light dawned on Louis and Marie Antoinette. Shortly afterwards, the Queen summoned her first lady-in-waiting, Madame Campan, and her secretary-librarian, the lady's father-in-law, "regarding us both as people sincerely interested in her happiness," and told them she had "finally become Queen of France, and hoped to have children soon."

Joseph counted his visit to France a success, and in terms of the Bourbon succession, so it was to prove. But in other respects, he had not helped his sister. Though he had impressed some of her subjects with his broad practical knowledge, he had offended many more with his personal arrogance and his lack of respect for protocol. Some courtiers thought him jealous of the natural and cultural glories of Louis' kingdom, and there may have been some truth in this: En route to France, Joseph had travelled through the Tyrol and Vorarlberg, Austria's *Vorland*, which he himself thought hardly worth keeping. These westernmost provinces, mountainous and sparsely settled, would have presented an extreme contrast to the far more densely populated French countryside, to say nothing of the environs of Paris, or the famed city of light itself. And though the Habsburgs possessed many fine palaces across their broad territories, there was nothing anywhere in the Monarchy to compare with the vast and splendid château of Versailles.

Like his youngest brother, Maximilian, and with less excuse, Joseph had embarrassed Marie Antoinette by "a frankness which often degenerated into rudeness." In public, he had spoken loudly and laughingly of his sisters in Parma and Naples, mimicking clumsy King Ferdinando and telling stories of Carolina locking him out of the bedroom. He had made a noisy fuss of Louis' thirteen-year-old sister, Elisabeth, saying he was thinking of marrying her, though no one took him seriously. According to Madame Campan, at one point he had actually grabbed her father-in-law "by the button of his jacket" to lecture him for a full hour on the sorry state of the French government, "a thing all the more blameworthy since an emperor should speak to a secretary-librarian only on matters relating to his occupational functions."

His plain manners and easy way of addressing his attendants had seemed mere affectation, especially since he failed to tip any of them.

Far worse for the Queen's reputation, however, was the widely held belief that she had given her brother "considerable sums" of money. It seems Louis himself had ordered this as a settling of some obligation between the two courts, but at Versailles and beyond, it was viewed as an outright gift. The young comte de Tilly, returning from England at this time, noticed "for the first time a strong impression of people disliking the Queen" because of it.

Joseph himself had retained quite a different feeling from his visit. Soon after his return to Vienna, the Empress relayed to Marie Antoinette what he had said about her. "And I don't betray him," she wrote, "in giving his own words, which I could never put so well: *I was sorry to leave Versailles, being sincerely attached to my sister. With her I found a kind of sweetness in life which I had renounced, but which, as I see, I still enjoy. She is lovable and charming. I spent hours and hours with her, without noticing the time passing. She was very moved at my departure, though she kept herself composed. It took all my strength to turn and leave her. . . .* If he found another woman like this," the Empress added, "he would be ready to marry for the third time. He is still thinking of going to see you again, which is most satisfying to me. If he doesn't want to stay with me, I would want him to be with his family, in France, Naples, or Tuscany"—though, noticeably, not in Parma.

# XVII

# 1777-1778

## In which Joseph attacks half of Bavaria, and Leopold attacks the whole family.

At about half past six on a January evening in 1777, a courier alighted outside the Hofburg with a letter for the Empress, who had just sat down to play a hand of cards. The letter contained news that the Elector Maximilian III of Bavaria, a determined opponent of inoculation, had died suddenly of a particularly virulent strain of "purple" smallpox. He had been childless, and his throne had now passed to a twelfth cousin once removed, a Rhineland prince with no particular interest in Bavaria.

Maximilian had also been the brother of Joseph's second, unloved wife; acquisition of his territory had been recognized as a possible future advantage of that match. Now, with the accession of the new ruler, Karl Theodor, just such an opportunity had arisen, for he wanted to swap the southern part of his Bavaria for the Habsburg territory of the Austrian Netherlands. Maria Theresia had reservations, grumbling that she "would rather have the Belgians as subjects than those Bavarian rustics," but in recent months, with the question of Poland long settled, she had allowed Joseph a greater involvement in foreign and military affairs, and he and Chancellor von Kaunitz found the new proposal interesting. Joseph disliked the bits and pieces of the Austrian Netherlands, non-contiguous territories far to the northwest, inherited by his grandfather from the Spanish in 1714. His plan for a single administrative model across the Habsburg territories would be easier to implement, he felt, if all the Monarchy's lands were geographical neighbours, as Austria and southern Bavaria would be. It was true the Austrian Netherlands were much richer but, being nearer to France and especially Prussia, they were strategically more vulnerable.

Early in 1778, a set of convenient (and apparently genuine) documents was unearthed in Vienna, proving a 350-year-old Habsburg claim to almost exactly the territory proposed, and within days, with no resistance from local forces, the Austrians were in possession of a substantial part of it. Joseph congratulated himself, but his precipitate occupation of southern Bavaria was about to provoke a war, for among Karl Theodor's nephews was Prince Karl August of Zweibrücken, the same Karl August who had loved, and lost, Joseph's sister Amalie ten years before. Though he had no objection in principle to his uncle's territorial swap, he had been nursing the humiliation of his rejected suit for a decade, with a recent unhappy marriage adding new pique to his long injured feelings. He now spied a chance for revenge, and appealed for help to the Prussians. King Friedrich II had just been celebrating, or lamenting, his sixty-sixth birthday. Though no longer in vigorous health, he was roused to anger by this sudden extension of territory on the part of his most formidable enemy. He at once promised Karl August his support.

Despite his army of 250,000, thoroughly reformed according to the treatise on the Prussian military written by his clever first wife, Isabella, Joseph's confidence was shaken, and he thought it wise to call for reinforcements. In February 1778 he appealed to Marie Antoinette for help, prodding her, "Remember you were born a German." Under the terms of the *renversement des alliances* which had led to her own marriage, she was to persuade Louis to send 24,000 men to Austria's aid, or failing the men themselves, enough money for Joseph to raise them elsewhere.

Eager to help her brother, and naively assuming that France's alliance with Austria would outweigh all other considerations, she approached her husband with some urgency, expecting him to comply with Joseph's request. But the French had been particularly displeased, the *renversement* notwithstanding, to see their historical ally, Bavaria, in league with their historical enemy, Austria. Louis' response was firm. "It is the ambition of your relatives that is going to disrupt everything," he told his wife. "They began with Poland, now it's Bavaria's turn. I am sorry about it for your sake. . . . This dismembering of Bavaria is being done against our will, and we do not approve of it."

Marie Antoinette returned a nervous apology to her brother, with a reasonable, if to his ears inadequate, excuse: France was now involved in the American war against Britain; there were no men and no funds to spare. Joseph declared himself "not satisfied with the Queen his sister, and most unhappy with the French court, an allied court which called itself a friend to Austria."

An anxious correspondence ensued, with Joseph and the Empress and Ambassador Mercy all pushing the Queen to change the King's mind, and Louis' own ministers repeatedly deceiving her into believing she had succeeded. At their head, in position if not in actual height, was Louis' slithery little minister of state, the comte de Maurepas, seventy-seven years old and guileful beyond Marie Antoinette's fathoming. "It's unbelievable," she said, "the talent the ministers here have for drowning everything in a flood of words." Hopelessly out of her depth, and ill served by the obtuse Mercy, she sent letter after deluded letter to Vienna, assuring her family of Louis' support. Confused by Maurepas' sophistry, she was also overwhelmed by pressure from her mother: "It would kill me if our alliance were to falter," the Empress had written; on reading this, the Queen turned pale. She continued to believe what she needed to believe: that France would support Austria's claim to Bavaria, and that the Prussians, daunted by this reinforcement, would simply acquiesce.

Among his own officers Joseph counted Marie Christine's old flame,

Prince Karl von Liechtenstein, plus two of his own brothers, twenty-two-year-old Maximilian and, later, an unwilling Leopold, and also brother-in-law Albert, himself a middling commander who nonetheless had no high opinion of Joseph's military prowess. The Empress made much of the danger facing the men of the family to continue the pressure on Marie Antoinette. If war should break out, she reminded her, "the Emperor and your brother and Prince Albert would be first in line: the very idea of it is almost enough to undo me, and if it doesn't kill me, it would make my life worse than death."

German born she may have been, but Marie Antoinette was also Queen of France. And in mid-April 1778, a new challenge arose to her divided loyalty: Her monthly period was late. "And I've never been late, in fact I'm always early," she wrote excitedly to her mother. "Yesterday I vomited a bit, which increases my hopes." The signs were correct: After eight years of marriage, she was finally pregnant. Joseph's advice had borne fruit, in the form—or so it was ardently hoped—of an heir to the throne.

The news was received in Vienna almost as rapturously as in France, though it did not stop the Empress' exhortations on the subject of Bavaria. But Marie Antoinette's choice had now effectively been made. She belonged to the French, as they swiftly recognized. The King, overjoyed, became attentive and tender, and his elderly aunts began to fuss over her relentlessly, smug in the imminent aggrandizement of their own status at court. The pregnancy gave Marie Antoinette herself a "coherence" beyond anything she had evinced in the past, as Mercy told the Empress. It brought about in her "the most advantageous changes in every sense." She even gave up playing billiards. And if confirmation of the Queen's loyalty to France were needed, when the Russians announced their own support of Prussia against Austria, she agreed to receive their ambassador.

In early July, Friedrich ordered his troops to invade Habsburg Bohemia, and Joseph responded by readying his own men for an attack on Prussia and Saxony. But both sides lacked good supply lines for fresh provisions, and on both sides, before they could get to firing any shots, the soldiers began to go short, and then to go hungry. For the next ten months, what might have been decided by generals in the field was instead quibbled and quarrelled over by diplomats in palace war cabinets and journalists in their newssheets.

Marie Christine made a contribution of her own to the paper battles. The outcome of the war was not her prime concern: She wanted Albert, her "most adored husband," safe at home, and even suggested giving three districts of Bohemia to the Prussians in order to achieve it the sooner, prompting a little jab from one of the *dames* at court: "Your Royal Highness may well be happy to give them away," said the lady, "since they don't actually belong to you."

Marie Christine's letters to Albert during these months of war reveal a tender, indeed passionate relationship. "It makes me really melancholy to think I can't come to you and fold you in my arms and press you to my heart," she wrote, "for I love you dearly as my beloved husband and madly and ardently as my lover and you know how I can love. There are moments when with all my religion and good sense I feel I can't bear it, I'm overwhelmed by despair that we're separated." There are many letters in this vein, attesting, after twelve years of marriage, to an intense bond between the two. With Marie Christine there is often a suggestion of exaggeration, even manipulation of the other party's feelings. So much she had practised with her mother, with dazzling success, over seventeen years, and the habit may have seeped into her dealings with her husband. But Albert at least believed her to be completely sincere, extolling her as "the best of wives."

As the months dragged on, Marie Christine blamed Kaunitz ever more loudly for starting the war in the first place. "She won't even have his name pronounced in front of her," wrote his indignant daughter-in-law Leopoldine—"which only goes to prove her very great ignorance of the affairs she wants to meddle in. She did everything she could to spare Saxony, when they've deliberately done so much to harm us." It was believed that the sacrifice of Albert's homeland of Saxony would be enough to secure a Prussian withdrawal, but that Marie Christine had persuaded the Empress to forbid it. Count Rosenberg came to Marie Christine's defence. "She isn't meddling at all," he said. "She's only worried about her husband."

Albert was in fact in little physical danger, at least not from actual fighting. But the Austrians' strategic and logistical weakness was cause enough for worry. Joseph began to lose his way; his generals became evasive. On leave in Vienna, one of them even confided that "the pernicious presence of the Emperor has prevented our success, where, without his interference, it would have been equally certain and brilliant." Always uneasy about the Bavarian plan, Maria Theresia finally went over her son's head and behind his back, and appealed to Friedrich directly. It was a revealing move, showing where ultimate power in the Monarchy still lay. Despite Joseph's outrage and his furious threats to continue the war, the Empress' intervention ensured it ended without much actual fighting, except perhaps behind closed doors at the Hofburg. Friedrich withdrew his troops, then Joseph withdrew his own. In due course, the two powers agreed to a peace in the Treaty of Teschen, with France and Russia as guarantors.

The treaty did bring Austria the farmlands and coal deposits of the Innviertel; but overall the Bavarian war was a defeat for Joseph, and it left him with a deficit of 100 million florins. The treaty had also given Russia, as a guarantor of the peace, a new legal standing in the affairs of the Holy Roman Empire, increasing its importance, whether ally or enemy. And since the most strenuous efforts of both sides in the long stalemate had been spent in requisitioning food from unwilling locals, it went ignobly down in Prussian history books as the "potato war," and in those of Austria as "the plum duff-up."

LEOPOLD HAD ONLY GRUDGINGLY taken part in Joseph's Bavarian venture. An overly methodical man himself, he thought the whole thing misconceived and fully on a par with too many of his brother's extravagant ideas. He had resisted coming to Vienna at all, but had been obliged to defer to the Empress' wishes. In the campaign itself he had played only a small part, spending most of the dark winter months at the Hofburg, sunk in a gloom of his own. He missed his family in Florence and, after thirteen years as ruler of his own Grand Duchy, resented having to take orders from his mother and brother, and he took his revenge in a series of private diatribes on everyone and everything around him. Written in Italian, in a secret code he had devised for himself, the pages are sprinkled with examples of old Tuscan *maldicenza*—the pleasure of saying nasty things about people.

Leopold had not needed to move to Tuscany to develop a facility in this. Though affectionate to his own children, he was otherwise of a cool and suspicious nature and quick to take offence. Count Rosenberg, who knew him well, said he had "the peculiar tic of writing down everything you said to him." Like his mother and his sister Carolina, whom he would at this point not have wanted to resemble, he was a continual, almost compulsive writer; the more than eleven hundred pages he produced during this unhappy stay in Vienna included the merciless *Stato della famiglia*, a fifty-page rant against his Hofburg family, written in code in a pink-covered workbook in the most direct language, almost as if he were telling them what he thought of them all.

In Leopold's *Stato*, almost everyone hates everyone else, everyone is jealous of someone, no one trusts anyone. No one is spared, though Albert and Maximilian come out relatively unscathed, the former "a good and honorable man," and the latter "a good person . . . gifted, but lazy," and not likely to amount to much. In Leopold's telling, Maximilian's lack of achievement at least endears him to Joseph, who loves him for recognizing "that he'll always be a second-rank subject."

Leopold took lunch every day with one or other of his sisters, either Marianna, or Marie Christine, or Elisabeth, apparently to ease them into his confidence and coax their real opinions out of them. It is an unattractive picture, made worse by the further use he made of Marie Christine, by far the most influential of the three, who dined every evening with her brother and his wife, Maria Luisa. To Marie Christine herself, this no doubt seemed quite natural, given the friendly footing they had lived upon during their many weeks together in Italy, but the viciousness of what Leopold was writing about her in private utterly belies any genuine warmth of feeling toward her.

Leopold sees Marie Christine as enveloped in and surrounded by hatred. She hates Marianna and Elisabeth, she hates Ferdinand and Beatrice because the Empress is fond of them, and she *really* hates Amalie in Parma, who is the object of their mother's constant concern. She is jealous of Marianna and particularly jealous of Elisabeth, "especially since she's begun to have some influence over the Empress." Marie Christine herself excites everyone's jealousy because of her closeness to their mother, and Joseph is afraid of her as well, for the same reason. Albert does not hate her, but she has him and all his family wound around her little finger. Count Rosenberg does not hate her either; indeed he is now entirely her creature, to the extent that "in the town they're saying she's having an affair with him." And as the coup de grâce, all Marie Christine's eight million Hungarian subjects hate her, too.

Marianna comes off a little better. She has no subjects, of course, and "no influence" anywhere, but all the same, she is talented and ambitious, and Joseph is rather anxious about this, imagining she is intriguing to advance her favourites at court. At just this time, the English traveller Henry Swinburne records that "the Archduchess Marianne is pleasing, and like a woman of the world," but Leopold finds her very withdrawn and always making a great show of her piety, "full of secrets and mistrust"—no doubt perceptive enough to mistrust Leopold himself—and "like the Empress, always serious and sad and ill." She is on very friendly terms with Amalie in Parma and, surprisingly, given her handsome personal income, is "constantly in debt to the salespeople," relying on her annoyed mother to bail her out. When not sad and ill and spending beyond her means, she is studying natural philosophy. She has even taken on a formal instructor, no less a person than Ignaz von Born, celebrated from Bavaria to Saint Petersburg for his scientific learning. The lean-faced Born is a Freemason, indeed a member of the secret, notoriously progressive Illuminati, and a frequenter, along with the composer Josef Haydn and the African scholar Angelo Soliman, of the Viennese lodge True Concord, of which Marianna herself is now a patroness—she reviews their list of members every year, and they have even dedicated a book of songs to her. Born has recently been appointed director of the Imperial Cabinet of Natural Curiosities; under his guidance she is studying mineralogy, chemistry, and the proto-geological science of *Montanistik*—mountain studies. And she is also preparing for her future life with the Elisabethan sisters in Klagenfurt, sending occasional consignments of furniture and pictures for her newly built palace and the little summer house nearby.

As for Elisabeth, she has no more sense than she ever had. She drives out regularly to visit other high-ranking ladies, and is everywhere feared for her sharp tongue and welcomed for her up-to-date gossip and entertaining stories. She is very friendly with her sister-in-law in Milan, Ferdinand's wife, Beatrice, and maintains a lively correspondence with her. She and Marianna don't really get on, but at times they do sit down together to complain about Marie Christine and their mother's favouritism toward her—and in fact even Swinburne reports that she and Albert "drain her prodigiously." The Empress disapproves of Elisabeth, but values her for the information she has about people at court and in the town. Most of Elisabeth's time, however, is spent petting and taking care of a tiny girl who has been left, anonymously, outside the door of her apartments. Without children herself, like her sister at Versailles, she has adopted one of the "surplus" children of the less well placed. For this little creature "she has an extraordinary fondness, and she is bringing her up with great devotion." A tender father himself, Leopold concedes at least this praise for his third sister, whose later letters reveal that she was, despite his coolness toward her, the one who loved him most.

For those away from Vienna, Leopold relies largely on old memories and the reports of others, though it is true he has had occasion to make his own assessment of his Milanese brother, Ferdinand, and his dismissal is brutal. "He is a weak man of small intelligence and little talent, mercenary, boring and workshy, with an unwarrantedly high opinion of himself. His wife has total command over him." Amalie in Parma is "very unhappy that her husband is a weak man," but her unhappiness is her own fault, the result of "her own extravagances and debts and bad behaviour." It seems to him that the Empress has absolutely given up on Amalie. As for Joseph, "he can't stand her."

Carolina is only a little happier than her sister in Parma, though Leopold admits she is "a good woman, if inexperienced and gullible and impatient and without anyone to advise her." He believes the Empress is rather annoyed with her, seeing that Carolina does not appreciate her interference in what she sees as her own affairs. And it seems Marie Christine may be attempting to step into the breach: She clearly takes an interest in Carolina and, surprisingly, receives frequent letters from King Ferdinando.

Leopold dismisses twenty-three-year-old Marie Antoinette, whom he has not seen since she was a child of nine, as "frivolous and thoughtless, given only to vanity and pleasures and outward show; but a good woman, even if her head has been turned by the customs and foolishness of that country. She's happy enough," he believes, "since the King loves her, but she has no influence in serious matters there."

But he reserves his sharpest thrusts for his brother Joseph, the Imperatore, an able man, certainly, but impulsive, furiously ambitious, and resentful of his mother's continuing grip on power. "He is full of the strongest, most violent, hardest despotism. He loves no one. He shows a friendly face only to those whose talents he needs, and afterwards he makes fun of them. He thinks his own talent will suffice to overcome any obstacle, and he despises everything that's not his own idea."

This was admittedly not a happy time for Leopold, but these unappetizing little tirades go well beyond his usual measured ways. While not without some truth, they are above all a projection of his own resentments and frustrations, here clouding his generally keen intelligence. It was his third visit to Vienna since his departure for Florence thirteen years before, and this time Leopold also noticed a marked change for the worse in his mother's health, which no doubt increased his anxiety about the approaching transfer of power to Joseph. The Empress was now sixty-one. Her breathing difficulties had increased to the point that even leisurely walking was hard for her: Her face would turn purplish and she would break out in perspiration.

She was often short of breath while sitting, too; it was an effort to continue embroidering her mourning chasuble, or even to speak for any length of time. She was constantly complaining of feeling hot, drinking endless glasses of iced lemonade, and keeping the windows open day and night, even in cold and windy weather. And despite her flushed colour after any exertion, she looked generally paler every day.

And she was afflicted now, too, by those common ailments of old age, poor hearing and forgetfulness. Leopold saw her as frustrated by her own physical weakness and always in a grouchy mood with everyone except Marie Christine. Though she adored Joseph, she wanted to control him, so that there were arguments whenever they were together, and he was not above criticizing or making fun of her opinions in public. She was constantly threatening to give up everything and retire but, like other observers, Leopold did not believe she would ever do so. And like so many others in the sad embrace of old age, she was often to be heard railing uselessly against the manners and mores of nowadays, and complaining that no one listened to her anymore.

# XVIII

# 1778-1780

In which Marie Antoinette gains a daughter, Carolina loses a son, and the Empress is lost to the world.

Just before the Christmas of 1778, in the presence of her husband and all his relatives, female and male, and "such a mixed crowd of people you'd have thought you were in a public square," Marie Antoinette gave birth to her first child. It was a daughter. Predictably, she was named Marie-Thérèse.

A delighted Louis presented his queen with a gift of 100,000 livres. But at the Hofburg, the news was received with only moderate satisfaction. The Empress had eleven living granddaughters already, four of them dutifully named for herself. Now the best Marie Antoinette had managed to do, after almost nine years of marriage, was to produce another one. In the midst of the celebrations, the dissatisfied grandmamma penned a hasty line to Beatrice in Milan, declaring she was "in no way content with this fifth Theresia." The twenty-three-year-old mother herself was happy enough. "Poor little thing," she sighed to her newborn, "you weren't wanted, but you won't be any less dear to me for that. A boy would have belonged more to the state. You will be mine. All my care will be for you."

In Naples, where Carolina was only weeks from another delivery of her own, anticipation of that event had been overshadowed by the death of her first son, whose birth, not four years earlier, had entitled her to a place, still informally denied her, in the Council of State. The little boy had died just two days before the birth of his cousin at Versailles, most likely from one of the infectious fevers which killed so many children of the time so suddenly. Carolina was devastated by his death. To her friend Martha Swinburne, wife of the travel writer Henry, she relayed "the dreadful blow that has taken from me my beautiful, dearest, perfect Carlo. This child had perfect health, and beauty and intelligence too, and he was perfectly robust. I lost him," she wrote, "in less than sixty hours. Grief of this kind is annihilating."

She had four children still living, three daughters and a son. To this little boy, fifteen-month-old Francesco, the mantle of dynasty now passed. And in the middle of January 1779 she gave birth again, to not one but two daughters. The delivery was difficult, nor were the twin girls to enjoy the "perfect health" of their late brother. Carolina was to have eleven more pregnancies, all arduous, some near fatal, with several of these children adversely affected by her increasingly poor health. She knew the cause of it, and shared it now with her brother Leopold. Ferdinando had been having an affair with a certain Madame Lusciano, from whom he had contracted syphilis. He had then infected Carolina, and she was to suffer the effects of it for the rest of her life.

THOUGH MARIE ANTOINETTE'S delivery of a daughter had been less than ideal, it had been enough to cement the Franco-Austrian alliance, and the Empress decided to mark it now by commissioning a portrait of her daughter at Versailles. The woman chosen to execute it, Elisabeth Vigée-Le Brun, was without formal training in studio or guild. She had learned her craft independently, guided by a number of painters who had recognized her talent, and for five years already she had been working professionally. A commission from the Queen of France was no small achievement. It was a triumph for the young artist to have been chosen ahead of her rival society portraitist, the more established Adélaïde Labille-Guiard, though the latter could afford to be gracious about it: a staunch advocate of women artists, she was soon to open her own teaching studio for female students at the Louvre. Madame Vigée-Le Brun was twenty-four years old and just pregnant with her first child. Marie Antoinette, also twenty-four and a new mother, was no longer the "very little & slender" girl looking "[not] above 12 Years Old" whom Lady Percy had observed at her wedding nine years before. She was now, as her admiring portraitist described her:

> . . . in all the splendour of her youth and beauty. She was tall, admirably well made, quite plump without being too much so. It's very difficult to give an idea, to someone who has never seen the Queen, of so many graces and such nobility united. Her features weren't regular; she had inherited from her family that long, narrow, oval face particular to the Austrians. She didn't have large eyes; they were almost blue in colour, with a sweet and intelligent expression. . . . But the most remarkable aspect of her face was the glow of her complexion. I couldn't render the effect of it as I would have liked: there were no colours to paint that freshness, those tones so very fine. I've never found them again on any other woman.

In her memoirs, Madame Vigée-Le Brun mentions the kind informality of Marie Antoinette's manner to her, but she was intimidated, nonetheless, by this first royal commission from life. Perhaps because of this, the portrait itself is rather stilted, yet the Queen was pleased enough with it to reengage her, with the happy result, over the next decade, of some thirty works, and a warm understanding between the two women.

Marie Christine had been sitting for a portrait, too, at Albert's request, with the celebrated Alexander Roslin. Marie Antoinette had heard about this from her sisters. "He did have quite a reputation here," she told her mother, "though some people say his talent wasn't really for portraits. Perhaps they were just jealous. He seems to be doing very well in Vienna." Roslin was a man who took his time, however. "She has had four sessions," the Empress replied, "each one three hours long, and it isn't finished yet. You dare not move or do the least thing the whole time." By contrast, Madame Vigée-Le Brun had worked swiftly: "You must try to do the head, especially the face, in three or four sessions of an hour and a half each, two hours at the most," she wrote, "since the model gets bored and impatient"—which may have been right: Certainly Roslin's florid rococo portrait shows Marie Christine looking distinctly grumpy.

Roslin was normally resident at the Louvre, where he had a grace-and-favour artist's apartment, and Marie Antoinette had assumed he was a Frenchman, but the painter actually hailed from Sweden. There were many of his compatriots at the French court. Their own gifted and dynamic king, Gustav III, was an ardent Francophile and, like Joseph, an autocratic proponent of Enlightenment ideas, who had recently ousted the conservative faction of nobles in his own parliament to initiate a radical programme of legal and economic reform. He was just thirty-two years old, and among his friends he counted the young Count Axel von Fersen, scion of a wealthy old Swedish family, who was currently enjoying an extended visit to Versailles. Marie Antoinette particularly enjoyed the company of young foreign visitors to the court, to an extent that at one point the comte de La Marck warned her this could harm her reputation. He later relayed the sad reply she made him: "It's true," she said, "but you see, they don't want anything from me."

Fersen had met the Queen five years before, passing through Versailles as part of his Grand Tour of Europe. "He was one of the handsomest men I've seen," the comte de Tilly recorded, "with one of those impassive faces that women don't dislike when they hope to animate them." The naturally courtly Fersen was a great lover of music, and he had served as a diplomatic attaché in Naples, so he knew Carolina, Marie Antoinette's favourite sister. All this had recommended him to the Queen. She had taken an immediate liking to him, and on his return to France in August 1778, had greeted him warmly. "Ah! here is an old acquaintance," she had said, and in the subsequent months, through the later stages of her pregnancy, a friendship had developed between the two, with Fersen soon included in her private circle.

Probably Marie Antoinette had fallen in love with him; certainly there was some flirtation on her part. "I often pay her my court at her card-games," the count told his father, "and each time she makes to me little speeches that are full of good-will. As some one had told her of my Swedish uniform, she expressed a wish to see me in it; I am to go Thursday thus dressed, not to court, but to the queen's apartments. She is the most amiable princess that I know."

Fersen and the Queen were both aged twenty-three. Inevitably, the amity between them aroused jealousy, not from the King, who had been closer to his wife since the birth of their daughter, and who seems to have been more often with her now at her private entertainments, but from other courtiers who felt excluded from them. In due course there were rumours of a scandal, so that by the spring of 1779, the Swedish ambassador, Count Creutz, felt obliged to inform King Gustav about it. "I ought to confide to Your Majesty," he wrote in his elegant Swedish—he was a celebrated poet—"that the young Count Fersen has been so well received by the queen that this has given umbrage to several persons. I own that I cannot help thinking that she had a liking for him; I have seen too many indications to doubt it. The conduct of the young count has been admirable . . . for its modesty and reserve."

Fersen found Marie Antoinette charming, but he seems to have had no thought of an affair with her, even had it been possible. In fact, he was doing his best to find a wife, and currently courting a Swedish heiress, so far with some success. And he had his military career to think of. Sweden was at peace, but the American war for independence from the British had been ongoing almost four years already: Along with thousands of other Swedish soldiers, Fersen now decided to join the French forces fighting with the Americans. "By thus departing," Ambassador Creutz continued, "he avoided all dangers; but it needed, evidently, a firmness beyond his years, to surmount that seduction. The queen's eyes could not leave him, during the last days, and they often filled with tears." The cosmopolitan Prince de Ligne, admittedly one of the Queen's devotees, protested the innocence of her relationship with Fersen. "Her so-called gallantry was never anything but a deep sense of friendship," he insisted, "which, perhaps, distinguished one or two persons, and a general coquetry of woman and queen which sought to please everyone." But the Prince was in a minority: Most courtiers at Versailles viewed the matter in the same sceptical light as the Swedish ambassador.

Marie Antoinette's disappointment at Fersen's departure was compounded by her failure to conceive another child, though, as she told her mother, "the life I am leading with the King gives me hope." The Empress was not sympathetic, especially since Carolina, with her twin daughters not yet a year old, was already five months pregnant again, though, as her mother told Marie Antoinette, "I fear she'll have another girl . . . and your daughter will soon be a year old. She needs a little brother, whom we're all impatient for."

> *Madame, I am quite in fashion; I have caught a cold, as my daughters and everyone else here has done, and as I have put off being bled for a month, I shall have it done at five o'clock to lessen the force of the cough. With my breathing difficulties, a cold is more troublesome. Do not think that I am ill. The Emperor has even gone hunting.*

Thus Maria Theresia's regular Monday letter to her daughter-in-law Beatrice in Milan. It was the middle of November, a chilly, gloomy season in Vienna, and the Empress was dismissing this latest indisposition as simply one more episode in her many years of feeling generally unwell. Marianna, far from well herself, believed her mother had caught the cold at a pheasant-shoot at Schönbrunn: It had been raining hard, and though the ladies had stood under a roof for protection, the Empress' feet had got very wet, and she had not changed her footwear for the rest of the evening. For some weeks already she had had catarrh, and now she had developed the cough, "very irritating, but not dangerous," as Marianna initially thought.

So it may have been for a sixty-three-year-old woman with normal lungs, but the Empress had long been tormented, not only by "my breathing difficulties," but also by a peculiar sensation of internal hardening. "I am turning completely to stone inside," she had often been heard to say. "I can feel it." And though she had always laughed about it, it was this that spelled the end for her now. As an autopsy was soon to show, her lungs were fatally congested, "with growths as hard as stones on both lungs, and the right lung hardly working at all." The cold the Empress had caught was merely the impetus to a last, desperate struggle for breath and life, with frightful episodes of near suffocation; it seems she could not in any case have survived much longer.

Maria Theresia lived nine days after her last Monday letter to Milan. It cannot be said that she did not suffer. But her deep Catholic faith sustained her: This, she believed, was the end of a mere earthly life; another life, infinitely better, awaited her. She showed no fear and no emotional distress. "I have done everything with the best intentions," she said. "I hope God will be merciful to me." To the last she heard daily mass, attended to matters of state, and talked with her children "just as if she had no other concerns but ours," as Marianna recorded. To Joseph, unusually, she spoke in French, "although generally she always spoke German with us."

Marianna and Elisabeth and Maximilian, all still living at the Hofburg, were with her constantly. Marie Christine and Albert arrived from Pressburg on Friday, the twenty-fourth of November. On Sunday the twenty-sixth, the Empress sent a note to Joseph, saying she wished to receive the last sacrament. Joseph demurred; he had not been present during the worst of her attacks, and felt this was unnecessary, "just women's hysteria." As for his beloved sister Josepha twelve years before, so now for his mother: He could not accept how gravely ill she was.

Maria Theresia insisted, and the sacrament was administered the following day. She became calmer and quite cheerful, astonishing them all. Even her breathing was easier. But in the night, her condition worsened. On Tuesday the twenty-eighth, all across the Monarchy, the churches began the forty hours of prayer for their empress—not for her recovery, which by now was held to be hopeless, but for her immortal soul. At the Hofburg, the doomed matriarch spoke words of comfort to her children. Joseph tried to reply, but was overcome, and could say nothing. He knelt and kissed her hand. "Leave the room," the Empress said, "it costs me too much to see you all like this," and the six of them were sent off to church.

Early on the morning of Wednesday the twenty-ninth, she called for Marianna, to speak to her alone. The Empress had never been enthusiastic about her plan to go to Klagenfurt, and now, in a failing voice, she made her daughter promise not to raise the subject, but to wait until Joseph spoke of it first; perhaps he would not do so at all, she said; "'perhaps everything will be different and he will want to keep you by his side.' I promised, reluctantly," Marianna recalled. "I really had to. . . . Then she blessed me again and kissed me, and called for Elisabeth, then Marie Christine."

Finally she asked for twenty-four-year-old Maximilian, for a quiet hour's talk. Though she had always underestimated her talented youngest child, she was fond of him, and even now felt a certain guilt about the celibate life that, at her own bidding, he was about to enter. Maximilian's sisters were all hardly out of the room when she sent to tell them they were not to return, not even to the antechamber, "where she could hear us coughing and snuffling." She did not want her daughters, she said, to see her die. Joseph stayed with her. In the afternoon, her physician brought her medicine, which she declined. "Thank you," she said, "but this is just meant to keep me here; I am not going to take it."

She had been sitting in a large armchair, propped up to ease her breathing. Quite suddenly, she struggled to her feet, took a few steps across to her chaise longue, and sank heavily onto it. Joseph tried to help her; she was lying uncomfortably, he said. "Yes," she replied, "but comfortably enough to die." Then she took three or four last shallow breaths, and was gone.

# XIX

# 1780-1781

In which countless tears are shed, and a certain number of new beginnings are made.

At Versailles, Louis stood with the black-edged letter from Vienna in his hand, unable to bring himself to inform Marie Antoinette. He had the Abbé Vermond tell her the next morning, waiting outside the room for a discreet quarter of an hour before going in himself to comfort her. The young Queen withdrew into mourning for the winter, leaving her rooms only to attend mass, speaking only with those closest to her, and writing only to her family. The poignant letter she wrote to Joseph has survived:

> *I am breaking down in tears as I write to you. Oh my brother, oh my friend! I can only recommend my sisters to you. They have lost even more than I have; they will be most unhappy. Adieu! I can no longer see what I'm writing.*

From her black-draped country house at Sala Baganza, Amalie was sending agitated messages to the *ayo* of her son, Ludovico, now turned seven and consequently, despite his epilepsy, in the care of male tutors in Parma. The loss of her mother seems to have reawakened the shock of her father's death, fifteen years before, and at thirty-four, Amalie felt orphaned. "It's absolutely the summit of misfortune. . . . To lose Father and Mother is something immense, particularly those such as I have lost," she wrote. "Our grief will increase every day."

But Marie Antoinette was right. It was her sisters at the Hofburg who had lost the most. Joseph did not want them there. Marianna was "like a harpy," he told Leopold, and though Elisabeth was "merely mad," he wasted no time in packing both of them off to their provincial abbeys. For good measure, he despatched as well all the other younger court ladies—"this female republic"—even offering, despite his general stinginess, to pay for their new accommodation, so eager was he to be rid of them. Only the elderly women were permitted to remain. "There's a lot of grumbling about it," he said, "but I don't care." According to Albert, Maximilian "had too much sense to ask to stay in Vienna." He set off for the turreted medieval castle of Mergentheim near Stuttgart, as Grand Master of the Teutonic Order, taking the place left vacant by his Uncle Karl, Franz Stephan's brother, who had died the previous summer.

Prince Karl's death had left a greater post vacant, too: that of governor of the Austrian Netherlands, with its seat in Brussels. Since the days of their formal betrothal, it had been intended that Marie Christine and Albert would eventually take over this "brilliant situation," as Albert called it, as joint governors. Maria Theresia had had time to sign the letters patent confirming these appointments, but now the couple hesitated. Joseph was making difficulties.

Of all the Habsburgs' territories, the Austrian Netherlands, with a population of some two million, was probably the most prosperous and the best administered. With most day-to-day affairs in the hands of stable provincial Estates, and an excellent minister plenipotentiary appointed from Vienna, Karl had had an easy time as governor, and Maria Theresia had seldom interfered. But in the six months since Karl's death, Joseph had made clear the new regime would be different: Where others saw, in each different province, time-honoured practices well adapted to local circumstances, he saw only endless examples of "the particularism he hated so much—nothing was done in the same way in more than one place." He wanted to standardize everything, with himself deciding the standards. Moreover, as his mother had done with the governorship of Hungary, he intended to make that of the Austrian Netherlands a largely representative post, keeping the reins of power to himself. He was planning major changes there, and had been talking openly and "in the most foolish and despotic way about what he wants to do with his officials in the Netherlands," as Leopold wrote in disgust. "He's going to take away their privileges and things like that."

He had already cancelled the allowance the Netherlands Estates had voted to cover the costs of the new governors' establishment in Brussels. Marie Christine and Albert were now to pay for this themselves. The income attached to the post had been reduced, and they were not to appoint any staff of their own but simply take over everyone who had worked for Prince Karl, so that Joseph would not have to pay any pensions for the latter. He even threatened the pair with a lawsuit over some land they had bought in Hungary.

The writing was on the wall. The joint governorship was not going to be the lucrative and interesting challenge they had anticipated. Recalling the wonderful time they had spent with Leopold's family, they now considered giving up all official positions and responsibilities and withdrawing to a luxurious private life in Italy. But friends persuaded them not to resign. If they did, Joseph would take it personally, and would only make things difficult for them, out of spite. They swallowed their pride, and consented to go to Brussels as arranged.

"**Marie Christine tells** me my sisters are behaving very thoughtlessly, telling everyone about everything. And she says the Queen of F. may be pregnant, and she says this would be the first miracle of our dear mother." Thus Carolina, writing privately in her diary. Marie Christine was still in

Vienna, since Joseph had forbidden her to go to Brussels before July 1781, by which time he would have paid his own visit to his new provinces in the northwest; disliking his genial Uncle Karl, the former governor, he had never been there before. Marie Christine's suspicions about their sister in France, incidentally, were correct: Marie Antoinette was two months pregnant, and this time, though she did not know it, with the longed-for son and heir.

Elisabeth and Marianna, not very surprisingly, had been complaining about Joseph's peremptory treatment of them—he intended they should be gone from Vienna even before the six months' formal mourning for the Empress had elapsed. As late as October, despite years of involvement with the Sisters in Klagenfurt and plans for her own residence there, there had still been some thought that Marianna might go to Innsbruck instead. But on the last day of 1780, just weeks after their mother's death, Joseph issued a patent despatching Elisabeth to Innsbruck, a place she had never yet been. And Marianna made her final decision to move to Klagenfurt, "hoping all the while that this would be delayed," and she might remain in Vienna after all, near her "friend." If he did try to persuade her to stay, as his wife or on any other terms, no record of it has come to light.

In March 1781, Joseph despatched a formal instruction to the governors of both provinces, specifying the powers, or rather lack of them, that his sisters were to have in their new residences. Though Marianna was to act as the Emperor's ceremonial representative, Elisabeth was not. Neither was to have any hand in the administration of the province, nor even any advisory position. They were to have no rights of decision over admission to the hospitals or any other charitable undertaking. They were not to be entitled to any service or provision from the people of the town, with respect to building or gardening, theatre or other entertainments, firewood, food or clothes. If either of them attempted to circumvent these instructions, the Emperor was to be immediately informed, and the governor would be held responsible. Paradoxically, they were still to be treated with all the respect owing to archduchesses of the House of Habsburg.

Toward the end of April, forty-two-year-old Marianna and thirty-seven-year-old Elisabeth left Vienna, with Joseph standing beside their carriages, as if to ensure their going. "The Archduchess Marianna left at seven in the morning for her Klagenfurt retreat," a courtier recorded. "The Emperor was present at her departure. She wept a great deal." A week later, it was her sister's turn. "Elisabeth has just this minute gone," Joseph wrote to Leopold, evidently wasting no time in reporting the satisfactory event. "She was crying and laughing at the same time."

**Marianna's journey down** to Klagenfurt in Carinthia lasted only three days, but it took Elisabeth and her train of fifty people a week to reach Innsbruck, much farther to the west, in the Tyrol—among the company, presumably, was the little girl she had adopted a few years before. Marianna's retinue was twice as large; she had sent most of them on ahead to ensure things would be properly prepared for her, though her astronomy-loving confessor Pater Richter and her personal physician, Anton von Störck, made the journey with her. Joseph, looking to save money as usual, had told the governors to arrange only a modest reception for his sisters. But they arrived flamboyantly enough, with a military escort and banners and plumes and cheering townspeople, Elisabeth driving through the Innsbruck triumphal arch, no longer of shaky wood and linen as it had been for Leopold's wedding, but rebuilt out of smooth ashlar stones salvaged from the old city walls. In Klagenfurt, the arch of the city gate had had to be broken apart to allow Marianna's high carriage to pass through. As was common at such an entry, she provided coins to be given to the townsfolk: Beggars from other villages were sent packing, with her 200 florins systematically distributed among the local poor. There were 14 florins left over, which the councilmen spent on drinking to her health.

Marianna and Elisabeth were both very welcome. Their presence brought prestige to the two provincial towns; it meant a lively court life, more public entertainments—including bravura sleigh rides in the frozen winters—

more visitors with large retinues and consequently more work for the craftsmen and tradespeople. For these subjects so distant from the capital, the dynasty itself now shone more brightly, and for Marianna and Elisabeth themselves, despite the official powerlessness insisted on by their brother, there was considerable benefit, too: Each of them now had a court of her own to preside over, with all the respect and freedom attendant on it. It was more than either one could ever have expected in Vienna. The English traveller Nathaniel Wraxall had observed that on the whole they had both led there "a gloomy, tedious life, immured in the Imperial Palace, almost destitute of society, obliged to attend their mother wherever she moves, and compelled to assist at ceremonies or exercises of devotion, as if they were nuns, rather than Princesses."

Marianna's new residence was not grand, but Elisabeth's, where Maria Theresia herself had thought of living, was a real Hofburg, a courtly palace, with rounded towers, a great marble-floored state hall—deprecatingly dubbed "the family room" by the Empress—and dripping chandeliers in all its handsome rooms, extravagantly furnished and bedecked with ancestral portraits. Where Marianna's palace was on the outskirts of the town, Elisabeth's was in the centre, dominating everything, as befitted a symbol of reaffirmed Hofburg power in the Tyrol. Marianna had had a hand in the design of her own new home—for years, on and off, she had been sending furniture and pictures to Klagenfurt—but Elisabeth's abode was the work of the Empress and her favoured architect, Nikolaus Pacassi. Like most of her sisters, with the exception of Marie Christine, Elisabeth had no taste for ceremony, and she accepted the splendour of her new surroundings now as more or less a stage setting for her own less formal way of living.

Though her foundation, and Marianna's, too, were exclusively for noble ladies, neither establishment was rich—the previous year, the convent hospital in Klagenfurt had actually run out of food, prompting an emergency delivery of meat, rice, and eggs from sympathetic burghers. So the two sisters quickly found themselves providing subsidies out of their own pockets. For their personal needs, however, they had money enough. At Joseph's instigation, their sisters and brothers had forfeited their own inheritance from the Empress to ensure Marianna and Elisabeth a comfortable income of 50,000 gulden per year—to be paid when they left Vienna. Though most of the siblings could afford to do this, hard-pressed Amalie no doubt took a few deep breaths before proffering her own share of the sacrifice.

CAROLINA HAD MOURNED her mother sincerely, withdrawing to the country, "my heart rent by the most natural sorrow," as she told Marie Antoinette, and for a single day—she even managed to stop Ferdinando going hunting. But alone among the sisters, she had rather benefited from the Empress' death. It gave her a measure of independence from the requirements of Habsburg politicking, and she began to think, too, that she might even be able to make some use of her powerful brother in Vienna, in a way she had not dared do with her mother. She had been surprised recently by an affectionate letter from Joseph, asking her to write to him more often, saying that, despite the many demands on his time, he would try to do the same, "and that if we were living closer he would be happy to establish himself as a member of my household—in short, a great many tender and obliging things." Without wishing to interfere in any personal matters, he said, he stood ready to help her in matters of government.

Carolina's husband was no more inclined than before to exert himself for his kingdom's welfare, and at twenty-eight, she felt it was time to renew her own efforts. At her instigation, an Academy of Sciences was founded in Naples, and she began to keep a comprehensive diary, recording the structure of her daily life and copying in large extracts from her correspondence. Though Tanucci was gone, she had not yet taken her seat in the Council of State: Ferdinando, ever wavering between relief and resentment at her keenness to engage in politics, had discouraged it. Now she insisted, and here she began to see at first hand the nobles' and churchmen's resistance to change that had stymied so many earlier attempts at reform.

She had always disliked Ferdinando's dependence on his father, and had recently scored a small personal victory in persuading him, against Carlos' wishes, to be inoculated against smallpox—losing, however, the greater battle to have their children inoculated: Seven of them were to die from the disease. More importantly for the kingdom at large, she now set in train the reform of the armed forces. Until now, Naples had relied on Spain for its defence; with no territorial threat for many decades, Tanucci had effectively ignored this otherwise vital aspect of government. Carolina saw it as a decisive step toward independence, and necessary, too, if the kingdom was to improve its standing on the European stage.

Naples and Sicily had long coastlines, yet at this point, their naval force was negligible. With no local expertise of any quality to call upon—the man currently in charge was the royal physician—she might have turned to Joseph for advice, but despite Austria's considerable coastal possessions, the Monarchy's own navy was not to be established for another five years. Instead, she approached her brother Leopold. Always on good terms with him, Carolina had by this time become probably his closest confidante, with a frequent correspondence between Naples and Florence revealing trust and reliance on her side, and concern and respect on his. His own Tuscan navy was commanded by the exceptional John Acton, a French-born Englishman in his early forties, who had made his reputation in action against Corsair pirates off the coast of Tunis. Carolina asked if she could "borrow" Acton for a limited time to help build up her own navy, and Leopold helpfully sent the man off southward, not suspecting he was never to return.

**In the months** since Maria Theresia's death, Marie Christine and Albert had been occupied with the transfer of their little court from Pressburg to the elegant city of Brussels, with its seventy-five thousand orderly and prosperous souls. They felt no great regret in leaving the more provincial Hungarian capital, where they had spent, as Albert kindly put it, "fifteen years of tranquillity." Much of that time, in fact, they had not even been there. Months of every year, particularly the winters, they had spent in Vienna. In the summers they had joined the rest of the imperial family at Schönbrunn or Laxenburg, and from time to time Albert had been required to accompany Joseph on his administrative and military travels to more distant parts of the Monarchy. They had been absent for almost a year during the Bavarian war, to say nothing of their long sojourn in Italy.

Above all, they had not had much to do in Pressburg. Representational duties had taken up time, but no real work of government had been left in their hands. And as far as court life went, Vienna, being so close, had drained much of the social and intellectual life they might otherwise have developed in their own capital. This at least they looked forward to furthering in Brussels. They had lost the reliable financial support of the Empress, and Joseph had reduced even the normal entitlements of their joint governorship, but Marie Christine complained about it to Leopold, and he sent her 200,000 gulden to soften the two pecuniary blows.

In early June 1781 they left Vienna, stopping en route with brother Maximilian in his new residence at Mergentheim, near Stuttgart. Once something of a misanthrope, at twenty-four, Maximilian had become a general favourite among his siblings. He was devoted to the Habsburg dynasty and also to its individual members—he had just returned from visits to Marianna and Elisabeth—but he generally kept his own counsel on their various foibles and failings. He thought Joseph wrong to want to force the Monarchy's territories into a single administrative mould, believing they were too diverse to be ruled in a single way, but his natural indolence had not quite disappeared, and he did not waste much breath in trying to dissuade his emperor brother. In his own charges he was dutiful without being overly ambitious. Clever, amusing, musical, he enjoyed these weeks of driving out and informal dining and conversation with Marie Christine, fifteen years his senior, and her genial husband. Of all his brothers and sisters, he was fondest of her.

They left him to sail down the Rhine to Coblenz, where they were met by half a dozen of Albert's many siblings, before crossing into the Flemish province of Brabant. And on the tenth of July they made their formal entry into Brussels, the celebrations concluding with a massive fireworks display.

Wonderful at first, this quickly got out of hand, leaving more than a hundred people injured—a presaging, could they have known it, of the troubles in store for them in their new realm: Unlike the fifteen they had spent in Hungary, their twelve oft-interrupted years in the Austrian Netherlands were to be anything but "years of tranquillity."

Their immediate difficulties were caused by Joseph, autocratically imposing all manner of political and social change, and also interfering and undermining the new governors at every turn. He could admire his sister and he was genuinely fond of Albert but, with his usual lack of perception and a dangerous lack of foresight, too, he had no idea how deeply he was offending them, nor how seriously he was exposing their territory to attack. Within months of their arrival, he ordered Prince Karl's summer palace and most of the country's fortifications to be dismantled and their materials sold, taking the proceeds for his own projects. In place of Karl's palace, he encouraged the pair to build a new summer residence at their own expense and, unconstrained at last, they set to this task eagerly.

It accorded well with their shared interest in art and architecture, and allowed Albert an opportunity to indulge his considerable talent as a draughtsman. They chose a pretty piece of land a half-hour's carriage ride from Brussels, where the ground rose somewhat to give a view over the city, and a nearby canal facilitated the delivery of the thousands of heavy bricks and stones that would be needed for the building, a princely neoclassical palace, to be named Schloss Schoonenberg-Laeken. Like Albert, its architect and interior designers were all Freemasons, and the forms and decorations of the palace played on many of the Brotherhood's signs and symbols: sun and moon, cube and globe, signs of the zodiac, and the egg, controlling the chaos of creation and encircling the soul of the world. Marie Christine was *connoisseuse* enough to appreciate it all: Though she had drawn nothing of her own since her marriage, she was confident enough of her youthful productions to display ninety-nine of them now in the public rooms of this grand new residence.

In Vienna, Joseph was gratified to learn that his sister and her husband were so actively occupied with the design and construction of their new summer palace. He knew that, thanks to the Empress' extravagant generosity, they could easily afford it without applying to him for funds, and he was confident it would keep them distracted from his own disruptive plans for their provinces.

MARIANNA HAD BY now been six months in Klagenfurt. The local people were pleased and proud to have an archduchess resident in their small town. In the Deaconess Xaveria Gasser, the convent chaplain, and her own confessor, she had found loyal friends. And, equally necessary to her active temperament, she had useful daily occupation in the small convent and hospital. But, with hands and mind busy with the day-to-day administration of convent and hospital, her heart was occupied, too, with the constant thought of her friend. "I was all the time hoping that if he came, God would take pity on me," she recorded in her *Confessions*—though what the Lord's pity should bring about, she did not say.

On the sixth of October 1781, he did come. It was Marianna's forty-third birthday, and the Sisters had arranged a public celebration of the occasion, with a hundred of the townsfolk erecting a small triumphal arch with lighted candles spelling out her name, to express their "love and gratitude for this precious gift from Heaven," as Sister Xaveria had it. Marianna was moved by the warmth of the reception. She turned away from the crowd to the Deaconess, surprising her by beginning to weep, and saying, "'I'm very happy here among you. I have never encountered such good and grateful hearts in any other place. I lived in Vienna for forty years, but no one there showed me they loved me.' And what's more," added Sister Xaveria, "she said this in the presence of a certain nobleman who had just come from Vienna and was admiring this modest little festival."

Marianna clearly meant this reproachful, not to say melodramatic, remark to be overheard by the "certain nobleman," who was surely the man she had loved so long. In itself, his presence shows that he must still have cared for her, too; he had travelled two hundred miles from Vienna, apparently in a private capacity, to be there on her birthday. And he stayed long enough to have a serious private conversation with her, in which he seems to have asked her to reconsider their relationship.

If the nobleman was a married man, he may have been asking her to leave Klagenfurt and live with him, presumably as his mistress. In this case it is clear why she would not have agreed—such a relationship would have been seen as scandalous and sinful. If the man was merely of modest birth or fortune, now that the Empress could not stand in the way, he may have overcome his hesitations, and decided to ask her to marry him. Perhaps, in the fifteen years since Marianna's descent into depression, he had married another woman, and since become a widower.

Whoever he was, and whatever he asked of her now, Marianna refused him. It cost her a mighty effort, as she relayed in her *Confessions*: "I cannot deny this was the greatest struggle, and it still is; of my own free will I had to tear myself from a passion I had never yet denied, where friendship, habit, sympathy, all were joined with love. But God gave me a supernatural strength, and I gave judgement against my friend, against my own heart. I gave it all up."

If the man was making a proposal of marriage, why did Marianna not accept him? She had a handsome income of her own. Perhaps she was still resentful of his having turned away from her so many years before. It may be that, given her age and poor health, she was afraid of an intimate life. Perhaps she did not want to return to Vienna, where none of her sisters remained to support her, nor indeed any brother but Joseph, who would certainly not welcome her. And she was exhausted, drained from the griefs and stresses of the previous months. It had been an enormous effort for her to break up her household, to disperse her large mineral and other scientific collections, and to pare her belongings down to the needs of a simpler life in the provinces. She may simply not have had the strength to make such another dramatic change in her life.

Perhaps she even felt herself too near death already, and feared the judgement to come. By sacrificing what she held most dear in this world, she might ensure her salvation in the next. If so, it is surprising that such religious heroism did not spur her to take vows as a professed nun. The Sisters of St Elisabeth seem to have thought of her already as one of them in this way, even commissioning a portrait of her dressed in their habit.

Indeed, after her friend's departure, she did her best to persuade herself that her end was upon her. She even had a small tomb built for herself in the crypt of the convent chapel, and had a slab of black marble brought from the Italian Tyrol to serve as her gravestone, and on it, all but the date of her death directly inscribed.

But in fact she was to spend the eight remaining years of her life not only administering the convent and hospital, but also hosting a lively secular court in Klagenfurt, entertaining visitors and personal friends, acting as patron of the local Freemasons' lodge, travelling to visit her sisters, and continuing her studies in the natural sciences, all the while thinking of the man she had sent away. "I know it would be much more final if I could erase him from my own heart," she confessed, "but I don't know how to do this. I don't quite trust myself yet to give up hope of our seeing each other again. I'm too weak for that, though I do try."

As far as is known, Marianna and her friend did not meet again. And though some telling hint may yet come to light, the nobleman's identity is still a secret.

# XX

# 1782-1785

In which Marianna enjoys a late view from the summit, Amalie outstays a welcome, and Carolina survives a conspiracy.

Marianna was now in her late forties, and she had grown happier, no longer beset by the romantic and religious passions that had once so tormented her. Her health was more stable than it had been, and on her weaker days, she was cared for devotedly by Sister Xaveria and the other nuns, all of whom thought the world of her. Her own rooms, light and airy, were on the eastern side of the little palace, overlooking her garden and the park, and blessed with the morning sun; there was even a balcony from which, wrapped up in woollen blankets, she could enjoy the peaceful view.

And she could feel a sense of satisfaction. Her years in Klagenfurt had been fruitful. The convent hospital now had thirty beds, and with financial help from Carolina, she had also established a pharmacy, managed by the nuns with advice from her personal physician, Anton von Störck, an expert on herbal plants and a founding father of medicinal homeopathy. Though Joseph had been closing convents and monasteries elsewhere—they were, in his view, insufficiently productive institutions, and moreover, some of them owned good confiscatable land—Marianna's Sisters of St Elisabeth were a nursing order, and so they had survived. Though an observant Catholic, Joseph insisted he knew "only two commandments, love of God and love of one's neighbour. It's much more laudable," he said, "to prepare medicine for a sick person than to spend the whole day praying and contemplating."

In fact he was keenly interested in the care of the sick, being at this time in the process of rebuilding the General Hospital in Vienna, and he had recently paid a brief visit to Marianna's establishment, where he had been surprised to find himself very satisfied with the organization and cleanliness of the whole, even remarking, "I've never seen such a nice little infirmary." He had spoken personally to each of the patients, and had then spent an hour with the Sisters themselves, "and he spoke to everyone in a very friendly way, particularly to the ones who'd come from other [closed] convents," the Deaconess Sister Xaveria recorded. "He stood in the middle of a swarm of nuns and talked a great deal about the abolition of the monasteries. 'Many people will curse me for it,' he said, 'and many will thank me.'" On his way out he had told Marianna he had been particularly pleased to find the nuns so bright and lively. "They're quite a different species from any I've seen elsewhere," he had said. Subsequently he had given Marianna money for additional hospital beds, at the same time annulling the gift by ending her institution's tax exemptions. His visit had flattered the nuns, but his was the greater benefit: They had given him ideas for his own larger-scale work and, what with the give and take, it had not cost him a penny.

Marianna had once said it would take "all her philosophy" to live in Klagenfurt, a country town of only two thousand souls. But she herself had brought it many changes. Her interest in literature and the natural sciences had acted as a magnet for other enthusiasts, encouraging well-read landowners in the countryside, for instance, to spend more time in the town. And every year, the celebrated Ignaz von Born came from Vienna to spend the month of August with her, discussing the latest fossil discoveries and experiments in electricity. She had long supported Born's lodge True Concord in Vienna, where the scientist had met Mozart—Born would later serve as model for the high priest Sarastro in the composer's *Magic Flute*. And it seems it had been Born's idea to establish a lodge in Klagenfurt, too. Just a short distance from the palace, it was named Beneficent Marianna in the Archduchess' honour, with her crown incorporated into its official seal. Though women were not formally admitted, the Brothers did host "evenings for sisters," and Marianna presumably attended at least some of these *Schwesterabende*.

Among his friends, Born numbered the writer Aloys Blumauer, whose clever and amusing essays against the power of the Church were then exciting discussion in intellectual circles across Europe. Perhaps surprisingly, Marianna herself made a point of reading his radical works. "I am only too aware of the weaknesses of our sex," she told her confessor, "and have always had the ambition to be as unlike a woman as possible in my way of thinking. I'm writing just out of my bath," she added with a marked lack of prudishness, "and I'll thank you to forget the Archduchess. I much prefer Marianna."

No doubt inspired by reports of Pompeii and Herculaneum, she had also developed an interest in archaeology, even investing 30,000 gulden—more than half her personal income for a year—in a dig on the site of the ancient town of Virunum, outside Klagenfurt. Many thousands of Roman objects were unearthed here, but of these Marianna kept only a few for herself, sending most of them to Carolina. Whether they were intended to complement or compete with the hoards being excavated near Naples, no comparison was ever made, since the ship carrying them was wrecked en route in the Adriatic, and the treasures disgorged by the earth were swallowed again by the sea.

Though Marianna was almost fourteen years older than Carolina, and the two had not been close during their Vienna years, with time they had grown more supportive of each other, exchanging letters regularly. With Amalie, Marianna had always had a special bond, and this had never weakened. She came often to Klagenfurt, staying a week or two each time, and developing a separate friendship with Marianna's deputy, Sister Xaveria—

Amalie's warm notes to the latter in her by now appalling handwriting are kept in the convent still.

The brothers visited, too, Maximilian the first to do so, Joseph always briefly, for a day or even just a few hours, Ferdinand with his heiress wife, Beatrice, appropriately leaving a generous donation behind them. But Leopold stayed longer, relishing the slower pace of life at his sister's unassuming residence, and surprised, it seems, to find himself enjoying her company. Mistress of her own life at last, Marianna had come into her own. Her health had improved, Leopold found, in the six years since he had seen her, and she had grown fatter. He made a satisfied tour of her hospital, lauded her choice of scientifically-minded friends, and even felt a touch of envy: Her pleasant days were full of interest and usefulness, yet free of the weighty responsibilities of state or family.

And it may even be that the Grand Duke—and perhaps his wife, pregnant with her fifteenth child—joined Marianna in her regular Sunday afternoon pastime, playing skittles with the nuns in her private garden.

**Joseph was on his way** to Naples, and "since I won't be in any particular hurry," he told Leopold, he intended to spend a day in Klagenfurt on his way. Since his previous visit to her well organized hospital, Marianna had risen in his esteem, though the same could not be said for Amalie, whom he had reluctantly agreed to meet toward the end of December 1783 in Rome. "As far as I can see I won't be able to escape her," he told Leopold. "I hope at least it's a short visit. She's very inconvenient for my plans." His brother had tried to reassure him. He had seen Amalie recently, and "I assure you," he replied, "you'll find her much more reasonable." On reaching Rome, however, Joseph learned she was still in "Napple," as he wrote it, and rather than being relieved, he found this too to be "most inconvenient." He liked Naples, and was fond of Carolina; Amalie's presence was bound to dim his pleasure in seeing both.

She had been there since mid-November, and so far had shown no sign of going. No doubt she appreciated the time away from her eccentrically religious husband, so distant from her in all aspects of their lives but sex: In May, at the age of thirty-seven, she had given birth to her seventh child, a second son among her five daughters, two of them twins, all of them as yet still living—over the next nine years she would have nine more children, including two further sets of twins.

Carolina was not particularly pleased to have her sister so long a guest. She herself had had a difficult year. In February, a series of immensely powerful earthquakes had destroyed the vital Sicilian port of Messina, the beautiful town itself "completely swamped," as she told Marianna, along with much of the surrounding agricultural land. Fleeing the quakes, the people had rushed to the beach, only to be drowned in their thousands by a huge tidal wave. "The King has lost so many people," she wrote—in fact some fifty thousand lives. "The survivors are in a pitiful state, they have no bread, no nothing, it's a total calamity, but we must bow our heads to God's will." Marie Christine had sent a helpful sum of money, and Marianna had responded with emergency supplies of Carinthian grain, but before they arrived, Carolina had been stricken with a nearer grief: While she had been battling to provide relief for the people of Messina, her own infant son, Giuseppe, had lain wracked by a smallpox fever. Summoned by his nurses, as she recorded in her diary, "I ran up the staircase and rushed into the room, he recognized me and grasped the finger I held out to him, I didn't leave him until his hands grew cold. Later, with the King's permission, I went again to see the still, cold body of my little boy, I kissed his hands, I held him, I kissed his feet with a terrible, painful tenderness, and then I asked him to pray for his afflicted mother." Within days, her four-year-old daughter was also dead. At thirty-one, of her ten children, she had lost four.

A visit from affable Maximilian helped to comfort her, and by the late spring, tempered by her strong religious faith and mellowed by a new pregnancy, Carolina's grief had grown quieter. A mid-May entry in her diary records an evening she and Ferdinando spent outside in the company of the handsome young Russian ambassador, later a celebrated patron of Beethoven, and himself a fair master of the violin. "I sat with the King on the balcony," Carolina wrote, "listening to Razumovsky playing."

She was fond of music and fond of the ambassador, too, as in due course, half of Europe was to hear.

On Christmas Day 1783, to her satisfaction, Carolina received word of Joseph's imminent arrival. With the ill feeling ever-increasing between herself and her father-in-law, King Carlos, she had been feeling the need of her brother's imperial support. She may also have been relying on Joseph's impervious outspokenness to give Amalie a hint to be gone. Indeed, Joseph had already begun, telling Leopold on Christmas Eve, "I've at least made her promise to go soon, because really it seems to me they've had enough of her." Just three days after Amalie's arrival, Carolina had been exaggeratedly doubting her sanity, telling Marie Christine, "She's so free of all proprieties, everyone feels entitled to behave toward her just as they like." Carolina herself was notably relaxed among people of lower rank than herself, but it seems Amalie had abandoned all distinctions, and her sister was no doubt seeking some sympathy for her exasperation with her, knowing how disapproving Marie Christine would be of the least unconventionality.

But Carolina's natural warmheartedness did not desert her. Despite constant severe headaches, and a sharp pain in her side—treated by electric shocks, which seemed to help—she spent much of every day with the rather lonely Amalie, and was considerate enough to accompany her on the usual tourist outings, which she had already made countless times, including the required visits to the ancient sites. For once, it seems, the objects being excavated were aesthetically uninspiring, "an ordinary jug, a vase with red blotches," a little statue, "almost unrecognizable," completely corroded and with a broken head, and "a great many enamelled glass buttons in the shape of little crowns," together with "flat sea pebbles and various pieces of stone or baked clay or plaster, which look very much like our plain buttons"—it seems they had stumbled into the shop of a long-gone haberdasher.

Amalie was still in Naples when Joseph arrived at New Year 1784. Her departure was to be on the fourth of January, and she had arranged to have an early breakfast with Carolina before setting off, but when the Queen woke she found a letter "with the news that she had left—this annoyed me." Amalie had not set off home to Parma, however, but had gone with Ferdinando to join a hunt at the royal lodge at Persano, sixty miles to the south, where a bad-tempered Joseph was obliged to meet them. Never a connoisseur of horseflesh, he is unlikely to have shared Amalie's delight in the elegant local bloodstock whose breeding had been set up by Carlos III in his younger days. By now she had her own stud farm at her little estate at Sala Baganza; there she had been crossing her fifty fine Parma horses with Arab and Hungarian stock, in the process becoming something of a celebrity in the business, with foreigners frequently turning up to see the results of her work and ask her advice. Marianna in Klagenfurt had benefited, too, receiving several beautiful gift-horses, and a few dogs as well, in token of the two sisters' hunting days together.

But with Amalie gone, Joseph did at least enjoy his stay. He was delighted with Carolina, though he saw her continuing sadness over the loss of her little son; he had even found the King much improved, if still mainly interested in hunting and fishing. But overall, things were not well in Naples. General affairs of government had long been left to the Queen, and though she was intelligent and diligent and genuinely interested in reform, she lacked the political skill to manoeuvre support, in her mother's clever way, or the authority to simply push things through, as Joseph himself would have done. Above all, the Kingdom's finances were in a poor state. It was not just a question of debt. The whole financial and fiscal system needed reforming, an age-old problem in Naples as in France.

Carolina had made an excellent decision in appointing John Acton to rebuild the royal navy, and his energy was such that he was soon working well beyond his original remit, even into the Kingdom's finances itself. William Hamilton, now Ambassador Sir William, praised him for it, but others were more critical of his efforts. A Sardinian envoy put the case succinctly: "Acton may be ideal for the marine and military affairs," he reported, "but he has little experience of finance. In this respect his sole virtue is a large foundation of honesty and impartiality, and his hands are untainted, a rarity here." With all his ability, Acton lacked any real competence in the management of a political economy, "which is what this country needs," the Sardinian concluded.

Most pressing was that recurrent problem of *ancien régime* Europe: taxation. Despite periodic attempts to improve things, taxes remained unfairly distributed, with nobles largely exempt and the poorest carrying the heaviest burden, with lawyers enriching themselves by playing both sides in a chaotic commercial system, and a modernizing, centralizing state turning in one direction after the next in search of steady revenues to pay for its broader reforms. Ferdinando referred all matters of state to his *maestra*, as he put it, but Carolina herself was personally no more able than Acton to reorganize the Kingdom's finances.

IN THE SPRING OF **1784,** at the age of thirty-two, Carolina became pregnant for the twelfth time. Her eleventh baby had been stillborn, and now, fearing a perilous delivery, she went so far as to make a will. But though the birth was not easy, the child arrived safely just before Christmas. It seems the Queen of France was very much in the thoughts of her sisters at this time: Just two months before, Amalie had borne her eighth child, whom she had named Antonietta, and Carolina now did the same. Marie Antoinette was her favourite sister, after all, if somewhat idle, at least as far as letter-writing was concerned: "Though your long silence is very hurtful to me," she had told her, "given the tender friendship I have had all my life and will always have for your dear person, I won't fail to write to you. . . . Do look after your precious health and think of our childhood and our friendship sometimes and don't forget me." At Easter 1785 Marie Antoinette herself gave birth to her third child, and she returned Carolina's compliment, though notably not Amalie's, in making her his godmother and naming him Louis-Charles, after her.

It had been seventeen years since Carolina had jumped out of her royal carriage in Vienna to clasp her little sister in a final embrace, before setting off for Naples. She was in a reflective mood, weakened by the latest birth and beset by the Kingdom's persistent challenges. And she had one very particular concern: Between herself and the musical Russian ambassador, Count Andrey Razumovsky, a certain closeness had developed, partly through political like-mindedness—pro-reform and anti-Spanish—but also because of their shared affection for imperial Vienna and a warm personal inclination on both sides. Their *amitié amoureuse*, however, is not likely to have been a love affair in the physical sense. Carolina had had and would continue to have many such enthusiasms for the men at her court, making easy work for detractors who sought, in the time-honoured way of attacking a powerful woman, to malign her as sexually immoral. Among them, not least was the Count Giuseppe Gorani, the professional muckraker who had already served up a similarly steamy dish about Amalie in Parma. But significantly, the comte de Damas, a long-standing friend of the Queen, insisted in his *Mémoires* that not one of her male favourites had ever "obtained the ultimate favours. This may sound incredible," he wrote, "but I am convinced of it."

Carolina was often indiscreet, however, in what she said and even what she wrote. And in her current enthusiasm, she had sent Razumovsky a number of letters compromising to herself. Realizing her mistake, she had sent First Minister Sambuca to request their return. Razumovsky had been reluctant to give them back, whether because he returned the Queen's feelings, or because he saw that her invectives against King Carlos might prove useful for Russian diplomacy. Whatever the case, Sambuca's suspicions had been awakened.

Though he had been her own protégé, appointed after her dismissal of Tanucci, in recent months Carolina herself had become wary of Sambuca, and she had been unwise to entrust this commission to him. Though she did not know it, he was in fact the leader of the "pro-Spanish"—effectively "anti-Queen"—faction, who had been meeting regularly at the residence of Carlos' ambassador, Herreira. Razumovsky was the first Russian ambassador ever appointed to Naples; until then, the Tsarina Catherine had entrusted that responsibility to her man in Madrid. Carlos disliked this sign of a new independence in Naples' foreign affairs and mistrusted Razumovsky's relationship with Carolina. Through Herreira, he had instructed Sambuca to find some way of forcing the Russian's recall. Seeing his opportunity, Sambuca had bribed Razumovsky's manservant to copy four of the letters for him, and had sent them post-haste to Madrid.

Carlos now sent an angry despatch to Catherine. The letters contained enough proof of "intrigues" to embarrass the Tsarina, who at once had Razumovsky packed off back to St Petersburg. Carolina retaliated by dismissing Herreira, an empty gesture, since he was quickly replaced. In Vienna and Florence, Joseph and Leopold threw up their hands in dismay, for nothing had been resolved: Naples was still at loggerheads with Madrid. Though in principle both brothers supported their sister in her push for more independence, they disapproved of her methods, finding them either too secretive, as with the Russian ambassador, or too fatuously dramatic, as with the Spanish.

In Razumovsky, Carolina had lost a firm political ally and perhaps her closest friend. She missed his intelligent and affectionate company, and her thoughts now turned to Leopold, so long a kindly advisor to her. She wanted a respite from the concerns and cabals of her court, and besides, there were marriage plans to settle, with a double match in the making between two of Leopold's Tuscan archdukes and two of her own Neapolitan princesses. She decided to go and see him. Without much discussion with the proposed host himself, and pointedly not informing King Carlos, her father-in-law and Leopold's, until it was too late for him to object, at the end of April 1785, she and Ferdinando and a substantial body of retainers set off from Naples on an extended visit to the north.

**Not for Carolina** the incognito all her siblings adopted to lessen the expensive and tiresome formalities of royal journeys. She and Ferdinando were to travel with full pomp and ceremony as King and Queen of Naples and Sicily. Carolina was particularly proud of the improvements she had brought about in the royal navy, so they went by sea to display one of their fine new ships, sailing up the Tyrrhenian coast to Livorno, before clambering into heavy coaches for the journey inland to Florence. Ferdinando had been reluctant to make so long a journey, but on board he was happy enough, fishing from the deck and shooting at seagulls. Once installed at the Palazzo Pitti, he would have the Boboli Gardens to wander about in, firing off his pistols at smaller birds.

En route they made a reluctant stop in Parma, as a courtesy to Amalie. It was a brief visit, and Amalie, four months pregnant with her ninth baby, does not seem to have wanted to see her sister go, in fact travelling the first part of her onward way with her. "We left Parma yesterday," Carolina wrote home. "It was very hard to leave my poor sister; she came with me in the carriage from Parma to Piacenza."

But if Amalie had wanted them to stay longer, Leopold was only half-pleased to see them at all. Though happy to show off his well administered and prosperous Grand Duchy and to encourage them toward reforms of the same kind, he surprised them by his rather distant manner. Though they had not realized it, he had been placed in an awkward position between his favourite sister and his brother the Emperor, to whom, formally, he owed obedience. Joseph had his own plans for Leopold's eldest son, Franz, now living with him in Vienna as "apprentice emperor," as the boy himself put it. Joseph had already selected a bride for Franz to suit his own political manoeuvring against Prussia: a Protestant princess from southern Germany, related by marriage to the Russian Tsarina. He had obliged the girl to convert to Roman Catholicism and had installed her in a convent in Vienna to await her fate. The composer Mozart had seen the Emperor—"Herr Ego," as he called him, with the Princess, "always kissing her hands, first one and then the other, and often both at once. I am really astonished," he told his father, "because she is, you might say, still a child."

Learning of Leopold and Carolina's alternative marriage plans, Joseph now decided to make his intentions clear to them both. A meeting was arranged for all three in Mantua, where, to Carolina's astonishment and Leopold's fuming resentment, Joseph not only dismissed their Florentine-Neapolitan project, but also reprimanded his sister for her noisy anti-Spanish posturing, and even announced his decision to demote his brother's independent Grand Duchy to a province of the Austrian Monarchy. Legally, he was within his rights to do so, and strategically, it made sense to gather all his neighbouring territories under a single governmental roof.

But Leopold had very different plans for Tuscany. He was already working on a constitution, on the model of Hungary's, that would keep the power of the sovereign in check—at least in theory. He was even planning to extend a parliamentary vote to every property-owning adult male, and in due course, as his brother's heir, to introduce the same in the Monarchy itself. Leopold's thinking was so advanced that even his loyal ministers were baffled by it; had he confided it to Carolina, she would have been amazed and alarmed. And it could not have been further from Joseph's contradictory stance of enlightened despotism: progressive change enforced by the reactionary means of the sovereign's unchallenged will. Joseph wanted to modernize Hungary, too, but to do so, he intended to discard most of the Hungarian constitution altogether, and bring the whole Kingdom under his direct personal rule. He gave orders that the royal crown of Hungary, until now held at Marie Christine's former home of Pressburg Castle, be brought to Vienna, a symbol of authority transferred.

It was useless to oppose his brother, as Leopold knew, though he parried the blow with a sharp retort, as he relayed to Marie Christine: "His Majesty obliged me to sign, in his presence, the act uniting Tuscany with the Monarchy after my death. I did it, but I told him that regardless of this piece of paper, whichever of us survived the other would do as he saw fit."

**Early in August 1785,** Carolina and Ferdinando arrived back in Naples, to a riotous welcome from their seven living children. With Antonia ("Toto") not eight months old, the Queen was already three months pregnant with her thirteenth baby. Though she suffered more in her many pregnancies than her mother had done, and sometimes objected to her husband's demands for sex, at no point did she consider her childbearing duty done. Even Maria Theresia had declared, after the birth of Leopold, her tenth child and third son, that she did not want any more children, "because I feel it weakens me and ages me greatly, not that I'd worry about that if it didn't make mental work harder for me." She had nonetheless encouraged her own daughters, at least in their early years of marriage, to produce a baby every year, and in time Carolina herself would do the same. For now, she delighted in her own motherhood, spending hours of every day with her children about her and recording daily details of their health, even while she struggled with the many intractable affairs of state.

Though Joseph liked Carolina and to a degree respected her, he had tired of her never-ending quarrels with Carlos, and for now had withdrawn his active support of her, instructing Leopold to do the same. The Neapolitan ministers were too lazy or too self-interested to be of use in any major programme of reform, but nonetheless Carolina was not alone. John Acton remained, an ally and a friend. Every day she consulted with him privately, her confidence in him as unshakeable as his loyalty to her. Inevitably, there were rumours that they were lovers, rumours fanned by the new Spanish ambassador, the caballero Las Casas, whose prime commission was no less than to bring about Acton's disgrace and have him run out of court.

Las Casas had been selected by Carlos' First Minister in Madrid, the conde de Floridablanca. A brilliant man and an energetic reformer within Spain itself, Floridablanca nonetheless nursed a hatred for the whole reforming Habsburg family. This was Joseph's opinion, and it is true that Floridablanca was fiercely hostile to Carolina at least. In his view, it was she who was masterminding Naples' emerging independence from Spain, and it was Acton who was making it practically possible. Floridablanca wanted to see Carolina discredited, banished from court, and locked away in a convent. As for Acton, if he could not be dismissed, the Spaniard was believed to be ready to have him kidnapped, or if necessary, eliminated.

Disgrace and dismissal seemed the safest way to begin, and Carolina herself opened the door to it. Though she was not having an affair with Acton, he was undeniably her favourite, and her manner with him, as with others, was often flirtatious: As Queen, she enjoyed the homage, even if diplomatically prompted, of many handsome men. The Razumovsky affair had revealed her susceptibility and her imprudence in putting pen to paper, but it had not stayed her hand, and once again, the duplicitous Sambuca had stepped in to undermine her. An ineffectual First Minister, he resented the influence enjoyed by the capable Acton, who had effectively taken his place. A little bribery and an easy theft had produced a new cache of letters handwritten by the Queen, this time to Acton. The Spaniards decided to put them to use.

With louche hints at their implication, Las Casas waved them before an outraged and hysterical Carolina and, brushing past her, packed them off to Carlos. Influenced, perhaps, by the situation in Madrid—by her own later admission, the Crown Princess had already borne nine children to men other than her husband—the King was only too ready to believe Carolina guilty. A stern missive was sent to Ferdinando, demanding he act immediately as befitted a betrayed sovereign and deceived husband: Acton must be dismissed and Carolina banished from court.

Ferdinando dithered. He did not believe there had been an affair, but he did not want to offend his father. He liked Acton, as indeed he liked anyone who removed responsibilities from his own shoulders. And besides, Acton was a good friend of Ambassador Sir William Hamilton, and Sir William was a frequent participant in Ferdinando's "Hunting and Shooting Parties," with their daily kills of 40 or 50 of "the largest and fiercest boars, as well as deer, hares, birds, foxes, wolves, and bears." The good opinion and company of such a genial gentleman, and such a good shot, could not be risked. He stood by his wife, foiling Carlos and Floridablanca, with the whole story making the rounds of all the courts of Europe. Las Casas was sent back to Madrid, to Marie Antoinette's feigned surprise: "I can't understand why the Queen didn't have him thrown out of the window at once," she remarked to her own Spanish ambassador.

Sambuca was despatched as well. "The marchese has been given a strong hint to proffer his resignation, and it has been immediately accepted," Carolina told the marchese di Gallo, her envoy at Turin—a restrained measure, in her view, "compared with what he might have feared." Indeed, with a less forgiving sovereign, Sambuca's treasonous behaviour could have cost him his life. Carolina pushed to have Acton appointed First Minister in his place, but this insult to his father Ferdinando would not countenance. Sambuca's handsome salary continued to be paid, and he returned to his native Palermo in the happy expectation of large ongoing revenues: long before, he had bought up, very cheaply, all the property of the despoiled local Jesuits.

# XXI

# 1786

## In which the tide begins to turn for Marie Antoinette.

*You will have been astonished by the dreadful story of Cardinal Rohan. Working with a certain Madame la Mothe, a first-rate adventuress, he took a diamond necklace worth 1,500,000 livres from the jeweller Boehmer, pretending it had been commissioned secretly by the Queen. He gave him a promissory note signed* Antoinette de France, *imitating the Queen's handwriting. This jeweller requested payment from the Queen. She was surprised to see the note and went straight to the King. The Cardinal has been arrested, and if they don't hang him, I don't know who'll ever be hanged again in France. I pity the Queen. She has to put up with all sorts of impertinence and bad will from that nation.*

The letter, written toward the end of August 1785, was from Marie Christine in Brussels to Eleonore von Liechtenstein in Vienna. The necklace in question was an elaborate looped arrangement of 647 diamonds, which the royal jeweller Boehmer had hoped to sell to Louis XV for his mistress Madame du Barry. The King and his lady were both long gone from Versailles, having never seen the piece; it had been left in the hands of an out-of-pocket and increasingly desperate Boehmer. Several times he had shown it to Marie Antoinette, hoping she would buy it, but, though the King was willing to negotiate, she herself had always rejected it, citing her many jewel-cases, already overflowing, and the country's own straitened financial circumstances. She advised Boehmer to break the necklace up and sell the stones individually.

At this stage of her life, Marie Antoinette was quite consciously domesticating her tastes; she was now the mother of three children, and turning thirty; in fact she was about to announce her own quasi-formal entry into middle-age, "upsetting the personal pride of quite a few people," as one baroness noted in her memoirs. All court ladies who had reached that age were from now on forbidden to wear feathers, flowers, or even the colour pink, "the Queen having indicated that she would not be wearing such things herself in future, since at her age it was ridiculous to do so. This resulted in a general wish," the baroness observed slyly, "to suppress all birth certificates."

As royal jeweller, Boehmer was often to be seen coming and going at Versailles, and it was known he was still trying to sell the fabulous necklace to the Queen—indeed, "he was complaining to all the world of his misfortune." A young woman living in one of the palace's smaller apartments, noble by rank if not by nature, and well versed in double-dealing, saw in this a money-making opportunity for herself. She was the comtesse Jeanne de la Motte, and she had already inveigled a goodly sum out of one of the less sagacious persons in her circle, the vain and venal Cardinal de Rohan, possibly one of her lovers, who had been neglecting his episcopal duties in Strasbourg for the entertaining life of the court. The Queen disliked Rohan: During a diplomatic sojourn in Vienna years before, he had made himself unpopular with her entire family by his unpriestly extravagance—and by his Derision of Maria Theresia's hypocritical weeping over the partition of Poland. But he was proud. He hailed from one of the grandest families in France, and he felt himself entitled to a place within Her Majesty's inner circle. Jeanne de la Motte had no such place herself, but by falsifying friendly little notes with the Queen's signature, she had managed to persuade the Cardinal that she did, and that moreover, she could ensure the same distinction for him. All could be managed with the help of the diamond necklace.

A correspondence ensued between Rohan and "the Queen"—in fact Madame de la Motte's current lover, Villette—which amounted to over a hundred letters. When one arrived stating that the Queen really did want the necklace, but at the moment could not afford the whole amount, Madame de la Motte convinced the Cardinal to serve as intermediary with the jeweller Boehmer, negotiating a payment-by-instalment. Boehmer himself, who as royal jeweller needed no intermediary with the Queen, was informed that, owing to the large sum involved, Her Majesty wished for the time being to keep the matter secret from the King, hence her use of a nobleman to act on her behalf. In a scene worthy of the most implausible stage play, a local prostitute was engaged to impersonate the Queen one dark night in a grove in the palace gardens, with the foolish Rohan accepting from her hand a personal note of thanks—and, suggestively, a rose.

The flattered Cardinal visited the jeweller. The jeweller was delighted. But, less gullible than Rohan, Boehmer wanted proof of the Queen's intention before he despatched the necklace to her. "Proof" was accordingly provided, in the form of a letter from the Queen, signed *Marie Antoinette de France*. In his relief at selling the necklace at last, Boehmer failed to notice that this was not the Queen's usual signature at all: As sovereign, she would have signed simply *Marie Antoinette*. But Boehmer was satisfied. He duly handed the necklace to the Queen's page—not a page at all, in fact, but Madame de la Motte's lover Villette. The piece was swiftly dismantled—in fact hacked apart with a kitchen knife—with the individual diamonds sold at bargain prices in Paris and London. As no theft had been reported, no suspicions were aroused.

Boehmer's eventual request for payment of the first instalment was dismissed by the Queen as nonsense, and she tossed his letter into the fireplace.

But his persistence brought the whole charade, very gradually, to light. The Cardinal was arrested and marched off to the Bastille, albeit to a luxury suite where he dined on oysters and champagne. The King then gave him the choice of admitting his guilt at once, in the hope of a royal pardon, or undergoing a trial by the *parlement de Paris*, not a parliament in the English sense but a high court to whom the King could delegate his own right, as sovereign, to make legal judgements. Seeing that the King already thought him guilty, Rohan opted for the latter. "From the moment of his arrest, I knew he wouldn't be appearing at court again," the Queen wrote to Joseph, "but this trial will last several months, and it could have other consequences."

She had spoken more prophetically than she knew. It had been generous but unwise of Louis to allow the Cardinal this choice, and the Queen had encouraged him for her own reasons: Confident of her innocence, she told Joseph, "I want every detail of this nightmare to be made absolutely clear in the eyes of the whole world." But a private confession might have contained the matter, with herself hardly mentioned at all. The trial was a public affair, and her name appeared at every turn, linked with all the letters and lies and impersonations, and tainted by association with the greed and duplicity of the perpetrators. It provided a focus for political machinations which undermined her standing at court and beyond. Perhaps worst of all, the fantastic story of her midnight rendezvous with Rohan in the garden grove was widely considered credible. The people of Paris, too ready to believe her guilty of lax morals, took the Cardinal's side. The men of the *parlement* cared little for Rohan himself, but they had their own reason to do the same: They were eager to exact a revenge on the monarchy, after Louis XV's curtailing of their power fifteen years before. Then they had been put in their place as servants of the crown. Now they welcomed the opportunity, handed them voluntarily by the present King, to humiliate the monarchy and declare their independence of royal judgement. Though Jeanne de la Motte was imprisoned and branded as a thief, the *parlementaires* found Rohan to be no more than an innocent dupe, and sentenced him only to exile from Paris. As he drove away into the countryside, crowds cheered him through the streets. A glow of popular fame shone round him, casting its shadow only on the Queen.

After the trial, Madame Campan found Marie Antoinette alone in her rooms, weeping and bewailing the vagaries of French justice. If even the Queen could find no impartial judges in a matter concerning her character and her honour, she asked, what hope was there for ordinary people?

THE COMTE DE MIRABEAU, a rising star in progressive political circles, was later to identify the diamond necklace affair as the prelude to the French Revolution. It revealed Louis' vulnerability vis-à-vis the Paris *parlement*, and a powerful ill will toward Marie Antoinette. In the earlier, childless years of her marriage, she had been spared public disparagement, with the blame laid on Louis for the lack of a Bourbon heir. But since then, though the King himself always defended her, she had become an ever more visible focus of grievance for his many dissatisfied subjects.

Perversely, Louis' own faithfulness as a husband had worked against her. In France, it was generally expected that the King would have many mistresses, and that his favourite among them would be designated *maîtresse-en-titre*, playing an acknowledged role at court and accruing wealth and influence along with her title. Though the King's wife might not rejoice at this, it gave her a measure of protection: The *maîtresse-en-titre* served as a lightning-rod, drawing attention and criticism away from the Queen personally and preserving the deference due her as a symbol of monarchy. Without the paradoxical shelter of a *maîtresse-en-titre*, Marie Antoinette herself had assumed that more precarious role. As a foreigner and a Habsburg, she was doubly exposed. Already, libellous and even obscene pamphlets had begun to circulate, berating her and accusing her of conducting illicit sexual affairs, including with her favourite, Madame de Polignac. In the public eye, she was no longer Her Majesty the Queen Consort, but simply *l'Autrichienne*—the Austrian.

The Swedish Count Axel von Fersen had remarked as much, returning to

Versailles finally after his years of service with the revolutionary armies in America. He had seen that the Queen received no public acclamation when she visited Paris in the spring of 1785, following the birth of her third child, Louis-Charles. Crowds of people had turned out to see her, but they had remained sullen and largely silent, with only occasional cries of *Vive la reine!* to be heard, apparently from individuals paid by the police. At court, indeed, it was rumoured that Fersen himself was Louis-Charles' father, since he had been at Versailles when the boy was conceived. But it is unlikely. The loudest whispers about it came from the mouth of Louis' brother Provence: As next in line to the throne, he had most to gain should the King's sons be declared illegitimate. Certainly, Fersen was a great favourite of the Queen, and always included in her private circle, but the King's own conjugal visits had continued as usual, and he gave no sign of doubting the child's paternity. Marie Antoinette had even drawn his attention to the rumours as evidence of increasing hostility toward her personally, and asked if she should stop seeing Fersen, but Louis had brushed this notion aside. He trusted his wife, and besides, he had other, very serious concerns.

The public coffers of France were empty. Indeed, they had been so since 1738. Long years of financial mismanagement, undertaxation of the country's wealth, the ruinous Seven Years' War, the loss of income from former colonies in Canada and India, all had contributed to the deficit. Not least, a vast sum had been conjured up to help the American revolutionaries in their war for independence from France's age-old enemy, Britain.

It had seemed to be worth doing, for economic reasons as well as political. Before the war, Britain's merchants had been doing very well out of trade with the Americans: Their finished goods, including robust practical furniture and agricultural tools, had been much in demand in the still pre-industrial colonies. Louis and his ministers had been confident that, following a British defeat, the Americans would swiftly and permanently transfer their custom to France, giving a hefty boost to trade revenues and gradually repaying the French war debt. Though France's Treasury had been in deficit for forty years already, Louis had insisted there should be no new taxes imposed to finance the American war. In consequence, most of the money had had to be borrowed, with the Director-General of the Treasury, the former banker Jacques Necker, maintaining confidence in the country's solvency and ensuring continuing credit by concealing the extent of the debt. Daringly, Necker had broken with ancient precedent in making public the Kingdom's accounts. Less daringly, or perhaps even more so, he had falsified them: By a mélange of arcane computing and outright deceit, he had made the huge deficit look like a comfortable surplus.

Above all, Necker had bet on a short war with Britain, probably only a single campaign. But there had been five campaigns, five years of fighting, and for the French, five years of borrowing money at increasingly high interest to fund their own involvement. To add insult to injury, the expected boost to trade receipts from America had not eventuated: The politically liberated colonists had remained commercially loyal to the British. And the new American government itself was in financial difficulty: After declaring independence, it had stopped its loan repayments to France, its largest creditor. A post-war British-French trade treaty had flooded French markets with cheap manufactured goods from England's more advanced industrial towns, putting hundreds of thousands of local people out of work. Even an attempt to reduce royal expenditures had miscarried by reducing work for the makers of luxury goods. Not least, a series of price-depressing overabundant harvests, followed by several years of bad weather and food shortages, had turned hard lives desperate for a growing population of peasants who, even at the best of times, had little or nothing to spare.

Necker was no longer at the head of the Treasury, though he remained influential. He had been replaced as Comptroller-General of Finances by the comte de Calonne, a protégé of the Polignacs, now venturing into higher politics without the Queen's support. After repaying his debt to them in sinecures and cash, Calonne had set in train a hefty programme of confidence-building public works—improving roads and canals, building factories and foundries, and encouraging investment in new enterprises. Some of the money for this came from French and international private sources but, ominously, much of it came from the already indebted crown, effectively borrowing from itself on the sophisticated Paris stock market, in the hope of future gains. "These temporary measures suspend the deficits and with inconceivable ease the complaining turns into applause," wrote Ambassador Mercy to Chancellor von Kaunitz in Vienna. "It is morally impossible for this anarchy to continue for long without producing some catastrophe."

MARIE ANTOINETTE HAD BEEN opposed to Calonne's appointment, having realized belatedly that his Polignac supporters had been abusing her friendship in their quest for money and position, and that her connection with that "voracious circle," as Mercy referred to them, was partly to blame for her public unpopularity. But for the moment, she had a more immediate concern: She was expecting again. In July 1786, she gave birth to a daughter, Sophie, named for one of Louis' aunts or, it was whispered, though Marie Antoinette had never met her, for the sister of Axel Fersen. The Queen had not wanted this fourth child. She did not want to be like Carolina, bearing one baby after the next—Amalie, too, had twelve children already, including newborn twin daughters. As Marie Antoinette told her brother, with two sons living, she considered she had fulfilled her dynastic duty, and for herself, she had a daughter: Marie-Thérèse was now seven years old. Joseph scolded his sister for her irresponsible attitude to childbearing, inveighing against "the young women nowadays who think it's fashionable to separate from their husbands, believing they've done their duty once they've had one or two children." But Louis took his wife's part, and there were to be no further pregnancies. From this point, apparently by mutual agreement, the King and Queen stopped sleeping together.

Despite much gossip at the time, and much speculation since, it does not seem that Marie Antoinette had already taken Fersen as her lover, or that she did so now. Certainly their relationship was one of some intimacy, but there is no evidence that it was consummated, and it may not have been sexual at all. Joseph thought his sister "rather prudish by nature"; more pertinently,

Fersen kept mistresses throughout the years of his friendship with Marie Antoinette, making a serious affair with her less likely. Comparing the Queen with the woman he was then living with, he later admitted he needed "both sacred and profane love," with "sacred love" not religious fervour, but the intensely idealistic passion of the early Romantics. Fersen was a staunch supporter of the monarchical system, with an inbred tendency to admire and even worship a beautiful queen. Marie Antoinette had been and probably still was in love with him. But if he felt the same for her, respect and caution would seem to have kept his physical desire, for the moment at least, in check.

AS IF HER HUMILIATION over the diamond necklace affair and the strain of an unwanted pregnancy had not been enough, in the early months of 1786 Marie Antoinette had also had to endure the nuisance of a visit from her bantam-sized brother Ferdinand and his matronly wife, Beatrice, travelling incognito from their residence in Milan. Piqued at being sidelined by Joseph's forced reforms in his own territory of Lombardy, Ferdinand had resolved to absent himself altogether, setting off on an extended European tour. But though in age only eighteen months apart, even in childhood brother and sister had not been close, and Marie Antoinette had made no particular effort for him at Versailles, delegating all arrangements to Mercy and keeping to her own rooms as much as courtesy allowed. The visit had remained formal, and she had been relieved to see Ferdinand and Beatrice go.

She had not been left in peace for long. Disconcerted by the diamond necklace affair, Joseph had sent Marie Christine to sound the terrain at Versailles. She arrived, together with Albert, in the summer of 1786, and she was no more welcome than Ferdinand had been. The two sisters had not seen each other for sixteen years, and since then, Marie Antoinette was convinced, Marie Christine had been relaying unfavourable reports of her from gazetteers and other gossips to the family in Vienna and elsewhere. Consequently, she was not disposed to like her. Like Carolina, who had warned her about their sister's snooping, she found Marie Christine personally intrusive, and very pointedly would not invite her to the *petit Trianon* in the park, this "little house the Queen had built for herself," as Albert described it, her own escape from the formalities of the court, and the place where she felt most at her ease. She went so far as to ask Mercy to keep her away, especially when Albert went deer hunting with Louis, telling him, "If it's at all possible, make it clear that I reserve those days for my own affairs and I like to be alone, so that she won't ask to come, because that would really be a nuisance to me."

On a visit to Paris, Marie Christine and Albert attended a session of the restive *parlement*, admiring a marvellously eloquent address by one of the advocates, sadly wasted on a good number of counsellors who spent the whole time "in a deep sleep." In the city streets, they saw many demonstrations of support for the King, but also much animosity toward the Queen, so much in fact that, though she did accompany them one evening to the entrance of the famous *Théâtre de la Ville*, she would not go inside to see the performance with them, "for fear of not being greeted as warmly as she used to be there."

Taking a meandering, scenic journey home to restive Brussels, they wrote to Joseph of their concerns over his intended reforms in the Austrian Netherlands, warning him of the resistance he would encounter, and offering to mediate, but they received only the brusque reply that "when it was a question of establishing a system that was for the common good, one must not allow oneself to be stopped by the opposition of corrupt or indifferent or lazy people." At the end of September they arrived home to find, as they had expected, few corrupt or indifferent or lazy people, but a very great deal of angry opposition to Joseph's plans for change.

# XXII

# 1787–1788

In which Marie Christine attempts to prevent revolution, Louis' burden shifts to Marie Antoinette's shoulders, and Carolina is assaulted by Ferdinando.

Toward the end of 1786, two edicts had been published in Joseph's name announcing sweeping ecclesiastical and educational reforms in his territories of the Austrian Netherlands. On the first day of January 1787, further edicts announced a radical centralization of government and bureaucracy. The existing layers of autonomous provinces and cities, with their own administrative and legal and commercial procedures, were now to be subsumed into a single Council of Government headed by one man personally appointed by the Emperor. But the complex old arrangements, developed piecemeal since medieval times, were not going to be easy to disentangle. For the moment, most officials simply shrugged and carried on as before.

The religious reforms, however, met with immediate resistance. Long under the yoke of His Most Catholic Majesty, the King of Spain, and with an unusual tradition of local involvement in the management of Church affairs, the Austrian Netherlands retained a deeply Catholic identity at every social level. Joseph's attack on the Church was thus felt viscerally. Young seminarians and monks dispossessed of their monasteries took to the streets, to be met by mounted dragoons, ordered in by the head of Joseph's new council, Count Belgiojoso, "an idiot Italian, crafty perhaps, but brainless," at least in the opinion of Chancellor von Kaunitz.

Joseph kept Belgiojoso in place nonetheless, and pressed on in his clumsy, determined way, forcing through immediate changes in the taxation of the provinces and in their laws and customs, not least abolishing the inherited sinecures which the nobles had for generations regarded "as part of the family silver" and reducing the number of lawyers—these two steps alone guaranteeing him a cadre of influential and highly skilled opponents. To Marie Christine, he had himself once praised the intelligence and competence of the Austrian Netherlands' provincial elites, ranking them far above those in any other part of his territories, and had he proceeded more sensitively now, he would no doubt have met with more success. As she recorded in the political journal she was keeping through these troubled months, "I'm convinced if we'd been allowed to speak to them earlier, things wouldn't have come to this extremity."

She and Albert were themselves in agreement with some of Joseph's reforms, but not with their hasty implementation. They saw and heard the daily resistance of the local people, and their indignant claims to the rights accorded them by their existing constitution, which had held the sovereign's power in check since 1356. Both of them sent complaining and explanatory letters to Joseph and to Kaunitz, pleading with the former to act less imperiously and with the latter to make him see reason. "The most restive are the poorer townsfolk who are looking to gain from a revolution or general pillage, and the peasants who've been stirred up by fears of military conscription," Marie Christine told Kaunitz. "But there's a frenetic spirit of liberty everywhere, among the women too." Even Marie Antoinette was chastened to hear of the difficulties her sister was facing. As Mercy reported to Joseph, "The present situation seems to have made her more sympathetic to the Archduchess than might have been predicted from her earlier sentiments."

Kaunitz remained unmoved. He had spent some time *en poste* in Brussels, and he waved away Marie Christine's appeal now as exaggerated. Joseph, dismissive of constitutions as getting in the way of his personal decisions, paid no attention at all to the letters. By now he had other affairs in hand. In the spring of 1787 he was in the Crimea with the Tsarina Catherine, celebrating Russia's annexation of the peninsula after its war of 1768–74 with Ottoman Turkey. By the treaty ending the war, the Ottomans had granted the solidly Muslim Crimea independence as a Tatar Khanate but, despite French protests, the Russians had taken control of the territory for themselves.

Joseph had made this journey with some reluctance, given Austria's alliance with France. But he needed Russia as a bulwark against Prussia, and secretly, he also hoped to gain some Turkish territory when, as seemed only a matter of time, the Russians dismembered the ailing Ottoman Empire entirely—Catherine was already planning to capture Constantinople. So Joseph had accepted her invitation to meet him in the newly claimed peninsula. And here, the emancipator of serfs and religious outsiders purchased a little Circassian slave girl, perhaps in memory of his own lost daughter, in any case to be brought up safely at his court.

Once returned to Vienna, he was surprised to find that everyone he encountered thought he should modify or at least delay his reforms in the Austrian Netherlands. His response each time was an obstinacy so ferocious, it was thought he might actually have become mentally unhinged. His friend Eleonore von Liechtenstein, having suggested a more temperate approach, exclaimed he had turned on her "looking like a lion about to devour me." In Brussels, Marie Christine had received "very strong representations from the local Estates, demonstrating the most determined defiance," with deputies "absolutely insisting on the dismissal of Belgiojoso and all foreigners from the management of local affairs." Joseph responded by sending more troops to Brussels, threatening to despatch his entire army of three hundred thousand men if necessary, and instructing Marie Christine and Albert to return to Vienna at once. But thousands of people were already in the streets, sporting cockades in the local colours of yellow and red, as distinct from the

Habsburgs' yellow and black—though Axel von Fersen, visiting at this time, observed some opportunistically wearing all four colours together.

The revolt of the Austrian Netherlands was an ambivalent phenomenon. Though defending their constitutional right to limit the sovereign's power, in itself a progressive stand and a key feature of Enlightenment political thinking, many of the rebels wanted to use that right to protect arch-conservative structures, such as noble privilege and the power of the Church. This paradox was reflected in the two main rebelling parties: the conservatives, who wanted a return to the status quo ante, and the French-influenced radicals, who wanted more democratic representation and secular voices added to the Estate of the Clergy. For the time being, both parties had agreed to mute their differences to form a united front against the Emperor.

Joseph still believed he could rely on his sister's popularity, and Albert's, to smooth over his rough-and-ready changes. But public sentiment had turned against the two once celebrated governors. Now they were suspected of playing a double game, pretending to temper Joseph's reforms while secretly supporting them absolutely. "The people's confidence in us is completely lost," Marie Christine recorded in her journal early in July 1787. An attempt to obey Joseph and leave the country seemed likely to trigger an armed uprising. "The uproar at the news of our departure was terrible," she continued. "It seems they absolutely will not allow us to leave." They were at least able to move from the tense city to their summer palace of Laeken, where they sheltered for eleven days before sneaking away in the middle of the night.

The Ottomans, in the meantime, objecting to the violation of their treaty, had demanded the return of the Crimea, and on the nineteenth of August, they declared war on Russia. Though he had no high opinion of "these cursed countries with all their diseases, plague and famine," Joseph felt that, given his private assurances to Catherine, he would soon have to send troops to defend her claim to them. To Leopold he remarked, with stunning obliviousness to the actual situation in his own territories, that at least there would be no need to send troops to the Austrian Netherlands, since he had "patched up the mess there."

His insouciance was all the more astonishing given the instability in the neighbouring Dutch Republic, where a years-long republican revolt against the ruling House of Orange had recently been put down by Prussian intervention. Problematically for Marie Christine and Albert, this had sent tens of thousands of defeated and radicalized Dutch citizens fleeing across the border, to enflame passions further in the Austrian Netherlands.

THE PRUSSIANS had saved the Dutch royal House of Orange, but the British had supported them, too. In consequence, on the doubtful premise that my enemy's enemy is my friend, the French monarchy had provided a brief display of military might, without any actual fighting, in support of the Dutch republicans. Among the officers now on leave from the inactive French regiments was Marie Antoinette's Swedish friend, Axel von Fersen, who arrived in Paris late in May 1787, in time to witness the closing sessions of the first Assembly of Notables. Fersen was impressed by the very fact of its quasi-democratic existence, telling his sister that nothing similar was likely to be seen again "in our days."

Louis had invented this Assembly to circumvent the opposition of the Paris *parlement* to his proposed financial reforms: This was critical, since the *parlement*'s jurisdiction extended far beyond the capital to cover half the country. The King and his Comptroller-General Calonne wanted to broaden the tax base and make it fairer: The current burden of taxation lay most heavily on the peasants and day labourers, with the nobles and bourgeois paying little tax and the clergy none at all.

In theory, the French monarchy was absolute, with the King supposedly receiving his authority directly from God and holding it by "divine right," so that Louis could dictate whatever laws he wanted. But in practice, he needed the *parlement* to register the legislation he decreed before it could take effect. If the *parlementaires* did not like it, they could refuse to register it. He could override them if necessary, standing on his prerogative as an absolute monarch, but this, in a time of increasing challenges to the very idea of absolutism, he was unwilling to do.

Marie Antoinette saw things differently. She had also grown up in an absolute monarchy, with her mother a source of apparently uncontested power and, indeed, an object of reverence because of it. She knew nothing of the many compromises the Empress had made behind the scenes to see her plans carried through with the least possible friction. With less excuse than his youngest sister, Joseph, too, had ignored the strategic give-and-take of his mother's long reign, and was behaving now as an out-and-out autocrat, expecting to be obeyed without question. Politically unsophisticated as she was, Marie Antoinette felt Louis should do much the same. She regarded the *parlement*'s refusal to register his reforms as similar to the anti-reform revolts in the Austrian Netherlands—as a failure of duty, tantamount to disobedience or even ingratitude, on the part of the sovereign's subjects.

But Louis was a reading man, well abreast of Enlightenment thinking about the role of kings and the increasing claims of ordinary people to political representation. He was not a democrat, but he sensed the changing balance between rulers and ruled. In temperament anything but imperious, he was ready to make concessions to see his reforms enacted. Hence his decision to convoke an Assembly of 144 "notable" men, all clergymen or nobles or wealthy bourgeois selected by himself. His hope had been that this Assembly would accept his reform plan, which could then be referred back to the *parlement* with the stamp of approval from a supposedly "popular" body.

In Vienna, news of the Assembly was greeted with derision. Joseph regarded it as a pseudo-democratic farce set up by Calonne to give himself a veneer of public support. Kaunitz was even more direct. "This ridiculous thing is an utter pantomime that the King's been obliged to adopt," he told Mercy. "It's—pardon my French—a piece of shit in every respect. There's only one way for the King to increase his revenues and that's in the reform of administrative abuses and the reduction of expenses."

The outcome of Louis' first Assembly proved, in any case, profoundly disappointing to him. The 144 carefully selected *notables*, supposedly a "popular" voice, had proved no more cooperative than the men of the *parlement* had been; indeed, in some cases, they were the very same individuals, and they included most of the country's printers and publishers, who had been able to manipulate the issues at hand in their own interests, obscuring the benefits to the less well placed that reforms might have produced. In the resentful and rebellious mood of the times, no one believed the King was seeking to improve the lives of his ordinary subjects. Though royal household expenditures amounted to a fraction of the state's budget, and interest on the national debt alone accounted for almost half, it was easier to blame the country's woes on an incompetent king and his profligate foreign queen. Louis had bowed to what seemed to him inevitable: He dismissed Calonne, and in his stead appointed the archbishop of Toulouse, Loménie de Brienne.

Brienne was an energetic man with a keen appreciation of his own talents, who liked to compare himself to those other great political Churchmen of France, Cardinal Richelieu and Cardinal Mazarin. He quickly came to dominate the cabinet of ministers at Versailles, but Louis, jealous of his easy influence over his colleagues, repeatedly withheld the authority he needed to act effectively. Within a few weeks, with no further progress made, Louis dissolved the Assembly of Notables altogether: In due course, he would dismiss Brienne himself, leaving the post of Comptroller-General perilously vacant.

"The King is still weak and mistrustful," Axel von Fersen reported to King Gustav in Sweden. "He has no confidence in anyone but the Queen, and it looks as though it's she who's doing everything, the ministers often go to her and inform her about all their business." But though Marie Antoinette's political stock may have risen at Versailles, in Paris, and in the country at large, she remained disliked and mistrusted. In a creative response to this, and no doubt recalling Maria Theresia's success in a similar role, she now sought to present herself not as a political actor but as Mother of the Children of France, and by implication, mother of the nation. It was an image that suited her instinctively, and it was rendered more plausible by her marked gain in weight over the previous few years. She was almost thirty-two, still attractive and still with her naturally stately bearing, but with the extra pounds, and now a soft double chin, she had begun to look quite matronly. Motherhood became her, which politicking had never done.

From Elisabeth Vigée-Le Brun, she had commissioned a large-scale portrait depicting herself in this motherly role, to be displayed at the Royal Academy in this same summer of 1787. But the voice of her previous ill repute proved too loud for the soft new melody. Though a fine and serious work, with the Queen dressed in quietly sumptuous red velvet and her children posed appealingly about her, the portrait failed spectacularly in its redemptive mission. The sudden death of her infant daughter Sophie in June had necessitated a partial repainting; the work was not ready in time for the August salon, and to its empty frame a malicious note was now attached, referencing Marie Antoinette's recently acquired sobriquet, *Madame Deficit*.

In the same month, hoping against hope, the King returned to the Paris *parlement* with an amended reform plan, and for once, he was supported by his often antagonistic brothers, Provence and Artois. But the plan was rejected on a formality: Only the Estates-General, said the *parlementaires*, was competent to approve it. That assembly, which had not met since 1614, represented the three "estates" or social orders of France: the Clergy, the Nobility, and the Commoners. Calling for the Estates-General was a way for the *parlement* to circumvent the King, as he had circumvented them by calling an Assembly of Notables. Moreover, many of the *parlementaires* had a right to sit in the Assembly of the Estates-General themselves: They were confident that, if the King did call it, they would dominate it anyway.

IT HAD BEEN CLEAR for some time that Louis was not well. Though only thirty-four, he had become clumsy and confused; he was unsteady on his feet and often fell asleep at council meetings. He was indecisive and inconsiderate; at times he even had lapses of reason. His cousin and enemy the duc d'Orléans, who may already have been seeking to dethrone Louis and set himself up as regent to the six-year-old dauphin, put it about that the King was a drunkard; certainly he was drinking more than usual, and eating more, too: Always big in stature, he had now grown fat. He was spending a lot of time hunting, seemingly in an effort to find distraction; in the evenings he would return exhausted, to closet himself with Marie Antoinette and weep.

The King's depressed and fragmented state of mind took its inevitable toll on the Queen. Weakened by the death of her infant daughter the previous summer, already anxious, with public opinion loudly against her and the health of the little dauphin deteriorating, she began having attacks of panic and breathlessness. In recent months, beset by troubles and with her husband overwhelmed, she had turned more frequently to her religious faith for consolation and guidance, and it was no doubt from this source that she drew the strength now to assume part of the responsibility that Louis could no longer carry. She stepped forward nervously and not without criticism from those who felt she should keep out of governmental affairs, but she began attending cabinet committees, and at one point, the King was even seen waiting in the salon at her little Trianon Palace while she consulted privately with ministers.

On one issue of vital significance, her stance may even have been decisive. In the autumn of 1788, the Council of State met to decide whether or not the number of commoners' representatives in the forthcoming Estates-General should be doubled. Traditionally, each Estate had three hundred members: Those of the First Estate stood for the country's one hundred thousand clergymen, those of the Second Estate its four hundred thousand nobles, with the three hundred men of the Third Estate representing the country's remaining nineteen or twenty million commoners, from the wealthy to the desperately poor. Though there was as yet no question of a truly balanced representation, a doubling of the Third Estate would at least give the commoners equal voting numbers with the other two Estates, provided each man's vote was counted individually. Louis favoured a doubling: He needed the commoners' support in pushing the clergy and nobles to pay new taxes. Behind the scenes, Marie Antoinette had been persuading other council members to this way of thinking. And at their final meeting in December 1788, she was, exceptionally, personally present to observe their compliance. The vote for doubling duly passed.

But on the whole, the Queen's belated arrival on the political scene achieved little. Lacking preeminent qualities of intellect and leadership, to say nothing of her inexperience, she was in no way equal to the task now at hand. "There are two major deficiencies ruining this monarchy," Mercy wrote to Joseph, "the lack of boldness and energy in the character of the sovereign or his representative, and the lack of money in the monarch's coffers. This second problem could be remedied, but as for the first, it seems it cannot."

JOSEPH WAS NOT unduly concerned about the unrest in France or even the continuing trouble in his own Austrian Netherlands. He had other things to think about. Since February 1788 he had been on campaign near Belgrade, leading his troops in a defensive stand against the Ottomans. With him had been Leopold's dour twenty-year-old son Franz and, for the first time in the history of the Austrian army, a substantial number of Jewish soldiers—Joseph's recent patents of religious toleration were beginning to take effect. But his campaign had not been going well: By the end of the year, without a single battle fought, he would have lost eighty thousand men, almost a third of his army, killed by disease or taken into Ottoman slavery. His war as Russia's ally was proving almost as costly as the Seven Years' War of his boyhood. Worse, the Hungarians who had provided most of his soldiers were not only resisting fresh conscriptions; urged on by the Prussians, they were actually plotting rebellion against the Monarchy and the establishment of an independent Hungarian state.

Carolina briefly considered coming to her brother's aid by sending troops into Ottoman Albania. That country could be speedily overrun, she was assured by Joseph's overreaching ambassador, and one of her young sons installed as its king. She still had ambition enough to envision herself acting independently on the international stage, though John Acton, her First Minister *manqué*, managed to dissuade her from this plan. But it was clear she was not well. "I think the same as you on the subject of the Queen of Naple's health," Joseph wrote to Leopold now. "I'm quite concerned about it, actually more about her than the illness itself, though that's very serious, but to turn her into a calm and moderate person you'd need to melt her down and start all over again." Always impulsive and often histrionic, Carolina had recently become excessively anxious as well, even convincing herself that a general European war was about to break out. And she was worried about her most dependable advisor. "We've had Acton very ill with a liver attack," she told Leopold. "It's the result of his sedentary life and his overworking. God forbid we should lose him."

But it was not Acton's malady that was of greatest concern. As Joseph had implied, Carolina herself was suffering from a serious illness, and not for the first time. She had syphilis, transmitted to her by her serially unfaithful husband. Worse, Ferdinando was in denial—not about the infidelities, but about the disease itself, for the best remedy of the day was slow and painful, and he did not want to undergo it. Late in July 1788, a week before giving birth to her fifteenth child, Carolina had "opened her heart" to Leopold, giving him the whole sorry story, much of it a repetition of earlier letters to him, but now with an appalling new turn.

She had known she was infected at the birth of her son Francesco eleven years before, and again five years later with her daughter Amalia: She herself, and both babies, had shown signs of the disease. Whether she had been repeatedly infected, or the symptoms of the same infection had been more or less apparent over the years, she did not know: Her physician thought the latter, and had now announced to Ferdinando "the absolute necessity of having the mercury treatment for a complete cure." Previously he had submitted only to baths, silk plasters, enemas, and suction cupping, and now he was refusing to take anything but teas made of "Indian wood." His gruesome symptoms were not abating. Carolina's own included fevers, fainting fits, painful bouts of urine retention, and an ulcerous sore in the vagina, giving a periodic green discharge. So she had relayed to Leopold, and so he now told Joseph.

The two brothers, themselves very much men of the world, took the existence if not the transmission of the infection in their stride, but the new turn of events shocked them both. Seven months pregnant and fearing for the baby's health, Carolina had refused to sleep with Ferdinando. "He wanted to force me," she told Leopold. "I was in tears. I pleaded with him to spare me, to consider he might infect the child, to consider his own state, he was dripping pus, to think how painful it would be for him, but I couldn't convince him." For four hours she had resisted, weeping and pleading. "Finally I gave him what he wanted and sacrificed myself, and as soon as the brutal act was finished, he started crying and shouting, cursing the act, saying it had been painful and had opened the ulcers and a thousand awful things like that. Even today," she concluded, almost two months later, "I can't understand why he demanded this sacrifice of me."

Leopold hardly knew what to advise her. "It's not easy," he replied. "I confess the whole thing has left me astonished, angry, shocked, indignant. The King should never have exposed himself to such a danger to his health"—the silk and fishskin condoms of the day would have protected him—"but after what happened his first duty was to cure himself and not risk your health and poison your deliveries and the health of his own children, but really the last scene is unbelievable, if we'd been private persons I can tell you I know what I'd have done . . ."

Ferdinando had accused Carolina of having given the infection to him, and had said the same to a Spanish spy. "He said that to pierce my soul," she wrote, "and how he succeeded! After twenty years of marriage and fourteen children, to think that of his wife." Leopold brushed this aside as pure calumny. It was well known in Florence, he said, that the King had caught the disease from his latest mistress, though it was possible the Spaniards had been circulating the contrary rumour, since "they're looking for every means of separating the King from you"—Ferdinando being infinitely more manipulable without his determined wife.

But the brother's gallantry had its limits. In the end he counselled resignation. "You have to spend your whole life with him," he wrote. "He's your husband and the father of your children. I can only advise you to put a good face on it and don't tell anyone about it, and once you've delivered this child make sure you're thoroughly and finally cured and insist the King do the same, properly for once, and don't sleep with him until he's fully cured, that's quite just and reasonable, but don't reproach him for this incident, and in future try not to leave him alone, follow him everywhere, so that he'll have no reason to pretend to suspect you, and so that your presence and authority will deter those who might inflame him against you."

Carolina was now only three weeks away from the delivery of her child. Of the fourteen she had already borne, she had seven daughters and two sons living. "I'd like to have a son," she told Leopold, "but a strong one, a healthy one, and I'm afraid the baby I'll bring into the world will be feeble and miserable and I'm even more afraid it will be another girl which I confess would really upset me." Late in August, the child arrived, a weak little boy. He lived only a few months.

Ferdinando did not undergo the proper cure that Leopold had advised. His symptoms worsened and his moods became ever more unpleasant. He called on one physician after the next, always hoping to hear better news, but each one told him the same: In order to be cured once and for all, he would have to submit to radical mercury treatment, in itself poisonous and potentially life-threatening. He refused, though for several months Carolina was at least spared the ordeal of having sex with him. But he insisted on watching her swallow the medicine prescribed for herself, "and he was most annoyed to see it didn't give me the troubles he'd had when he took it, painful urination and so on."

Toward the end of the year it seemed she had recovered, with the physicians recommending a resumption of her wifely duties, "but I'm very afraid I'll be the sacrificial victim since I'm convinced the King is not cured. He thinks he is and he won't hear the word mercury pronounced, he flies into a fury if anyone mentions it. He says he vehemently, furiously desires to sleep with me, and for the love of peace I can't deny him any more; I'm only waiting until my courses come and then I'll be fulfilling my cruel duty once again. . . . It's only to you, my dear brother, that I dare tell all this."

This letter, marked *top secret*, reveals a brutal aspect of Ferdinando's immature and irresponsible character, but it shows, too, how very little a woman of this time was worth, even a mother of princes, even, perhaps, in her own estimation. No letter of this period survives from Carolina to any of her sisters, but none of them in any case could have given her advice much different from Leopold's. She might have protected herself by withdrawing to a convent, but that would have meant giving up the almost hourly contact with her children which formed the bedrock of her emotional life. She devoted herself instead to keeping the whole matter from them, "concealing, palliating, suffering everything so the children don't notice anything, so they won't lose respect"—for their father, and perhaps for herself as well.

Leopold had relayed the ongoing details of the affair to Joseph. He was disgusted with Ferdinando, but felt he could do nothing to help. He had recently returned to Vienna after nine fruitless months on campaign against the Ottomans. Much of that time he had been ill, and he was still weak and feverish. "It's so excessively cold here," he wrote to Carolina, "I don't yet dare go outside."

# XXIII

# 1789

In which an oath sworn on a tennis court changes history, the royal family is forced from Versailles, and Marianna goes to her eternal rest.

In the spring of 1789, France's failing monarchy reached the point of no return. At the beginning of the year, Louis had summoned a meeting of the Estates-General for early May. The Estates had not met since 1614; the 175 years since then had been years of comparatively strong absolute monarchy in France, and it was a measure of Louis' weakness as king that he was summoning them now. The call was answered by some twelve hundred men, representing all regions of the twenty-eight million people of France. They were to decide on questions of financial and other reforms that the Paris *parlement* and Louis' special Assembly of Notables had failed to decide.

The meeting was held in a newly constructed hall near the palace of Versailles, and as Louis entered, dressed in a suit of gold cloth, he was greeted with cries of *Long Live the King!* from all the assembled men. Behind him walked Marie Antoinette, once again grown thin and looking older than her thirty-three years, despite her dauntless white gown laced with silver, and the white heron plume in her hair—though, significantly, no necklace. She was drained from the stresses of the previous months, above all the wasting consumption of her seven-year-old son, the dauphin Louis-Joseph. Besides, the present assembly represented many forces opposed to her husband's authority, and she had long feared it.

The Estates' first duty was to verify that the deputies present were those who had been duly elected. This should have been a formality, and indeed, for the Clergy and Nobles, it was, but the Commoners delayed, insisting on one clarification first: Should the verification of each individual deputy be reported, that is, by head, or simply that of their Estate as a whole, that is, by order? It made a difference, for with the recent doubling of the representatives of the Third Estate, there were now about as many men in the Commons as in both the other Estates together. The procedure for verification was sure to be a precedent for the subsequent voting procedure: If voting was carried out by order, the First and Second Estates could be expected to vote together, and outvote the Third; if it was by head, the Third Estate would be likely to prevail. The delay lasted almost three weeks, during which time strenuous efforts were made by all parties to reach an agreement, but on the twenty-sixth of May the discussions ceased: They had reached an impasse.

On the third of June, the determined Commoners invited the Clergy and Nobles to join them in a combined verification by head. It was an extraordinary invitation, potentially overturning the ancient divisions of the Kingdom to create a single body representing all Frenchmen together. Though this was a clear challenge to the monarch's authority, the Commoners' sympathies were still overall with Louis, and they looked to him now, declaring they would accept no intermediary between the King and his people. It was a moment for decisive leadership, but at this critical point, Louis absented himself. He withdrew to his private rooms in the palace, doubling the guard on the doors to ensure the importuning deputies could not force their way through to him, and eventually betook himself with his family to the smaller château of Marly. It was not weakness or fear that had driven him to this, but grief, for on the fourth of June, covered in sores and wracked with pain, the little dauphin had died.

In her memoirs, lady-in-waiting Henriette Campan says it was believed at Versailles that Marie Antoinette preferred her robust and lively younger son, four-year-old Louis-Charles, to his sickly elder brother. But others tell of her constant tenderness to the long ailing boy, and of his great attachment to her. "He begged her to dine in his room with him the other day," another court lady reported. "Alas, she swallowed more tears than bread." The death of a son, less than a year after the death of an infant daughter, was a bitter blow to the Queen, who, as Joseph had said, was more a mother than anything else. As for Louis, pressed repeatedly to receive deputies from the Third Estate, he could only utter the pitiful reply, "Are there no fathers among them?"

The dauphin's body was interred with those of his Bourbon ancestors in the Basilica of Saint-Denis in Paris, and his heart at the Benedictine convent of Val-de-Grâce. As First Prince of the Blood, Louis' cousin the duc d'Orléans was expected to accompany the latter relic on its journey, but in a further attack on the King, he excused himself, pleading his duties as a deputy of the Nobles' Estate. It was the least of his occupations. Half the radical pamphlets of Paris were being sold, safe from police interference, from the grounds of his splendid Palais Royal, which had become a quasi-headquarters for the politically disaffected. A Freemason and a longtime opponent of absolutism, he favoured a constitutional monarchy along British lines, with power effectively in the hands of the Third Estate, who saw him as one of their own heroes—he supported their demand for election verification "by head." Louis distrusted his charismatic cousin, while Marie Antoinette regarded him with an intense dislike that was just as intensely returned.

On the seventeenth of June, emboldened by the defection of nineteen priests to their ranks, and led by the comte de Mirabeau, defector in spite of himself—the nobles of his province had rejected him—the Third Estate declared themselves the true representatives of the people of France, under a new name, the National Assembly, and "by this act alone gave birth to representative democracy in Europe."

To this momentous event there was no public response from the two usurped Estates, and even Louis was at first remarkably relaxed about it—"It's only a phrase," he said. But three days later, when the Third Estate arrived at their usual place of meeting, they found the doors locked and guarded, by order of the King. One of their number, a certain Doctor Guillotin, suggested they meet instead at the nearby royal tennis court, indoors in the manner of the day. There, squashed in amid a crowd of spectators, they swore not to disperse until the King had granted France a constitution "fixed upon solid foundations"—effectively, by recognizing their power and limiting his own, starting with voting not only "by head," but also "in common," with all three Estates combined in a National Constituent Assembly.

Three days of frantic meetings ensued. Ironically, a deputation arrived at Marly from the Paris *parlement*: Seeing the revolutionary writing on the wall, they were at last ready to agree to the reforms they had so long rejected. But as they now saw, it was too late. They had been overtaken by events partly of their own making.

Louis was inclined to concede combined voting, and Necker, who had regained his post as Director-General of the Treasury, suggested the King might even ignore the Assembly's declaration and himself instruct the three Estates to join together, so arriving at the same position while preserving his sovereign authority. Marie Antoinette initially also supported combined voting, but was gradually persuaded against it by the King's brother Artois. With an extraordinary interruption of the Council of State and an emotional appeal to the rights of his children, she managed to change Louis' mind, and to convince him, tragically, to present a set of lesser changes as a charter, issued and amendable only by the King, rather than in the form of a constitution, drafted and equally amendable by the Assembly.

On the grey and drizzly twenty-third of June, Louis returned to Versailles, to cheers from the First and Second Estates, but silence from the Third. Necker, not wanting to seem complicit in the announcement to come, had tactically absented himself, giving rise to angry suspicions that he had been dismissed. The King's long efforts to work with the Third Estate to raise the taxes of the other two had come to an end. In a historic statement, Louis announced that a constitutional monarchy was to be established—not, however, with one Assembly, as the Commoners had demanded, but in partnership with the Clergy and Nobles. If those present would not accept this, he would declare it on his own sovereign authority.

Louis believed that, in establishing a constitution, and voluntarily ceding a great deal of power, he was making a heavy personal sacrifice. He was an absolute monarch, after all, and in the eyes of the law, which he respected, he was entitled to remain so. But in practice he had lost real authority long before, as the deputies knew. The Third Estate saw his action now as a betrayal, and henceforth turned against him.

Louis instructed the deputies to disperse: The three Estates were to meet the next day in their traditional form, separately, each in the hall allocated to it. The Assembly flatly refused, and general uproar ensued. In letters to Joseph and Kaunitz, Mercy described the next three days as "the most violent crisis I have seen in this country," with France "in the most imminent danger of famine, bankruptcy and civil war." The King's cousin Orléans took this opportunity to abandon the Second Estate, going over to the Assembly with some fifty other noblemen. On the twenty-seventh of June, prompted by a fearful Marie Antoinette, and in a last attempt to maintain at least the illusion of royal authority, Louis did as Necker had suggested: He commanded the rest of the Nobles, and all the Clergy, too, to join them. Though it was now renamed the Legislative rather than Constituent Assembly, since it could enact laws of its own without the King's seal, from this point the existence of a single-chamber Assembly was official.

After this meeting, several thousand people swarmed to and even into the palace of Versailles, challenging the bodyguards, looking for their hero Necker. For half an hour Marie Antoinette pleaded with him not to resign: Without his reassurance, she feared, the crowd would become violent. Necker went out to them, to rapturous acclaim, and eventually they dispersed, but the vulnerability of the royal family was clear. Even Orléans took fright, and began to seek a reconciliation with the King. Louis gave orders for troop reinforcements to be brought in from the provinces.

Since the spring of 1789, there had been intermittent riots in Paris and beyond. Shortage of bread was the prime impulse behind most, but it was soon combined with political protest, particularly in the capital. Louis had acted to provide more grain, but delivery of relief supplies from further north was blocked by military conflict, for Sweden and Russia were at war. The grain depots of Paris had been ransacked, and on the thirtieth of June, a mob four thousand strong attacked the Abbaye prison in Saint-Germain-des-Prés. Within a few days, there were thirty thousand soldiers near Versailles, half of them not French at all but Swiss and German regiments, with Axel von Fersen hoping, in vain, that his own regiment would be sent to join them. Foreign soldiers, it was presumed, would be less susceptible to the radicalism fast spreading among the locals—and, as others believed, less hesitant to control the French populace by force. A major insurrection in Paris seemed imminent, but it was to defend Versailles from its overflow, rather than to attack the capital itself, that the troops had been summoned. Within this *cordon sanitaire*, transferred if necessary to the château de Compiègne—to which the crown jewels were now removed—Louis could guide the Assembly through the implementation of the constitution he had announced on the twenty-third of June.

But the Treasury's Director-General Necker had not been present at that meeting. He did not support that constitution. Clearly, he would have to be replaced by a minister who did. On the eleventh of July, while dining peaceably with his family, the people's hero received a letter from the King, informing him, in remarkably friendly tones, that he had been dismissed. "The departure of Necker," Mrs. Swinburne wrote to her husband, "was the signal of explosion." By the twelfth of July, the capital was out of control. An English resident, driving fearfully along the rue St Honoré, was horrified by a bloody head thrust through the window of her carriage, at which sight, she said, "I screamed and fainted away, and had I not had an English lady with me, who had courage enough to harangue the mob, and to say that I was an English patriot, they certainly would have murdered me."

With extremists urging the people to violence, the city's small royal force withdrew altogether. On the fourteenth of July, some eighty thousand people, sporting cockades and banners in Orléans' colours of blue, white, and red, broke into the huge military edifice of the Invalides. They seized thirty thousand muskets and several cannon, before surging to the weakly defended fortress of the Bastille, where the powder for the muskets was stored. Once a feared prison, it now contained only a handful of inmates. They were at once set free, but the governor was set upon and killed. Mutineers from Louis' *Gardes françaises* showed the rioters how to use the muskets, and they began their rampage in search of further victims, with the governor's head affixed to a pike before them.

"We are living years in a few days here, or rather in a few hours," the Spanish ambassador wrote to his alarmed First Minister Floridablanca, himself a supporter of political reform. "The taking of the Bastille lasted less than two hours."

And on the last day of July, a peg-legged American businessman—supposedly, a perilous leap to escape a jealous husband had cost him a limb—sent a private letter to his friend George Washington, Esquire. One of the celebrated Founding Fathers and an outspoken opponent of slavery, Gouverneur Morris was nonetheless a decided elitist by temperament and conviction, and he deplored French ideas of pure democracy advocating the transfer of political power to the uneducated, as he told the newly inaugurated President:

> *This Country is at present as near to Anarchy as Society can approach without Dissolution. . . . You may consider the Revolution as compleat; that is to say the Authority of the King and of the Nobility is compleatly subdued, but yet I tremble for the Constitution. They have all that romantic Spirit and all those*

*romantic Ideas of Government which, happily for America, we were cured of before it was too late.*

THOUGH THE ROYAL AUTHORITY had been "compleatly subdued," as Morris put it, the people of Paris still wanted to see their king. Locked in council at Versailles, Louis could not decide what to do. The Baron de Breteuil, a protégé of the Queen's who had replaced Necker and was now Comptroller-General of Finance, urged the royal family to transfer the court to the eastern city of Metz, some two hundred miles from volatile Paris, where there was a strong citadel: From this safety the King might negotiate a new constitution, retaining a powerful role for himself. Marie Antoinette supported this idea, but the Commander of the King's forces felt his troops could not be trusted to escort the royal family and, as the duc de Provence insisted, if the throne were left vacant, it might be claimed by the King's cousin Orléans, now being fêted in Paris.

The historically-minded Louis was also keenly aware of what King Charles I had done when challenged 140 years before in England: He had abandoned his capital, and in the end it had cost him his life. He decided to stay, but commanded his brothers to leave France, along with the Polignacs and other courtiers close to him. Provence flatly refused to go, but Artois, having begged Louis on his knees to flee with them, took the road to Brussels, spitting with anti-revolutionary bile. Marie Christine was not pleased to see him there. By now her own supporters were being denigrated as "royalists," and his presence only added fuel to the smouldering local fire.

Breteuil fled, too, supposedly disguised as a monk. In his haste he neglected to resign his post, so that, although the Assembly immediately reinstated Necker, the King and Queen both continued to regard the Baron as the legitimate minister, and their own prime representative outside of France. Breteuil's escape was mimicked by hundreds of terrified aristocrats, who now rushed for the borders dressed in their servants' clothes, a first wave of indignant and burdensome émigrés whom Carolina would soon be describing as "pestilential vermin." They included Marie Antoinette's favourite Gabrielle de Polignac, into whose hand the weeping Queen pressed a purseful of gold coins—a loan, she said, to be repaid in happier times.

That lady's place as governess to the royal children, eleven-year-old Marie-Thérèse and four-year-old Louis-Charles, was taken, after some hesitation, by the formidable duchesse de Tourzel, a staunch believer in royal authority as ordained by God, who referred to the two children now in her care as "divinities." Marie Antoinette had need of her, for most of her friends were gone and, if Madame de Tourzel is to be believed, "Most of the royal family's servants had been won over by the agitators and were acting as spies, passing on the most precise details of what they were doing."

Among the few allies who remained was the Queen's lady-in-waiting, Madame Campan, and her first friend, the Princesse de Lamballe, who insisted on remaining with her despite being urged to flee. Axel von Fersen also stayed, and from this point he spent ever more time with the Queen. In his memoirs, the comte de Saint-Priest, who remained as head of the King's Household, writes that these *rendez-vous* caused a public scandal, insinuating that the two were lovers, but neglecting to mention his own grievances against them both: that the Queen had declined to support him for the position of Foreign Minister and, more tellingly, that his much younger wife was herself embarrassingly in love with Fersen. As the latter had told his sister in Sweden, "She has become crazy over me. There is no kind of humiliation to which she has not submitted herself . . . everything a woman can offer a man."

Louis did present himself to the people of Paris, to the Queen's distress: She believed they intended to arrest or even assassinate him. He was not in danger, though his bodyguards were prevented from accompanying him beyond a certain point. But he was met with cries of *Vive la nation!* until he agreed to the constitutional demands of the Assembly and accepted a cockade in the blue, white, and red of his enemy Orléans, already metamorphosed into the revolutionary tricolour. At that point the cries changed to *Vive le roi!*

> *My dear Sister, The ambassador will send you all the news from here; I don't have the strength to do it myself. But don't think I'm lacking in courage; I assure you I have plenty, and you need much more of it to endure the continual humiliation and difficulties that we're constantly subject to, than you would if you were in immediate danger. . . . If only our sorrows and misfortunes can lead to a happier future for my poor child after us. Praise heaven he is only four years old, he will get used to the way he will have to live, and never know exactly what we were. . . . I love him with a passion. . . . His sister is with me almost all day now, and I'm very pleased with her. All in all if we were just ordinary private people, we would be perfectly content in ourselves.*

So Marie Antoinette wrote to Carolina, late in the summer of 1789. The Neapolitan ambassador had already sent his report of "the appalling shock that has overturned this monarchy for a century at least." And though Marie Antoinette felt in no immediate danger, the ambassador did not agree. "The situation now is more violent than ever," he had continued. "We are on the brink of a second revolution that will be more ferocious than the first. The royal family is already in the custody of the people, and it makes me tremble to think of them completely abandoned into their hands."

Though the royal family was still at Versailles, it was true they could not have left easily. The King spent the rest of the summer in anxious negotiation with the National Assembly, who had begun drafting their historic *Declaration of the Rights of Man and of the Citizen*, while the Queen remained largely in retirement, in constant attendance on her children. But since the spring, ever louder rumours had been spreading of a royal flight abroad, or even of the King's abduction by counterrevolutionaries. The radical lawyer-turned-journalist Camille Desmoulins was claiming the Queen was plotting to join her brother Joseph to encourage an attack on France. Others thought Marie Antoinette might be returned to Vienna against her will. "I'm always afraid they'll force her to leave or oblige the King to send her away," Leopold now told Marie Christine, "because they're deliberately spreading horrific slanders to stir up the people against her, even in the provinces, saying she's sent all the money to Vienna, she's behind all the taxation, she's caused poverty everywhere etc."

In Paris, the unrest showed no sign of abating. Mobs of armed men were joined by thousands of angry women demanding bread for their families. Silver from the royal household was melted down to pay for more, but much more was not to be had. Calls grew louder from all political factions for the King to come to the capital. In Paris, it was believed, he could more easily be observed; he would be better placed to address the government's divisions, and might even be able to increase supplies of grain. Meanwhile, denunciations of the King and, more especially, the Queen continued at Orléans' Palais Royal, with agitators looking for an opportunity to force an open confrontation.

They found it in the standard banquet hosted in Versailles' little opera house on the occasion of a change of garrison. It was nothing out of the ordinary. The King and Queen had not even expected to make an appearance, but had relented in response to the soldiers' enthusiasm to see them. It was an army dinner, with many toasts and raucous singing, which the anti-royalist press, led by Desmoulins, swiftly decried as a sacrilegious orgy defaming *la Nation* and the revolutionary tricolour.

It may have been Orléans himself—certainly Marie Antoinette believed so—who on the fifth of October incited the marketwomen of Paris to march the twelve miles to Versailles, in rain and dense fog, to demand bread from the King in person. Their arrival was terrifying. Seven thousand strong, many were armed with scythes or pitchforks, pikes, muskets or daggers.

Urged on by *agents provocateurs* paid by Orléans, they roared for the Queen, shouting they would make cockades out of her entrails. The Versailles *Garde nationale*, loyal to the Assembly, began a skirmish with the King's bodyguards, with a general *mêlée* avoided only by the arrival of the *Garde nationale* from Paris, under the command of the marquis de La Fayette, now sporting the less aristocratic moniker of plain Monsieur Lafayette. By evening, the situation appeared to have been brought under control, and at two o'clock in the morning, the household finally went to bed, the King and Queen to their separate apartments.

But the women had not dispersed. They were bivouacking outside, under what shelter they could find. At half past five, through an entry left treacherously unlocked, a group of them broke into the palace. They killed two guards and cut off their heads, then made for the Queen's apartments, meting out the same fate to the guard outside. Hearing his last cries of "Save the Queen!" her ladies-in-waiting had locked the inner doors. They had time to rush her in her nightshift to the King's apartments, before the women burst in and slashed the fabrics of her bed to pieces.

Lafayette had slept through it all, but once woken, he was quickly able to drive the women out to the rest of the throng, now clamouring for the King and Queen. They appeared, together with their daughter and the little dauphin. The people shouted for the children to retreat, before aiming their muskets at the Queen.

She did not move. Seeing the bravery of this dishevelled figure, draped in a yellow dressing-gown, the volatile crowd sent up a new cry: "*Vive la reine!*" One loud voice shouted, "The King to Paris!" and at once it became the demand of thousands.

Louis agreed to go, seeing this as the only way to avoid further bloodshed, but he insisted, unnecessarily, that his family go with him; it seems he expected to calm the people by this show of trust in them. The four of them rode in a single carriage, together with Louis' twenty-five-year-old sister, Elisabeth, and the governess, Madame de Tourzel, with Axel von Fersen following behind. Arriving six hours later at the Hôtel de Ville, Louis was handed the keys to the city, without apparent irony on the mayor's part, before being driven on to the Tuileries palace, adjacent to the Louvre on the right bank of the Seine.

One of the royal pages later described the Tuileries as "that prison disguised by the name of palace," but it was not a prison, and the royal family, at this point, were not considered prisoners. An extension of the vast Louvre, the Tuileries had once been the official Paris residence of the King, but since the building of Versailles a hundred years before, it had fallen largely into disuse. Some of the rooms had been let out to private occupants, and in the early days of her marriage Marie Antoinette had occasionally stayed there after a late night in the capital, but though the gardens remained a popular place for the public to stroll, by now the palace itself was hardly habitable: unheated, with no staff and no functioning kitchens, and not even enough beds. For the first few nights, the royal family's attendants—half the court officials had followed them—had to sleep on chairs.

The men of the Assembly, since October meeting in Paris by public demand, were well aware of the situation. They quickly voted the handsome sum of 280,000 livres and employed some eight hundred workmen to have parts of the palace refurbished, with good furniture transferred in the meantime. The King's apartments, on the first floor, soon included an atelier for his locksmithing. The Queen had six rooms on the ground floor, overlooking the terrace, and the children slept here with her—"I prefer to have them near me," she said. In due course her bedroom would be elegantly redecorated in blue and silver, with marble and gilding and precious woods. She had four thousand books brought from her own library at Versailles, and at this early stage, perhaps expecting to make it their primary residence, she and Louis even began to discuss a major renovation of the whole Tuileries palace.

Fersen was a frequent visitor; he had given up his Versailles house and taken rooms nearby. His real importance now was as an intermediary between the royal family and those loyal to them, including his own King Gustav III. Marie Antoinette was nervous about sending letters, as she told

Marie Christine, currently with brother Maximilian in Bonn. The Queen's antipathy to her had evidently softened, as she reveals in this, the only one of her letters that survives among Marie Christine's papers:

> *How good you are, my dear sister; your letter moved me to tears; yes, it's impossible that anyone could disapprove of two sisters assuring each other of their friendship and asking for and giving news of each other, and I wouldn't have hesitated, but I don't want anyone in the postal service to come across my handwriting; it's so easy to copy it and add something to a letter that I have to take the greatest precautions; that kind of wickedness is the only thing I'm afraid of, since I defy the universe to find I've done anything really wrong. . . . Adieu my dear sister, I embrace my brother and brother-in-law with all my soul; think of me sometimes and tell yourselves, when the three of you are all together, that there exists a heart that, though far away from you, is always united to you by the truest feelings of tenderness and attachment and gratitude.*

Fersen at least could move freely in and out of the palace, even if others could not. Indeed, Lafayette had instructed that the entrance he used be left unguarded, though not unobserved. It seems he was hoping to gather evidence to have the Queen tried for adultery, which might necessitate a divorce. Fersen was at the palace almost every day, encoding and delivering countless messages, and at times even drafting the Queen's letters himself. The King's portly brother Provence, who had refused to go into exile, refused equally to stay at the Tuileries with the rest of the royal family. He decamped instead to the palais de Luxembourg, leaving his sister Elisabeth to voice their shared principles of inflexible reaction.

Despite his apparent acceptance of the calmed situation, Louis was by no means resigned. Six days after arriving in Paris, without even informing those of his ministers who remained, he sent a secret letter to his cousin the King of Spain, "head of the second branch of the Bourbon family, to deposit in your hands my solemn protest against all those acts contrary to royal authority which have been extracted from me by force since the 15th of July of this year, and at the same time, to accomplish the promises I made in my declarations of the 23rd of June."

The men of the Assembly had already begun drafting a new constitution to establish France as a constitutional monarchy, with the King's powers limited by a directly elected body meeting in a single chamber, without distinction of Estate. Though Louis appeared to accept this, he had not abandoned hope for a continued *ancien régime* monarchy in partnership with the Clergy and Nobles, and he expected his cousin to assist him in regaining his royal authority with a view to implementing it. But the King of Spain was no longer the formidable Carlos III, who might have taken such steps. For ten months already he had lain in his tomb, and his throne was now occupied by his lumbering and dimwitted son, Carlos IV, spouting the decisions of his wife, Maria Luisa, sister of Amalie's husband Don Ferdinando. The shocking news arriving from France had weakened Spain's reformist First Minister Floridablanca and turned the court reactionary, but despite much monarchical huffing and puffing by the royal pair, neither of them was to prove of any help to Louis or his family.

*I was pleased to see the Emperor's letter. He seems to be getting better and better. At the same time I was very sorry to hear of your sister Marianna's illness. I know how much pain this will give you.*

Thus Ferdinando to Carolina, on the twentieth of November, 1789. But though his sentiments were kind, the King's news was out of date on both counts. For Joseph's condition was in fact worsening, and the very day before, at the age of fifty-one, Marianna had come to the end of her mortal life.

She and Carolina had been good friends. If their relationship was not quite so close as Marianna's with Amalie, it had perhaps been more equal, without the mother-and-daughter overtones of the other. She had been accustomed to writing to Carolina every three weeks or so, and she also seems to have told her of her hopes of marriage, and not necessarily to her "friend": after her death, mentioning the newly widowed Elector Karl Theodor of Bavaria, who, at seventy, was seeking to marry again, Carolina told her daughter, "I think Marianna would have accepted him willingly." Very little of the sisters' long correspondence has survived, but it was the inveterate epistolarian Carolina who had kept Marianna informed of much family news, particularly about the reluctant letter-writing Queen of France, who had at least asked that her Vienna letters be forwarded to Klagenfurt. Through Marianna's eight years at the convent there, she had repeatedly received money for the hospital and other practical help from Carolina. In a period of famine only the year before, she had sent large shipments of grain from Naples for the hungry people of Carinthia; now she announced a donation to the convent of 1,000 florins annually, to be paid for the rest of her own life.

Given her unsteady health, Marianna had long been prepared for death, specifying the details of her own burial shortly after her arrival in Klagenfurt. Since then, with the help of her court ladies, she had been embroidering a set of ecclesiastical vestments in black, white, and gold silk, works of great beauty, to be worn by the celebrants at her own Requiem Mass. In the same Christian resignation and hope of salvation, Maria Theresia had once embroidered such vestments for herself.

Like her mother, Marianna had suffered for years from her damaged lungs, breathing with ever more difficulty. She, too, had grown fat until, hardly able to walk, she was spending her days in a cushioned wooden wheelchair. But quite suddenly, in the early autumn of 1789, she had lost a great deal of weight. Soon she had been unable to leave her bed, and in the first week of November, wearing a plain nightshirt of her mother's, she had received the last sacraments.

In the morning of the nineteenth of November, Sister Xaveria sent for a priest. Marianna was well enough to converse with him, through tears on both sides; she had been feeling worse every day, and had asked the Sisters not to pray for her recovery, but rather that she should have "a happy hour of death." She weakened throughout the course of the day, with the Sisters tending to her constantly. "Deaconess, you know something about the sick," she said to Sister Xaveria. "What do you think, will I really die today?" "To console her," replied her deeply religious friend, "I told her I found her much worse than she had been yesterday."

It was the feast-day of Saint Elisabeth, the founder of their Order. "I hope she'll be good enough to take me hence today," Marianna remarked. "I'll forgive her if she comes late this evening. They'll be celebrating her name day in heaven, and she won't have much time before then." She asked whether the post had arrived. "I only want to know how the Emperor is," she said, "and Marie Christine in the Netherlands, and the Queen of France"—all three, as she knew, in poor and perilous circumstances. There were indeed letters from the first two. Her chamberlain read them to her.

Though her stoical mood did not fail, Marianna's last hours were not easy. "Can the last agony be worse than this?" she asked Sister Xaveria. "Oh, I feel I'm going to suffocate any moment." The good Sister reassured her she was approaching her end "with very swift steps." And at eight in the evening, Marianna kissed her hand in farewell to her physicians and the weeping Sisters, and took her final leave.

Though she might have been laid to rest in the imperial crypt in Vienna, she had chosen instead to be buried in the little convent chapel, with a space reserved beside her for the loyal Sister Xaveria. As she had requested, there had been no autopsy and no embalming: Indeed, her chamberlains had been instructed to pour lime over her face, to hasten its disintegration. They duly did. Her body, as yet uncorrupted, which the Sisters regarded as a miracle, was dressed in a shift of her own making, embroidered with grey silk thread that had been her mother's. The funeral took place three days after her death, with no one present but the Sisters and the local clergy. But eight nuns carried her coffin afterwards through the town, so that the people could mourn her, and they did so "with indescribable wailing, loud sobs and weeping," before the coffin was brought back to the chapel to be interred. On the simple wall-stone had been engraved only Marianna's name, and the epitaph she had given herself: A sinner.

**Marianna had already** made a will before her departure from Vienna in 1781, but in the weeks before her death she had composed a new and very different one in which, apart from a few small family bequests, she left most of her personal fortune to the Elisabethan Sisters, and the rest to the poor—they included, in her understanding, the impoverished nobles of the district. Joseph, aware he was nearing his own end, was charitable enough to waive the death duties on her bequests.

Sister Xaveria had had a portrait of Marianna's body made lying on her funeral bier, and now offered to have three copies made of it—for Amalie, Carolina, and Elisabeth—without apparently thinking of Marie Christine or Marie Antoinette. Amalie was glad to accept, but Carolina and Elisabeth declined the grim memento. Carolina sent a lyrical demurral: "Her image will live indelibly in my soul," she wrote. "It's too painful for me," said her straightforward sister.

Amalie was deeply affected by Marianna's death. The closest of all her sisters in their Vienna girlhood, she had also been the most frequent visitor to the Klagenfurt convent, developing friendly ties of her own with some of the nuns. She was now a melancholy and restless forty-three, "continually needing a change of situation," as the Spanish minister at Parma reported to Madrid. Amalie had reason enough for melancholy: Of her sixteen children, seven had already died; in the past year alone, she had lost four daughters, two within the last two months. Parma did have an heir, though of the three sons she had borne, only sixteen-year-old Ludovico remained. She and Don Ferdinando now spent very little time together, and even if his conjugal visits to her country house at Sala Baganza continued, she had probably passed the age of childbearing. "My dear sister is happy," she told Xaveria Gasser, "but we are unhappy, since we have lost her."

Amalie requested a rosary or prayer-book of Marianna's, "and please do let me know if I can be helpful to you in anything," she wrote, "since my sister recommended you to me." But her big blue lapis lazuli rosary beads had already been sent to Marie Christine, who had asked for them. They had once belonged to Maria Theresia, who had given them to her eldest daughter the evening before her death; Marianna had then given them to Xaveria the evening before her own. Learning this, Marie Christine offered a little half-heartedly to send them back for Xaveria to keep for herself, "if you request it," but as this was accompanied by a present of fifty ducats, Xaveria did not ask for their return.

Marie Antoinette, no doubt still overwhelmed by her quasi-incarceration in the Tuileries, does not seem to have written to Sister Xaveria at all. She had never replied to the chamberlain who had kept her informed of the progress of Marianna's last illness and of her death. Late in December, Ambassador Mercy was obliged to respond on her behalf.

"THE EVENTS IN France are of a nature and a kind that have never happened since the world has existed, they've never been heard of in any history," Joseph wrote to Carolina. "It makes me shudder. If I could know my sister was 100 leagues away from there, or with me, if I could carry her out of there on my back I would do so, then they can do what they want, I don't care, I could watch all their indignities quite calmly, but as it is I am not easy for a moment, her health and her fate are of the keenest concern to me. I am beset by constant anxiety, I can't be of any help to her, for her own good I even have to avoid anything that could look as if we were sharing information." Carolina herself, normally very stout-hearted, admitted, "In her place I would be dead, I would never have had her courage."

Joseph loved Marie Antoinette, but Joseph was nearing his end. His place as emperor would soon be taken by forty-two-year-old Leopold, who had not seen his sister for more than twenty-four years, when she was a child of nine. He had not been close to her in his boyhood, and he had had no opportunity to get to know her as she became a wife, a mother, and a queen. Had Joseph lived, his strong feeling for her would surely have informed his official reaction to her predicament, and may even have made a difference to her fate. Leopold was genuinely concerned for her safety, asking Marie Christine even now to "let me know what you can of the Queen. I know the ferocity the whole nation bears toward her and the infamies they've blamed on her for so long." But his lack of any deep personal connection to Marie Antoinette meant that he viewed the upheaval in France, and her plight within it, through primarily political eyes. His assessment of the situation now, at the end of this momentous year of 1789, remained cool and formal. He foresaw a difficult period for the French, but not for himself or others. As he told Carolina, "This state of affairs in France won't finish soon without a civil war and inconveniences for my sister, the rest is nothing, since that will leave them useless for years and they won't be able to meddle and intrigue any further in the affairs of Europe . . ."

Even in the brief remainder of Leopold's life, he was to have ample time to realize his mistake.

# XXIV

# 1789-1790

In which a second United States is founded, Leopold becomes Emperor, and six cousins enter into marriage.

Marie Christine and Albert had not wanted to return to Brussels. The volatile situation they had so anxiously escaped showed no sign of settling. Once again, as before their appointment as governors, they had considered withdrawing to a private life in Italy and, as a last resort, Albert had even volunteered to join the Emperor on his campaign against the Ottomans. But early in 1788, following the grand imperial wedding of his nephew Franz, Joseph had sent them unceremoniously back to Brussels. Despite all the unrest, he still expected to exploit what he believed was their continuing general popularity to push through his reforms. By now, however, the pair were impossibly compromised. Throughout the nine provinces, two contradictory but equally correct opinions were held about them: They opposed the high-handed implementation of the reforms, and at the same time, they would not do anything to prejudice the House of Habsburg.

Joseph had confused things further by appointing two new ministers, each with full independent authority and answerable only to himself: the Military Commandant d'Alton, a trigger-happy Irishman who Marie Christine thought "horrible, a foreigner with no heart for the Monarchy." Replacing the "idiot Italian" Belgiojoso as minister plenipotentiary was the intellectual lightweight, or so Marie Christine regarded him, Count Ferdinand Trauttmansdorff. The Count was instructed to tread softly in his dealings with the Estates, but at the same time he was to respond to any open resistance with unrestrained force. In the new year of 1788 he had done precisely that, firing on demonstrators and killing several of them. Though this had not brought the Estates around to Joseph's way of thinking, it had intimidated them into voting 4 million florins to fund his Ottoman campaign.

Marie Christine and Albert had heard this news while on their way back to Brussels. They had been in Bonn, visiting brother Maximilian in the modest townhouse he preferred, despite the half-dozen palaces in his possession since assuming his grand titles of Prince-Bishop of Münster and Prince-Elector Archbishop of Cologne a few years before. Always stout, at thirty-one, Maximilian had become positively portly, his appearance not improved by the shabby grey frock-coat he habitually wore—though in mitigation, he did have two spares. He kept a lively court all the same, and was very popular with the townsfolk; he had even acquired a mistress in the literary-minded German wife of the boorish English ambassador. Maximilian was on very good terms with his sister and brother-in-law: They had stayed with him before and would soon do so again, for Joseph's unhappy *mélange* of intransigence, neglect, and sudden violence was to ensure a deteriorating situation in their Netherlands territories. Though they no longer held any real power there, they dutifully continued to keep the Emperor informed, "putting ourselves at your feet," as Marie Christine told him, not without a grimace.

Through 1788, the unrest had continued. In June, the clergy and nobles of the wealthy province of Brabant had flatly refused to pay their taxes. Joseph's response was that force would bring them to their senses. D'Alton had swiftly put down the riots wherever they broke out; townsfolk had pelted soldiers with stones; more lives had been lost. Powerless and ignored, Marie Christine and Albert had withdrawn again to their country residence of Laeken. Toward the end of the year, the Brabant Commoners Estates had cancelled the subsidies they had voted for the Ottoman campaign.

Marie Christine had received her brother's angry response. "They want to profit from the fact that I'm at war," he had written. "They think I need money and they'll be able to wring concessions out of me because of it. I'm far from doing anything of the kind. I am firmly and irrevocably determined not to give in." He had not done so, and the result had been more bloodshed. The Estates had relented, temporarily, but Joseph was exhausted. His summer campaign had gone badly; the exceptionally cold winter, and his worsening health, had driven him back to Vienna.

By the beginning of 1789 he was coughing blood. "I take drugs and drink goat's milk every morning," he told his sister, "but it makes no difference. I lead the life of a woman in childbed. I go nowhere except to the princess [Eleonore] von Liechtenstein. The slightest movement leaves my heart pounding." Though it had been clear for some time that he was ill—his courtiers believed with venereal disease—it seems he had contracted tuberculosis during his months in the damp and insalubrious army camp. In April 1789, apparently close to death, he received the last sacraments—in public, in the Habsburg manner. To his own surprise and everyone else's, he made a good recovery. But there was no question of his returning to a field command for the summer campaign. In his place, and possibly revealing a lack of mental clarity, he appointed the infirm seventy-eight-year-old Hungarian Marshal Hadik, who could no longer even mount a house—already Maria Theresia, more than a decade before, had deemed him too fat to fight. In the event Hadik lasted only a few months, before being replaced by Marshal von Laudon, almost equally old and infirm, being "subject to violent disorders of the stomach and bowels, which frequently threaten his life." But Laudon's long experience carried him through, and from this time on the tide turned for Joseph's army; by autumn the Austrians had captured the Ottomans' prize fortress of Belgrade.

The war may have prevented Joseph from containing the revolt in the Austrian Netherlands, but in Count Trauttmansdorff's opinion, his illness had been even more significant. It simply seemed he could not live long, and the rebels believed, correctly, that his brother and heir Leopold had quite different views on how the territory should be governed. "It's useless to force even something good on people," he told Marie Christine. "They need to be persuaded of its usefulness. If you use force you lose their hearts and minds, and in the long run you gain nothing."

By now the two were in regular correspondence on these very subjects, penning their letters in lemon juice to avoid detection, though Leopold pressed his sister to use code instead, "since with lemon juice it often happens that I can't easily read what you've written." Joseph suspected this but, though weak and failing, he would not relent. Utterly determined to see his reforms implemented, he had set about "reviving and exacerbating almost every possible grievance in every province." Predictably, the protests had resumed. Early in June 1789, he delivered to the Estates a "classic assertion of Enlightened despotism," telling them, "I do not need your consent for doing good." The Estates found themselves surrounded by Austrian troops. Trauttmansdorff announced that the Emperor had abrogated their constitution and the deputies could consider themselves dismissed. It was effectively an absolutist coup d'état, and the result was revolution.

> *I've received your letter. The same courier brought me news of the unbelievable events in France. It's incomprehensible how things could have gone so far. When they read it in the history books, they won't believe it. We can only hope this example doesn't turn the heads of our people.*

So wrote Joseph, at the end of July 1789, to Marie Christine at Laeken. It is an extraordinary passage, revealing how little he had grasped of her situation. Impervious to all warnings from his allies and all protests from his enemies, even in mid-September he was still talking of making a state visit to Brussels, as absolute sovereign.

Trauttmansdorff had encouraged his complacency by dismissing rumours of a force of emigré rebels amassing on the border. Both men were stunned when, late in October, insurgents attacked a vital fortress near Antwerp, ransacking its arsenal and taking the local governor prisoner. Though the insurgents were eventually driven back into Holland, Joseph told Marie Christine and Albert that if further attacks looked likely, they should return to Vienna. Bravely if nervously, not wanting to give the appearance of Austrian defeatism, they only moved back to the capital from their country palace of Laeken.

The rebels had their strongest support in the towns, rather than the countryside, and it was in the town of Turnhout, near Antwerp, that their most significant victory was won. Judging correctly that they could not defeat the more numerous Austrians in open battle, they withdrew into the town itself, and there, after five hours of street fighting, with the townsfolk hurling missiles from behind barricades, they routed Joseph's troops. This late October triumph was enough to inspire a general uprising. By mid-November, most of the country was in rebel hands, and rebel forces were marching toward the capital.

Hopelessly belatedly, Joseph instructed Trauttmansdorff to reinstate the constitution, rescind the ecclesiastical reforms, and get Marie Christine and Albert out of the capital as quietly as possible, "on the reasonable pretext of concern for their personal safety." Not that he was really afraid for them; rather, it seems he thought they might turn to the rebels, and claim sovereignty of the country in his place. Marie Christine resisted going, telling Trauttmansdorff stoutly that "I was not afraid, he did not know me, I was not like other women, fearful and faintheartened, it was a question of our reputation not to leave inopportunely, and we were resolved not to go unless the government and the army went with us." Only when the Minister threatened force did she and Albert consent to leave, "and you can imagine how outraged we were," she told Leopold, "when we saw the despatches he sent, saying we had fled, which made us look like [those French aristocrats]."

All their efforts, and all Joseph's, too, had come to nought. Early in January 1790, following a triumphant entry into Brussels, the assembled representatives of the eight rebel provinces of the Austrian Netherlands declared the establishment of a new republic, the United States of Belgium.

"The state of the Monarchy is terrible," Leopold had written to Carolina the previous summer. "War, bad harvests, no end to the different innovations, it's enough to make you dizzy." The eruption of a volcano in faraway Iceland had darkened skies and left harvests failing all over Europe, while Joseph's hasty reforms had caused unrest not only in the Austrian Netherlands but in Hungary, Bohemia, and elsewhere. In Elisabeth's Tyrol, despite repeated prohibitions, the old Catholic practices—religious processions, the clothing of statues, continuous bell-ringing in bad weather—were carried defiantly on. Riots had broken out in many towns, including Vienna itself.

Chancellor von Kaunitz, now seventy-nine, slowed by age and hampered by deafness and his own nervous repulsion for illness of any kind, had had little recent contact with the ailing Joseph. This had only further confused the already unsteady government. Ambassadors in Vienna reported home that only the Emperor's death could save the situation, and Kaunitz seems to have agreed. When Joseph finally expired, at five o'clock in the bitter cold morning of the twentieth of February, 1790, the Chancellor coolly remarked, "That was very good of him."

Joseph had died with no family or friends around him. Though Leopold's son Franz had been living and working alongside him for six years, there had been no friendship between them: Franz, just turned twenty-two, was a cold-tempered young man, and his position had been compromised, in any case, by the tension between his father and uncle. Between Franz's very winning young wife and Joseph there had been genuine fondness, but only days before the Emperor's death, the Archduchess herself had died in childbirth. Joseph's nearest sibling, Elisabeth, could have been called from Innsbruck, but he had made no attempt to summon her, and she may in any case not have agreed to come. She had attended a vigil for him at her own church while he lay in extremis, but they had never been close, and she had not forgotten how ruthless he had been in driving her out of Vienna after their mother's death. He was at least sincerely mourned by his two favourite sisters, Marie Antoinette and Carolina, with the latter lamenting the "double loss of a brother and a friend," and the latter, in the mantle of Neapolitan Catholicism, fretting that he had fixed the last of his strength on affairs of state, rather than preparing for his final judgement with a good steady priest.

Joseph had brought many freedoms to his subjects, abolishing serfdom, emancipating Protestants and Jews, even allowing a limited freedom of the press, but he left behind him the reputation of a despot. An intelligent and questioning man, he had seen the enlightened writing on the walls of his time but, temperamentally too well suited to the habits of autocracy, he had been unable to read between the lines. Determinedly progressive in the ends he had sought, he had been no less determinedly conservative in the means he had taken to achieve them. Though others saw it, and even warned him of it, Joseph never understood this fatal contradiction at the heart of his reign. He saw that he had failed, but he did not see why. And he left his own sad and no doubt too harsh epitaph on a life of strenuous striving for change: "Here lies Joseph II," he declared his tombstone should read, "a prince who failed in everything he undertook."

It was now only a matter of time, and of elaborate and expensive organization, before Leopold, already King of Hungary and Bohemia, ascended the throne of the Holy Roman Empire. The formal agreement of the Empire's seven Electors was not in doubt. The Elector of Cologne, indeed, was Leopold's own music-loving brother Maximilian, who now commissioned the composition of two cantatas, one for Joseph's mourning ceremony and one for Leopold's coronation, from a certain Ludwig van Beethoven, a nineteen-year-old viola player in Maximilian's court chapel orchestra in Bonn. Neither of these, Beethoven's first major commissions, was really fulfilled, but the commission itself did prove useful: Though the first cantata was not ready in time, and the second proved too difficult for the orchestra to play, one or other of them came to the attention of Joseph Haydn, who considered it promising. He felt it might be worth inviting the young man to meet him in Vienna.

En route from Florence to Vienna, in their new life as the imperial family, Leopold's wife, Maria Luisa, and twelve of their children made a stop in Innsbruck to see an excited Elisabeth, "overwhelming my grand-mamma's heart with joy," as she told "my King, friend, patriarch and dear brother whom I love and trust and esteem"—in short, Leopold. Elisabeth, now forty-six, was as devoted to the new Emperor as she had been unenthusiastic about the last. Her lively and self-deprecating letters to him, written in a clear if inelegant hand—"I don't have the patience to dictate; I prefer to write myself"—show that the years had not dimmed her wit, but they also hint at a rather lonely life, without much purpose. Though intelligent, she had never had many personal enthusiasms, such as Marianna's interest in science or Amalie's horse-breeding, and she makes no mention of regular drawing or music-making, as Carolina and Marie Antoinette do. But she was interested in the theatre and, perhaps ill advisedly, even invited the great German dramatist Goethe to attend a couple of local productions during his visit to Innsbruck at this time. A comedy followed by a melodrama, they were presumably not to his taste; he left no mention of them in his memoirs, though his travelling companion did describe them in hers as "badly acted."

Elisabeth had little power as governor of the Tyrol—Joseph had made sure of that—and by now she was minimally involved with her *Damenstift*, but even duties at court could be onerous and expensive. Leopold's ascension required a celebratory reception for almost five hundred people—and a banquet, too, "most copious," as she told her brother, "for these Tyrolians love eating well, and drinking. I'll send you a summary of what it all cost. We tried to economize as much as possible." And as always at the start of a new reign, there were appointments to be made, "and I see that to make one person happy, you have to disappoint and disoblige countless others buttering you up for the same place. The little vanity of having the title of Governor isn't worth the trouble you have to put up with."

Leopold's response to his sister's adoring missives, if businesslike, was always kind, and while he lived, she received more money for the *Damenstift* and more attention from Vienna than she had in a decade. And she loved his children dearly, as she made clear in her letters to him. *Basta!* she concluded, laughing, after pages of laudatory and affectionate description of each of them in turn. Like Marie Christine, she had a particularly soft spot for Karl, now eighteen, and destined for military fame. "Karl is charming, polite, socially adept, wanting to do good and make everyone happy, even the ordinary people," she told his father. "In a word he's a boy who'll succeed wherever you place him because of his manner and his kind heart."

And Amalie was eyeing Leopold's second son, Ferdinand, as a possible husband for one of her daughters but, as so often in her dealings with the family, her efforts now were in vain. Though Leopold would have agreed to a match—he was keen to extend his family's influence in Italy—he had just confirmed the young man's betrothal to Carolina's second daughter.

CAROLINA HAD ACTUALLY laughed out loud when she read that the wife of her nephew Franz had died. In slight mitigation, she had never met the girl, but she was callous enough to say to the envoy who had brought the letter, and who reported the whole story to Chancellor von Kaunitz, that the path was now clear for her eldest daughter to marry Franz herself. This had been her original plan, and Leopold's, too, before Joseph had intercepted it. Now it was resurrected, and a grand double wedding set for September 1790 in Vienna: The two eldest cousins, Franz and Teresa, would marry alongside the two second eldest, Ferdinand and Luisa. In due course, there would be a third alliance between the two families, but for the moment there was enough to arrange. The event would coincide with Leopold's formal accession to two of his three thrones, as Holy Roman Emperor in Frankfurt and as king of Hungary in Pressburg; his Prague coronation as King of Bohemia was to take place the following year.

Elisabeth had immensely enjoyed the visit of Leopold's family to Innsbruck in May, and she planned now to meet up with Carolina and her brood while en route to Vienna. "The Queen of Naples has told me all about the triple alliance, and I congratulate you," she wrote to Leopold in July. "There are no hearts anywhere like those of you two. . . . I've written to her today that I'll see her at Ljubljana, where they'll make a break in their journey. What joy to see a sister again, after nineteen years of separation!" She found her "just as she was in Vienna, still admirable and adorable. I opened my heart to her." The two shared a birthday on the thirteenth of August, with Elisabeth turning forty-seven and Carolina thirty-eight, but the younger sister's greater worldly experience evidently impressed the elder, "and in future so that I won't be always bothering you I'll write to her," Elisabeth told Leopold, "but never without reason. I trust you both completely, as you both deserve."

Though there had been concerns that Leopold might eventually capture all seven temporal and spiritual electorates for various of his ten surviving sons, thanks to the diplomatic efforts of brother Maximilian, himself the Elector of Cologne, and also to Leopold's own reputation as a man bent on peace rather than war, he had duly been elected. Leopold had had the good sense not to push his advantage and have his son Franz crowned King of the Romans, and hence assumed heir to the Holy Roman Empire, at the same time. Indeed, before the election result had been formalized, he had been adroit enough to present the planned trip—not to Frankfurt itself but to a pretty town upriver—as merely the occasion for a family gathering: Though few were taken in by the tactic, many appreciated the tact.

The Vienna wedding festivities had already taken place when the family set off for Frankfurt on the third of October 1790. It was quite a troop. With

Leopold travelled Maria Luisa and their five eldest sons, two of them with their new brides, "who are neither beautiful nor sociable, but who will be good, I hope," as their mother remarked. Indeed, Elisabeth Vigée-Le Brun, who had just painted both brides, remarked that though Teresa, the elder girl, possessed "her mother's features, so similar to those of our charming Queen in France, Louisa was extremely ugly, and pulled such faces that I was most reluctant to finish her portrait"—one or other of these facts not unconnected, perhaps, with the many months subsequently required for the consummation of her marriage.

Carolina herself, after a miserable pregnancy, had just given birth to her sixteenth child, "a magnificent Leopoldo, strong as a bull," and she was relieved "to be able to bend and move about again." To avoid excessive ceremony, she and Ferdinando were travelling in recognized incognito as the Count and Countess of Castellamare, and Marie Christine and Albert as plain Monsieur and Madame Beyle: They had come with Maximilian from Bonn, where they had been living, in his pretty château of Poppelsdorf, since their hurried departure from Brussels ten months before. Albert's brother Clemens was also present as Elector of Trier. Elisabeth and Amalie and Ferdinand did not join the party—the two latter had recently seen Leopold in Mantua, with Amalie finding their brother looking "rather haggard," as she told Marie Christine.

Nor of course was Marie Antoinette present. Whether she might have been is a moot point: She wanted at any rate to emphasize that she and her family were not free. The Assembly, for their part, wanted to demonstrate the contrary, and to this end had allowed the royal family to spend the summer of 1790 at the Queen's personal château of Saint-Cloud near Paris. Here, on the third of May, with Louis depressed and ineffectual in his own apartments, Marie Antoinette had slipped out into the palace gardens for a covert meeting with one of the Assembly's leaders. It had been brokered by Ambassador Mercy with the comte de Mirabeau, now prudently known, in revolutionary circles at least, as simple Monsieur Raqueti.

Formerly acting in raucous unison, the Assembly was by now beginning to split into more or less radical parties, though as yet none was advocating the actual abolition of the monarchy. All agreed that Louis was to be central in the forthcoming *Fête de la Fédération*, a grand celebration of the accomplished Revolution and the establishment of a constitutional monarchy, led by the elected Assembly itself. But many aspects of the new regime had still to be decided. Louis needed a strong voice to press his claims to continued authority in strategic areas. The powerful Mirabeau, as Mercy knew, was his best hope.

Forty years old, a large, loud man and a brilliant orator, a noble among the commoners, disfigured by smallpox but very attractive to women, Mirabeau arrived at Saint-Cloud in the blaze of his present Assembly glory and with a strong whiff of his sulphurous past. Author of obscene volumes, an indefatigable womanizer, more than once a prisoner, even sentenced to death for abduction, and always in debt, he had survived by his powerful intellect and his protean ability to manoeuvre among diverse people and in ever-changing circumstances. Marie Antoinette is said to have been horrified by the very mention of his name, but she was steely enough now to meet him in person, and in secret, to negotiate a path forward. She agreed to pay his many debts and provide him with a comfortable monthly income. In return he would press the King's case in the Assembly and speak for him abroad.

Hence Mirabeau's arrival in Frankfurt, and his long interview with Leopold, in the course of which, according to the American Morris, Mirabeau "pressed him to undertake a Counter Revolution in France, but [the Emperor] smiled and told him that it was an impracticable Project. He thinks the Administration in France was so bad as to occasion and justify a Revolution." Morris' information was not quite correct: Mirabeau did not want a return to the status quo ante, but favoured a constitutional monarchy along British lines. But Leopold did feel his sister and her husband should accommodate themselves to the new regime. And if France should be weakened by infighting or even civil war, so much the better for Austria. The *renversement des alliances* linking the two had long outlived its usefulness.

Leopold's coronation as Holy Roman Emperor took place in Frankfurt's red-stone Cathedral of St Bartholomew. A quarter-century before, in the same austere church, he himself had made fun of the old-fashioned ceremonies attending Joseph's coronation as King of the Romans. In the intervening years Europe had witnessed a great surge of anti-monarchical feeling, so that now, in Frankfurt itself, a local critic felt safe enough to publish his own caricature of the "tasteless puppet-theatre" of the proceedings. "The Emperor's regalia looked as if it had been put together from pieces bought at a flea-market," he wrote. "The throne looked like a chicken-crate. When they placed the crown on the imperial head, drums and trumpets thundered out: Tiddly-pom, tiddly-pom, tiddly-pom-pom-pom!"

Despite this, the ceremony impressed two very young men present: Leopold's eldest son and heir, twenty-two-year-old Franz, and an elegant, musical, extraordinarily self-assured student of law and political science from the University of Strasbourg—Count Clemens von Metternich, just seventeen years old. It was here that the two were introduced, with Metternich's father easily flattering the heir to the imperial throne, long more used to badgering and ridicule from his recently deceased Uncle Joseph. The shrewd efforts of Metternich *père* were to bear handsome fruit, with Franz later appointing the still young Clemens Austria's Foreign Minister and then Chancellor: He was to wield great influence, with ever greater fame, for almost forty years.

In any case, Leopold's progressive reputation as Grand Duke of Tuscany had preceded him, and his coronation was a public relations success, with even the radical press praising him. A celebratory mass was performed by musicians brought from Vienna, under the baton of court opera director Antonio Salieri. Mozart was in Frankfurt, too, but not in any official capacity. He had paid his own way in order to perform two of his piano concertos, neither of them new. Such a gathering of nobles was an unmissable opportunity to present himself as composer and musician: At thirty-four, he still needed sponsors. A long-ago attempt by brother Ferdinand to employ the "young *Salzburger*" at his Milan court had been foiled by Maria Theresia herself: "I don't know what you want him for," she had told her son tersely.

"I don't believe you need a composer . . . I say this so you won't take on these useless people. . . . They lower the tone of your employ, running about the world like beggars." Fortunately for the composer, Maria Theresia was now beyond all objecting, and music-loving Maximilian was directly at hand, and all ears.

MARIE CHRISTINE HARDLY recognized Pressburg when her carriage rolled into the town in November 1790 for Leopold's coronation as King of Hungary. It was almost a decade since she had lived there, and instead of the ordinary French-style clothes she remembered, most people were now dressed in striking Hungarian folk costumes. Joseph's heavy-handed reforms had led to the public burning of his decrees; conscription for his Ottoman campaign had provoked violent resistance. His standardizing mission for the Monarchy had produced, paradoxically, a surge of incipient nationalism among the Hungarians.

The Magyar nobles were its clear beneficiary. Leopold had been obliged to rescind not only Joseph's changes, but also those his mother had made decades before, in 1765. The old Hungarian constitution, ignored by Maria Theresia to centralize power in her own hands and overtly dismissed by Joseph, was now reinstated: The office of locally elected Palatine, which the Empress had abolished to appoint Albert as her governor, was reestablished; the taxes Joseph had extracted from the nobles were annulled, and all commoners and foreigners were forced out of local positions of power. As Austria retreated, and the nobles gathered up the wealth and power left behind, the ethnically diverse townsfolk and peasants were obliged to console themselves with a defensive and ill defined sense of "Hungarianness," a burgeoning thorn, nonetheless, in the Monarchy's side. The nobles were indulgent enough to elect as their Palatine Leopold's fourth son, twenty-eight-year-old Alexander. In return, their king appeared at his coronation dramatically dressed in Hungarian costume—as did all the rest of his family, including the King of Naples.

Returned *en famille* to Vienna, with Albert unwell, Marie Christine managed to offend Carolina mightily by giving unwanted advice to her daughters and their new husbands, and by commandeering Ferdinando in the evenings to persuade him to her way of thinking about various family matters. "And I was so uneasy about her influence on him," Carolina later wrote, "that I turned up at her rooms myself, and that put a stop to it."

Leopold's pragmatic compromising did much to calm the Monarchy's restless lands, and it also lessened conflict beyond them. Though Russia's war with the Ottomans continued, Austria's involvement now ended, and Prussia's support for the Belgian revolutionaries was stopped. Brother Maximilian had had a clever hand in this, turning the Holy Roman Empire's many other states against the mediocre Prussian King Friedrich Wilhelm II, who had assumed quasi-leadership of the Empire to undermine Austria for his own purposes. At the end of July 1790, at Reichenbach in Silesia, Leopold restored the Belgians' old constitution and offered a general amnesty to all the rebels. Marie Antoinette applauded him. "It's most gracious," she wrote, "to be able to grant pardon without spilling a drop of your subjects' blood"—graciousness being the quality Franz Stephan had long ago urged on his children as rulers.

Leopold's amnesty offer was genuine, and quickly accepted by the Belgian peasantry, who had resented interference in their old religious practices, now restored, but were less interested in the political issues that had motivated many townsmen. But among the latter, and within the governing Estates, the country was so factionalized that hardly any policies could be agreed upon, let alone implemented: Most provinces had been stumbling on in a more or less civilized chaos. Following a brief show of Austrian force, the territory slipped uneasily back into the Monarchy's fold, with Leopold's third son, twenty-nine-year-old Archduke Karl, becoming hereditary sovereign, and Marie Christine and Albert grudgingly accepted as joint governors once more. With no children of their own, they now formally adopted Karl, making him heir to their titles and fortune, and returned unwillingly to Brussels, "to begin again on our arduous path," as Marie Christine told Eleonore von Liechtenstein. "It's thornier than it used to be. As if to punish me for my sins, the Netherlands is flooded with Frenchmen of every kind."

That number was soon to be further increased, for annexation by France was not far away.

# XXV

# 1791-1792

*In which the French royal family escapes and is recaptured, a sullen twenty-four-year-old ascends the imperial throne, and France declares war on Austria.*

The French royal family had been considering the possibilities of retreat even before their forced departure from Versailles in October 1789. Their various advisors had produced any number of plans for their removal to Metz or Compiègne or Normandy or Luxembourg, by force of arms or by cover of night, with or without foreign help. Louis had long dismissed them all, preferring to make the best of things as they now were and continuing with a semblance of the old court life, including even the presentation of debutantes—though his attendants, and indeed the debutantes, were now drawn from a wider section of society. But Marie Antoinette had taken a keen interest in the various plans to leave. Like Fersen and others loyal to the King, she misjudged the deep social dissatisfaction across the country, believing the revolutionary agitation was being driven by a small number of determined extremists in Paris, and that in the provinces she and her family would find safety and even military support; in addition, a flight to the east would bring them close to her brother's forces in the Austrian Netherlands.

It was only in July 1790, with the promulgation of the Civil Constitution of the Clergy subordinating the Roman Catholic Church to the national government, that Louis had realized that for him personally, the Revolution had passed the point of compromise. He had been forced to sanction the Civil Constitution, provoking an outcry from the Pope and flat refusals to comply from more than half the clergy of France. Even his elderly aunts Adélaïde and Victoire, both now approaching sixty, took this moment to exile themselves to Rome: En route, local revolutionaries detained them for a time, which the ladies spent pleasantly playing piquet with a handy priest while others further up the chain of command debated their significance or otherwise to the Revolution.

Sanctioning the Civil Constitution had stricken Louis' religious conscience. For months he doubted whether he was even entitled to make the Easter communion required of all Roman Catholics—it seems he did so, in April 1791, but secretly. And it was at this point that he finally agreed to a plan of escape, one long in the making, its chief architect Axel von Fersen. An envoy was sent to Naples to ask Carolina for the loan of a million ducats to fund it. Just returned from the family's own costly wedding and coronation travels, Ferdinando had sent him packing, though Carolina herself had had her doubts, as she admitted to Leopold: "My husband won't hear a word of it, and quite rightly, and anyway that amount of money can't be found so easily or so quickly. . . . But it's true, it's not very pleasant to think we'll be blamed for sacrificing these sovereigns"—meaning as yet their liberty, rather than their lives. In the end, the royal family was lent a fraction of the sum by Fersen himself, his sympathetic Italian mistress, of whose existence the Queen was not aware, and the children's governess, Madame de Tourzel.

Marie Antoinette was evidently confident the venture would prove successful. She had spent much of the early spring organizing a wardrobe for the exile, undeterred by the insistence of her lady-in-waiting Madame Campan that such preparations were useless, that "the Queen of France would find undergarments and gowns everywhere. I would go out alone and almost in disguise to buy these things or have them made up for her and the children," Madame Campan recorded. The clothes were smuggled out to Brussels in a travelling chest, supposedly as a gift for Marie Christine. In Brussels, an astonished Mercy, *en visite*, also received crates of porcelain and other belongings of the Queen. She had even sent her hairdresser to wait for her at one of the staging-posts en route to Montmédy.

All the same, the royal family did not intend to leave France, as Louis' brothers and so many others had done. By contrast, they needed to show they were not abandoning the country, and were not implacably opposed to all aspects of the Revolution—though how true this was rather changed according to the shifting circumstances. By escaping from the Tuileries, they at least expected to arrive at a better place, literally and figuratively, from which Louis could negotiate with the Assembly, which was gradually splitting into more or less radical factions which it seemed might be played off against one another: Fersen and Mercy thought Louis should simply pretend to support and even lead the Revolution in order to manipulate them.

The Assembly had proposed a new constitution, which Louis had provisionally agreed to, despite being privately opposed to it. But in July it was to be formalized into law, and this he was determined not to accept. If he could reach a safe place, far enough from Paris but still within French borders, he believed he could achieve a revised constitution, reserving certain powers for himself, and a place for the Clergy and Nobles as well. Louis had no expectation of a return to *ancien régime* absolutism, though Marie Antoinette, less politically attuned than her husband, still had hopes of it. She was even nursing plans of vengeance, which she imputed, incorrectly, to the King as well, telling Mercy they would "pardon those who have been merely led astray . . . [and] exempt from the pardon the revolutionary leaders, the city of Paris unless it returns to the old dispensation, and everyone who has not laid down his arms by a certain date." Mercy thought the whole escape plan perilous and unlikely to succeed. He knew there would be no practical help from Leopold, at least until he had extricated Austria from the Ottoman war. Her brother's caution was frustrating to Marie Antoinette; in time it would embitter her toward him.

"The voyage," as the King and Queen referred to it, was by now almost an open secret, even beyond France. With some exaggeration of local ignorance, an envoy from Amalie's Duchy of Parma reported immediately afterwards: "The royal family's escape was rumoured throughout the whole of Europe, but it wasn't even suspected in Paris itself. The London papers announced they would depart at the end of June. They said the Parisians had no idea what was happening in their own city."

In fact it was the twenty-first of June when they left, soon after midnight, their separate carriages rolling out into streets bizarrely icy on this very morn of midsummer. Louis' sister Elisabeth, rather a gossip in Marie Antoinette's view, had been told the details only the afternoon before. Accompanied by a handful of trusted guards and servants, the royal party were themselves in disguise, with Madame de Tourzel as a foreign baroness, Louis as a valet, and Marie Antoinette as governess to her children: Six-year-old Louis-Charles, dressed as a girl, was soon asleep on the floor of the carriage. Fersen served as coachman for this first stage, to the city gate of Porte-Saint-Martin. Here they met up with Madame Elisabeth, who tripped over her little nephew as she climbed in to join them—happily, he did not cry out. Fersen left them, expecting to meet up with Louis at Montmédy, "if he is fortunate enough to reach it," as he told his father. With a new coachman, they then drove eastwards for some five hours, every moment afraid of being recognized, and twice delayed by the horses stumbling on the muddy ground, and a snapped harness needing to be mended. As day broke, they reached Châlons-sur-Marne, a hundred miles from Paris, and here they were indeed recognized, fortunately by royalists, "who praised God they had seen the King, and wished him Godspeed," as twelve-year-old Marie-Thérèse was later to record.

Near Châlons, they were to rendezvous with a mounted guard of forty men who would escort them further, but they found no one. Their delays had cost them several hours; the guards had assumed the mission had been aborted and had left, sending confused messages onward alerting other sympathizers, including the vital suppliers of fresh horses, to relax their guard or abandon their posts entirely.

Anxious and frightened, the royal party had no choice but to travel on alone. At eight in the evening, they arrived at the post station of Sainte-Ménehould, and here a glimpse of Louis aroused the suspicion of a young official named Drouet. Uncertain, he allowed the carriage to proceed, but his superiors, hearing the story an hour later, sent him and others in pursuit of it. A false turn in the road had taken the royal carriage astray, delaying the party further, and it was nearing midnight when they arrived, desperately in need of new horses, at the sorry little town of Varennes.

They found no horses, though they were in fact there. The town, one side built on a steep hill, was bisected by a river. Across the bridge, concealed by a small castle, a royal regiment stood waiting for them. They had posted no lookout, and had not seen the carriage arrive. They were only alerted by the noisy approach of Drouet and his men, and now found their tardy rush to assist the royal party obstructed by a heavy furniture wagon, overturned on the bridge. On the other side, with fire bells ringing, the townsfolk surrounding them, and armed men levelling their muskets, the royal party were trapped.

They were more or less obliged to accept the hospitality of a local official, who placed half his modest house at their disposal. But they were not under arrest, and indeed, the town quickly filled with the various contingents of guards who had been intended as their escorts. Trained military men, all armed, they might still have staged a rescue and set the royal party safely on their way, but unconscionably, no one thought to do so. Even the King failed to call his own men to do their duty, and save him. While Marie Antoinette organized beds for the children, Louis simply flopped into an armchair, and waited for the dawn.

With it arrived emissaries from the Assembly, covered in dust from their hard ride from Paris. They brought orders that the King was to return at once. He meekly requested a delay, owing to the fatigues of the previous day, but this was denied. Only the Queen vented her frustration and anger that their own subjects should dare to dictate to Louis and herself. She flung the papers down on the bed where her little son was sleeping. Exhausted and oblivious, he slept on.

"THEY WERE CAPTURED SCARCELY four miles from the border," a tearful Marie Christine told Eleonore von Liechtenstein two days later. "If they had taken another road, they would have been saved." Perhaps. But as Marie Antoinette had seen, they had enemies in the provinces, too. As she later told Mercy, "There is not a single town, not a regiment on which we can rely." This was in the east of the country, at least. Had they travelled westwards, they might in fact have found support: There a Catholic and royalist army would soon be raised. And it seems the King's plan to renegotiate the constitution to his advantage was not so far-fetched: On learning of the journey, the moderate majority of the Assembly had organized a deputation to follow him to Montmédy and open discussions with him there; they had been about to set off when news of the arrest arrived.

The flight from Paris to Varennes had taken twenty-two hours. The return took almost four deeply uncomfortable days. There were now eight people crammed into the two-bench carriage: on one side the King and Queen, with Assembly representative Barnave between them, and little Louis-Charles in his mother's lap. Facing them, representative Pétiot sat in the middle, with Elisabeth and Madame de Tourzel on either side, taking turns to balance Marie-Thérèse on their knees. The weather had turned hot, so that the windows were kept open, and the roads—and soon the clothes of all the travellers—were thick with dust. Abusive crowds hindered their passage and hounded them at every stop.

At half past six in the evening of the twenty-fifth of June, the carriage arrived at the gates of Paris, before being driven around the city walls: To drive through the streets was impossible, "for fear of being shot at from a window," as the Spanish ambassador Fernan Nuñez, an eyewitness, reported to Madrid: "An immense crowd stood hurling abuse at the King and his royal spouse; the Queen was the principal object of the people's fury; they held her responsible for all the misfortunes of the past and even for this current flight."

Lafayette and others of his National Guard forced a way for them through the hostile crowd, some of whom, Fernan Nuñez was informed, were planning to attack the Queen. Though obliged to defend them, Lafayette had no sympathy for his captives: He insisted all bystanders keep their hats on to demonstrate their lack of respect; those without hats were required to cover their heads with whatever grubby rag might come to hand. Once arrived at the Tuileries, "the King could hardly climb out of the carriage, he was so utterly exhausted, but the Queen stepped down proudly and nobly."

Within the palace, they found no ministers and no servants awaiting them, but only a deputation from the Assembly, who now read to Louis, from a decree of that very morning, the terms of his arrest. Outwardly, he appeared in reasonable spirits. He thanked Barnave and Pétiot for accompanying them on the return journey, and several times invited them to dine with him that evening, a grace they declined. Though the six-year-old dauphin was jumping up and down excitedly, his sister, old enough to understand the situation, sat quietly weeping. Madame Elisabeth, as always, retained her composure, and the Queen even attempted to joke with an unresponsive Barnave about the cramped journey back to Paris. She did not know that a short walk away, near the Palais Royal, the bloody head of a woman was being paraded through the streets on the end of a pike, an incitement to the people of Paris to an act of atrocity. For though the head was made of cardboard, it was modelled on her own.

And during the night, little Louis-Charles awoke from a dream in which he was being eaten alive by wolves.

# 1791-1792

*Of one thing I am certain, of pitying the Queen; which was so generally felt here as soon as the reverse of her escape was known, that I was told that, if money could serve her, an hundred thousand pounds would have been subscribed in a quarter of an hour at Lloyd's coffee-house.*

Thus the elderly Horace Walpole, writing to a friend from London. He had seen Marie Antoinette in her early days at Versailles, and he retained bright memories of her grace and charm. At least Louis' brother Provence and his wife had made a successful escape to Marie Christine's court in Brussels, where Artois now joined them, "and I wouldn't be at all surprised," noted his lieutenant, "if in a little while there were certain people who thought the King's arrest wasn't such a great misfortune." It seems Provence may already have been thinking of taking the throne for himself, and Artois may have approved the thought. Also in Brussels was Axel von Fersen, who was observed to be "in despair, though trying to bear up."

In Paris, Fersen was correctly numbered among those responsible for the escape. A week after the recapture, Marie Antoinette sent him a hasty letter via a chain of emissaries. "Don't come back here, not on any pretext," she wrote. "They know it was you who got us out of here. If you come here, you are lost." Later in the same day, she smuggled out another note, revealing her still passionate feelings for him. "I can tell you that I love you and have time for no more than that. Tell me where I should send the letters I'm able to write to you, for I can't live without that. Adieu, most beloved and most loving of men. I embrace you with all my heart."

Fersen worshipped the Queen and also loved her, though it seems not quite as she loved him. He had devoted himself to her family's cause, but at this very time he was engaged in an affair with a former ballet dancer, an affair he was to continue for a further six years. He needed, as he said, both sacred and profane love.

The royal family's recapture was in any case not the desperate event Fersen evidently thought it, though it did polarize opinions, including in the fracturing Assembly. While this body now suspended all Louis' monarchical functions, such as they had become, and set about completing the new constitution limiting his powers, which he would soon accept, at least publicly, a majority of deputies agreed that the monarchy would have to continue in some form in order to legitimize the government's authority and maintain law and order. In an attempt to salvage the King's reputation with the public, they even announced he had not tried to escape at all but had been kidnapped, with the commander of the Montmédy fortress, now safely in exile, loyally accepting the blame. The story was largely accepted on pragmatic grounds: Though Louis personally had forfeited a great deal of public trust, most people feared chaos would ensue if the King were not somehow reintegrated into the government.

For the Assembly itself had weakened. For some time it had been losing sway to "the clubs" of Paris, rival political associations of extremists and moderates, unconstrained by the need for compromise. The uncontainable Mirabeau had recently died, overcome by the twin excesses of revolutionary labour and *volupté*, and a coterie of fierce young lawyers, hardly over thirty, were the clubs' emerging leaders: Barnave and Pétion, who had travelled with the royal family back from Varennes, were among the moderates who wanted a constitutional monarchy. But there was also a talented minority of hardline "Jacobins," taking their name from the club they frequented in a former Jacobin monastery, and now, for the first time, they began to demand a republic, with no king at all. Prominent among them were Georges Danton and Maximilien Robespierre, allies now, though destined for fatal discord. They carried with them the "popular movement" of *sans-culottes*—mostly members of the petty bourgeoisie rather than the very poor, their name deriving from the trousers the men wore instead of *culottes*, the knee-breeches of the propertied classes. In mid-July, a lethal encounter between extremists and moderates at the Paris park of the Champs de Mars hardened the political battle-lines, with republicans on the one side, and on the other the constitutionalists, supported by the armed force of Lafayette's National Guard, and of course the King.

**Louis himself believed** the Revolution had already played itself out: "The Assembly is now reaching its end," he told Leopold soon after his recapture, writing in his tiny, squeezed handwriting. "Every kind of government is destroyed, the clubs have seized all authority, even above the Assembly." He expected the other sovereigns of Europe to exert pressure on the French to put him back on his throne, if not as an absolute monarch, then at least within a constitutional monarchy. He considered he had made a considerable personal sacrifice in renouncing his royal prerogative and, referring to himself as "the King," denounced "the countless outrages perpetrated on Himself and His family."

Certainly, Fersen's King Gustav III of Sweden had vowed to support Louis to the hilt, and he now tasked Fersen with rousing other sovereigns to similar action. It had been almost twenty years since Gustav himself, then just twenty-six years of age, had staged a coup d'état in Sweden to restore an absolute monarchy, albeit an enlightened one: Like Joseph, he believed in using reactionary means to achieve progressive ends. Gustav wanted to form a league of princes to invade France, though Fersen was doing his best to persuade him that the threat of force alone, from an armed congress led by Leopold, would be enough to bring the French to heel. Ferdinando in Naples, "pierced with indignation" at the King's recapture, also urged the Emperor to "employ without delay the most effective means to reclaim his liberty, and above all his honour, which is necessarily connected with that of every sovereign." Louis himself expected his brother-in-law the Emperor to "take every measure his generous heart suggests to come to the aid of the King and the Kingdom of France." But Leopold was overtaxed already with the Belgian revolution and multiple revolts elsewhere in the Monarchy, to say nothing of the unconcluded Ottoman war. Marie Antoinette had a clearer idea of what he might be ready to do: He had revealed his priority in October 1790 when he had transferred Ambassador Mercy to The Hague for international discussions about the fractious Belgian provinces. Though she overestimated Mercy's personal attachment to her, telling Leopold "his feelings for me are those of a father for his child and I conceal nothing of my feelings from him," he had been her mainstay at Versailles for more than two decades.

Marie Christine and Albert had just returned to Brussels after a tour of the country, and they were only half-reassured by what they had encountered. Though the old pre-Josephine provincial structures had been reconfirmed, Leopold was still trying to introduce certain legal reforms that were clearly unwelcome in some regions, notably among the commoners of the Third Estate. He had wanted to recall some of his Habsburg troops to boost the threatened force against France, but Marie Christine, fearful of renewed rebellion in the Austrian Netherlands, insisted she could not spare any of them. "My dear brother," she told him, "I tell you again and I cannot repeat it often enough, our safety and the holding of these provinces depends on our troops; the least reduction of them is impossible, and I don't mean just for the moment, I mean for years to come."

And there was still the threat of invasion from France, particularly with so many Frenchmen already in the country. The revolutionaries among them were encouraging local anti-Habsburg feeling, while the many counterrevolutionary émigrés in Brussels stood as a permanent pretext for France to declare war on those sheltering them. A French count at Marie Christine's court remarked on the terrible state of the Archduchess' nerves at this time. She was "anxious and embittered about everything and in despair at having to be in this country," he told his wife. She seemed to be in constant fear, and in an effort to contain anti-Habsburg protests, had ordered a number of arrests, which the count thought counterproductive, but which Leopold endorsed.

His policy was to hold the line in the Austrian Netherlands until things should settle, and as for France, simply to wait for the reverse. In due course, he believed, and Louis' recent letter had lent weight to this, France would descend into chaos, at which point Austria and the other Great Powers might profitably intervene. Prussia, Russia, and England thought along similar lines. Though Louis wanted to avoid it at any cost, a civil war in France, with the resultant breakdown of commerce and trade and a withdrawal from foreign ventures, would by no means be to their disadvantage.

But most of the counterrevolutionary émigrés, notably the King's brothers Provence and Artois, wanted Leopold to lead a military invasion of France to restore the *ancien régime* and, in the event of Louis' incapacity, to establish Provence, at the very least, as regent to little Louis-Charles. Marie Christine put it succinctly in a letter to her brother: "It's absolutely clear they want to provoke a war and drag you into it. And their goal is visibly not what the King could have proposed." "They're doing more harm than good," Leopold replied.

The comte d'Artois in particular was making a nuisance of himself, doing the rounds of the courts to drum up support for armed intervention and the establishment of his brother as regent. "He has a good heart but he can't be trusted, he's surrounded by too many of the wrong people," Marie Antoinette told Leopold. "We thank you for not receiving him." Elisabeth in Innsbruck was not sure whether to receive him or not. He had announced he would not come to the town unless she did, so she arranged a neutral dinner and theatre visit for him and his entourage, "and I chatted with them about [his wife's home city of] Turin and of Venice, and I said not a word about politics," as she informed her adored brother. "I think you're doing the right thing by going *pian piano* as the Italians say in all this business"—a reference to his strategic temporizing. "And whoever loves and serves my Leopold"—which Artois clearly did not—"has my approval already."

It did not help that the princes were not the only émigrés supposedly acting on Louis' behalf, or that the plans and instructions smuggled out from the Tuileries were rarely consistent. The immovably absolutist views of Louis' sister Elisabeth were provoking constant arguments within the small circle of Tuileries captives. The Queen had her own personal envoy whom she used, despite Louis' doubts and the princes' outright opposition, as a spokesman for the whole royal family. And she was also in disingenuous correspondence with the moderate deputy Barnave, persuading him, for a time at least, that she supported his plan for a constitutional monarchy.

Axel von Fersen, too, was making his own approaches to other courts, all the while pleading for clearer instructions from the King. Leopold initially welcomed his pragmatism and plainspokenness, but gradually he came to mistrust him, realizing Fersen wanted him to restore Louis as an absolute monarch in the enlightened mould of his own King Gustav in Sweden. Leopold's cooling toward Fersen and his determination to avoid armed conflict frustrated Marie Antoinette. "The King and I understand we must act with prudence," she wrote to him, "but my dear brother, under certain circumstances too much delay could mean everything is lost. The revolutionaries are making such headway and so quickly, we think it's dangerous not to take a stand against them. They want to subvert the whole Kingdom. And it's very likely that if order is not restored in France, in the long run you won't have complete control of Brabant [in the Austrian Netherlands], and these venomous principles will spread to every country in Europe." Even Maximilian had written, in his elegant handwriting, to tell Leopold of a band of restless Breton émigrés arrived in Bonn, "not courtiers but brave soldiers very keen to fight for the King" as soon as they receive the signal. Maximilian himself was ready to contribute men and money, but Leopold, "the Chief and protector of the whole Empire," would have to provide the leadership.

There were few fighting men among the émigrés in Naples. Instead, most of them, as Carolina complained, were "useless people, nobles, lords, loafers, both unpleasant and unwelcome." In principle, the Kingdom needed craftsmen and other productive workers, but in practice, those who had arrived were fatally tainted, "talking about Reason, sowing the seeds of revolution, hairdressers, valets, cooks, every head filled with agitation. I wish they could have been kept right out of Italy and not be coming here to disturb our tranquillity. As for the [French] King, I despise him from the bottom of my heart. He has no soul"—meaning, presumably, no faith in his divine right to rule as an absolute monarch.

**Early in July 1791,** Leopold called on the sovereign powers of Europe, great and small, to demand the release of the French royal family. The call met with little active response, but it did bring about a crucial rapprochement, for the first time in half a century, between the Habsburgs and their old enemy, Prussia. Toward the end of August, at the palace of Pillnitz near Dresden, persuaded by, of all unlikely contenders, the generally ridiculed comte d'Artois, Leopold and Friedrich Wilhelm II issued a joint declaration. Abjuring expansionist ventures at each other's expense, they also insisted the royal family be set at liberty and monarchical government be restored in France, threatening invasion otherwise, though only on the almost impossible condition that all the other European Powers would join forces with them. The point of the declaration was to exert pressure on the French, whose country they regarded as a mayhem of "anarchy compounded by bankruptcy." Whatever Artois may have wanted, neither Leopold nor Friedrich Wilhelm had any intention of actually sending in the troops: Their policy, for the moment, was to bark and not bite. "With God's help I will manage to avoid war," Leopold had told Carolina the year before. "I'll never wage it on anyone. To maintain peace in Europe is my most fervent wish."

Louis' hasty brothers almost managed to undermine him. Boosted by money from the Tsarina Catherine, they published a wholly precipitate announcement of an imminent invasion of France. Marie Christine criticized this sharply, for which Leopold thanked her. "I know the French princes and their circle very well," he told her. "They're only looking after their own interests, and they want to involve me and others in their affairs to achieve their own ends and carry out all their ill considered, reckless, inexcusable plans. Keep their pretensions reined in and don't believe anything they say." The princes had appealed to Leopold to reprimand Marie Christine, but she was sure of her brother's support. "To give you a good laugh," she had already sent him copies of their strategic suggestions. "I'm not surprised and I'm not concerned," she told him now. "I knew they were criticizing me, but I can't complain as I'm in good company, since they're criticizing you, too."

Though Marie Antoinette had also been urging her brother, as well as the Kings of Spain and Sweden, toward an armed congress, Louis himself now lent wind to the peace-lovers' sails by accepting the establishment of a constitutional monarchy. Though his sincerity was doubtful, it suited Leopold to believe he had accepted the current state of the Revolution and the new, constrained role it had brought about for himself. This obviated the need for any further military threats, and gained him time—for privately, it seems, he was already reassessing his strategy of maintaining peace. "The cowardice and weakness of our good Louis XVI will get us off the hook," a delighted Chancellor von Kaunitz declared in Vienna. Leopold thought the princes and other émigrés should accept the amnesty the new Assembly had offered them. They should go home and wait for the Revolution to burn itself out, then reform the system themselves, from within.

Though Marie Antoinette kept protesting, he considered it best to ignore her letters for a time. In despair, she appealed to the Russian Tsarina. The King, she said, had been coerced into accepting the new constitution. But Catherine was more concerned about Poland, where war had broken out between the promoters of a new, liberal constitution, led by the King himself, Elisabeth's long-ago suitor Stanisław Poniatowski, against conservative nobles supported by Russia. As in France, Naples, Hungary, and so many other places in Europe, Poland's nobles were resisting paying their fair share of the country's taxes. Catherine was less interested in taxes than in keeping Stanisław and his reformers under her own thumb, and in carving further territory out of Poland for herself. She would not spare troops for another king's quarrel. Besides, she regarded Louis with contempt, and his family as doomed.

In Paris in the autumn of 1791, the Assembly met for the first time under the new constitution. It was entirely new: None of its 745 members had served previously, and very few this time were nobles or clerics. The Jacobin Robespierre had instigated this ostensibly to prevent the entrenchment of cliques of power, but the new body of inexperienced men was no more united than its predecessor had been.

The imperial city of Vienna witnessed three equally noteworthy events that same season. At the Theater auf der Wieden, Mozart's last, fantastical opera, *The Magic Flute*, premiered to exuberant acclaim, with the composer himself conducting and his wife's sister in the dazzling role of Queen of the Night. In December, feverish and in pain, still struggling to finish his great *Requiem*, Mozart died at the age of just thirty-five. His death inspired a flurry of memorial services and concerts of his music, and a generous donation from Maximilian to his widow and her two little boys. And in the same month, at the Hofburg palace, Carolina's daughter Teresa gave birth to her first child, named Maria Luisa after her paternal grandmother, the Empress. In time she would become an empress herself, as the wife of a former artillery officer from the rocky island of Corsica.

> *Thank you for your warning about Fersen. I don't trust him one inch either and in fact I won't talk to him about state affairs. . . . In public I make clear my attachment to the Queen, which indeed I do feel, and I pity her, but no further. It's true I'm having to sacrifice all my pride, since they're saying I'm stupid or indifferent or whatever, but it's only your approval and happiness that count for me. . . . Like you, I think the King and Queen are being poorly advised at the moment, and it will be difficult, not to say impossible, to help them as they wish.*

Marie Christine was writing to Leopold in the middle of February 1792. She had been sending letters constantly, even two or three times a day, passing him information on affairs in France and seeking his counsel on the still alarming situation in the Austrian Netherlands. "We're at open war with the Estates in Brabant," she told him now. "It's unbelievable the bad faith, the chicanery, the sophistry they'll use to escape any kind of order or obedience or rule." Moreover, the malcontents were receiving money from the French Assembly, who needed a friendly or at least unstable neighbour to prevent invasion of their own country from the north.

But now, more than ever, Leopold needed that territory to be secure. That very month he had signed a secret defence treaty with the newly amicable Prussians, agreeing to aid each other in the event of attack, and sealing the pact by reviving Joseph's plans of 1778 and 1784 to swap the Austrian Netherlands, far from Austria's heartlands, for neighbouring southern Bavaria. Friedrich "the Great" had then opposed this, but his nephew Friedrich Wilhelm II was prepared to accept it now, in return for more Polish territory for himself. And if, on this third attempt, the old Bavarian Elector Karl Theodor were to gain the Netherlands province at last, he wanted it at least to be at peace.

And on the question of peace in Europe as a whole, Leopold had by now changed his mind. Though he had consistently dismissed the "absurd projects" of Louis' brothers, which seemed only likely to make things worse for the captive royal family, he now felt an invasion of France would not only rein in the revolutionary extremists, it would very likely win Austria valuable territory—including, satisfyingly, his father's quondam Duchy of Lorraine, in French hands for more than fifty years. Marie Antoinette had long feared just such a venture, believing it would be enough to turn the revolutionaries into regicides. Had she known it, her many letters to Leopold and others urging an armed congress and no more, arduously produced and despatched with the greatest difficulty, had served in the end no purpose at all.

Marie Christine herself was still "anxious and in despair," as the émigré count had observed six months before. Albert's intelligent help notwithstanding, it was only Leopold who could make the decisions and issue the instructions she could act upon. But at this very point, she received the ap-

Gala evening at the Hofburg: "In Vienna, at court and in the private palaces of the aristocracy, it was all pleasure and gaiety."

Franz Stephan, Maria Theresia, and their children: "The Empress introduced to me, with an inexpressible grace, all the archduchesses one after the other, and the young archdukes; this family is the loveliest thing you can imagine."

Marianna at twenty-seven, spiritual and scientific: "I felt I loved her more than the others," her mother said.

Grand Duke and Emperor in 1769: Joseph (right) admired his younger brother, but Leopold disliked Joseph's autocratic temperament.

Albert at thirty-three. Amiable and capable, a general family favourite, but the Empress denied him any real power.

Marie Christine at twenty-four: A *grande dame* in the making, she positioned herself artfully as her mother's favourite.

Marie Christine and Albert (left) display prints from their Italian journey to the family: Maximilian, Marianna, Elisabeth, Maria Theresia (seated), and Joseph.

Elisabeth before and after her illness: The beauty of the family. "She only wants to be liked by some guardsman or prince, she . . . cultivates nothing else." But smallpox destroyed her marriage prospects.

Chancellor von Kaunitz: The vain but formidable "first minister of all the first ministers of Europe," he arranged the sisters' marriages.

Marianna helps the widowed Empress with her correspondence. A portrait of the late Franz Stephan hangs on the wall behind them.

Amalie in her twenties: Fractious and unpredictable, but with "something very touching . . . that is hard to resist."

Don Ferdinando of Parma. From a distanc[e] he appeared an ideal prince, but he prove[d] disappointing as both ruler and husband[.]

Guillaume du Tillot, marchese di Felino, Parma's first minister. From the outset, Amalie was his determined enemy.

A sad Amalie with her family in 1776. Of her fifteen children, only the four eldest would live to adulthood.

Josepha at the keyboard, by Liotard. Her mother found her flighty and dissembling; others felt she had "the best qualities of both her parents."

The three youngest sisters: Josepha (centre), Carolina (left) and Antonia. The latter two were particularly close.

TOP LEFT: *Il re nasone*, Ferdinando IV of Naples, "King Bignose."

TOP RIGHT: Carolina at seventeen: "Of all my daughters," the Empress said, "she is the most like me."

MIDDLE: Ferdinando and Carolina in 1783, with six of their eighteen children, painted by Angelika Kauffmann. The Queen wanted the artist to remain in Naples to teach her daughters.

BOTTOM LEFT: Marchese Bernardo Tanucci. He was determined to maintain Naples' dependence on Madrid, but Carolina proved his nemesis.

The diminutive Ferdinand and his statuesque wife, the duchessa Beatrice d'Este, tactfully seated.

Archduke Ferdinand: The least talented and best behaved of all Maria Theresia's children.

Archduke Maximilian: After an unpromising start, he proved an able ruler and a devoted family member.

The dauphin Louis in 1771: Introverted, indecisive, and "a complete sexual incompetent."

Marie Antoinette at fifteen: "Very tenderhearted," but "a featherbrain who . . . cannot make use of her advantages."

The eighteen-year-old Maximilian embarrassed his sister with his prudish disdain for the extravagance of the Versailles court.

Count Axel von Fersen: "So well received by the queen that this has given umbrage to several persons"—though the King was not among them.

The Queen of France, painted by Elisabeth Vigée-Le Brun in 1787, presents herself as mother of the nation. But it was not enough to salvage her public reputation.

Marie Antoinette, "the Widow Capet," imprisoned in 1792. She met her end with grace and dignity.

Amalie in later life, “cast aside like a pebble, living on the charity of the Emperor.” But friends remembered her kindness of heart.

Archduke Karl, talented military commander and Marie Christine's adopted son. His name was the last word she spoke.

Alexander Roslin's "grumpy" 1778 portrait of Marie Christine. "She had four sessions, each one three hours long. . . . You dare not move . . . the whole time."

Marianna in 1781: It took "all her philosophy" to leave Vienna for Klagenfurt, but she led a lively and purposeful life there.

Elisabeth in 1781: "The ugliest . . . and wittiest princess in the world."

Carolina in 1791, with John Acton, her capable and honest first minister, "a rarity" in Naples. She borrowed him from brother Leopold and never gave him back.

Carolina exasperates her son-in-law, the Emperor Franz, on a prolonged visit to her daughter Teresa in Vienna in 1802.

The young Emperor Franz in 1810: Conservative and opportunistic, he helped his family only grudgingly and finally capitulated to Napoleon.

Emperor Napoleon I (Napoleon Bonaparte) in 1814: Carolina resisted him fiercely, but called him "the greatest man . . . in centuries. . . . If he dies," she said, "they should make a powder out of him and give a dose of it to every ruler."

Carolina's granddaughter Marie Louise paints her new husband, Napoleon. By her marriage, she had made Carolina "the devil's grandmother."

Albert in 1812: The passions of his old age remained his mistresses, cautious hunting, and his great art collection.

Carolina in 1813. "All the hardships of fate seem to have weighed her down."

palling news of his sudden death in Vienna, at the age of just forty-four. Weakened by a recurrence of the old gastric problem that had plagued him at the long-ago time of his wedding, he had succumbed within only a few hours. "On the first of March the Emperor began to vomit with terrible spasms and threw up everything he took in; at half past three in the afternoon, while vomiting, he died, in the presence of H. M. the Empress." So his physician recorded. It had happened so suddenly that it was suspected he had been poisoned—by Jesuits, said some; by French agents, said others—but those who knew him blamed his demise on the frenetic pace of work he had kept for decades, only increased since his election as Emperor, and on the demands on his health of his many marital infidelities. Leopold's death was so unexpected that his son Karl, now living in Brussels, simply refused to believe it until Marie Christine gently took him aside and assured him in person that it was so.

She herself was grief-stricken. "It's too dreadful a blow," she wrote to Eleonore von Liechtenstein, "too heart-numbing, it strikes too many points. In our brother and sovereign we have lost a real friend." Not even her beloved Albert could console her. From Bonn, she summoned her favourite brother, Maximilian. "His friendship," she said, "is a salve for my wounded heart."

In the months of her captivity, Marie Antoinette had learned to mistrust Leopold, and her feelings toward him had soured. Elisabeth, by contrast, had adored him, and Amalie too had loved him for his reliable consideration of her, often when she was shunned elsewhere. But for Marie Christine, and for Carolina, too, his loss was of a different order. They had been in constant correspondence with him, and they had depended on him for years as a friend and advisor, to a degree that their sisters had not known. "I wasn't expecting it in the least," Carolina wrote to the marchese di Gallo in Vienna, now her ambassador there, "and when they said to me, 'There is bad news,' I thought of some massacre in France, never of this cruel catastrophe."

Leopold's widow Maria Luisa did not survive him long. "Sensitive, nervous, always a little depressive," her husband had described her. And at forty-six, after sixteen pregnancies, she was no longer physically strong. Her lungs suffering from "the sharp, cold air" of the Viennese spring, she died just two months later.

Leopold had not thought the men of the fractious French Assembly would initiate a war. But for those of them who sought one, his death lent wind to their sails. The assassination of the Swedish King Gustav III a fortnight later, by a literal stab in the back at the Stockholm Opera House, added to their confidence by eliminating another stalwart counterrevolutionary leader. They decided to gather France's restive armed forces into a new revolutionary army, destined for military action abroad. This, they believed, would keep them in control of the many soldiers who were not yet supporters of the Revolution at home. Moreover, victory on the battlefield would be followed by exactions and war booty, refilling the depleted national coffers. And victory seemed likely. The Assembly was sure the conflict would remain regional, since no major Power had responded to Leopold's call for an armed congress—they did not know of his secret defence treaty with Prussia. The well armed British wanted to remain neutral. And Leopold's successor, his eldest son, Franz, was an inexperienced twenty-four-year-old, not even officially elected head of the Holy Roman Empire, whose many composite states had as yet no leader.

Louis thought the gathering of so many soldiers would give the royalist majority among them, such as he believed it to be, an opportunity to put an end to the Revolution once and for all, and restore him fully to his throne. Though privately he hoped to avoid a war of aggression abroad, the Assembly was keeping him abreast of certain campaign plans, and these Marie Antoinette relayed—treacherously, in the eyes of the French who later learned of it—to Mercy and Fersen. On the twentieth of April 1792, Louis, under duress, mumbling and stammering and with tears in his eyes, appeared before the Assembly to propose a revolutionary war abroad. To avoid provoking the other German states, war was declared only on Franz as the new king of Hungary and Bohemia. The proposal was at once accepted, to wild cheering from the crowded public gallery.

. . .

THE FIRST TARGET of the French revolutionary army was the neighbouring Austrian Netherlands; an invasion force was assembled in only ten days. But France itself was nearing a state of civil war; there would have been occupation enough to employ the troops at home, especially in the streets of the capital. On the twentieth of June, an armed crowd assailed the Tuileries, overpowering the guards and breaking into the palace. Among the witnesses, in Paris in search of a new artillery commission, was the twenty-two-year-old Napoleone Buonaparte. He was appalled at the licence given the crowd: The forces of law and order appear to have deliberately taken their time to arrive. Inside the palace, with Madame Elisabeth held at knife-point and the Queen cowering behind a huge table with the dauphin, the King was forced to appear at a window wearing the red Phrygian cap of the revolutionaries. Though his wife felt he showed "firmness and an impressive strength," Buonaparte thought otherwise. *Che coglione!* he is said to have muttered, as he watched Louis swig from a bottle of wine to toast the health of his captors—*What an arsehole!*

Louis himself had believed for some time that his assassination was imminent, and had even received the last sacrament in preparation for death. By the end of this day, Marie Antoinette was convinced of the same. In a coded letter written in invisible ink and smuggled out by her hairdresser, she told Fersen, "I'm still alive, but it has been a terrible day! Now it's not me they want most, it's the very life of my husband. They're not concealing it any longer."

At the Assembly, the Jacobins announced that unless the monarchy was abolished, the Tuileries would be attacked again: Even the date was specified, the tenth of August 1792. The palace guard was vastly increased to some forty-five hundred men—though of two thousand aristocrats summoned, only three hundred answered the call. Tension and fear increased on both sides when a manifesto was received from the Duke of Braunschweig, *generalissimo* of the Prussian forces, Austria's ally, that if the Tuileries was attacked again, or if any member of the royal family harmed, the city of Paris would be destroyed and any person resisting put to the sword. Marie Antoinette had long urged a threat of this kind, and it seems that both Fersen and Artois had had a hand in the manifesto's composition, but though intended to intimidate the revolutionaries, it only served to outrage and embolden them.

On the tenth of August, the Tuileries was stormed again. This time the armed mob—organized, it seems, by the Jacobin leader Danton—was twenty thousand strong. Buonaparte saw them near the palace, one man brandishing a head on a pike. Accosted by a rough group, the well dressed young officer at once began shouting *Vive la nation!* to signal his loyalty to the Revolution. But the sights he saw that day were enough to shatter his youthful faith in the goodwill of "the people," and it was not to return.

Resistance evidently being futile, the royal family, with their friends and loyal servants, quickly left the palace for the nearby *Manège*, meeting-place of the Assembly. In their haste, they left many incriminating papers behind, and Louis forgot to instruct his thousand Swiss Guards to abandon the defence of the Tuileries: By the time he remembered to do so, they had killed or wounded several hundred of the attackers. His order arriving at last, the insurgents turned on the Guards, killing them to a man, before—or even after—mutilating their bodies, then ransacked the palace.

The royal family passed two fearful and hungry days in a single small room attached to the *Manège*, while the Assembly, still partly sympathetic to them, discussed where they should go now that the Tuileries was uninhabitable. Eventually the decision was given over to the Paris Commune. Since 1789 the city's governing body, the Commune was by now dominated by hardline Jacobins, who ordered the family and their attendants to the immense medieval fortress of the Temple, two miles distant.

The Temple had belonged to the King's brother Artois, and within its ancient walls a sumptuous palace had been built, where the comte had lived. For a few hours the royal family thought this was to be their new abode, but soon enough they were led through the gardens to the forbidding Great

Tower. Marie Antoinette had always been repelled by its grim, high walls, and had repeatedly asked her brother-in-law to have it demolished. Now it was to be converted into a prison for herself and her family; in the meantime, they were to be housed in a series of mean little rooms in the adjoining Little Tower. They were at least permitted to take daily exercise in the courtyard, and were even given money to buy clothes and a few other necessities, for they had fled the Tuileries with nothing.

Those who had fled with them did not remain in the Temple. Though the servants were set free, the nobles, including the children's governess, Madame de Tourzel, and the Queen's friend, the Princesse de Lamballe, were taken to other prisons in the city. But the dauphin's clever valet, thirty-three-year-old Jean-Baptiste Cléry, managed to have himself reassigned as valet to the King. And together with Louis' chef Turgy, he was to prove a lifeline for the family, mitigating many small hardships and, importantly, smuggling coded messages in and out on their behalf, little notes in hats and gloves and biscuit boxes, or simply by a slowly agreed sign language. The Temple was a large complex of buildings with some two hundred guards and many servants and other officials. There were enough cautious royalists among them to help Cléry, but also to add risk in the fragile chains of trust. More than once, sympathizers gave themselves away or simply changed their minds.

Within a week of the family's transfer to the Temple, France was invaded. By the end of August, Prussian troops had broken through revolutionary defences to take the vital eastern fortress of Verdun, with its commander committing suicide to avoid the dishonour of surrender. The path to Paris now lay open to the Prussians, and panic seized the city. On the second of September, the Commune, with the Duke of Braunschweig's threat to kill all resisters ringing in their ears, called the citizens to arms, but without organization, the call resulted in a rampage. Nobles, priests, anyone suspected of counterrevolutionary sympathies fell victim to the terrified and murderous mobs. Fuelling the paranoia, the quondam revolutionary hero Lafayette called on his National Guard to turn against their own citizens: Their refusal sent him fleeing for his life to Brussels. Believing the royalists recently imprisoned would join the invading forces against them, the mobs attacked the city's prisons, killing more than a thousand inmates, most of them ordinary criminals. Among the victims was the Princesse de Lamballe.

On the afternoon of the third of September, Marie Antoinette and Louis were seated at a table in their cell playing backgammon, when they heard a tremendous commotion outside the Tower. One of the guards went to the window to see, and suddenly pulled the curtains shut. A number of soldiers appeared at the door asking for Louis to go to the window but, as young Marie-Thérèse later wrote in her memoirs, the guards would not allow it. Louis asked what was the matter. "Well, monsieur," replied a young soldier, "since you want to know, they want to show you Madame de Lamballe's head." For two hours the guards and soldiers argued, with one of the former hanging his tricolour sash across the door to emphasize their loyalty to the Revolution, until it was agreed that six of the killers could parade around the Tower sporting the bloody head at the end of a pike, on condition that they left the Princess' naked body at the door—they had wanted to drag it around as well. The ghastly sight appearing at the window, Marie Antoinette fainted. The guard who had displayed the tricolour coolly asked Louis to pay him for it.

The bloodlust spread to dozens of other towns, and once sated, the chaos remained. In Paris, the unguarded storehouse for the crown jewels was robbed for six consecutive nights before anyone noticed, while the Prussians continued their westward march. But at Valmy in the Champagne, on the twentieth of September, the heroic attitudes of French volunteer forces shouting *Vive la nation!* and singing the "Marseillaise"—and perhaps concern to save his men for a fight for more territory in Poland—persuaded Braunschweig to call off his attack with scarcely a shot being fired beyond a few listless cannonballs: Having advanced only two hundred paces, his army stopped, and the Duke called a council of war.

Though it was the French who left the field that night, in drenching rain, their quasi-victory at Valmy was claimed as a triumph for the Revolution. In the event, it proved to be no less. The dramatist Goethe, travelling with the Prussian army, declared it "the beginning of a new epoch in the history of the world." Though hardly a battle at all, Valmy revealed the determination of the French revolutionaries, and the half-heartedness of their Coalition opponents. From this point on, the Revolution was secured. Despite some defeats, the armies of France would remain in the ascendant for a generation.

WITH THE NEWS FROM VALMY came the end of France's monarchy. The very next day, the country was declared a republic, and the single-chamber Assembly, now renamed the Convention, set about drafting another new constitution. This time Louis did not even have to make a pretence of agreeing with it, since he was not consulted. He had become a private citizen, and was now known, at least in his prison, by the name of Louis Capet, the surname taken from a long-ago ancestor.

As for his queen, she was now Citizeness Antoinette Capet. "I tremble continually for my poor sister," Carolina told her ambassador Gallo in Vienna. "Only a miracle can save her."

# XXVI

# 1792–1793

*In which the French capture the Austrian Netherlands, two show trials take place in Paris, and Louis and Marie Antoinette meet their end.*

On the nineteenth of November 1792, aflame with a sense of history in the making, the Convention in Paris issued an Edict of Fraternity, calling on the common people of all countries in Europe to rise up against their princes and churchmen and take the government into their own hands. The Convention was in confident mood. The Prussian invasion from the east had been stopped. And after five months of fighting in the northern borderlands, France had wrested the Austrian Netherlands from the Habsburgs. A series of early Austrian victories had been upended by increasing experience on the part of the volunteer French forces, and by indecisiveness and opportunism among the Belgians themselves.

Albert had been in the field at the head of a small army, with the Archduke Karl alongside him. On Franz's orders, Marie Christine had remained in Brussels, charged with keeping the uncooperative Estates in the Habsburg camp, but it was no easy task—as the sister of Marie Antoinette, she was a ready target for Jacobin calumny, and when the French town of Lille was besieged, she was even supposed to have begun the cannon-firing herself.

With French victories mounting, Franz transferred such power as might now be exercised from his aunt to the Count von Metternich, father of the precocious Clemens, who was already serving in Brussels. Having secured vital state papers, Marie Christine began packing up her own most valuable possessions.

Early in November 1792, she had fled Brussels for an army camp near Maastricht, where she was reunited with Albert and Karl. Here she had hoped to stop, but the townspeople were in revolutionary mood, and there were French troops closing in behind them. Though Albert was ill, they could not stay. They hastened across the German border and on to the gabled medieval town of Münster, to take refuge once again with brother Maximilian; here they were to pass the winter. Though Albert recuperated only slowly, Marie Christine's nerves were gradually calmed by the unflamboyant German town and its plain-speaking people. Long entranced by high French culture, she had in recent years learned to see a tawdriness in its sparkle. And though some of her finest works of art, and most of Albert's prized library, were lost in a wreck off the stormy Friesian coast, two other richly laden ships arrived safely in Hamburg, to provide eventual consolation.

**If the month** of November 1792 had carried Marie Christine to a place of temporary safety, for Marie Antoinette and her family, it had brought only more peril. In the first week of December, the Convention set about preparing a case against Louis, for treason, as France's former head of state.

Both the preliminary hearing, at which Louis heard for the first time the charges against him, and the trial itself, on the twenty-sixth of December, were held before a packed public gallery, in the Convention's usual hall of meeting. Louis had made a will beforehand, believing he would be murdered on his way there. There was no prosecutor and no judge but, keenly aware of the criticism faced by the regicides of the English King Charles I in 1649, the deputies were careful to allow a proper defence, though only ten days for its preparation. The two elder counsel ensured their arguments would be heard in the huge hall by engaging a brilliant young lawyer of notably loud voice to present them.

The defence, partly on the grounds of unconstitutionality, was legally solid and eloquently made—Louis had instructed his counsel to avoid any emotional appeals. But the papers he had left behind at the Tuileries provided clear evidence of his collusion with the military powers now attacking France: A guilty verdict was inevitable, and indeed, apart from a few abstentions, unanimous. A further motion that the verdict be put to the people for approval was easily defeated. As for the sentence, almost half the 721 Convention members present voted for imprisonment or exile or even deferred execution. They were defeated by only five votes—according to one assessment, by only a single vote. Louis was condemned to death, the sentence to be carried out within twenty-four hours. Among those voting for immediate execution were his own ambitious cousin, the duc d'Orléans, now strategically presenting himself as Citizen Philippe Égalité (Equality). After learning of the sentence, Louis surprised his guards by eating a hearty dinner. They had thought he would try to kill himself.

With so little time left, and with all the Powers of Europe antagonistic to France, there was nothing their leaders could do to plead for clemency. Touchingly or pathetically, Amalie had written weeks before from her little Duchy of Parma to the King of still neutral Spain, apparently urging him to intervene. But the secretaries had been unable to decipher her by now diabolical handwriting, and had marked the letter illegible. It would in any case have had no effect.

Louis was permitted to confess to a priest of his own choosing and to see his family, from whom he had been separated since their arrest almost four months before. This he did, on the twenty-first of January, the morning of his execution. This final meeting was private, but it was observed by the King's valet Cléry, through the glass window of a side door. Cléry watched as Louis told them of his impending execution; he saw Marie Antoinette sway with shock, then break down weeping. The little dauphin wrapped his arms fiercely around his father's knees, while Louis spoke to him of God, and urged him to pardon those who had condemned him. He then gave details of his trial, his words relayed, years later, by the only survivor of that harrowing scene, his daughter, Marie-Thérèse. Louis remained with his family for almost two hours. As he turned to go, Marie-Thérèse fell at his feet in a dead faint.

Two days later, the American Gouverneur Morris, now his country's minister plenipotentiary in Paris, wrote to Secretary of State Thomas Jefferson in Philadelphia:

> *The late King of this Country has been publicly executed. He died in a manner becoming his Dignity. Mounting the Scaffold he express'd anew his Forgiveness of those who persecuted him and a Prayer that his deluded people might be benefited by his Death. On the Scaffold he attempted to speak but the commanding Officer, Santerre, ordered the Drums to be beat. The King made two unavailing Efforts but with the same bad Success. The Executioners threw him down and were in such haste as to let fall the Axe before his Neck was properly plac'd so that he was mangled.*

The news was reported the following day in the *Gazette de France*, and so matter-of-factly that, when it reached Naples more than two weeks later, Carolina had to read it three times before she fully understood what had happened. In London, Prime Minister Pitt denounced Louis' execution as "the foulest and most atrocious deed which the history of the world has yet had occasion to attest." In St Petersburg, the Tsarina Catherine fell physically ill on hearing the news. The revolutionary spirit was abroad in Poland, too, and as ruler of more than a third of that cynically partitioned land, she now felt the threat personally. In shock, she took to her bed.

She did not stay there long: With her customary energy she was soon despatching troops to her new territories to the west, with no intention, however, of sending them as far as France. First, there was more of Poland to be devoured.

**Marie Christine heard** of Louis' execution on the way to Vienna, where she and Albert had been summoned by their emperor-nephew Franz. The news added shock and grief to an already dreadful winter journey of four hundred miles through snow and mud, with Albert still unwell, and only sporadic news of their adopted son, Karl, who had returned to active service in the Austrian Netherlands. In Augsburg, far to the south, they stopped to rest a few days. Here Albert's brother Clemens had fled to escape French forces advancing on his Prince Bishopric of Trier. Elisabeth, too, had made a cold and bumpy journey from Innsbruck through the Tyrolean mountains down to the flat land of Augsburg to see them. Unlike her younger sisters, she was on easy good terms with Marie Christine: Perhaps, as with so much else in her life, Elisabeth no longer took her too seriously. She was generally eager to meet up with family members, and she may have been seeking some special reassurance now, after the appalling news from France. In Innsbruck itself, an English lord was setting up a club, apparently without irony, to promote revolutionary ideology among the young. And whether prompted by this or not, the forty-nine-year-old Archduchess had given instructions for a sepulchre to be built for herself at the city's cemetery.

Though Marie Christine and Albert were en route to Vienna, it was in no way certain where they would now live. Officially, they were still joint governors of the Austrian Netherlands, assuming the territory could be won back from the French. Even in Albert's home city of Dresden, they had no residence of their own. Long before, they had talked of retiring to Italy, and it now seemed to an alarmed Carolina that they might seek to reestablish themselves near her, or with her empress daughter Teresa, Franz's wife, in Vienna. "Put plainly, I wish my sister every good fortune," she told Teresa, "but not with me. I hope she won't come here at all, or just make a brief stop in Naples. Venice, Rome, Pisa are all better places to visit," she said, implausibly, "but where will she settle? In Styria, in Graz, in Ljubljana? The best place would be Saxony, because if she's in Hungary, or even worse, in Vienna, you'll never have a moment's peace. I'm quite decided—to lose my peace and quiet for the rest of my life, my health wouldn't stand it and I don't want it, and your dear father knows her as I do, and he thinks the same."

Carolina thought Marie Christine might remain several months in Vienna, and she warned Teresa not to allow herself to be manipulated by her aunt and not to take her into her confidence. If there were outbursts of anger, these were only staged to provoke a reaction, she wrote, "but when she wants to she can be very insinuating and pleasant and that's when you need to keep your distance if you're to avoid trouble."

Marie Christine and Albert reached the imperial city in mid-March, in time for the formal celebrations of the Emperor's twenty-fifth birthday. There were still some familiar faces in the new court—Count Rosenberg and the eighty-two-year-old Prince von Kaunitz, only just retired from the Chancellorship, and Eleonore von Liechtenstein, now a widow—but it was not a happy reunion, for all that. As Carolina had feared, Marie Christine began trying to gain some ascendance over the twenty-year-old Teresa, "but if you and your dear husband remain firm, and just take note of all her gossip about different women and men, but don't lend it any credence, after three or four months you'll be left in peace, because once she sees that with all her efforts she can't get through to you, she'll give up and she'll go."

In the event it was only a matter of weeks before Marie Christine "gave up and went." Never confident of their loyalty to him, and perhaps now influenced by the warnings of his mother-in-law, Franz accused his aunt and uncle of dereliction of duty in Brussels and, despite his own transfer of executive power to Count Metternich, even of desertion. Though their governorships had been lifetime appointments, guaranteed by Maria Theresia, Joseph, and Leopold, he now abrogated them, together with the handsome salaries they encompassed.

Outraged, the pair departed for Albert's home city of Dresden, from where Marie Christine despatched a series of sharp letters to her nephew, demanding the money owed them. Even through their years in Brussels, there had been many payments missed, and Marie Christine, as an imperial daughter, was personally entitled to a substantial additional sum and a residence in Vienna. Taken aback, Franz at once offered them half the money owed: Recognizing the many demands on the imperial purse in the current state of war, they accepted. As a residence he returned to them the little Palais Tarouca, their home in the days of the old Empress. It was not empty, but as yet they were still in Dresden: They might take possession of it on the death of its current inhabitant, an elderly minister in conveniently poor health. Marie Christine was pacified. Albert, still not quite recovered from his illness and now fifty-five, settled in, as he thought, to a bookish retirement.

The Belgian Estates had been mistaken in expecting the victorious French to respect their constitution. The invasion force lacked provisions of its own and, despite objections from one of its generals, the earnest Charles Dumouriez, had been simply living off the Belgian people and confiscating from the Church anything that could be turned into cash. It now seemed to the Belgians that the French were bent on destroying their Catholic traditions, and a resurrected loyalty to Austria ensued among them. The French derided them as too mired in "superstition and ignorance" to make reliable revolutionaries, but the loss of their support was enough to give the Austrians a swift and important victory at Neerwinden, near Brussels, in March 1793, with the Archduke Karl in a commanding role. Within weeks, the French army was routed, with one of its generals guillotined in Paris and Dumouriez himself defected to the Austrians to avoid the same fate.

Franz rewarded his brother Karl by appointing him the new governor-general of the reclaimed Austrian Netherlands; the dashing twenty-one-year-old Prince received a hero's welcome as he rode into liberated Brussels. The Belgians' treasured constitution was reinstated but, though Karl personally supported it, the Estates had cause enough to doubt the young Emperor's good faith. They accepted the return of Austrian power and agreed to cooperate, but they went on grumbling.

**Louis' execution had** brought about the creation of an armed Coalition against France. Austria and Prussia were now joined by Spain and Britain, the latter more concerned about commercial threats than revolutionary ideology. Austria's forces were drawn from its many crown lands, including some recently reclaimed by the Ottomans. In Innsbruck, Elisabeth fêted a free band of Serbian soldiers still loyal to the Habsburgs with wine and bread and cheese, inviting a display of their traditional dancing in the main square: Half the people of the town turned out to watch them caper in their broad trousers and red cloaks and caps, pistols still tucked into their belts.

Naples, short of money and, despite its new navy, unprepared for war, remained as yet neutral, and anxious to avoid further provoking the French: A refusal to receive an ambassador from the new Republic had resulted in French ships appearing at Naples in mid-December 1792, demanding money and help with repairs, and threatening to declare war if it was denied; with no adequate means of defending themselves, the Neapolitans had been compelled to a resentful acquiescence. Now, in these restive months of spring, with grain stocks low, the new harvest yet to ripen, and the price of food rising "from one day to the next, with the poor crying out," it seemed an invasion force might meet little resistance from the common people, or even from some of the ruling class: To Carolina's horror, the twenty-four-year-old Grand Duke Ferdinand III of Tuscany, her own nephew and son-in-law, had been the first sovereign in all of Europe to recognize the French Republic.

But if Naples was hungry, France was hungry, too, and for the moment, Carolina hoped this might be enough to prevent the revolutionary forces from turning toward her territory. "If famine really takes hold there, and it's already being felt quite sharply in France, their courage and strength and capacity to fight may fail," she wrote to Franz, "and Italy will be left in peace."

Further north, in the Duchy of Parma, Amalie too seemed concerned to prevent a French invasion, or to quell the very modest revolutionary stirrings in her own duchy, or to help Marie Antoinette escape, or to achieve something else entirely: As so often with her sister's near impenetrable handwriting, Carolina was not sure. Amalie had sent her a mysterious parcel containing twenty-four boxes arranged in a circle, and "the whole thing looks to me like a code," she told Gallo in Vienna. "At first I thought it contained garden seeds, it was so light"—Carolina's vast garden at Caserta was famous—"but it looks as if it's locating and outlining military developments. I wanted to send it to my daughter or the Emperor and I could do that quite innocently, pretending I thought it was full of toy soldiers. But I'm not good at dissembling, and as I say, I think it's a code. So I'm sending it to you."

Amalie may have been seeking some kind of reconciliation with Carolina, whom she knew to be following military affairs with keen interest. The latter's seven months at Leopold's court, and the marriage of her two daughters with his sons, had caused a rupture between the two sisters. "Since my sojourn in Vienna I'm no longer on terms of friendship or confidence with her," Carolina continued. "I'm sorry for her when she's unhappy, and I'll gladly help her, but at the same time I will prevent any kind of intrigue that could be dangerous or malicious. The loss of the Netherlands seems to me misfortune enough without adding to it with intrigues and secret messages to God knows who."

Amalie seems to have received no response to her cryptic parcel. No one in Vienna was able to make any more sense of it than anyone in Naples had been. But Carolina's cautious neutrality was soon interrupted. In April, the British secretly approached Ferdinando, offering a handsome bribe and a promise to defend his coasts for the duration of the war against France, if he opened his harbour to their fleet. In mid-July 1793, prompted by Sir William Hamilton, Ferdinando signed the proffered treaty of alliance, and Naples became a British naval base. Soon afterwards, the Neapolitans sighted the warship *Agamemnon* sailing into their beautiful bay, on the bridge its brilliant, impulsive thirty-five-year-old Commander Horatio Nelson, soon to be viewed by Carolina as the saviour of the Kingdom.

Carolina's active temperament was in no way suited to the watching and waiting of political neutrality. "In our hearts," she told Franz, "we have wanted to fight since the very beginning, but without any guarantee of safety for our states it would have been imprudent, even criminal. The business of last December [with the French ships] proves the truth of that." The long imprisonment of the royal family had made caution even more necessary, with opponents of the French government fearing to provoke it to violence against them. But much had changed since Louis' execution. Carolina no longer had any real hope that her sister would survive. It seemed only a question of time before Marie Antoinette herself and her young son, too, would be led to the guillotine.

Assuming fourteen-year-old Marie-Thérèse, with no claim to the throne, would be spared, Carolina was making plans to "reclaim the girl," as she told Gallo, "and the King agrees. Where should she go after the massacre of her parents? I think I'm the only one who wants to and the only one who should take her in as my daughter, and if I can, establish her as just that. The only difficulty is for Francesco," her eldest son, now fifteen, who was currently betrothed, indeed married by proxy, to his cousin Clementina, daughter of the late Leopold. Carolina evidently hoped to have the ceremony annulled and marry him instead to Marie-Thérèse. Marie Antoinette herself also seems to have expected her own execution, as Carolina described, relaying the news she had received from Paris: "Every moment, at every sound, every cry, every time someone comes into her room, my unhappy sister falls to her knees and starts praying and preparing herself for death."

In fact it was not certain that "the Widow Capet," as she was now known, would be executed at all. While the more radical members of the Convention urged it, others suggested she might be ransomed for a huge sum, or exchanged for French prisoners of war, or simply locked away in a convent or banished from the country. The English revolutionary firebrand Thomas Paine, famous for his support of American independence and now, despite his complete ignorance of the French language, an elected member of the Convention, even proposed she be exiled to the new United States.

Fersen believed she might still be rescued. The King's execution had brought more countries into the Coalition against France, though without the bellicose Gustav III, Fersen's own homeland of Sweden remained outside: Duke Karl, the new Regent, was now suggesting the Count be appointed to England. He resisted the move. "I would be forced to leave [my mistress] Eleanore," he confided to his diary, "and to go far away from Her [the Queen] and French affairs, which give me the opportunity of serving Her and contributing to Her liberation. I was so much the more disconsolate since the Duke had said my mission here had become superfluous." But in mid-March, with the Archduke Karl's defeat of the French army at Neerwinden, hopes for the captive royal family had risen: Fersen soon found himself Sweden's ambassador to the eight-year-old Louis XVII. Though the appointment was somewhat hollow, since he could not even visit the boy, he was at least permitted to stay on the European continent.

After the Prussian retreat at Valmy late in 1792, tens of thousands of volunteer soldiers, believing France's borders to be secure, had simply left their battalions and drifted home. The Convention had responded in February 1793 with an attempt to recruit three hundred thousand men, volunteers if possible, otherwise by force. This had been widely resisted. The price of bread was rising sharply, with regional hunger turning people desperate. Unwarranted arrests and ongoing executions without trial led to fierce political polarization and a surge in counterrevolutionary violence. France had entered a state of civil war.

In April 1793, with Catholic and royalist armies forming in the Vendée and other western regions of the country, and shifting foreign alliances threatening it from outside, the Convention appointed an emergency Committee of Public Safety, a rotating group of twelve men, to serve only one month at a time, to direct the course of all military action. While executive power officially remained with the Convention, the Committee was to serve as its wartime cabinet. It quickly assumed a wider importance, with Jacobin influence increasing steadily within it. Though without any official leader, it was at first dominated by Georges Danton, despite his being already suspected of profiteering. He was soon superseded by the "incorruptible" revolutionary purist, Maximilien Robespierre, whose name was to become a byword for the Reign of Terror, which intensified at this point in the Revolution. But he had not been its only instigator, and it was not entirely to end with his fall.

In mid-July, one of the Convention's most prominent Jacobin members, Jean-Paul Marat, was assassinated at his home in Paris. It was Marat who had urged the King's trial after the storming of the Tuileries, and he was widely believed to have encouraged the prison massacres of the previous September. Marat had suffered from a serious skin condition which often obliged him to conduct his work from a bath of sulphurous medicinal water, and it was here that he had met his end, stabbed to death with the single blow of a kitchen knife. His assassin was the petite twenty-four-year-old Charlotte Corday, who had travelled from Normandy on her own initiative, determined to avenge the massacres and to prevent the civil war she believed Marat to be fomenting. After the deed she had simply remained in the bathroom, awaiting her own arrest, and certain execution.

Marat's assassination intensified the government's response to the counterrevolution. Citizens were urged to destroy all symbols of monarchy, and even to desecrate royal tombs. A *levée en masse*, compulsory conscription, more than trebled the number of men under arms to some eight hundred thousand: France now had fifteen revolutionary armies.

Marie Antoinette, still in the Temple Tower, found a lurid new light cast upon her as the figurehead of reaction. The conditions of her daily life grew worse. Her books and writing materials were taken away, and with the jailers afraid of being thought sympathetic, small things, such as the herbal drinks and fresh flowers that her servant brought in, were now denied her. And her linen was changed less frequently, a sad humiliation for a woman of thirty-seven, whose monthly periods had become heavy to the point of haemorrhage. Bitterest of all, eight-year-old Louis-Charles had been moved to a different cell. "They have taken her son from her," Carolina told Gallo in Vienna. She had not made it easy for them, blocking their path to his bed for over an hour, insisting they would have to kill her first. Only when the Commune officials threatened to kill both the children and her sister-in-law Elisabeth had she relented, weeping and exhausted. "This will have been a dreadful blow for my most unhappy sister," wrote Carolina. "I hope it will bring about her end. For a long time now I have been reduced to wishing her a natural death as the happiest thing that could befall her."

In the first week of August 1793, in the middle of the night, Marie Antoinette was awoken by officers of the Convention, come to transfer her from the Temple Tower to the Gothic prison of the Conciergerie near Notre Dame; here she was to await trial as a common criminal. Obliged to dress in front of the four men, permitted to take only a few clothes and a bottle of smelling salts in case she should faint, she was driven through Paris to the Île de la Cité, and finally led into a small cell, "damp and fetid, without a stove or fireplace," with a canvas bed, a rough table and chair, and a bucket. Two men were to guard her day and night, and she was not permitted to leave the cell at all, not even to wash her clothes in an outside fountain, as the other women prisoners did. High in the wall of the cell was a small iron grille through which she could be observed, and many new-made citizens came to see her, paying the prison authorities for a glimpse of their fallen queen. A few clumsy attempts by royalist sympathizers to free her only made things worse: She was transferred to an even smaller cell, her ration of precious candles was reduced, and her interrogations lengthened; they were conducted almost in darkness, the faces of her accusers obscured.

Early in September, at a secret overnight meeting of the Committee of Public Safety, it was decided she must die. Her pitiless nemesis was the journalist Jacques-René Hébert, celebrated in his persona of everyday ironmonger "Old Duchesne" for his crude and clever tirades against the royal family and all aristocrats. Though originally in favour of a constitutional monarchy, Hébert had always written savagely about Marie Antoinette, accusing her of every sort of sexual license and blaming the desperate state of the Kingdom's finances on her personal extravagances. Having failed to become an elected deputy, he still craved political recognition, and he found it in the Committee of Public Safety, thrusting himself forward to demand the execution of the Queen. He was not alone in wanting this, though others doubted a jury would find her guilty, or that her offences warranted the death penalty. Hébert concocted a plan to ensure both.

He had already done a great deal to paint the Queen as a debauched nymphomaniac, cuckolding the King with both men and women and in the most depraved ways, and though this picture had wide currency in France and well beyond, there had never been any evidence to prove it. Hébert now suggested exploiting the eight-year-old dauphin in order to provide some.

The little boy was in a frighteningly vulnerable position. Wrenched from his mother's arms three months before, he had been given into the hands of a near-illiterate former shoemaker and owner of a cheap eatery, fifty-seven-year-old Antoine Simon, now a Commissioner of the Paris Commune, who was to "re-educate" the child, turning him into a committed citizen of the new republic. Simon had been a poor shoemaker and a worse businessman, and he had transformed his bitter resentment of those more privileged into a fanatical devotion to the Revolution. This, and his evident manipulability, had brought him to the attention of Hébert, and hence to his current appointment. Though a coarse and even violent man, Simon had treated Louis-Charles at first with reasonable care, but goaded by Hébert, he had quickly turned abusive.

Hébert's plan was to turn the child against his mother and lead him to incriminate her. Louis-Charles was taught to swear and blaspheme and to call Marie Antoinette and Elisabeth whores. He was force-fed disgusting food and alcohol, and several times threatened with the guillotine, which caused him to faint in terror. He was given pornographic books and also, it seems, encouraged to masturbate—a significant aspect of the charges that were to be brought against his mother. Those prison guards who objected to the ongoing brutality kept silent out of fear: One commissioner who did complain was arrested. Cursed, beaten, kicked, the boy had become desperately nervous; gradually he stopped speaking at all.

The testimony Hébert needed was drafted by his own hand. On the sixth of October, following a questioning by officials of the Commune, it was given to Louis-Charles to sign. The child was drunk. After agreeing that his mother was sworn to bring down the Revolution, he confessed that she and his aunt had together taught him to masturbate, and that his mother had forced him to have sex with her. He then signed Hébert's prepared statement to that effect.

**Marie Antoinette's trial** began on the fourteenth of October 1793. In a touching gesture of defiance, she had put her now white hair up a little higher that morning, but her frail and haggard appearance still shocked the crowds packed into the public galleries, long used as they were to thinking of her as the personification of glamorous vice. Before the five judges and the twelve-man jury of a revolutionary tribunal, she sat in silence as the charges of counterrevolutionary conspiracy were read out. One of the jurors later described her as seeming to be lost in a world of her own, "moving her fingers, as when one plays on the Piano." To speak against her, forty-one "witnesses" had been engaged. For her defence she had been assigned two experienced counsel, one of them Claude Chauveau-Lagarde, who had recently defended Marat's assassin, Charlotte Corday; despite that failure, and despite having very little time to prepare his case, he was later to be interrogated as a suspected counterrevolutionary for defending Marie Antoinette too well.

There was never any doubt, including, it seems, in her own mind, that she would be found guilty. But the trial was also an exercise in the humiliation of a proud woman, and a vortex for the hatred of a foreigner in time of war. Repeatedly her loyalty to France was questioned, and though she always insisted on it, calmly and firmly, there was more than enough in the

Tuileries letters to show her support for Austria's armies. Over the years, she had learned to think of herself as French and to resist pressure over questions of patronage, telling Mercy that "it wasn't right for the court of Vienna to be nominating ministers for the court of Versailles"—which the ambassador had regarded as a "bizarre scruple." But in the cataclysm of the Revolution her first instincts had reasserted themselves. "Oh! God defend my fatherland and you!" she had exclaimed to Leopold, from "all the monsters and the misfortunes" besetting France.

Now, above all, she was concerned for her son, Louis-Charles, since his father's execution recognized him in royalist circles, and even in the new republic of the United States of America, as Louis XVII. The Convention, of course, regarded him in no such terms. To them he was simply Charles Capet, imprisoned for the sins of his fathers, if too young to be tried for any of his own. They had not wanted to kill him outright for fear of provoking sympathy for the counterrevolution, and besides, he was likely to serve as useful leverage in future dealings with foreign powers. Few deputies were likely to have been aware of the level of brutality to which he had been subjected over the past three months. Certainly his mother was not: Had she been, it would likely have brought about the "natural death" that Carolina had felt was now "the happiest thing that could befall her."

But in the course of the trial it became clear to Marie Antoinette that through this beloved child she was to be publicly defiled as a perverted woman and a vicious mother. To Hébert's charge of incest itself, she did not deign to respond, instead declaring fiercely that "nature itself repudiates any reply to such an accusation against a mother, as I call on every mother present to assert." From the shocked public audience came a sudden surge of sympathy for her, with Robespierre condemning Hébert for a fool whose machinations would lead to her acquittal after all.

Throughout the two days of the trial, faced with accusations sweeping from the treasonous to the ludicrous, her comportment remained dignified. At times she was openly defiant. Asked whether she regarded those with whom France was currently at war as her enemies, she replied, "I regard as my enemies all those who can harm my children." Once or twice she undercut her interrogator with a quick remark. Charged with treating her son at table as if he were a king, she snapped, "Did you see that yourself?"—which he had not. But she also lied, most obviously about being in contact with foreign powers. And the Tuileries letters proved she was lying.

The defence counsel Chauveau-Lagarde had too sanguinely prepared the Queen to expect only life imprisonment, but when the verdict was announced, at half past four in the morning of the sixteenth of October, it was followed by a sentence of death, to be carried out that day. Marie Antoinette made no response other than to bow her head. But while being led back to the Conciergerie, she broke down in tears. Recovering herself swiftly, she observed to her guards they would see no such weakness on her way to the scaffold.

Once returned to her cell, she sat down to write a last letter, not to her daughter, to whom she believed no letter would be delivered, but to her sister-in-law, Elisabeth, who had been imprisoned with her for so long. In it, she begged pardon for any harm she may have done "without wishing to." She also asked that her son be reminded of his father's last injunction, "that he should never seek to avenge our death!"—doubly important for Louis, still hoping to avoid civil war in France, and for himself, hoping for pardon at the divine judgement he believed he would soon face. Concerning the accusation her son had made against Elisabeth herself, "Forgive him, my dear sister," she wrote. "Think how young he is, and how easy it is to make a child say whatever you want him to, even if he doesn't understand it. The day will come, I hope, when he will feel all the more the value of your goodness and tenderness." She died, she said, in the Roman Catholic religion of her fathers, and bid farewell to her sisters and brothers and her friends—"Let them know at least that until my last moment I thought of them."

Her servant, Rosalie, came to her at seven o'clock, and helped her to change her underclothes, which were sodden with blood. The guards did not even turn their backs, though they did grudgingly grant her a moment's privacy to crouch over a bucket in the corner. The Queen had been seventy-six days in the Conciergerie, but when she was taken from her cell, Rosalie gave no curtsy and made no adieux. She simply watched her go, then ran to her room to weep and pray for her.

At eleven o'clock, dressed in a plain white shift and bonnet, with hands bound behind her and hair cut short so as not to blunt the blade of the guillotine, Marie Antoinette was brought to the prison gates. Though the King had been driven to the scaffold in a carriage, for his queen there was only a tumbril, a rough cart into which she now climbed, quickly and unaided, to be driven through the streets to the place of execution.

Twice she was approached by priests offering to accompany her, but she ignored them both, as she had said she would, not wishing to compromise their safety. Jeered and insulted by the Parisians as she passed, she gave no sign of noticing them, but maintained a firm composure. The volatile Jacobin painter Jacques-Louis David, who months before had voted for her husband's death, saw Marie-Antoinette now in the tumbril and quickly sketched her with mouth clenched and eyes downcast, but other witnesses, equally hostile, depicted her expression as calm and tranquil as the cart rattled slowly toward the Place de la Révolution.

They were surprised to see the lightness of her movements as she got down from the cart and climbed up to the scaffold. Her hands still bound, she pulled off her bonnet herself and walked quickly toward the guillotine, past the executioner Sanson, scion of a long line of Paris axemen and hangmen, the man who had killed her own husband. As she went, she accidentally trod on his foot. "I beg your pardon, monsieur," she said to him, "I didn't mean it."

Shortly afterwards, and for the last time, the Ambassador of Parma despatched his weekly report from Paris to his First Minister:

> *Your Excellency will have learned from the newspapers that the royal sovereign has died with great courage. Not for a single moment did she abjure her great soul and the illustrious blood of the House*

*of Austria. . . . The power of the Jacobins has reached its highest degree; it is useless to defy it.*

**On the nineteenth of October**, three days after Marie Antoinette's execution, Vienna's foremost newspaper reported in its foreign pages that a society of art lovers in Spain was reproducing an important collection of copper etchings, and from Germany came news of a string of victories for the Prussian army. From France itself, there was nothing to report. The next edition, published on Wednesday the twenty-third, reported from the Dutch Republic that Prince William of Orange had completed his inspection of the country's military forces, and from Russia, that a monument was to be erected in memory of the late Prince Potemkin. From France, there was still nothing to report.

On Wednesday the twenty-sixth, the Sultan of Morocco denounced the "anarchic despotism" now prevailing in France, and from that country itself, readers learned that military reverses were leading to riots, and that propertied people of both sexes were being driven out of their houses and even arrested. But there was still no news of Marie Antoinette.

A despatch, uncertain, finally arrived in Vienna on the twenty-ninth of October, thirteen days after her death. A Neapolitan prince, visiting the city as part of his Grand Tour of Europe, relayed it to a friend in Bavaria: "An agent has brought the news that the Queen has been killed," he wrote. "Some say on the eleventh—others say on the seventeenth. This rumour has led to a terrific fury here against everything that even looks French. . . . My God! What a barbaric century. The poor Queen, what an end fate had in store for her."

And in Naples, on the third of November, Carolina had been penning a note about a lively family reunion of the day before, when she was interrupted by the arrival of a courier. "I was here," she later continued, "in the middle of my letter, when I received the appalling news that my most unfortunate sister has ended by being torn apart. May God have taken pity on her in the last moments." She did not know that Marie Antoinette's body had been left lying on the bare ground, with its severed head beside it, while the men who should have buried it lingered over their midday bread, nor that their indifference had made time for the ghoulish Madame Tussaud to take a wax cast of the head before it was tossed into the common grave.

Carolina, eight months pregnant with her eighteenth child, and just recovering from one of the convulsive seizures which had begun to plague her, was prostrate with exhaustion and grief. But her immediate concern was for her sister's immortal soul, that God would have given her "the supernatural strength to forgive her villainous executioners," for like her late husband, it was only in doing so that could she expect mercy at her own last judgement. Hence Carolina was anxious to know every detail of Marie Antoinette's last hours. This, for the present, no one could tell her, but in time she would learn of the dignity and piety with which her sister had gone to her death, achieving at the last, after a life of erratic endeavour, a moment of human greatness.

# XXVII

# 1794-1797

In which a Jacobin plot in Naples is thwarted, Amalie's Parma is sold to the French, and an unknown Corsican makes his name.

The execution of Louis and Marie Antoinette turned a great many supporters of the Revolution determinedly against it, within France and beyond. From its early pinnacle of hopeful reform it seemed to have descended into violent chaos. Even foreign governments which had once observed complacently as the country's competing commercial structures disintegrated were now in fear of revolution spreading to their own borders. In Austria and Hungary, if latent Jacobin tendencies were monitored with a certain dilatoriness, active conspirators were arrested and their leaders put to death.

But for the would-be revolutionaries of Naples, the news from France inflamed rather than cooled Jacobin sympathies. Tempers and voices and fists were raised, until the "patriots," as they called themselves, split into two factions, with the histrionic names of *Romo* (*Repubblica o Morte*) and *Lomo* (*Libertà o Morte*). The *Romo* faction (a Republic or Death!) wanted the complete abolition of the monarchy; the *Lomo* faction (Liberty or Death!) wanted a constitutional monarchy, but significantly, not with the present King and Queen. Both parties agreed to work together until the revolution should be accomplished, at which point, supposedly, further discussion would suffice to allow a new Neapolitan state to be established that was acceptable to both. For now, the action to be taken was clear enough: They were to "capture the castles, rouse the rabble, burn the arsenal and docks, and massacre the royal family and their ministers." Money was dispersed among the poor folk of Naples to buy their support or at least their acquiescence; agitators were sent out to provoke insurrection in the provinces. Weapons were collected, leaders appointed, tactics agreed, and a day fixed for the uprising: the thirtieth of March, 1794.

Rumours of the plot circulated for weeks, but were largely dismissed as mere talk. Many among the Kingdom's nobility and gentry, jealous of the central place played by the foreigner John Acton in their government, were not displeased to hear of an underground wave of dissatisfaction. Unlike the common people, they did not revere their king, and neither did they love his queen, though they feared her influence. In any event, they assumed any change in government was likely to be in their favour. Even the Chief of Police, Luigi de' Medici, half agreed with them. Though he owed his position to Carolina—he was the brother of her favourite, the marchesa de San Marco—he had many friends among the conspirators, with two of them, indeed, living in his house. Whatever his motivation, he was slow to apprehend them, and they were astonished to find him presiding over a court of seven judges when eventually he did act, bringing fifty-three of them to trial.

Some of the leaders had followed a hint to escape, while others had not deigned to flee, considering themselves immune from prosecution as Medici's friends. He proved a slow and scrupulous judge, but with dozens of conspirators denouncing their fellows, and 124 volumes of cross-examined evidence emerging after months of trial, convictions were inevitable. Though two men were acquitted, most were exiled or imprisoned, and three were condemned to death.

The Queen they had plotted to kill now pleaded for their lives. "I have done all I possibly can to persuade the King to spare them," she wrote to Gallo in Vienna, "but in vain. He just says, 'If they had only wanted to take my life and the lives of my family, I would have been quite ready to pardon them, but they swore to destroy all religion, every constitution, and the State, and that I cannot excuse. The judges have condemned them unanimously and I owe it to the State and to the public safety to carry out the sentences.'" On the eighteenth of October, "the sad day of execution of our three unfortunate Jacobins," the men were publicly hanged in the palace square. Carolina refused to attend. "In spite of their crimes, I am wretched and really tormented to think of their youth and their despairing families," she wrote. "I dare not go out or even go near the window, the sight of them rends my heart."

The crowd of spectators was vast all the same, but remained orderly until the very end, when it seems a musket shot was fired—it was never established by whom. A horse bolted, panicking those standing nearby. A few random shots from the guards provoked a general stampede; more firing left dozens of people wounded, and six dead. But there was no rounding on the guardsmen, and no attempt to storm the palace. If the people of Naples really wanted a revolution, the Chief of Police afterwards remarked, they had missed a perfect opportunity.

IN FRANCE, WHERE PALACES had been stormed repeatedly, large areas remained still in the grip of civil war. In the western region of the Vendée, a ruthless "pacification" of a Catholic and monarchist rebellion had begun that would incur some four hundred thousand deaths. To the south, too, in the strategic Mediterranean port of Toulon, the townsfolk had maintained their fealty to the Bourbons, raising the *fleur-de-lys* in the name of the seven-year-old Louis XVII, and forcing the local Jacobins into hiding. In retaliation, revolutionary troops had been besieging the town for more than four months, through the autumn of 1793, with an Anglo-Spanish fleet and Neapolitan land forces aiding the loyalists. Both sides desperately needed Toulon, for it was a vital place, a natural harbour defended by a chain of forts, and a major naval arsenal, home to a third of France's warships.

The plan to besiege the city had come from a twenty-four-year-old Corsican officer, grudgingly appointed to replace a wounded superior. He had seen that, on so well fortified a city, a traditional attack with swords and muskets could not succeed; only sustained artillery bombardment could break through its defences. Though still sensitive about his inexact French, the young Napoleone Buonaparte, "the most active and obstinate of all the officers," as an English civilian observed, had confidence enough to commandeer munitions from all the surrounding towns, and charisma enough, despite being "a little ill looking fellow with sallow complexion," to draw his conscript soldiers into a keen fighting body. A final fierce and massive attack in mid-December had secured not only his victory but an absolute rout of his opponents, with the Spaniards fleeing "in the most cowardly manner" and the English commander, forced to surrender, soon locked in a Paris prison.

Carolina's own troops had acquitted themselves poorly. They abandoned Toulon and made haste back to their own kingdom, "leaving the whole of Italy exposed to invasion," as she lamented to her empress daughter Teresa in Vienna. They were followed by thousands of French moderate republicans, fleeing the vicious reprisals of their Jacobin compatriots. They were little more welcome in Naples. Carolina mistrusted their politics, and resented having to feed and house them when her own people were already in difficult straits. "We can't keep them prisoners, and we'll have to keep a constant watch on them," she wrote. "It's really a bad addition to Naples. Why can't the English take them for their colonies?"

Teresa was pregnant for the third time, and Carolina was advising her to massage her stomach and sides with perfumed water to prevent miscarriage. Her own eighteenth child was just two months old, "and she had to be pulled out of my body, I was too weak and sick and old to do it myself." The baby, herself big and strong, was named Elisabetta, after her aunt in Innsbruck, who declared herself enchanted with the compliment. And to her mother's relief, this child was to be her last. Carolina was forty-one, still suffering from convulsions, seemingly a legacy of the syphilis she had contracted from Ferdinando. Only a few days before, she had collapsed, remaining unconscious for a full hour, so alarming the court that a priest had been called to administer the last rites. She was exhausted, ill, and beset with difficulties, but nothing could stop her letter-writing, especially to Teresa. "Just imagine," she said, "I was fifteen years old and your dear father seventeen when I arrived in Naples, and we were all alone. If I were nearer to you I would tell you the story of my life and a thousand other things, so you could learn from my experience and avoid the mistakes I've made. . . . I'd give anything in the world to be able to come to you by balloon and just look after you and keep you company, but with no one knowing who I was, so I wouldn't have to see any of those dreadful émigrés."

Marie Christine and Albert had not returned to Brussels, even after its recapture by the Austrians, soon indeed to be reversed. They had spent the whole of 1793 in Dresden, and in January 1794 they made their way back to Vienna, with 230 servants, to reestablish their home there. They found Maximilian already ensconced in a snug little country house in Hetzendorf, near Schönbrunn: French troops were by now too close to his own city of Bonn. They were delighted to see him, though he was the bearer of unexpected tidings: Franz was forming a new imperial army with soldiers from the many German states of the Holy Roman Empire and an auxiliary force of French émigrés, and Albert was to be their overall commander. Not deigning or not daring to tell his uncle himself, Franz had delegated that task to Maximilian. Albert set off dutifully to defend the Rhineland.

In the autumn he was joined by Marie Christine. She was feverish and dejected, but as the winter drew on they moved to warmer quarters in Heidelberg, and here her mood was lifted by the arrival of the Archduke Karl, though he was himself unwell and had come to seek help from the renowned local physicians, famed throughout Europe for four hundred years already. Though they no doubt advised him now according to the best current theories, it is probably through his aunt's own simple daily care that Karl gradually regained his health. It was vital for her that he should, for, as she told a military friend, "It is my dear son who keeps me most attached to this world. He is the centre of my concerns and my sorrows and my joys."

But as Karl improved, Albert declined, albeit not physically. He had proved only a middling military commander, and in the spring of 1795 Franz instructed him to send the troops he still commanded to other Coalition generals: his army now disintegrated, and with it, a part of himself. In a state of deepening despondency, he submitted his resignation from the imperial forces; Karl, now recovered, carried the letter personally to his brother in Vienna. "And so," recorded the Duke, "with a heavy heart, I turned away from the path I had followed with ambition and devotion since my youth."

Among the fifty thousand French monarchists released from Albert's army was the comte d'Artois, who was now seeking a place to live. Franz approached his Aunt Elisabeth in Innsbruck, inviting her to provide a home for Artois, his tiny, long-nosed wife, and her sister, plus their three adult children and some thirty attendants. Elisabeth was startled by the request and not at all eager to comply. Artois had the reputation of being demanding and troublesome, and in any case, as she told Franz's wife, Teresa, in her rambling handwriting, "Sacred Majesty, it's impossible, I have only a dozen rooms, and as we know he's not a good solid Austrian, I'm afraid I'm useless at all that intriguing. . . . There are two houses in town, but do please tell your husband there's no room at court, I beg you my dear niece, do tell him, I'm fifty-two years old, I want a peaceful existence."

There was at least room again in the little palace in Vienna that Franz had granted Marie Christine and Albert after their dismissal from Brussels. The ailing old minister inhabiting it had finally given up the ghost. In May 1795 they moved back in.

BY NOW, A SUCCESSION of military successes abroad and unrelenting measures against its internal opponents had eased the pressure on the revolutionary government in Paris. The country was no longer in immediate danger: There was less need now for the ferocity of the Terror to keep the counterrevolution at bay. Many of those who had accepted or even helped to drive it had turned against its most prominent prosecutors, including the Jacobin leader Robespierre; in July 1794 he had been arrested and brought with twenty-one other men before the revolutionary tribunal. Given the passage of his own law, written only weeks before, prohibiting any legal defence for those accused, he and all the others had at once been condemned to death. Less brave than Marie Antoinette, Robespierre had attempted to shoot himself to avoid a public execution. He had failed, inflicting a serious wound to his jaw, and had been led in agony to the guillotine.

Though the mass executions ended soon afterwards, a great many individual Jacobin supporters were vengefully hunted down and killed, as the Revolution entered its final phase. In October 1795, the once feared Committee of Public Safety was abolished and the unified Convention replaced by a two-chamber Directory, with a strict separation of powers between the law-making *legislatif* and the implementing *executif.* It was to last four years, until the coup d'état perpetrated by the Corsican artillery officer, hero of Toulon, who would by then be the greatest general in Europe.

**Marie Antoinette had been wise** to address her last letter to her sister-in-law Elisabeth. This devout princess, still in her twenties, had proved an invaluable support through the griefs and horrors of four captive years. Despite her rigid reactionary views, at times unhelpful as others struggled to respond to a dangerous and unstable situation, her personal loyalty had never wavered, and her strong religious faith had brought comfort and even purpose to their most despairing hours. Left alone with her fourteen-year-old niece, she had created a daily routine of handwork and reading and prayer for the girl. This Marie-Thérèse had kept to, so maintaining a measure of structure and indeed mental stability even after her aunt's removal. She had not been informed when Elisabeth was guillotined in May 1794, nor did she know that her mother had met the same end until the late summer of 1795, by which time negotiations for her own release were underway.

No such good fortune was allotted to her brother Louis-Charles, who had died two months before. Insulted and maltreated for two anguished years, unaware of his mother's execution and constantly pleading to see her, the boy had declined from day to day, and irrevocably. "If only we are the only ones to suffer, and our sorrows and misfortunes can lead to a happier future for my poor child after us!" Marie Antoinette had written to Carolina long before. "This idea sustains my courage, but at other moments when I hold him in my arms, I am distraught to think he may be just as unfortunate as we are." It was as well she had never known what her beloved son endured. In the spring of 1795, his vicious keeper, Simon, had been dismissed, but the humane attentions of more sympathetic men had been too late to save him. In June, just ten years old, he had finally succumbed, leaving a pitiful, unfinished scratching on the wall of his cell: *Maman, I beg you—*

In late December of the same year, his traumatized sister was discreetly released. The Directory had hoped this would bring about a peace treaty with Austria, but Franz refused: He was not ready to stop the war and had no intention of recognizing the French Republic, which a treaty would have required. Under cover of darkness and with the porous incognito of Charlotte-Antoinette, Marie-Thérèse was carried to the Swiss city of Basel. Just turned seventeen, she descended from the carriage with the tremulous query, "Am I really safe now?"

A further eastward drive of 250 miles brought her, on New Year's Day 1796, to Elisabeth's palace in Innsbruck. The fastidious girl was not pleased to meet her bluff and disfigured old aunt, who further disconcerted her with news that she was soon to be married to her cousin the Archduke Karl: In due course, it was planned, they would ascend the restored throne of France together. Karl himself, now twenty-four, was not averse to the match: Marie-Thérèse's portraits showed a pretty blonde girl, with the drama of her background lending her an alluring romantic light. Had he met her in person, "Her eyes, her big azure blue eyes, so beautiful!" as another admirer declared, might have settled the matter for him.

Carolina had written to her niece, inviting her to think of her as a mother, and the girl had replied without enthusiasm, but touching her aunt's heart nonetheless by telling her, "My mother often spoke to me of you, she loved you more than her other sisters." Marie Christine, from her own palace near the Hofburg, took a good deal of trouble now to insinuate herself with Marie-Thérèse, possibly thinking of Karl, or simply considering it politic to cultivate a possible future Queen of France: Either way, it was wise to annul some of the prejudices the girl might have acquired from her mother, who had never been unequivocally fond of this intrusive and high-handed sister.

Perhaps, with no children of her own, Marie Christine was simply fond of the girl. Certainly they shared an insistence on court formalities that most at the Hofburg preferred to dispense with; in any case, Marie-Thérèse responded sincerely to her. She also got on particularly well with Franz, rather to the chagrin of his wife, Carolina's daughter, Teresa, who had until then enjoyed a close and happy five years of married life with him. There was no suggestion of any flirtation between the young Emperor and his rather prim French cousin. Rather, their conservative political views accorded very well: In the decades to come they would maintain their friendship, with the politics of both ossifying into the downright reactionary.

Marie-Thérèse was to remain three years in Vienna—a wistful Axel von Fersen would visit her once to pay his respects—and it would be twenty years before she returned to France, as the wife of her cousin the duc d'Angoulême, son of the comte d'Artois and his long-nosed comtesse. Though the duc had inherited the tiny stature and bizarre nose of his mother, he was a decent and sensible man, and the marriage was to prove a happy one.

**Early in March 1796,** France's Army of Italy welcomed a new commander, just twenty-six years old: General Napoleon Bonaparte, now writing his name in the French manner. Like hundreds of other young Frenchmen, he had been promoted swiftly: With a cadre of experienced aristocrats having fled into exile or been simply lynched in the streets, the revolutionary armies had from the outset had an unusually young and overwhelmingly proletarian officer corps, and over the previous four years of war, this had been further depleted by the guillotining of many officers, with battlefield defeats transmuted into counterrevolutionary treason.

The Army of Italy, a supposed force of sixty thousand soldiers, was in reality smaller by ten or even twenty thousand men. Of these, only a few could properly be called soldiers at all. Most were rough peasant or mountain boys, conscripts or volunteers, the latter as often for lack of alternative as for any real revolutionary ardour. Conditions in the army were unlikely to inspire them in that respect; pay was in arrears, food was scarce and poor, supplies were nonexistent. Lacking tents, they slept in the open; lacking hats, they wrapped handkerchiefs around their heads; lacking boots, they wove themselves shoes of straw; many of them even lacked trousers.

Little wonder, then, that cries of *Vive le roi!* could now and then be heard among them. And it is a measure of Bonaparte's sagacity and confidence that he at once appointed a much older and more experienced man as his chief of staff: the forty-two-year-old Captain Berthier, an engineer and cartographer who had fought in the American Revolutionary War. The combined competence of the two men, and their willingness to exact whatever they needed from local populations, ensured that, once out of the mountains, they would lead a well equipped and successful campaign onward to Rome and further south.

All roads from northern Italy to the Papal States passed through the little Duchy of Parma. With subsidies from France long ceased, Don Ferdinando had for some time been financially dependent on his brother, King Carlos IV of Spain. Since his own withdrawal from the Coalition against France, Carlos had imposed a state of neutrality on Parma. Don Ferdinando had chafed against this—he had until then been secretly providing money and provisions to Austrian soldiers in Lombardy—but he was in no position, either financially or militarily, to act against it. With the Austrians themselves defeated at the vital battle of Lodi in May 1796, Don Ferdinando could do nothing to prevent the French from crossing the Po River southward into his territory of Piacenza, and setting up a garrison there.

Fortunately for him and Amalie and the rest of the Duchy's ruling classes, the Directory had instructed that Parma should be treated with exceptional indulgence: It was not to become a "satellite republic" like other occupied lands, with local institutions overturned in favour of a quasi-French revolutionary establishment. France needed Spain to remain neutral, and the five men of the Directory had allowed themselves to be persuaded by the Spanish First Minster, Manuel de Godoy, to let the sleepy conservative dogs of Parma lie.

Bonaparte was quick all the same to take what he could from the Duchy. Having looted the public coffers of Piacenza, he feigned preparations for an attack on the capital itself. It would have been quite impossible for Don Ferdinando to attempt any resistance with his tiny local forces—"my peaceable army," as he called it, and which others dubbed, perhaps no less affectionately, "the little fatso's troopers." Instead, pawning the crown jewels to raise ready cash, he bought the French off with "a huge bribe in silver, corn, oats and other victuals, sixteen hundred horses, and twenty works of art" of Bonaparte's choice. Nonetheless, of the soldiers Bonaparte marched into Milan a few days on from Parma, most were in rags and many, even among the officers, were still barefoot.

By the time they arrived, Amalie's brother Ferdinand had fled the city with Beatrice and their seven surviving children. He had expected to find refuge in Vienna, but the Emperor Franz, without giving any reason, would not allow it. All Ferdinand was granted was a strange half-meeting outside the city with Albert and a rather frail Marie Christine, who accompanied the disappointed family a little part of their journey on to the Moravian city of Brno. From here at least Ferdinand would be closer to his favourite brother, Maximilian, the companion of his boyhood. The "pretty little miniature" of thirty years before was now a corpulent man in his forties, so broad indeed that the ever whimsical Maximilian, himself legendarily fleshy, challenged him to a waist-measuring contest—and narrowly won.

IN THE MIDDLE of May 1796, General Bonaparte entered Milan in triumph, cheered by pro-French local Jacobins and Italian patriots glad to see the Habsburgs routed. Socially prominent families made haste to accommodate the newcomers, who repaid them by looting their city treasury and the famously rich Milanese banks. Though most of the money made its way back to the Directory in Paris, theft beyond the army's daily needs was increasing, with some officers openly bent on personal enrichment. Bonaparte was learning to plunder for himself as well, and by now felt confident enough to ignore instructions from the Directory when he chose. These included a new command to capture Rome and Naples and send home a fabulous booty of artworks and Roman antiquities for the vast palace-turned-museum, the Louvre. Bonaparte knew his army's strength would not stretch so far. He asked for reinforcements, and in the meantime, on his own initiative, negotiated first a truce and then a treaty of neutrality with both powers, frightening them into paying huge exactions to persuade him to do what he wanted to do in any case.

Carolina did not trust Bonaparte, but the Neapolitans could only accept his terms, for they had lost two powerful allies. With Spanish warships now threatening their fleet, the British were withdrawing from the Mediterranean. An abashed Sir William Hamilton had arrived at court to convey the news. With him came the beautiful Emma Hart, formerly his mistress, before that the mistress of his nephew, and now his own lady wife. Despite her *demi-monde* background, Emma was fast becoming one of Carolina's closest friends. She had visited Marie Antoinette in the Tuileries in September 1791, and had brought a letter, supposedly the last, from the Queen to Carolina; this in itself would have been enough to ensure her an interested welcome. Hamilton's bad tidings were further darkened by news from Moscow: The Tsarina Catherine had died, and the new Tsar Paul I had snapped his mother's friendly ties with Austria and moved closer to neutral Prussia, so strengthening France's strategic position.

Though Ferdinando and Acton disagreed, Carolina was determined that, despite the current unfavourable situation, active military opposition to France must sooner or later be resumed. "A war now would ruin us," she told Gallo in Vienna, "but the neutrality they imagine is a chimera." She even believed she was about to be assassinated by agents of the Directory, who regarded her, not incorrectly, as the greatest obstacle left to their control of southern Italy. "It wouldn't be enough to push me out of the Council and put me back in my place as a woman," she wrote. "I expect a little shot in the back, or a blow on the head or a dose of poison. I'm surprised they didn't start with that."

And she was dismayed to be obliged now to host the two aunts-in-law of her lost sister, Marie Antoinette, both now in their mid-sixties. From threatened Rome the road-stained carriages of pugnacious Madame Adélaïde and podgy Madame Victoire rolled up to her huge country palace of Caserta, from which fifty families had had to be displaced to accommodate them, for they insisted on maintaining the same formalities and privileges they had once enjoyed at Versailles. They had brought with them few possessions and no money at all, but seventy-two personal attendants, "people of every quality and colour," as Carolina told Teresa, exasperatedly, "split into two groups and fighting like cats and dogs. It's an absolute and utter nuisance to me," she wrote, "but from the duties of hospitality, there's no escaping."

In April 1797, again without consulting the Directory, Bonaparte signed a preliminary peace with Franz's Holy Roman Empire—represented, bizarrely, by Carolina's ambassador, the marchese di Gallo, whom the ambitious General rather liked, considering him a potential ally. The French had advanced to within a hundred miles of Vienna, causing general panic and a great deal of packing up and riding off, but their resources were near exhaustion, and they could not risk an attempt on the imperial capital itself. The armistice claimed the Austrian Netherlands and much of northern Italy for France, and in return handed the Austrians control of Venice, which, however, they were not to keep for long. In a clear indication of his high political confidence, Bonaparte informed the Directory that if they declined the terms he had specified, he would resign his military commission and devote his energies to a career in civil life. This threat to their own position they understood at once: In October 1797, to jubilation in France and throughout Franz's Empire, the peace was formally ratified in the Treaty of Campo Formio.

# 1794-1797

. . .

**Marie Christine was among** the few who could not wholly welcome the news of peace. Though it did rescue her cherished adopted son, Karl, from the perils of the battlefield, it seemed to her that too much had been given for too little gain. Austria had been humiliated. Revolution was everywhere in the ascendant. "I can't help thinking of all the blood spilt," she wrote to a military friend. "So many good men wounded and killed. In the midst of all the rejoicing I feel sad and distressed. I can only applaud the peace with a heavy heart and with my eyes full of tears."

She and Albert had spent the summer of 1797 in Teplice in northern Bohemia. It was a spa town, known for its hot springs, and they had gone there in the hope of restoring Marie Christine to health, for the anxieties and challenges of the previous ten years had sadly undermined her, and since waving Ferdinand's family on their way to Brno, she had been suffering from serious abdominal pain and periodic attacks of fever. She was now a wan fifty-five years old, and her physicians had persuaded her to pass the season sipping and bathing in the mineral waters, and taking gentle walks in the fresh country air. It did her good, and her condition was further improved by a congenial sojourn afterwards with Albert's family in nearby Dresden.

In October the pair made their way back to Vienna, where, to their delight, they were joined by Karl, just turned twenty-six and a celebrated war hero. With the Italian campaign at an end and the Austrian Netherlands now a French province, his emperor-brother had appointed him governor and general commandant of Bohemia, allowing him a month's leave to see his adoptive parents. Marie Christine at once attempted, without success, to buy a princely residence for him in Prague. She adored Karl, and was delighted to have him with her through the autumn, but by Christmas 1797 he was on his way to his new post: She and Albert drove with him seventy miles north, as far as the little Renaissance town of Znojmo. They returned to Vienna to spend a rather sombre winter, punctuated by a few lacklustre balls. The spirit had gone out of the place, and the heart was going out of them, too.

# XXVIII

# 1798

## In which Bonaparte's army sails for Egypt, Marie Christine departs this earthly life, and Carolina flees to Sicily.

Unlike Ferdinando, who had returned to his daily hunting with relief and relish, Carolina had accepted the peace of Campo Formio only as a temporary measure, "to give us a little respite, time to form a ministry, to put a few things in order." Though she did not trust Bonaparte, she admired him enormously, and rhapsodized to Gallo, "He is the greatest man to have appeared in centuries. I'm only sorry he's serving such a detestable cause. I would like to see the fall of the Republic, but the continuation of Bonaparte. I wish him good fortune and glory, as long as it's not at our expense. I say if he dies, they should make a powder out of him and give a dose of it to every ruler, and two to every one of their ministers, then things would be on a better footing. Happy the country with such a sovereign!" she concluded, with a thought, perhaps, of what her own harebrained husband might have been, if fortified with a dose of Corsican powder.

Carolina's instinct for a man of military competence was timely, for she had been right about Bonaparte: While Ferdinando was out hunting and John Acton was contemplating an early retirement in Shropshire, French forces had seized Rome and looted the Vatican, with their energetically anti-clerical commissioner personally tearing the rings from the fingers of the aged Pope before despatching him to captivity in France. With a revolutionary republic declared only 150 miles away, the Army of Italy looked set to begin a confident march to Naples. But the Directory, nervous of Bonaparte's popularity, had other plans for him. Britain was the only major power still at war with France: The time seemed ripe for an invasion. They summoned him to Paris and placed him in command of a new Army of England, little more than muddled groups of regular soldiers, conscripts, and volunteers. Having inspected a series of coastal forts and ports, Bonaparte himself insisted an invasion was impracticable, but he set to work nonetheless to form his motley troops into a genuine army.

The Foreign Minister, the adaptable Charles-Maurice de Talleyrand, capably serving the Directory now as he had once served the Monarchy and would soon serve Napoleon's Empire, had instead been pushing for an invasion of Egypt. Revolutionary France, arthritically conservative in certain respects, was looking for new colonies to replace those lost to Britain—Canada in the Seven Years' War and the valuable plantation islands of the Caribbean in campaigns of recent years. Egypt, currently under loose Ottoman control, appeared as low-hanging fruit. The twenty-eight-year-old Bonaparte was easily inspired by the idea of a *mission civilisatrice*, whereby he would bring to the Egyptians the values of the European Enlightenment in imposed exchange for antiquities beyond value. Perhaps he had a thought, too, of the great Alexander, two thousand years before, turning away from the sure conquest of Babylon to mount his expedition to India.

By March 1798 he was transforming his Army of Italy into the Army of the Orient. In mid-May, poorly equipped but fired with enthusiasm, they set sail.

. . .

**In this hopeful springtime,** fifty-six-year-old Marie Christine had made a tiny journey of her own. She was feeling better. The pains in her stomach had lessened, and she had been able to eat a little more; her mood, and Albert's, had consequently lifted. They decided to renovate their little palace, and for the months of that work, rented the Kaunitz family's lovely garden *palais* in Mariahilf, just outside Vienna. The old Chancellor himself was no longer there, indeed for four years his face had not been seen at all other than through the window of a wooden coffin in a Moravian country church, but his residence was itself a perfect reminder of the elegance and discernment he had brought to all his undertakings. It was now abloom with colour and fragrance, and Marie Christine spent much of her time walking slowly there, or simply sitting and gazing out at the low wooded hills beyond. As June approached she improved further. She began to read and write again, and was even able to pay the briefest of visits—just a few minutes—to the sisters Eleonore von Liechtenstein and Leopoldine von Kaunitz, both now living in Vienna. But by midsummer she was declining. The pain had returned and she could scarcely eat at all; her personal physician summoned six of his *confrères*, who pronounced an ulcerated stomach; all agreed she could not live long.

Whatever Albert, in his desperation, may have hoped, Marie Christine did not deceive herself; she had requested the last sacrament some time before. In the morning of the twenty-third of June, she received a few visitors, and in the evening was herself driven to pay her respects to her emperor-nephew Franz and his wife, Carolina's daughter Teresa. The girl was fond of her, and kissed her now tearfully, assuring her of her prayers. Marie Christine returned to Mariahilf, and there spent a difficult last night, mitigated only by the physicians' opium and the constant presence of her husband.

She was fully conscious through the whole of the next day, and even managed to write a few letters and arrange some last gifts of charity. Sitting up in bed as the sun set that evening, she took Albert's hand and kissed it. Her beloved Karl was still in Prague, but her thoughts were with him, and his name was the last word she spoke.

Marie Christine was buried three days later, having lain in an open coffin in the Hofburg chapel. Eleonore von Liechtenstein had had courage enough to view the body of her old friend and long-ago rival for her husband's attentions. "It was the only time I've ever seen a corpse without being horrified," she said later. "Instead, I was suffused with a deep feeling of peace." As court protocol dictated, the Emperor and Empress absented themselves from the funeral service. Neither was Albert there. He had left Mariahilf on the night of his wife's death, and taken private refuge with a friend in the nearby countryside.

Of all Marie Christine's siblings, it was Maximilian, himself now very ill and overwhelmed by depression, who mourned her the most. Only he had been really fond of her. Informed of her death, he wrote sadly, "My sister's battle has ended, and she has at last been released from this world. She is to be envied, but not so those who remain behind, who now have only one more reason to grieve."

Albert's grief was terrible, and it was to last for the rest of his long life. Inconsolably, he carried on for some time as if she had not died at all, renovating her apartments in their Vienna residence in the French fashion she had so admired, with walls decorated in gold paint and hung with Gobelin tapestries brought from the palace they had built together at Laeken. From the great Venetian sculptor Antonio Canova, a fellow Freemason, he commissioned a memorial to "the best of wives" for the imperial family's Church of St Augustine, and it stands there still in graceful mourning, a symbol of its paradoxical time, a Deist monument to a devout but tolerant Catholic in a temple of her ancient faith.

Knowing her death to be imminent, Marie Christine had written a last letter to her "dear, cherished husband" of thirty-two years, to be opened after she was gone. "How can I find the way to tell you what I think, what I feel for you. Oh, I have seen only too clearly your deep sorrow, your suffering; that is what makes our parting so difficult. If I have deserved esteem or regret in the eyes of the world, it is only because of you. You have made me what I am. You were my guiding star, the only person I wanted to be worthy of." He should seek consolation, she said, in philosophy, in religion, and in the embrace of the family, and she asked him to turn most particularly to Karl, "the precious heirloom left to us both, to support him with your good counsel. May you be happy. May the angel of consolation find you now. A thousand farewells, my beloved husband!"

Though Albert was to live another thirty years, he ended his long and detailed memoirs now, with Marie Christine's death. But some time later, aware, no doubt, of the ambivalence her family had felt toward her, he added a postscript, in which the pride and presumption that others had seen in her was exculpatorily transformed. "Her extraordinary spiritedness," he wrote, "often misled the judgement of people who did not know the beauty and greatness of her lofty soul. This spiritedness was never turned against me; to me she expressed it only in a particular way that made her ever more dear to me. And her matchless devotion and love for me, unwavering until her death, was manifest in the most touching manner even in her last moments. . . . After that, how could I ever find words to describe the state in which I found myself at that terrible time? How could I express what I felt then and what I shall feel all my life for this adorable, unique woman!"

Albert had been dazzled, even perhaps a little blinded by his passion for Marie Christine, but it may be, too, that he, and he alone, had known and loved not only the woman she was, but also the woman that, through the thirty years and more of her life with him, she had sought to be.

**Bonaparte had set sail,** but to his enemies, and even to some of his own troops, his destination was as yet unknown. Some thought he was headed for England or Ireland, others for Naples or Malta. Horatio Nelson, recently promoted to Rear Admiral, shrewdly suspected he might be making for Alexandria, with a longer-term view of attacking British possessions in India. He set off in pursuit, actually reaching the Egyptian port before the French, but finding nothing, he immediately turned back to Sicily for reprovisioning. Had he stayed only a few hours in the harbour, his war fleet might have met Bonaparte with cannon fire.

The fifty thousand French troops disembarked to begin their military expedition, with an initial victory against Ottoman Mamelukes followed by repeated disasters, the whole to be mitigated, in their own eyes at least, by the looting of invaluable ancient artefacts for their new museum of the Louvre. In due course, the news reached Sicily, and late in July 1798 Nelson set sail a second time for Alexandria, this time finding the undermanned French fleet at anchor in nearby Aboukir Bay. Under cover of night he surrounded them, with half his ships between them and the shore, and the rest blocking their escape to sea. The result was catastrophe for the French and a tremendous victory for Nelson.

With two of his ships in need of repairs and refitting, he headed for Naples, well equipped with shipyards after John Acton's years of building up the kingdom's navy. Formally, Naples was still a neutral power, but few who witnessed Nelson's near-hysterical welcome there could have believed it.

It was a welcome beyond exuberance, in fact near to hysteria. Five hundred boats and barges packed with dignitaries and elated locals rowed several miles out to meet the damaged *Vanguard*. Dozens of guitarists were squashed in among them, lending a rough coherence to the Neapolitan renditions of "Rule Britannia" and "God Save the King" that burst out repeatedly from one vessel or the next. From the crowded shore, fishermen released thousands of caged birds all at once in an ancient ritual of rejoicing. Wine flowed freely, kisses were bestowed willy-nilly, and anyone or anything appearing remotely French was jostled or smashed or spat upon.

Carolina was not to be seen. She had been ill for some days and was not up to leaving her rooms; of late she had begun taking opium, supplied to her by Emma. But her joy in the victory was real enough, and she declared the British Union Jack the finest flag in the universe. The Hamiltons were rowed out to the

*Vanguard* alongside the rest of the royal family, with Ferdinando greeting the Admiral effusively as his "deliverer," and insisting on inspecting the battered ship, in his suit of velvet and lace, to the last intrusive detail. As for Emma, her meeting with Nelson has passed into legend. Helped up from her barge to the accompaniment of a fifteen-gun salute, at the sight of him she raised her arms to the heavens, exclaiming, "Oh God, is it possible!" and collapsed on him in a swoon, probably staged, though just possibly genuine. For it had been some years since Nelson was last in Naples, and Emma had not expected to see the conquering hero as he was now, one-armed, one-eyed, with a deep wound across his forehead, and yellowed with malaria. Certainly another lady, having clambered aboard in the heat and effort of the last weeks of pregnancy, set eyes on the disfigured little Admiral and fainted in good earnest.

Though his preference was for a quiet hotel, Nelson was pressed to take up his abode at the Hamiltons's Palazzo Sessa, with his own name and *veni, vidi, vici* blazing in a giant illumination of three thousand candles fixed to its facade. At least from inside he had a wonderful view of the bay.

Nelson was personally less flattered than frustrated by the extravagant celebrations laid on for him, regarding them as a waste of time when, as he reported to his superiors in London, "Three months would liberate Italy." He began to urge an immediate attack on the French in Rome, telling Carolina, "The boldest measures are the safest," and by the last week of November the Neapolitans were ready to march, the Queen spurring them on from her horse in a riding-habit of royal blue with a gold *fleur-de-lys* at her neck and a long white plume in her general's hat. To the already indifferent regular regiments had been added twice as many forced conscripts, most of them peasants, some of them barefoot, all of them untrained and unwilling to fight.

In Rome, they were swiftly routed, their King taking flight on horseback and Acton following ignominiously in a cart drawn by mules. Ferdinando was welcomed back to Naples with the usual cries of *Viva il re!* sprinkled with taunts of *veni, vidi, fuggi*—I came, I saw, I scarpered.

Ten thousand disciplined French troops had already crossed the border into his kingdom, and Acton insisted the whole royal family flee Naples for the island of Sicily. At first both King and Queen resisted the idea, trusting to the *lazzaroni*, the city's large underclass of beggars, thieves, and day labourers, all fiercely attached to king and religion, to defy the unbelieving, republican French. "I can count on the people," Carolina told Gallo. "The egotistical, degenerate class is the aristocracy." But when a crowd thousands strong surrounded the palace demanding weapons to defend themselves against the French, her heart quailed. Like Marie Antoinette and Louis before them, she and Ferdinando appeared on the palace balcony, succeeding by their presence in pacifying the crowd, but, terrified they would be taken hostage, they distributed no weapons. Carolina saw the departure of her family now as their own flight to Varennes, an escape for their lives, "to keep from having our heads cut off."

Fearful of an uprising, unsure of their own armed forces, the royal family made their plans to sail on Nelson's ship, the *Vanguard*, with other, less highly ranked escapees directed to the vessels of "the very heterogeneous armada assembled under Nelson's command," crewed by whoever could be found to serve. On the very cold night of the twenty-first of December, 1798, the Admiral and Hamilton slipped away from a reception to escort the royal family and their entourage from the palace via a secret passage to the harbour.

Their departure was felt as a double abandonment by the people of Naples. They had long regarded the British as their sole military protection against the French, and they were now bereft as well of their king's talismanic presence among them. Though their queen held less symbolic power, it was she who wept and wailed to leave them now, histrionic even among the practicalities of flight. "My soul is more than despairing," she sobbed. "If I don't die of sorrow now, I'll never die."

In fact she was closer to death by drowning, for the storm that arose now, after two days at anchor waiting for the last of Naples' English colony to board, was the worst Nelson had experienced in his near three decades in the navy. Everyone, including the Admiral himself, who in all those years had never acquired good sea-legs, was prostrate with seasickness—everyone, that is, except Emma, who ministered to all and sundry with stouthearted competence, while

Sir William lay in his cabin, two loaded pistols in his hands, resolved not to die "with the guggle-guggle-guggle of the saltwater in his throat." The Viennese ambassador took his own more religious precautions, casting overboard his bejewelled snuff-box, decorated as it was with a miniature portrait of his naked mistress, "for he considered it highly impious to keep about his person so profane an article, when (as he thought) on the verge of eternity."

And though Carolina had been lamenting "the terrible, cruel loss of our beautiful kingdom, our honour and reputation, all that matters to us, and my son's inheritance," all this was now surmounted by the pitiful death of her six-year-old son, Alberto. So rough was the passage that he and his eight-year-old brother, Leopoldo, had been tied into their beds with skeins of wool. But where Leopoldo was big and exceptionally strong, his father's "little bull," Alberto was a delicate child, and in recent days he had been ailing. A thunderous barrage of wind and wave, enough to snap the ship's topmast, threw him into convulsions; with his mother unable to get up from her mattress on the floor, he perished in the arms of the loyal Emma. Carolina was forty-six years old. Of her eighteen children, Alberto was the tenth she had lost, and the blow was a heavy one, for, as she said, "Nature made me a mother; the queen is only a gala-dress, which I put on and off."

Carolina's grief was such that she could not join the King for the formal welcome that awaited them, in driving snow, on the quay at Palermo. Escorted by Nelson, she went directly to the Palazzo Colli, a summer residence, "remarkable for its ugliness," unheated and totally unprepared, that had not seen a royal visit in fifty years. Ferdinando was not concerned. Above all he had been anticipating good hunting on the island—midwinter was just the season for woodcock. But Carolina took to her rickety bed, and for a few days her attendants feared she might never rise from it. One of her daughters was later to say that the Queen's use of opium increased at this point; and she began to show signs of an unusual equivocation, making decisions with difficulty and frequently changing her mind.

Ferdinando had never shown much interest in sovereign power, and he made no effort to regain it now. Despite repeated pleas from loyalists in the capital itself, and constant urging from Carolina, he was not to return to Naples for two and a half years. His first edict in Palermo, far from a declaration instituting the city as the kingdom's new capital, as many had hoped, was an announcement appropriating all the island's hunting-grounds to himself: He was to spend the rest of his stay making use of them.

Toward the end of January 1799, preparing a path for the French forces en route from Rome, Neapolitan republicans had formally deposed Ferdinando and established the Parthenopean Republic—named for the alluring siren Parthenope of ancient Greek *Neapolis*. The French troops had met with fierce resistance all the same on their entry into Naples. The *lazzaroni* were royalists to a man and, though poorly armed and scarcely disciplined at all, it had taken the invaders three days and nights of hard street fighting to contain them.

The French made little effort, all the same, to install any kind of revolutionary government in the former kingdom. The Directory in fact declined to recognize the new republic, even refusing to meet a representative delegation who arrived soon afterwards in Paris. Their ambitions remained military and financial, rather than political; they had neutralized a hostile power, now they began to demand impossible exactions, installing a rapacious regent to squeeze them out of the resisting local people. Thereafter resentment of the French grew swiftly.

> *It's perishingly cold here, it never stops snowing and all the streets and rooftops are white, an extraordinary thing in Palermo. I've never been so cold in my life, there's not a single window or door that shuts properly and the rooms have no carpets and no fireplaces. It's enough to kill you.*

Carolina was writing to Gallo from the freezing Palazzo Colli. For her, the flight to Palermo had been effectively a tactical retreat to higher ground, and now, daily or even hourly, she had been besieging the Russians and Ottomans and especially the Emperor with desperate letters, trying to organize resistance in Naples and a better defence for Sicily. News from the mainland she was receiving regularly, having long before installed a network of informers who passed on their messages through the fishermen working off the coasts.

Ferdinando had taken no part in her efforts. He was thoroughly enjoying himself, "delighted to be safe, tormenting the rest of us with petty economies, going to the theatre, going off hunting," as Carolina told Gallo—indeed, even planning a palatial new hunting-lodge near Palermo. He was relishing his recovered role of merry monarch, and was finding as well a new sense of himself as patriarch, for once able to dismiss the exhortations of his domineering wife without second thoughts, since almost everyone around him disagreed with her, too. She had become isolated, and she exacerbated her isolation by withdrawing to her rooms in the palace, writing compulsively and seeing few people apart from her children.

The English trio, or rather triangle, of Nelson and the Hamiltons were also in Palermo; they remained loyal to Carolina, though she saw less of them than she had done in Naples. Though short of money, they had rented a spacious *palazzo* of their own and were enjoying an extravagant social life there, with Emma and the hero of Aboukir by now engaged in a fully fledged love affair, and Sir William patriotically indulging them both.

At the turn of the new year of 1799, Tsar Paul I of Russia and Sultan Selim III, the latter outraged by Bonaparte's invasion of Ottoman Egypt, answered Carolina's prayers by joining Naples and the British in a second Coalition against France. Nelson took a tearful leave of Emma to search the Mediterranean, looking for French ships to do battle with.

And at the chilly Palermo court, an unlikely hero emerged in the person of Cardinal Fabrizio Ruffo, fifty-four years old and a native of the loyalist province of Calabria, who now volunteered to raise an army to overturn the Parthenopean Republic and drive out the French. Carolina was hesitant, saying, "I don't care for red hats in affairs of state," but Ruffo, though no soldier, did have military credentials of a kind: He had once headed the Pope's own Ministry of War. A relieved Ferdinando, himself unwilling to engage in anything more combative than a day's hunting, dubbed him minister plenipotentiary, and in the first week of February Ruffo departed, with a total force of eight men, all but one of them civilians.

His success was almost miraculous. Equipped with hardly more than a large banner with the royal arms on one side and on the other the Christian exhortation *In hoc signo vinces*, Ruffo created his army, appealing to the clergy to spread the insurrectionary word and confiscating whatever he needed to raise the necessary funds. Within days of his arrival on the mainland he had eighty followers; by the end of the month he had seventeen thousand; within two he had ninety thousand. He called them the *sanfedisti*, the soldiers of the Holy Faith, and he had judged his compatriots correctly, for *King* and *Religion* were conjuring cries in a land where every peasant, no matter how poor, "had a crucifix on one side of his bed and a gun on the other," as his secretary reported. Dismissing his own noble status, the Cardinal made himself one of them, eating the same food, fighting alongside them, inspiring them with constant talk of *guapperie*—Calabrian deeds of valour. They attached themselves to him with terrible ferocity, killing any man who wavered in his cause, and rampaging pitilessly through every town that offered resistance.

The republicans in the provinces were quickly overcome, though not without summary executions and brutalities on both sides. Ruffo's *sanfedisti* entered the capital in mid-June 1799. They found the republican government collapsing under the weight of its own disagreements, its leaders already in flight. Vitally, almost all the French were gone, recalled to northern Italy to face troops from Austria, newly reengaged in the war. A small force of disciplined Russians and a smaller force of undisciplined Ottomans had arrived to support Ruffo, and the latter, together with his own large and motley army of peasants, labourers, ecclesiastics, and outright criminals now broke out of his control and ran riot in the city, gleefully plundering and killing, until the Russian regulars regained the upper hand.

And later in the year, in Paris, a greater revolution also came to an end. On the ninth of November, the "18th Brumaire Year VIII" of the republican calendar, the thirty-year-old General Bonaparte achieved a bloodless change of power, replacing the Directory by a three-man Consulate, with himself First Consul of France. He and his wife, Josephine, took up residence in the Tuileries palace, with the lady not quite at ease, reflecting on the fate of its last occupants, Louis XVI and Marie Antoinette.

**Ferdinando and Carolina** were more than lavish in rewarding those who, in their view, had regained their kingdom for them. The Hamiltons were showered with diamonds, and Nelson, with funds diverted from the hospital at Palermo, became Duke of the Sicilian domain of Bronte, though Cardinal Ruffo, as the original and most daring of their saviours, might have deserved that more: He received in any case a substantial estate and plenty of money, too.

Consolation was needed, for in the same month of February 1800, Sir William learned that, after thirty years as British representative in Naples, he was being recalled. He and Emma had just returned from a five-week Mediterranean cruise with Nelson on board his *Foudroyant*. The news threw Emma into a fury and Carolina into hysterics, and it cast Sir William himself, by now very much an *Inglese italianizzato*, into depression and fitful illness. Nelson was dismayed, and not only on his friend's behalf, for he, too, was now relieved of his command and ordered home. His open affair with Emma, and his apparent acquiescence to every last wish of the King and Queen of Naples, had exposed him to "ridicule and censure" from his superiors at the Admiralty and in other influential circles in London. A "tiny minuet of courteous insolence" ensued, in which both Admiral and envoy attempted to delay the inevitable, but each met in reply only an aureate disregard.

# XXIX

# 1800-1804

In which a challenging family reunion takes place in Vienna, Amalie meets a lonely end in Prague, and two new empires are conjured into being.

Hamilton's distinctly unwelcome replacement, who arrived in Palermo early in April 1800, was the twenty-nine-year-old Arthur Paget, debonair son of an English peer: Sir William, still persuading himself that his own absence would be only temporary, actually tried to prevent him from presenting his credentials. Acton treated him civilly, but Ferdinando, whom Paget described as "a sad Poltroon," was irritated by the Englishman's insistence that he return at once to Naples. Paget saw, correctly, that though the Queen also disliked him, she no longer had any influence, and she saw, equally correctly, that he regarded himself, "with his imperious manner and tone," as effectively now in charge. "It's clear he wants to make us feel all the weight of his country's power," she told Gallo. Indeed, Paget himself had told his father, "the Plan is I fancy to give me *the entire management of everything* in the Mediterranean, Adriatic, Archipelago, etc., etc.," adding, with the confidence of the well financed imperialist, "I am of opinion that nothing useful or good can be effected but by the introduction and direct interference of Foreigners."

Carolina made up her mind to leave Palermo. Knowing that the King's popularity in Naples did not necessarily extend to herself, she decided instead to make the long journey to the city of her birth, taking upon herself a double mission of national and family politics. Naples had long been on indifferent terms with Vienna, and she wanted, as she told Gallo, "to try to find a way of reestablishing the entente between our two courts." Moreover, she still had three unmarried daughters: Apart from the unattached Archduke Karl in Prague, whom she had not lost sight of, at the Hofburg itself there were five young archdukes, brothers of the Emperor. Three of their siblings were already married to children of hers, and she was eager to match three more. On the ninth of June 1800, they set sail in Nelson's *Foudroyant*.

There was tremendous excitement when the Queen and the Admiral and their various companions drove into the courtyard of the summer palace of Schönbrunn at ten in the evening of the fourteenth of August, 1800. Carolina's second daughter, Luisa, who had fled the approaching French troops in Tuscany with her husband, the Grand Duke Ferdinand, was the first to greet them. "She threw herself into mamma's arms and then into ours," wrote her sister Amalia, who had begun to keep a personal diary. "Then she led us into a little glass room and by means of a machine we went up to the next floor"—a reference to the lift the girls' grandmother, Maria Theresia, had had installed decades before, once her broadened girth and narrowed lungs had made it impossible for her to climb the stairs. The young Emperor Franz, though ambivalent toward his Aunt Carolina, had ordered a sumptuous supper, and he remained, amicably enough, to eat with them all.

Albert and Maximilian and the rest of the extended family came to greet them the following day. Carolina was on good terms with both brother and brother-in-law, and it was a happy meeting for all three, now well into middle age, and friends for forty years: They had not been together since the time of Leopold's coronation and the grand double wedding, a decade before. Albert was rather aged by his sad two years of widowhood, and since his return to Vienna he had not managed to gain any official appointment that might have absorbed his steady talents. But he was renovating his palace and expanding his collection of prints and drawings, and he had evidently found a close companion in Marie Christine's former Mistress of the Household, the Countess Mansi: Whenever he received a family visit, the Countess was present as a matter of course.

Maximilian, with Franz's rather reluctant permission, had been living at the Hofburg since the end of April. He had been seriously unwell for some time, and in fact had requested permission the year before to come to Vienna to consult the city's celebrated physicians. The Emperor had sent a stony refusal, leaving Maximilian to write out a painstaking description of his many symptoms and send it to the medical men—to no avail. With time, and repeated requests, Franz had relented, allowing his uncle to return at last to the imperial city he loved and had long missed.

But though Maximilian continued to carry out official work for his Electorate of Cologne and the Order of Teutonic Knights, the now appalling state of his health was clear for all to see. Carolina's daughter Amalia described him a week after their arrival, at a celebratory dinner for her mother's forty-eighth birthday: "He's monstrously fat, it's really painful and quite frightening to see him. Imagine, he can hardly move, he eats like a wolf, and he always falls asleep at dinner and snores. Archduke Johann is aware of this and is always kind enough to sit next to him and wake him up."

Gallo had recently resigned his diplomatic position in Vienna, and Carolina had wanted him to stay on as her friend and advisor. But he had already decided to move to Paris. Having spent a good deal of time at the imperial court, he knew the Queen's political mission to be hopeless. Franz had his own plans for Italy—Carolina suspected he wanted to extend Austria's southern frontier all the way to Rome—and his own exigencies for negotiation with the other Coalition powers and with France itself. It was a delicate and dangerous time for Austria, and the Emperor did not want his aunt interfering. And had she known it, he was determined that her personal mission, to marry her daughters to his brothers, was also doomed to fail.

But with the presence of so many young people, and the entertainment-loving, and indeed entertainment-providing Emma Hamilton in residence, it was a lively summer sojourn, reviving memories for the older family members of the days of their youth, in the time of Maria Theresia. Even Sir William began to recover his health and spirits through his many relaxed afternoons spent fishing, content as he was to leave Emma to monopolize the Admiral's days. "She leads him about like a keeper with a bear," remarked an English countess, disdaining the vulgarity of this jumped-up Lancashire lass. But the Viennese were not exercised about Emma's less than courtly ways, and though now very fat, she still managed to captivate audiences with her posed classical "attitudes" and also with her lovely singing. On one occasion she was accompanied by no less a master than Josef Haydn, now sixty-eight and everywhere famed and fêted, but nonetheless "modest and sensible," at least in conversation with one musical observer, who pronounced the duet "grand." After six weeks in Vienna, the colourful English trio prepared to drive to Prague, to celebrate Nelson's forty-second birthday at the residence of the Archduke Karl.

Emma's departure coincided with the arrival of a no less flamboyant solo performer, the Archduchess Elisabeth, now fifty-seven. She had not been in Vienna since her half-laughing, half-tearful departure nineteen years before, and she had not come directly from Innsbruck. For the past few weeks she had been in an alpine valley in the medieval town of Bruneck, where she had retreated twice before. This was in fact the fourth time she had fled Innsbruck, each flight mirroring the advance of French troops in her province of Tyrol. In 1796 they had been held off, with Elisabeth herself urging the townsfolk to resistance; in 1797, nearly victorious, they had been beaten back, forcing Bonaparte to abandon a projected advance on Vienna. But the General had not given up. By the summer of 1800, the Tyrol was effectively under French occupation, and Elisabeth had fled again, at first half-heartedly, for a mere ten days, but now more decidedly, spurred by the knowledge that Carolina was in Vienna. She had not wanted to go there before, reckoning, correctly, that her nephew would not welcome her. But Franz did not like Carolina either, and she had not been deterred. Elisabeth made up her mind to join her, and by the end of September she was comfortably installed near Schönbrunn, at the charming baroque palace of Hetzendorf.

Over the years her smallpox disfigurement had been worsened by the growth of three lumpy goitres, which she kept generally concealed beneath a white silk neckerchief. Seeing her now, the baronne du Montet, a fifteen-year-old French émigrée residing in Vienna, described her as "the ugliest, most cutting, most terrifying and wittiest princess in the world." Elisabeth had once moved with grace, but, though she still held her head high, at fifty-seven she was stooped and short and very fat, and accompanied everywhere, to comic effect, by a lady-in-waiting extremely tall and thin. And though the years had not dimmed the sharp edge of Elisabeth's tongue, Carolina's daughter Mimi reported that "she can be very sweet when wants to be. It's a pleasure to see how fond she is of mamma. In spite of everything, it's impossible not to like her." Indeed, always eager and not often able to be part of the family circle, Elisabeth was fond of almost everyone, and almost everyone was fond of her, at least for the first few months. Mimi and her two sisters were sending regular letters back to the family in Naples, and from these emerges a picture of an entertaining old *Tante Liesl*, saying just what she thinks, ignoring the proprieties, and making them all laugh.

Waiting with Albert for their carriage, she catches him yawning and slaps him with her fan. On a stroll in the Augarten, her wig is blown off by a gust of wind, and she plumps herself down on the path, refusing to budge until someone retrieves it. She whisks off her neckerchief to reveal her three big goitres, and begins rolling them around in her throat, exciting a general repelled fascination. With the smallest children, she gets down on all fours on the carpet and starts growling, pretending to be a bear. And gradually she oversteps the limits. Mimi has very dark eyes, she observes; she doesn't really belong to the family; everyone else's are light—and she gets up with her lorgnette to examine each of the thirty pairs in the room with her.

Carolina was the only person able to keep her to some degree in check, and in time even this influence faded; Elisabeth's teasing and clever retorts became less amusing and more obnoxious. The younger family members started to retaliate, mimicking her and calling her names; one afternoon, when she spilt coffee on her gown and called for water, two of the boys tipped full carafes over her, and she began slapping her shawl at their faces, calling one of them "a little shit." (She called his emperor-brother "the boor.")

Franz spent as little time as he decently could in Elisabeth's company, and also in Carolina's—he even suggested she should leave Vienna and join her brother Ferdinand in Brno, and at one point, anxious about French forces supposedly approaching, she did consider this. Franz eventually permitted her to stay provided she made no attempt to arrange any marriages. He resisted all his aunt's attempts to influence him on political matters as well, though he did ask his Uncle Maximilian's advice on one crucial issue: Bonaparte had made Austria an offer of peace. Maximilian opposed it, fearing that, with Prussia now determinedly neutral, all the smaller German states, including his own ecclesiastical fiefs, would be left defenceless. Franz signed a treaty anyway, removing both French and Austrian troops from Elisabeth's Tyrol, confirming French possession of the Austrian Netherlands, and forcing Austria to abandon its grand plans for expanding further into Italy, indeed to relinquish all its existing Italian possessions, including the Grand Duchy of Tuscany.

In Naples, without Carolina to oppose him, King Ferdinando quickly followed suit, signing his own peace with France, and ceding further territory. This enabled the French to establish an entirely new Kingdom of Etruria out of the shards of Austrian and Neapolitan possessions in northern Italy, and it effectively deposed Amalie's husband, Don Ferdinando. Their eldest son, Ludovico, was installed as the puppet king of Etruria. He had no expectation now of inheriting his father's Duchy of Parma, since the French had claimed that, too. The peace treaties of early 1801 left Britain the only remaining power in the war against France, raising fears of invasion in the island state, itself newly renamed, after the defeat of an Irish rebellion, the United Kingdom of Great Britain (England, Wales, and Scotland) and a still resisting Ireland.

# 1800-1804

. . .

As the spring of 1801 approached, Maximilian's dropsy and "murrain" grew worse, his skin swelling with fluid and infectious erysipelas spots appearing on his feet. By April he could hardly get out of bed, and by June, the heat of the city had driven him out to Hetzendorf in the countryside, to Gall Hof, the cooler country house of a friend, opposite the little palace. But, ever dutiful, he made one painful journey back to Vienna to initiate his nephew Karl, in a ritual eight hundred years old, into the ranks of the Order of Teutonic Knights, of which he himself was Grand Master. Even so, the ceremony had to be delayed until he was able to manage the five-mile carriage ride into the city.

It was a splendid event, with all the family in attendance, and the knights themselves, including Albert, in long white cloaks embroidered with black crosses. Karl himself first entered dressed as an abbé, his long hair touching his shoulders, before reappearing "in full armour from the olden days, with a rosary in his hands. After the [hymn] *Veni Creator Spiritus* he lifted his visor and the Grand Master dubbed his face with his naked sword . . . then he dubbed him on the head and then on his left shoulder, creating him a knight."

It was the last formal act of Maximilian's life. On the twenty-sixth of June, he attended a family dinner hosted by Elisabeth at Hetzendorf Palace, teasing and joking in his old convivial way, though at times he had difficulty making himself understood. But, toward midnight, he suffered a stroke, and within hours he was dead.

Elisabeth, who had made no small number of petty enemies, now had to endure rumours that she had poisoned him, though no motive was ever posited, and no one else at the dinner had even felt unwell. The rumours were mere spite, since Maximilian's health had been so poor for so long, and his death had been every day expected. He was laid to rest in the crypt of the Capuchin friars, near the tombs of his mother and father and Marie Christine and Josepha and Leopold and Joseph and other lesser known imperial figures, all of them evoking a "religious horror" in the younger Habsburgs obliged to attend the gloomy rite.

Elisabeth departed for Innsbruck three months after Maximilian's death, in October 1801. She had been more than a year in Vienna, and no one was sorry to see her go: "the sooner, the better," as one of Carolina's daughters remarked. By now she had irritated or offended almost everyone, with a streak of real malice eventually surfacing as she tried to set one family member against another, "which hopefully she won't succeed in doing," as another reported. "Mamma and all of us are afraid of her now and try to avoid her." On the tenth of the month she arrived back in Innsbruck, to celebrations both civil and military; thanks to the treaty signed earlier in the year, the soldiers were no longer on active service.

Before she left Vienna, Elisabeth had managed to extract from the Emperor the promise of 1,000 florins per annum for her *Damenstift*. It was a mere pittance, and on return, she discussed the issue with the Deaconess of the *Damenstift*, the Countess Cavriani, a relative of Amalie's friend in Parma. To both it was clear the sum would not even be enough to cover the existing deficit. Without further personal resources, and with Elisabeth unwilling to press her nephew for more, they set to work to rein in expenses, laying down some hopeful new rules: From now on, all provisions were to be weighed and kept in a locked room to prevent theft by the servants; to prevent waste, the *Dames* were to give a day's notice of their intention to dine in-house; they would no longer be served in the big kitchen, with its huge fireplace, but in a small closed room that was easier to heat; and there would be no more expensive provender such as young geese and venison.

It was a reasonable effort, but it was wartime, and inflation was soaring. Elisabeth's Mariatheresienstift sank further and further into debt.

CAROLINA AND HER FAMILY remained a further nine months in Vienna, her own days made much the pleasanter by the arrival of her old friend, the musical Count Andrey Razumovsky. He had been reappointed Russian ambassador by Tsar Alexander I, newly enthroned after the assassination of his father, Paul I, just months before. Razumovsky was delighted to be back in Vienna and delighted to spend his ample leisure time with Carolina. They were the same age and held many political views in common, and she had hopes the Count would influence the Tsar to her benefit. Their bond all the same was primarily personal, though there is no evidence of the sexual relationship rumoured by the Queen's enemies. It is true she was very fond of him. "Every conversation with you is balsam to my heart, since in you I have a true and loyal friend," she told him, "in a time when I have no other."

For once, she may not have been exaggerating. In many respects, Carolina was now alone. Brother Leopold, her mainstay in all matters moral and political, was long gone, as were her two closest sisters, Marie Antoinette and the supportive Marianna. Her husband, once easily swayed, had taken to ignoring her; John Acton, for so long an ally, had turned against her, too. Gallo, grown wary of her headstrong enthusiasms, was strategically distancing himself. The Emperor disliked her, and even his wife, her own eldest daughter, Teresa, was behaving toward her with a decided coolness: Though her four other girls adored her, none seems to have been able to serve as a real confidante for her now.

To add to her troubles, she had contracted typhus, with her physicians attempting to combat the fever by making four incisions into her abdomen, including one into the intestine. It left her "in an appalling state," though it was not enough to prevent her writing to Tsar Alexander, urging him to support Ferdinando's reassertion of power in Naples. This appeal fell on deaf ears, and by the late spring, Franz had determined to stop his own. Before setting off for an extended sojourn in Pressburg to attend the Hungarian Diet, he instructed Carolina to make her preparations to be gone, and as she told her other daughters, even Teresa "behaved very impertinently" toward her. The imperial couple were to return to Vienna in June, and the Queen and her family were to depart immediately afterwards.

Carolina's dual political and familial mission had failed, and she wept farewell to her two eldest daughters, but her real sadness now was in having to leave Count Razumovsky, her very dear friend and, perhaps, the man she now loved. "Had fate not decreed our separation, you would have made my happiness," she wrote to him on the point of departure. "Feelings like this are all the more precious for being so rare."

A miserable journey by coach to the Austrian port was followed by a hardly more cheerful sea voyage, enlivened somewhat by an ongoing family beetle-hunt, no very difficult thing on the infested bark. They arrived in Naples on the seventeenth of August 1802, returning to the royal palace for the first time in "three years, seven months and twenty-seven days." Carolina was hardly back, and "overwhelmed with things to organize," when she learned of the sudden death of Amalie's husband near Parma. By the treaties of 1801, he had been forced to cede control of his duchy to the French, though he had refused to leave, and they had retaliated by keeping him, and Amalie, too, under a loose house arrest. Not long before, Don Ferdinando had survived an assassination attempt by an unhappy patriot wielding a dagger: An opponent of the death penalty, he had not only pardoned his attacker, but had also helped him flee. But the Duke's death now, at fifty-two, after no particular illness, spurred renewed talk of assassination, this time by poison and on orders of the French, wanting to take final control over Parma. It was not true and indeed would hardly have been necessary, since the process was already well under way. France in general, and Bonaparte in particular, was in comfortable mood, savouring victory and even peace: Owing to a series of treaties, for the first time in ten years, the country was not at war with anyone, and the First Consul, following a vote unrevolutionarily limited to property owners, had been granted, at the age of thirty-two, tenure for life.

Don Ferdinando was buried in October 1802 in the Abbey church of Fontevivo, in the white and black habit of the Dominican friars, joining at last, if only in death, the brotherhood he had so long revered. Amalie had already written to Franz, asking for refuge. Her letter reveals great anxiety and also, perhaps, a trace of paranoia: Though it is true the French wanted her gone, subsequent letters suggest there were dozens of "souls" who remained her friends and whom, presumably, she could trust. "Your Majesty can imagine how I am placed here," she wrote, "and You would do me a great service in sending me someone who could help me, as I am surrounded by my own enemies and those of my House. I am in great confusion, without a soul I can trust." And, no doubt hoping for a sympathetic familial embrace, she signed herself, "Your very faithful Aunt Amalie."

The steely Franz did not offer her any haven in Vienna. Instead, he suggested she betake herself to the Hradčany Castle in Prague, where, as a daughter of the late Queen of Bohemia, she had the right to reside. Amalie was now fifty-six. Of the sixteen children she had borne, six were still living: Her only surviving son, Ludovico, was in Florence, on the throne of Bonaparte's invented Kingdom of Etruria; her eldest daughter, Carolina, was in Dresden, a princess of Saxony and the mother of seven young children. And in Parma itself, there were four other daughters, all nuns or soon to make their professions, who wanted to remain in their Parma convents.

In her doubtful Italian, Amalie now wrote to Parma's treasury minister, Carlo Formenti, reminding him that, by the terms of Don Ferdinando's will, she was now the Duchy's regent, though in fact the position was already being assumed by a French administrator. The substance of her letter was in any case in the postscript: "I'll tell you the truth," she wrote. "I would like four thousand *zecchini*, that I'll return directly, because I intend to pay my debts, but that sum would be a comfort to me in my widowed state. I'll give it back immediately." Formenti was a man of some wealth and a good deal of generosity. He had long been subsidizing Don Ferdinando from his own personal funds, and he knew Amalie was without means; she was even known to be borrowing from her servants. He supplied her with the 4,000 *zecchini*, surely aware, despite her emphatic assurances, that he was unlikely to see them again. More surprisingly, on the twenty-fourth of October, the very day she was escorted out of the Duchy by French soldiers, he lent her a further 42,000 in gold and silver pieces. Perhaps he harboured hopes that this greater sum might in time be honoured by her relatives of the House of Austria.

At Piacenza, together with a handful of personal servants, she boarded a small boat that would carry her down the great Po River to Venice. Here she took lodgings at a modest inn, ironically named the *Scudo di Francia* (Shield of France). Amalie immediately sent to Formenti, not his 4,000 *zecchini*, but a further request: He was to have her "paintings, books, porcelains and other works of art" sent to the inn, "and from there I'll let you know where I'm going. I'll send you a list of the value of my effects at Sala, and since there'll be some money left over, as I calculate, I would ask you to pay three months' wages to the boatmen who brought me to Venice when they arrive back in Parma: I'll send you their names. If there's anything left over, keep it for yourself as part of what I owe you, which I'll repay in instalments. *Addio*."

Amalie spent three weeks in Venice, arriving in Prague just before the snowy Christmas of 1802. Though she had arrived from a place of legendary splendour, she cannot have remained dispassionate as she approached the more quietly impressive Bohemian capital, which she had not seen before. "This city is extremely beautiful when seen at a distance," an English traveller had written of it. "It is situated on two or three hills, and has the river Mulda [Moldau] running through the middle. . . . The houses are all of white stone, or stucco, in imitation of it, and all uniform in size and colour. . . . A great part of the town is new, as scarce a single building escaped the Prussian batteries, and bombardment during the blockade, in the [Seven Years' War]. A few churches and palaces only, that were strongly built, and of less combustible material than the rest, were proof against their fury; and in the walls of these, are still sticking innumerable cannon balls and bombs."

Among the churches and palaces "strongly built" was the Hradčany Castle, a vast complex a thousand years in the making, enclosing the Cathedral of St Vitus and the royal palace itself. Amalie's apartments were here, probably in a modern wing recently added to the old Gothic-Renaissance edifice, and they were no doubt grand, as befitted a daughter of the late Queen. But they were by no means provided simply "by grace and favour." Apart from the servants she had brought from Parma, she was obliged by protocol to engage an entire local staff as well, including a handsomely paid personal physician, to whom she was to have frequent recourse, and a Master of the Household, paid at positively noble rates. Even had she wanted to curtail her spending, she was hardly able to do so. It was a chilly and rather lonely refuge: Amalie continued to correspond with dozens of people in other places, but in the city of Prague itself, she seems to have known no one.

CAROLINA WAS FEELING pleased with herself. She had achieved quite a coup with the double match of son Francesco and daughter Antonia ("Toto") with two of their Spanish Bourbon cousins, an attempt to reaffirm the often shaky friendship between Naples and Spain. Francesco had captured Isabel, the only unmarried Spanish Infanta, and Toto had landed Fernando, Prince of Asturias, heir to the throne: One day she would be Queen of Spain. No one in Naples had known Isabel or Fernando. As was conventional, their portraits had been delivered during the negotiations, and as was conventional, these were assumed to be somewhat flattering. But in fact they had been, both of them, grotesque misrepresentations, as eighteen-year-old Toto had been learning in Madrid, and as Carolina discovered in Naples now, in the October of 1802, as the thirteen-year-old Infanta, "a tiny little person, fat as a ball," waddled out from her ship on little bow legs, looking overwhelmed by the entire proceedings.

She spoke only Spanish, and that very little, responding to all approaches with a silly giggle. Carolina thought at first she must be deaf, then realized she was simply the victim of an appallingly bad education: She did not even know there were other countries in the world besides Spain and Naples. Her new mother-in-law was dismayed. "It's a crime to bring children up like that," she wrote to Count Razumovsky in Vienna, adding that even her four-year-old granddaughter was more advanced. But, characteristically, she at once set to work to improve things. "We'll get teachers for her," she announced. "At least her face is pleasant enough. Poor Francesco is bewailing his misfortune. They say her brother's even more brainless."

Indeed they did, and as Toto had seen, neither was he compensated by any physical attributes that might have drawn her to him. "Every day I find him uglier and stupider and grosser," she wailed. The Crown Prince Fernando was fleshy to excess, with a squeaky voice and the manners of a wayward child. Though already eighteen years old, he would not manage to consummate the marriage for almost a year, with his anguished wife concealing from her family his persistent grim attempts in the meantime. "Francesco and I thought we were choosing two divinities," she wrote home, "and instead we've got two cabbage sprouts . . . I am desperate." "Poor Toto is a slave in bitter chains," her sister Amalia noted sadly. "The only thing she wants now is to die quickly. I think God can only have permitted these two marriages as punishment for our sins."

Distressed, Carolina told Razumovsky she would reproach herself for the rest of her life for allowing her children to be connected with "these cretins." She believed Fernando's education had been deliberately neglected in order to keep him in tutelage to the thirty-five-year-old First Minister Manuel Godoy, lover of the fifty-one-year-old Queen and, it was said, father of half a dozen of her fourteen children. But remorse was useless. In time, and with the help of his sister Amalia, who kindly took Isabel under her wing, Francesco at least was to develop a steady relationship with his gradually more refined wife; they would eventually have twelve children. Toto, however, was to be granted her tragic wish: Within four years she would be dead, poisoned, or so Carolina was to insist, by her malevolent mother-in-law, the Queen of Spain.

THE QUEEN OF SPAIN was certainly not fond of Toto, and she had also had her reservations about her daughter Isabel's marriage to Toto's brother, Crown Prince Francesco of Naples. With an eye to the shifting balance of power in Europe, and no doubt prodded by her first minister Godoy, whose enthusiasm for Bonaparte had been growing, she had been angling for a match between the bow-legged Isabel, rumoured to be Godoy's own daughter, and the First Consul himself. Bonaparte was in fact already married, but had no children: Though his wife, Josephine, had a son and daughter from a previous marriage—her first husband had been guillotined during the Terror—a fall from a collapsing balcony had left her apparently unable to bear more. And she was nearing forty. Bonaparte, wanting an heir, was widely believed to be contemplating divorce and an alliance with one of the great royal families. But he hesitated. Despite her many infidelities, and his own, he loved Josephine and wanted to remain with her—but for that she would need to bear him a son. While he considered alternative possibilities in the 1802 interlude of peace, she began a desperate search for cures to help her conceive.

As the new year of 1803 turned, Bonaparte could congratulate himself that his military and political exploits had pulled France out of the mire of revolution and placed it at a historical zenith. With some thirty-seven million inhabitants, it was by far the most populous country in Europe, "dominant in western Europe, checking Habsburg influence in Germany and excluding that of Britain from most of the Continent"—with the persistent exception of Naples and Sicily, and the important island base of Malta, from which the British maintained control of the central Mediterranean.

With no inherited position to speak of, Bonaparte regarded his position of national leadership as justified only by military glory. But within the army, he had many enemies, both more and less revolutionary than himself. Those he had personally commanded in battle remained fiercely loyal, but rumours were rife of plots to depose or even assassinate him. Early in 1804, a conspiracy of just this kind was uncovered, and its leader identified, not unambiguously, as the young duc d'Enghien, a Bourbon prince of the blood and former commander of counterrevolutionary forces in Germany. D'Enghien was arrested, tried, and found guilty, with a widespread expectation of pardon and perhaps banishment, including, it seems, on his own part. Instead, at two o'clock in the morning, beside the open grave already dug for him, the Duke was executed by firing squad.

It was said of France's foreign minister, the mercurial Talleyrand, who was not without blame in the affair, that he came to regard this execution as worse than a crime—it was, he said, a mistake, since it unleashed outrage across Europe and in time would lead four other powers to join Britain, already at war, to form a third Coalition against France. But among the French, on the whole, Bonaparte was little criticized for d'Enghien's execution: After so many years of upheaval, the people wanted stability, and stability required the determined stamping out of conspiracies, proven or suspected. Bonaparte found his position actually strengthened, and this was to embolden him, within the next few months, to take the final, sacrilegious step from First Consul for life to hereditary emperor.

"On Friday the troops swore an oath of fidelity to the newly appointed Emperor Napoleon. They say it was a boring ceremony." Thus a minor nobleman in Parma, at the end of May 1804, to Amalie in Prague. Numbed by the sudden loss of their duke Don Ferdinando and worn down by a season of hunger, the Parmense had submitted to French authority without much resistance. Their passivity was not to last, though unlike in the old battle for independence from Spain and Austria, they would find no would-be leader this time in their spirited duchess.

For Amalie was dying, tormented by painful swellings, the probable sign of a failing heart, and, like her mother, stricken by a rheumatism in her arm that was so severe she could hardly move it. But it was her left arm, and Amalie was right-handed. She continued to write, and her friends in Parma and elsewhere continued to reply, attesting to a fondness for her of which there is little trace in the correspondence of her Habsburg family. Among these dozens of letters are many from former servants or people she has helped, and they address her warmly; she is "my adored royal patroness," and "like a tender mother." Nor was she forgotten by Marianna's Sisters of St Elisabeth in Klagenfurt, whom she had visited often.

She knew her death was approaching. In great detail, she dictated a will, then another, then a codicil, leaving a year's wages to all her servants, past and present, and some fifty handsome legacies to various charities and individuals. In intention, she was as generous now as she had always been, though whether these many bequests were ever paid is a moot point, given that she was still in debt. Now a widow, she was entitled to reclaim the dowry of 70,000 florins that had been paid to Vienna by the King of Spain on her marriage to his nephew Don Ferdinando, and she wrote to Franz, asking him to divide the money and pay it to her daughters and granddaughters, but it seems this was never done.

Numerous letters survive from these last weeks of Amalie's life from her two eldest daughters, Antonia and Carlotta, in their Parma convents, and from these it is clear she was still writing to each of them every few days. Antonia's letters suggest a warm bond with her mother, with Amalie sending her a vast quantity of silk embroidery threads for the liturgical vestments she was making with the other Ursuline nuns: "It's absolutely magnificent, and excellent for our work, it's so kind of you to have sent it. All my companions send their thanks and assure you they'll be praying for you." Day after day Antonia chats on about a special choral mass, a local murder by drowning, the early summer heat: "I hope the warm weather does you good, you're always better in the heat than in the cold, but from what you tell me I see your arm's getting worse. It must be unbearable, I wish I could do something to comfort you. . . . Get someone else to write if it's too tiring for you."

Carlotta's letters also express an affection for her mother, but they are blunt and rather gloomy, without the lively intelligence of her sister's: "It's not good to see you're still getting worse and are near to death, I'm really sorry about that. . . . I've also been a bit unwell with a fever, I think because of my period. . . . I won't forget to pray for you though my prayers aren't worth much. I kiss your hand. With the deepest respect."

On the ninth of June 1804, Amalie received the last sacraments. Two days later, remembering the anniversary of Marie Christine's death six years before, she thoughtfully wrote to Albert. He was taking a cure in Baden when he received the letter, and he wrote back immediately: "I am so sorry, my very dear sister-in-law, to hear your sad news, especially concerning your own health, and I am all the more moved and touched that still, in this dreadful situation, you have the goodness to think of me. In this I recognize your very kind heart." He expected to be in Prague in the autumn, and assured her he would then thank her in person, but even these written thanks may not have reached her, for three days after he penned this letter, Amalie died. As she had long been ill, there was no obduction, but her heart was removed and placed in a gold and silver urn to be sent to Vienna; it was interred in the Loreto Chapel of the imperial family's Church of St Augustine, the scene of her sad proxy wedding, thirty-five years before. Her body was laid to rest in the Cathedral of St Vitus, within the Hradčany Castle.

Amalie had died at the age of fifty-eight, unmourned in Vienna where, in all the years of her loveless marriage, she had never been permitted to return. Her siblings, with the exception of Marianna and, possibly in later years, Elisabeth, had found her demanding and exasperating, though Carolina did feel some belated pity for her now, writing of her in the days after her death as a person "cast aside like a pebble, living on the charity of the Emperor, a frightful truth but no less true for that." But it was not the whole truth. In Parma itself, where she had been popular for her informality and for the generosity she could so rarely afford, Amalie was commemorated fondly. In August, in the chapel of her country house at Sala Baganza, a solemn vigil and mass were held to pray for her soul, with music especially composed by the 'cellist Alfonso Savi, once a member of her court orchestra, the soprano solos written, perhaps, with her own lovely voice still in his memory.

"I WOULD LIKE to see the fall of the Republic, but the continuation of Bonaparte," Carolina had told Gallo, seven years before. Now her wish had been almost granted. On the freezing morning of the second of December, 1804, the brilliant little General was crowned Napoleon I in the Paris Cathedral of Notre-Dame. To avoid, or rather to compound confusion, he had taken the title "Emperor of the French," supposedly enabling the reestablishment of the monarchy without abolishing the sovereignty of the people: Formally, the French Republic was to continue, albeit with a hereditary ruler at its head.

Napoleon was driven by a personal sense of almost divinely ordained destiny, but he had hoped, too, that in practical terms his assumption of this novel throne would unite the still fractious French of left and right, Christian and unbeliever. Instead, it divided them further, provoking outrage and ridicule as, swamped in his "carnavalesque" coronation robes, he paraded among the people, no longer citizens but, after fifteen years of bloodshed and hardship, subjects once again. The diplomats of France were obliged to present their credentials a second time at the courts where they resided. In Naples, the French Minister Alquier, a fierce republican who had voted for the execution of Louis XVI, could not conceal his discomfort at the demotion from *citoyen* to subject. Carolina savoured his humiliation, replying to his speech with numerous pointed references to "the Emperor, *your master*."

In Vienna, Franz had responded to the new Empire of the French by declaring his own new Empire of Austria, though he had taken care to secure Napoleon's approval first. The revolutionary wars had left France in control of many German states that had formally been part of the Holy Roman Empire, effectively a Habsburg fiefdom for three and a half centuries. Franz feared it might be dissolved entirely, or even that Napoleon might take it over himself. He needed to protect his own status as an emperor, and the Habsburgs' continued standing as an imperial family. As yet still Franz II of the Holy Roman Empire, on the eleventh of August 1804 he had proclaimed himself Franz I of Austria as well, incidentally fulfilling his Uncle Joseph's old dream of bringing all the disparate crown lands and territories of the Habsburgs under centralized control.

Napoleon had gained a crown, but he had not quite put aside his officer's bicorne hat. On campaign he had always worn it sideways, aligning the corners with his small shoulders, rather than in the customary forward-backward style. It had made him instantly recognizable on the battlefield, and perhaps broadened his silhouette as well. He was soon to put the crown aside to don this hat again. Franz's reign as dual-emperor would last not quite two years.

## XXX

# 1805-1810

*In which an ancient empire vanishes, Elisabeth bids a final farewell, and Carolina becomes the devil's grandmother.*

The Emperor Napoleon was not amused. Amid the pomp and circumstance and glittering uniformed dignitaries of his imperial coronation, no special envoy from the Kingdom of Naples had been seen. The British, with whom he was already at war, had also failed to send a representative, as had the Russians and the Swedes, but that was less offensive to him, for they were his declared enemies, while with Naples he had long been expecting the conclusion of a formal alliance. For over a year already, since his first overture had been rebuffed, he had had tens of thousands of troops stationed on the Kingdom's mainland, and since then he had been determinedly ignoring Carolina's pleas for them to be withdrawn in return for a guarantee of neutrality and a huge monthly indemnity of 400,000 florins.

Ferdinando had left the matter up to his wife. He was bent on returning to Sicily, to continue his preferred life as a country gentleman. "I regard the Kingdom of Naples as lost," he told John Acton, and when the French insisted Acton himself should leave Naples, believing him to be essentially serving the King of England, Ferdinando shrugged his shoulders and agreed. Acton himself, nearing seventy, put up little resistance. His wife, not quite twenty, had two small children and was soon to have a third; retirement with his flourishing family to a fine house in Palermo was a perfectly satisfactory prospect for the once unassailable First Minister. Besides, his influence had faded along with the King's interest in ruling. He was not on good terms with the Queen, and would have had no place in the government she now held in eager but unsteady hands.

Nervous of an official French annexation of Naples and suspicious of British designs on Sicily, in September 1805 Carolina signed a hasty treaty with the Russians, very much to their advantage. Though she had only weakened one yoke to strengthen another, since the Russian generals, like the British, were evidently "more disposed to dictate than discuss," she had not been mistaken in her instinct to find a second ally, since the British wanted Sicily for themselves and were supporting its royal family only insofar as it served their interests. And the danger was real: Napoleon had finally agreed with Carolina to withdraw his troops from Naples, only to give instructions behind her back for a full invasion of the Kingdom.

In the previous month of August he had abandoned all pretence of an invasion of the British Isles, and renamed his supposed "Army of England" the *Grande Armée*. Now, in September, the Austrians invaded his ally Bavaria, and Napoleon ordered his army to march out to challenge them. The months the men had spent training together had turned them into a fighting force 180,000-strong, with a powerful *esprit de corps* and a firm loyalty to their commanders, all promoted on proven merit, and to Napoleon himself. It enabled them to progress inland at a remarkable pace, despite poor provisioning; they lived off the land as they went, at times even going without food, but morale remained high and there were few desertions. En route, Napoleon himself even had time to attend a performance of Mozart's *Don Giovanni* in Stuttgart. By mid-October, following a series of swift and brilliant victories, he had captured fifty thousand Austrian soldiers, and on the thirteenth of November, he took up residence at the palace of Schönbrunn.

The road into Vienna had been almost a *promenade* for his troops. The city was poorly defended, and the townsfolk had put up no resistance. "The lower classes in this city are still deeply attached to the Habsburgs," noted the émigré comte de Damas, but there had been no one to motivate them: The Emperor Franz and his family had already left the city, almost in secret. "The upper classes are far from having the same feeling," Damas continued. "Their attachment is just a habit, and they're only committed as far as it serves their personal interests." As the Milanese had done, so now the Viennese accommodated themselves to the presence of the French, entertaining their officers and converting their cooks to the pleasures of *la cuisine française*.

Napoleon did not intend to stay long at Schönbrunn. Despite his own recent successes in the field, he had been unnerved by the destruction in October of his fleet at Trafalgar—it had cost the British not a single ship, though Admiral Horatio Nelson had paid with his life. Napoleon knew the Prussians were considering entering the Coalition against him, and he was also under pressure from his own government in Paris, where the cost of the renewed war had caused a financial crisis and the near default of the Bank of France. He needed a quick and decisive victory on the battlefield to boost the nation's morale. Within a week he had left Schönbrunn for Moravia.

The combined armies of Austria and Russia, with their emperors at their head, were concentrated at Olmütz, and Napoleon set up camp at Brno, fifty miles distant. In between the two cities lay the little town and large baroque château of Austerlitz, ancestral seat of the Kaunitz family, whose flat and gently sloping lands stretched out beyond it, parts of them ideal for battle. Through a series of military feints, interspersed with false offers of an armistice, Napoleon drew the combined armies onto the terrain that best suited his own smaller force, anticipating the enemy's tactics and preparing a devastating response. The Battle of the Three Emperors was fought, and unequivocally decided, over nine wintry hours on the second of December 1805, one year to the day after his coronation at Notre Dame.

Napoleon himself regarded Austerlitz as his finest victory. It ended the Third Coalition against France, and it also brought to an end another cooperative institution of much longer standing: the Holy Roman Empire, "the soft heart of Europe" that had served for a thousand years as "a self-balancing mechanism" for the interests and ambitions of the German peoples. Napoleon made no attempt to seize its crown for himself, as Franz had feared he might. Instead, he pressured eighteen of its constituent states, excluding the Great Powers of Prussia and Austria, to form a new union of mutual defence, the Confederation of the Rhine, with himself as its protector. Franz, until then Holy Roman Emperor, accepted the *fait accompli*, dissolving the Empire by his own decree.

That ancient crown was by no means all he had lost. With the Peace of Pressburg that followed Austerlitz, the French had taken control of a vast swathe of Austria's crown lands as well, including Bohemia, leaving only restless Hungary and parts of the territory further east once seized from Poland. Elisabeth's Tyrol was ceded to France's ally Bavaria, prompting her to flee Innsbruck for the sixth time, and the last. Austria had already lost its remaining Italian territories, with Napoleon annexing his own creation, the Kingdom of Etruria, from Amalie's grandson, and declaring himself hereditary King of Italy.

In Naples, Carolina's daughter Amalia recorded the situation succinctly in her journal: "In the evening we received confirmation of the armistice, and of the almost complete ruin of the Austrian Monarchy."

Carolina had been slow to recognize Napoleon's new Kingdom of Italy. Even Ferdinando was moved to protest, though only within his own court. "My Kingdom is also part of Italy," he complained to Acton. "What's to be our fate?"

It was not too soon to ask. The Kingdom of Naples was important to Napoleon because it included the island of Sicily, and Sicily was only a hundred miles north of Malta: With their capture of that strategic archipelago in 1800, the British had taken control of the central Mediterranean, a bulwark against French ambitions. Moreover, Napoleon was not content simply to co-opt existing princes into his own newly created states: Many of them he wanted to replace with people of his own choosing—indeed, members of his own family—to build a European dynasty of his own. He had four brothers and three sisters living, and of these, only thirty-year-old Lucien, a staunch revolutionary since his boyhood, had resisted his brother's overturning of the hard-won republic.

As his Viceroy in the Kingdom of Italy, Napoleon had appointed Josephine's twenty-four-year-old son, Eugène de Beauharnais. Now, seeking a wife for him, and taking his cue from the old Habsburg precept of avoiding war by marrying wisely, Napoleon approached the court of Naples, where two young princesses, Mimi and Amalia, remained unmarried: Twenty-three-year-old Amalia, three years younger than her sister, was his choice. Carolina's response was one of outrage at his presumption. To Gallo in Paris, who had served as an intermediary in the affair, she wrote privately that "an alliance with this new reigning family, who come from the mountains of Corsica, would be the lowest imaginable, and deserving of general scorn. Any ordinary little gentleman would be preferable." Napoleon's reply to her refusal, no doubt sharpened by *parvenu* pique, was no more charitable: "Tell her in my name," he instructed his emissary, "that when a woman gets old and ugly, the only thing left for her is to throw herself into the embrace of piety. . . . I will not leave her dynasty enough land to bury themselves in." Carolina later described how she had "crumpled up this letter in indignation after reading it," and even as she told the story, as a sympathetic observer relayed, "her expressive eyes flashed, her pale face was suffused with crimson: it was indeed the glance of an outraged Queen."

"I CAN SEE Italy cut up like a cake," Carolina complained to Gallo, "to give fiefdoms and principalities to every new sovereign." She believed, correctly, that Napoleon was now on the point of invading Naples. It did not occur to her that she herself might have prevented this by allowing him to join his family with hers. Instead, all the while protesting her neutrality, she had been securing defensive treaties with the British and the Russians, and surprisingly, given the many spies at her court and the British envoy's tendency to indiscretion, she had managed for some time to keep this a secret. When Napoleon discovered the deception, he wrote to her personally, accusing her of indulging in a love affair with England and of "treating affairs of state like affairs of the heart," and prophesying that she would lose her throne and bring her family to ruin, with her children "wandering through all the countries of Europe, begging from their relatives."

In fact the arrival of the two foreign forces in Naples in November 1805 was not unwelcome to him. It gave him the public pretext he wanted to proceed with his invasion, and by the end of the year, his troops were on their way. They marched preceded by the glory of their great victory at Austerlitz, frightening both the British and the Russians: With the new year hardly turned, both abandoned the Neapolitans to their fate. On the tenth of January 1806 they began their evacuation, with Ferdinando, hunting-rifle in hand, applauding their good sense: Resistance, in his view, was futile. He himself went off on a final wild-boar hunt, swearing to leave not a single animal alive for the French to kill; on the twenty-third of January, he set sail for Palermo.

Carolina insisted on staying in Naples. She was determined to head a resistance, even if it led her to the same fate as that of the young duc d'Enghien, which she would regard, she told Gallo, as "a real honour for me." Though her younger son Leopold was only fifteen, she urged him to take up arms alongside his brother, the Crown Prince Francesco, and the pair set to at once, trying to expand their small standing army, just twelve thousand strong. But as their father had predicted and their mother now realized, the task was hopeless. In the city itself, the propertied classes simply closed their doors, preferring stability to the uncertainty of resistance, and without their old leader Ruffo, the tough *sanfedisti* could not be spurred to action: The Cardinal himself was now in Paris, sent by Carolina, belatedly, to beg Napoleon for peace. Even the *lazzaroni* could not be moved. Their king, after all, had once again deserted them.

"I may have miscalculated," Carolina wrote to Gallo in the last week of January, "but I was guided by the purest and truest motives. In the end I am the victim of my feelings. It has been God's will." Thus she comforted herself as she boarded ship for Sicily once again in mid-February. She and Ferdinando had abdicated "by a solemn and irrevocable act which, while destroying us politically, will allow us to vegetate peacefully for the remaining years with which Providence will chastise us," and she imagined her eldest son, Francesco, "the grandson of Carlos III and Maria Theresia, at Bonaparte's feet, receiving a crown seized from his parents. . . . But," she added, with precipitate confidence, "this heavy sacrifice must fulfill all the political intentions of the Emperor of the French."

It did not. Within weeks a far heavier sacrifice would be demanded. By the day of Carolina's flight, forty thousand French troops under Napoleon's brother Joseph, more lawyer than soldier, had already crossed the border; in March Napoleon declared him, rather than Ferdinando's son, the new King of Naples. Under threat of arrest, Francesco and Leopoldo took their own quick passage to Sicily, where their father and mother still reigned, as a lesser king and queen.

Despite her talk of "vegetating," Carolina had no intention of giving up the fight. In her penultimate letter to Gallo, she told him she would publish a personal attack on Napoleon "as soon as I get to Sicily," and if he did not treat her family with due consideration, she said, "I will strike back. . . . I don't want to have to reproach myself. I will have done everything and tried everything, everything."

She would have been wiser to say nothing at all. Had she been more circumspect, she might have seen, in the evasions and withdrawals of the previous five years, a change in Gallo's point of view. For after twenty years of correspondence, some fourteen hundred confidential letters, her "dear old friend" had finally thrown in his lot with the enemy and was passing her every word to the French. And when Joseph Bonaparte formed his first royal government in Naples in the spring of 1806, Gallo was at his side, sporting his credentials as newly appointed Foreign Minister.

# 1805-1810

. . .

**Though the city** of Naples had capitulated with barely a fight, Joseph Bonaparte still had more than enough to do to control other parts of his new kingdom. In the fortress-port of Gaeta and across the region of Calabria, resistance continued until July, when a string of French victories sent the rebels and their British backers retreating to Sicily. It gave Joseph time, at last, for a coronation, but there was to be no resting on his laurels: Napoleon, determined to bring the entire Mediterranean under his sway, was urging his brother to seize Sicily as well.

Ferdinando had long abandoned any idea of reclaiming his mainland kingdom, and of the many British envoys and military men protecting him now in Sicily, most thought he was wise to have done so. Carolina, however, would not give up; she believed the mainland should and could be wrested back from the French. The organized military forces of French émigrés, vacillating Neapolitans, and half-hearted Englishmen having proved no match for Joseph's army, she transferred her support to a popular insurrection in the always restless province of Calabria. Glad to have something active to do, and rather relishing the aspect of intrigue in the whole affair, she agreed to fund the venture out of her personal pockets, albeit no longer very deep, and secretly appointed as its leader the distinguished if controversial Admiral Sir Sidney Smith or, as she called him, *Schmidt*.

Smith was a man in Carolina's own mould: determined, impulsive, not afraid to offend his comrades or indeed his superiors. He was dashing enough to have sparked the jealousy of Admiral Nelson himself. Smith personally disagreed with Britain's priority of keeping Sicily even at the cost of relinquishing the mainland; early in July 1806, he landed a force of irregulars in Calabria.

His inept little army was soon beaten back, though not without having tied down a large French force, so helping to prevent the invasion of Sicily. Nonetheless, at the turn of the new year of 1807, his superiors in London recalled him, and Carolina was left effectively isolated in Palermo. Still she would not give up. With Ferdinando literally, as metaphorically, gone fishing, she was able to fill the government with men who would not oppose her, and she continued to harangue the British in Sicily, and their masters in London, to reclaim the whole kingdom for her husband and her son. "Her Sicilian Majesty, with great susceptibility of temper, of a lively, imaginative and active and enterprising spirit, does not, or perhaps does not choose to, see the difficulties which oppose the attainment of any favourite object," the British ambassador reported, diplomatically, of the wilfully determined Queen.

This bedrock trait of her character had helped Carolina through decades of trials and sorrows. Combined with her fierce loyalty and her tenderness and generosity to those she loved or favoured, it had allowed her a certain influence, albeit erratic. Many of her efforts over the years had been interrupted by Ferdinando's brief and impulsive forays into government, but it was her own stubbornness that defeated her now. In due course Ferdinando would reclaim his throne, but for the moment that formed no part of Britain's plan, and her insistence that it should do made the British impatient with her. They began to think it would be easier if she were gone.

> *Your grandchildren are happy in the midst of their misfortune, since [the Empress] Ludovika cares for them as if they were her own, she attends all their lessons, in short everyone agrees that my sister-in-law Beatrice has brought her up very well.*

Thus Elisabeth to Carolina, early in the summer of 1808. She was in Vienna again, driven from her home in Innsbruck by the ever-changing fortunes of war. This time there was to be no returning. Her own palace was now largely empty, a mere occasional residence for the new Bavarian ruling family, with Innsbruck itself demoted once again from Habsburg imperial seat to provincial town, a pretty way-station en route to places more important.

She had left in a mood of resignation rather than alarm, having had time enough to pack her smaller treasures, and confidence enough to leave instructions for the larger ones to be sent after her. It seems she had intended to go to the northern provincial capital of Linz, but French troops were already threatening that area: Napoleon himself would soon be in residence at the city's beautiful Landhaus. She had gone instead to the Hungarian region of Pest, perhaps at the Emperor's own suggestion, since he had not been eager to have her in Vienna. Early in February 1806, she had turned up anyway.

"Aunt Elisabeth arrived on the 4th," the then Empress Teresa had written to her mother in Naples. "I find her just the same as ever except she's less well, her heart beats fast and she has palpitations that last half the day until she's almost unconscious. Because of her health she wanted to stay in town, and I think afterwards she'll go to Linz, but she's the same, she says the most incredible things. I try and I'll continue to try to ensure the children don't see her unless they're with me, and then as seldom as possible." Teresa and Franz had nine living children, the eldest, Marie Louise, a demure fourteen.

Brother Ferdinand and Beatrice had also arrived in Vienna, and were living rather splendidly in a private *palais* a few steps from the Hofburg. Beatrice's enormous wealth had fallen into French hands along with her land in Lombardy, but Ferdinand had been able to claim a portion of his own inheritance, provided long before by his astute father, the industrialist-Emperor Franz Stephan, and this had allowed them to purchase a handsome residence in the centre of the town. With them had come their four unmarried sons and their youngest child, eighteen-year-old Luigia, known since her arrival in the imperial capital as Ludovika, and still struggling to impose the strictures of the German language on her flowing native Italian. The exile imposed on so many of her wider family by the advance of Napoleon's armies had given her a marked prejudice against all things French. She was sympathetic to Elisabeth's plight, and a kind of friendship seems to have sprung up between them; certainly her aunt thought highly of her.

Beatrice held court at home in very grand style, though for the Christmas season of 1806, the festivities had been muted, since Ferdinand was gravely ill. Had Maximilian been alive to suggest a second waist-measuring contest with his brother, he might this time have lost, for Ferdinand's stomach was now massively swollen with cancerous fluid. On the twenty-fourth of December, surrounded by his family, he had died, at the age of fifty-two. After six weeks' official mourning and a rather longer period of notable grumpiness, for she had genuinely loved him, his fifty-eight-year-old widow, Beatrice, had turned her considerable energies toward her daughter Ludovika's prospects of marriage. They had soon been enhanced beyond all expectation; indeed, shortly after her twentieth birthday, she had replaced her cousin Teresa as Franz's wife, and become the new Empress of Austria.

Teresa had fallen ill in the freezing winter months of early 1807, contracting an infection of the lungs that had developed into pleurisy. Her every breath painful, she had been treated with frequent bleeding, which had served only to weaken her. She was thirty-four years old and pregnant with her twelfth child. Early in April, the stress of her condition, aggravated by the misguided medical practice of the day, had brought on a miscarriage; Teresa herself had lived just seven more days. Her distraught husband, who had had to be forcibly restrained as her body was taken for burial, had fled the court soon afterwards.

Carolina had been hardly less afflicted than Franz, experiencing Teresa's death as a divine punishment, perhaps for her long-ago rejoicing at the death of Franz's first wife, which had opened the path for Teresa herself. "I am stunned by this cruel and unexpected blow, the early death of the daughter I loved so dearly. . . . God has chastised me," she wrote. "I am incapable of doing anything."

The Emperor Franz, by now a severe forty years of age, was not temperamentally inclined to remain long a widower. In the first month of the new year of 1808, he had married his third wife, Ferdinand and Beatrice's daughter Ludovika, with an émigré comte remarking, "The ease with which this sovereign takes on one woman after another must be encouraging for all the unmarried princesses of Europe"—indeed, in due course there would be a fourth wife, too. The French had opposed the marriage, the fiancée being a constant supporter of continuing the war against them, and Prince Clemens von Metternich, now, at thirty-four, Austria's Foreign Minister, had also had reservations, and for the same reason. But Franz was not to be deterred: Ludovika was young and pretty and lively, and usefully, from the contemporary dynastic point of view, his cousin. It seems he had even fallen in love. Early in 1808 he had married her.

Elisabeth had been present, though not at the marriage ceremony itself, and she was proud enough to tell Carolina, the only one of her sisters still living, how considerate she had been in absenting herself from that event: The bride's mother, Beatrice, "as dowager Archduchess would have had to walk after me, and knowing her as I do, she would not have appreciated that, so I pretended it was too much for me in my state of health and only appeared at the ball. Here I had to take precedence of her, which put her in a bad mood. As you know, the old girl's always standing on her dignity and the Emperor brushes that aside and that starts her grumbling."

Elisabeth herself, at sixty-four, was six years older than "the old girl" Beatrice, to whom she had shown a kind consideration, but she had now to summon the energy for another strenuous move. On the eighteenth of May she arrived in Linz. From Count von Khevenhüller, a relative of her mother's old court chancellor, she had rented a private house in the centre of the town. It was large, as it needed to be, since ahead of her arrival she had sent a staff of fifty people to make it ready for her, and even so, "having spent sixty-four years of my life in royal residences, I find it rather odd."

Elisabeth had never been inclined to do much more than she had to, and she did not do much now. She had at least the excuse of her age and infirmities, and she had no court to hold, and no formal responsibilities. She spent her days in amicable chatter, and her evenings at the theatre, newly built in the fashionable Empire style, and happily just across the street from her house. It was a pastime she had always enjoyed, and it now became her principal interest.

Her health did not improve. The heart palpitations continued, and in the summer of 1808, around the time of her sixty-fifth birthday, she was obliged to move from her central *maison particulière* to Linz Castle, no longer an imperial residence but, since the wars against the French, a military hospital. And here, in the grand Renaissance edifice of white stone overlooking the Danube River, on the twenty-second of September, she died. In Innsbruck, the city she had still regarded as her home, the local newspaper printed the following epitaph for her: "On this day in Linz died the Archduchess Elisabeth, so highly esteemed by the Tyroleans and especially by the people of Innsbruck, in which city she had lived for many years, making herself greatly loved."

It was probably true enough. Elisabeth had not accomplished much in the twenty-five years of her life there, but neither had she done much harm. Naturally disinclined to exert herself, she was hopelessly unsuited to the arduous work of government in which she might have been involved. But neither had she been overbearing or even distant from the people of the province. She had lent importance to their capital and personally attended all the regular entertainments of balls and feasts and shooting contests expected of an imperial representative, always with her own easy manner and, as far as possible, without undue ceremony. To the poor she had been generous, and to the higher echelons of her little society she had proved a bountiful and amusing hostess. And she had been warmly family-minded, relishing every contact with the children of her sisters and brothers, and if at times that contact could be sharp-edged, it had never been without affection. A family of her own might have softened her, but that possibility her disfigurement had precluded.

**Napoleon was back in Vienna.** His path into the imperial city had not been so easy as in 1804. This time the great gates had remained closed to him, and to gain entry he had been obliged to bombard the old town centre, setting parts of it ablaze. One volunteer patrolling the defensive city walls was the eighteen-year-old Franz Grillparzer, as yet merely an indebted law student, later to become one of the century's finest dramatists; with the bombardment intensifying, he had clambered down into a dark old cellar to find, sheltering there, an artist already at the peak of his fame: Ludwig van Beethoven.

By mid-May 1808 Napoleon had taken up restless residence at Schönbrunn, aware of Austrian forces, led by Marie Christine's adopted son, the Archduke Karl, massing for battle across the Danube. Though there was little time for diversions, he did visit the Habsburgs' family church of St Augustine to see the beautiful Canova monument to Marie Christine that Albert had commissioned a few years before. Napoleon was an admirer of the great Venetian sculptor, and had already posed for a marble statue of himself, not unequivocally, as Mars the Peacemaker. He and a group of his officers arrived at the church at nine in the evening, with a posse of nuns carrying flaming torches to illuminate the monument, "and in this light it glowed alone, leaving the rest of the vast church in a dark and fantastical obscurity." The attendant priest later relayed that, after gazing at the work for some time, Napoleon was heard to sigh, *Vanity of vanities, all is vanity!* before turning away and quickly leaving.

Barely a week after his arrival at Schönbrunn, he was once again in the field, this time on the floodplain of Aspern-Essling, across the Danube from Vienna. Until now, Austria's armies, still basically fighting on eighteenth-century principles, had not performed particularly well. Consequently, though his troops were outnumbered, Napoleon was in confident mood. But the Archduke Karl had learned from his previous encounters with the French. Though his troops were still organized under a central command, rather than with the devolved structures which allowed the French to respond to events more swiftly, they were now better prepared for Napoleon's less rule-bound tactics. Throughout the battle, however, Karl remained cautious, committed to defensive actions. This prudent strategy was not enough to rout the French, but it was enough to deny Napoleon a victory—for the first time in thirteen years.

This at least was the Austrians' view of the battle, though its outcome had in fact been indecisive, with both sides claiming a victory of sorts. For Napoleon, it was chastening nonetheless, and it was to be more than a year before he attempted to redeem himself, early in July 1809, at Wagram, to the west of the capital. Once again he faced the Archduke Karl, and once again the result was indecisive.

The battle of Wagram was the largest Napoleon had ever waged; with constant use of artillery, it had resulted in exceptionally heavy casualties, even more on the French side than the Austrian. Karl was obliged to retreat all the same. He withdrew his men into Bohemia, with the French in pursuit, and the two armies met in a final skirmish, again indecisive. On his own initiative, without consulting his brother the Emperor, Karl then proposed an armistice; perhaps surprisingly, Napoleon accepted. Though his generals urged him to finish off the Austrians, he silenced them, saying too much blood had been spilt already. He had been fighting for twenty-five years, and he was about to turn forty. It was time, he felt, for a spell of peace.

Franz, who was in Hungary, was furious when he heard of the armistice. Long jealous of Karl, he now demoted him from Generalissimo: Over the remaining twenty-six years of his reign, he would ensure his brother never again held an active command. He himself was lucky to keep his throne: Napoleon had initially thought of forcing him to abdicate, but Karl had declined the treasonous honour of replacing him on the Habsburg throne. A demoralized Franz returned to Schönbrunn without fanfare, but the people of Vienna set to rejoicing anyway. They also felt it was time for a spell of peace.

EVEN WITHOUT A RESOUNDING military victory abroad, Napoleon's position in France seemed unassailable. Still, he needed a son. Though his wife could no longer bear children, he had proven he was not infertile: Through the machinations of his sister Caroline, who disliked Josephine and wanted to see her replaced, he was now the father of an illegitimate daughter. And though his love for Josephine was real, his ambition to found a dynasty of his own was greater. In mid-December 1809, the couple, both in tears, announced their intention to divorce, with a concocted story of their marriage having never been quite legal in the first place: Napoleon was obliged to pay a fine of six francs for this supposed failure of civic and religious duty.

There was now the question of whom he should marry, a young woman, obviously, and one in good health, and also a princess, the daughter of an ancient House whose name would legitimize his own newly conjured title of emperor. His first preference was for a Russian archduchess: The Tsar had two marriageable sisters, and such a match would bolster his uncertain alliance with that Empire. But the girls' mother held the power of veto, and the idea of the upstart Napoleon as a son-in-law was more than she could countenance.

Encouraged by the ever-available Talleyrand, the imperial *divorcé* turned instead to Austria and the Emperor's eldest daughter, Marie Louise, ideally aged at just eighteen. Talleyrand met with Count Metternich, each of them concerned to prevent further military escapades on Napoleon's part, and each convinced that a fresh marriage with the promise of a family would be just the thing to achieve it. The proposal was made and accepted, and on the very same day the articles of marriage were drawn up, modelled, without superstitious reservations on the bridegroom's part at least, on those of Louis and Marie Antoinette. Though many in France disliked this echo of that unhappy alliance, Talleyrand persuaded Napoleon that it could equally be viewed in the spirit of expiation for the crime of the late Queen's execution, and as a means of reconciling the rest of Europe to a new royal dynasty in France.

Marie Louise was Franz's daughter by his second wife, Teresa, and thus Carolina's granddaughter. Nine years before, when Napoleon's divorce was first mooted, Carolina had told Gallo she would rather kill her daughters than lower them to marry him, even if he were king of the whole world. "He's a man of unequalled ability and courage and energy, made great by his own talent and success," she had written, "but nonetheless he's an absolute scoundrel and a usurper. *Basta*. We'll see how that all turns out."

Carolina's two daughters had in the meantime married other men. And on this prospect for her granddaughter, she was not consulted, learning of the match, as she complained indignantly to Franz, "from the gazette." Far from her usual greeting of *My very dear brother and triple-nephew*, she had begun this letter with a simple *Monsieur*, and she declared it was to be her last, for the Emperor's abandonment of all the ties of family and duty and religion had imposed on her from now on, as she said with august theatricality, "an eternal silence." It did not apply to other correspondents, however, to whom she now gave vent to her feelings. "The Emperor, once a man of religion," she told her envoy at his court, "is daring to give His daughter as an adulterous Concubine to a villain tainted with every crime and atrocity . . . because it's not a marriage, since he has another wife . . . I am well enough acquainted with the Emperor's pettiness of mind, though I wouldn't have expected this." All the same, on the eleventh of March 1810, Marie Louise was married to Napoleon in Vienna, with her Uncle Karl standing as proxy bridegroom.

Soon afterwards Franz added insult to injury by recognizing Napoleon's brother-in-law Joachim Murat as the King of Naples in Ferdinando's stead, and by addressing Carolina, in his belated letter informing her of her granddaughter's marriage, as the Queen of Sicily. The letter was returned unopened, with a note to the effect that no such person existed.

Marie Louise herself seems to have hoped to bring about a truce between her father and her grandmother. She had probably been encouraged by her stepmother Ludovika, to whom she was close. "My very dear Grandmamma," the bride wrote shortly after the wedding, "I kiss your hands a thousand thousand times. . . . You will perhaps have heard that I am the wife of the Emperor Napoleon. You will easily imagine, dear Grandmamma, what this step costs me. It is only the obedience I owe to my father that could have brought me to make this great sacrifice. . . . I cast myself at your feet, dear Grandmamma, and dare to ask for your blessing."

There is a note of pride in the letter, all the same. "The wife of the Emperor Napoleon" slipped easily into her new role, and he in turn grew fond of her, though without the deep love he had felt for Josephine.

Carolina concluded she must accept the blow as a divine punishment for some or other failing. But, she said, after all the trials of her long life, this was the hardest to bear: to have become, like the old figure of German fairy tale, "the devil's grandmother." A year after the wedding, after a long and difficult labour, Marie Louise gave birth to Napoleon's longed-for son.

# XXXI

# 1811-1814

In which Napoleon's star falls,
and Carolina embarks on her very last voyage.

Carolina was no longer quite in Palermo. For some months she and the rest of the family had been living thirty miles inland at the palatial hunting lodge of Ficuzzi, which Ferdinando had commissioned soon after their arrival in Sicily in 1799. This lavish undertaking, begun despite protestations of poverty, had been a clear sign from the outset of his intention to stay on the island. Carolina's ill-considered attempts to reclaim the mainland since then had come to nothing. After three years, Joachim Murat and Napoleon's sister Caroline still reigned as King and Queen of Naples, and of Sicily, too, though the latter in name only, with the British fleet protecting the island, ostensibly for Ferdinando, if actually for themselves.

In contrast to most other regions of Europe, in Sicily the Napoleonic wars had brought about something of an economic boom. This was largely owing to the British, who had been subsidizing the government—or, as it turned out, the royal family—with some 350,000 pounds per year. Ferdinando, without any qualms, had diverted a good deal of the money for his own building projects and hunting sprees, and Carolina had been using her share for the large network of spies and secret agents she employed to stir up resistance to the French—not very effectively, since their chief was keeping much of the money for himself. But in the wake of the direct subsidies had come substantial private loans and investment capital that had found a broader way through the local economy, increasing commerce, providing more regular work, and contributing to a real improvement in the daily lives of ordinary Sicilians.

The French economy, however, was struggling, the ironic consequence of years of Napoleon's own efforts. His blockade of British merchant trading since 1806 had led to shortages in Europe, pushing wartime inflation even higher, particularly for the Russians. With little industry of their own, they had suffered most from the lack of imported goods: Apart from anything else, to the indignation of many sable-clad grand dukes and duchesses, the cost of champagne had quadrupled. As Tsar Alexander's popularity had waned under the economic strain, so his alliance with France, insisted upon despite much opposition in his councils, had begun to wane as well. Napoleon's marriage with an Austrian princess had also given Alexander pause, and there was the question of Poland, no longer in existence as a kingdom in its own right, but the subject of much hope among Polish patriots and other nascent nationalists. A restored Poland would mean a major loss of territory currently held by Russia; the bordering Grand Duchy of Warsaw was widely viewed as the heart of a future independent Polish kingdom, and it was already a client state of France. The Tsar was fearful and, as Metternich reminded Napoleon, "Russia acts only out of fear. She fears France, she fears our relations with France, and with fear generating more fear, she will act."

Metternich blamed Alexander for initiating the disaster that followed. Napoleon had no interest in the eventual restoration of an independent Poland, though he pretended to be when he needed Polish soldiers for his war in Spain and Portugal, with the dream of their own kingdom as a later reward. The Tsar insisted that Napoleon sign a pledge to prevent this, but Napoleon demurred. Alexander lifted his blockade of British trade, compounding the damage to France by imposing tariffs on French goods coming into Russia. Napoleon responded by seizing several vital ports. Alexander mobilized his army.

In the spring of 1812, on the pretext of protecting his Grand Duchy of Warsaw from Russian trespass, Napoleon installed himself with a massive entourage in Dresden, near the Duchy's border. He did not intend to invade Russia in the sense of launching a military attack. He did not want to capture Russian territory, or indeed to wage war on the Russians at all. He regarded Alexander as "less an enemy to be defeated than an ally to be brought back to heel." He wanted him to reinstate the blockade, to put pressure on the British so they would be forced to sue for peace in the Iberian Peninsula, and that draining war could be brought to an end. Over the ensuing weeks, he sent successive envoys from Dresden to negotiate with the Tsar. All returned empty-handed. To everyone but himself, war now seemed inevitable.

By the summer, still deluding himself that Alexander would back down, Napoleon was leading a vast new *Grande Armée* across the Nieman River into Russian territory, and toward catastrophe.

THOUGH THE ORDINARY people of Sicily were enjoying the financial fruits of British protection, the nobles were feeling aggrieved. Until now, in the too frequent practice of the *ancien régime*, and with the reliable protection of the King, they had never had to pay a fair share of taxes. But Ferdinando had recently changed his mind, or rather, Carolina had changed it for him. With the British subsidies swallowed by their private priorities, the royal couple needed further funds for the army and navy. The nobles, doing well now through rising agricultural prices and new industrial ventures, were the obvious source: They would have to pay more tax.

The Sicilian Parliament, most of them nobles, had several times been summoned to discuss the matter, and each time they had met, they had become less loyal to the King as their feudal lord, and more determined to achieve a constitution that would free them from what they were coming to view as his "arbitrary" decisions. Its members were not so much taking a French-style stand against absolute monarchy, although for a section of them, that played a part. Rather, most wanted to benefit themselves by having more control over the law: They wanted to abolish feudalism not in order to liberate the island's many peasants from an outdated, impoverishing social system, but in order to convert the large areas of inalienable, family-owned land into a commercial commodity that could be sold for ready cash, with the courts, naturally in their pockets, enabling the transactions.

The parliamentarians were led by the sixty-six-year-old Prince Giuseppe di Belmonte, "an immensely vain and somewhat slippery character," whom Carolina regarded with hostility. Though she supported reform in general, she was utterly opposed to any initiative coming from anyone but the King himself. Hers was an attitude of despotism, albeit cautiously enlightened. In the constitution demanded by the Parliament, she saw the seeds of revolution, the eventual overthrow of the monarchy and—in her more dramatic moments—her own head upon the block.

The parliamentarians had a second grievance, and it had cost Carolina much of their potential support. She had always prioritized the needs of the mainland Kingdom of Naples, and had stacked the Sicilian ministries and bureaucracy with highly paid Neapolitans loyal to herself. These were men with little interest in the island who intended to return to Naples as soon as the French had been driven out; naturally enough, the locals wanted them to go now, and to take the abandoned positions for themselves.

Belmonte and his allies had long sought support from the many British consuls and vice-consuls who were by now effectively in charge of the Sicilian economy. Proud of their own customs, the British were inclined to agree that some form of constitutional monarchy was the best path to take toward a modernized, more prosperous Sicily. But, as their outgoing ambassador had reported home to London, "No minister will be able to stand, unless supported by Great Britain, against the pernicious influence of the Queen. . . . My successor should find himself empowered to control her influence."

In early March 1811, a new ambassador had arrived in the person of Lord

William Bentinck, thirty-six years old, lately governor of the Indian province of Madras, Lieutenant-General of the army, and, from July, minister plenipotentiary in Sicily. Bentinck was a young man from an old family: His father, the Duke of Portland, had twice been prime minister. His political instincts were reformist, not so much further than Carolina's had been before the excesses of the French Revolution and, in particular, the execution of her sister. But by now there was no chance of their views coinciding. And though both believed a British-style constitution was too exotic a plant to flourish in Sicilian soil, Carolina had seen through the nobles' democratic posturing to their aim of enriching themselves, while Bentinck was quickly brought around to Ferdinando's way of thinking: that any kind of constitution would be better than the out-and-out revolutionary alternative he feared was brewing. Ferdinando had been further encouraged by the promise, in the event of a constitution being adopted, of a civil list pension worth half the island's national revenue. "They are sending us a viceroy, not an ambassador!" Carolina is said to have exclaimed, when she read the extent of Bentinck's powers; to which Ferdinando supposedly retorted, "What difference does it make to me and my subjects? We shall only have a master instead of a mistress."

Carolina's attitude to the British had changed markedly since the days of Admiral Nelson and Sir William Hamilton. She was now convinced that their "protection" of Sicily from the French was merely an excuse, that they were working with the nobles to push Ferdinando and herself aside, "all so they can get control of all Sicily's resources." She was not quite correct. Though the British were supporting the rebellious nobles with money and occupying troops, and Bentinck and one or two other consuls periodically thought they should take over the island formally as a protectorate of some kind, the British government had no interest whatsoever in doing so. And though the facts of the case are cloudy, Carolina's misreading of this situation seems to have led her into, or near to, a plot to drive the British out by force of arms, and even possibly into a conspiracy with the French.

Certainly there was a plot, a rather perplexing one, with hundreds of people working undisentangleably for and against one another, changing sides according to an increased chance of success or an increased offer of pay. Supposedly, "the French proved the most unscrupulous, the British the cleverest, the Queen's spies the most unreliable, and she herself the loser overall." Incriminating letters were found addressed to Carolina, letters for which she first disclaimed responsibility, and then insisted were fakes. No clear proof of her involvement was ever found, but neither was she ever fully exonerated. Even her old friends felt unsure of her. "The confused way she's writing says more about the state of her mind and the worries oppressing her than it does about what's really happening," noted the émigré comte de Damas, a long-standing supporter. "She seems to have been pushed to the edge by the way the English are treating her."

Carolina's typically impulsive behaviour had been becoming ever more erratic. Her temper was shorter, her judgement poorer, and her arguments often muddled. When Ferdinando's Jesuit confessor, a critic of the Queen, died suddenly of an apparent fit, it was rumoured she had had him poisoned. And when her eldest son, the Crown Prince Francesco, fell ill after eating a hearty meal, it was believed she had done the same to him. She had been furious when the British had appointed Francesco regent in place of his father, and though it seems unlikely she would have tried to murder him, it is a measure of how odd her behaviour had become that even the young man himself took to avoiding her.

Carolina was now sixty years old. Her mind may have been distempered by a lingering syphilitic or other venereal infection, or it may be that the onset of senility had turned her native determination to a volatile stubbornness. She had recently suffered a stroke, lying unconscious for twenty-four hours; her apparent recovery from this may not have been as complete as had been thought. But she had also been so unwell for so many years, and for so many years had forced herself to carry on, frequently in pain and never far from exhaustion, that she had driven herself into an opium addiction. "Her imagination travels a vast distance in the twinkling of an eye, without her mind being able to concentrate on the same subject," the comte de Damas observed. For whatever reason, this "uncommonly clever woman," as Bentinck himself described her, had become incapable of further reasoned effort.

For Bentinck and the parliamentarians, the main thing was to push Carolina out of the government councils where, through patronage and old loyalties, she still held considerable sway. Bentinck's word was effectively law on the island, but still, he could hardly arrest the Queen. Instead, in flowery letters full of sharp little thorns, he advised her, repeatedly and forcefully, to leave. Her presence in the councils, he said, was not helpful to the running of government or the well-being of the people. She would be wise to retire, at least "to a more remote part of the island," before she made things worse.

Carolina made no move to go, but she did write to her nephew Franz, testing the waters for a possible place of asylum "with my dear husband the King and [son] Leopold or with Leopold alone." After some delay, Franz agreed, in principle, to help "in case of misfortune or necessity," as if neither had yet befallen them. He could not refuse her some kind of refuge, though he was particularly careful not to suggest Vienna, where he certainly did not want her. He had never been fond of her, she was no longer his mother-in-law, and for years already he had disagreed with almost all her political actions. And all reports reaching him confirmed that in recent months she had become more difficult and more demanding than ever, to say nothing of her opium addiction.

As usual, Ferdinando had been content to allow others to make most of the important recent decisions for him, but he was not unaware of how things stood. He understood well enough the obstacle his wife presented, not only to the current government of his son, but to his own eventual return to the throne. In due course, he felt, others would achieve his wishes for him: The French would be defeated and the British would have no further interest in Sicily; then, with luck, the rebellious nobles would undo themselves by their own internal disagreements. Until then, he was satisfied to bide his time, a passive state of affairs which he knew the Queen would never tolerate.

At the beginning of March 1813, referring to himself as "your old companion who loves you tenderly, and who has admired and does admire and will always admire you," Ferdinando told her that, "for the well-being of our family and that of our beloved subjects," she must leave. Her precarious health would provide excuse enough for her departure, and he suggested a move from chilly inland Ficuzza to a warmer coastal area of wine and olive groves and good sea air. "Dearest wife," he continued, "you have religion and intelligence and wisdom enough to know what you must do to allow me, when it is possible, to do my duty freely and calmly. Be gracious enough not to force me to beg you, and if this is, as it is, a sacrifice for you, offer it to God, and do it for the love of your always most affectionate companion Ferdinando."

The King's letter achieved what no number of British threats could have done: They removed Carolina's last hope of support; she realized, with a mixture of sorrow and outrage, that she must leave Sicily. "After all the sacrifices I have made over forty-five years, you have been persuaded to sacrifice me by a handful of revolutionary subjects who have known how to flatter your own false pride, and by a flitting fear of Bentinck," she told Ferdinando now. But she would not go humbly, "making any ridiculous excuses about my health when I have to undertake a lethally dangerous voyage. I am a Sovereign," she insisted, "and the wife of an independent Sovereign, and I do not want to give to the whole of Europe the horrible example of being driven out and insulted by a brute"—presumably Bentinck. "I am decided, I am utterly and absolutely decided to go, but I will not go like someone who has been evicted, but with all consideration owed to me by my state and my birth, as I am entitled to. My conscience and my honour demand no less."

Conscience and honour also demanded that Bentinck should pay off her debts and retrieve her jewels from pawn before she departed. He did so readily, using British secret service funds: Now that he no longer had to pursue the Queen's network of spies, he had money from that source to spare.

CAROLINA SAILED IN MID-JUNE 1813 from the western port of Mazara, travelling not as Queen but as the less protocol-demanding Countess of Castellammare, with only a modest train of servants. With her as personal companions went her burly son Leopold, just turning twenty-three; his former tutor, the émigré marquis Charles de Saint-Clair, who was one of her own favourites; and an elderly lady-in-waiting. No one else from the family was there to farewell her—"as if I were just going to the country for a few days," she remarked bitterly—but the townsfolk at least sent her off with song and dance and many praises, belatedly discovering their devotion to her, or simply enjoying the spectacle. Three thousand British soldiers also attended her departure, as if she might yet try to flee back to Palermo. Their commanding general, ashamed of the ridiculous show of force he had been ordered to stage, absented himself until she had sailed.

The Queen's departure did not solve Sicily's problems. Before she had even reached the port, Bentinck himself had left for the war ongoing in Spain, eager to escape the thorny entanglements of politics for the simpler challenges of soldiering. Even with his assiduous oversight, the new constitutional government had been rent with discord, and he had been naive to expect it to function smoothly without him. In his absence, rival factions grew noisier and less cooperative, refusing the payment of necessary funds. Palermo erupted in riots; the government resigned and Crown Prince Francesco appointed a populist replacement; Ferdinando himself considered fleeing the island. In October, Bentinck returned to face the chaos he himself had unwittingly promoted; at the end of the month, he declared martial law.

He was a chastened man. His military venture in Spain had not been a success, and he was gracious enough now to admit he had made a grave political error, too. As Carolina had foreseen and he had feared, an English-style constitution, even supposedly adapted to local circumstances, was not practicable in Sicily. From now on, he would stand behind Ferdinando's throne, even to the point of antagonizing his own government in London. For the new Prime Minister, Lord Castlereagh, the island in the Mediterranean was still strategically important. Its king and queen, however, were not.

Carolina's journey from Sicily to Vienna took eight months. Owing to French control of much of the continent, a direct route was impossible, and there were constant delays caused by sea-storms, snow-storms, quarantines, and a good deal of waiting about for letters. From palatial receptions to isolated farmhouses, the journey provided a shifting reflection of the splendid way of life that had once been Carolina's and the restraints to which she had been reduced. She sailed first to the lovely Greek island of Zante, Homer's "woody Zakynthos," and here she read news-sheet reports, issued by Napoleon, of Ferdinando's dispossession and her own banishment, the price they had paid for their long and foolish loyalty to perfidious Albion. In mid-September she arrived in Constantinople, where she was royally fêted by the reforming young Sultan Mahmud II, who showered her with sumptuous gifts in the old Ottoman style—great silver bowls, beautiful shawls and brocades of gold, perfumes and balsams of amber and attar of roses, dainty treasures of crystal and precious stones. Many of her already small entourage left her here, preferring the hardships of an overland journey to the hazards of further travel by sea, but Carolina was determined to sail as far as she could, and she now chartered a merchant vessel to carry her on to the port of Odesa. Early in November, after a rough passage along the Black Sea coast, she arrived in the wide harbour, and there, on board ship, she remained for six cramped weeks, obliged to wait out the usual period of quarantine, for plague had been reported in the area, and not even a queen could be guaranteed free of it. The important deep port of Odesa, "the pearl of the Black Sea," for centuries an Ottoman seat, had been recently lost, by the fortunes of war, to Russia. Its governor, all the same, was a Frenchman, a scion of the illustrious Richelieu family, who had personally served Marie Antoinette and Louis in the days of the *ancien régime*. The quarantine once lifted, Richelieu did his utmost to honour and entertain the Queen, but more precious to Carolina than Paisiello operas and Goldoni comedies would surely have been the time she spent conversing with the duc of her beloved lost sister.

She was heartened, too, by news arriving of the great Coalition victory over Napoleon at the Battle of the Nations at Leipzig. After years of on-and-off alliances, Austria, Russia and Prussia, supported by Sweden and Britain, had agreed to form a united force against the Emperor of the French. In mid-October 1813, the once invincible general, his own army depleted by the terrible toll of his futile Russian venture, had been overwhelmed by a massive Coalition force of 360,000 men, with his Polish regiments, still possessed by the hope of reviving their own kingdom, fighting heroically to the end.

Leipzig was the greatest of all the many battles of the Napoleonic Wars; with more than half a million men engaged, it would stand for a century as the largest battle fought in Europe. For Napoleon, it marked the beginning of the end, with the Sixth Coalition subsequently overrunning other parts of his Empire, and his allies, one after the other, falling away. "It won't be long before he's completely finished," Carolina's son Leopold wrote in the journal she had asked him to keep of their travels, "and then the good times will be back for us, and we'll all be able to enjoy them together." Though Leopold's jubilation was precipitate, the outcome of Leipzig did force Napoleon to retreat. By mid-November he was at the château of Saint-Cloud outside Paris, still convinced, despite assurances of the French people's loyalty to him, that only a decisive victory in the field could keep him on the throne. It was this belief, that his political power could not be maintained without ever-fresh military laurels, that would in due course induce him to leave the comparative safety of France to seek battle again, and to lose.

The news of the victory at Leipzig was accompanied by two further despatches, one even more welcome to Carolina, the other much less so.

From Ferdinando came a letter granting her full authority to negotiate on his behalf with the Coalition powers on the future of the Kingdom of Naples and Sicily. But the second letter informed her that, despite Napoleon's defeat and his withdrawal to France, his brother-in-law Joachim Murat had returned to Naples, and still as king. Murat himself, a gifted cavalry commander who had been at Leipzig fighting against the Coalition, had not been party to all the intrigues that had made this return possible. Between them, his astute wife, Caroline, and her former lover, Prince Metternich, had arranged that he could keep the throne if he agreed to abandon Napoleon and join the Austrians in their ongoing fight to regain northern Italy. Though the formal agreement guaranteeing Murat the throne was soon to be signed, Carolina was hopeful that, with her new plenipotentiary standing, she might yet save it for Ferdinando.

The new year of 1814 found her little caravan travelling westward through the frozen landscape toward Hungary, and here she received an unpleasant missive from her nephew the Emperor: If she continued her journey, she was to come no closer to the imperial capital than a distance of six miles—the standard proscription of exile from court. Having read this instruction, as one of her travelling companions recorded, the Queen drew herself up with a "grave and majestic" expression; her very stature "seemed to have increased." Without a word she stepped into her carriage and waved the coachmen on toward the Austrian border.

Through Galicia they travelled and on to the capital city of Lviv, claimed long before in the first partition of Poland by a disingenuous Austria. Strapping Leopold, just turned twenty-four, was in his element, entertained extravagantly by the Countess Goëss at her beautiful, and beautifully peopled, residence. "God knows," he wrote in his journal, "these Polishwomen are almost all devilishly lovely and agreeable. And every single person is wild for Poland to become an independent kingdom again." Carolina was disconcerted to find that everyone in Lviv assumed she was on her way to Pressburg, but reassurance awaited her. In Brno, just seventy miles from Vienna, she was met by her own Ambassador Ruffo, who told her that, despite the instructions of the Emperor and Metternich that she was not to be received in the city, the resolute young Empress Ludovika had had apartments prepared for her opposite the Hofburg itself. Franz and his Foreign Minister were away, in the train of the Coalition armies marching, for the first time, toward France itself. In their absence, the Queen of Sicily was to be welcomed with all the honour befitting the last surviving daughter of the great Maria Theresia.

> *I cannot express what an impression it made on me to see the Queen of Naples, the sister of Marie Antoinette. How stooped and aged she looks! All the hardships of fate seem to have weighed her down: beneath that heavy crown her head is bent and white.*

Carolina was at the Hofburg theatre, observed by the émigré baronne du Montet and a thousand other people of Vienna. She had arrived ten days before, worn out from her tremendous journey, with Leopold and the marquis de Saint-Clair still loyally in tow. It was grey wintertime, a sad season to return to the home of her girlhood, with the "charm and softness" of the city she loved unchanged, but her many brothers and sisters all vanished.

Albert was there at least, her first and fondest brother-in-law, seventy-five years old now, still kind and congenial, still turning up at the social events and regimental revues he had always so enjoyed. Since his retirement from the army twenty years before, he had been denied any active role in military or political affairs, but he had his passions yet: his art collection, his mistresses, and not least, his hunting, though by now "he was so stiff he had to be hoisted up into his saddle," like one of the knights of old. Sister-in-law Beatrice was there, too, a loud-voiced *grande dame*, mother of the Empress now as Carolina had once been, sumptuously dressed at every hour of the day, and expecting the same of every lady who visited her, though it is unlikely the new arrival, with her preference for ease over elegance, made much effort to oblige.

She was delighted to be close again to her cherished Russian friend, Count Razumovsky, now retired from the diplomatic service and settled permanently in Vienna in his magnificent neoclassical *palais*. It was the grandest of settings for the city's musical life, with the Count himself always present, and by now as famous for his patronage of the great Beethoven as for his immense wealth and extravagant *soirées*.

But the greatest joy of Carolina's return was her grandchildren, six of them still in the imperial city, none of whom she had seen before. "Nature made me a mother," she had once said; "the queen is only a gala-dress, which I put on and off." And in May, a great-grandchild arrived in Vienna as well, Carolina's first, already three years old, a little Napoleon, the son of Marie Louise and the Emperor of the French. Whatever she may have thought of his father, Carolina adored this little boy, calling him her *petit Monsieur*, though she was not above berating his mother for failing to accompany her husband in his exile on the island of Elba, as was her duty, in Carolina's view, as his wife. In fact, Marie Louise had at first wished to do so, but had been prevented by her father, Franz, with Carolina declaring she should have torn up her sheets and climbed out the window to join him. But the girl had accepted the new turn of events and returned gladly enough to Vienna. She was soon involved in a love affair with the one-eyed Field Marshal Count von Neipperg, forty years old to her twenty-two, a veteran of many battles against her husband: In time, she would marry him.

For the summer of 1814, all the young people were to be at Schönbrunn, several miles outside the city, and Carolina wanted to be nearer to them. She wrote to Franz, asking his permission to move there: The Emperor was with the Coalition armies in occupied Paris, where Louis-Stanislaus, the comte de Provence, had formally ascended the throne as Louis XVIII. Franz refused her request, with the dubious excuse that seeing her there himself, as he soon expected to do, would be too painful a reminder of her daughter, his beloved second wife, now more than seven years deceased. He suggested instead that she go to nearby Hetzendorf, the little palace where Elisabeth had stayed on her return to the imperial city.

The move suited Carolina. Hetzendorf was cooler and less formal than the apartments she had had in Vienna. "The air here has done me a great deal of good," she told her son Francesco in Palermo, a few days after her sixty-second birthday. "I was quite unwell when I came here but I'm stronger now and my appetite has improved"—and she concluded with a longing for the plums then ripening in the Sicilian heat. Francesco was writing regularly to her, addressing her always as *Mia Carissima Mamà*, all thought of her once having poisoned him evidently forgotten. Still she was not satisfied that he was keeping her properly informed of all the political comings and goings in the kingdom, not that it would have made much difference, for as she herself said, "The Congress is beginning here, so many sovereigns and their ministers arriving who will decide the fate of Europe, and our own."

Almost everyone in Vienna believed that Ferdinando would soon regain his Neapolitan throne, though Metternich, concerned to maintain some French weight in the European balance, wanted Joachim Murat to keep it. With full powers to negotiate, and encouraged by the well informed Razumovsky, Carolina still expected to have a hand in the decision herself, and Metternich, knowing the Emperor's susceptibility to persuasion, did his best to prevent her from meeting privately with Franz. He need not have troubled himself. There was no love lost between them; their first meeting, at Schönbrunn in June, had been brief and awkward, and Franz had soon afterwards betaken himself to the mountains, to wait out the heat of the summer until the dignitaries should arrive at the end of September. Aunt and nephew were not to meet again.

On the eighth day of that month, a large packet of letters arrived from Naples and Sicily, and Carolina spent the day, as she had spent so many days, reading and responding to them. She was in good spirits, and she worked until late, retiring for the night at half past eleven, and asking not to be woken before seven in the morning, as she needed rest and wanted to sleep a little longer than usual. In her evening prayers, as had for some years been her habit, she invoked the protection of a Neapolitan saint against the peril of sudden death, that could steal away her chance of repentance and consequent salvation. It seemed then that she slept. But just before two o'clock, her maid, in the adjoining room, was awoken by a noise, as of a groaning, coming from the Queen's chamber. She rushed in to find her lying on the floor, her mouth open, and her lifeless hand outstretched toward the servant's bell. She had suffered a stroke.

HEARING OF NAPOLEON'S abdication in June 1815, Ferdinando, out tuna-fishing in a bright Sicilian bay, was to throw himself face-down in his boat, praising the Almighty in a loud voice for his final deliverance. His relief at the news of his wife's death now, if quieter, was no less deeply felt. For decades, Carolina had been a challenge incarnate to his every inclination; now, he said, he could do as he pleased at last. Though he declared a respectful six months' public mourning, he was quick to arrange a secret marriage to his compliant mistress, a plump and pretty widow, twenty years younger than himself. Rumours of it leaked out, causing a scandal, but true to form, Ferdinando did not care.

The extravagant social demands of the huge Vienna Congress reduced the official period of mourning for the Queen to just six weeks there: As the baronne de Montet observed, "It was bad form to attend a ball dressed in black." The obsequies were swiftly arranged and not very grand, as Carolina had herself requested. Her sorrowing son Leopold had suggested the observance of a particular Neapolitan practice—lavish fare to be set out on a table beside the body, in case the deceased should be inclined to partake of a last meal—but this had been omitted in favour of less southern protocols. There was no obduction or embalming, according to Carolina's stated wishes, though her heart was removed and placed in a small casket; the body was then exposed for three days in the Hofburg chapel, before its interment in the imperial crypt.

"I went to see her this morning," wrote the baronne de Montet. "There were lots of people there, but only out of curiosity, and no one of distinction. The Queen seemed to me extremely small; she was dressed very simply in a black taffeta dress with a lace bonnet and collar, and shoes of silver cloth.

The coffin, quite plain, was on a high catafalque and surrounded by giant candles that were drooping in the heat. The Queen's body lay on a silver cloth; and on a black velvet cushion, to her right, there was a pair of white gloves and a fan: it's an old custom."

"Of all my daughters," Maria Theresia had said, on the eve of Carolina's marriage, "she is the most like me." As a girl, she had shown the same intelligence and stamina, the same sense of duty and the same strength of will, and in her womanhood she had developed the same piety, the same devotion to her children and her wider family, and not least, the same loyalty to her philandering husband. Like the Empress, too, Carolina had faced challenges enough but, unlike her mother, she had not been surrounded, all her life, by men and also women of experience and probity to advise and, where necessary, to provide disinterested opposition.

"How unfortunate they are, those whom destiny endows with authority without the self-discipline to resist their first impulses, and among them there has never been one so unfortunately split than this poor queen," observed the comte de Damas. "She was born to confuse and aggravate everything she involved herself in, all with an excellent heart and the best intentions in the world."

There had been much in Carolina of her great mother, but one trait, vital for an effective ruler, she had lacked: She had never learned to master her intense "first impulses." Though these had been always perceptive and generally well-meaning, at times admirable and even courageous, through forty-five years of reign and revolution and refuge, her political impulses, at least, had seldom been wise. "No one misses the Queen of Naples," Prince Talleyrand wrote to the restored King of France, "and her death seems to have put Prince Metternich quite at his ease."

It was true that Metternich was relieved, but otherwise, Talleyrand was mistaken. He himself had been put out by Carolina's death; he had been counting on her support against Metternich on the issue of the Naples throne.

And if her husband's grief was less than exemplary, she was sincerely mourned by the children and grandchildren who had been the emotional heart of her life, and by her loyal circle of friends. A letter survives from her niece the Empress Ludovika, written to one of Carolina's daughters. "Oh, my dearest friend, we have lost the best, the most tender of mothers," Ludovika began. "You will forgive me if I say *we*, but given the filial devotion I had for her, I feel I may call myself her affectionate daughter. Her death was so unexpected. . . . She had never been so well, she was contented and happy to be in her homeland, surrounded by her grandchildren. . . . She believed in the possibility of happiness again, she believed her family would regain all their lost rights. . . . Our dear Leopold is beside himself, overcome with grief. . . . And the poor marquis was in the most dreadful state, he was sincerely attached to her."

The "poor marquis" de Saint-Clair had spent the entire night before the interment on his knees before the coffin, keeping vigil. He was thoughtful or credulous enough to write to Ferdinando, in a superfluous attempt to console him. It is not known whether Ferdinando was moved to reply.

# EPILOGUE

"The city of Vienna is the best vantage point of all for watching the spectacle, and the last act cannot be far off."

The "spectacle" was the momentous Congress of 1815, the fabulous, glittering, "dancing Congress" of Vienna, though the last act was further off than the comte de Damas had suspected at its opening in the previous October. It was a historic gathering of all the powers of Europe, great and small, come together to redraw the map of their continent after two decades and more of near-continuous war. The treaties signed here, settling territorial claims and installing broadly stable, conservative governments, would provoke resistance and revolution in almost every land, but they would guarantee a peaceful balance of power in Europe that would last, more or less, for a hundred years.

In the first month of the new year of 1815, the dancing stopped for a day to allow a mass of remembrance, conducted by *Hofkapellmeister* Antonio Salieri, to be held for King Louis XVI and Queen Marie Antoinette at St Stephen's Cathedral. On the same day, a royal funeral service was held at the Basilica of Saint-Denis in Paris, and the earthly remains of the King and

Queen were interred in the cathedral crypt, near their little son Louis-Charles. The bodies had been exhumed a few days before from the common graves into which they had been cast, with the writer Chateaubriand, standing alongside the pit as Marie Antoinette's skull was unearthed, recognizing "the jaw of this daughter of kings" from the memory of her pronounced Habsburg smile.

At the end of the following year of 1816, Ferdinando IV of Naples and III of Sicily finally reclaimed his birthright, the renamed Kingdom of the Two Sicilies, with himself its King Ferdinando I. The constitution so long and so bitterly fought over was abolished, provoking new reform struggles and a military revolt that brought the kingdom, in 1821, under direct Austrian control, finally burying Carolina's dream of independence.

In that same year, the deposed Emperor Napoleon, shabbily treated for six years by his British captors, died ill and almost unattended on the distant Atlantic island of Saint Helena. His widow, Carolina's granddaughter Marie Louise, refused to accept the embalmed heart he had bequeathed her. From the victorious powers gathered in Vienna she had received the coronet of Parma, former duchy of her great-aunt Amalie, and here she spent more than three decades in benevolent and practical public work, outliving her son Napoleon, Duke of Reichstadt, by fifteen years. She is remembered in Parma with respect and fondness to this day.

And had Amalie been able to glimpse the future, as she lay dying in the castle at Prague in 1804, longing for her home, a smile of consolation might have been seen to cross her lips. For, almost two centuries later, on an autumn evening in Vienna, the embalmed body of an ancient lady was carried to the thirteenth-century "giant gate" of St Stephen's Cathedral. Encased in a coffin of cedar wood adorned with an imperial crown, mounted on the funeral catafalque of the Habsburgs, it had been drawn through the streets and squares of the town by eight slow-stepping horses. As it lay in state, in the old imperial tradition, an orchestra and choir performed the great Mozart Requiem, composed while Amalie herself had sat sorrowing in her lonely country house at Sala Baganza. The body was then interred in the Imperial Crypt, near the Habsburgs' now legendary ancestress, Maria Theresia.

The woman carried through Vienna in 1989, home at last from her own long exile, was Amalie's great-great-great-granddaughter Zita. Eleven years a wife, eight times a mother, sixty-five years a black-clad widow, she had been as well, for two brief summers, the very last Empress of Austria.

# ACKNOWLEDGMENTS

I would like to express my thanks to the directors and staff of the following libraries, archives, and residences:

In Vienna: Director Thomas Just and his colleagues at the Haus-, Hof- und Staatsarchiv; the staff of the Österreichische Nationalbibliothek am Heldenplatz; the ÖNB Musiksammlung; the ÖNB Augustinerlesesaal; and the ÖNB Sammlung von Handschriften und alten Drucken. Also, Dr. Christoph Metzger, Chefkurator at the Albertina, and his colleague Alexandra Iby at the Studiensaal. My thanks are also due to Dr. Gerhard Stradner, former curator of the KHM Musikinstrumente, for his information about historical musical instruments. I would particularly like to thank Dr. Markus Langer and Susanne Gaugl at Vienna's Hofburg, and Judit Alberti at Schloss Laxenburg, for their very kind personal guidance on my visits to these palaces.

Many images for the book have been provided by courtesy of the Universität für angewandte Kunst Wien (the University of Applied Arts Vienna), and I would like to thank Veronika Loiskandl and her colleagues for their help with these. Three images are by courtesy of the Bundesmobilienverwaltung of the Austrian Bundesministerium für Wirtschaft, Energie und Tourismus, and here I must thank Ingrid Blümel, Christine Stallbaumer, and their colleagues. Several images have also been provided by courtesy of Schloss Belvedere, and I express my thanks here to Carmen Müller and her colleagues. I would also like to thank Alice Hundsdorfer-Zhou for her help with images from the Albertina collection, and Natalie Maierhofer for her help with those from the Kunsthistorisches Museum.

In Klagenfurt: Claudia Köstenbaumer at the Kunsthaus Marianna; Dr. Robert Kluger of the Bischöfliches Ordinariat; the staff of the Kärntner Landesarchiv; Sister Hildegard Poroutz at the Elisabethinenklosterarchiv; and Mag. Franz Lamprecht, director of the Elisabethinenstiftung Klagenfurt. I am particularly grateful for the latter's courtesy in providing many images for the book.

In Innsbruck: Martin Ager and his colleagues at the Tiroler Landesarchiv; Christian Reiter and his colleagues at the Archiv der Stadt Linz.

In Brixen/Bressanone: Kathrin Zitturi and staff at the Hofburg Diözesanmuseum.

In Hungary: Attila Kárpáti and his colleagues at the Magyar Nemzeti Levéltár (National Archives of Hungary) in Budapest. I would also like to express my special thanks to Anne Marshall Zwack for her kind hospitality during my stay in that city.

In Czechia: Jan Kahuda and his colleagues at Knihovna Chodovec (the National Archives) in Prague. At Nelahozeves: Library and Archive Curator Soňa Černocká and her colleagues, and Visitor Coordinator Šárka Šulejová. I would particularly like to thank the Lobkowicz family for permission to access their collections at the Lobkowicz Library and Archives at Nelahozeves Castle. Special thanks are also due to Jan Bednař for his help with queries in the Czech language.

In Italy: Dott. Gaetano Damiano, Dott. Imma Ascione, Dott. Barbara Orciouli, and their colleagues at the Archivio di Stato di Napoli. Special thanks are also due to Dario Castellano. In Parma, Director Dott. Graziano Tonelli, archivist Alberta Cardinali, and their colleagues at the Archivio di Stato di Parma; Director Paula Cirani, Dott. Grazia Maria de Rubeis, Maria Elisa Agostino, and their colleagues at the Biblioteca Palatina. I would like to express my particular thanks to Dr. Franz Koessler for his invaluable help on my visits to Italy.

## ACKNOWLEDGMENTS

In Sweden: One image has been provided by courtesy of the Nationalmuseum Stockholm, and I express my thanks here.

In the US: The staff of the Houghton Library, Harvard University.

Living in Vienna, I have benefited from much thoughtfulness and generosity on the part of many local people. I would like to acknowledge them here: Prof. Dr. Thomas Angerer, Dr. Paul Asenbaum, Gertraud Auer Borea d'Olmo, Elisabetta Carrel, Christophe Coin, Dr. Peter Fuhring, Dr. Claudia Haas, Dr. Roswitha Juffinger, Robert Neumüller, Dr. Andreas Obrecht, Dr. Franz Pichorner, Tanja Star-Busmann, Dr. Gerhard Stradner, and Dr. Gudrun Swoboda.

Eighteenth-century German-language manuscripts are written in *Kurrentschrift*, which requires special training to read. I would like to express my special thanks to Patrick Fiska for his indispensable help with these handwritten texts. Here I must also thank Adam Zamoyski and Sylwia Lorek for their help with Polish sources. I would also like to thank Dr. Stephen Paterson for reading the manuscript. My thanks are owing, too, to my agent Markus Hoffmann, of Regal Hoffmann & Associates, and to my editor at Viking/Penguin, Terezia Cicel.

Finally, I must give my thanks—many, many thanks—to my always inspirational, always encouraging, very dear husband, Philipp Blom.

# NOTES

## PROLOGUE

xi **"After a long and arduous journey":** *Wiener Zeitung*, 35, February 4, 1814, 139.

## INTRODUCTION

1 **On a broad plain:** Vienna lies on the Pannonian Basin, between the Carpathian Mountains and the Alps.

1 **"old Gothic building":** Charles Burney, *The Present State of Music in Germany, the Netherlands, and United Provinces: Or, The Journal of a Tour Through Those Countries, Undertaken to Collect Materials for a General History of Music*, vol. 2 (London: Becket, 1773), ch. VIII, 84, September 1, 1772.

2 **Her father, the Emperor Karl VI:** This was the Pragmatic Sanction, allowing a daughter to inherit the Monarchy's lands in the absence of male heirs. It was signed in 1713 by France, Spain, Prussia, Britain, and other powers, and by Hungary in 1723.

2 **"neither holy, nor Roman":** Peter H. Wilson, *The Holy Roman Empire: A Thousand Years of Europe's History* (London: Penguin, 2017), 2.

3 **"a woman you could call":** Barbara Stollberg-Rilinger, *Maria Theresia. Die Kaiserin in Ihrer Zeit. Eine Biographie* (München: C. H. Beck, 2017), 458.

3 **"all pleasure and gaiety":** Albert Kasimir of Sachsen-Teschen, *Mémoires de ma vie: 1780–1798*, Albertina K.S. D-2267, II, 1759–60, 204.

3 **"The war going on elsewhere":** The Seven Years' War, also known as the Third Silesian War in Germany and the Third Carnatic War in India and Pakistan, lasted from 1756 to 1763. It subsumed the French and Indian War (fought against Britain on the American continent), which had started in 1754. Within the Holy Roman Empire, it was effectively a civil war between Prussia and Austria and their respective allies.

4 **40 million florins:** One florin was roughly equal to one gulden or one pound sterling.

4 **"argued about this":** Graf Otto Christoph von Podewils, *Friedrich der Grosse und Maria Theresia: diplomatische Berichte*, ed., Carl Hinrichs, trans., von Gertrud Podewils-Dürniz (Berlin: R.v. Decker's Verlag, G. Schenck, 1937), 61, January 18, 1747.

5 **already gone to God:** Three daughters had died in infancy: Elisabeth (1737–40), Carolina (1740–41), and another Carolina (1748). The very promising Karl (1745–61) and Johanna (1750–62) had died in early youth.

6 **"loveliest thing you can imagine":** Edmond et Jules de Goncourt, *Portraits intimes du XVIIIe siècle*, vol. 2 (Paris: E. Dentu, 1857–58), 172, June 12, 1766.

6 **on a piebald pony:** The portrait hangs in the Elisabethinenkloster, Klagenfurt.

# NOTES

7 **Princess Caroline von Trautson:** Née Baroness von Hager (1701–93).

7 **Jean-Étienne Liotard of Geneva:** I am grateful to Gertraud Auer Borea d'Olmo for drawing my attention to these Liotard pastels.

8 **Prince Anton Wenzel von Kaunitz-Rietberg:** 1711–94.

8 **"arrogantly aristocratic house":** Alexandrine de la Boutetière de Saint-Mars, baronne de Fisson du Montet, *Souvenirs de la baronne du Montet, 1785–1866*. 3me éd. (Paris: Plon, 1914), 31.

8 **"in front of it":** Podewils, *Berichte*, 142, September 17, 1756.

8 **"first ministers of Europe":** Goncourt, *Portraits*, vol. 2, 169.

9 **Half a century before:** In the War of the Spanish Succession (1701–14). For a summary, see Veronica Buckley, *Madame de Maintenon: The Secret Wife of Louis XIV* (London: Bloomsbury, 2008), ch. 18.

## CHAPTER I

13 **During her childhood:** Rudolf Khevenhüller-Metsch und Hanns Schlitter (eds.), *Aus der Zeit Maria Theresias. Tagebuch des Fürsten Johann Joseph Khevenhüller-Metsch, Kaiserlichen Oberhofmeisters*, vol. 4 (Wien: Adolf Holzhausen, 1907–1972), 77, April 9, 1757.

13 **Countess Maria Walpurga Lerchenfeld:** Née von Trauttmansdorff (1714–70). "I loved most of all": Alfred von Arneth (ed.), BKuF IV, no. III (Wien: W. Braumüller, 1881), 105–6, s.d. (April 1757); and Elisabeth Badinter, *Les Conflits d'une mère*: *Marie-Thérèse d'Autriche et ses enfants* (Paris: Flammarion, 2020), 80, April 1757 (to Count Emanuel Silva-Tarouca).

14 **"pierce her lungs":** Badinter, *Conflits*, 81, April 23, 1757.

14 **at ease in herself:** Marianna's work can be seen in Vienna today at the Albertina Museum and the Akademie der Bildenden Künste. I am grateful to Peter Fuhring of the Fondation Custodia in Paris for his help in locating these drawings. The original book of engravings is lost, but two copies made by Adauctus Voigt are held in the Münzkabinett of Vienna's Kunsthistorisches Museum.

14 **"completely in delights":** Adolf Innerkofler, *Eine grosse Tochter Maria Theresias, Erzherzogin Marianna in ihrem Hauptmonument dem Elisabethinerinnenkloster zu Klagenfurt* (Innsbruck: Im Verlage der Vereinsbuchhandlung, 1910), 53, "Selbstbekenntnis."

15 **"played so often":** Innerkofler, *Eine grosse Tochter*, 57.

16 **"displays his passion quite openly":** Albert Kasimir of Sachsen-Teschen, *Mémoires de ma vie: 1780–1798*, Albertina K.S. D-2267, II, 1759–60, 206.

16 **"common people under control":** HHStA Tagebücher Zinzendorf, IX, March 5, 1764.

17 **"just as the first":** Innerkofler, *Eine grosse Tochter*, 57, *Selbstbekenntnis*.

17 **"enchanted me even more":** Albert, *Mémoires* II, 203–4.

18 **had been brothers:** Albert's maternal grandfather, Holy Roman Emperor Joseph I (1678–1711), was the elder brother of Marie Christine's maternal grandfather, Karl VI (1685–1740).

18 **"loved her to the point":** Badinter, *Conflits*, 27.

19 **"more than the others":** Badinter, *Conflits*, 77.

19 **"sweetness of her manner":** Alfred von Arneth, GMT VII, Anm. 346, 534, November 1, 1766.

19 **"your adorable arse":** Elisabeth Badinter (éd.), *Isabelle de Bourbon-Parme, "Je meurs d'amour pour toi" Lettres à l'Archiduchesse Marie-Christine, 1760–1763* (Paris, 2008), 119–202.

19 **"gracious and winning condescension":** Nathaniel William Wraxall, *Memoirs of the Courts of Berlin, Dresden, Warsaw, and Vienna, in the years 1777, 1778, and 1779*, vol I (London: A. Strahan, 1800), 334.

20 **Joseph should never see:** See Barbara Stollberg-Rilinger, *Maria Theresia: Die Kaiserin in Ihrer Zeit, Eine Biographie* (München: C.H. Beck, 2017), 932, fn142.

20 **"distant and haughty":** Wraxall, *Memoirs*, vol I, 334.

20 **"full of porridge":** Rudolf Khevenhüller-Metsch und Hanns Schlitter (Hg.), *Aus der Zeit Maria Theresias. Tagebuch des Fürsten Johann Joseph Khevenhüller-Metsch, Kaiserlichen Oberhofmeisters*, vol. II (Wien: Adolf Holzhausen, 1907–1972), 358, October 9, 1749.

20 **"one of your subjects":** Charles de Moüy, (éd.), *Correspondance inédite du roi Stanislaus Auguste Poniatowski et de Madame Geoffrin, 1764–1777* (Paris: Plon, 1875), December 7, 1764.

21 **"cultivates nothing else":** Alfred von Arneth (ed.), MTuJ I, 199 f, September 14, 1766.

22 **a possible match:** See Emmanuel Rostworowski, *Popioły i korzenie. Szkice historyczne i rodzinne*. (Znak: Kraków: 1985), 68–69. I am grateful to Sylwia Lorek for her translation of this text.

# NOTES

## CHAPTER II

24 **"I would prefer":** Alfred von Arneth (ed.), BKuF IV, no. VII (Wien: W. Braumüller, 1881), 284, February 24, 1764.

24 **in Austria was Jansenist-dominated:** See Peter Hersche, "War Maria Theresia eine Jansenistin?," *Österreich in Geschichte und Literatur* 15 (1971): 14–25.

25 **"regarding him as our master":** Arneth, BKuF III, 6, end June 1769.

25 **"not yet had the smallpox":** Arneth, BKuF IV, no. VII, 284, February 24, 1764.

25 **"red spots; bad teeth":** Derek Beales, *Joseph II*, vol 1: *In the Shadow of Maria Theresa, 1741–1780* (Cambridge: Cambridge University Press, 1987), 85, November 13, 1764.

26 **less energetic muses:** Elisabeth sang the role of Melopomene, muse of tragedy; Josepha sang Euterpe, muse of music; and Carolina sang Erato, muse of love poetry.

26 **court of Louis XIV:** *Le triomphe de l'amour*, composed almost a century before with music by Jean-Baptiste Lully and choreography by Isaac de Benserade.

26 **"to general admiration":** Rudolf Khevenhüller-Metsch und Hanns Schlitter (Hg.), *Aus der Zeit Maria Theresias. Tagebuch des Fürsten Johann Joseph Khevenhüller-Metsch, Kaiserlichen Oberhofmeisters*, vol. VI (Wien: Adolf Holzhausen, 1907–1972), 78, January 24, 1765.

26 **"trees at Schönbrunn":** MNL P298-8-8a, no. 66, March 8, 1766.

27 **"but his voice is":** Khevenhüller, *Tagebuch*, vol. VI, 113–14, July 17, 1765.

27 **"return from Innsbruck":** Arneth, *BKuF* II, no. IX, 359, n.d. (1765).

27 **"whole world is watching you":** Alfred von Arneth, GMT VII, Anm. 351, 350, 534, n.d. (1765).

28 **"I was everyone's confidante":** Adolf Innerkofler, *Eine grosse Tochter Maria Theresias, Erzherzogin Marianna in ihrem Hauptmonument dem Elisabethinerinnenkloster zu Klagenfurt* (Innsbruck: Im Verlage der Vereinsbuchhandlung, 1910), 53, *Selbstbekenntnis*.

28 **"he notices everything":** Arneth, *BKuF* II, no. IX, 359–60, n.d. (1765).

28 **"as a true friend":** Elisabeth Badinter, *Les Conflits d'une mère: Marie-Thérèse d'Autriche et ses enfants* (Paris: Flammarion, 2020), 22, September 4, 1765.

29 **"befall the Emperor":** Khevenhüller, *Tagebuch*, vol. VI, 103–4, July 4, 1765.

29 **no prince of the family resident there:** Archduke Sigismund Franz von Habsburg (b. 1630) had died in Innsbruck in 1665.

29 **"their masters' visit":** Arneth, *GMT* VII, Anm. 238, 521, n.d. (1765). Not included in Arneth, *BKuF*.

29 **"read all about it there":** Khevenhüller, *Tagebuch*, vol. VI, 103, July 4, 1765.

30 **"Thank God we have":** Arneth, *BKuF* IV, no. V, 457, March 6, 1765.

30 **"on his mother's orders":** Khevenhüller, *Tagebuch*, vol. VI, 103, July 3, 1765.

30 **"with considerable relish":** Khevenhüller, *Tagebuch*, 105, July 4, 1765.

31 **Italian Duchess Beatrice d'Este:** Duchessa Maria Beatrice Ricciarda d'Este (1750–1829).

31 **"a great deal this year":** Arneth, *BKuF* III, no. VIII, 72, June 14, 1765.

33 **"part of the family":** Arneth, *BKuF* III, no. VIII, 110, July 15, 1765.

33 **"Act of Copulation":** Khevenhüller, *Tagebuch*, vol. VI, 118–19, August 2–3, 1765.

34 **"excess of goodness":** Khevenhüller, *Tagebuch*, vol. VI, 115, July 22, 1765.

35 **brought "almost violently":** Khevenhüller, *Tagebuch*, vol. VI, 126, August 18, 1765.

36 **"my own father":** Badinter, *Conflits*, 22, September 4, 1765.

36 **spiritual and temporal life:** HHStA FA, K. 54 fol.1–58; Franz Stephan, *Instruction pour mes enfans tant pour la vie spirituelle que la temporelle*, n.d. (1752).

37 **"sexual morals or bigotry":** Alfred von Arneth (ed.), *MTuJ* III, 342; Joseph, *Memorandum of 1765*.

38 **"Even the sun":** Arneth, *BKuF* IV, no. XI, 464–65, November 9, 1765.

38 **the Empress Widow:** In old Austrian German, *die Kaiserin Wittib*.

38 **"lost its appeal for her":** Barbara Stollberg-Rilinger, *Maria Theresia: Die Kaiserin in Ihrer Zeit, Eine Biographie* (München: C.H. Beck, 2017), 521.

## CHAPTER III

39 **by the Spanish crown:** By the Treaty of Aix-la-Chapelle (Aachen), October 18, 1748, which ended the War of the Austrian Succession.

40 **"the faithful Tillot":** Charles Nisard, *Guillaume du Tillot: Un Valet Ministre et Secrétaire d'État, épisode de l'histoire de France en Italie, de 1749 à 1771* (Paris: Paul Ollendorff, 1887), 55–56, n.d., (late July 1765).

40 **"whatever he wanted":** HHStA HA 23-XII, July 1771.
40 **"the subsidized prince":** Wolf, Adam. *Aus dem Hofleben Maria Theresias,* Wien 1859, S. 201.
40 **Silesian Duchy of Teschen:** Teschen (Cieszyn) is today in southern Poland.
41 **"a week ago":** Alfred von Arneth (ed.), *MTuJ* I, no. LXIII, 153, November 14, 1765.
41 **"has been inexpressible":** Arneth, *MTuJ* I, no. LXIII, 153, November 14, 1765. The garden is now Vienna's Augarten.
41 **"touching her only in bed":** HHStA FA Sbde 7, November 14, 1765. Arneth omits this passage.
41 **Hungarian capital of Pressburg:** Pressburg, or Pozsony in Hungarian, is now Bratislava, the capital of Slovakia. As Carnuntum, it was the capital of the ancient Celts.
42 **"necessary understanding of things":** Albert Kasimir of Sachsen-Teschen, *Mémoires de ma vie: 1780–1798,* vol. VI, Albertina K.S. D-2267, 4–5.
43 **"gratitude for this nation":** Adam Wolf, *Aus dem Hofleben Maria Theresias (*Wien: Gerold, 1859) 353, n.d.
44 **"the Hungarians weren't as distinguished":** HHStA Tagebücher Zinzendorf VI, October 6, 1761.
46 **"will not deny me this":** Alfred von Arneth, GMT VII, Anm. 343, 533, September 4, 1754.
46 **"plenty of opportunity":** MNL P298-8-8a, no. 130, n.d.
46 **"over this Prague business":** MNL P298-8-8a, no. 24, January 14, 1766.
46 **"extraordinary for a lover":** MNL P298-8-8a, no. 30, January 19, 1766.
47 **"Could you have any friend":** MNL P298-8-8a, no. 41, February 16, 1766.
47 **"talking about you":** MNL P298-8-8a, no. 43, February 18, 1766.
47 **"sufficiently mistress of myself":** MNL P298-8-8a, no. 40, February 16, 1766.
47 **"loves more genuinely":** MNL P298-8-8a, no. 43, February 18, 1766.
47 **"compel her on this":** Arneth, Alfred von Arneth, GMT VII, Anm. 344, 534, February 12, 1766.
48 **"will not be so great":** MNL P298-8-8a, no. 46, February 20, 1766.
49 **"very angry with her":** MNL P298-8-8a, no. 48, February 24, 1766.
49 **"on a separate sheet":** MNL P298-8-8a, no. 34, February 13, 1766.
49 **"had been different":** MNL P298-8-8a, no. 19, January 11, 1766.
49 **"the other Empress":** MNL P298-8-8a, no. 63, March 6, 1766.
50 **"quite upset about it":** MNL P298-8-8a, no. 65, March 7, 1766.
50 **"[Vienna's] so-called Diarium":** Rudolf Khevenhüller-Metsch und Hanns Schlitter (Hg.), *Aus der Zeit Maria Theresias. Tagebuch des Fürsten Johann Joseph Khevenhüller-Metsch, Kaiserlichen Oberhofmeisters,* vol. VI (Wien: Adolf Holzhausen, 1907–1972),175, April 5, 1766.
50 **"layers of Brussels lace":** Khevenhüller, *Tagebuch* VI, 173, April 2, 1766.
50 **"the banquet as well":** Pressburger Zeitung, nr. 29, 6, April 9, 1766.
51 **"Altenburg in Hungary":** Khevenhüller, *Tagebuch* VI, 174, April 5, 1766.
51 **"my own early marital happiness":** Arneth, *BKuF* IV, no. XV, 474, May 1, 1766.
52 **"country fair and amusements":** Khevenhüller, *Tagebuch* VI, 176, April 9, 1766.

## CHAPTER IV

53 **"by myself, alone":** Adolf Innerkofler, *Eine grosse Tochter Maria Theresias, Erzherzogin Marianna in ihrem Hauptmonument dem Elisabethinerinnenkloster zu Klagenfurt* (Innsbruck: Im Verlage der Vereinsbuchhandlung), 55–57, *Selbstbekenntnis.*
54 **"all my good intentions":** Innerkofler, *Eine grosse Tochter,* 55–57, *Selbstbekenntnis.*
54 **her "blameworthy passion":** Innerkofler, *Eine grosse Tochter,* 53, *Selbstbekenntnis.*
55 **"I gathered a circle":** Innerkofler, *Eine grosse Tochter,* 56, *Selbstbekenntnis*
55 **other "natural curiosities":** Michèle Galand (éd.), *Journal secret de Charles de Lorraine, 1766–1779* (Bruxelles, Hayez, 2000), 470, December 28, 1778.
56 **"I had to turn up":** Innerkofler, *Eine grosse Tochter,* 56, *Selbstbekenntnis.*
56 **"Amalie would be more welcome":** Alfred von Arneth (ed.), BKuF IV, no. XIX (Wien: W. Braumüller, 1881), 479, July 11, 1766.
56 **"establishment in the Tyrol":** Alfred von Arneth, GMT VII, Anm. 491, 551, December 7, 1765.
56 **"greater need of your direction":** Arneth, *BKuF* IV, no. XIII, 115, n.d. (1763).
57 **"would accept the position":** Elisabeth Badinter, *Les Conflits d'une mère: Marie-Thérèse d'Autriche et ses enfants* (Paris: Flammarion, 2020), 108, January 21, 1763.
57 **generally "very obliging":** Arneth, BKuF III, no. I, 4, late June 1769.

# NOTES

57 **"I am afraid of her":** Évelyne Lever, *Correspondance de Marie-Antoinette (1770–1793)* (Paris: Tallandier, 2005), 131, January 16, 1773.
57 **"hard to resist":** Arneth, BKuF III, no. I, 4, late June 1769.
27 **Countess Sophie Amalie von Enzenberg:** Née Baroness Schrack (1707–88).
57 **these two "hunting sisters":** Arneth, BKuF II, no. V, 355, n.d. (1761?).
57 **"wild boar this year":** Alfred von Arneth (ed.), MTuJ I, no. LXX, 18, December 19, 1765.
58 **"regard her as someone who is ill":** Arneth, BKuF II, no. V, 355-6, n.d. (1761?).
58 **"lock myself away alone":** Badinter, *Conflits*, 37–38, December 23, 1748, to Count Emanuel Silva Tarouca.
59 **"seem[ed] to get better":** Rudolf Khevenhüller-Metsch und Hanns Schlitter (Hg.), *Aus der Zeit Maria Theresias. Tagebuch des Fürsten Johann Joseph Khevenhüller-Metsch, Kaiserlichen Oberhofmeisters*, vol. I (Wien: Adolf Holzhausen, 1907–1972), 222, June 11, 1744.
59 **"I've had too much experience":** Badinter, *Conflits*, 100, October 27 and September 23, 1763, to Countess d'Herzelles.
61 **"as perfect happiness":** Arneth, BKuF IV, no. XIX, 479, July 11, 1766.
61 **"baptize her at once":** Khevenhüller, *Tagebuch* VI, 235, May 16, 1767.
62 **"the most extreme agitation":** Arneth, GMT VII, Anm. 448, May 27, 1767.

## CHAPTER V

63 **the French King Louis XIII:** Josepha through her paternal grandmother, Élisabeth d'Orléans (1676–1744), and Ferdinando through his paternal grandfather, Felipe V of Spain, the former duc d'Anjou (1683–1746).
63 **"I will be forever happy":** ASN:AB Tanucci 1.12, 246–47, May 16, 1767.
64 **"love to the Princess Belmonte":** Egon Caesar Corti Conte, *Ich, eine Tochter Maria Theresias. Ein Lebensbild der Königin Marie Karoline von Neapel.* (München: Bruckmann, 1950), 26. Carolina's original note about this, once in the Munich archive, was destroyed in World War II.
64 **gossip at court about it:** See Henry Swinburne, *The Courts of Europe at the Close of the Last Century*, vol. I, ed., Charles White (London: Colburn, 1841), 351.
64 **an elder sister:** Archduchess Maria Johanna Gabriele (1750–1762).
64 **"behind the scenes":** Arneth, Alfred von (Hg.), BKuF no. XIV (Wien: W. Braumüller, 1881), 116, October 13, 1763.
64 **"something rough about her":** Arneth, BKuF IV, no. XIV, 116 f, October 13, 1763.
65 **"She is nicely formed":** Rudolf Khevenhüller-Metsch und Hanns Schlitter (Hg.), *Aus der Zeit Maria Theresias. Tagebuch des Fürsten Johann Joseph Khevenhüller-Metsch, Kaiserlichen Oberhofmeisters*, vol. VI (Wien: Adolf Holzhausen, 1907–1972), 273, October 15, 1767.
65 **"in such miserable condition":** Corti, *Ich, eine Tochter*, 24, August 26, 1767, Embassy Secretary Anton von Binder to State Chancellor von Kaunitz.
66 **"protection and will":** ASN:AB, Tanucci, vol. 23, 108v, May 16, 1767. The Jesuits were expelled from the Kingdom of Naples and Sicily during the night of October 20–21, 1767. They fled to Corsica.
66 **"on pain of death":** J. Lacouture, *Jesuits: A Multibiography*. (Washington, DC: Counterpoint, 1995, 286.
67 **"with a vast force, extending everywhere":** ASN:AB Tanucci vol. 23, 60v, May 16, 1767.
67 **remained loyal to the Jesuits:** Marianna and Elisabeth had kept Franz Richter. After her marriage Marie Christine had chosen the rather fierce Upper Austrian Ignaz Parhammer, once confessor to Franz Stephan.
67 **"delivery of the bride-Queen":** ASN:AB Tanucci 23, 186, May 16, 1767.
67 **"pitiful condition and completely dilapidated":** Corti, *Ich, eine Tochter*, 23, March 2, 1767.
68 **"for this one morning":** ASN:AB Tanucci 23, 52v., May 16, 1767.
68 **"now habitual melancholy":** ASN:AB Tanucci 22, 38, October 11, 1766, to Carlos III.
68 **"in my declining age":** ASN:AB 1–13, 163, October 8, 1767, to the duca di S. Elisabetta.
69 **"to embrace her as she left":** Alfred von Arneth, GMT VII, Anm. 449.
69 **"goodness of her heart":** Arneth, GMT VII, Anm. 449, May 27, 1767, to Starhemberg.
69 **"the smallpox poison":** Barbara Stollberg-Rilinger, *Maria Theresia: Die Kaiserin in Ihrer Zeit, Eine Biographie* (München: C.H. Beck, 2017), 505.
69 **"The small-pox, so fatal":** Lord Wharncliffe, (ed.), *The Letters and Works of Lady Mary Wortley Montagu*, vol. 1 (London: George Bell and Sons, 1908), 184, April 1, 1717, to Miss Sarah Chiswell.

## NOTES

71 **"globules of blood":** Arneth, GMT VII, Anm. 452, May 27, 1767. Report of Venetian ambassador Paolo Renier.

72 **"residence of the imperial family":** Swinburne, *Courts* I, 334.

72 **"enchantment and pleasure":** Albert Kasimir of Sachsen-Teschen, *Mémoires de ma vie: 1780–1798*, vol. II, Albertina K.S. D-2267, 222.

75 **"a head taller":** *ibid.*, no. XVIII, 80, n.d. (end July 1766).

75 **"little sister-in-law":** *ibid.*, no. XIX, 82, September 9, 1766.

75 **Gluck's "lugubrious" tragedy:** Khevenhüller, *Tagebuch* VI, 269–70, October 5, 1767.

76 **"to the lowest priority":** Khevenhüller, *Tagebuch* VI 270, October 5–6, 1767.

77 **"to let the pustules erupt":** Khevenhüller, *Tagebuch* VI 272, October 10 and 14, 1767.

77 **"infected Viennese air":** Khevenhüller, *Tagebuch* VI 276, October 23, 1767.

78 **"the poisonous exhalations":** Khevenhüller, *Tagebuch* VI 274, October 15, 1767.

### CHAPTER VI

80 **"in sight of the mountain":** William Hamilton, *Observations on Mount Vesuvius, Mount Etna, and Other Volcanoes: In a Series of Letters, Addressed to the Royal Society* (London: T. Cadell, 1774), 21 ff., December 29, 1767, to the Earl of Morton.

80 **"far more to be feared":** Évelyne Lever, *Correspondance de Marie-Antoinette (1770–1793)* (Paris: Tallandier, 2005), 363, September 1, 1779, to Marie Antoinette.

81 **"a smoaked glass":** Hamilton, *Observations*, 21 ff.

81 **"make her well soon":** ASN:AB 1–13, 180v, October 20, 1767.

81 **"his attachment for the Archduchess":** LRRA P. 16/21, no. 24, February 29, 1768, to Leopoldine von Kaunitz.

81 **"the same bad kind":** Arneth, Alfred von (Hg.), BKuF III, no. XXVI (Wien: W. Braumüller, 1881), 88, October 28, 1767.

82 **"in His hands":** Elisabeth Badinter, *Les Conflits d'une mère: Marie-Thérèse d'Autriche et ses enfants* (Paris: Flammarion, 2020), 31, October 24, 1767.

82 **"the same illness":** Arneth, BKuF III, no. XXVII, 89, November 3, 1767.

83 **"very much changed":** Rudolf Khevenhüller-Metsch und Hanns Schlitter (Hg.), *Aus der Zeit Maria Theresias. Tagebuch des Fürsten Johann Joseph Khevenhüller-Metsch, Kaiserlichen Oberhofmeisters*, vol. VI (Wien: Adolf Holzhausen, 1907–1972), 278, November 22, 1767.

83 **"my declining age":** ASN:AB 1–13, 163v, October 8, 1767, to the duca di S. Elisabetta.

83 **"as nearly equivalent":** ASN:AB 1–13, 186v, October 27, 1767, to Carlos III.

83 **"this cruel disease":** Egon Caesar Corti Conte, *Ich, eine Tochter Maria Theresias. Ein Lebensbild der Königin Marie Karoline von Neapel.* (München: Bruckmann, 1950), 29, October 23, 1767, to the Marqués Jerónimo de Grimaldi.

84 **"bless our good intentions":** Conte, *Ich, eine Tochter Maria Theresias*, 29–30, November 2, 1767.

84 **"she has been ill enough":** Arneth, BKuF IV, no. XIII, 50, November 3, 1767, to Count Anton Thurn.

84 **"Austrian danger of the smallpox":** ASN:AB 1–13, 212v–213, November 17, 1767.

84 **"much more beautiful":** Badinter, *Les Conflits*, 119, November 16, 1767.

85 **"a numerous progeny":** Alfred von Arneth, GMT VII, Anm. 494, 551, November 18, 1767.

85 **"the most like me":** Arneth, GMT VII, XXV, 488, March 23, 1768.

86 **"only a child herself":** Arneth, GMT VII, Anm. 493, March 23, 1768.

### CHAPTER VII

87 **"I am very fat":** Arneth, Alfred von (Hg.), BKuF Iv, no. VIII (Wien: W. Braumüller, 1881), 521–22, August 7, 1769, to Countess Edling.

88 **"She didn't like":** Adolf Innerkofler, *Eine grosse Tochter Maria Theresias, Erzherzogin Marianna in ihrem Hauptmonument dem Elisabethinerinnenkloster zu Klagenfurt* (Innsbruck: Im Verlage der Vereinsbuchhandlung), 77, *Relation*.

88 **"useful to them":** Arneth, BKuF I, no. XXI, 71, October 1, 1771, to Ferdinand.

88 **"doesn't know how to play":** Rudolf Khevenhüller-Metsch und Hanns Schlitter (Hg.), *Aus der Zeit Maria Theresias. Tagebuch des Fürsten Johann Joseph Khevenhüller-Metsch, Kaiserlichen Oberhofmeisters*, vol. VI (Wien: Adolf Holzhausen, 1907–1972), S. 149, October 28, 1765.

90 **"French culture and manners":** *ibid.*, S. 281, December 29, 1767.
90 **"a grand match for him":** LRRA P. 16/21, LK to EL, no. 21, January 26, 1768.
91 **"won't have the same ideas":** Alfred von Arneth (ed.), MTuJ, no. XXVI, 68–69, April 1, 1764, to MT.
91 **"for the Prince's amusement":** Alfred von Arneth, GMT VII, Anm. 525, 554, Précis of March 3, 1768.
91 **"If he married his sister":** LRRA P. 16/21, LK to EL, no. 21, January 26, 1768.
92 **"Since he had not the means":** Albert Kasimir of Sachsen-Teschen, *Mémoires de ma vie: 1780–1798*, vol. VI, Albertina K.S. D-2267, 22.
92 **"I did not hesitate":** Arneth, GMT VII, Anm. 529, 554, March 5, 1768.
94 **"Archduchess Elisabeth would require":** HHSTA Nachlass Nenny, K. 2, December 5, 1770.
94 **"Her Royal Highness":** HHSTA Nachlass Nenny, K. 2, March 4, 1771.
94 **"secrecy will be maintained":** HHSTA Nachlass Nenny, K. 2, December 5, 1770.
95 **"we can wait for everything else":** Arneth, BKuF IV, no. XIV, 50, January 24, 1768, to Count Anton Thurn.
95 **"really moving spectacle":** LRRA P. 16/21, EL to LK, no. 22, February 18, 1768.
96 **"never be too many of them":** HHStA FA SV 7-1, September 8, 1768. Arneth omits this letter.
97 **"save her while there was still time":** Arneth, *BKuF* I, Letter IV, 29, October 19, 1769.

## CHAPTER VIII

98 **"The King of Spain remaining":** Carl Schütz, Anna Maria archeducessa Austriae. *Schau- und Denkmünzen, welche unter der glorwürdigen Regierung der Kaiserinn Koeniginn Maria Theresia gepräget worden sind.* (Wien: Krauss, 1782), Part 2, CCVI, 278.
99 **exponents of the art:** Jakob Schmutzer, first director of Vienna's Imperial Academy of Copper Engravers, and Schmutzer's pupil Friedrich Brand.
99 **"exactly after the originals":** Schütz, *Schau- und Denkmünzen*, Preface.
99 **elderly French numismatist:** Valentin Duval (1695–1775).
100 **"One feels sorry for her":** Arneth, Alfred von (Hg.), BKuF IV, no. XIV (Wien: W. Braumüller, 1881), 50, January 24, 1768, to Count Anton Thurn.
100 **"an army of labourers":** Friederike Hausmann, *Herrscherin im Paradies der Teufel. Maria Carolina, Königin von Neapel.* (Munich: C.H.Beck, 2014), 35–36.
100 **"most miserable savages":** Girolamo Imbruglia (ed.). *Naples in the Eighteenth Century: The Birth and Death of a Nation State* (Cambridge: Cambridge University Press, 2000), 74.
101 **"the other one [Josepha]":** Elisabeth Badinter, *Les Conflits d'une mère: Marie-Thérèse d'Autriche et ses enfants* (Paris: Flammarion, 2020),133.
101 **"to seek and follow my advice":** Arneth, BKuF II, no. XXI, 378, n.d. (end December 1775).
102 **"he will be handsome enough":** Arneth, BKuF III, no. XXVIII, 91, January 7, 1768.
102 **"his life's companion":** Badinter, *Conflits*, 140, July 26, 1768, to Mme Bentinck.
102 **"I love my children":** Badinter, *Conflits*, 28, September 25, 1768.
102 **"I have just been united":** HHStA FK A, Karton 51-10-3, April 7, 1768.
104 **the actual "delivery":** Arneth, BKuF IV, no. XIV, 50, January 24, 1768, to Count Anton Thurn.
104 **"with my late sister":** Badinter, *Conflits*, 128, October 15, 1767.
104 **"will do for my dear sister":** HHStA FK A, K. 51-10-4, 7, April 17, 1768.
106 **"is very strong and never cries":** HHStA FK A, K. 51-10-4, 9, May 2, 1768.
106 **"But above all," she wrote:** HHStA FK A, K 9v-10, May 2, 1768.
106 **"I love her tenderly":** HHStA FK A, K 11-11v, s.d. (early May 1768).
107 **the ancient Appian Way:** Albert Kasimir of Sachsen-Teschen, *Mémoires de ma vie: 1780–1798*, vol. VIII, Albertina K.S. D-2267, 434.
108 **"whole happiness of her life":** Egon Caesar Corti Conte, *Ich, eine Tochter Maria Theresias. Ein Lebensbild der Königin Marie Karoline von Neapel.* (München: Bruckmann, 1950), 52, May 9, 1768.
108 **"I would not witness":** HHStA FA SB 7-1, May 13, 1768.
108 **"roughly and very reluctantly":** Corti, *Ich, eine Tochter*, 56.
109 **"never does anything I want":** Alfred von Arneth, GMT VII, Anm. 514 and 515, 573.

# NOTES

## CHAPTER IX

110 **"My very dear grandson":** Philippe Amiguet, *Lettres de Louis XV à l'Infant Ferdinand de Parme* (Paris: Grasset, 1938), 110, August 1, 1768.

110 **"threw herself at the Empress' feet":** Elisabeth Badinter, *Les Conflits d'une mère: Marie-Thérèse d'Autriche et ses enfants* (Paris: Flammarion, 2020), 111, January 4, 1769. Le comte de Canale to King Victor-Amadeus of Sardinia.

111 **"The tales they tell":** Alfred von Arneth, GMT VII, Anm. 532, 555, April 30, 1768.

111 **the first, Auguste de Keralio:** Marquis Auguste Guy Guinement de Keralio (1715–1805).

111 **sharp-eyed Étienne Bonnot de Condillac:** 1714–80.

111 **"seek the Archduchess Elisabeth":** BPP, ms Parmense 574, 281, June 17, 1768.

112 **"*your personal opinion* as well":** Badinter, *Conflits*, 112–13, February 11, 1769. Italics original.

113 **"let things take their course":** Arneth, Alfred von (Hg.), BKuF IV, no. XXVII (Wien: W. Braumüller, 1881), 490, June 22, 1768.

113 **"when it is consummated":** Amiguet, *Lettres de Louis XV à l'Infant Ferdinand de Parme*, 115, October 10, 1768.

113 **"Her fate is without question":** Elisabeth Badinter (éd.), *Isabelle de Bourbon-Parme, "Je meurs d'amour pour toi," Lettres à l'Archiduchesse Marie-Christine, 1760–1763* (Paris, 2008), Lettre 28, f. 303–304, 82–83, February 1761?.

115 **"addressed his complaints to his crucifix":** Charles Nisard, *Guillaume du Tillot: Un Valet Ministre et Secrétaire d'État, épisode de l'histoire de France en Italie, de 1749 à 1771* (Paris: Paul Ollendorff, 1887), 71–72.

118 **"match with the King of France":** Alfred von Arneth (ed.), MTuJ I, no. CXX, 281–82, May 30, 1769.

119 **"a great deal of embarrassment":** Arneth, MJK II, no. 163, 339, November 1, 1768.

119 **"*her face did not displease him*":** Arneth, MJK II, no 166, 348, December 29, 1768, to Kaunitz. Italics original.

120 **"struck with their appearance":** Lady Mary Coke, *The Letters and Journals of Lady Mary Coke, 1756–1774*, vol. III (Bath: Kingsmead Reprints, 1970, first published 1889), 313, November 4, 1770.

121 **"Her Majesty will never agree":** Arneth, GMT VII, Anm. 400, 540, February 24, 1769, to Kaunitz.

121 **"What a misfortune":** Arneth, MTuJ I, no. CXX, 281–82, May 30, 1769.

121 **"though there one is amused":** Arneth, MJK II, no. 167, 350, January 4, 1769.

## CHAPTER X

123 **"people of this kind are very rare":** Arneth, Alfred von (Hg.), BKuF III, Letter II (Wien: W. Braumüller, 1881), 37–43, n.d. (early April, 1768).

123 **"silly little headstrong thing":** ZLKN P. 16/21, LK to EL, no. 44, June 2, 1768.

123 **"I'm always obliged to go, too":** ZLKN P. 16/21, LK to EL, no. 52, June 23, 1768.

123 **"worst ladies of the court":** Elisabeth Badinter, *Les Conflits d'une mère: Marie-Thérèse d'Autriche et ses enfants* (Paris: Flammarion, 2020),169, October 4, 1768. (Original missing from LRRA P. 16/21.)

124 **participant in a ladies' lodge:** The lodge of *Saint Jean du Secret et de la Parfaite Amitié*.

124 **"most thoughtless girl":** Badinter, *Conflits*, 169, October 3, 1768. (Original missing from LRRA P. 16/21.)

124 **called it "shameful":** LRRA P. 16/21, LK to EL, no. 119, July 20, 1769.

125 **"or anyone else of this":** Badinter, *Conflits*, 168–69, September 23, 1768?

125 **"to see you again":** NKCR:M, AC 11, no. 23, December 18, 1768 and January 5, 1769.

125 **"I could die of shame":** NKCR:M AC 11, no. 23, January 1, 1769.

125 **"thin and ill":** NKCR:M AC 11, no. 23, February 11, 1769.

125 **"Amalie is behaving very badly":** LRRA P. 16/21, EL to LK, no. 21, February 11, 1768.

126 **"some kind of hussar":** Egon Caesar Corti Conte, *Ich, eine Tochter Maria Theresias. Ein Lebensbild der Königin Marie Karoline von Neapel.* (München: Bruckmann, 1950), 721, October 20, 1768. Munich original lost.

126 **"between his teeth":** Corti, *Ich, eine Tochter*, 722, April 21, 1769, Joseph to MT.

127 **"no honourable man would take":** LRRA P. 16/21, LK to EL, no. 95, 502, February 28, 1769.

127 **Ferdinando's father, King Carlos:** From 1734–59 he was Carlos VII of Naples and Carlos V of Sicily. From 1759–88 he was Carlos III of Spain.

128 **"her greatest admirer":** Arneth, BKuF I, no. IV, 29, October 19, 1769.

129 **"distinguish him among a thousand persons"**: Corti, *Ich, eine Tochter*, Appendix, 730–31 and 738, April 21, 1769, *Relation de Naples.*
130 **"command of temper"**: Derek Beales, *Joseph II.* Vol 1: *In the Shadow of Maria Theresa, 1741–1780*, vol. I (Cambridge: Cambridge University Press, 1987), 261.
130 **"he doesn't stink"**: Corti, *Ich, eine Tochter*, Appendix, 731, April 21, 1769, *Relation de Naples.*
131 **"with the King than with him"**: Alfred von Arneth (ed.), MTuJ I, no. CXVII, 266, May 16, 1769.
131 **"my own son"**: Philippe Amiguet, *Lettres de Louis XV à l'Infant Ferdinand de Parme* (Paris: Grasset, 1938), 131, May 29, 1769.
132 **"live very agreeably in Parma"**: Arneth, MTuJ I, no. CXVII, 266-8, May 16, 1769.
132 **"whatever comes into her head"**: HHStA HA 23-III, August 15, 1769, to Knebel.
132 **Princess Caroline von Trautson**: Née Baroness von Hager (1701–93).
133 **"translating word for word"**: Arneth, BKuF III, late July 1769.
134 **"once again it was the Archduke Ferdinand"**: Schutz, *Schau- und Denkmünzen*, Part 2, 295, CCXV.
134 **"he will be taller"**: Arneth, BKuF III, no. XL, 103, July 25, 1769.
134 **"not entirely easy about her state of health"**: Arneth, BKuF IV, no. XXIX, 492, July 19, 1769.

## CHAPTER XI

136 **"people lining the streets"**: Wienerisches Diarium, no. 52, 7, Sonnabend den 1. Heumonat [Juli] 1769, Österreichische Nationalbibliothek.
137 **"who adores her"**: Elisabeth Badinter, *L'Infant de Parme* (Paris: Fayard, 2008), 90–91, fn, July 21, 1769.
137 **"full of it, I hope"**: Philippe Amiguet, *Lettres de Louis XV à l'Infant Ferdinand de Parme* (Paris: Grasset, 1938), 134, July 17, 1769.
137 **"*healthy offspring*"**: Badinter, *L'Infant*, 56. Italics original.
137 **"with instructions for their use"**: Amiguet, *Lettres*, 135–36, July 29, 1769.
138 **"pull it back properly"**: Amiguet, *Lettres*, 136–39, August 28 and September 25, 1769.
138 **"though the scandal would be"**: Arneth, Alfred von (Hg.), BKuF IV, no. II (Wien: W. Braumüller, 1881), 68, n.d. (October 1769), to Rosenberg.
139 **"doing your best to enjoy yourself"**: Amiguet, *Lettres*, 140, October 23, 1769.
139 **"Perhaps next week we'll know more"**: Amiguet, *Lettres*, 144, December 11, 1769.
139 **"The present Royal Family of Parma"**: Lady Anna Riggs Miller, *Letters from Italy: describing the manners, customs, antiquities, paintings, &c. of that country, in the years MDCCLXX and MDCCLXXI: to a friend residing in France*, vol. I (London: Edward and Charles Dilly, 1777), 278, November 20, 1770.
140 **"fine courtesan, a lover of every beautiful"**: Umberto Benassi, *Guglielmo du Tillot: Un ministro riformatore del secolo XVIII*, vol. XIX (Parma: Presso la R. Deputazione di Storia Patria, 1919), 246.
141 **"there are a hundred troubles"**: Arneth, BKuF III, no. I, 3–13, n.d. (late June 1769).
141 **"the ones to demand it"**: Arneth, BKuF IV, no. II, 69, n.d. (October 1769).
142 **"They say you have blindly submitted"**: HHStA HA 23-VI, 45v–46v, September 19, 1769.
143 **"My mother hates me"**: Elisabeth Badinter, *Les Conflits d'une mère: Marie-Thérèse d'Autriche et ses enfants* (Paris: Flammarion, 2020), 114, September 6 and October 6, 1769.
143 **"every time the post arrives"**: Badinter, *Les Conflits*, 181, April 1770.
143 **"as your majesty is at Vienna"**: Badinter, *Les Conflits*, 190, September 23, 1769.
143 **"conventions of the Houses of Bourbon"**: Arneth, BKuF IV, no. III, 77, March 1772.
144 **"the future of my dauphine"**: Arneth, BKuF III, 14 fn1, August 15, 1769.
145 **"the only person"**: Badinter, *Conflits*, 115, January 9, 1770.
146 **"for our departed patients"**: Robert Kluger, *Die bishöfliche Residenz in Klagenfurt, 1769–1981* (Klagenfurt: Verlag des Geschichtsvereines für Kärnten, 2020), 35.

## CHAPTER XII

147 **"in the years before the wedding"**: Alfred von Arneth, *Geschichte Maria Theresias*, vol. VII (Wien: W. Braumüller, 1863–79), 419.
148 **"by being entertained"**: Simone Bertière, *Marie-Antoinette l'insoumise* (Paris: Éditions de Fallois, 2002), 77.
148 **"parties awaiting her in France"**: Adam Wolf, *Fürstin Eleonore Liechtenstein, 1745–1812, Nach Briefen und Memoiren ihrer Zeit* (Wien: Carl Gerold's Sohn, 1875), 74, December 21, 1769.
148 **"I have always had"**: HHStA FK A, K. 51-10-4, 32v–33, August 13, 1768.

149 **"slim and slender":** Arneth, Alfred von (Hg.), BKuF III, no. XXXVII (Wien: W. Braumüller, 1881), 99, November 27, 1768.

149 **"to be read by everyone":** Georges Girard, *Correspondance entre Marie-Antoinette et Marie-Thérèse* (Paris: Grasset, 1933), 24, April 21, 1770, *Instruction.*

150 **"less attached to her":** Elisabeth Badinter, *Les Conflits d'une mère: Marie-Thérèse d'Autriche et ses enfants* (Paris: Flammarion, 2020),138, May 4, 1770, to Mme Bentinck.

150 **"then arose not only tears":** Thomas Carlyle, *The French Revolution: A History* III, book IV, ch. 7 (London: Chapman and Hall, 1842), 243.

151 **"She was weeping":** Suzanne Burkard (éd.). *Mémoires de la baronne d'Oberkirch sur la cour de Louis XVI et la société française avant 1789.* (Paris: Mercure de France, 2000), 58.

152 **"she wore the young princess out":** Jean Chalon (éd.), *Mémoires de Madame Campan, première femme de chambre de Marie-Antoinette* (Paris: Mercure de France, 1988), 52.

152 **"in a day or two":** Philippe Amiguet, *Lettres de Louis XV à l'Infant Ferdinand de Parme* (Paris: Grasset, 1938), 154, May 14, 1770.

152 **"Marie Antoinette's tender heart":** Adolphe Fourier de Bacour (éd.), *Correspondance entre le comte de Mirabeau et le comte de La Marck pendant les années 1789, 1790 et 1791*, vol I (Paris: Le Normant, 1851), 30.

154 **"Look of her former profession":** James Greig (ed.), *The Diaries of a Duchess: Extracts from the Diaries of the First Duchess of Northumberland* (London: Hodder and Stoughton, 1936), 110–16.

154 **"without her headaches":** Amiguet, *Lettres,* 160, August 6, 1770.

154 **"subdued and reserved character":** Évelyne Lever, *Correspondance de Marie-Antoinette (1770–1793)* (Paris: Tallandier, 2005), 52, July 14, 1770.

155 **"unless he's hunting":** Lever, *Correspondance*, 141, April 18, 1773.

155 **"gentle and amusing":** Lever, *Correspondance*, 45, May 4, 1770.

155 **"he was not ignorant":** Lever, *Correspondance*, 53, July 14, 1770.

155 **"small and child-like":** Lever, *Correspondance*, 289, June 29, 1777.

155 **"do not approve of":** Lever, *Correspondance*, 64, December 1, 1770.

155 **"the body of a woman":** Lever, *Correspondance*, 60, November 1, 1770.

156 **"she will dare to do a lot":** Lever, *Correspondance*, 64, December 1, 1770.

157 **"It is not the custom here":** Amiguet, *Lettres,* 157–58, July 2, 1770.

158 **"I'm writing now":** Lever, *Correspondence*, 75, May 8, 1771.

159 **"clearly in love":** Lever, *Correspondence*, 94, October 31, 1771.

159 **"jealous of her marriage":** Lever, *Correspondence*, 99, December 18, 1771.

159 **"I would have taken her for myself":** Amiguet, *Lettres,* 178–79, May 12 and 20, 1771.

159 **"has not been consummated at all":** Lever, *Correspondance*, 81, June 21, 1771.

159 **"these princes are simply too young":** Lever, *Correspondance*, 84, July 9, 1771.

160 **her "elevated soul":** Charles Nisard, *Guillaume du Tillot: Un Valet Ministre et Secrétaire d'État, épisode de l'histoire de France en Italie, de 1749 à 1771* (Paris: Paul Ollendorff, 1887), 286, July 23, 1771, Durfort to d'Aiguillon.

160 **"set free of him":** HHStA HA Kaiser Franz, K. 23-XII, 4, July 1771, to MT.

161 **"I saw Du Tillot":** Amiguet, *Lettres*, 205, June 13, 1772.

161 **"I cannot tell you":** Lever, *Correspondance*, 108, June 13, 1772.

## CHAPTER XIII

162 **"a good deal of melancholy":** Alfred von Arneth, (Hg.), BKuF III, no. LXXIII (Wien: W. Braumüller, 1881), 133, March 9, 1772.

163 **"I want my freedom":** Charles Nisard, *Guillaume du Tillot: Un Valet Ministre et Secrétaire d'État, épisode de l'histoire de France en Italie, de 1749 à 1771* (Paris: Paul Ollendorff, 1887), 254 ff.

163 **"Madame the Infanta":** Elisabeth Badinter, *Les Conflits d'une mère: Marie-Thérèse d'Autriche et ses enfants* (Paris: Flammarion, 2020), 192, April 29, 1772.

164 **"dead to me":** Badinter, *Conflits*, 192, May 4, 1772.

164 **"tenderness and amity":** Arneth, BKuF I, no. VI, 32 ff, December 19, 1772.

165 **"how happy I would have been":** Arneth, BKuF IV, nos. XXXV and XLIV, 503 and 510, February 7 and 20, 1771.

165 **"some sort of embroidery":** Lady Mary Coke, *The Letters and Journals of Lady Mary Coke, 1756–1774*, vol. III (Bath: Kingsmead Reprints, 1970, first published 1889),353, January 10, 1771.

165 **"There is only God's great mercy":** Arneth, BKuF IV, no. XLIV, 510, February 20, 1771.
166 **"leaf by leaf":** Adam Zamoyski, *Poland: A History* (London: Collins, 2015), 194.
166 **from the Foreign Ministry:** Choiseul's 1770 dismissal was the apex of the Falkland Islands crisis. Spain and England both wanted sovereignty over this strategically important territory in the South Atlantic. Choiseul had favoured supporting Spain in a war with England, but Louis XV wanted peace. The decision led the English to believe France would not support the Americans militarily in their bid for independence.
166 **"horror and disgust":** Arneth, BKuF I, no. CXXVI, 226, August 26, 1773. The figure of some 2,600,000 includes the populations from the 2nd and 3rd Partitions in 1793 and 1795.
167 **"away from here":** Barbara Stollberg-Rilinger, *Maria Theresia: Die Kaiserin in Ihrer Zeit, Eine Biographie* (München: C.H. Beck, 2017), 634. See also 636 ff. for her expulsion of the Jews from Prague in 1744–46.
167 **"begin to explain to her":** Évelyne Lever, *Correspondance de Marie-Antoinette (1770–1793)* (Paris: Tallandier, 2005), 138, March 17, 1773.
167 **"rupture between my two families":** Alfred von Arneth, und Auguste Mathieu Geffroy (Hg.), *Correspondance secrète entre Marie Thérèse et le comte de Mercy-Argenteau, avec les lettres de Marie Thérèse et Marie Antoinette*, vol. I, no. XXX (Paris: Didot, 1874), 322, July 17, 1772.
167 **"lend herself to anything":** Arneth, *Correspondance secrete*, vol. I, no. XXXII, 329, July 18, 1772.
168 **"between mother and son":** Badinter, *Conflits*, 187, October 5, 1771.
169 **"to make a wife happy":** Arneth, BKuF I, no. CLXXI, 274, May 4, 1774, to Ferdinand.
169 **"being so unreasonable":** Arneth, BKuF II, no. LXXXIII, 462, May 29, 1780.
169 **"the immortal Sovereign":** Carl Schütz, Anna Maria archeducessa Austriae. *Schau- und Denkmünzen, welche unter der glorwürdigen Regierung der Kaiserinn Koeniginn Maria Theresia gepräget worden sind.* (Wien: Krauss, 1782), Part 1, CLXXI, 232.
170 **"happy days came to an end":** Arneth, BKuF IV, no. I, 443, May 1, 1766, to Count Ignaz Cassian Enzenberg.
170 **"increase by the day":** Arneth, BKuF IV, no. XXXV, 503, February 7, 1771.
171 **"she brought it on herself":** Arneth, BKuF IV, no. CLXXXVIII, 297-8, September 1, 1774.
171 **"a little intrigue":** LRRA P.16/23, KL to EL, no. 22, July 21, 1772.
171 **"advancing his prospects":** LRRA P.16/23, EL to KL, no. 19, July 29, 1772.
171 **"be of some benefit":** LRRA P.16/23, KL to EL, no. 22, July 21, 1772.
172 **"the veil of friendship":** LRRA P.16/23, EL to KL, no. 19, July 29, 1772.
172 **"do as I please":** LRRA P.16/23, EL to LK, no. 16, July 15, 1772.
172 **"how the mood takes him":** LRRA P.16/23, EL to KL, no. 13, July 11, 1772.
172 **"He's a funny specimen":** LRRA P.16/23, EL to LK, no. 19, July 29, 1772.
172 **"not in him to act like other people":** LRRA P.16/23, KL to EL, no. 23, July 31, 1772.
173 **"She has been bled":** Arneth, BKuF I, no. XCV, 178, January 28, 1773.
173 **"In spite of her illness":** La Rocheterie, Maxime de & le marquis de Beaucourt (éds.), *Lettres de Marie Antoinette: Recueil des lettres authentiques de la reine publié pour la société d'histoire contemporaine.* (Paris: Au Siège de la Société, 1895–96), I, 43, February 15, 1773.
173 **"This fasting food":** Lever, *Correspondance*, 141, April 18, 1773.
175 **"one day nearer my deliverance":** Adolf Innerkofler, *Eine grosse Tochter Maria Theresias, Erzherzogin Marianna in ihrem Hauptmonument dem Elisabethinerinnenkloster zu Klagenfurt* (Innsbruck: Im Verlage der Vereinsbuchhandlung), 61–72, February 24 to April 10, 1773, Asketisches Tagebuch.
175 **"I have finished":** Arneth, BKuF I, no. CXXVI, 226, August 26, 1773.
176 **"resumes his correspondence with them":** Arneth, BKuF I, no. CXIX, 217-8, July 15, 1773.
176 **"a child of peace":** Alfred von Arneth, GMT VII, Anm. 574, SS. 558-9, July 10, 1773.
176 **"even ugly, which she never was":** Arneth, BKuF IV, no. XLI, 508, October 16, 1773.
177 **"there are arguments":** Philippe Amiguet, *Lettres de Louis XV à l'Infant Ferdinand de Parme* (Paris: Grasset, 1938), 170, January 7, 1771.
177 **"the new King Louis XVI":** Jean Chalon (éd.), *Mémoires de Madame Campan, première femme de chambre de Marie-Antoinette* (Paris: Mercure de France, 1988), 74.

## CHAPTER XIV

178 **"his other qualities":** Georges Girard, *Correspondance entre Marie-Antoinette et Marie-Thérèse* (Paris: Grasset, 1933), 129, September 7, 1774.

178 **"Infidels, and Free Thinkers":** Nathaniel William Wraxall, *Memoirs of the Courts of Berlin, Dresden, Warsaw, and Vienna, in the years 1777, 1778, and 1779*, vol. II (London: A. Strahan, 1800), 326–27.

178 **"the example style attached":** Alfred von Arneth, (Hg.), BKuF II, no. I (Wien: W. Braumüller, 1881), 337, n.d. (April 1774).

179 **"produce heirs to the throne":** Jean Chalon (éd.), *Mémoires de Madame Campan, première femme de chambre de Marie-Antoinette* (Paris: Mercure de France, 1988), 106.

179 **"to the mother and the child":** Évelyne Lever, *Correspondance de Marie-Antoinette (1770–1793)* (Paris: Tallandier, 2005), 225, August 12, 1775.

180 **"which I believe is necessary":** Girard, *Correspondance*, 160, September 15, 1775.

180 **"son of that stranger on the throne":** Maurice Lever, *Pierre-Augustin Caron de Beaumarchais*, vol. II (Paris: Fayard, 1999), 422–24, *Dissertation extraite d'un plus grand ouvrage*.

180 **"too much attached to her":** Girard, *Correspondance*, 160, September 15, 1775.

180 **"her constant care":** Campan, *Mémoires*, 106.

181 **presented to her as a gift:** In 1787 Jean Amilcar (1781–96) was purchased from slavers by the Chevalier de Boufflers, who wanted to save the boy from the transatlantic crossing to America. He was able to begin training as an artist in Paris before his early death from illness.

182 **"jealous people as there are courtiers":** Suzanne Burkard (éd.). *Mémoires de la baronne d'Oberkirch sur la cour de Louis XVI et la société française avant 1789.* (Paris: Mercure de France, 2000), 286, June 13, 1782.

182 **"makes the people very restless":** Lever, *Correspondance*, 228–29, September 18, 1775.

182 **"end up one day their victim":** Lever, *Beaumarcharchais*, II, 424, *Dissertation*.

183 **"never see each other again":** Girard, *Correspondance*, 141, March 17, 1775.

183 **"where the heat is considerable":** Arneth, BKuF II, 343, April 20, 1775, *Continuation*.

184 **"Spanish court etiquette":** Erzherzog Maximilian Franz (Graf von Burgau), *Tagebuch 1775–1776*. HHStA Este 176, 81–81v, April 20 & 91v–92v, May 10, 1775.

184 **an illegitimate daughter:** See Giuseppe Bertini, *L'Appartamento del Duca Ferdinando a Colorno dipinto da Antonio Bresciani* (Parma: TLC, 2000), 17.

184 **"the honours of paternity":** Bertini, *L'Appartamento* 116.

185 **"She buys a horse":** Henry Swinburne, *The Courts of Europe at the Close of the Last Century*, vol. I, ed., Charles White (London: Colburn, 1841), 305–6.

188 **"ignorant or penurious owners":** Gianni Nigrelli, "*Un collezionista Mantuano a Parma nel secondo settecento: Il marchese Guido Cavriani (1735-1791) e la sua raccolta di stampe*," Accademia Nazionale Virgiliana di Scienze Lettere e Arte, Atti e Memorie, Nuova serie, vol. XXXV (2017), p 65.

189 **"a very good walker":** Albert Kasimir of Sachsen-Teschen, *Mémoires de ma vie: 1780–1798*, vol. IX, Albertina K.S. D-2267, 512.

189 **"does not yet reassure me":** Arneth, BKuF II, no. XXXII, 401, February 19, 1776.

190 **"for kindness and charity":** Albert, *Mémoires* VII, 265–66.

190 **"of most interest to me":** Arneth, BKuF II, no. XXXIII, 401–2, February 26, 1776.

190 **"I have Gust sent":** Mary Webster, *Johann Zoffany, 1733–1810* (New Haven, CT: Yale University Press, 2011), 326.

## CHAPTER XV

191 **"undertaken at all":** MNL P298-8-8a-no. 64, March 6, 1766.

193 **"contradicted that infinitely":** Albert Kasimir of Sachsen-Teschen, *Mémoires de ma vie: 1780–1798*, vol. VIII, Albertina K.S. D-2267, 402–3, 407, 434–39, 446.

193 **"I developed a serious fever":** HHStA EC Nachlass II, 1786–93, March 9, 1793.

193 **"beyond all expression":** Albert, *Mémoires* VIII, 443–46.

194 **"All of us were always together":** Egon Caesar Corti Conte, *Ich, eine Tochter Maria Theresias. Ein Lebensbild der Königin Marie Karoline von Neapel.* (München: Bruckmann, 1950), 406, November 27, 1802. Carolina's twelfth child, Antonia, to her fifth, Francesco.

194 **"if you die or burst":** Harold Acton, *The Bourbons of Naples (1734–1825)* (London: Methuen, 1956), 179.

194 **"I still bear the scars":** Alessandro Coletti, *La regina di Napoli. La vita appassionata di Maria Carolina, protagonista di splendori e miserie del Settecento napoletano* (Novara: Agostini, 1986), 62.

194 **"My dear sister writes":** Joseph J. Gerning, *Reise durch Oesterreich und Italien*, vol. I (Frankfurt: Willmann, 1802), 267.

195 **"fear for his health":** Albert, *Mémoires* VIII, 445–46.

199 **"other exalted Masons":** Acton, *Bourbons*, 180.

200 **"very affecting to see":** Albert, *Mémoires* IX, 523–26.
200 **The current ministers:** First Minister Count Giuseppe Sacco and Finance Minister the Marchese Canossa.
201 **"the only friend I have":** Idelfonso Stanga, *Maria Amalia di Borbone, duchessa di Parma, 1746–1804* (Cremona: Nuova, 1932), 88.
201 **"who wishes me well":** Stanga, *Maria Amalia*, 56.
202 **"but never in Vienna":** Alfred von Arneth (Hg.), BKuF III, nos. CLXXVIII & CLXXXII (Wien: W. Braumüller, 1881), 229 and 233, April 29 and May 27, 1776.
202 **"same as she does":** Stanga, *Maria Amalia*, 73, n.d. (1776?).
202 **"is to do nothing":** Charles Nisard, *Guillaume du Tillot: Un Valet Ministre et Secrétaire d'État, épisode de l'histoire de France en Italie, de 1749 à 1771* (Paris: Paul Ollendorff, 1887), fn92.
203 **"all have our weaknesses":** Arneth, BKuF II, no. XXI, 380, n.d. (end December 1775).
203 **"to live, and not die":** Stanga, *Maria Amalia*, 76.

## CHAPTER XVI

204 **"intended for her use":** Albert Kasimir of Sachsen-Teschen, *Mémoires de ma vie: 1780–1798*, vol. X, Albertina K.S. D-2267, 640–41.
205 **"very expensive and interesting":** Alfred von Arneth (Hg.), BKuF III, no. CLXXXVIII (Wien: W. Braumüller, 1881), 237–38, July 15, 1776.
205 **"suffering from the heat":** Arneth, BKuF no. CXCL, 241, August 5, 1776.
205 **While "the Tuscans":** Arneth, BKuF no. CXCVI, 245, September 9, 1776.
206 **"not as much as Elisabeth, but still":** Arneth, BKuF no. CXCI, 241, August 5, 1776.
206 **"my dogs stink":** Idelfonso Stanga, *Maria Amalia di Borbone, duchessa di Parma, 1746–1804* (Cremona: Nuova, !932), 74, August 30, 1776.
207 **"heavy and inanimate":** Harold Acton, *The Bourbons of Naples (1734–1825)* (London: Methuen, 1956), 181–82.
207 **"managed this affair very cleverly":** Évelyne Lever, *Correspondance de Marie-Antoinette (1770–1793)* (Paris: Tallandier, 2005), 267, December 16, 1776.
207 **"impolitic and blundering":** Acton, *Bourbons*, 182.
209 **"stuffed with straw":** Moses Tyson and Henry Guppy (eds.), *The French Journals of Mrs. Thrale and Doctor Johnson* (Manchester: Manchester University Press, 1932), 125, October 19, 1775.
209 **"above all no gambling":** Lever, *Correspondence*, 225 and 292, August 31, 1775 and August 30, 1777.
209 **star of the *Comédie française*:** Lever, *Correspondence*, 278, April 16, 1777. The actress was Louise Élisabeth Contat, who would create the role of Suzanne in Beaumarchais's *Marriage of Figaro* in 1778.
209 **"in my private room":** Lever, *Correspondence*, 294, September 10, 1777.
209 **"not to torment him about it":** Lever, *Correspondence*, 298, October 2, 1777.
210 **"of assistance to her":** Alfred von Arneth (ed.), MTuJ II, no. CCLI, 123ff, November 24, 1776.
210 **"to give you good advice":** Lever, *Correspondence*, 269, January 2, 1777.
210 **"What discussions we'd have":** Arneth, MTuJ II, no. CCLIV, 130, April 29, 1777.
210 **"not even Kaunitz sees those":** Lever, *Correspondance*, 181, June 16, 1774.
211 **"of which she is in such need":** HHStA FA SB 7, 309, April 29, 1777.
212 **"took great advantage of this":** Adolphe Fourier de Bacourt (éd.), *Correspondance entre le comte de Mirabeau et le comte de La Marck pendant les années 1789, 1790 et 1791*, vol. I (Paris: Le Normant, 1851), 24 ff.
212 **"hard erections apparently":** HHStA FA SB 7, May 11, 1777.
212 **"two absolute incompetents":** HHStA FA SB 7, June 9, 1777. This letter not published by Arneth.
213 **"his occupational functions":** Jean Chalon (éd.), *Mémoires de Madame Campan, première femme de chambre de Marie-Antoinette* (Paris: Mercure de France, 1988), 148–56.
214 **"disliking the Queen":** Alexandre de Tilly, *Mémoires du comte Alexandre de Tilly, pour servir à l'histoire des moeurs de la fin du XVIIIe siècle*, vol. II (Paris: Chez les marchands de nouveautés, 1828), 95.
214 **"France, Naples, or Tuscany":** Lever, *Correspondance*, 289 and 293, June 29 and August 30, 1777.

## CHAPTER XVII

215 **"those Bavarian rustics":** Derek Beales, *Joseph II.* Vol 1: *In the Shadow of Maria Theresa, 1741–1780*, vol. I (Cambridge: Cambridge University Press, 1987), 397.

216 **"you were born a German":** Elisabeth Badinter, *Les Conflits d'une mère: Marie-Thérèse d'Autriche et ses enfants* (Paris: Flammarion, 2020),183.
217 **"we do not approve of it":** Évelyne Lever, *Correspondance de Marie-Antoinette (1770–1793)* (Paris: Tallandier, 2005), 311–12, February 18, 1778.
217 **"called itself a friend to Austria":** Adolphe Fourier de Bacourt (éd.), *Correspondance entre le comte de Mirabeau et le comte de La Marck pendant les années 1789, 1790 et 1791*, vol. I (Paris: Le Normant, 1851), 34.
217 **"a flood of words":** Lever, *Correspondance*, 321, May 5, 1778.
217 **"if our alliance were to falter":** *Correspondance*, 308, February 1, 1778.
218 **"make my life worse than death":** *Correspondance*, 313, February 19, 1778.
218 **"increases my hopes":** *Correspondance*, 318–19, April 19, 1778.
218 **"advantageous changes in every sense":** *Correspondance*, 323, May 5, 1778.
219 **"most adored husband":** Adam Wolf, *Marie Christine, Erzherzogin von Österreich* (Wien: Carl Gerold's Sohn, 1863), 261, n.d., 1778.
219 **"don't actually belong to you":** LRRA P. 17/24, LK to EL, no. 88, September 29, 1778.
219 **"despair that we're separated":** Wolf, *Marie Christine* II, 263, June 2, 1778.
219 **"the best of wives":** From the memorial monument sculpted by Canova after Marie Christine's death.
219 **"so much to harm us":** LRRA P. 17/24, LK to EL, no. 88, September 29, 1778.
220 **"worried about her husband":** LRRA P. 17/24, LK to EL, no. 88, September 29, 1778.
220 **"certain and brilliant":** Nathaniel William Wraxall, *Memoirs of the Courts of Berlin, Dresden, Warsaw, and Vienna, in the years 1777, 1778, and 1779*, vol. II (London: A. Strahan, 1800), 214.
220 **"the plum duff-up":** *Zwetschgenrummel.*
221 **"everything you said to him":** HHStA Tagebücher Zinzendorf XXIII, February 7, 1778.
222 **and "no influence":** Adam Wandruszka, *Leopold II. Erzherzog von Österreich, Großherzog von Toskana, König von Ungarn und Böhmen, Römischer Kaiser*, vol. I (Wien: Herold, 1963–65), 347–52.
222 **"a woman of the world":** Henry Swinburne, *The Courts of Europe at the Close of the Last Century*, vol. I, ed., Charles White (London: Colburn, 1841), 342.
222 **"serious and sad and ill":** Wandruszka, *Leopold II*, vol. 348.
223 **Imperial Cabinet of Natural Curiosities:** Forerunner of Vienna's Naturhistorisches Museum, the Museum of Natural History.
223 **"drain her prodigiously":** Swinburne, *Courts*, vol. I, 341.
223 **"total command over him":** Wandruszka, *Leopold II*, vol. I, 349–53.
224 **"debts and bad behaviour":** HHStA FA SB Karton 15, Allegato di no. 1
224 **"he can't stand her":** Wandruszka, *Leopold II* vol. I, 347.
224 **"she has no influence":** HHStA FA SB Karton 15, Allegato di no. 1.
224 **"everything that's not his own idea":** Wandruszka, *Leopold II*, vol. I, 343.

## CHAPTER XVIII

226 **"in a public square":** Jean Chalon (éd.), *Mémoires de Madame Campan, première femme de chambre de Marie-Antoinette* (Paris: Mercure de France, 1988), 170.
226 **"this fifth Theresia":** Alfred von Arneth (Hg.), BKuF III, no. CCXCVII (Wien: W. Braumüller, 1881), 337, December 28, 1778.
226 **"care will be for you":** Campan, *Mémoires*, 173–74.
227 **"Grief of this kind is annihilating":** Henry Swinburne, *The Courts of Europe at the Close of the Last Century*, vol. I, ed., Charles White (London: Colburn, 1841), 234–35.
228 **"in all the splendour":** Élisabeth Vigée Le Brun, *Mémoires d'une portraitiste* (Paris: Éditions Scala, 1989), 41.
228 **"very well in Vienna":** Évelyne Lever, *Correspondance de Marie-Antoinette (1770–1793)* (Paris: Tallandier, 2005), 310, February 13, 1778.
228 **"She has had four sessions":** Lever, *Correspondance*, 314, March 6, 1778.
229 **"bored and impatient":** Inès de Kertanguy, *Madame Vigée-Le Brun* (Paris: Perrin, 2000), 60.
229 **"they don't want anything from me":** Adolphe Fourier de Bacourt (éd.), *Correspondance entre le comte de Mirabeau et le comte de La Marck pendant les années 1789, 1790 et 1791*, vol. I (Paris: Le Normant, 1851), 33
229 **"they hope to animate them":** Alexandre de Tilly, *Mémoires du comte Alexandre de Tilly, pour servir à*

*l'histoire des moeurs de la fin du XVIIIe siècle*, vol. II.(Paris: Chez les marchands de nouveautés, 1828), 118.

230 **"most amiable princess that I know":** Baron de Rudolf Maurits Klinckowström, *Le comte de Fersen et la cour de France. Extraits des papiers du comte Jean Axel de Fersen* (Paris: Firmin-Didot, 1877), xxxii–xxxiii, August 20 and November 19, 1778.

230 **"its modesty and reserve":** Katherine Prescott Wormeley (trans.), *Diary and Correspondence of Count Axel Fersen, Grand-Marshal of Sweden, Relating to the Court of France* (London: William Heinemann, 1902), 12–13, August 26 and November 19, 1779.

231 **"sought to please everyone":** Wormeley (trans.), *Diary and Correspondence of Count Axel Fersen*, 13–19.

231 **"the life I am leading":** Lever, *Correspondance*, 369, December 15, 1779.

231 **"we're all impatient for":** Lever, *Correspondance*, 368–69, December 1, 1779.

231 **"the Emperor has even gone hunting":** Arneth, BKuF III, no. CDX, 443, November 20, 1780.

232 **"spoke German with us":** Adolf Innerkofler, *Eine grosse Tochter Maria Theresias, Erzherzogin Marianna in ihrem Hauptmonument dem Elisabethinerinnenkloster zu Klagenfurt* (Innsbruck: Im Verlage der Vereinsbuchhandlung), 76–84, *Relation*.

232 **"just women's hysteria":** Hans Wagner, "Historische Lektüre vor der Französiche Revolution: Aus den Tagebüchern des Grafen Karl von Zinzendorf," in *Mitteilungen des Instituts für Österreichische Geschichtsforschung*. Sonderband (Wien; Köln; Weimar, 1880), 36, January 26, 1781.

233 **"to see you all like this":** Innerkofler, *Eine grosse Tochter*, 83.

233 **"comfortably enough to die":** Innerkofler, *Eine grosse Tochter*, 84–85.

## CHAPTER XIX

234 **"no longer see what I'm writing":** Alfred von Arneth (Hg.). *Marie Antoinette, Joseph II, und Leopold II: Ihr Briefwechsel*, vol. V (Leipzig: K. F. Köhler, 1866), 22, December 10, 1780.

235 **"Our grief will increase every day":** Idelfonso Stanga, *Maria Amalia di Borbone, duchessa di Parma, 1746–1804* (Cremona: Nuova, 1932), 79, December 5 and 7, 1780, to the marchese Prospera Manara.

235 **"but I don't care":** HHStA SB 7-9, March 28 and January 3, 1781.

235 **"to ask to stay in Vienna":** Albert Kasimir of Sachsen-Teschen, *Mémoires de ma vie: 1780–1798*, vol. XII, Albertina K.S. D-2267, 1.

235 **Grand Master of the Teutonic Order:** In 1780 Maximilian became Hochmeister des Deutschen Ordens and Coadjutor of the prince-bishoprics of Münster and Cologne. In 1784 he would become prince-bishop of Münster and prince-elector archbishop of Cologne.

235 this **"brilliant situation":** Albert, *Mémoires* XII, 1.

236 **"the same way in more than one place":** T. C. W. Blanning, *Joseph II* (London & New York: Longman, 1994), 117.

236 **"take away their privileges":** Adam Wandruszka, *Leopold II. Erzherzog von Österreich, Großherzog von Toskana, König von Ungarn und Böhmen, Römischer Kaiser*, vol. I (Wien: Herold, 1963–65), 343.

236 **"Marie Christine tells me":** HHStA EC Nachlass I, 1777–85, 94, March 18, 1781, *Diary*.

237 **"this would be delayed":** Adolf Innerkofler, *Eine grosse Tochter Maria Theresias, Erzherzogin Marianna in ihrem Hauptmonument dem Elisabethinerinnenkloster zu Klagenfurt* (Innsbruck: Im Verlage der Vereinsbuchhandlung), 57.

238 **"She wept a great deal":** HHStA Tagebücher Zinzendorf XXVI, April 23, 1781.

238 **"She was crying and laughing":** HHStA FA SB 7, April 30, 1781.

239 **"nuns, rather than Princesses":** Nathaniel William Wraxall, *Memoirs of the Courts of Berlin, Dresden, Warsaw, and Vienna, in the years 1777, 1778, and 1779*, vol. II (London: A. Strahan, 1800), 332.

240 **"the most natural sorrow":** HHStA EC Nachlass 1, 1777–85, 98, January 2, 1781.

240 **"tender and obliging things":** HHStA EC Nachlass 1, 1777–85, 93, February 8, 1781, *Diary*.

240 **from her correspondence:** Transferred from Naples to Munich for safekeeping before Garibaldi's incursion of 1860, most of this diary was destroyed by Allied bombing in 1944. Corti had been able to access it in the 1930s for his 1950 biography.

241 **"fifteen years of tranquillity":** Albert, *Mémoires* XII, 3.

244 **"God would take pity on me":** Albert, *Mémoires* XII, 57, *Selbstbekenntnis*.

244 **"modest little festival":** Albert, *Mémoires* XII, 95–96, *Klostergeschichte*.

246 **"I'm too weak for that":** Albert, *Mémoires* XII, 57–58, *Selbstbekenntnis*.

# NOTES

## CHAPTER XX

248 **"quite a different species":** Adolf Innerkofler, *Eine grosse Tochter Maria Theresias, Erzherzogin Marianna in ihrem Hauptmonument dem Elisabethinerinnenkloster zu Klagenfurt* (Innsbruck: Im Verlage der Vereinsbuchhandlung), 107, *Klostergeschichte*.
249 **named Beneficent Marianna:** *Zur wohltätigen Marianna*. See Rudolf Cefarin, *Kaernten und die Freimaurerei. Eine kulturhistorische Studie* (Wien: Saturn, 1932), 74–124.
249 **exchanging letters regularly:** Carolina's correspondence with Marianna was destroyed by Allied bombing of Munich in 1944. A handful of extracts survive in HHStA EC Nachlass I.
250 **"She's very inconvenient":** HHStA HA SB 8-2, December 4 and November 17 and 24, 1783.
250 **"much more reasonable":** HHStA HA SB 8-2, November 29, 1783.
250 **be "most inconvenient":** HHStA HA SB 8-2, December 24, 1783.
251 **"bow our heads to God's will":** HHStA EC Nachlass I, 1777–85, February 8, 1783.
251 **"his afflicted mother":** HHStA EC Nachlass I, 1777–85, February 19, 1783.
252 **"listening to Razumovsky playing":** HHStA EC Nachlass I, 1777–85, May 14, 1783.
252 **"had enough of her":** HHStA HA SB 8-2, December 24, 1783.
252 **"just as they like":** Egon Caesar Corti Conte, *Ich, eine Tochter Maria Theresias. Ein Lebensbild der Königin Marie Karoline von Neapel.* (München: Bruckmann, 1950), 119, November 25, 1783.
252 **"our plain buttons":** M. Pagano, *I diari di scavo di Pompei, Ercolano e Stabia di Francesco e Pietro La Vega (1764–1810)*. Raccolta e studio di documenti inediti (Roma: L'Erma di Bretschneider, 1997), 80.
253 **"this annoyed me":** Cinzia Recca, *The Diary of Queen Maria Carolina of Naples, 1781–1785: New Evidence of Queenship at Court* (London: Palgrave Macmillan, 2017), 249.
254 **"what this country needs":** Harold Acton, *The Bourbons of Naples (1734–1825)* (London: Methuen, 1956), 197–98.
254 **"don't forget me":** HHStA EC Nachlass I, 1777–85, October 19, 1782.
255 **"I am convinced of it":** Acton, *Bourbons*, 487.
257 **"Parma to Piacenza":** HHStA K.52-2, June 19, 1785.
257 **"still a child":** Derek Beales, *Joseph II.* Vol 1: *In the Shadow of Maria Theresa, 1741–1780*, vol. II (Cambridge: Cambridge University Press, 1987), 129, December 5, 1781.
258 **"as he saw fit":** Adolf Beer (Hg), *Leopold II., Franz II und Catharina: Ihre Correspondenz* (Leipzig: Duncker & Humblot, 1874), 219, July 7, 1789.
259 **"mental work harder for me":** Elisabeth Badinter, *Les Conflits d'une mère: Marie-Thérèse d'Autriche et ses enfants* (Paris: Flammarion, 2020),76.
260 **"foxes, wolves, and bears":** Kate Williams, *England's Mistress: The Infamous Life of Emma Hamilton* (New York: Ballantine Books, 2006), 134, n.d.
261 **"out of the window at once":** Corti, *Ich, eine Tochter*, 140.
261 **"he might have feared":** M.-H. Weil et le marquis de Somma Circello (éds.), *Correspondance inédite de Marie-Caroline, Reine de Naples et Sicile, avec le marquis de Gallo*, vol. I (Paris: Émile Paul, 1911), no. 2, 2–3, n.d. (between December 27, 1785, and January 4, 1786).

## CHAPTER XXI

262 **"You will have been astonished":** Adam Wolf, *Marie Christine, Erzherzogin von Österreich*, vol. II (Wien: Carl Gerold's Sohn, 1863), 247–48, August 24, 1785.
263 **"suppress all birth certificates":** Suzanne Burkard (éd.). *Mémoires de la baronne d'Oberkirch sur la cour de Louis XVI et la société française avant 1789.* (Paris: Mercure de France, 2000), 540.
263 **"of his misfortune":** Jean Chalon (éd.), *Mémoires de Madame Campan, première femme de chambre de Marie-Antoinette* (Paris: Mercure de France, 1988), 237.
265 **"have other consequences":** Alfred von Arneth, *Marie Antoinette, Joseph II und Leopold II: Ihr Briefwechsel*, no. XLV (Leipzig: K. F. Köhler, 1866), 101, December 27, 1785.
265 **"eyes of the whole world":** Arneth, *MAJL*, no. XLIV, 93–94, August 22, 1785.
265 **fifteen years before:** See T. C. W. Blanning, *The French Revolution: Class War or Culture Clash?* (London: Macmillan, 1997), 32.
268 **former banker Jacques Necker:** Being neither a Roman Catholic nor a French subject, Necker could not be named Comptroller-General.
269 **"producing some catastrophe":** Arneth, *CSMJK* II, no. 54, 106, March 10, 1786.
269 **that "voracious circle":** Arneth, *CSMJK* II, no. 54, 106, July 14, 1787.

269 **"one or two children":** Arneth, *CSMJK* II, no. 8, 13, April 1, 1786.
270 **"both sacred and profane love":** H. Arnold Barton, *Count Hans Axel von Fersen: Aristocrat in an Age of Revolution* (Boston: Twayne, G. K. Hall, 1975), 73.
271 **"used to be there":** Barton, *Count Hans Axel von Fersen* 111.
271 **"indifferent or lazy people":** Barton, *Count Hans Axel von Fersen* 94.

## CHAPTER XXII

273 **"crafty perhaps, but brainless":** Arneth, *CSMJK* II, no. 57, 110, July 28, 1787.
273 **"part of the family silver":** Adam Wolf, *Marie Christine, Erzherzogin von Österreich*, vol. I (Wien: Carl Gerold's Sohn,1863), 248.
273 **"to this extremity":** Marie Christine, *Journal des Mois Avril Mai Juin Juillet*, MNL P 299-1.5. A.1:28.1787, May 31, 1787.
273 **"among the women too":** MNL P299-1.5. A.1:28.178.105, June 9, 1787.
273 **"her earlier sentiments":** Arneth, *CSMJK* II, no. 54, 105, July 14, 1787.
274 **"looking like a lion":** Adam Wolf, *Fürstin Eleonore Liechtenstein, 1745–1812, Nach Briefen und Memoiren ihrer Zeit.* (Wien: Carl Gerold's Sohn, 1875), 195.
274 **"management of local affairs":** MNL P 299-1.5. A.1:28.1787, *Journal*, July 1 & June 30, 1787.
275 **"not allow us to leave":** MNL P 299-1.5. A.1:28.1787, *Journal*, July 7, 3 & 4, 1787.
276 **"patched up the mess there":** Arneth, *JuL* II, 115, August 30, 1787.
276 **"in our days":** H. Arnold Barton, *Count Hans Axel von Fersen: Aristocrat in an Age of Revolution* (Boston: Twayne, G. K. Hall, 1975), 74.
277 **"reduction of expenses":** Arneth, *CSMJK* II, no. 39, 74, February 7, 1787.
278 **"about all their business":** Arneth, *CSMJK* II, no. 39, 113, December 27, 1787.
280 **the Council of State:** *Le Conseil des dépêches.*
281 **"it seems it cannot":** Arneth, *CSMJK* II, no. 68, 133, October 18, 1787.
282 **"start all over again":** HHStA EC Nachlass II, 1786–93, April 10, 1786.
282 **"we should lose him":** HHStA EC Nachlass II, 1786–93, September 3, 1787.
283 **"this sacrifice of me":** HHStA EC Nachlass II, 1786–93, July 22, 1788.
283 **"what I'd have done":** HHStA EC Nachlass II, 1786–93, July 29, 1788.
283 **"of his wife":** HHStA EC Nachlass II, 1786–93, July 22, 1788.
284 **"inflame him against you":** HHStA EC Nachlass II, 1786–93, July 29, 1788.
284 **"really upset me":** HHStA EC Nachlass II, 1786–93, August 9, 1788.
285 **"won't lose respect":** HHStA EC Nachlass II, 1786–93, December 18, 1788.
285 **"yet dare go outside":** HHStA EC Nachlass II, 1786–93, December 12, 1788.

## CHAPTER XXIII

288 **"more tears than bread":** Jean Chalon (éd.), *Mémoires de Madame Campan, première femme de chambre de Marie-Antoinette* (Paris: Mercure de France, 1988), 559, fn. 133.
288 **no fathers among them:** Simone Bertière, *Marie-Antoinette l'insoumise* (Paris: Éditions de Fallois, 2002), 571.
288 **"representative democracy in Europe":** Munro Price, *The Fall of the French Monarchy. Louis XVI, Marie Antoinette and the baron de Breteuil* (London: Pan Books, 2013), 56.
289 **"only a phrase":** John Hardman, *The Life of Louis XVI* (New Haven & London: Yale University Press, 2023), 313.
289 **"fixed upon solid foundations":** Bertière, *Marie Antoinette*, 573.
290 **"famine, bankruptcy and civil war":** Évelyne Lever, *Correspondance de Marie-Antoinette (1770–1793)* (Paris: Tallandier, 2005), 483–84, July 4, 1789.
291 **"signal of explosion":** Henry Swinburne, *The Courts of Europe at the Close of the Last Century*, vol. II, ed., Charles White (London: Colburn, 1841), 83.
292 **"would have murdered me":** Grace Dalrymple Elliott, *During the Reign of Terror: Journal of My Life During the French Revolution* (New York: Sturgis & Walton Company, 1910), 33.
292 **"less than two hours":** Albert Moussez, *Un Témoin ignoré de la Révolution: Le comte de Fernan Nuñez* (Paris: Édouard Champion, 1924), 65, August 10, 1789.
293 **"was too late":** Beatrix Cary Davenport (ed.), *A Diary of the French Revolution by Gouverneur Morris 1752–1816, Minister to France During the Terror*, vol. I (Boston: Houghton Mifflin, 1939), 171, July 31, 1789.

294 **as "pestilential vermin":** HHStA EC Nachlass II, 1786–93, Sept 22, 1789.
294 **"what they were doing":** Duchesse de Tourzel, *Mémoires de Madame la duchesse de Tourzel, gouvernante des enfants de France de 1789 à 1795* (Paris: Mercure de France, 1986), 22.
294 **"can offer a man":** H. Arnold Barton, *Count Hans Axel von Fersen: Aristocrat in an Age of Revolution* (Boston: Twayne, G. K. Hall, 1975), 72.
295 **"content in ourselves":** HHStA EC Nachlass II, 1786–93, September 1 and 18, 1789.
295 **"abandoned into their hands":** HHStA EC Nachlass II, 1786–93, August 10, 1789.
296 **"caused poverty everywhere etc.":** [Adolf] Beer (Hg.), Leopold II., Franz II. und Catharina: Ihre *Correspondenz* nebst einer Einleitung: zur Geschichte der Politik Leopold's II (Leipzig: Duncker and Humblot, 1874, 219, July 7, 1789.
298 **"the name of palace":** Cécile Berly, "Le palais des Tuileries et Paris, ou l'affirmation de la reine politique (6 octobre 1789–10 août 1792)," in Jean-Christian Petitfils (éd.). *Marie-Antoinette. Dans les pas de la reine* (Paris: Perrin, 2020), 211.
298 **"have them near me":** Petitfils (éd.). *Marie-Antoinette*, 214.
299 **"attachment and gratitude":** La Rocheterie, Maxime de and le marquis de Beaucourt (éds.). *Lettres de Marie Antoinette: Recueil des lettres authentiques de la reine publié pour la société d'histoire contemporaine*, vol. II (Paris: Au Siège de la Société, 1895–96), 173–4, May 29, 1790.
300 **"the 23rd of June":** Albert Moussez, *Un Témoin ignoré de la Révolution: Le comte de Fernan Nuñez* (Paris: Édouard Champion, 1924), 228 fn (Archivo historico nacional, Madrid, Papeles de Estado 3942, liasse 2).
300 **"I was pleased to see":** ASN:AB, Caserta, November 20, 1789.
301 **"accepted him willingly":** HHStA SB 56-3, September 16, 1794.
303 **"loud sobs and weeping":** Adolf Innerkofler, *Eine grosse Tochter Maria Theresias, Erzherzogin Marianna in ihrem Hauptmonument dem Elisabethinerinnenkloster zu Klagenfurt* (Innsbruck: Im Verlage der Vereinsbuchhandlung), 133–34.
303 **"It's too painful for me":** Innerkofler, *Eine grosse Tochter*, 148, 129.
303 **"a change of situation":** Idelfonso Stanga, *Maria Amalia di Borbone, duchessa di Parma, 1746–1804* (Cremona: Nuova, 1932), 60.
304 **"if you request it":** Innerkofler, *Eine grosse Tochter*, 149–50.
304 **"we were sharing information":** HHStA EC Nachlass II, 1786–93, October 26 and November 2, 1789.
304 **"never have had her courage":** HHStA EC Nachlass II, 1786–93, November 23, 1789.
305 **reaction to her predicament:** See Egon Caesar Corti Conte, *Ich, eine Tochter Maria Theresias. Ein Lebensbild der Königin Marie Karoline von Neapel.* (München: Bruckmann, 1950), 163, fn3.
305 **"blamed on her for so long":** Beer, *Correspondenz*, 219, July 7, 1789.
305 **"in the affairs of Europe":** HHStA EC Nachlass II, 1786–93, December 3, 1789.

## CHAPTER XXIV

307 **"no heart for the Monarchy":** Derek Beales, *Joseph II.* Vol 1: *In the Shadow of Maria Theresa, 1741–1780*, vol. II (Cambridge: Cambridge University Press, 1987), 610.
307 **"at your feet":** Adam Wolf, *Marie Christine, Erzherzogin von Österreich*, vol. II (Wien: Carl Gerold's Sohn,1863), 252, April 27, 1788.
308 **"not to give in":** Wolf, *Marie Christine*, 4–5, January 8, 1789.
308 **"leaves my heart pounding":** Wolf, *Marie Christine*, 282–83, November 17 and December 16, 1788.
308 **"frequently threaten his life":** Nathaniel William Wraxall, *Memoirs of the Courts of Berlin, Dresden, Warsaw, and Vienna, in the years 1777, 1778, and 1779*, vol. I (London: A. Strahan, 1800), 339. Laudon (1717–90) was born in eastern Livonia, now Latvia.
309 **"what you've written":** Beer, *Correspondenz*, 209–10 & 220, March 8 & July 7, 1789.
309 **"for doing good":** Beales, *Joseph II* II, 593 and 605.
309 **"the heads of our people":** Wolf, *Marie Christine* II, 16, July 29, 1789.
310 **"their personal safety":** Hanns Schlitter (Hg.), *Geheime Correspondenz Josefs II. mit seinem Minister in den österreichischen Niederlanden Ferdinand Grafen Trauttmansdorff, 1787–1789* (Wien: Adolf Holzhausen, 1902), no. 219, 441, October 26, 1789.
311 **"those French aristocrats":** Adam Wolf (Hg.), *Leopold II und Marie Christine. Ihr Briefwechsel 1781–1792* (Wien 1888), (Wien: Gerold, 1867), no. LI, 66ff, November 25, 1789.
311 **"make you dizzy":** HHStA, EC Nachlass II, 1786–93, August 4, 1789.

## NOTES

311 **"very good of him":** Viktor Bibl, *Kaiser Joseph II. Ein Vorkämpfer der grossdeutschen Idee* (Vienna & Leipzig, 1943), 292.
312 **"of a brother and a friend":** AJL 122, May 1, 1790.
312 **"everything he undertook":** See Beales, *Joseph II* II, 639, fn1.
313 **"trust and esteem":** HHStA FK K. 26-2-2, April 15 and 22, 1790.
313 **"prefer to write myself":** HHStA FK A, K. 51-9-2, April 28, 1791, to the Comte Lehrbach.
313 as **"badly acted":** Steiger, *Goethes Leben* III, S. 89.
313 **"economize as much as possible":** HHStA FK K. 26-2-2, July 1, 1790.
314 **"the trouble you have to put up with":** HHStA FK K. 26-2-2, August 1, 1790.
314 **"his kind heart":** HHStA FK K. 26-2-2, April 1790.
314 **between the two families:** Also in 1790, Carolina's son Francesco was betrothed to Leopold's daughter Clementina; they married in 1797.
315 **"as you both deserve":** HHStA FK 26-2-2, July 8 and August 1, 1990.
316 **"who will be good, I hope":** M.-H. Weil et le marquis de Somma Circello (éds.), *Correspondance inédite de Marie-Caroline, Reine de Naples et Sicile, avec le marquis de Gallo*, vol. I (Paris: Émile Paul, 1911), no. 8, 17, July 26, 1790.
316 **"reluctant to finish her portrait":** Elisabeth Vigée-Le Brun, *The Memoirs of Elisabeth Vigée-Le Brun*, trans, Siân Evans (London: Camden Press, 1989), 148 and 112.
316 **"strong as a bull":** HHStA EC Nachlass II, 1786–93, July 2, 1790, and HHStA SB 52-3, May 24, 1791.
316 **"move about again":** HHStA EC Nachlass II, 1786–93, April 27, 1790.
316 looking **"rather haggard":** Hanns Schlitter (Hg.), *Briefe der Erzherzogin Marie Christine, Statthalterin der Niederlande, an Leopold II, Nebst einer Einleitung zur Geschichte der franz. Politik Leopolds II* (Wien: Fontes rerum austriacarum, 1894), 108, June 2, 1790.
317 **"justify a Revolution":** Beatrix Cary Davenport (ed.). *A Diary of the French Revolution by Gouverneur Morris 1752–1816, Minister to France During the Terror*, vol. II (Boston: Houghton Mifflin, 1939), 36, October 27, 1790.
318 **"The Emperor's regalia":** Adam Wandruszka, *Leopold II. Erzherzog von Österreich, Großherzog von Toskana, König von Ungarn und Böhmen, Römischer Kaiser*, vol. II (Wien: Herold, 1963–65), 306.
318 **two of his piano concertos:** K459 in F, no. 19 (1784) and K537 in D, no. 26 (1788) the "Coronation."
319 **"about the world like beggars":** Alfred von Arneth (Hg.), BKuF I, no. XXXVII (Wien: W. Braumüller, 1881), 93, December 12, 1771. Italics in the original.
320 **"put a stop to it":** HHStA EC Nachlass II, 1786–93, March 9, 1793.
320 **"a drop of your subjects' blood":** HHStA FK K. 26-2-3, 306, December 19, 1790.
321 **"Frenchmen of every kind":** Wolf, *Marie Christine* II, 99, May 31, 1791.

### CHAPTER XXV

323 **"sacrificing these sovereigns":** Corti, *Eine grosse Tochter*, S.178, June 4, 1791.
323 **"the Queen of France would":** Jean Chalon (éd.), *Mémoires de Madame Campan, première femme de chambre de Marie-Antoinette* (Paris: Mercure de France, 1988), 338.
324 **"laid down his arms by a certain date":** La Rocheterie, Maxime de and le marquis de Beaucourt (éds.). *Lettres de Marie Antoinette: Recueil des lettres authentiques de la reine publié pour la société d'histoire contemporaine*. 2 vols. Paris: Au Siège de la Société, 1895–96, no. CCXCV, 218, February 3, 1791. Trans. in John Hardmann, *The Life of Louis XVI* (New Haven and London: Yale University Press, 2023), 383–84. Lever does not include this letter.
325 **"The royal family's escape":** Emmanuel-Henri, vicomte de Grouchy et Antoine Guillois (éds.), *La révolution française. Racontée par un diplomate étranger. Correspondance du Bailli de Virieu, Ministre Plénipotentiaire de Parme, 1788–1793* (Paris: Flammarion, 1903), 271, June 27, 1791.
325 **"fortunate enough to reach it":** Évelyne Lever, *Correspondance de Marie-Antoinette (1770–1793)* (Paris: Tallandier, 2005), 542, June 22, 1791.
325 **"wished him Godspeed":** M. de. Barghon-Fortrion, *Mémoires de Marie-Thérèse, duchesse d'Angouleme* (Paris: La Mode nouvelle, 1858), 9.
327 **"would have been saved":** Adam Wolf, *Marie Christine, Erzherzogin von Österreich*, vol. II (Wien: Carl Gerold's Sohn,1863), 106, June 25, 1791.
327 **"There is not a single town":** John Hardman, *Marie Antoinette: The Making of a French Queen* (New

Haven & London: Yale University Press, 2019), 232, October 31, 1791. Neither La Rocheterie nor Lever includes this letter.

327 **news of the arrest arrived:** See Hardman, *The Life of Louis XVI,* 380 ff, 397 f; Munro Price, *The Fall of the French Monarchy. Louis XVI, Marie Antoinette and the baron de Breteuil* (London: Pan Books, 2013), 202.

328 **"for this current flight":** Albert Moussez, *Un Témoin ignoré de la Révolution: Le comte de Fernan Nuñez* (Paris: Édouard Champion, 1924), 276, June 26, 1791.

328 **"proudly and nobly":** Ernest Daudet (éd.), *Lettres du comte Valentin Esterhazy à sa femme, 1784–1792* (Paris: Plon, 1907), 237, June 26, 1791.

329 **"at Lloyd's coffee-house":** Margery Weiner, *The French Exiles 1789–1815* (London: John Murray, 1960, 13.

329 **"trying to bear up":** Daudet, *Lettres du comte Valentin Esterhazy*, 238, June 27, 1791.

329 **"I embrace you with all my heart":** Lever, *Correspondence,* 545, June 29, 1791 (2 letters).

330 **he would soon accept, at least publicly:** On September 14, 1791.

331 **"Himself and His family":** HHStA FK K. 26-2-3, July 1791.

331 **"that of every sovereign":** HHStA EC Nachlass II, 1786–93, July 15, 1791.

331 **"the King and the Kingdom of France":** HHStA FK K. 26-2-3, July 1791.

332 **"his feelings for me":** HHStA FK K. 26-2-3, May 29, 1790.

332 **"for years to come":** Schlitter, *Briefe,* 118, 2nd letter of June 16, 1791.

332 **"to be in this country":** Daudet, *Lettres du comte Valentin Esterhazy*, August 4, 1791, 244.

333 **"It's absolutely clear they want to provoke":** Hanns Schlitter (Hg.), *Briefe der Erzherzogin Marie Christine Statthalterin der Niederlande an Leopold II. Nebst einer Einleitung zur Geschichte der franz. Politik Leopolds II* (Wien, 1894), 234, January 13, 1792.

333 **"more harm than good":** HHStA FK K. 26-2-3, March 14, 1791.

333 **"for not receiving him":** Lever, *Correspondence*, 523, February 27, 1791.

333 **"has my approval already":** HHStA FK K. 26-2-2, February 7, 1791.

334 **"every country in Europe":** HHStA FK K. 26-2-3, February 27, 1791.

334 **"the whole Empire":** HHStA FK K. 26-2-5, January 6, 1791.

335 **"He has no soul":** HHStA EC Nachlass II, 1786–93, September 22, 1789.

335 **"anarchy compounded by bankruptcy":** T .C. W. Blanning, *The French Revolutionary Wars, 1787–1802* (London: Arnold, 1996), 63.

335 **"my most fervent wish":** HHStA EC Nachlass II, 1786-93, February 25, 1790.

335 **"don't believe anything they say":** Beer, *Correspondenz*, 221, August 30, 1791.

336 **"they're criticizing you, too":** Schlitter, *Briefe*, 159 and 194, August 21 and October 20, 1791.

336 **"get us off the hook":** Price, *The Fall,* 242.

337 **"Thank you for your warning":** Schlitter, *Briefe*, 245–46 and 249, February 12 and 14, 1792.

338 **"order or obedience or rule":** Schlitter, *Briefe*, 202, November 26, 1791.

338 **the "absurd projects":** Schlitter, *Briefe*, 159, August 21, 1791.

339 **"in the presence of H. M. the Empress":** HHStA HA Stammbaum K. 1A-33, March 1, 1792.

339 **"for my wounded heart":** Wolf, *Marie Christine* II, S. 128.

339 **"this cruel catastrophe":** M.-H. Weil et le marquis de Somma Circello (éds.), *Correspondance inédite de Marie-Caroline, Reine de Naples et Sicile, avec le marquis de Gallo*, vol. I (Paris: Émile Paul, 1911), no. 17, 37, March 24, 1792.

340 **"sharp, cold air":** Beer, *Correspondenz*, 211, June 4, 1789.

341 **"they're not concealing it any longer":** Lever, *Correspondance*, 794, n.d.

344 **"Madame de Lamballe's head":** Marie-Thérèse, *Mémoire écrit par Marie-Thérèse-Charlotte de France sur la captivité des princes et princesses ses parents depuis le 10 août 1792 jusqu'à la mort de son frère arrivée le 9 juin 1795. Publiée sur le manuscrit autographe appartenant à Madame la Duchesse de Madrid* (Paris: Plon, 1892), 68.

345 **"new epoch in the history of the world":** Blanning, *Revolutionary Wars,* 78. Blanning's reference is Goethe, *Campagne in Frankreich,* (Weimar, 1898), vol. xxiii, 74.

345 **"Only a miracle can save her":** Weil, *Correspondance* I, no. 27, 48, October 9, 1792.

## CHAPTER XXVI

348 **according to one assessment:** See Gerard Carney, "The State Trials of Louis XVI and Marie Antoinette," *Owen Dixon Society* eJournal, 1 (2017): 1–24, 11.

349 **"The late King of this Country":** Beatrix Cary Davenport (ed.), *A Diary of the French Revolution by Gouverneur Morris 1752–1816, Minister to France During the Terror*, vol. II (Boston: Houghton Mifflin, 1939), 601–2, January 25, 1793.
349 **"occasion to attest":** Munro Price, *The Fall of the French Monarchy. Louis XVI, Marie Antoinette and the baron de Breteuil* (London: Pan Books, 2013), 328.
351 **"give up and she'll go":** HHStA EC Nachlass II, 1786–93, March 9 and 12, 1793.
352 **"superstition and ignorance":** Janet L. Polasky, *Revolution in Brussels, 1787–1793* (Brussels: Palais des Académies, 1982), 210.
353 **"the poor crying out":** HHStA EC Nachlass II, 1786–93, July 20, 1793.
354 **"be left in peace":** HHStA EC Nachlass II, 1786–93, April 6, 1793.
354 **"God knows who":** M.-H. Weil et le marquis de Somma Circello (éds.), *Correspondance inédite de Marie-Caroline, Reine de Naples et Sicile, avec le marquis de Gallo*, vol. I (Paris: Émile Paul, 1911), no. 44, 95–96, February 2, 1793.
355 **"proves the truth of that":** HHStA EC Nachlass II, 1786–93, July 16, 1793.
355 **only difficulty is for Francesco":** Weil, *Correspondance* I, no. 45, 100, February 9, 1793.
355 **"preparing herself for death":** Weil, *Correspondance* I, no. 49, 106, March 5, 1793.
356 **"here had become superfluous":** Alma Söderjhelm, *Fersen et Marie-Antoinette. Correspondence et journal intime inédits du comte Axel de Fersen* (Paris: Kra, 1930), 286, March 13, 1793. Trans. in H. Arnold Barton, *Count Hans Axel von Fersen: Aristocrat in an Age of Revolution* (Boston: Twayne, G. K. Hall, 1975), 171–72.
358 **"happiest thing that could befall her":** Weil, *Correspondance* I, no. 69, 141, July 27, 1793.
358 **"without a stove or fireplace":** Deborah Cadbury, *The Last King of France. Revolution, Revenge and the Search for Louis XVII* (London: Fourth Estate, 2002), 112.
360 **"plays on the Piano":** Thomas Carlyle, *The French Revolution: A History*, vol. III (London: Chapman and Hall, 1842), book IV, ch. 7, 241.
361 **"court of Versailles":** Alfred von Arneth und Auguste Mathieu Geffroy (Hg.), *Correspondance secrète entre Marie Thérèse et le comte de Mercy-Argenteau, avec les lettres de Marie Thérèse et Marie Antoinette, publiée avec une introduction et des notes par le chevalier Alfred d'Arneth et A. Geoffroy*, vol. II (Paris: Didot, 1874), 80, March 1, 1787.
361 **"monsters and the misfortunes":** Alfred von Arneth, *Marie Antoinette, Joseph II und Leopold II. Ihr Briefwechsel*, no. LXXV (Leipzig: K. F. Köhler, 1866), 136, August 17, 1790.
361 **"every mother present to assert":** Gérard Walter (éd.), *Le procès de Marie-Antoinette, 23–25 vendémiaire an II (14–16 octobre 1793). Actes du tribunal révolutionnaire* (Bruxelles: Éd. Complexe, 1993), 61.
362 **"Did you see that yourself?":** *Le procès de Marie-Antoinette*, 31 and 60.
362 **"I thought of them":** Évelyne Lever, *Correspondance de Marie-Antoinette (1770–1793)* (Paris: Tallandier, 2005), 820–22, October 16, 1793.
363 **"Your Excellency will have learned":** Emmanuel-Henri, vicomte de Grouchy et Antoine Guillois (éds.), *La révolution française. Racontée par un diplomate étranger. Correspondance du Bailli de Virieu, Ministre Plénipotentiaire de Parme, 1788–1793* (Paris: Flammarion, 1903), 477, October 21, 1793.
364 **"in store for her":** Christian, Steeb, *Die Grafen von Fries. Eine Schweizer Familie und ihre wirtschaftspolitische und kulturhistorische Bedeutung fuer Oesterreich zwischen 1750 und 1830* (Bad Voeslau: Stadtgemeinde, 1999), 143.
364 **"on her in the last moments":** Weil, *Correspondance* I, no. 83, 157, November 3, 1793
365 **"her villainous executioners":** HHStA EC Nachlass II, 1786–93, Folder 171-345, November 5, 1793.

## CHAPTER XXVII

367 **"royal family and their ministers":** Harold Acton, *The Bourbons of Naples (1734–1825)* (London: Methuen, 1956), 272.
368 **"rends my heart":** M.-H. Weil et le marquis de Somma Circello (éds.), *Correspondance inédite de Marie-Caroline, Reine de Naples et Sicile, avec le marquis de Gallo*, vol. I (Paris: Émile Paul, 1911), no. 138, 245–46, October 18, 1794.
369 **"fellow with sallow complexion":** Catherine, Hyde, Marchioness Broglio Solari, *Letters of the Marchioness Broglio Solari, Containing a Sketch of Her Life, and Recollections of Celebrated Characters, with Notes* (London: William Pickering, 1845), 112.
369 **"most cowardly manner":** HHStA EC Nachlass II, 1786-93, December 10, 1793, Esterhazy to Thugut.
369 **"take them for their colonies":** HHStA EC Nachlass II, 1786-93, January 10-13, 1794, to Teresa.

# NOTES

369 **"too weak and sick and old":** HHStA EC Nachlass II, 1786-93, 1786-93, December 10, 1793.

370 **"those dreadful émigrés":** HHStA EC Nachlass II, 1786-93, 1786-93, May 12, 1792, & 1794-96, January 18, 1794.

370 **"my sorrows and my joys":** Adam Wolf, *Marie Christine, Erzherzogin von Österreich*, vol. II (Wien: Carl Gerold's Sohn,1863), 146, June 27, 1793, to Delmotte.

371 **"ambition and devotion since my youth":** Albert Kasimir of Sachsen-Teschen, *Mémoires de ma vie: 1780–1798*, vol. XVII, Albertina K.S. D-2267, 255.

371 **"a peaceful existence":** HHStA SB 56-1, Book 156, June 26, 1794

373 **"as unfortunate as we are":** HHStA EC Nachlass II, 1786–93, September 18, 1789

373 **"Am I really safe now?":** Charlotte Pangels, *Die Kinder Maria Theresias: Leben und Schicksal in kaiserlichem Glanz* (München: Georg D. W. Callwey, 1980), 259.

373 **"azure blue eyes, so beautiful":** Alexandrine de la Boutetière de Saint-Mars, baronne de Fisson du Montet, *Souvenirs de la baronne du Monte, 1785–1866* (Paris: Plon, 1914), 18.

373 **"than her other sisters":** Egon Caesar Corti Conte, *Ich, eine Tochter Maria Theresias. Ein Lebensbild der Königin Marie Karoline von Neapel.* (München: Bruckmann, 1950), 231.

376 **"little fatso's troopers":** Pangels, *Die Kinder*, 320–21.

377 **"the neutrality they imagine is a chimera":** Weil, *Correspondance* I, no. 248, 489, October 15, 1797.

378 **"I expect a little shot":** Weil, *Correspondance* I, no. 214, 396–97, August 28, 1796.

378 **"there's no escaping":** Corti, *Ich, eine Tochter*, 243, February 21, 1797.

379 **"eyes full of tears":** Wolf, *Marie Christine* II, 181.

## CHAPTER XXVIII

380 **"such a sovereign":** M.-H. Weil et le marquis de Somma Circello (éds.), *Correspondance inédite de Marie-Caroline, Reine de Naples et Sicile, avec le marquis de Gallo*, vol. I (Paris: Émile Paul, 1911), no. 248, 489–90, October 15, 1797.

383 **"deep feeling of peace":** Adam Wolf, *Marie Christine, Erzherzogin von Österreich*, vol. II (Wien: Carl Gerold's Sohn, 1863), 186.

383 **"one more reason to grieve":** Max Braubach, *Maria Theresias Jüngster Sohn Max Franz, Letzter Kurfürst von Köln und Fürstbischof von Münster* (Wien, München: Verlag Herold, 1961), 449–50.

383 **her ancient faith:** Canova based his monument for Marie Christine on his unfinished mausoleum for the painter Titian in the Basilica di Santa Maria dei Frari Gloriosa dei Frari in San Polo in Venice.

384 **"my beloved husband":** Wolf, *Marie Christine* II, 188–89.

384 **"adorable, unique woman":** Albert, *Mémoires* XVII, 268–69.

386 **"boldest measures are the safest":** Harold Acton, *The Bourbons of Naples (1734–1825)* (London: Methuen, 1956), 316.

387 **"degenerate class is the aristocracy":** Harold Acton, *The Bourbons of Naples (1734–1825)* (London: Methuen, 1956), 235.

387 **"our heads cut off":** Harold Acton, *The Bourbons of Naples (1734–1825)* (London: Methuen, 1956), 233–34.

387 **"under Nelson's command":** David Constantine, *Fields of Fire: A Life of Sir William Hamilton* (London: Weidenfeld & Nicolson, 2001), 222.

387 **"I'll never die":** Weil, *Correspondance* I, 544, December 21, 1798.

388 **"the verge of eternity":** Acton, *Bourbons*, 331.

388 **"my son's inheritance":** Egon Caesar Corti Conte, *Ich, eine Tochter Maria Theresias. Ein Lebensbild der Königin Marie Karoline von Neapel.* (München: Bruckmann, 1950), 296.

388 **"put on and off":** Flora Fraser, *Beloved Emma: The Life of Emma, Lady Hamilton* (London: John Murray, 2003), 222.

388 **"for its ugliness":** Auguste Creuzé de Lesser, *Voyage en Italie et en Sicile, fait en MDCCCI et MDCCCII* (Paris: Didot l'Aîné, 1806), 105.

389 **"enough to kill you":** Weil, *Correspondance* II, 19, January 12, 1799.

390 **"red hats in affairs of state":** Corti, *Ich, eine Tochter Maria Theresias*, 302.

391 ***In hoc signo vinces*:** In this sign you will conquer.

392 **"minuet of courteous insolence":** Terry Coleman, *Nelson: The Man and the Legend* (London: Bloomsbury, 2002), 230.

# NOTES

## CHAPTER XXIX

393 **"a sad Poltroon":** David Constantine, *Fields of Fire: A Life of Sir William Hamilton* (London: Weidenfeld & Nicolson, 2001), 247.

393 **"his country's power":** M.-H. Weil et le marquis de Somma Circello (éds.), *Correspondance inédite de Marie-Caroline, Reine de Naples et Sicile, avec le marquis de Gallo*, vol. I (Paris: Émile Paul, 1911), nos. 344 and 345, 152 and 155, April 20 and 21, 1800.

393 **"interference of Foreigners":** Harold Acton, *The Bourbons of Naples (1734–1825)* (London: Methuen, 1956), 444–46. Italics original.

394 **"between our two courts":** Weil, *Correspondance* II, no. 344, 151, April 20, 1800.

394 **"and then into ours":** Suzanne d' Huart, (éd.), *Journal de Marie-Amélie, reine de France* (Paris: Perrin, 1981), 33, August 14, 1800.

395 **"wake him up":** Egon Caesar Corti Conte, *Ich, eine Tochter Maria Theresias. Ein Lebensbild der Königin Marie Karoline von Neapel.* (München: Bruckmann, 1950), 350, August 21, 1800. The original letters from Carolina's daughters in Vienna in 1800–1801 were destroyed in Munich during World War II. Extracts may exist in HHStA EC Nachlass IV–IX.

396 **"a keeper with a bear":** Constantine, *Fields*, 250.

396 **pronounced the duet "grand":** Roger Fulford (ed.), *The Autobiography of Miss Knight, Lady Companion to Princess Charlotte* (London: William Kimber, 1960), 73–74.

397 **"wittiest princess in the world":** Alexandrine de la Boutetière de Saint-Mars, baronne de Fisson du Montet, *Souvenirs de la baronne du Monte, 1785–1866* (Paris: Plon, 1914), 19.

397 **"not to like her":** Corti, *Ich, eine Tochter*, 360, November 18, 1800.

398 **emperor-brother "the boor":** Charlotte Pangels, *Die Kinder Maria Theresias: Leben und Schicksal in kaiserlichem Glanz* (München: Georg D. W. Callwey, 1980), 262–63.

398 **his own peace with France:** The Treaty of Aranjuez of 1801. Spain was also a signatory.

399 **"creating him a knight":** Huart, *Journal*, 44, June 11, 1801. The *Veni Creator Spiritus (Come, Creator Spirit)* is an early medieval hymn.

400 **a "religious horror":** Huart, *Journal*, 37, November 2, 1801.

400 **"the sooner, the better":** Corti, *Ich, eine Tochter*, 381.

400 **"try to avoid her":** Corti, *Ich, eine Tochter*, 367.

401 **"I have no other":** Corti, *Ich, eine Tochter*, 393.

401 **"in an appalling state":** Corti, *Ich, eine Tochter*, April 9, 1802.

401 **"behaved very impertinently":** Corti, *Ich, eine Tochter*, 53, March 1, 1802.

402 **"for being so rare":** Corti, *Ich, eine Tochter*, 393, June 12, 1802.

402 **"things to organize":** Weil, *Correspondence* II, no. 434, 333, August 23, 1802.

403 **"faithful Aunt Amalie":** HHStA HA Stammbaum K. 1A-32, October 9, 1802.

403 **"give it back immediately":** Nullo Musini, *Un amministratore privato di Casa Borbone e un carteggio inedito di Maria Amalia e di Luisa Maria* (Parma: *Biblioteca dell' Aurea Parma, Nuova Seria no. 26*, 1930, IX).

404 **"repay in instalments. *Addio*":** Musini, *Un amministratore private*, 6.

404 **"cannon balls and bombs":** Daniel E. Freeman, *Mozart in Prague* (Minneapolis, MN: Bearclaw, 2013), 33–34, quoting Dr. Burney.

405 **"even more brainless":** Corti, *Ich, eine Tochter*, 402.

406 **"stupider and grosser":** Corti, *Ich, eine Tochter* 407.

406 **"I am desperate":** Huart, *Journal*, 65–66, October 10, 1802.

406 **"punishment for our sins":** Corti, *Ich, eine Tochter*, SS. 404-5.

406 **with "these cretins":** Corti, *Ich, eine Tochter*, 402.

407 **"dominant in western Europe":** Zamoyski, Adam. *Napoleon: The Man Behind the Myth* (London: William Collins, 2018), 337.

408 **four other powers:** The other Third Coalition powers were Austria, Russia, Naples, and Sweden.

408 **"On Friday the troops swore":** HHStA HA SB 68a-1-2, May 28, 1804.

408 **"like a tender mother":** HHStA HA SB 68a-1-2June 2 and 11, 1804.

409 **"too tiring for you":** HHStA HA SB 68a-1-1, June 1, 5, 8, 19, and 22, 1804.

409 **"with the deepest respect":** HHStA HA SB 68a-1-1, June 1, 4, and 11, 1804.

410 **"your very kind heart":** HHStA HA SB 68a-1-1, June 15, 1804.

410 **"no less true for that":** Weil, *Correspondance* II, no. 482, 488, June 30, 1804.

410 **French Republic was to continue:** The Republic of France continued formally until 1809.

411 **swamped in his "carnavalesque":** Zamoyski, *Napoleon*, 369.
411 **"the Emperor, *your master*":** Acton, *Bourbons*, 511. Italics in the original.

## CHAPTER XXX

412 **"the Kingdom of Naples as lost":** Egon Caesar Corti Conte, *Ich, eine Tochter Maria Theresias. Ein Lebensbild der Königin Marie Karoline von Neapel.* (München: Bruckmann, 1950), 442.
413 **"to dictate than discuss":** Harold Acton, *The Bourbons of Naples (1734–1825)* (London: Methuen, 1956), 534.
414 **"their personal interests":** Jacques Rambaud (éd.) *Mémoires du comte Roger de Damas, Vienne de 1806 à 1814, suivis de lettres inédites de Marie-Caroline, Reine de Naples, au comte Roger de Damas* (Paris: Plon-Nourrit et Cie, 1914), 109.
415 **"a self-balancing mechanism":** T. C. W. Blanning, *The French Revolutionary Wars, 1787–1802* (London: Arnold, 1996), 273.
415 **by his own decree:** Franz dissolved the Holy Roman Empire on August 6, 1806.
415 **Peace of Pressburg:** Signed on December 26, 1805.
415 **King of Italy:** That is, parts of the northern peninsula, with regions as far south as Rome also under his direct control as *departements* of France's Empire.
415 **"ruin of the Austrian Monarchy":** Suzanne d' Huart, (éd.), *Journal de Marie-Amélie, reine de France* (Paris: Perrin, 1981), 88, January 10, 1806.
415 **"What's to be our fate?":** Corti, *Ich, eine Tochter*, 466.
416 **"would be preferable":** M.-H. Weil et le marquis de Somma Circello (éds.), *Correspondance inédite de Marie-Caroline, Reine de Naples et Sicile, avec le marquis de Gallo*, vol. II (Paris: Émile Paul, 1911), no. 509, 580, May 5, 1805.
416 **"enough land to bury themselves in":** Corti, *Ich, eine Tochter*, 471.
416 **"an outraged Queen":** Acton, *Bourbons*, 635.
416 **"every new sovereign":** Weil, *Correspondance* II, no. 509, 580, May 5, 1805.
417 **"begging from their relatives":** Waltraud Maierhofer, Gertrud M. Rösch, and Caroline Bland (eds.), *Women Against Napoleon: Historical and Fictional Responses to his Rise and Legacy* (Frankfurt am Main, New York: Campus Verlag, 2007), 63.
418 **"dear old friend":** Weil, *Correspondance* II, nos. 543–44, 670–74, January 26, 1806, and Corti, *Ich eine Tochter*, 515, January 30, 1806. Underlining in the original.
420 **"any favourite object":** Weil, *Correspondance* II, 568, 572, and 576.
420 **"brought her up very well":** HHStA EC Nachlass III, 1806–1814, June 12, 1808.
421 **"as seldom as possible":** HHStA EC Nachlass III, 1806–14, February 8, 1806.
421 **in the centre of the town:** The Modena Palais in the Herrengasse.
422 **"incapable of doing anything":** Alberto Lumbroso (a cura di), "Lettere inedite di Maria Carolina, Regina delle Due Sicilie (1806–1809)," *Miscellanea Napoleonica*. Serie III–IV (Roma: Modes e Mendel, 1898), 461–539, no. XVIII, 488, May 10, 1807.
423 **"unmarried princesses of Europe":** Rambaud, *Mémoires*, 35.
423 **"I find it rather odd":** HHStA EC Nachlass III, 1806–1814, June 12, 1808.
423 **just across the street from her house:** At Theatergasse 50.
424 **"making herself greatly loved":** Carl Unterkircher, *Chronik von Innsbruck* (Innsbruck: Verlag der Vereinsbuchhandlung, 1897), September 22, 1808 (Innsbrucker Zeitung Nr. 81.)
425 **"dark and fantastical obscurity":** Alexandrine de la Boutetière de Saint-Mars, baronne de Fisson du Montet, *Souvenirs de la baronne du Monte, 1785–1866* (Paris: Plon, 1914), 148–49.
427 **"how that all turns out":** Weil, *Correspondance* II, no. 414, 275, December 21, 1801.
428 **"an eternal silence":** Corti, *Ich, eine Tochter*, 773, April 7, 1810. As a fellow sovereign, Franz was Carolina's "brother." He was also three times her "nephew," being the son of her brother Leopold and of her cousin Maria Luisa, and the son-in-law of her brother Ferdinand.
428 **"wouldn't have expected this":** Corti, *Ich, eine Tochter*, 768–69, March 22, 1810, to Ruffo.
428 **"dare to ask for your blessing":** Corti, *Ich, eine Tochter*, 771–72, n.d. (March 1810).

## CHAPTER XXXI

430 **"she will act":** Adam Zamoyski, *Poland: A History* (London: Collins, 2015), 493–94.
431 **"brought back to heel":** Zamoyski, *Poland*, 512.

# NOTES

432 **"somewhat slippery character":** Denis Mack Smith, *A History of Sicily: Modern Sicily After 1713* (London: Chatto & Windus, 1968), 349.

432 **"control her influence":** Harold Acton, *The Bourbons of Naples (1734–1825)* (London: Methuen, 1956), 602–3, July 28, 1810.

433 **"a master instead of a mistress":** Acton, *Bourbons*, 604.

433 **"all Sicily's resources":** Egon Caesar Corti Conte, *Ich, eine Tochter Maria Theresias. Ein Lebensbild der Königin Marie Karoline von Neapel.* (München: Bruckmann, 1950), 782, December 5, 1812.

434 **"she herself the loser overall":** Friederike Hausmann, *Herrscherin im Paradies der Teufel* (München: Beck, 2014), 249.

434 **"the English are treating her":** Jacques Rambaud (éd.) *Mémoires du comte Roger de Damas, Vienne de 1806 à 1814, suivis de lettres inédites de Marie-Caroline, Reine de Naples, au comte Roger de Damas* (Paris: Plon-Nourrit et Cie, 1914), 225–26, March 11, 1812.

435 **"concentrate on the same subject":** Acton, *Bourbons*, 550.

435 **"uncommonly clever woman":** Corti, *Ich, eine Tochter*, S662.

435 **"remote part of the island":** Corti, *Ich, eine Tochter*, 774, March 16, 1812.

436 **"will always admire you":** Corti, *Ich, eine Tochter*, 783, March 2, 1813.

436 **"that of our beloved subjects":** ASN: AB 3. X 251.

436 **"affectionate companion Ferdinando":** Corti, *Ich, eine Tochter*, 783–84, March 2, 1813.

436 **"demand no less":** Corti, *Ich, eine Tochter*, 784–85, n.d. (early March 1813).

437 **"to the country for a few days":** Corti, *Ich, eine Tochter*, 674.

439 **against the Emperor of the French:** At the Treaty of Töplitz of September 9, 1813.

439 **"enjoy them together":** Corti, *Ich, eine Tochter*, 683.

440 **"seemed to have increased":** Acton, *Bourbons*, 636–37, quoting the comte Armand de Saint-Priest.

440 **"an independent Kingdom again":** Corti, *Ich, eine Tochter*, 686.

441 **"her head is bent and white":** Montet, *Souvenirs*, 99.

441 **"hoisted up into his saddle":** Montet, *Souvenirs*, 224.

443 **"my appetite has improved":** ASB:AB Volume Lettere di S.M. la Regina 1814, 4.1.386, August 22, 1814.

443 **"the fate of Europe, and our own":** ASB:AB Volume Lettere di S.M. la Regina 1814, 4.1.386, September 8, 1814.

444 **"dressed in black":** Montet, *Souvenirs*, 224.

445 **"it's an old custom":** ASB:AB Volume Lettere di S.M. la Regina 1814, 4.1.386, September 10, 1814.

445 **"best intentions in the world":** Rambaud, *Mémoires*, 229, March 11, 1812.

445 **"quite at his ease":** Emmanuel de Waresquiel (éd.), *Mémoires du Prince de Talleyrand, suivis de 135 lettres inédites du Prince de Talleyrand à la duchesse de Bauffremont (1808–1838)* (Paris: Robert Laffont, 2007), 492, September 25, 1814.

446 **"sincerely attached to her":** Maurice Fleury, "Lettres de Marie-Louise, Impératrice d'Autriche," *Le Carnet historique & littéraire*, 1 juillet, 1899, 36–38, 27 septembre, 1814.

## EPILOGUE

447 **"the last act cannot be far off":** Rambaud, Jacques (éd.), *Mémoires du comte Roger de Damas, Vienne de 1806 à 1814, suivis de lettres inédites de Marie-Caroline, Reine de Naples, au comte Roger de Damas* (Paris: Plon-Nourrit et Cie, 1914), ii.

448 **"daughter of kings":** François-René de Chateaubriand, *Mémoires d'outre-tombe*. vol. I, V (Paris: Gallimard, 1951), 8, 167.

449 **last Empress of Austria:** The Italian Princess Zita of Bourbon-Parma (1892–1989) married Karl von Habsburg-Lothringen in 1911. After the assassination of the Archduke Franz Ferdinand in Sarajevo in June 1914, Karl became heir to the imperial throne. As Karl I, he reigned from the death of his great-uncle Franz Joseph in 1916 until his own abdication and the dissolution of the Austrian Empire in 1918.

# BIBLIOGRAPHY

## NOTE ON THE SOURCES

The known manuscript sources for a work of this kind are distributed across public and private archives in many cities, and I am most grateful to all those who have made these documents available for my consultation.

Eighteenth-century German-language manuscript sources are written in *Kurrentschrift*, which requires special training to read. I would like to express my particular thanks to Patrick Fiska for his indispensable help with these handwritten texts.

Some of the Budapest sources pertaining to Marie Christine and Albert were damaged or destroyed by fire during the Soviet incursion of 1956. A complete handwritten copy of Albert's seventeen-volume, still unpublished *Mémoires* is kept in Vienna's Albertina. Many sources relating to Maria Carolina, including much of her personal diary, were transferred for safekeeping from Naples to Munich in 1860, before the arrival of Garibaldi's "Redshirts," his army of unification. Egon Conte Corti and his researchers were able to make copies of those sources in the 1930s, before their destruction in the Allied bombing of Munich in 1944. Nine cartons of these copies, mostly in French and Italian, are held today in Vienna's Haus-, Hof- und Staatsarchiv. Some are published, though almost all in German translation, in Corti's 1950 biography.

Special thanks are due to the Lobkowicz family for permission to access the famous, still unpublished Liechtenstein-Kaunitz correspondence at Nelahozeves Castle in Czechia. I would also like to thank Adam Zamoyski for his helpful references to Polish sources, and to Sylwia Lorek in Vienna for her translations of these.

## UNPUBLISHED PRIMARY SOURCES

ALB: Albertina Bibliothek, Vienna:

K.S.D-2267, Albert Kasimir von Sachsen-Teschen. *Mémoires de ma vie*, 17 vols. Vols 2, 6–10, 12–17

ASL: Archiv der Stadt Linz:

Archiv der Stadtpfarre Linz, Armenwesen I, f. 26

# BIBLIOGRAPHY

ASN: Archivio di Stato di Napoli:

Archivio Borbone:

Carte Medici, Fasc. 13, f. 1–3

Corrispondenza Tannuci, 1.12, 1.13 (1767)

Corrispondenza di S. M. la Regina colla Famiglia Imperiale di Austria, Sezione I, Fasc. 92

Trattati e Pienipoteri dati a S. M. la Regina di felice memoria, Fasc. 95

ASP: Archivio di Stato di Parma:

Carteggio Borbonico, Busta 951

Carteggio Borbonico Interno, Buste 960a, 960b

Carteggio Farnesiano e Borbonico Estero (Germania), Busta 100, 1760–1803, Casa d'Austria

Carte Dutillot, Viaggi, V 49–55

Casa e Corte Borbonica, Buste 26, 27, 29

MS 27, Antonio Sgavetti, *Diario* 1746–71, vols 12 and 13

BPP: Biblioteca Palatina, Parma:

MS Palatino. 464, f. 15–17. Duca Ferdinando di Borbone, *Storia della mia vita*

Carteggio Paciaudi, Cass. 73–75, 77, 80–82, 84, 86–88, 90, 94

EKK: Elisabethinenklosterarchiv, Klagenfurt:

Twenty-one letters from the Archduchess Amalie to Xaveria Gasser, 1783–90

HHStA: Haus-, Hof-, und Staatsarchiv, Vienna:

EC Nachlass, Egon Conte Corti Nachlass, K. I (1750–85), K. II (1786–96), K. III (1806–14)

Estensarchiv 176, Tagebuch über die Reisen des Erzherzogs Maximilian im Jahren 1774 und 1775

Familienarchiv Haan 7

Familienarchiv Sammelbände 7, 8, 26-1, 2; 51, 68a

Familienkorrespondenz A, K. 26-2 (f. 1–5, 14); K. 27-11; K. 51-9, 10, 11, 14; K. 52-2, 3, 4, 14; K. 68-1, 2;

Handarchiv Kaiser Franz, K. 9-1-4; K. 23, I–XVII

Kabinettsarchiv Niederlande Q5 (AKA 36), 1774

Nachlass Nenny, Karton 2, Fasz. I, 1770–71

Obersthofmarschallamt 216, 2–3

Privat- und Familienfonde, General-Direktion, K. ÄR 2-4

Stammbaum K. 1–33

Vertrauliche Akten 70, f. 1

Zinzendorf, Graf Karl Ludwig, *Tagebücher*, Bde 2, 3, 6, 8, 24, 48

HOU: Houghton Library, Harvard University:

MS Eng 196.5, 2.72, Correspondence Emma Hamilton with Horatio Nelson

KLA: Kärntner Landesarchiv, Klagenfurt:

AT-KLA 457-B-284 F St

Gubernium Graz K. 514m, Fasz. 8 (1781–83)

# BIBLIOGRAPHY

K. RLh 98: Folder L183, f 33, 1–36 (1770–71)

MNL: Magyar Nemzeti Levéltár (National Archives of Hungary), Budapest:

P 298-8-8a, Letters from the Archduchess Marie Christine to Albert, 1765–66

P 298-16, Marie Christine, *Italienreise, 1776*

P 299-1.5 A.1:28, Marie Christine, political journal, 1787

P 299-1.5. A.1:28.178.105, Letters from Marie Christine to Kaunitz, 1787

LRRA Roudnická Lobkowiczká knihovna (Lobkowicz Family Archive), Nelahozeves:

P. 16/18, P. 16/21, P. 16/23, P. 17/24, P. 17/33, Liechtenstein-Kaunitz correspondence

NKCR:M Národní knihovna České republiky (National Library of the Czech Republic), Prague:

AC Acta Clementina 11, Nr. 23, Metternich Family Archive, Maria Carolina-Kaunitz correspondence

TLA Tiroler Landesarchiv, Innsbruck:

Archiv des K.u K. Damenstiftes:

DIA K. 1, Pos. I/1–24; Pos. I/1/3 a (2)

DIA K. 3, Pos II/1a–23; II/2; II/3; II/5; II/6; II/9

## OTHER ABBREVIATIONS

BKuF: Arneth, *Briefe der Kaiserin Maria Theresia an ihre Kinder und Freunde*

EL: Princess Eleonore von Liechtenstein

GMT: Arneth, *Geschichte Maria Theresias*

LK: Countess Leopoldine von Kaunitz

MAJL: Arneth, *Marie Antoinette, Joseph II und Leopold II: Ihr Briefwechsel*

MJK: Arneth, *Correspondance secrète du comte de Mercy-Argenteau*

MTuJ: Arneth, *Maria Theresia und Joseph II: Ihre Correspondenz*

## PUBLISHED PRIMARY SOURCES


Amiguet, Philippe. *Lettres de Louis XV à l'Infant Ferdinand de Parme*. Paris: Grasset, 1938.

Andrés, Juan (Giovanni Andres). "*Vita del Duca di Parma Don Ferdinando di Borbone, scritta in lingua spagnola e voltata in italiano da Monsignore Giovanni Rossi, Parme, 1849.*" Bertini, Giuseppe. *L'Appartamento del Duca Ferdinando a Colorno dipinto da Antonio Bresciani*. Parma: TLC, 2000, 79–90.

Arneth, Alfred von (Hg.). *Maria Theresia und Joseph II: Ihre Correspondenz sammt Briefen Joseph's an seinen Bruder Leopold*. 3 Bde. Wien: Gerold, 1867–68.

Arneth, Alfred von und Auguste Mathieu Geffroy (Hg.). *Correspondance secrète entre Marie Thérèse et le comte de Mercy-Argenteau, avec les lettres de Marie Thérèse et Marie Antoinette, publiée avec une introduction et des notes par le chevalier Alfred d'Arneth et A. Geoffroy*. 3 Bde. Paris: Didot, 1874.

Arneth, Alfred von (Hg.). *Briefe der Kaiserin Maria Theresia an ihre Kinder und Freunde*. 4 Bde. Wien: W. Braumüller, 1881.

Arneth, Alfred von (Hg.). *Marie Antoinette, Joseph II und Leopold II: Ihr Briefwechsel*. Leipzig: K. F. Köhler, 1886.

Bacourt, Adolphe Fourier de (éd.). *Correspondance entre le comte de Mirabeau et le comte de La Marck pendant les années 1789, 1790 et 1791*. 3 vols. Paris: Le Normant, 1851.

Badinter, Elisabeth (éd.). *Isabelle de Bourbon-Parme, "Je meurs d'amour pour toi," Lettres à l'Archiduchesse Marie-Christine, 1760–1763*. Paris: 2008.

# BIBLIOGRAPHY


Barghon-Fortrion, M. de. *Mémoires de Marie-Thérèse, duchesse d'Angouleme*. Nouvelle ed. Paris: La mode nouvelle, 1858.

Bauer, Wilhelm, Otto Eric Deutsch, und Joseph Heinz Eibl (Hg.). *Mozart: Briefe und Aufzeichnungen*. Erweiterte Ausgabe, hg. von Ulrich Konrad. Kassel: Bärenreiter, 1962.

Beer, Adolf (Hg.). *Leopold II., Franz II., und Catharina: Ihre Correspondenz nebst einer Einleitung: zur Geschichte der Politik Leopold's II.* Leipzig: Duncker and Humblot, 1874.

Bouillaguet, Pierre et J. A. Dainard (Dir. de l'éd.). *Correspondance de Madame de Graffigny*. 15 vols. Oxford: Voltaire Foundation, 1985–2016.

Burkard, Suzanne (éd.). *Mémoires de la baronne d'Oberkirch sur la cour de Louis XVI et la société française avant 1789*. Paris: Mercure de France, 2000.

Burney, Charles. *The Present State of Music in France and Italy: Or, The Journal of a Tour Through Those Countries, Undertaken to Collect Materials for a General History of Music*. London: Becket, 1771.

Burney, Charles. *The Present State of Music in Germany, the Netherlands, and United Provinces: Or, The Journal of a Tour Through Those Countries, Undertaken to Collect Materials for a General History of Music*. 2 vols. London: Becket, 1773.

Chalon, Jean (éd.). *Mémoires de Madame Campan, première femme de chambre de Marie-Antoinette*. Paris: Mercure de France, 1988.

Chateaubriand, François-René de. *Mémoires d'outre-tombe*. 2 vols. Paris: Gallimard, 1951.

Choiseul, duc de. *Mémoires du duc de Choiseul 1719–1785*. 2e ed. Paris: Plon, 1904.

Cléry, Jean-Baptiste. *Journal de ce qui s'est passé à la Tour du Temple, pendant la captivité de Louis XVI, roi de France*. London: L'Imprimerie de Baylis, 1798.

Coke, Lady Mary. *The Letters and Journals of Lady Mary Coke, 1756–1774*. 4 vols. Bath: Kingsmead Reprints, 1970 (first published 1889).

Condillac, Étienne Bonnot de. *Cours d'étude pour l'instruction du Prince de Parme, aujourd'hui son altesse royale l'infant D. Ferdinand, Duc de Parme*. Genève: Dufart, 1789.

Creuzé de Lesser, Auguste. *Voyage en Italie et en Sicile, fait en MDCCCI et MDCCCII*. Paris: Didot l'Ainé, 1806.

Criscuolo, Vittorio. *I democratici e la revoluzione oscurata (1796–1797)*. In Alba Mora (a cura di). *Un Borbone tra Parma e l'Europa. Don Ferdinando e il suo tempo (1751–1802)*. Reggio Emilia: Edizioni Diabasis, 2005, 289–334.

Criste, Oskar. *Erzherzog Carl von Österreich. Ein Lebensbild im Auftrage seiner Enkel, der Herren Erzherzoge Friedrich und Eugen*. 3 Bänder. Wien und Leipzig: Wilhelm Braumüller, 1912.

Davenport, Beatrix Cary (ed.). *A Diary of the French Revolution by Gouverneur Morris 1752–1816, Minister to France During the Terror*. 2 vols. Boston: Houghton Mifflin, 1939.

Daudet, Ernest (éd.). *Lettres du comte Valentin Esterhazy à sa femme, 1784–1792*. 2 vols. Paris: Plon, 1907.

De Nicola, Carlo. *Diario napoletano, 1798–1825*. 3 vols. Napoli: Soc. Napoletana di storia patria, 1906.

Élisabeth de France. *Mémoires de Madame Élisabeth de France, soeur de Louis XVI*, annotés et mis en ordre par Barghon Fort-Rion, François de. Paris: Vaton, 1858.

Elliott, Grace Dalrymple. *During the Reign of Terror: Journal of My Life During the French Revolution*. New York: Sturgis & Walton Company, 1910.

Fulford, Roger (ed.). *The Autobiography of Miss Knight, Lady Companion to Princess Charlotte*. London: William Kimber, 1960.

Galand, Michèle (éd.). *Journal secret de Charles de Lorraine, 1766–1779*. Bruxelles: Hayez, 2000.

Gasser, Xaveria. "Klostergeschichte." In Innerkofler, Adolf. *Eine grosse Tochter Maria Theresias, Erzherzogin Marianna in ihrem Hauptmonument dem Elisabethinerinnenkloster zu Klagenfurt*. Klagenfurt: Druckerei Carinthia, 1993.

Gerning, Johann Isaak von. *Reise durch Oesterreich und Italien*. 3 Bänder. Frankfurt: Friedrich Wilmans, 1802.

Girard, Georges. *Correspondance entre Marie-Antoinette et Marie-Thérèse, présentée et annotée par Georges Girard*. Paris: Grasset, 1933.

Gorani, Giuseppe. *Mémoires secrètes et critiques des cours, des gouvernemens et des moeurs des principaux etats de l'Italie*. Paris: Buisson, 1793.

Greig, James (ed.). *The Diaries of a Duchess: Extracts from the Diaries of the First Duchess of Northumberland*. London: Hodder and Stoughton, 1936.

Grouchy, Emmanuel-Henri, vicomte de, et Antoine Guillois (éds.). *La révolution française. Racontée par un diplomate étranger. Correspondance du Bailli de Virieu, Ministre Plénipotentiaire de Parme, 1788–1793*. Paris: Flammarion, 1903.

Huart, Suzanne d' (éd.). *Journal de Marie-Amélie, reine de France*. Paris: Perrin, 1981.

Khevenhüller-Metsch, Rudolf und Hanns Schlitter (Hg.). *Aus der Zeit Maria Theresias. Tagebuch des Fürsten Johann Joseph Khevenhüller-Metsch, Kaiserlichen Oberhofmeisters.* 8 Bde. Wien: Adolf Holzhausen, 1907–1972.

Lever, Évelyne. *Correspondance de Marie-Antoinette (1770–1793)*. Paris: Tallandier, 2005.

Ligne, Charles-Joseph, Prince de. *Fragments de l'histoire de ma vie*. Ed. Jeroom Vercruysse. 2 vols. Paris: Honoré Champion, 2000–2001.

Lumbroso, Alberto (a cura di). "Lettere inedite di Maria Carolina, Regina delle due Sicilie (1806–1809)." *Miscellanea Napoleonica*, Serie III-IV. Roma: Modes e Mendel, 1898.

Maria Anna (Marianna), Archduchess. *Selbstbekenntnis, Asketisches Tagebuch, und Relation*. In Innerkofler, Adolf. *Eine grosse Tochter Maria Theresias, Erzherzogin Marianna in ihrem Hauptmonument dem Elisabethinerinnenkloster zu Klagenfurt*. Klagenfurt: Druckerei Carinthia, 1993.

Miller, Lady Anna Riggs. *Letters from Italy: Describing the Manners, Customs, Antiquities, Paintings, &c. of That Country, in the Years MDCCLXX and MDCCLXXI: To a Friend Residing in France*. 2nd ed. 3 vols. London: Edward and Charles Dilly, 1777.

Miot de Melito, comte André-François. *Mémoires*. 3 vols. Paris: Michel Levy Frères, 1858.

Montet, Alexandrine de la Boutetière de Saint-Mars, baronne de Fisson du. *Souvenirs de la baronne du Montet, 1785–1866*. 3e éd. Paris: Plon, 1914.

Mousset, Albert. *Un témoin ignoré de la Révolution: Le comte de Fernan Nuñez, Ambassadeur d'Espagne à Paris (1787–1791)*. Paris: Edouard Champion, 1924.

Moüy, Charles de (éd.). *Correspondance inédite du roi Stanislaus Auguste Poniatowski et de Madame Geoffrin, 1764–1777*. Paris: Plon, 1875.

Mueller von Asow, Hedwig and E. H. (eds.). *The Collected Correspondence and Papers of Christoph Willibald Gluck*. Translated by Stewart Thomson. London: Barrie and Rockliff, 1962.

Palumbo, Raffaele (a cura di). *Carteggio di Maria Carolina Regina delle due Sicilie con lady Emma Hamilton. Documenti inediti, con un sommario storico della reazione borbonica del 1799, ricavato dei documenti e corredato di note ed allegazioni*. Napoli: Jovene, 1877.

Piozzi, Hester Lynch. *Observations and Reflections Made in the Course of a Journey Through France, Italy, and Germany*. 2 vols. London: Strahan & Cadell, 1789.

Podewils, Graf Otto Christoph von. *Friedrich der Grosse und Maria Theresia: diplomatische Berichte*. Hg. Carl Hinrichs, Übersetzt von Gertrud Podewils-Dürniz. Berlin: R.v. Decker's Verlag, G. Schenck, 1937.

Pressburger Zeitung, founded 1764. Österreichische Nationalbibliothek.

Rambaud, Jacques (éd.). *Mémoires du comte Roger de Damas, Vienne de 1806 à 1814, suivis de lettres inédites de Marie-Caroline, Reine de Naples, au comte Roger de Damas*. Paris: Plon-Nourrit et Cie, 1914.

Ricci, Paolo (a cura di). *Diario napoletano, dicembre 1798–dicembre 1800. I Giorni della storia 3*. Milano: Giordano, 1963.

Saint-Priest, le comte de. *Mémoires. Règnes de Louis XV et de Louis XVI*. Publiés par le Baron de Barante. Paris: Calmann-Lévy, 1929.

Schlitter, Hanns (Hg.). *Briefe der Erzherzogin Marie Christine Statthalterin der Niederlande an Leopold II. Nebst einer Einleitung zur Geschichte der franz. Politik Leopolds II*. Wien: Fontes rerum austriacarum, 1894.

Schlitter, Hanns (Hg.). *Geheime Correspondenz Josefs II, mit seinem Minister in den österreichischen Niederlanden Ferdinand Grafen Trauttmansdorff, 1787–1789*. Wien: Adolf Holzhausen, 1902.

Schütz, Carl & Anna Maria archeducessa Austriae. *Schau- und Denkmünzen, welche unter der glorwürdigen Regierung der Kaiserinn Koeniginn Maria Theresia gepräget worden sind*. Wien: Krauss, 1782.

Söderhjelm, Alma. *Hans Axel Graf v. Fersen et Marie-Antoinette: Correspondance et journal intime inéd. du Comte Axel de Fersen*. 2e. éd. Paris: Kra, 1930.

Swinburne, Henry. *The Courts of Europe at the Close of the Last Century*. Edited by Charles White. 2 vols. London: Colburn, 1841.

Tanucci, Bernardo. *Lettere di Bernardo Tanucci a Carlo III (1759–1776)*. R. Mincuzzi (a cura di). Roma: Istituto per la Storia del Risorgimento Italiano, 1969.

Tilly, Alexandre de. *Mémoires du comte Alexandre de Tilly, pour servir à l'histoire des moeurs de la fin du XVIIIe siècle*. 2e éd., 3 vols. Paris: Chez les marchands de nouveautés, 1828.

Tourzel, la duchesse de. *Mémoires de Madame la duchesse de Tourzel, gouvernante des enfants de France de 1789 à 1795*. Jean Chalon (éd.). Paris: Mercure de France, 1986.

Tyson, Moses and Guppy, Henry (eds.). *The French Journals of Mrs. Thrale and Doctor Johnson*. Manchester, England: Manchester University Press, 1932.

Verdile, Nadia (a cura di). *Un anno di Lettere coniugale: Da Caserta, il carteggio inedito di Ferdinando IV con Maria Carolina.* Caserta: Spring Edizione, 2008.

Vigée-Le Brun, Elisabeth. *Mémoires d'une portraitiste.* Paris: Éditions Scala, 1989.

Walter, Gérard (éd.). *Le procès de Marie-Antoinette, 23–25 vendémiaire an II (14–16 octobre 1793). Actes du tribunal révolutionnaire.* Bruxelles: Éd. Complexe, 1993.

Waresquiel, Emmanuel de (ed.). *Mémoires du Prince de Talleyrand, suivis de 135 lettres inédites du Prince de Talleyrand à la duchesse de Bauffremont (1808–1838).* Paris: Robert Laffont, 2007.

Weil, M.-H. et le marquis de Somma Circello. *Correspondance inédite de Marie-Caroline, Reine de Naples et Sicile, avec le marquis de Gallo*, 2 vols. Paris: Émile Paul, 1911, reprinted 2019.

Wharncliffe, Lord (ed.). *The Letters and Works of Lady Mary Wortley Montagu.* 2 vols. London: George Bell and Sons, 1908.

Wienerisches Diarium, 1703–79. From 1780 renamed Wiener Zeitung. Österreichische Nationalbibliothek.

Williams, Helen Maria. *Letters Written In France in the Summer of 1790, to a Friend in England.* 4th ed. London: T. Cadell, 1794.

Wolf, Adam (Hg.). *Leopold II und Marie Christine: Ihr Briefwechsel, 1781–1792.* Wien: Gerold, 1867.

Wormeley, Katherine Prescott (trans.). *Diary and Correspondence of Count Axel Fersen, Grand-Marshal of Sweden, Relating to the Court of France.* London: William Heinemann, 1902.

Wraxall, Nathaniel William. *Memoirs of the Courts of Berlin, Dresden, Warsaw, and Vienna, in the years 1777, 1778, and 1779.* 2nd ed., 2 vols. London: A. Strahan, 1800.

Wraxall, Nathaniel William. *Historical Memories of My Own Time, from 1772–1784.* 2nd ed., 2 vols. London: Cadell & Davies, 1800.

## SECONDARY SOURCES

Acton, Harold. *The Bourbons of Naples (1734–1825).* London: Methuen, 1956.

Arneth, Alfred von. *Geschichte Maria Theresias.* 10 Bde. W. Braumüller, Wien 1863–1879.

Badinter, Elisabeth. *L'Infant de Parme.* Paris: Fayard, 2008.

Badinter, Elisabeth. *Les Conflits d'une mère: Marie-Thérèse d'Autriche et ses enfants.* Paris: Flammarion, 2020.

Balázs, Éva H. *Hungary and the Habsburgs, 1765–1800: An Experiment in Enlightened Absolutism.* Budapest: Central European University Press, 1997.

Barea, Ilsa. *Vienna: Legend and Reality.* London: Pimlico, 1992.

Barton, H. Arnold. *Count Hans Axel von Fersen: Aristocrat in an Age of Revolution.* Boston: Twayne: 1975.

Bassett, Richard. *For God and Kaiser: The Imperial Austrian Army.* New Haven & London: Yale University Press, 2016.

Beales, Derek. *Joseph II.* Vol. 1: *In the Shadow of Maria Theresa, 1741–1780*, vol. 2: *Against the World, 1780–1790.* Cambridge: Cambridge University Press, 1987 and 2009.

Beales, Derek. *Enlightenment and Reform in Eighteenth-Century Europe.* London and New York: I. B. Tauris, 2005.

Becquet, Hélène. *Marie-Thérèse de France, l'orpheline du Temple.* Paris: Perrin, 2012.

Benedik, Christian, Klaus Albrecht Schröder (Hg.). *Die Gründung der Albertina. Herzog Albert und seine Zeit.* Ostfildern: Hatje Cantz, 2014.

Benedik, Christian, Hellmut Lorenz, und Anna Mader-Kratky (Hg.). *Die Wiener Hofburg 1705–1835. Die kaiserliche Residenz vom Barock bis zum Klassizismus.* Wien: Verlag der Österreichischen Akademie der Wissenschaften, 2016.

Bédarida, Henri. *Parme et la France de 1748 à 1789.* Paris: Honoré Champion, 1928.

Beerli, Frieda. *Die Kinder der Kaiserin: zwölf farbige Bildnisse der Kinder Maria Theresias von Liotard, Jean Etienne, 1702 1789.* Wiesbaden: Insel-Verlag, 1955.

Benassi, Umberto. *Guglielmo du Tillot: Un ministro riformatore del secolo XVIII.* Parma: Presso la R. Deputazione di Storia Patria, Parma, Nuova Seria, vol. XIX, 1919.

Berly, Cécile. "Le palais des Tuileries et Paris, ou l'affirmation de la reine politique (6 octobre 1789–10 août 1792)." In Petitfils, Jean-Christian (éd.). *Marie-Antoinette. Dans les pas de la reine.* Paris: Perrin, 2020, 211–29.

Bertière, Simone. *Marie-Antoinette l'insoumise.* Paris: Éditions de Fallois, 2002.

Bertini, Giuseppe. *L'Appartamento del Duca Ferdinando a Colorno dipinto da Antonio Bresciani.* Parma: TLC, 2000.

Best, Geoffrey. *War and Society in Revolutionary Europe 1770–1870.* Stroud, Gloucestershire: Sutton, 1998.

Blanning, T. C. W. *Joseph II.* London & New York: Longman, 1994.

# BIBLIOGRAPHY


Blanning, T. C. W. *The French Revolutionary Wars, 1787–1802.* London: Arnold, 1996.

Blanning, T. C. W. *The French Revolution: Class War or Culture Clash?* London: Macmillan, 1997.

Boulant, Antoine. "La Conciergerie." Dans Petitfils, Jean-Christian (éd.). *Marie-Antoinette. Dans les pas de la reine.* Paris: Perrin, 2020, 249–64.

Braubach, Max. *Maria Theresias Jüngster Sohn Max Franz, Letzter Kurfürst von Köln und Fürstbischof von Münster.* Wien, München: Verlag Herold, 1961.

Buckley, Veronica. *Madame de Maintenon: The Secret Wife of Louis XIV.* London: Bloomsbury, 2008.

Bürgschwentner, Joachim. "Von der Äbtissin zur Ersatzlandesmutter. Erzherzogin Maria Elisabeth in Innsbruck (1781–1806)." Barth-Scalmani, Gunda et al. (Hg.). *Forschungswerkstatt. Die Habsburgermonarchie im 18. Jahrhundert.* Bochum: Jahrbuch der Österreichischen Gesellschaft zur Erforschung des Achtzehnten Jahrhunderts, Band 26, 2012, 59–65.

Bürgschwentner, Joachim. "Krankheit, Äbtissin, Flucht: Stationen Erzherzogin Maria Elisabeths," in Zedinger, Renate (Hg.). *Innsbruck 1765. Prunkvolle Hochzeit, fröhliche Feste, tragischer Ausklang.* Das achtzehnte Jahrhundert und Österreich: Jahrbuch der Österreichischen Gesellschaft zur Erforschung des Achtzehten Jahrhunderts, Band 29. Bochum: Winkler, 2015, 143–59.

Cadbury, Deborah. *The Last King of France. Revolution, Revenge and the Search for Louis XVII.* London: Fourth Estate, 2002.

Calaresu, Melissa. "*The Patriots and the People in Late Eighteenth-Century Naples.*" In *History of European Ideas*, vol. 20, nos 1–3, 1995, 203–9.

Carney, Gerard. "The State Trials of Louis XVI and Marie Antoinette," 2017. Owen Dixon Society eJournal, Curtis University Law School, 2017, 1: 1–24.

Carrai, Guido. *Maria Amalia, Duchessa di Parma e Piacenza 1746–1804.* Prague: Eleutheria, 2018.

Cefarin, Rudolf. *Kaernten und die Freimaurerei. Eine kulturhistorische Studie.* Wien: Saturn, 1932.

Clark, Christopher. *Iron Kingdom: The Rise and Downfall of Prussia, 1600–1947.* London: Allen Lane, 2006.

Coleman, Terry. *Nelson: The Man and the Legend.* London: Bloomsbury, 2002.

Coletti, Alessandro. *La regina di Napoli. La vita appassionata di Maria Carolina, protagonista di splendori e miserie del Settecento napoletano.* Novara: Agostini, 1986.

Colletta, Pietro. *Storia del Reame di Napoli dal 1734 sino al 1825.* 4 vols. Napoli: Libreria scientifica, 1953 (first published in 1834).

Constantine, David. *Fields of Fire: A Life of Sir William Hamilton.* London: Weidenfeld & Nicolson, 2001.

Cont, Allessandro. "Il potere della tradizione. Guillaume Du Tillot e la questione della nobiltà." In "Nuova Rivista Storica" 100, no. 1 (2016), 73–106.

Corti, Egon Caesar, Conte. *Ich, eine Tochter Maria Theresias. Ein Lebensbild der Königin Marie Karoline von Neapel.* München: Bruckmann, 1950.

Craeybeckx, J. "The Brabant Revolution: A Conservative Revolt in a Backward Country?," *Acta historiae neerlandica*, 4 (1970): 49–83.

Craveri, Benedetta. "*Salons francesi e salotti italiani: proposte di confronto*" in Betri, Maria Luisa (ed.), Elena Brambilla (a cura di), *Salotti e ruolo femminile in Italia tra fine Seicento e primo Novecento.* Venezia: Marsilio, 2004, 539–44.

Cremer, Annette C., Matthias Müller, und Klaus Pietschmann (Hg.). *Fürst und Fürstin als Künstler. Herrschaftliches Künstlertum zwischen Habitus, Norm und Neigung.* Berlin: Lukas Verlag, 2018.

Cremer, Annette C., Anette Baumann, und Eva Bender (Hg.). *Prinzessinnen unterwegs: Reisen fürstlicher Frauen in der Frühen Neuzeit.* Berlin and Boston: De Gruyter, 2018.

Croce, Benedetto. *Storia del Regno di Napoli.* 2nd ed. Milano: Adelphi, 2005. Originally published in 1924.

D'Alconzo, Paola. "Facing Antiquity, Back and Forth, in Eighteenth-Century Naples," in *Music in Art* 40, no. 1–2, 2015, 9–43.

Daguenet, Patrick. *Les séjours de Marie-Antoinette à Fontainebleau, 1770–1786.* Fontainebleau: Les Éd. de Belleombre, 2016.

Darnton, Robert. *The Revolutionary Temper.* New York: W. W. Norton, 2024.

Davies, Norman. *Vanished Kingdoms: The Rise and Fall of States and Nations.* New York: Viking, 2011.

Davis, John. *Naples and Napoleon: Southern Italy and the European Revolutions, 1780–1860.* Oxford: Oxford University Press, 2006.

Deinhardt, Wilhelm. *Der Jansenismus in Deutschen Landen. Ein Beitrag zur Kirchengeschichte des 18. Jahrhunderts.* München: Verlag Josef Kösel & Friedrich Pustet, 1929.

De Smedt, Helma. "Living Apart Together: Socio-Economic Changes in the Southern Netherlands Within the Habsburg Monarchy in the 18th Century," Heppner, Peter Urbanitsch and Renate Zedinger (eds.). *Social Change in the Habsburg Monarchy.* Bochum: Winckler, 2011, 37–59.

# BIBLIOGRAPHY


Dimond, Peter. *A Mozart Diary: A Chronological Reconstruction of the Composer's Life, 1761–1791*. Westport, CT: Greenwood Press, 1997.

Drei, G. *Visita a Parma dell'imperatore Giuseppe II, Distinta relazione della venuta, dimora e partenza da questa città di Parma da S. M. Imperiale Giuseppe II ecc*. AP, 1938.

Duindam, Jeroen. *Vienna and Versailles. The Courts of Europe's Dynastic Rivals, 1550–1780*. Cambridge: Cambridge University Press, 2003.

Eichert, Joachim. "*Dr. Philipp Gaggl, der letzte Leibarzt der Erzherzogin Maria Anna*." Carinthia, Klagenfurt, 2002, 363–68.

Engels, Amelie. *Maria Anna, eine Tochter Maria Theresias, 1738–1789*. PhD Fiss., Universität Wien, 1965.

Evans, R. J. W. *The Making of the Habsburg Monarchy 1550–1700: An Interpretation*. Oxford: Clarendon Press, 1998.

Evans, R. J. W. *Austria, Hungary, and the Habsburgs: Essays on Central Europe c. 1683–1867*. Oxford: Oxford University Press, 2008.

Farr, Evelyn. *Marie-Antoinette and Count Axel Fersen: The Untold Love Story*. London & Chester Springs, PA: Peter Owen, 2013.

Farr, Evelyn. *I Love You Madly: Marie-Antoinette and Count Fersen: The Secret Letters*. London & Chester Springs, PA: Peter Owen, 2016.

Felder, Alois. "*Eine unbekannte Habsburgerin in Linz*." *Blickpunkte: Kulturschrift Oberösterreich*. Linz: Veritas Verlag, Jg. 46 (1996), H. 2, S. 28–31.

Félix, Joël. *Louis XVI et Marie-Antoinette. Un couple en politique*. Paris 2006.

Filangieri, R. "L'archivio della real casa di Borbone in Napoli," in *Archivio storico italiano* 111 (1953), 295–301.

Ford, Franklin L. *Europe 1780–1830*, 2nd ed. London: Longman, 1989.

Fosca, François. *Liotard (1702–1789)*. Paris, 1928.

Fournoux, Amable de. *Marie-Caroline, reine de Naples*. Paris: Pygmalion, 2014.

Fraser, Antonia. *Marie Antoinette: The Journey*. London: Weidenfeld & Nicolson, 2001.

Fraser, Flora. *Beloved Emma: The Life of Emma, Lady Hamilton*. London: John Murray, 2003.

Fräss-Ehrfeld, Claudia. "*Noch nie habe ich ein so niedliches Spital gesehen: Die Elisabethinen und Erzherzogin Maria Anna*," *Klagenfurt 500. Bulletin Sonderheft Erstes Halbjahr* 2018, *Geschichtsverein für Kärnten*.

Freeman, Daniel E. *Mozart in Prague*. Minneapolis, MN: Bearclaw, 2013.

Frenzel, Monika. "*Eine landschafliche Idylle im Innsbrucker Hofgarten*." In Zedinger, Renate (Hg.). *Innsbruck 1765. Prunkvolle Hochzeit, fröhliche Feste, tragischer Ausklang*. Das achtzehnte Jahrhundert und Österreich: Jahrbuch der Österreichischen Gesellschaft zur Erforschung des Achtzehten Jahrhunderts, Band 29. Bochum: Winkler, 2015, 343–48.

Furlani, Silvio und Adam Wandruszka. *Österreich und Italien. Ein bilaterales Geschichtsbuch*. Wien: Jugend u. Volk, 2002.

Gates-Coon, Rebecca. *The Charmed Circle: Joseph II and the "Five Princesses," 1765–1790*. West Lafayette, IN: Purdue Press, 2015.

Geffroy, M. A. "*Les lettres du comte Axel Fersen*," *Revue d'histoire diplomatique*, no. 2, 1888, 90–99.

Gepp, Christian. "Maria Amalia e l'influenza di Vienna." In Alba Mora (a cura di), *Storia die Parma V. I Borbone: fra Illuminismo e rivoluzioni*. Parma 2015, 215–34.

Gepp, Christian und Stefan Lenk. "*Reisen aus Staatsräson. Die Brautfahrten der Erzherzogin Maria Carolina 1768 und der Erzherzogin Maria Amalia 1769*," in Cremer, Annette C., Anette Baumann, und Eva Bender (Hg.). *Prinzessinnen unterwegs: Reisen fürstlicher Frauen in der Frühen Neuzeit*. Berlin and Boston: De Gruyter, 2018, 171–90.

Giegl, Gabriele. *Musik in der Familie Maria Theresias*. Diss., University Wien, 2002.

Giglioli, Constance. *Naples in 1799: An Account of the Revolution of 1799 and of the Rise and Fall of the Parthenopean Republic*. London: John Murray, 1903.

Girault de Coursac, Paul et Pierette. *Louis XVI et Marie Antoinette. Vie conjugale, vie politique*. Paris: OEIL, 1990.

Goldstone, Nancy. *In the Shadow of the Empress: The Defiant Lives of Maria Theresa, Mother of Marie Antoinette, and Her Daughters*. London: Weidenfeld & Nicolson, 2021.

Goncourt, Edmond et Jules de. *Portraits intimes du XVIIIe siécle*. 2 vols. Paris: E. Dentu, 1857–58.

Gossi, Herbert. *Der Graf F. C. Mercy-Argenteau als Vermittler zwischen Maria Theresia und Marie Antoinette*. Diss., University Wien, 2000.

Gottsman, Andreas (Hg.). Römisch Historische Mitteilungen, Band 60, Wien: Verlag der Österreichischen Akademie der Wissenschaften, 2018.

# BIBLIOGRAPHY


Graffigny, Françoise de. *Ziman et Zenise, suivi de Phaza, comédies en un acte en prose*. Paris: BNF Hachette, 2016.

Hamilton, William. *Observations on Mount Vesuvius, Mount Etna, and Other Volcanoes: In a Series of Letters, Addressed to the Royal Society*. London: T. Cadell, 1774.

Hampson, Norman. *The Enlightenment: An Evaluation of Its Assumptions, Attitudes and Values*. London: Penguin, 1990.

Hanák, Péter (Hg.). *Die Geschichte Ungarns. Von den Anfängen bis zur Gegenwart*. Budapest: Corvina, 1988.

Hardmann, John. *Marie Antoinette: The Making of a French Queen*. New Haven and London: Yale University Press, 2019.

Hardmann, John. *The Life of Louis XVI*. New Haven and London: Yale University Press, 2023.

Harsanyi, Doina Pasca. *French Rule in the States of Parma, 1796–1814: Working with Napoleon*. London: Palgrave Macmillan, 2022.

Hartmann, Gerhard. *Die Kaiser des Heiligen Römischen Reiches*. Vierte Auflage. Wiesbaden: Marixverlag, 2016.

Haslinger, Ingrid. *Küche und Tafelkultur am kaiserlichen Hofe zu Wien: zur Geschichte von Hofküche, Hofzuckerbäckerei und Hofsilber- und Tafelkammer*. Bern: Benteli, 1993.

Hanzl-Wachter, Lieselotte. *Hofburg zu Innsbruck. Architektur, Möbel, Raumkunst. Repräsentatives Wohnen in den Kaiserappartements von Maria Theresia bis Kaiser Franz Joseph*. Wien: Böhlau, 2004.

Hausmann, Friederike. *Herrscherin im Paradies der Teufel*. München: Beck, 2014.

Hengerer, Mark. "Baroque Architecture in the Former Habsburg Residences of Graz and Innsbruck." In Cohen, Gary B. and Franz A. J. Szabo. *Embodiments of Power: Building Baroque Cities in Europe*. New York and Oxford: Berghahn Books, 2008.

Heppner, Peter Urbanitsch and Renate Zedinger (eds.). *Social Change in the Habsburg Monarchy*. Bochum: Winckler, 2011.

Herman, Heinrich. "Maria Anna, Erzherzogin von Oesterreich." *Carinthia*, Jahrgang 53, 1863.

Hersche, Peter. "*War Maria Theresia eine Jansenistin?*" *Österreich in Geschichte und Literatur* 15 (1971): 14–25.

Hersche, Peter. *Der Spätjansenismus in Österreich*. Wien: Verlag der Österreichischen Akademie der Wissenschaften, 1977.

Hertel, Sandra. "Die Dame die den Brief zerreißt: Die Inszenierung der zeichnenden Erzherzogin Marie Christine." In Cremer, Annette C., Matthias Müller, und Klaus Pietschmann (Hg.), *Fürst und Fürstin als Künstler*. Berlin: Lukas Verlag, 2018, 219–30.

Hohenauer, L. F. "Das Elisabethinerinnenkloster." *Carinthia* I, 1820.

Huart, Suzanne d'. "*Vraies ou fausses? Les lettres de Marie-Antoinette.*" *L'Histoire*, no. 51 (1982): 91–93.

Iby, Elfriede, Martin Mutschlechner, Werner Telesko, und Karl Vocelka (Hg.). *Maria Theresia 1717–1780. Strategin—Mutter—Reformerin*. Wien: Amalthea, 2017.

Imbruglia, Girolamo (ed.). *Naples in the Eighteenth Century. The Birth and Death of a Nation State*. Cambridge: Cambridge University Press, 2000.

Innerkofler, Adolf. *Eine grosse Tochter Maria Theresias, Erzherzogin Marianna in ihrem Hauptmonument dem Elisabethinerinnenkloster zu Klagenfurt*. Innsbruck: Im Verlage der Vereinsbuchhandlung, 1910.

Jenkins, John S. "Mozart and the Castrati," *Musical Times* 151, no. 1913 (Winter 2010): 55–68.

Johnston, R. M. (éd.). *Mémoire de Marie Caroline Reine de Naple intitulé de la révolution du royaume de Sicile par un témoin oculaire bien instruit des faits, et qui en a soigneusement receuilli les détails*. Cambridge, MA: Harvard University Press; London: Henry Frowde; Oxford: Oxford University Press, 1912.

Judge, Jane. "Provincial *Manifestes*. Belgians Declare Independence, 1789–1790." *De Achttiende Eeuw* 47 (2015): 127–45.

Judge, Jane C. *The United States of Belgium: The Story of the First Belgian Revolution*. Leuven: Leuven University Press, 2018.

Kernbauer, Eva, Aneta Zahradnik (Hg.). *Höfische Porträtkultur. Die Bildnissammlung der österreichischen Erzherzogin Maria Anna (1738–1789)*. Berlin and Boston: De Gruyter, 2016.

Kertanguy, Inès de. *Madame Vigée-Le Brun*. Paris: Perrin, 2000.

King, David. *Vienna 1814: How the Conquerors of Napoleon Made Love, War, and Peace at the Congress of Vienna*. New York: Three Rivers Press, 2008.

Klinckowström, Rudolf Maurits, baron de. *Le comte de Fersen et la cour de France. Extraits des papiers du comte Jean Axel de Fersen*. Paris: Firmin-Didot, 1877.

Klingenstein, Grete und Franz A. J. Szabo (Hrsg.). *Staatskanzler Wenzel Anton von Kaunitz-Rietberg 1711–1794: Neue Perspektiven zu Politik und Kultur der europäischen Aufklärung*. Graz and New York: Andreas Schnider, 1996.

Kluger, Robert. *Die bischöfliche Residenz in Klagenfurt 1769–1981. Vom Schloss Erzherzogin Maria Anna zum Gurker Bischofssitz.* Klagenfurt: Verlag des Geschichtsvereines für Kärnten, 2020.

Kolb, Franz. Das Tiroler Volk in seinem Freiheitskampf 1796–97. Innsbruck, Wien, München: Tyrolier Verlag, 1957.

Kopplin, Monika. *Japanische Lacke: Die Sammlung der Königin Marie-Antoinette.* München: Hirmer Verlag, 2001.

Körner, Günther (Hg.). *750 Jahre Stadt Völkermarkt: Beiträge zu Geschichte und Gegenwart Völkermarkts.* Völkermarkt: Stadtgemeinde Völkermarkt, 2001.

Koschatzky, Walter (Hg.). *Maria Theresia und ihre Zeit. Eine Darstellung der Epoche von 1740–1780 aus Anlass der 200. Wiederkehr des Todestages der Kaiserin.* Salzburg, Wien: 1979.

Koschatzky, Walter and Selma Krasa. *Herzog Albert von Sachsen-Teschen, 1738–1822, Reichsfeldmarschall und Kunstmäzen.* Wien, 1982.

Kovács, Elisabeth. "*Die ideale Erzherzogin. Maria Theresias Forderungen an ihre Töchter.*" Mitteilungen des Instituts für Österreichische Geschichtsforschung 94 (1986): 49–80.

Lacour-Gayet, Michel. *Marie-Caroline, reine de Naples: Une adversaire de Napoléon.* Paris: Tallandier, 1990.

Lacouture, Jean. *Jesuits: A Multibiography.* Washington, DC: Counterpoint, 1995.

Langer, Ellinor. *Die Geschichte des Adeligen Damenstiftes zu Innsbruck.* Innsbruck: Universitätsverlag Wagner, 1950.

La Rocheterie, Maxime de et le marquis de Beaucourt (éds.). *Lettres de Marie Antoinette: Recueil des lettres authentiques de la reine publié pour la société d'histoire contemporaine.* 2 vols. Paris: Au Siège de la Société, 1895–96.

Lendvai, Paul. *The Hungarians: A Thousand Years of Victory in Defeat.* Princeton: Princeton University Press, 2004.

Lenotre, G. *La captivité et la mort de Marie-Antoinette.* Paris: Perrin, 1908.

Lever, Evelyne. *Marie Antoinette.* Paris: Fayard, 1991.

Lynch, John. *Bourbon Spain, 1700–1808.* Oxford: Basil Blackwell, 1989.

Macartney, Carlile A. *Hungary: A Short History.* Edinburgh: Edinburgh University Press, 1962.

Mack Smith, Denis. *A History of Sicily: Modern Sicily After 1713.* London: Chatto & Windus, 1968.

Madariaga, Isabel de. *Russia in the Age of Catherine the Great.* London: Phoenix, 2002.

Madariaga, Isabel de. *Catherine the Great: A Short History.* New Haven, CT: Yale University Press, 1990.

Maierhofer, Waltraud. Gertrud M. Rösc, and Caroline Bland (eds.). *Women Against Napoleon: Historical and Fictional Responses to His Rise and Legacy.* Frankfurt am Main and New York: Campus Verlag, 2007.

Mallet du Pan, Jacques. *Correspondance inédite du Mallet du Pan avec la Cour de Vienne (1794–1798)*, 2 vols. Paris: Plon, 1884.

Mansel, Philip. *The Court of France, 1789–1830,* Cambridge: Cambridge University Press, 1988.

Marchi, Adele Vittoria. *Parma e Vienna: Cronaca di 3 secoli di rapporti fra il ducato di Parma Piacenza e Guastalla e la corte degli Asburgo.* Parma: Artegrafica Silva, 1988.

Martus, Steffen. *Aufklärung: Das Deutsche 18. Jahrhundert. Ein Epochenbild.* Hamburg: Rowohlt, 2018.

McPhee, Peter. *The French Revolution 1789–1799.* Oxford: Oxford University Press, 2002.

Mora, Alba (a cura di). *Un Borbone tra Parma e l'Europa. Don Ferdinando e il suo tempo (1751–1802).* Reggio Emilia: Edizioni Diabasis, 2005.

Mora, Alba (a cura di). *Storia di Parma V. I Borbone: fra Illuminismo e rivoluzioni.* Parma: Monte Università, 2015.

Moussez, Albert. *Un Témoin ignoré de la Révolution: Le comte de Fernan Nuñez.* Paris: Édouard Champion, 1924.

Muratori-Philip, Anne. *Madame Royale, fille de Louis XVI et de Marie-Antoinette.* Paris: Fayard, 2016.

Musini, Nullo. *Un amministratore privato di Casa Borbone e un carteggio inedito di Maria Amalia e di Luisa Maria.* Parma: *Biblioteca dell' Aurea Parma, Nuova Seria no. 26* (1930, IX), 1–10.

Nagel, Susan. Marie-Thérèse: *The Fate of Marie-Antoinette's Daughter.* London: Bloomsbury, 2008.

Natter, Tobias G. (Hg.). *Angelika Kauffmann. Ein Weib von ungeheurem Talent.* Boca Raton, FL: VLM Press, 2007.

Nigrelli, Gianni. "*Un collezionista mantovano a Parma nel secondo settecento: Il marchese Guido Cavriani (1735–1791) e la sua raccolta di stampe,*" Accademia Nazionale Virgiliana di Scienze Lettere e Arte, *Atti e Memorie*, Nuova serie, vol. 85 (2017).

Nisard, Charles. *Guillaume du Tillot: Un Valet Ministre et Secrétaire d'État, épisode de l'histoire de France en Italie, de 1749 à 1771*, 2e éd. Paris: Paul Ollendorff, 1887.

# BIBLIOGRAPHY


Noflatscher, Heinz und Jan Paul Niederkorn (Hg.). *Der Innsbrucker Hof. Residenz und höfische Gesellschaft in Tirol vom 15. bis 19. Jahrhundert.* Archiv für Österreichische Geschichte 138. Wien: Verlag der Österreichischen Akademie der Wissenschaften, 2005.

North, Jonathan. *Nelson at Naples: Revolution and Retribution in 1799.* Stroud: Amberley, 2018.

Nougaret, Christine. "Marie-Antoinette dans les fonds des archives nationales," *Annales historiques de la Révolution française*, 338, 2004, 129–36.

Obendorfer, Fritz. "Briefe der Erzherzogin Maria Anna an Anselm von Edling," *Blaetter zur Gesch. und Heimatkunde der Alpenlaender*, no. 11 und 12, Graz 1910.

Oezel, Zigdem. *Die Kunstpatronage von Königin Maria Carolina (1752–1814). Repräsentation, Kulturtransfer und Gabentausch zwischen Neapel und Wien.* Diss., University Wien, 2023.

Paciaudi, Paolo. *Descrizione delle feste celebrate in Parma l'anno 1769. Per le auguste nozze di sua altezza reale l'infante Don ferdinando colla reale archiduchessa Maria Amalia.* Parma: Stamperia reale, 1769.

Pagano, M. *I diari di scavo di Pompei, Ercolano e Stabia di Francesco e Pietro La Vega (1764–1810).* Raccolta e studio di documenti inediti. Roma: L'Erma di Bretschneider, 1997.

Palmer, Alan. *Metternich: Councillor of Europe.* London: History Book Club, 1972.

Pangels, Charlotte. *Die Kinder Maria Theresias: Leben und Schicksal in kaiserlichem Glanz.* München: Georg D. W. Callwey, 1980.

Petitfils, Jean-Christian. *Louis XVI.* 2 vols. Paris: Perrin, 2010.

Petitfils, Jean-Christian (éd.). *Marie-Antoinette. Dans les pas de la reine.* Paris: Perrin, 2020.

Pitt-Rivers, Françoise. *Madame Vigée Le Brun.* Paris: Gallimard, 2001.

Plaschka, Richard Georg, Grete Klingenstein et al. (Hg.). *Österreich im Europa der Aufklärung. Kontinuaität und Zäsur in Europa zur Zeit Maria Theresias und Josephs II.* Internationales Symposion in Wien, 20–23 Oktober 1980. 2 Bänder. Wien: Bundesministerium für Wissenschaft und Forschung, Österreichische Akademie der Wissenschaften, 1985.

Polasky, Janet L. *Revolution in Brussels, 1787–1793.* Brussels: Palais des Académies, 1982.

Praschl-Bichler, Gabriele und Gerd Wolfgang Sievers. *Kaiserliche Küche: die Rezepte der Habsburger.* Graz: Stocker, 2010.

Price, Munro. "Mirabeau and the Court: Some New Evidence," *French Historical Studies* 29, no. 1 (2006): 37–75.

Price, Munro. *The Fall of the French Monarchy. Louis XVI, Marie Antoinette and the baron de Breteuil.* London: Pan Books, 2013.

Radlecker, Kurt. *Gottfried van Swieten: eine Biographie.* Diss., Universität Wien, 1950.

Rao, Anna Maria. *La Repubblica Napoletana del 1799.* Roma: Tascabili Economici Newton, 1997.

Rapp, Christian and Nadia Rapp-Wimberger (Hg.). *300 Jahre Freimaurer. Das wahre Geheimnis.* Wien: Österreichische Nationalbibliothek, 2017.

Recca, Cinzia. "Maria Carolina and Marie Antoinette: Sisters and Queens in the Mirror of Jacobin Public Opinion," *Royal Studies Journal* I (2014): 17–36.

Recca, Cinzia. *The Diary of Queen Maria Carolina of Naples, 1781–1875: New Evidence of Queenship at Court.* London: Palgrave Macmillan, 2017.

Reinalter, Helmut. *Die historische Entwicklung Tirols von der älteren Regierungszeit Maria Theresias bis zum ersten Franzoseneinfall 1796.* Diss., Universität Innsbruck, 1970.

Rostworowski, Emmanuel. *Popioły i korzenie. Szkice historyczne i rodzinne.* Kraków: Znak, 1985.

Rothenberg, Gunther E. *Napoleon's Great Adversary: Archduke Charles and the Austrian Army, 1792–1814.* Staplehurst: Spellmount, 1995.

Rudan, Othmar. "*Erzherzogin Maria Anna in Klagenfurt, 1781–1789: Palais und Kloster vereint*," *Carinthia* 1.170, Klagenfurt, 1980, 185–260.

Schissel von Fleschenberg, Otmar. "*Die Rückkehr der Erzherzogin Maria Elisabeth Josepha nach Innsbruck 1797*," *Forschungen und Mitteilungen zur Geschichte Tirols und Vorarlbergs* 5 (1908), 55–57.

Schissel von Fleschenberg, Othmar. "*J. F. Primissers Begrüssungen der Erzherzogin Maria Elisabeth 1797 und 1801*," *Zeitschrift des Ferdinandeums für Tirol und Vorarlberg* 3, no. 54 (1910): 358–62.

Schlossar, Anton. *Erzherzog Johann von Österreich. Sein edles Leben und segensreiches Wirken, mit Benutzung des handschriftlichen und künstlerischen Nachlasses des Erzherzoges.* Graz und Wien: Styria, 1908.

Scholz-Michelitsch, Helga. *Georg Christoph Wagenseil. Hofkomponist und Hofklaviermeister der Kaiserin Maria Theresia.* Wien: Wilhelm Braumueller, 1980.

Siemann, Wolfram. *Metternich: Strategist and Visionary.* Translated by Daniel Steuer. Cambridge, MA: Harvard University Press, 2019.

Smith, Digby. *The Greenhill Napoleonic Wars Data Book.* London: Greenhill Books; Pennsylvania: Stackpole Books, 1998.

Sodano, Giulio e Giulio Brevetti (a cura di). *Io, la Regina. Maria Carolina d'Asburgo-Lorena tra politica, fede, arte e cultura*. Palermo: Quaderni, 2016.

Solnon, Jean-François. *La Cour de France*. Paris: Fayard, 1987

Stanga, Idelfonso. *Maria Amalia di Borbone, duchessa di Parma, 1746–1804*. Cremona: Nuova, 1932.

Stangl, Waltraud. *Tod und Trauer bei den österreichischen Habsburgern 1740–1780. Dargestellt im Spiegel des Hofzeremoniells*. Diss., Universität Wien, 2001.

Steiger, Robert und Angelika Reimann. *Goethes Leben von Tag zu Tag. Eine dokumentarische Chronik*, 8 Bänder, Zürich und München: Artemis Verlag, 1984.

Stollberg-Rilinger, Barbara. *Maria Theresia: Die Kaiserin in Ihrer Zeit, Eine Biographie*. München: C.H. Beck, 2017.

Sugar, Peter F. (ed.). *A History of Hungary*. London: I. B. Tauris, 1990.

Szabo, Franz A. J. "Prince Kaunitz and the Balance of Power," *International History Review* 1, no. 3 (July 1979): 399–408.

Szabo, Franz A. J. *Kaunitz and Enlightened Absolutism 1753–1780*. New York: Cambridge University Press, 1994.

Tamussino, Ursula. *Des Teufels Grossmutter. Eine Biographie der Königin Maria Carolina von Neapel-Sizilien*. Wien: Deuticke, 1991.

Tresoldi, Lucia. *La biblioteca privata di Maria Carolina d'Austria, regina di Napoli*. Roma: Bulzoni, 1972.

Tropper, Peter G. (Hg.). *300 Jahre Elisabethinen in Klagenfurt: 1710–2010*. Klagenfurt: Konvent der Elisabethinen zu Klagenfurt, 2010.

Unterkircher, Carl. *Chronik von Innsbruck*. Innsbruck: Verlag der Vereinsbuchhandlung, 1897.

Valentin, Hellwig. *"Aufklärung und Freimaurerei in Kärnten,"* *Geschichtsverein für Kärnten*, Sonderheft 2019, 15–18.

Vehse, Eduard. *Geschichte der deutschen Höfe seit der Reformation. 8. Theil: Geschichte des österreichischen Hofs und Adels und der österreichischen Diplomatie*. Hamburg: Hoffman und Campe, 1852.

Venturi, Franco. *Italy and the Enlightenment*. London: Longman, 1972.

Vial, Charles-Éloi. *"L'avant-dernière étape: Marie-Antoinette au Temple."* In Jean-Christian Petitfils (éd.). *Marie-Antoinette. Dans les pas de la reine*. Paris: Perrin, 2020, 231–48.

Wachter, Friederike. *Die Erziehung der Kinder Maria Theresias*. Diss., Universität Wien, 1969.

Wandruszka, Adam. *"Die Religiosität Franz Stephans von Lothringen."* *Mitteilungen des Österreichischen Staatsarchivs* 12 (1959): 162–73.

Wandruszka, Adam. *"Il 'Principe filosofo' e il 'Re Lazzarone': Le Lettere del granduca Pietro Leopoldo sul suo soggiorno a Napoli nel 1768,"* *Rivista Storica Italiana*, 72–73 (Settembre 1960), 501–10.

Wandruszka, Adam. *Leopold II. Erzherzog von Österreich, Großherzog von Toskana, König von Ungarn und Böhmen, Römischer Kaiser*. 2 Bde. Wien: Herold, 1963–65.

Waresquiel, Emmanuel de. *Juger la reine. 14, 15, 16 octobre 1793*. Paris: Tallendier, 2016.

Webster, Mary. *Johann Zoffany, 1733–1810*. New Haven and London: Yale University Press, 2011.

Weissensteiner, Friedrich. *Die Töchter Maria Theresias*. Wien: Kremayr & Scheriau, 1994.

Weissensteiner, Friedrich. *Die Söhne Maria Theresias*. Wien: Kremayr & Scheriau, 2004.

Wheatcroft, Andrew. *The Habsburgs: Embodying Empire*. London: Penguin, 1996.

Williams, Kate. *England's Mistress: The Infamous Life of Emma Hamilton*. New York: Ballantine Books, 2006.

Wilson, Peter H. *The Holy Roman Empire: A Thousand Years of Europe's History*. London: Penguin, 2017.

Witt-Dörring, Christian. *Die Möbelkunst am Wiener Hof zur Zeit Maria Theresias*. Diss., Universität Wien, 1978.

Wolf, Adam. *Aus dem Hofleben Maria Theresia's*. Wien: Gerold, 1859.

Wolf, Adam. *Marie Christine, Erzherzogin von Österreich*. 2 Bde. Wien: Carl Gerold's Sohn, 1863.

Wolf, Adam. *Fürstin Eleonore Liechtenstein, 1745–1812, Nach Briefen und Memoiren ihrer Zeit*. Wien: Carl Gerold's Sohn, 1875.

Zamoyski, Adam. *The Last King of Poland*. London: Weidenfeld & Nicolson, 1997.

Zamoyski, Adam. *Rites of Peace: The Fall of Napoleon and the Congress of Vienna*. London: Harper, 2007.

Zamoyski, Adam. *Poland: A History*. London: William Collins, 2009.

Zamoyski, Adam. *Phantom Terror: The Threat of Revolution and the Repression of Liberty 1789–1848*. London: William Collins, 2015.

Zamoyski, Adam. *Napoleon: The Man Behind the Myth*. London: William Collins, 2018.

Zedinger, Renate. *Die Verwaltung der Österreichischen Niederlande in Wien (1714–1795). Studien zu den Zentralisierungstendenzen des Wiener Hofes im Staatswerdungsprozess der Habsburgermonarchie*. Wien, Köln, Weimar: Böhlau Verlag, 2000.

Zedinger, Renate. *Franz Stephan von Lothringen (1708–1765): Monarch, Manager, Mäzen*. Wien: Böhlau, 2008.

Zedinger, Renate und Wolfgang Schmale (Hg.). *Franz Stephan von Lothringen und sein Kreis*. Bochum: Jahrbuch der Oesterreichischen Gesellschaft zur Erforschung des achtzehnten Jahrhunderts, Bd. 23, 2009.

Zedinger, Renate (Hg.). *Innsbruck 1765. Prunkvolle Hochzeit, fröhliche Feste, tragischer Ausklang*. "Das achtzehnte Jahrhundert und Österreich: Jahrbuch der Österreichischen Gesellschaft zur Erforschung des Achtzehten Jahrhunderts," Band 29. Bochum: Winkler, 2015.

Zedinger, Renate. *Maria Luisa de Borbón (1745–1792). Grossherzogin der Toskana und Kaiserin in ihrer Zeit*. Wien: Böhlau, 2022.

Zoller, Franz Carl. *Geschichte und Denkwürdigkeiten der Stadt Innsbruck und der umliegenden Gegend von den ältesten Zeiten bis zur Erlöschung der österreichisch-tirolischen Linie mit Erzherzog Sigmund Franz*. 2 Bände. Innsbruck: Wagner, 1816 und 1825.

Zöllner, Erich. *Österreich im Zeitalter des aufgeklärten Absolutismus*. Vienna: Österreichischer Bundesverlag, 1983.

# LIST OF ILLUSTRATIONS

# LIST OF ILLUSTRATIONS

# INDEX

# INDEX

# INDEX

# INDEX

# INDEX

# INDEX

# INDEX

# INDEX

# INDEX

# INDEX

# INDEX

# INDEX